Encyclopedia of Western Atlantic Shipwrecks
and Sunken Treasure

Encyclopedia of Western Atlantic Shipwrecks and Sunken Treasure

by Victoria Sandz
with Robert F. Marx

McFarland & Company, Inc., Publishers
Jefferson, North Carolina, and London

LIBRARY OF CONGRESS CATALOGUING-IN-PUBLICATION DATA

Sandz, Victoria, 1958–
Encyclopedia of western Atlantic shipwrecks and sunken
treasure / by Victoria Sandz with Robert F. Marx.
p.   cm.
Includes index.

ISBN-13: 978-0-7864-2902-8
ISBN-10: 0-7864-2902-X
(softcover : 50# alkaline paper) ∞

1. Underwater archaeology—Atlantic Ocean—Encyclopedias.   2. Shipwrecks—
Atlantic Ocean—Encyclopedias.   3. Treasure-trove—Atlantic Ocean—
Encyclopedias.   4. Atlantic Ocean—Antiquities—Encyclopedias.
I. Marx, Robert F., 1933–   II. Title.
CC77.U5S27   2006   909'.0963—dc21   2001031611

British Library cataloguing data are available

Manufactured in the United States of America

Cover photograph ©2001 Index Stock

*McFarland & Company, Inc., Publishers
Box 611, Jefferson, North Carolina 28640
www.mcfarlandpub.com*

Encyclopedia of Western Atlantic Shipwrecks and Sunken Treasure

by Victoria Sandz
with Robert F. Marx

McFarland & Company, Inc., Publishers
Jefferson, North Carolina, and London

LIBRARY OF CONGRESS CATALOGUING-IN-PUBLICATION DATA

Sandz, Victoria, 1958–
Encyclopedia of western Atlantic shipwrecks and sunken
treasure / by Victoria Sandz with Robert F. Marx.
p.   cm.
Includes index.

ISBN-13: 978-0-7864-2902-8
ISBN-10: 0-7864-2902-X
(softcover : 50# alkaline paper) ∞

1. Underwater archaeology—Atlantic Ocean—Encyclopedias.   2. Shipwrecks—
Atlantic Ocean—Encyclopedias.   3. Treasure-trove—Atlantic Ocean—
Encyclopedias.   4. Atlantic Ocean—Antiquities—Encyclopedias.
I. Marx, Robert F., 1933–   II. Title.
CC77.U5S27 2006   909'.0963—dc21   2001031611

British Library cataloguing data are available

Manufactured in the United States of America

Cover photograph ©2001 Index Stock

*McFarland & Company, Inc., Publishers
Box 611, Jefferson, North Carolina 28640
www.mcfarlandpub.com*

For Capt. George H. Reid
and Evelin Reid
—Victoria L. Sandz

To my grandson Robert,
a future treasure hunter
—Robert F. Marx

Contents

Introduction

Since the beginning of recorded time, man has crossed the oceans. Ships of every description have been used to explore new territories, conquer nations and transport goods. They have been used for trading, piracy, slavery, emigration and conducting business between continents. Wars have also been fought at sea, both above and below the surface.

The thousands of shipwrecks that have accumulated in the Western Atlantic are an historical graveyard of information covering several centuries of man's existence. One of the best examples is the S.S. *Central America*, a U.S. steamship that is currently being salvaged off the Carolina coast. The *Central America* sank in the 19th century during an extremely powerful hurricane. The gold coins, bars, nuggets and dust it carried were produced during the "California Gold Rush," one of the most defining eras in America's history. The foundering of the *Central America* and the loss of its commercial gold shipments set off a wave of financial difficulties.

The enormous amount of treasure lost over the centuries also chronicles world events. Between 1492 and 1820, over 2,000 Spanish treasure galleons sank while carrying treasure from the New World back to Spain. During this period, an average of 17.5 million pesos of gold and silver was shipped back to Spain each year. An unregistered amount of gold, silver and emeralds was also smuggled out of the New World to avoid paying the king's taxes. It has been said by some that more treasure lies on the ocean floor than will ever be harvested from the land in the next 200 years.

Primitive navigation methods led to the foundering of the large number of ships in the Western Atlantic. It wasn't until 1736 that a method for determining longitude was finally established. Previously, ships traveling between the Americas and Europe would sail up the Florida Coast to Cape Canaveral, then turn east for Bermuda. From there they would follow the same latitude past the Azores and on to their European destinations. During this time, many ships ran aground on the treacherous reefs scattered along the way.

The effects of nature also contributed to a great number of shipwrecks in the Western Atlantic. Technology that allows mariners to track seasonal hurricanes and global weather patterns wasn't available until recently.

Oceanography was also rudimentary until World War II. During the war, the United States Navy conducted a substantial amount of research to plan successful maneuvers of landing craft. These were the first major studies undertaken on the effects of wind, waves and currents near landmasses.

The vast number of ships wrecked in the Western Atlantic were from countries all around the Western Hemisphere. Some shipwrecks have been located and identified while many others still remain unaccounted for.

This work is the summation of many years of research carried out by Robert F. Marx, the world's preeminent authority on shipwrecks, treasure hunting and underwater archaeology. Mr. Marx has traveled around the world for over 45 years, researching in archives, libraries and museums. He is accredited with locating and excavating the city of Port Royal, Jamaica, that sank in 1692 in a devastating earthquake. Mr. Marx is also responsible for locating thousands of other significant shipwrecks worldwide. This book combines the information Mr. Marx has collected from those many depositories, creating a single reference source of known shipwrecks and treasures in the Western Atlantic for historians, students, recreational divers and treasure hunters.

Unfortunately, both man and nature have destroyed many shipping documents over the years. Many of the Spanish records containing information on New World treasure shipments were lost due to natural disasters. In

1

1551, the House of Trade building in Seville was destroyed by fire. In 1962, a flood destroyed many more documents in the Archives of the Indies of Seville.

In 1670, Henry Morgan was responsible for burning Panama City to the ground, thus destroying all shipping and trade documents up until that time. The humid Panama climate has destroyed many more documents since then.

The complete archives in Cartagena and Bogota, Colombia, were also destroyed during the War of Independence. The Mexican War of Independence claimed many of the shipping documents in Veracruz and Mexico City.

Europe has lost valuable records as well. Portugal lost its shipping records in 1755, when the Casa de India Depository of Historical Documents sank into a Lisbon river during an earthquake. Other shipping records were lost during World War II due to fire caused by bombings in London, Paris, Rotterdam and Amsterdam.

The main archives in Lima, Peru, were destroyed twice by earthquakes in the 18th century. Very few Dutch shipping documents exist concerning the New World other than what can be found in the Spanish or British depositories.

Many more shipping documents lie bundled and uncataloged in numerous archives. Other bundles of documents have been found to be mislabeled. Researchers will not have access to scores of shipping documents until archives catalog them.

When using the information in this encyclopedia it should be remembered that all information regarding Spanish shipwrecks was obtained from original documents. Where vital information is missing on a shipwreck, it could not be found in the original documents.

The exact locations of shipwrecks may have been vague in original documents. In the early days, this would apply mainly to Spanish shipwrecks, where few place-names could be found on many charts. The names of locations have been changed in this book to the modern day name where possible.

The dates of shipwreck losses have also been converted to the modern day calendar. In 1582, Pope Gregory XIII ordered that ten days of that year be omitted to bring the calendar and sun into correspondence again, creating the Gregorian calendar, which is in use today. All the Protestant nations continued to use the old calendar for many years before changing over. England didn't make the change until 1752.

Finding no reliable means to convert the value of the monetary units used in the old days to our present-day monetary system, the values of treasures and cargoes are stated in the terms in which they are described in the old documents. It should also be noted that ships carrying treasure from the New World were often loaded with contraband, sometimes four or five times the amount shown on the ship's manifest.

Salvaging of a shipwreck was attempted whenever possible. Although some records of salvage efforts do exist, there are no records of illegal salvage operations that may have occurred over the years.

Excavating shipwrecks found in shallow water has gone on for several centuries. However, the latest advances in underwater technology have made both the discovery and excavation of deep-ocean shipwrecks now possible. In this book we have included the latest equipment and technology being used along with the personalities of those who have left their mark on the business of treasure hunting and underwater archeology.

Today, the investments a person can raise are the only barriers that exist as we travel farther into the deep seas and back into history.

Part I
DICTIONARY

Aerial Survey An aerial search may be the most efficient way to begin searching for a shipwreck if the search area is large. This type of survey can help in locating ballast piles, cannon and anchors. Some wrecks that are completely covered over with sand can also be identified by an aerial survey. Sand generally darkens over a shipwreck site where a great deal of metal, such as large cannon, is located due to the iron oxide formed. Small solitary coral reefs or several small patch reefs may also indicate a shipwreck where coral began to grow on parts of the wreck located above the sand.

Both helicopters and light, small planes offer advantages and disadvantages when searching from the air. Although a helicopter with floatation gear can land on a suspected target it has a number of drawbacks, one of which is the expense. Since the helicopter has the ability to hover over a spot it may seem to be an ideal way to check out a suspected site, but the downdraft from its rotors roils the water, obliterating visibility. A single engine, high wing plane such as a Cessna 172, with the doors removed, is a practical choice. The best time to perform an aerial search is between 10:00 A.M. and 2:00 P.M. on a clear day when the sun is high enough for deep light penetration into the water. Polarglasses should be used to eliminate reflections from the surface of the water. Once a promising area is sighted, the plane will circle several times for confirmation before a buoy or other transponder is dropped. When flying alone, the best method to fix a position is with the Global Positioning System (GPS). Flying several timed compass headings from the site to stationary landmarks is another method, but isn't very accurate.

It is often impossible to establish the precise position of a shipwreck without the aid of a surface vessel, even when sighted from the air. The vessel can be directed to a suspected area by radio, and divers can immediately investigate. A boat can make the placement of buoys or transponders over a site much easier as well. A more economical method for an aerial search is by balloon, which is attached to the stern of a boat. The balloon is filled with either helium or hot air and towed through a

An aerial view of sunken buildings in the Bahamas.

planned search pattern. When something has been spotted the balloon can be hauled down and the boat stopped. For the best results, the sea should be flat calm and the observer at an altitude of between one hundred and five hundred feet. Either buoys or sonar transmitters can be dropped over a site and by using sonar-receiving equipment the position can be easily located.

Airlift An airlift is a tool commonly used in excavating a shipwreck buried in sand or mud. However, the airlift is not effective when a wreck is lying under a deep layer of sand. It operates by forcing compressed air supplied from a surface vessel or float to the ocean bottom through a hose. The hose is attached to the base of a pipe and positioned over the excavation site. As the compressed air rises in the pipe it creates suction, drawing the sand and sediment away from the excavation area. There should be a control valve on all airlift tubes so that the diver can control the amount of air entering the tube. When removing overburden, the airlift is run at full power to remove as much sediment as possible. When areas containing artifacts are reached, however, the speed of the suction is reduced to permit the diver to grab artifacts before they are sucked up by the tube or damaged by striking against its bottom. Two wires can be attached across the bottom of the metal tube in opposite directions, which permits only the smallest artifacts to be sucked up. The spill from the top should be directed onto a floating screen or onto a boat or barge containing a screen. One of the advantages of using the airlift on muddy or silty bottoms is that the spill can be directed and carried away by the current. Thus, underwater visibility isn't affected. The airlift cannot be used effectively in water less than fifteen feet deep. The difference between atmospheric pressure on the surface and water pressure on the bottom is not sufficient to create enough suction in the tube. Nor is the airlift useful on shipwreck sites that are widely scattered or buried under deep, sedimentary deposits. In these situations, the work can be accomplished in a fraction of the time with a prop-wash.

The following chart indicates the diameters of tubes and hoses required at various depths and the amount of air pressure and volume of air needed to work efficiently.

Under no circumstances is an airlift

Airlift Diameter (inches)	Hose Diameter (inches)	Max. Depth to be used (feet)	Air Volume (cubic feet per minute)	Air Pressure (pounds per sq. inch)
3	½	40	20– 40	50
3	½	65	30– 50	75
3	½	90	10– 60	100
4	¾	40	30– 50	50
4	¾	65	40– 60	75
4	¾	90	50– 70	100
6	1 ¼	40	75–100	50
6	1 ¼	65	100–125	75
6	1 ¼	90	125–150	100

An airlift being used to remove the overburden on a shipwreck site.

with a diameter larger than six inches recommended. They are difficult to control and artifacts can be destroyed or lost in them. This occurred during a six-week excavation of the sunken city of Port Royal by the noted explorer Edwin Link in 1959 when a 12-inch diameter airlift was used.

Alvin   The Alvin is a deep submersible vehicle that was originally launched in 1964 with an operational depth of 1,829 meters (6000 feet). It was later modified to reach depths of 4,000 meters. The submersible has two manipulator arms and can carry a crew of three. In its career it has seen both military and commercial use. In 1966, two years after it was launched, the United States Navy used the Alvin to successfully retrieve a hydrogen bomb. Four hydrogen bombs had spilled when an Air Force B–52 bomber collided with a jet tanker during refueling operations off the coast of Spain. Three fell on land and were easily retrieved, but the fourth fell into the ocean. It was located in March 1966. While retrieving the two-ton bomb, a cable snapped and the bomb fell again. It was relocated and retrieved nine days later in water 300 feet deeper. Two years later, during a research operation off Cape Cod, the

lowering cables on the surface broke and the Alvin sank in 5,000 feet of water. The three-man crew escaped during the few seconds it remained afloat. The United States Navy authorized the money for the Alvin's recovery. The submersible vehicle Aluminaut performed the task of recovering her in the same manner that the Alvin had used to lift the hydrogen bombs. In 1986, the Alvin was used in motion picture filming of the operation to salvage the *Titanic* and in the operation itself. A small tethered remote-operated vehicle (ROV) called Jason Jr. was wed to the Alvin, enabling the recovery of objects inside the *Titanic*.

Anchors   From the time of the Vikings until about 1825, all anchors were hand-forged from several pieces of iron. After this period many were cast in one piece. The stocks were made of wood until the middle of the 19th century, when they were replaced by iron bars. The first mention of chains being used on an anchor occurred in 1817 and referred to an English warship. The number and size of anchors a ship carried depended on her size and type. Since anchors were routinely lost, many extras were carried onboard.

There weren't any regulations as to

the number of anchors a ship must carry until 1579, when the King of Spain issued an order stating that ships over 100 tons and going to the Tierra Firme must carry five anchors and those going to Mexico must carry seven. The first mention of their sizes occurred in 1620, when a galleon of 500 tons carried seven anchors on a voyage to Veracruz; one of a ton weight, two of 1,800 pounds, two of 1,600 pounds, one of 450 pounds and one of 350 pounds. In 1709, an order was issued that the total weight of anchors on all Spanish warships must be equal to five percent of the total weight of the ship. After 1634, French merchantmen were required to carry a minimum of four large anchors and at least six on warships. One large French warship lost in a hurricane in the Caribbean near the end of the 17th century was carrying ten anchors at the time, while another, lost during the same hurricane, had only two available, resulting in her loss when both anchor cables parted and she wrecked on a reef. In 1688, English warships were required to carry the following number of anchors: a ship of 2,000 tons, known as a first-rater, carried nine anchors weighing a total of 17 tons; a second-rater of 1,500 tons carried nine weighing a total of 12½ tons; a third-rater of 1,000 tons carried six weighing a total of 8½ tons; a fourth-rater of 700 tons carried six weighing a total of 5½ tons; and a fifth-rater of 500 tons carried five weighing a total of 4½ tons.

The grapple or multiarmed iron anchor is believed to have been developed by the Greeks and was used until modern times. Various sizes and shapes can be seen in religious illuminated works of the medieval period and in paintings of the 15th and 16th centuries. In the New World they were widely used during the first half of the 16th century on smaller vessels. Some were erroneously identified as grappling hooks, which were used when boarding an enemy vessel. With the introduction of the iron anchor with a wooden stock, there were very few changes or improvements until the 19th century.

Records in 1514 list anchors by name and show that the *Henri Grace Adieu* had four bower anchors, four destrelles, one shot anchor and a cadger or kedge

The submersible Alvin under tow. *Courtesy of the U.S. Navy.*

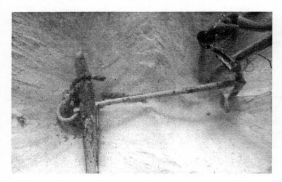

Spanish anchor recovered from a galleon lost in 1551.

anchor. By the time of Elizabeth I, anchors had taken on their present names of bower, sheet, stream and kedge. Bower anchors were for ordinary use such as mooring and were stored in the bow for ready use, hence their name. Sheet anchors were heavier and used in emergencies such as to prevent a ship from grounding on a lee shore. Stream anchors were small anchors used mainly as stern anchors or to supplement the bowers. Kedge anchors were the smallest and used for light work such as maneuvering a vessel, bringing around the head for example, and sometimes for navigation, where it was rowed out ahead of the ship and having the ship hauled up to it when the vessel was becalmed or being steered through hazardous waterways. Another type of anchor used throughout this period was the mooring anchor, which is easily identified since it has one of its arms bent back to the vertical shank or stem. It was generally attached to permanent mooring buoys in an anchorage, the good arm digging into the bottom and the other bent back to prevent damage to a vessel tying up to the mooring.

With a few exceptions, most anchors of the 16th and 17th centuries had curved arms. However, as larger anchors were made the straight-arm variety was introduced; they were used first by the English and soon after by other nations. The flukes were generally the shapes of equilateral triangles and about half the length of the arms. The anchor ring was usually smaller in diameter than the fluke. The use of rope wrapping on the rings, then in general use, most likely dates back to

antiquity. *Mainwaring's Seamen's Directory*, first published in 1622, states that the shank is twice as long as one of the flukes plus half the distance between the tips of the flukes. The anchor stock was more or less the length of the shank, except in Portuguese and Spanish anchors where it was 25 to 40 percent longer. The stock was made from timbers bound with iron hoops which were driven on when heated.

Caution should be exercised when using anchors to identify a shipwreck. There have been many instances where anchors have been recovered from the sea, after having been lost through snagging on other anchors or cables, or when vessels had to get under way in a hurry and had insufficient time to raise anchor. Once raised many were used again on totally different ships, sometimes centuries later. During hurricanes and bad storms it was also the practice to cast anchors, and sometimes cannon, overboard to lighten ship and prevent capsizing. In many instances, contemporary or later salvors are known to have thrown over anchors on shipwreck sites to lighten ship in order to be able to carry more of the salvage materials on their vessels. A good example of this involved a 1648 Dutch merchantman, lost near Memory Rock in the Bahamas, which had a 19th century anchor on top of its ballast pile. Beneath another section of the ballast were numerous 19th century spirit bottles. This seems to indicate that the site was worked by salvors in the 1800s, since the water was too shallow to be used as a normal anchorage.

Archaeomagnetic Dating This method for dating clay objects is based on the knowledge that the intensity and direction of the earth's magnetic field varies over the years. Clay contains magnetic minerals such as hematite and magnetite. When heated or fired these minerals will assume the direction and proportional intensity of the magnetic

field that surrounds them and continue to hold them after the clay has cooled. By measuring these quantities, the age of a clay piece can be reckoned if the changes in the earth's magnetic field are known for the location where the piece was fired.

Small Spanish olive jar.

Artifacts, Preservation of Proper preservation is one of the weakest aspects of shipwreck exploration for both commercial salvors and archaeologists. There are fewer than one hundred persons working worldwide in this specialized field and there are very few facilities where this type of work is done. Treasure salvors have very limited access to these laboratories in the United States due to the fact that they are controlled by academic archaeologists. Most preservation laboratories in universities or government agencies will only handle materials from projects in which they are directly involved. Treasure hunter Mel Fisher set up his own preservation laboratory where technicians developed new methods for cleaning and preserving artifacts. A number of foreign governments have sent their people there for training. The International Artifact Conservation and Research Laboratory Inc. of Belle Chasse, LA, a commercial laboratory, has served both the private and public sectors since 1987.

Raising and restoring the *Vasa*, sunk in the Atlantic and now on display in Sweden, has been the most ambitious restoration program thus far attempted in this field worldwide. When the *Vasa* was raised in 1961, there were no conventional techniques available to preserve

The raising of the *Vasa*.

Bronze astrolabe c.1600.

such an enormous ship and the hundreds of thousands of artifacts found as well. Preserving this ship became a proving ground in which most of the preservation methods used today were developed. Unfortunately, preservation of the *Vasa* itself has proved a dismal failure. Now, three and a half centuries after she sank and almost four decades since she was brought to the surface, the 64-gun flagship is in serious trouble again. As soon as the *Vasa* was raised, the oak hull was impregnated with polyethylene glycol (PEG) to keep the wood from shrinking as it dried. It now appears that the PEG was not applied properly and a great deal of the hull is deteriorating. Experts fear that the *Vasa* will be lost if a solution isn't found.

The preservation experts today who are raising other shipwrecks face a similar dilemma. Even smaller objects preserved by experts over the years are in deplorable states of deterioration today. Several small iron cannon found at Port Royal and turned over to the Conservation Laboratory of the Smithsonian Institution are today only iron fragments and dust like particles that can be seen in their plastic tombs. Preservation techniques are constantly improving, but far more research is necessary before there can be any certainty that

something preserved today will last forever or even another 50 years. Although the methods described in this volume are the best and latest for a wreck salvor to use in cleaning and preserving their finds, it is strongly recommended, whenever possible, to seek the services of a preservation expert. Over the years, divers have destroyed treasure and unique artifacts in their efforts to clean and preserve them. Even large objects such as iron and cannon begin to disintegrate quickly when left exposed to air. Any shipwreck artifact that requires preservation must be kept wet, preferably in salt water and exposed to air as little as possible. Since water is heavy and large amounts of it are very heavy, immersion is not always practical for large objects or when there is a great deal of material. In this case, they can be wrapped in plastic wrap or placed in an airtight plastic bag or container. Large items can also be transported from the salvage vessel to a laboratory in wooden barrels or boxes containing moist sawdust.

Astrolabe   An astrolabe is a bronze navigation instrument used on ships during the colonial period to find a vessel's latitude by calculating the position of the sun at high noon or the North

Star at night. Fewer than 70 exist in the world today. Several have sold in auctions in recent years for more than $200,000.

B   **Ballast**   Locating a ballast pile may indicate a shipwreck. Ballast of various types was often carried onboard wooden ships to stabilize them. Old Spanish and Portuguese ships carried round ballast rocks ranging from several ounces each to two hundred pounds. Since most ships took on their ballast in ports or harbors, most of which had rivers or streams emptying into them, the round "pebble" or "river rock" ballast was the most common type used. Mariners also preferred the naturally round rocks since they wouldn't pierce the ship's wooden hull. The larger rocks were usually placed over the lowest deck. The smaller rocks were then used to fill in the spaces between the larger ones. On some of the early French and English ships, a substantial amount of ballast rock was cemented together with mortar for use as permanent ballast. It is not known whether ships of other nationalities followed this practice.

There were many instances where river rock was not available and ships were forced to use other types of rock. A late 16th century wreck salvaged in Bermuda contained flint rock for bal-

Location of the ballast pile from the wreck of the *San Pedro. Courtesy of the Florida Keys National Marine Sanctuary.*

last. Documents dated 1570 tell of a Spanish merchantman sailing from Cuba to Spain with copper ore for ballast. Another Spanish ship sailing in 1638 from Venezuela to Spain used saltpeter for ballast and yet another sailing from Cadiz to Venezuela in 1760 used gypsum rock. As early as 1614, there are mentions of Spanish ships carrying bars of iron from Spain to America as ballast, but this was done only when iron was being carried for sale or use in the New World colonies. From 1700 onward, English warships used bar-shaped pigs of iron as ballast, a practice that took hold with French warships from 1707 onward.

A shipwreck site may not have any ballast on it at all for several reasons. When ships carried heavy cargoes they did not take on ballast in order to avoid being dangerously overweight. When ballast rocks were scarce, sand was used. Also, on small vessels the limited space below deck necessitated an alternative means of carrying ballast. Therefore, as casks and barrels containing water, beer, wine, vinegar and so on were consumed, they were filled with seawater. This method permitted quick and easy lightening of a ship during a storm. The casks and barrels could either be emptied into the bilge and pumped

overboard, or they could be easily jettisoned, unlike with ships carrying ballast in the form of rocks or pig iron. On the other hand, finding a ballast pile does not always indicate a shipwreck, especially when it is discovered near or in a port or harbor. Ships occasionally sailed without cargoes requiring large loads of ballast to stabilize them. Before or after entering a port where a heavy cargo was to be loaded, most and sometimes all of the ballast was thrown overboard. If the ship remained in the same position when this operation was under way, the ballast pile would resemble one at a shipwreck site. If the ship were swinging at anchor, the ballast would be scattered, as it is on a wreck site where the ship was badly broken up and the ballast strewn over a large area. In an age when all mariners were not overly concerned about sanitation, the Spaniards had the reputation for having the dirtiest ships afloat. Since many seamen and the poorer passengers lived below deck on these long voyages, a great amount of fish, animal, and fowl bones, broken pieces of ceramic, glassware and other debris was thrown into the hold with the ballast. Thus these items would be thrown overboard with the ballast rock and might now lead a salvor to believe that

the ballast pile is indeed associated with a shipwreck.

Bar Shot Bar shot and chain shot were used primarily during sea battles to destroy the sails and rigging of enemy vessels. The first mention of bar shot was by the Dutch in 1619. Some bar shot was made by attaching an iron bar measuring six to twelve inches in length between two round shot. Other types were made with two halves of a round shot and some with round disks. The Dutch introduced chain shot in 1666, with a chain replacing the iron bar of the bar shot.

Barshot was used for destroying the sails and rigging of sails.

Bayonets Bayonets were introduced by the Spaniards in 1580, but not adopted by the French until 1647 and the English until 1690.

A Civil War bayonet and rifles recovered from a blockade-runner.

Dutch bellarmine jugs dating from between 1650 and 1720.

Bellarmine Jugs   These types of jugs found on a wreck site can be dated fairly accurately. They were manufactured in Germany from a type of ceramic known as stoneware, and ranged in capacity from one pint to five gallons. The clay used in manufacturing them contained flint and was fired at a much higher temperature than utilityware. Bellarmine jugs were coated with a salt glaze, which gives them a distinctive whitish-gray interior and brownish exterior. Most of the necks of the jugs were decorated with a human face, which had its origin in a caricature of the Spanish Cardinal Bellarmine. Some have armorial medallions on the bodies. They were mainly used by the Dutch.

Botany   Botanists can help identify the origin of vegetable material found on an underwater site. Several black beans from a test core on the Columbus wreck site were identified as a type grown only in Spain. At another site, a botanist identified several tobacco leaves found on the shipwreck as coming from Venezuela, thus helping to identify the ship.

Brass, Preservation Methods   Brass objects suffer very few effects from being immersed in salt water. Calcareous deposits on large objects can be removed

by tapping with a rubber mallet. Smaller objects can be cleaned by immersion in a bath consisting of ten percent nitric acid and 90 percent fresh water, followed by washing in running water for a short time. The acid bath is used to remove any green patina found on these objects; this can also be accomplished by the discreet use of steel wool.

Brass navigational dividers from one of the 1715 fleet shipwrecks.

Bronze, Preservation Methods   Bronze objects suffer very few effects from being immersed in salt water. Calcareous deposits on large objects can be removed by tapping with a rubber mallet. Smaller objects can be cleaned by immersion in a bath consisting of ten percent nitric acid and 90 percent fresh

water, followed by washing in running water for a short time. The acid bath is used to remove any green patina found on these objects; this can also be accomplished by the discreet use of steel wool.

 Canister Shot   The French introduced canister shot, a type of cannon projectile, in 1745. Soon afterward it was put into use by other nations. It consisted of a thin cylindrical wooden or metal can containing various shaped objects, such as glass fragments, nails, tacks, musket balls or small pebbles.

Cannon   Finding cannon may aid in locating a shipwreck. However, this may not be the case unless other items such as anchors and ballast are found as well. Often when a ship was in danger of capsizing during a storm, or ran aground on a reef or shallow area, some or all of its cannon were thrown overboard to lighten it. Cannon were sometimes used as ballast on ships as well, and occasionally jettisoned when not needed. Over 200 cannon have been discovered in a relatively small area off the eastern end of Bonaire Island. It was found that ships traveling from Holland anchored in this area to load salt from the island. The cannon were thrown over when the ships took on the cargo. Cannon have also been found in large numbers near old forts in the Caribbean.

At times, a cannon can be useful in identifying the size, type and approximate date of a ship, but not always the nationality. Cannon manufactured in many different countries were sometimes carried on a single vessel. During the second half of the 16th century, the majority of cannon carried on Spanish ships were made in England and Holland. A large percentage of cannon the Spanish carried during the 17th and 18th centuries were of foreign manufacture as well. Many ships belonging to other European countries also carried cannon of foreign manufacture, most of which were obtained when they captured foreign ships.

The wreck site of the *San José*.

Various types of cannon were carried throughout the centuries. During Columbus's voyages, he armed his ships with two types of cannon— Lombards and Versos; the latter were also called swivel guns. As early as 1504, some of the larger Spanish ships sailing to the New World were carrying bigger cannon mounted on two-wheeled wooden gun carriages. One merchant *nao* sailing to Santo Domingo in 1504 carried: one bronze Demiculverin, 11 feet, 2 tons, and firing a 12-pound ball; four iron cannon Serpentines, 8 feet, 2½ tons, and firing a 40 pound ball; one bronze Saker, 7 feet, 1,200 pounds, and firing a 6 pound ball; and three Versos of unknown size and weight, firing a 4 pound ball. In 1552, a royal order was issued which stated that all Spanish merchant ships sailing to the New World had to carry the following amounts of armament. A ship of 100 to 170 tons must carry one bronze Saker, one bronze Falconet, six iron Lombards, and twelve iron Versos. A ship of 170 to 220 tons must carry one bronze Demiculverin, one bronze Saker, one bronze Falconet, eight iron Lombards and 18 iron Versos. A ship of 220 to 320 tons must carry one iron Demiculverin, two bronze Sakers, one

bronze Falconet, ten iron Lombards and 24 iron Versos. A treasure galleon of between 400 and 600 tons was required to carry all bronze cannon, comprising 30 to 50 Culverin cannon, four to six Demiculverins, two to four Sakers, four Falconets and an unknown number of Versos. The Culverins were the main armament for fighting against enemy ships.

Around 1570, Spanish ships began carrying larger numbers of iron cannon due to the scarcity of copper needed to manufacture sufficient bronze Culverins and other types of cannon. The largest was called plain Cannon. It fired a 40-pound ball, was 17 times its bore diameter in length, and weighed 6,200 pounds. The Demi-Cannon was also used at this time. Small vessels frequently used several other types of cannon such as the Pasavolante, Moyana and Esmeril. During the 16th and 17th centuries,

the Pedrero was occasionally carried on Spanish ships. With the exception of the Lombards, which went out of use near the end of the 16th century, all the cannon described above remained in use until the beginning of the 19th century, when Carronades replaced most of the larger cannon on Spanish ships. In 1599, the Spaniards apparently had a sufficient supply of bronze cannon, as all 12 galleons in the Tierra Firme Armada carried only bronze cannon. In 1605, a royal order stated that all treasure galleons and the *capitana*s and *almiranta*s (lead ships) of the *flotas* (fleets) must carry only bronze cannon.

Cannon Shot The basic cannon projectile was round shot, generally made of iron, but sometimes of stone or lead. The size of the shot used for each cannon was one-quarter inch smaller in diameter than the caliber of the cannon. Since there was no difference in the appearance of the round shot made by all the countries, the only information that can be obtained from those salvaged from a shipwreck is the caliber of the cannon that used them; this becomes important in the event that the cannon has been previously salvaged. The following table gives the average weight of iron round shot in relation to its size.

Diameter (inches)	Weight (lbs. & ozs.)	Diameter (inches)	Weight (lbs. & ozs.)
2	1 & 2	5 ¼	20 & 1
2 ¼	1 & 9	5 ½	23 & 2
2 ½	2 & 2	5 ¾	26 & 6
2 ¾	2 & 14	6	30
3	3 & 12	6 ¼	34
3 ¼	4 & 12	6 ½	38
3 ½	6 & 1	6 ¾	42
3 ¾	7 & 5	7	48
4	8 & 5	7 ¼	53
4 ¼	10 & 10	7 ½	58
4 ½	12 & 10	7 ¾	64
4 ¾	14 & 14	8	71
5	17 & 5	8 ¼	78

Bar shot and chain shot were used primarily during sea battles to destroy the sails and rigging of enemy vessels. The first mention of bar shot was by the Dutch in 1619. The Dutch then introduced chain shot in 1666, with a chain replacing the iron bar of the bar shot. Two types of antipersonnel shot were also used—grape shot and canister; the latter was sometimes called case shot. The earliest mention of grapeshot was in 1556 aboard English ships. Canister shot was introduced by the French in 1745. It is not known in which period the incendiary carcass shot first came into use, only that it was in use during the second half of the 17th century. Carronade shot was much like carcass shot but did not contain any combustible matter or have holes in it.

Cannon, 16th Century English The principal cannon carried on English ships during the 16th century are given below with their average weights and measurements.

Name	Weight (lbs.)	Length (feet)	Caliber (inches)	Shot Weight (lbs.)
Robinet	200	5	1 ¼	1
Falconet	500	4	2	2
Falcon	800	6	2 ½	2 ½
Minion	1,100	6 ½	3 ½	4 ½
Saker	1,500	7	3 ½	5
Demiculverin	3,000	10	4 ½	9
Bastard Culverin	3,000	8 ½	4 ½	11
Culverin	4,000	11	5 ½	18
Demi-Cannon	5,000	9	6 ½	30
Cannon	7,000	12	8	60

B

The cannon described above in table B remained in use until the beginning of the 19th century, when Carronades replaced most of them.

Cannon, 17th Century English The principal cannon carried on English ships during the 17th century are given in table A with their average weights and measurements.

Name	Weight (lbs.)	Length (feet)	Caliber (inches)	Shot Weight (lbs.)
Robinet	120	3	1 ¼	¾
Falconet	210	4	2	1 ¼
Falcon	700	6	2 ¾	2 ¼
Minion	1,500	8	3	4
Saker	2,500	9 ½	3 ½	5 ¼
Demiculverin	3,600	10	4 ½	9
Culverin	4,000	11	5	15
Demi-Cannon	6,000	12	6	27
Cannon	7,000	10	7	47
Cannon Royal	8,000	8	8	63

A

Of the above mentioned English-made cannon, the Robinet, Falconet, Falcon, Minion, Saker, Demiculverin and Culverin were generally made of bronze. Other types, regardless of size, were generally made of iron. The numbers and types of cannon carried on English merchantmen depended on the size of the ship and the availability of armaments, as cannon were scarce in England.

An ornate iron English cannon dated around 1650.

Cannon, 18th Century English The principal cannon carried on English ships during the 18th century until the introduction of the Carronades, are given below in table C along with their average weights and measurements.

Name	Weight (lbs.)	Length (feet)	Caliber (inches)	Shot Weight (lbs.)
Robinet	150	3 ½	1 ¾	½
Falconet	700	4 ½	3	3
Falcon	800	6	3 ¼	4
Minion	2,000	7 ½	3 ¾	6
Demiculverin	2,600	8	4 ½	9
Culverin	3,200	9	4 ½	12
18-Pound Cannon	3,900	9	5 ⅓	18
24-Pound Cannon	4,600	9	5 4/5	24
32-Pound Cannon	5,500	9 ½	6 ½	32
42-Pound Cannon	6,500	10	7	42

C

The Carronade was introduced on English ships in 1779. The numbers and types of cannon carried on English merchantmen depended on the size of the ship and the availability of the armaments, as cannon were scarce in England. This random approach applied to English warships until the middle of the 18th century when the Admiralty issued an order specifying the numbers and types of cannon that must be carried on their ships. In 1762, a first-rater of 100 cannon carried thirty 42 pounders, twenty-eight 24 pounders, thirty 12 pounders, ten 8 pounders and two 6 pounders. A second-rater of 90 cannon carried twenty-six 32 pounders, twenty-six 18 pounders, twenty-six 12 pounders, ten 8 pounders and two 6 pounders. A third-rater of 74 cannon carried twenty-eight 32 pounders, thirty 24 pounders, fourteen 9 pounders and two 6 pounders. A fourth-rater of 50 cannon carried twenty-two 24 pounders, twenty-two 12 pounders and ten 6 pounders. A fifth-rater of 36 cannon carried twenty-six 12 pounders, and ten 6 pounders. A sixth-rater of 28 cannon carried twenty-four 9 pounders and four 6 pounders. The Carronade replaced most of the large-caliber cannon on ships of all nations from 1800 onward.

Cannon, Dutch Dutch cannon were very similar to those of the English and French. They used bronze cannon almost exclusively on all of

Diver removing coral growth from an iron cannon on an English wreck in the Bahamas.

their ships, including the majority of their large merchantmen. Many Dutch ships carried cannon made in the Orient; they had trading posts there and obtained the cannon in trade.

Coauthor Robert F. Marx, third from left, identifying two mid–16th century breech-loading swivel guns.

Cannon, French French cannon were very similar in size, shape and weight to the English cannon, but were generally lavishly marked with decorations, especially those cast in bronze. The numbers and types carried on their merchantmen and warships varied greatly until 1643, when the king issued an order concerning the armament on all French ships. Merchantmen sailing to the New World were required to carry the following numbers and sizes. A ship between 200 and 300 tons must carry six Demiculverins of 2,400-pound weight; twelve Sakers of 1,600-pound weight; two Minions of 1,000-pound weight; one Falconet of 300-pound weight; and one Robinet of 200-pound weight. The ships of larger sizes had to carry the same except for the Demiculverins, which increased in number and weight with the size of the ship. A 300-ton ship carried nine Demiculverins of 3,000-pound weight and a 500-ton sip carried 16 Demiculverins of 3,200-pound weight. A 700-ton ship carried 22 Demiculverins also of 3,200 pound weight. All French first and second-raters were required to carry only bronze cannon; one-quarter of the cannon on all the smaller French warships were required to be of bronze, and the remainder of iron.

Cannon, Identification of Most bronze and iron cannon were struck with dates at the time they were founded. Many also carried the coat of arms of the monarch of the country of manufacture. For instance, the English cannon were struck with a crowned rose during the Tudor period and the initials GR (*Georgius Rex*) during the reign of King George I. These marks have survived on bronze cannon, but have disappeared on many iron cannon that have been discovered. Along with other distinctive characteristics, they can be used to date the cannon when dates have been lost. All European nations have artillery museums with experts who can generally date the pieces to within 50 years. In the United States, the Smithsonian and the South Street Seaport Museum in New York have experts who can aid a salvor in identifying and dating cannon. Various books have been published on cannon, but the majority are written in foreign languages and are difficult to obtain in the United States.

Cannon, Portuguese Portuguese cannon differed vastly in shape from any of the others manufactured in Europe. Many of those carried on Portuguese ships were actually manufactured in India or in other Portuguese Far East possessions. The Artillery Museum in Lisbon is one of the best cannon museums in the world.

Carbines A carbine, a type of firearm, was introduced by the English during the second half of the 16th century. Similar in appearance to a musket, it was much smaller and fired a lead ball weighing less than an ounce. The firing mechanisms on carbines changed at the same time they did on muskets, pistols and harquebuses. In 1517, a German invented the wheel lock that replaced the matchlock. Another improvement on the firing mechanism was introduced around the end of the 16th century when the flintlock superseded the wheel lock. The flintlock remained in continuous use on all firearms until about the 1820, when the percussion lock replaced it. Although it was invented near the end of the 16th century, some nations did not use the flintlock for many years. It was not used on a large scale in France until 1670.

Carbon Dating Carbon dating using radiocarbon 14 (or C-14) is a method of dating an old object but is limited to organic material such as wood, bone, charcoal, peat, shell and plants. It was conceived by the noted nuclear physicist W.F. Libby, who discovered that all organic material absorbs C-14 from the earth's atmosphere until it dies, then the absorption ceases and the C-14 is lost from the material at a known rate over time. By measuring the amount of C-14 remaining in the material, scientists can determine the length of time that has elapsed since the object died. Only small samples of the material are required for this test. Anyone planning to use this method should keep the material wet until the tests are performed. Many universities have facilities for C-14 dating. There are also a number of commercial laboratories that can perform this testing as well. Testing takes from two to six weeks. The main disadvantage in using this is its imprecision in dating due to a plus or minus factor in years. When C-14 dating is used on items that are many thousands of years old, the plus or minus factor is of little significance, but when items are several hundred years old, this factor is critical. Furthermore, in many cases the date of wooden hulls obtained by this method will have no relationship to the date of the wreck; the ship may have been many decades old when it sank. In addition, the ambiguous date obtained from C-14 testing would relate to the time when the tree that supplied the timber was cut. There are many instances where a ship was constructed of timbers from other ships, which in turn could have been constructed from the timbers of even older ships.

Carcass Shot   Carcass shot was an incendiary cannon projectile, consisting of a hollow cast-iron ball filled with combustible materials. When fired, flames streamed out through small holes in the side of the ball. It is not known in which period this projectile first came into use, only that it was in use during the second half of the 17th century.

Carronade Shot   Carronade shot is a cannon projectile, which consisted of a hollow cast-iron ball but did not contain any combustible matter or have holes in it.

Carronades   This type of cannon was introduced on English ships in 1779. It was easily recognizable from cannon of earlier years because of its large bore diameter and short length of only three to six feet. Carronades fired balls weighing 9, 12, 24, 32, 42 and 68 pounds. Those made up until 1800 had low trunnions; after 1800, the trunnions were centered. After 1825, many of them had no trunnions but were mounted with lugs on the gun carriages. The Carronade replaced most of the large-caliber cannon on ships of all nations from 1800 onward.

Chain Shot   Bar shot and chain shot were used primarily during sea battles to destroy the sails and rigging of enemy vessels. The Dutch introduced chain shot in 1666, with a chain replacing the iron bar of the bar shot.

Circular Sweep Search, Visual   Once the search boat reaches the vicinity of a likely target, a heavy anchor is dropped on a line. Another line is attached to some part of the anchor. If the search is to be visual this second line is marked at intervals so the diver knows how far to space each circle they will make. If the underwater visibility is only five feet in each direction, each mark on the line should be spaced about eight feet apart. The marks can be made by knotting or tying a piece of cloth to the line. The diver starts the search by swimming a complete circle around the anchor while holding the first mark. They then move out further in progressively larger circles until the target has been located. When the target is large, a faster method is for the diver to swim out to the far end of the search line. Holding the line taut, the diver swims a large circle, the circumference depending on the length of the line. Once the target is snagged by the line, the diver still holding the line taut, swims back toward the anchor until he runs into the target. He quickly drops a small marker buoy, which serves until a larger buoy can be dropped from the search vessel.

Clay Pipes   White clay smoking pipes can be valuable for establishing the date, but not the nationality of a

The maker's initials on clay smoking pipes can be used to identify and date the place of manufacture.

shipwreck. Almost all were manufactured in either England or Holland and were exported all over Europe. Most clay pipes can be dated to within ten years of the date of manufacture, with the exception of a few that were manufactured in Virginia and Jamaica. Unlike many other items discovered on shipwrecks, the fragile clay pipes did not last long in everyday use, so those found on a wreck will date very closely to the time the ship was lost.

Europe did not learn about the use of tobacco until after the discovery of the New World. Columbus and his men saw Indians on various Caribbean islands smoking cigars. Later explorers in North America saw Indians smoking tobacco from clay pipes. The Spaniards began cultivating and exporting tobacco to Spain from the colonies near the end of the 16th century. Most of the tobacco imported into Spain was sold to England since the Spanish Catholic Church prohibited the use of tobacco until the beginning of the 19th century. On his voyage to the West Indies in 1565, John Hawkins gathered a large amount of tobacco and introduced it into England upon his return. The first mention of the manufacture of clay pipes in England occurred in 1573. By the end of the 16th century the use of tobacco and clay pipes was widespread both in England and Holland. By 1619, there were so many manufacturers of clay pipes in England that they incorporated into a guild, with Dutch pipe makers doing the same in 1660. Pipes

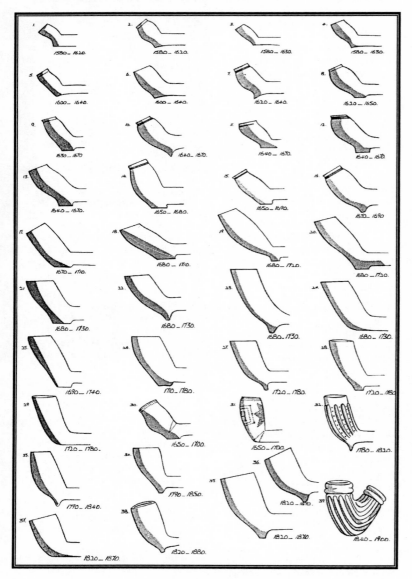

Data used for dating clay pipes.

of the pipe bowls increased in proportion. As the size increased, the shapes of the bowls changed as well, making it possible to date the pipe within ten or 20 years of manufacture. A majority of pipes manufactured in England were marked with either the initials or full name of the manufacturer. Records exist in England listing 3,400 pipe makers from the year 1600 forward. Some of the earliest pipes had the pattern of the fleur-de-lis or of rosettes etched on them. Later types bore oak leaves, grapes, flowers, anchors and myriad other designs. From the end of the 18th century to the middle of the 19th century, decorations on pipes became much more elaborate. Some pipes were adorned with busts of the British monarchs, mermaids, or a coat of arms. Practically nothing is known about the markings on pipes made in other European nations until well into the 19th century. The same applies to the red clay pipes believed to have been produced in Virginia or Jamaica. Discovery of a large number of pipes on a shipwreck usually identifies the wreck as an English or Dutch ship. However, small numbers have been discovered on a few Spanish shipwrecks. Tobacco stoppers, generally made of brass or pewter, are first mentioned in records as being used in 1640. Many contain distinctive markings that can help establish a date or place of manufacture. Coauthor Robert Marx discovered the largest collection of clay pipes ever found in the sunken city of Port Royal, Jamaica where he brought up over 12,000.

Clay Pipes, Preservation Method
Calcareous deposits can be easily removed from clay pipes. After recovery they should be air-dried, which actually decreases the pipe slightly in size, causing the calcareous deposits to fall off on their own. Various stains can be removed by washing with a mild detergent and soft brush. Repairing or piecing together all types of ceramics is relatively simple. Clean the joints of any foreign bodies and cement them together with Durofix or Elmer's Glue. The pieces should be held in place by tape or placed in a sandbox while the glue is drying.

were first produced in Denmark in 1655 and in Switzerland in 1697. Very little is known concerning the dates they were first manufactured in other European nations. It is believed that a small number were being manufactured in Virginia and Jamaica in the late 17th century, but it wasn't until the beginning of the 19th century that the United States began manufacturing clay pipes on a massive scale.

Clay pipes have many distinctive features that can aid in dating them. When smoking came into vogue in England and Holland, the cost of tobacco was high due to the fact that it was purchased entirely from Spaniards. Consequently, pipe bowls were small. After the English began cultivating tobacco in the New World and exporting it to England, the cost became progressively less. Thus, the size

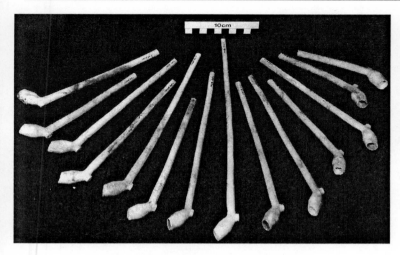

Dutch clay smoking pipes from a wreck lost in 1629.

Spanish piece of eight dated 1684.

Closed-Circuit Television This system is used when it is necessary to visually search an extensive area in deep water. The television cameras, with strong lights if the water is dark or dirty, is mounted on a small platform, similar to a sea sled, and is towed through the water by a surface vessel.

Cofferdam Cofferdams have been used to excavate and reconstruct various shipwrecks. After the perimeters of the shipwreck are determined, a wall is constructed around the site. The water and mud overburden covering the site are removed with a combination of pumps, dragline buckets and shovels. The ship is first mapped *in situ* and then taken apart and reassembled in a permanent exhibit.

Coinage, Dating Very little is known about the earliest coins minted in the New World. Several documents mention that private persons minted their own gold and silver coins in Mexico City as early as 1528, but nothing is known about their descriptions or how long this practice continued. In 1535, a mint was established in Santo Domingo where copper maravedi coins were first minted. Practically nothing is known about this coin, except that it was also minted at Mexico City and Panama City, among other places, and was used until the beginning of the 19th century. Very few

were stamped with distinctive markings such as dates, mintmarks or assayer's initials. Some, minted in Santo Domingo from the second half of the 16th century, had an anchor on one side and a fort on the other. Others, minted there in 1636, had a fort on one side and two ships on the other. Occasionally, maravedi coins minted in Spain bearing dates and other marks have been discovered on shipwrecks. The known denominations of these coins were 8, 4 and 2 maravedis. However, they may have been minted in other denominations as well. Their actual buying value was limited and they were basically used as small change in the New World. A silver one-real coin was worth 34 maravedis and an eight-real coin or piece of eight was worth 272 maravedis. Silver coins were officially minted at Mexico City in 1536; Lima in 1568; Potosi in 1572; Bogota in 1622; Guatemala City in 1733; and Santiago (Chile) in 1751. It is believed that they were also minted at Cartagena and Panama City for short periods at various times during the 17th century. The basic silver coin was the eight-real piece, which weighed an ounce. Other real denominations were the 4, 2, 1, ½ and ¼ coins, smaller in size and weight. Gold coins were first officially minted at Cartagena in 1615; Bogota, 1635; Mexico City, 1679; Lima and Potosi, 1697. They were also minted for a six-month period during the year

1698 and again after 1750 at Cuzco, Peru. The gold coins are of the same size and weight as the silver and are in denominations of 8, 4, 2, 1 and ½ escudos. Although the screw press was used to mint round milled coins in England as early as 1610, it was not used in Spanish-America until 1732, when the first round milled coins were made at the Mexico City mint. The Lima mint did not produce round milled coins until 1752, and the other mints at even later dates. Prior to 1732, almost all the gold and silver coins minted in the New World were not round in shape but of many irregular patterns. However, there were some exceptions. The silver coins minted in Mexico City during the first 20 or 30 years of operation were almost perfectly round and over the years all the mints made small numbers of perfectly round gold and silver coins. The round gold coins were known as royals and are quite rare. It is believed that each mint made several royals each year and sent them to the king to show that they were capable of producing good coinage. The irregularly shaped gold and silver coins were called cobs, a name probably derived from *cabo de barra*, which means "end of a bar." These coins were made by pouring molten metal on a flat surface in long thin strips. After the metal cooled, pieces of the approximate size and weight for the desired coins were cut from the strip, then trimmed to their proper weight. The planchet was then placed between two dies and struck with a heavy hammer. Since one or both sides of the coin were not perfectly flat the dies only marked the highest surfaces of these sides. This resulted in the majority of the cob coinage not having full die marks. The coins made at the Mexico City mint during the 17th and 18th centuries are of poor quality and show faulty die marks and are the most difficult to date. Other mints appeared to have exercised a higher quality of workmanship, as larger amounts of both their gold and silver coins have been found with fuller die marks in addition to bearing dates. There are other means by which coins can be dated fairly accurately when dates are not shown. The majority of them have the shield or coat of arms of the monarch on the obverse side, so the coin can be dated to the period in which the particular king reigned. From 1772 to 1825, the end of Spanish rule in America, both the gold and silver coins carried the portrait of the Spanish king. All coins were also marked with the initials of the assayer and cover the period in which a particular assayer was in charge of a mint. On small numbers of coins the reigning monarch's name or initials were also marked. The place in which a coin was minted can be determined from the mintmarks on each coin. The letter L for Lima; P, Potosi; M, Mexico City; C, Cartagena; G, Guatemala; S, Santiago; and NR, Bogota. When the mintmarks are not visible on the coin, the place where it was minted can be identified by its die markings. Almost all of the Mexico City coins had a Jerusalem cross on the reverse side, as did some of the Bogota and Cartagena minted coins. The Lima and Potosi minted coins had a plain cross with the arms of Castile and Leon on their reverse sides. Generally the place in which it was minted can be identified even if only a small amount of the die is visible, making a coin one of the best markers in unraveling the mystery of a shipwreck. Platinum had no intrinsic value in the old days and was sometimes used illegally in the production of silver coins.

Contraband   During Spanish rule of the New World, contraband, such as gold, silver and jewels, was often carried onboard a ship but not listed on the ship's manifest to avoid paying the king's and church taxes. Many differ-

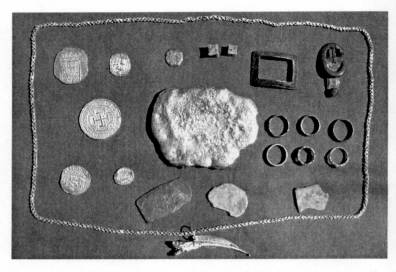

Contraband gold disk in center is not marked to signify that the taxes have been paid to the king or church.

ent ingenious ways were used to smuggle treasures back to Spain and Portugal. In 1606, customs officials in Cadiz were suspicious when they saw two large anchors that had been painted. They proved to be made of solid gold. Gold bars were sometimes covered with copper and listed as copper ingots on the manifests.

Copper, Preservation Methods
Objects made from this metal suffer very few effects from being immersed in salt water. Calcareous deposits on large objects can be removed by tapping with a rubber mallet. Smaller objects can be cleaned by immersion in a

A stack of copper cooking kettles found on a British merchant ship lost off Boston c. 1880.

bath consisting of ten percent nitric acid and 90 percent fresh water, followed by washing in running water for a short time. The acid bath is used to remove any green patina found on these objects; this can also be accomplished by the discreet use of steel wool.

Coring Device   Coring devices are used to determine the overall perimeters and depth of a shipwreck when it is buried in mud or silt. They can also be effective on sandy bottoms or even in soft coral growth. Those used by marine geologists are driven into the sea floor by explosives or other equipment operated by a surface vessel. A coring device used by divers can be much simpler. It may consist of four-foot sections of four-inch-diameter iron tubing. One diver holds the tube vertically on the sea floor while another drives it into the sediment by hitting the top of the tube with a heavy sledgehammer. As the section sinks into the sediment another section is attached and the operation continues. Lifting bags are then used to pull the tube out of the sea floor. Before the coring device is pulled out a rubber plug is inserted into the top of the coring tube to maintain suction in it. This keeps the sediment and artifacts intact while the tube is removed from the sea floor. Once aboard a vessel or onshore, the sample in the tube is recovered by removing the plug, holding the tube almost vertically and gently shaking. Artifacts such as wood, glass, flint, iron nails, tacks, small ballast rock, ceramic shards, animal bones, and beans can be recovered and the exact stratigraphic depth determined. When using a coring tube in coral growth, the bottom of the tube needs to maintain a sharp edge for cutting, often requiring the tube to be sharpened for the operation.

Cox, Harry   The late Harry Cox was a native Bermudan and prosperous businessman who spent his time prowling the Bermuda reefs in a relatively relaxed manner. Over the years, Cox spent weekends taking friends and sometimes tourists to an area of the reefs he called "wreck country," where he had pinpointed more than 15 old wrecks. It was on such an excursion in 1968 that he discovered a richly laden Portuguese treasure ship, lost in the second half of the 16th century.

Cox and friends were returning from a day spent recovering bottles from an 18th century English merchant shipwreck when he made this, the greatest discovery of his life. As they headed for port, one man was hanging on to a line from the rear of the boat, scanning the bottom through a facemask for signs of a wreck. He spotted a few scattered ballast stones

Harry Cox holding a bronze astrolabe. *Courtesy of the Bermuda News Bureau.*

and despite the appearance of evening clouds on the horizon Cox stopped to investigate. While everyone donned diving gear, his friend surfaced with an elephant's tusk. Everyone but Cox returned to the boat after thoroughly combing the area and turning up nothing more than ballast stones and a few pottery shards. As he tells it, Cox "had a feeling that there was something great down there," so he continued searching in the rapidly darkening water. He fanned in a small sand hole on a nearby reef with his hand and uncovered a silver coin. Fanning faster, he soon found two gold coins and a large, solid-gold bracelet. He surfaced shouting, "Gold, gold!" The others quickly grabbed their fins, masks and tanks and threw themselves overboard. In the next 45 minutes, before it became pitch black and their air was consumed, they recovered treasure valued at more than $200,000. The find included a number of gold bars, pieces of gold jewelry, a massive ten-foot double-linked gold chain, an elaborate gold manicure set, silver items and a brass mariner's astrolabe. One of the many pieces of jewelry discovered that afternoon was a magnificently worked gold ring with a large empty socket. Cox vowed he would find the stone that had once graced the ring. Two years later, working on a million to one chance, he actually did find it—a breathtaking five-carat emerald that fit the empty socket perfectly. Cox went back to the wreck site many times afterward and found an assortment of additional artifacts but the bulk of the treasure came up on that first thrilling dive. This seems to indicate that Cox had found the area of the reef where the vessel had struck and dropped some of her contents, but not the main body of the wreck.

D   **Decompression Chamber**   A portable decompression chamber should be carried onboard a shipwreck salvage boat to treat cases of the bends, or it should be available onshore. A doctor versed in diving medicine is an essential member of a team working in deep water.

Delftware   This type of pottery was manufactured in every country and used mainly by the upper and middle

Delftware cup made in Holland.

classes. The English, Dutch and most other northern European countries called it delftware. However, in France and Italy it was called faience and in Spain and its New World possessions majolica. It was generally made of the same clay as utilityware but was coated with a glaze of tin oxide, which appeared white in color after firing. The surface of the glaze was then decorated in a wide range of colors and designs. Most of the pieces were manufactured in Europe. Some of the later pieces made in the New World have distinctive maker's marks on them which can be used to establish the object's date and place of origin. Experts should be consulted to aid in identification of all unmarked pieces.

Demiculverin   This type of cannon fired balls weighing from seven to 12 pounds. They were 25 to 40 times their bore diameter in length and weighed between 3,000 and 4,000 pounds.

Dendrology   A definite method for determining the date and origin of wood samples is through the science of dendrology. Experts in this field can not only identify the kind of wood and its country of origin, but in many cases even narrow it down to what part of a country the wood came from. This information is an aid in establishing where a ship was built and was one of the ways that the two Columbus shipwrecks in St. Ann's Bay were positively identified. Dendrologists are able to date most wood samples precisely by

Diver exploring timbers of a 16th century galleon that wrecked in Bermuda.

Coauthor Robert F. Marx, removing coral growth from a large cannonball.

the number of their tree rings. They are able to determine the origin of a sample through its tree-ring pattern which reflects the localized climatic conditions prevailing during the life of the tree from which the wood came. Catalogues of such tree-ring patterns pertaining to specific geographic areas have been compiled stretching back thousands of years, and by an examination of these catalogues, dendrologists can usually find a match for their sample. For ships built in Western Europe, however, this method has restricted application. The climate fluctuated there so much over the centuries that the ring patterns are too variable from one region to the next to have been mapped effectively.

Electronic Positioning Devices By using the Global Positioning System and a computer printout, these devices can tell a person their exact position at all times in relation to beacons they have set up ashore or on offshore towers or buoys. However, they must set up the same transmitting beacons in the exact same places to return to a precise position at a point in the future. These systems also enable a person to make their search pattern runs without using any buoys. Some even

give indications of drift caused by currents or the wind. Their only restrictions are their rental or purchase costs, which are prohibitive for anything but a professional operation.

Esmeril This type of cannon was used on small Spanish vessels. Very little is known about the Esmeril except that it remained in use until the beginning of the 19th century. It was sometimes used as a signal gun.

Falconets A type of cannon that fired a three- or four-pound ball. They were 30 to 36 times their bore diameter in length and weighed between 1,500 and 2,500 pounds.

Ferrous Metals Approximately 95 percent of all metal objects discovered on a shipwreck consist of iron, whose highly corrodible nature presents some of the most challenging problems for preservation. In many cases cast-iron objects corrode into a crystalline form and are so totally destroyed that only powdered oxide remains. Wrought iron objects are not as prone to corrosion, probably because they have a greater nickel content. The same applies to steel, which has a high nickel content. The amount of metal remain-

ing in an object can best be determined by its weight or by testing with a magnet. If the object has no magnetic attraction, it has been completely oxidized. This can also be determined by x-ray photography or a fluoroscope when laboratory facilities are available.

Ferrous Metals, Preservation Methods The first step in the treatment of ferrous metals, iron or steel, is the removal of any exterior calcareous encrustation. This can only be attempted when a substantial amount of the original metal remains in the object. These deposits can best be removed on large objects like cannon by gently tapping with a hammer or other tool. Small, delicate objects can be cleaned in an ultrasonic electrical bath or chemically. The chemical process consists of a bath in a solution of ten percent nitric acid and 90 percent water, with several washes in fresh water to remove the alkalis. The object must then be treated by electrochemical reduction. It should be placed in a bath consisting of ten percent sodium hydroxide and 90 percent water and soaked for a period of four to eight weeks. The object is then removed and reimmersed in a new bath of the same solution, following which the entire object is covered with zinc chips or surrounded by zinc plates. The solution will begin to bubble soon after the zinc

Sixteenth century cannon being put into a large electrolyte reduction bath.

is added to the bath. This will continue throughout the two to four weeks the object is kept in the bath. Upon removal the object will be covered with a white coating, which can be removed by placing the item in another bath consisting of five percent sulfuric acid and 95 percent fresh water. The next step is to place the object in a running-water bath for at least a week and then in a bath of distilled water for another week. The bath should then be tested to make sure it is free of both alkalis and chlorides. If it is not free of these elements, then more baths in distilled water are required until there are no traces left. The object is then dried, preferably in a high temperature oven.

After drying it can be coated with paraffin wax or a clear synthetic plastic or lacquer to seal its exterior and prevent further corrosion.

When little or nothing remains of the original ferrous material, an item can be treated by one of the following two methods. The first method is to embed the object in a plastic resin, such as Selectron 5,000. The object must first be thoroughly dehydrated, either by heat or the alcohol process, otherwise it will continue to disintegrate inside the plastic blocks. This can be a lengthy process if the mass is large, as only very thin layers of the plastic can be placed in the mold containing the object. The second method is to make an exact plaster replica of the object. By x-raying the object, its size and location in the encrusted conglomerate can be determined. Then the conglomerate is cut in half with a diamond saw. The two halves will be hollow inside where the original object was and will serve as the mold into

 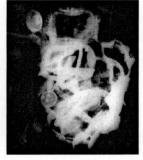

Left: Coral-encrusted conglomerate containing dozens of artifacts. *Right:* An X-ray of the same conglomerate that included crucifixes, buckles, buttons, coins and jewelry.

which the plaster is placed to make the replica. A variation on this method is to drill a hole into the conglomerate and force the plaster compound into the cavity of the conglomerate. After hardening, the exterior encrustation can be removed by grinding or hand tools.

Fisher, Mel The late Mel Fisher was one of the most successful and controversial treasure hunters in the Western Atlantic. He was also one of the earliest pioneers in the diving industry. Mel's interest in diving began very early in his life when he made his first dive helmet out of a bucket, some hose line and a bicycle pump. In 1950, he opened California's first dive shop in a shed on his chicken ranch. He was responsible for making some of the very first underwater movies. Mel went on to open Mel's Aqua Shop in Redondo Beach and produce some of the first wet suits ever made.

After meeting treasure hunter Kip Wagner in 1964, Mel and his wife Deo moved to Florida to treasure hunt on a full-time basis. Mel and Kip formed Universal Salvors, which later changed its name to Treasure Savors Inc. Mel's first recoveries were from the 1715 Spanish treasure fleet. After that he moved on to the Florida Keys to search for the *Atocha*, a Spanish galleon belonging to a treasure fleet that sank

The famous treasure hunter Mel Fisher.

during a hurricane in 1622. The *Atocha* was said to have carried treasure worth $200 to $400 million in gold, silver and jewels and locating her was to become Mel's ultimate lifetime goal. He found several of the 1733 fleet shipwrecks while searching for the *Atocha*, and then, in 1973, Mel's company finally discovered a silver bar that matched the records of the *Atocha*'s manifest. Two years later, Mel's son Dirk found nine of *Atocha*'s bronze cannons. Dirk, his wife Angel and diver Rick Gage were lost when their salvage vessel capsized and sank less than a week after discovering the cannon. Mel Fisher continued his efforts to find the *Atocha* after the tragic accident.

It wasn't until 1985, after 16 years of searching, that Mel's divers finally discovered a reef of silver bars that led to the "motherlode" of the *Atocha* treasure. From the initial impact zone, the ship had bounced along in the hurricane for 12 miles before the main hull finally sank. The State of Florida soon stepped in and changed its definition of "State Waters," thereby claiming ownership of the *Atocha* wreck and her precious cargo. The battle with the State finally ended seven years later in the United States Supreme Court. Mel was awarded the treasure and artifacts from the *Atocha* along with the treasure from the other wrecks he had discovered while searching for it.

Fisher's greatest finds included a gold plate and gold cup used to detect poisoned wine, a heavy gold priest's chain, the only known example of a "cinta" necklace or belt, a 17th century navigator's astrolabe, and an enormous number of Colombian emeralds that had been smuggled aboard the *Atocha*. Mel's group was also responsible for locating and recovering artifacts from the *Henrietta Marie*, one of the few wrecks of slave ships ever discovered in the Western Hemisphere. He enjoyed a lifetime of successful treasure hunting. Mel Fisher's company, Treasure Salvors Inc., continues to salvage treasure from the *Atocha*.

G **Ghost Wreck**   A shipwreck that does not exist and which originated in the imagination of a

Painting of a galleon foundering during a hurricane.

writer is known as a "ghost wreck" by professional treasure hunters and archaeologists. The information on these wrecks is occasionally based on information gathered from other poorly researched books instead of authentic research carried out in national archives, shipping registers and government agencies. Hundreds of thousands of dollars have been wasted by both professional treasure hunters and amateurs who have searched for shipwrecks based on this false information instead of actual research.

Glass   Glass bottles are often used to establish the date of a shipwreck. Their shape changed quite often and can usually be dated to within ten years of their manufacture. The Phoenicians and the Egyptians, who first made glass, crafted many exquisite objects. At the time of Columbus's discovery of America, Venice was the center of European glass manufacturing, specializing in drinking glasses and decanters. Glass factories were founded in Antwerp in 1550 and in London in 1557. Another was founded in Jamestown, Virginia in 1608, which went out of business in 1624. A glass factory was started in Salem, Massachusetts in 1632, making bottles to transport rum and cider to the West Indies and England. The next glass-

works to open was in Brussels in 1662, and soon after others were founded in Spain, France, Holland and Germany.

Glass bottles that contained any type of liquor were generally called "wine bottles." The first known manufactured bottles were those made in Salem in 1632. The exact date they were manufactured elsewhere is not known, but it is believed that they were made in England around 1650. Other European nations were not manufacturing wine bottles until well after 1700. At least 95 percent of all wine bottles discovered on 17th and 18th century shipwrecks are of English manufacture, since the English produced them on a large scale and exported them all over Europe. Wine bottles manufactured in Holland are very similar in appearance to their English counterparts but those made in other European countries have their own distinctive characteristics, permitting nationality to be established. Some bottles bear the dates of manufacture and others bear identification seals of the persons for whom they were made such as the owner of a tavern. Bottles were sealed with wax-covered cork until near the end of the 17th century, when brass wire was used to hold the corks in place. Late in the 18th century, copper wire came into general use to secure the corks. All

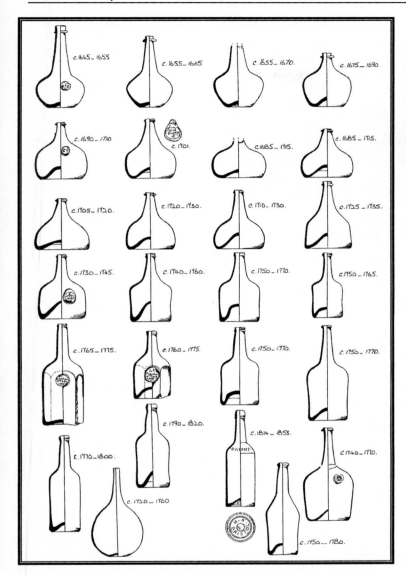

Data used for dating bottles.

Dutch bottles dating from 1720.

bottles were blown by hand until the second decade of the 19th century, when they began to be manufactured in molds. Thus, any bottle discovered with mold marks or with the maker's or owner's name molded on it must date from after 1810.

Glass plate used for windows and mirrors was first made in England in 1673. Glasses found on shipwrecks can be identified by sending photographs and measurements of the items to the Corning Glass Museum. Dr. Robert Brill, of Corning, has also developed a method of dating a shipwreck by counting the number of layers of weathered crust on the glass fragment. This can establish the length of time the glass has been under the sea.

Glass, Preservation Methods
Glass is affected to varying degrees in the ocean, depending on its composition. Optical glass generally survives in a good state of preservation but the exterior is occasio: ally found pitted. White-lead glass objects, such as plate glass, wine glasses, tumblers and pharmaceutical vials or medicine bottles are generally found free of calcareous deposits, though most will be covered with a thin coating of lead oxide or sometimes iron oxide when discovered in close association with iron objects.

To preserve an item, it should be placed in a ten percent solution of nitric acid for the time required to remove the lead oxide. If iron oxide is present, a five percent solution of sulfuric acid should be used to remove the oxide, then the item should be given several thorough washings in distilled water. If the item shows signs of flaking on its exterior after drying, it should be coated with several layers of clear plastic spray, such as Krylon. As a rule, most bottles postdating 1750 require very little preservation. Sediment inside the bottle can be removed with careful use of a high-pressure hose or various types of tools, such as a wire or an icepick. Exterior calcareous growth can be removed by tapping gently on the bottle with a rubber mallet or by immersion in a bath consisting of 0.2 percent solution of sulfuric acid for several hours or as long as a week, depending on the amount of growth on it. The bottle must then be thoroughly washed in several baths of fresh water, or distilled water when available, until the glass is free of alkalis. The litmus-paper test is the best way to determine if the glass is free of

Late 18th century round English rum bottles and a square Dutch bottle.

alkalis. Upon drying, the surface of some bottles may tend to look dull or to develop a very thin layer of pearly iridescence in spots. No further treatment is necessary, although the iridescent material, if especially fragile, may tend to flake off. Preservation of badly decomposed glass (which is the state of most bottles predating 1750) is difficult. However, if the glass is not impregnated in some way, it is very likely that the exterior weathering crust will crumble away when it dries out. Most bottles predating 1750 can be cleaned and preserved with a 0.2 percent solution of sulfuric acid which removes the calcareous growth and stains. Depending on the fragility of the bottle, a high-pressure hose or probe can be used to remove the sediment inside. Then it must be thoroughly rinsed in distilled water until free of all alkalis. Without the bottle drying completely, it must then be bathed in alcohol (wood, denatured ethyl or rubbing) which tends to remove the remaining water without causing the decomposition crust to crumble away. After that it must be air-dried for a short period and finally impregnated with several coatings of clear spray lacquer. However, coauthor Marx discovered that this method does not preserve the more

badly decomposed bottles, such as those he recovered at Port Royal. After several months the glass began flaking under the lacquer coatings and in many cases the bottles completely disintegrated. To prevent this, he followed the same procedure as described above, except that instead of coating the bottles with lacquer, he immersed them for a week or two in a solution of 50 percent distilled water and 50 percent vinyl acetate, the same material used in making the glue for bookbinding. Vinyl acetate is marketed as padding cement. After removing the bottle, the excess solution was wiped off with a slightly damp cloth, then air-dried in a cool area. After completely drying, the glass was coated with several layers of lacquer. For mending or piecing together broken glass or bottles, there are a number of convenient epoxy cements that can be used. The most important step in cementing glass is cleaning the surfaces to be joined.

Grape Shot The earliest mention of grapeshot, a type of cannon projectile known as antipersonnel shot, was in 1556 aboard English ships. It consisted of 20 to 50 small cast-iron balls of one to two inches in diameter held in place between two or more wood or metal disks connected to a central rod. The

balls were lashed to the frame with cords or leather. The cylindrical projectile was covered with canvas and coated with wax, paint or pitch.

Gurr, Tom If perseverance and determination could be converted into money, Tom Gurr would be a millionaire. He has encountered a multitude of problems and frustrations trying to make a livelihood from treasure hunting, yet he has always been able to overcome them and continue at the profession he loves. Gurr began spear fishing and lobstering along Florida's east coast while skin diving was still in its infancy. He made his own fins, mask and spear gun before diving equipment was available on the market.

Gurr became interested in treasure hunting and explored the Florida Keys part time for many years. It wasn't until 1966, however, that he finally succumbed to "treasure fever" on a grand scale. He met an old sea captain who spun yarns of treasure ships that he had seen in his youth. For two years, the old man led Gurr on one wild goose chase after another searching for shipwrecks, which were never found. Gurr began to doubt the old man's knowledge and sincerity. Questioning him concerning his method of pinpointing the location of a wreck, Gurr discovered that he was using a water tower and several other prominent objects ashore, which were not even in existence when he claimed to have discovered the wrecks. Confronted with these facts, the old man conveniently suffered a coronary attack and was rushed to the hospital. Gurr was reluctant to give up without a shadow of success and felt he owed something to the crew of divers who were eager to continue with him.

During this period, Gurr ran across an article about the *San Fernando*, one of the 1733 fleet shipwrecks from which two amateur divers "claimed" to have salvaged over $50,000 worth of treasure. Gurr discovered that the wreck was in international waters and up for grabs for anyone who wished to salvage it. Gurr and his divers worked the wreck for many months, but with very little to show for their efforts. Later, he learned that the Spaniards had thoroughly salvaged the wreck and what little they had missed had been picked up over the years by many other divers, including Art McKee. Mel Fisher contracted Gurr to salvage four different shipwrecks during the next eight months while Fisher's Treasure Salvors Company searched for the elusive *Atocha*. The wrecks did not produce much of value. During the salvage efforts, Gurr located an American Civil War Blockade-runner, which also yielded little of value.

Later, while working for Art McKee on the *Capitana* wreck, Gurr located another wreck a few miles away in international waters. The wreck was later identified as the *San José de las Animas*, a 326-ton Spanish merchantman belonging to the 1733 fleet. Gurr recovered between $100,000 and $500,000 in treasure and artifacts. Several weeks later, the State of Florida Conservation board claimed that Gurr was working illegally in Florida waters and tried to board his salvage vessel. Gurr's crew deterred their efforts. The following day, the United States Coast Guard came alongside and customs officials boarded, thoroughly searched the vessel, and left without an explanation. After contacting his congressman, Gurr found that someone had maliciously informed customs that the salvage boat was being used as a drop-off vessel for exiles making raids against Cuba and that there was a large cache of weapons and munitions onboard. Gurr finally received an official apology from both the Coast Guard and Florida officials. This wasn't the end of the difficulties he would encounter concerning the *San José*. Gurr was summoned to court, where a judge ruled that the State's three-mile limit no longer measured out from the existing coastline, but rather from the farthest submerged reef offshore. When he demanded a hearing in the Federal District Court in Miami, the judge granted his request but ordered an injunction prohibiting further salvage work. He also demanded that Gurr turn over everything that he had recovered from the wreck to the State. When Gurr refused, he was summoned on contempt of court charges

and threatened with six months in Federal prison if he did not comply with the Federal Court decision. When he asked for a new trial, he was given the same judge and demands, which left him no choice, as he didn't have the funds to continue the legal battle.

After Gurr's trial was over, State officials approached him and offered to discontinue legal action and grant him a lease to complete salvage of the *San José* for a 50 percent split of the items recovered. Normally Florida only receives 25 percent of items salvaged in State waters. They also offered him an exclusive exploration and salvage lease covering a large area of the Florida Keys. When Gurr finally received

Tom Gurr holding an Indian metate recovered from the Spanish wreck of the *San José*.

the contract, the exploration areas were only one-tenth the area promised by the State and the exclusive rights now read nonexclusive. Once again, he was forced to seek legal assistance and fight for his rights, but to no avail. Without the funds to continue the legal battle he was forced to accept the contract. Months later, but too late for Gurr, the Federal Government would declare Florida's extension of her State-owned waters illegal. Gurr subcontracted the remaining salvage efforts on the *San José* to the Real Eight Company, then run by coauthor Robert Marx.

The salvage of the *San José* was completed four months later, despite numerous attempts by State officials and pirate divers to impede the operation. On several occasions the State refused to make any effort to stop the theft or damage done by those pirate divers. Once the salvage was com-

pleted the State made no effort to have a division of items recovered, nor did it give Gurr any reasons why it would not do so. With investors breathing down his neck Gurr threw all of his finds back into the sea, which was documented on national television. Soon afterwards, diving at night, he recovered all the treasure and artifacts. Several years later, he tried to sell some of them. He was arrested and only avoided going to prison by agreeing to turn over everything recovered from the wreck.

Tom Gurr ultimately quit the treasure hunting business and became a lay missionary in Panama.

 Hand Grenades Hand grenades were used on ships as early as 1467 and remained in use until the middle of the 19th century.

They were made in many forms, but were usually round, made of various metals, glass, or ceramic and filled with gunpowder. A small hole held a fuse that was lit before the grenade was thrown. Very few have been found on shipwrecks.

Harquebuses, Matchlock Matchlock harquebuses, introduced in the 14th century, were generally five or six feet long, weighed as much as 60 pounds and fired an iron or lead ball ranging from half an inch to an inch in diameter. The disadvantage in using this weapon was the necessity of keeping the match lit to fire it or having the means to light it when needed. In 1517, a German invented the wheel lock to replace the matchlock. Another improvement on the firing mechanism was introduced around the end of the 16th century when the flintlock superseded the wheel lock. The flintlock remained in continuous use on all firearms until about 1820, when the percussion lock replaced it. Although it was invented near the end of the 16th century, some nations did not use the flintlock for many years. It was not used on a large scale in France until 1670. The firing mechanisms on muskets, carbines and pistols changed at the same time as those of the harquebuses.

Hydrolift A hydrolift is also known as a transfer tube, underwater dredge or gold dredge. It was first developed to aid prospectors in recovering placer deposits of gold, which collected in crevices on river bottoms. The hydrolift consists of a six-foot length of four- to six-inch-diameter metal or plastic tube that has a 90° bend on the working end of it. A water jet from a surface pump is attached at the apex of the outside bend. The water jet is pointed straight up the centerline of the tube and forces the flow along the length of the tube. This creates a venturi effect, causing sediment and small objects to be sucked through the tube and discharged several feet away. The spill is either directed into a screen basket so that small artifacts can be found, or a diver is stationed at the exhaust end to cull for artifacts as they

are spewed out. The hydrolift is useful for making test holes in sediment more than six feet deep. It can remove about one and a quarter as much sediment as an airlift that has the same diameter tube. The hydrolift has a limited application in very shallow areas where it might be the only feasible excavation tool.

Jason Jr. Designed, built and operated by Woods Hole Oceanographic Institute (WHOI), Jason Jr. is a small prototype of the ROV named Jason. Jason Jr. (or J.J. as it is called) was wed to the Alvin, a deep-sea submersible vehicle owned by the United States Navy and operated by WHOI and used during the exploration and filming of the salvaging of the *Titanic* in 1986. Later, J.J. was aboard a barge when it sank near Ecuador, but was retrieved. J.J. is the size of a small end table and weighs 160 pounds. It has one tilting color video camera, one still camera and strobe, two canted horizontal thrusters and a manipulator arm.

Jet, Air The air jet is a probe tool used to locate objects buried under sediment. It is mainly used when there are no other alternatives available during a site survey. A surface compressor forces air into the top of a metal pipe

through a hose, permitting the diver to blow away small amounts of sediment as he pushes it deeper into the sediment. In skilled hands, a diver using an air jet can determine the nature of buried objects such as stone, wood or metal. Usually a small lift bag is used to retrieve the pipe.

Jet, Water A water jet is a specialized tool that is used in limited circumstances in excavation of a wreck site. It is similar to an air jet, except that it pumps high-pressure water instead of air down to the bottom to blow away sand and sediment from a site. It can be useful in removing overburden that may pile up around the lip of a hole being dug with an airlift or prop-wash. On wreck sites where there is a thick covering of eel grass, the jet is useful in breaking up the matrix holding the grass, which thereby enables an airlift or prop-wash to dig more effectively. It is also capable of digging tunnels under a ship to be raised, which was the method used on the *Vasa*, lost in 1628 in Stockholm Harbor. In areas where sediment is only a few feet deep, the water jet can excavate faster than an airlift, yet not as fast as a prop-wash. However, as the water jet can be a great deal more powerful than the air jet, there is always the danger of the high pressure blowing objects away. The device usually

A diver using a water jet to remove overburden covering a wreck.

Johnson-Sea-Link, used for work on deep water wrecks.

followed by placement in a running-water bath for several hours. Softness of the metal is usually caused by pieces bending and losing their original shape when the shipwreck occurred.

Liftbags Liftbags are used to bring heavy objects to the surface during shipwreck salvage. They are also very useful for removing large amounts of ballast from a wreck site. The bags are attached to an object with the open end down. Compressed air is then introduced into the bag, displacing the water. Most bags have a plunger dump valve at the top of the bag to control the ascent of the object. Since seawater weighs approximately 64 pounds per cubic foot, a two-cubic-foot capacity liftbag can lift 128 pounds and a three-cubic-foot-bag can lift 192.

Lombards This type of cannon was made of forged-iron strakes running the length of the barrel and held together by iron bands spaced four to six inches apart. They were in use from the beginning of the 15th century until the end of the 16th century. The piece was opened at both ends and a breech lock loaded with powder was wedged against the back end of the piece after a ball was inserted. The cannon was

decreases visibility so drastically that it can only be used effectively when a current is flowing, which can carry the turbid water away. To overcome the excessive pressure problem, a small high-pressure pump can be run from a surface float or vessel to force water into a special nozzle fitted to the working end of the water jet hose. The nozzle has small water jets that counteract part of the water flow to limit the tendency of the hose to recoil. The nozzle should have a valve that allows the operator to control the water pressure of the jet.

Johnson-Sea-Link I & II These manned submersibles are used for deep water exploration and can also be used to locate and excavate shipwrecks. A Johnson-Sea-Link was used on the famous *Monitor* shipwreck as well as one of the 1715 shipwrecks located in 1,200 feet of water off the coast of St. Augustine, Florida. They have also been used on many other deep-water shipwrecks. The vehicle is equipped with manipulator arms, video cameras and a 70mm still camera. An excavation tool called a thruster was mounted on the bow of the vehicle, which allowed salvors to excavate the 1715 fleet wreck mentioned above.

L

Laws *see* **Shipwreck Laws**

Lead, Preservation Methods Lead objects suffer very little from long immersion in salt water, other than accumulating a thin coating of lead oxide on the surface. This can be easily removed in a bath of ten percent acetic acid and 90 percent fresh water

Liftbag being used to recover a cannon from the *Queen Anne's Revenge. Courtesy of Diane Hardy, N.C. Archives and History.*

mounted on a wooden cradle and carried on the main deck of a ship. These pieces varied from six to 12 feet in length, weighed from 500 to 2,000 pounds and fired a ball of stone between four and ten inches in diameter. The weight of the stone depended on the type of rock used in making the ball. A distinctive feature of this type of cannon was the absence of trunnions, which made it unlike any other cannon used at later dates. In 1552, some were made with trunnions.

Magnetometer Magnetometers are the main search tool used universally to detect shipwrecks in shallow water, especially those buried under sediment or coral, and for shipwrecks where a visual search is restricted for whatever reason. They are also used for confirming what a target is when it has been picked up on side scan sonar and the sonar operator is not sure whether it is a shipwreck or a pile of rocks.

Magnetometers were first developed during World War II to detect enemy submarines, but today they are often used in locating shipwrecks. The instrument detects gradients in the earth's magnetic field produced by local concentrations of ferromagnetic materials, such as cannon, anchors or any ferrous metal objects found on a wreck. There are four types of magnetometers, each working on a different principle: the rubidium, proton, cesium and differential fluxgate. The usual method of operating a magnetometer is to tow it behind the boat at speeds from two to ten knots, depending on the sensitivity of the instrument and the size of the object being sought. On several occasions, large metal shipwrecks have been located by using a magnetometer in a helicopter. With this method, the sensing probe of the meter is lowered until it is just above the surface of the water.

To conduct a magnetometer survey, a search pattern is sometimes set up using buoys, which can be quite time consuming. The survey vessel then runs out and is kept on course by an operator using a hand-held radio. In recent

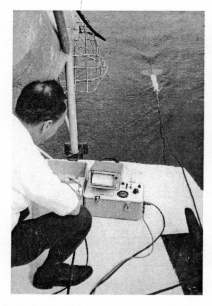

A technician using a magnetometer which detects the presence of iron or steel.

years, most salvors have switched to various electronic navigation systems such as the Motorola Mini-Ranger, which eliminates the need for buoys and for a person to direct the course the boat must follow. A magnetometer survey of the search area is produced either on a graph or computer screen. When searching for large targets such as cannon or anchors in shallow-water areas, the sensing probe is pulled along near the surface between speeds of five to ten knots. When the amount of detectable ferrous metal is suspected to be small, the sensing probe is pulled close to the sea floor and the width of each search lane narrowed considerably. An example of this is a wreck of a ship that carried bronze cannon, which do not register on the magnetometer, or a ship that may have lost all its anchors in another area before wrecking. A target such as a Civil War blockade-runner, that may have had as much as 100 tons of iron used in its construction, can be detected at a distance of 400 to 600 feet. An older shipwreck with a large number of cannon and anchors may be detected from 250 to 300 feet away if the iron objects are confined in a small area. When the wreck has been scattered and large

ferrous articles are spread over a large area, each piece is usually detected individually at a maximum range of 100 feet. In a case where a shipwreck has only a small amount of ferrous material such as cannonballs, tools, weapons and bits of rigging, the location can be detected only if the sensing probe passes within 30 or 40 feet of the site. If very small items are widely scattered, the probe must come within ten or 15 feet to detect them. Of the various types of magnetometers, the Differential Flux Gate has several important features that many others lack. It operates at full efficiency regardless of geographic location, problems resulting from orientation in the earth's magnetic field are eliminated, and it is unaffected by ignition interference or atmospheric conditions. The control unit is watertight and operates to a depth of 200 feet. It also has negative buoyancy and can be operated by a diver in an underwater environment when it is equipped with an optional sensing probe. Indications of magnetic anomalies are provided both visually and aurally with this instrument. Power is provided by the power case and is generated by rechargeable nickel cadmium cells. The total drain is approximately 4.5 watts, and the device will provide 20-hour operation between charges. A charger operating from 115v AC, with overcharge protection and under voltage protection, is also part of the power case. However, many professional treasure hunters prefer using the proton-precession magnetometer as it requires less maintenance and is easier to use. Like sonar instruments, this magnetometer can be run continuously under most sea conditions. On the east coast of Florida and in the Florida Keys alone, treasure hunters have found more than 500 shipwreck sites in the past 30 years. Magnetometers have been used to locate many of these along with other types of submerged objects, such as airplanes and pieces of military equipment. However, the magnetometer is not practical for sites buried under the sea floor, such as ancient shipwrecks and sunken buildings, which have little or no ferrous materials on them.

Mapping a Shipwreck By mapping and recording all the information gathered during the survey of a site, the salvor can determine the overall extent of the wreck site. This can also help establish the cause of the sinking, which can be useful in determining whether the ship is the one the salvor is looking for and whether it has been salvaged by contemporary divers. Mapping can also help determine the ship's size, tonnage and number of cannon it carried. Measuring the length of the keel (when it exists), and estimating the amount of ballast the ship carried or discovering the number and size of cannon onboard can also do this. Mapping information concerning the construction of the ship, how and where the cargo was carried and other pertinent data are of historical value to archaeologists as well. In many cases, the most likely area for finding treasure on a wreck is the stern section; most of the treasure onboard Spanish treasure ships was carried there. If the wreck was not badly scattered, mapping can help locate this part of the ship, provided it sank in deep water and has not been disturbed by man or nature over the years.

The method used to map a site depends on many factors including underwater visibility, current, depth and distance from shore. When underwater visibility is good, the sea floor is more or less level, and the wreck is contained in a relatively small area; the grid system commonly used by land archaeologists works well. This system involves marking off and numbering squares, and plotting the squares on a chart. Another less expensive and less time consuming method used in lieu of the grid system establishes a datum point, a point in the center of the wreck. A chain is attached at the datum point and artifacts can then be located by noting the compass bearing on the azimuth circle and measuring the distance from the datum point to the object. This works well on wrecks where the bottom is not uniformly level. If the wreck site is close to shore, the best method is to erect shore mark-

ers and plot the position of the markers on a chart. Compass bearings taken from the shore markers towards the top of the airlift tube when an item is recovered will indicate the position of the item. Another method for a wreck near shore involves plotting the degree of angle between at least three landmarks using a sextant. By taking the water depth and state of tide into con-

Diver using underwater theodolite to map a wreck site.

sideration, how deep the wreck is can also be determined. Mapping a shipwreck site that is scattered over a large area and not close to shore is the most difficult to accomplish. A datum point is usually established with a sextant and good electronic equipment, and then a buoy is placed over the datum point. Two other datum points are established forming a triangle from which to take compass bearings of artifacts found on the site. Bearing should be taken with a surveyor's transit or theodolite, which are more precise than a compass. Divers place buoys over major artifacts and bearings can be taken from shore points. If a site covers a very large area such as several square miles, it is gridded off on the site chart into many sections and a datum point is established in the center of each section as it is excavated. Another method involves using a GPS unit, connected to a laptop computer. This system calculates the latitude and longitude, plots positions and generates maps and dispersion patterns of the shipwreck. By entering the information into the computer the salvor can have instant data showing the exact locations where objects are found, and maps showing areas where excavation has been completed and areas that have been missed. A simple device called a plain table, which is similar to a surveyor's transit, can be used to map a wreck site in clear water. The device has two units: a form of underwater drawing table and a siting mechanism. The siting tube is made of plastic or

metal and is about ten inches long and two inches in diameter. Two wires are stretched at both ends of the tube, crossing each other and resemble a telescope but without magnification. The siting device is mounted on a base plate and a mark is made on the front of the plate corresponding to the line of site of the device. A pipe connected to the bottom of the base plate is fit into a hole in the middle of the drawing table in such a way that it can rotate three hundred sixty degrees (360°). An azimuth circle is then marked off in degrees and attached or painted on the top of the table, and the siting device and base plate are enclosed inside. Underwater photography can be used in mapping a wreck site if visibility is good and the wreck is contained in a small area. Generally the wreck is first marked with a grid system and plotted. A grid frame is then used to hold the camera and photos are taken of each grid square. Photographic mosaics of wreck site where large sections of the ship exist can yield important data for archeologists. Technology such as the Sonic High Accuracy Ranging & Positioning System (SHARPS) provides fast and accurate three-dimensional acoustical mapping of a shipwreck site. Four transceivers are used: three are positioned in a triangular arrangement while a diver holds the fourth. The three stationary transceivers that track the one held by the diver are connected to the surface by a coaxial cable and feed the data into a control unit, which then passes the information into a computer. Each time an artifact is to be plotted, the diver activates a transmitting button, which relays the information to the surface through the other three transceivers. The precise position is recorded with x, y and z coordinates. During this operation a map is traced on a computer screen and stored for later use or printed out on recorder paper.

Marx, Robert F.   Robert F. Marx, the world's preeminent authority on shipwrecks, underwater archaeology and treasure hunting, began his highly successful career early. He started out as a helmet diver at the age of 13 and found his first gold on a California Gold Rush shipwreck two years later. While in the United States Marine Corps, he became the director of the U.S.M.C. Diving School in Vieques Island, Puerto Rico. During the past fifty years, he has worked on shipwrecks and sunken cities in over 60 countries and located more than 2,000 shipwrecks. Throughout his long career, Marx has lived an adventurous and sometimes dangerous life. He has been shipwrecked, left to swim three miles to shore with his wife after having his boat stolen, had his plane sabotaged before takeoff, and been bitten by sharks twice.

In 1960, while living in Seville and researching shipwrecks in the Spanish archives, Marx found more than 15,000 pages dealing with the *Maravillas*—the second-richest Spanish ship lost in the New World—along with a copy of her original manifest. He also came across a book published in Madrid in 1657 by one of the survivors of the shipwreck. The man's account was so vivid that Marx felt as though he had been onboard the *Maravillas* when it wrecked. He was determined to find the galleon, but to that point, almost everyone of note in the treasure hunting business had searched for the *Maravillas* and failed to find her. The *Maravillas* became known as Marx's Phantom Wreck during the next 12 years. In 1962, he co-organized and acted as navigator for the historical re-creation of Columbus's 1492 voyage aboard the *Niña II*, which sailed from Spain to San Salvador.

Two years later, he organized and captained the voyage of a 10th century Gokstad Viking ship in which he was shipwrecked during the maiden voyage. Undaunted, in 1969 aboard the Viking ship he went on to make the voyage from Ireland to Gibraltar. Marx's most important project, though, was excavating the sunken city of Port Royal in Jamaica, which he worked on full-time between 1964 and 1968. The famous pirate haven had fallen into the sea during an earthquake in 1692. Marx recovered over two million artifacts from the sunken city and was able to match artifacts with historical documents about the town, thus proving the city actually existed. In 1972, Marx finally located his Phantom Wreck, the *Maravillas*. He recovered tons of silver bars, thousands of silver coins, gold disks, uncut emeralds and tons of other artifacts. The most stirring find was a silver plate bearing the coat of arms of Dr. Ribadeneyra, author of the book that had led him to begin his search for the treasure galleon. There is a timeworn saying that "treasure is trouble" and the *Maravillas* treasure proved to be no exception. Soon after reaching port, Marx was notified that the Bahamian government had rescinded his salvage permit. When Marx went to Nassau, he learned that news of the find had leaked out and other treasure hunters wanted to cash in. Rumors which inevitably plague any treasure operation were circulating that Marx had found more than five tons of gold, as well as the Golden Madonna and had spirited it all away so as to cheat the Bahamians. No amount of reasoning persuaded the Bahamian officials otherwise. Unable to produce what he had not found, Marx was forbidden to continue work. Not only did he lose his rights to the rest of the treasure, but had to wait four years to get his share of what he had recovered.

Marx has written 52 books and published over 700 scientific reports and popular articles on underwater archaeology. He has lectured professionally for more than 45 years throughout the United States and in 42 foreign countries on the subjects of underwater archaeology, maritime his-

Coauthor Robert F. Marx with 300 pounds of Spanish silver coins found on the *Maravillas* wreck.

tory, treasure hunting and travel. His goal is to educate others on the importance of underwater archaeology and preservation of historical shipwrecks that are being destroyed by dredging and landfill operations, fishing nets, beach restoration, and harbor operations.

McKee, Art   The late Art McKee was one of the first to work on shipwrecks in modern times. As a boy, growing up in New Jersey, he read many stories about sunken treasure. When he graduated, Art decided to become a deep-sea helmet diver. The first job he landed was repairing a bridge. His first discovery of a shipwreck occurred on the next job, where he was hired to retrieve an anchor, and finding old rum bottles and ceramic shards fueled his passion for treasure hunting. In 1934, Art moved to Florida. He took a position as the recreational director for the city of Homestead, which he soon quit, to work as a full-time diver. Art McKee's greatest discovery occurred a short time later when he was hired to work as a diver on a wreck: he found several cannon

Art McKee with the first type of diving helmet used to salvage wrecks in the 1930s.

A diver using an underwater metal detector.

and 1,800 gold doubloons. Unfortunately, he received only his diver's wages and a few token pieces of the treasure.

In 1937, while working on a pipeline job in the Florida Keys, Art discovered an old wreck that produced several artifacts. An old fisherman had told him of a pile of stones with corroded pipes on top, which he soon located and identified as a shipwreck. Art brought up from the wreck several cannon balls, four badly sulfated silver pieces of eight and a gold escudo coin stamped 1721. He later identified the wreck as the *El Rubi*, known as the *Capitana*, the flagship of the 1733 fleet, which sank in a hurricane. Her original cargo consisted of over five million pesos in treasure that had been completely salvaged according to the records. Art McKee and his partners searched the Florida Keys for the next ten years, locating more than 75 shipwrecks, at least 30 of which he was able to identify as cannon wrecks. He watched salvage divers bring up old cannon and anchors to use as scrap metal during World War II. He understood the loss of these historical and archaeological artifacts and data, and attempted to stop the plundering but was unsuccessful. In 1949, Art opened the first public museum in the world devoted entirely to such treasure. Over the years, his quest for sunken treasure took him all over the Caribbean. Many of the salvors active today began their careers by working for Art

and learning the ropes from him.

Merlin The ROV Merlin was a technical marvel when it was completed in 1990 at a cost of more than two million dollars. It contains three video cameras capable of providing 180° of underwater vision, and three 70mm still cameras for taking pictures of artifacts *in situ* which can be digitized and stored in a computer for later mapping of a site. It is equipped with two manipulator arms, suction pumps, water jets to remove bottom sediment and a number of other revolutionary devices. The ROV was designed by Gordon Richardson to work on the Dry Tortugas shipwreck, sister ship of the famed *Atocha*, lying in 1,400 feet of water. With the Merlin, thousands of artifacts were recovered from this 1622 wreck while meeting the most stringent archaeological standards. Even small objects such as pearls and rats' teeth were brought up. Since the Merlin was built, much smaller and less expensive ROVs have been developed and are currently in use for deep-water shipwreck and offshore oil work.

Metal Detector Underwater metal detectors are used by salvors to detect the presence of all metals, both ferrous and nonferrous. A metal detector is usually used on a shipwreck site once its perimeters have been established. It can locate smaller concentrations of coins and other metallic artifacts and treasure. It is also used to locate large objects such as bronze cannon when a subbottom profiler is not employed during the wreck survey. The depth a detector can detect metal depends on the power of the device, the size of the object, and the depth of the object in the sediment or coral. The main dis-

advantage of a metal detector is its depth of penetration. It can detect a cannon—either iron or bronze—only to a depth of eight to ten feet; small individual coins of any metal, only to 15 inches deep.

Metallography Scientists specializing in this field can use atomic absorption spectrography and other means to determine the exact origin of the minerals and metal alloys in metal artifacts or objects such as ore pieces. This will not necessarily establish the nationality of the sunken ship, but can help. Metallography is especially helpful when metal fastenings used in a ship's construction are found, since they were normally manufactured in a shipyard near the source of the raw materials.

Moyana This type of cannon was used on small Spanish vessels. The cannon fired an iron ball weighing from six to ten pounds and remained in use until the beginning of the 19th century.

Muskets Muskets were introduced in 1521 and were the largest guns fired by a single man. Some were as long as ten feet and weighed over 100 pounds. Due to its size and heavy recoil, the musket had to be supported by a yoke-shaped rest. The average size of the ball was one inch in diameter. They gradually decreased in size over the years and by 1690 the average musket was about five feet in length. From

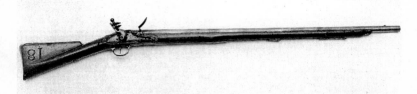

British flint lock musket. *Courtesy of the Metro Museum of Art.*

around 1700 onward, the name "musket" was used to identify any type of firearm shot from the shoulder. The firing mechanisms on muskets, carbines and pistols changed at the same time as those of the harquebuses. In 1517, a German invented the wheel lock that replaced the matchlock. Another improvement on the firing mechanism was introduced around the end of the 16th century when the flintlock superseded the wheel lock. The flintlock remained in continuous use on all firearms until about 1820, when the percussion lock replaced it. Although it was invented near the end of the 16th century, some nations did not use the flintlock for many years. It was not used on a large scale in France until 1670.

N **Navigational Instruments** The navigational instruments used at the time of Columbus consisted of astrolabes and quadrants to establish latitude, nocturnals to establish the approximate time of night, and a compass and dividers to mark off distances on charts. Around the middle of the 16th century, the cross-staff or Jacobstaff came into general use. The sextant was invented simultaneously in 1732 by John Hadley in England and Thomas Godfrey in Philadelphia, but did not come into general use until around 1750. Several brass astrolabes and a number of dividers have been recovered from shipwrecks; however, none of the other instruments mentioned above have been found with the exception of several sextants dating from the 19th century. Quadrants and cross-staves probably have not been found on wreck sites due to the fact that they were made of wood and may

have either floated away or been devoured by seaworms. It is rather strange that nocturnals have not been discovered since they were made of brass. The same applies to compasses whose housings were usually made of lead or other nonmagnetic metals. Establishing the place and date of most

navigational instruments is best left to an expert, since very few reference books on the subject are available to the average underwater explorer. Several astrolabes have been found on shipwreck sites dating from over 100 years prior to the ships being lost. These were most likely handed down from fathers to sons. The majority of all astrolabes found throughout the colonial period were of Portuguese manufacture.

Nemo The manned submersible was designed by the Columbus-America Discovery Group to excavate the S.S. *Central America*. Instead of survey and sampling work, the revolutionary six-ton submersible was designed to

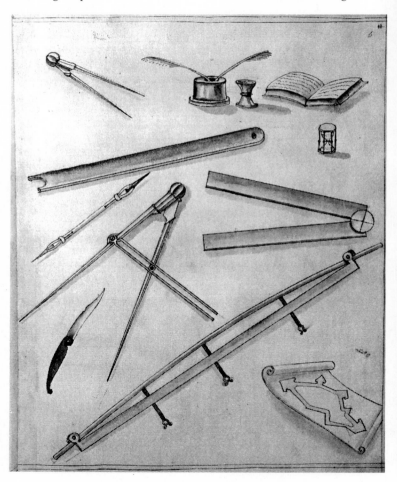

Navigational instruments used aboard ships c. 1500.

perform heavy salvage work on the deep ocean wreck. It is capable of picking up a half-ton anchor or retrieving coins as small as a dime.

Nonferrous Metals Nonferrous metals are always recovered in a far better state of preservation than ferrous metals. Gold is almost always recovered as bright and shiny as the day it was lost and doesn't require any

Silver bar from the *Maravilla* wrecked in 1656.

preservation treatment. Silver is affected to varying degrees underwater, depending on conditions. Silver that has been protected by electrolysis will survive intact sometimes with only a superficial amount of corrosion. When large amounts of silver coins or items are found together, the majority will often be in a very good state of preservation. However, silver coins not protected by electrolysis from other metals, even other silver coins, may be converted to silver sulfide. Pewter is generally found in a good state of preservation with very little cleaning required. Likewise, lead, copper, brass and bronze objects are also affected very little by salt water. Occasionally, though, these metals may be found badly corroded and the only means of preservation is to imbed the object in plastic. Cleaning the various metals requires slightly different processes which are discussed separately in this book.

Olive Jars Olive jars were carried on all Spanish ships and on many ships of other nationalities. They resembled the amphoras of the Greeks and Romans and were used to carry liquids as well as solids. Spanish olive jars were manufactured in Seville and the surrounding countryside and exported all over Europe and to the New World. They were made of the type of clay used in utilityware and usually had a gray exterior. They were often used to smuggle contraband objects such as gold ingots, coins and jewelry. The contraband was placed in the bottom of the jar and covered with molasses or other liquids or solids which customs officials were not likely to want to probe. The approximate date of a vessel can be obtained from its shape and from the maker's mark found on some of them. The maker's initials can be seen on many of the

spanish Olive Jars.

C. 1500 _ 1580.

C. 1580 _ 1780

C 1780 _ 1850

Data used for dating Spanish olive jars.

Large Spanish olive jar recovered from a ship lost in 1571.

necks of olive jars. A maker can be identified by consulting documents in the Notary Archives in Seville.

Organic Artifacts, Preservation Methods Organic materials such as sisal or hemp fibers, beans and pods, tortoise shell, hair, textiles, leather, horn, bone, and paper, will generally disintegrate upon drying if the proper preservation treatment is not employed. Sometimes organic materials such as wood or bone are completely preserved by saturation of iron oxide, which occurred while they were lying close to iron objects under water. They tend to become mineralized and hard in texture.

All items of organic material recovered from salt water must be bathed in fresh water from two to four weeks, depending on its size, to remove all sea salts before preservation treatment can be attempted. If possible, the bath should consist of running water, which will flush away the sea salts as they are leached from the objects. Large items, like wooden ship's timbers, can be placed in a freshwater stream or river, provided the water is not contaminated by industrial waste. If a running-water bath cannot be provided, water should be changed at least daily.

To preserve organic animal materials, they must first be thoroughly dehydrated in successive baths of alcohol to remove all water: the first bath should consist of 40 percent alcohol and 60 percent water; the second of 60 percent alcohol and 40 percent water; the third of 100 percent alcohol. The length of each bath depends on the size of the object. It may take an hour for a small fragment of leather and several hours for a bone object weighing several pounds. Next, the object must be placed in two successive baths of xylene: in the first for a week, and in the second for four weeks. Paraffin chips should be added until a saturated solution of paraffin is obtained. After the object is removed from the second bath and allowed to solidify by air drying, a small amount of paraffin crystals may remain on the exterior. These can be removed by heating the object in an oven at about 500 degrees F until the excess crystals melt off, or by brush-

ing the object with a fine-bristle brush. Very fragile organic animal materials, such as small objects of ivory or horn, which may suffer from treatment in the above manner can be preserved by embedding them in clear plastic blocks after they have been dehydrated.

Organic vegetable materials such as wood, sisal and hemp fibers, textiles, paper, and beans and pods, can also be preserved by the previously described method for organic animal materials. However, there are several other methods that can be used. The alum and glycerin process has been used with good results, especially on wood, because the alum crystallizes and replaces the water in the wood, which prevents it from shrinking or losing its original shape. After all foreign matter has been removed from the object, it is immersed in a boiling solution containing equal parts by weight of alum, glycerin and water. As soon as the object is placed in the bath, the bath is removed from the heat source and allowed to cool slowly. The object should remain in this bath from one to two days, depending on its size. After the object has hardened and been air dried, it should be coated with a solution of 50 percent turpentine and 50 percent linseed oil. The polyethylene glycol process has also proven to be quite successful. The great advantage of this process is that dehydrating the object before it is immersed in its chemical bath is not required. Preservatives are sold commercially under the trade names of Polywax and Carbowax. Polyethylene glycol is a polymer formed by the condensation of ethylene glycol into a wax-like water-soluble preservative. The length of time that the object must remain in the chemical bath varies from four hours to several weeks, depending on the type of Polywax or Carbowax used and the size of the object.

Padrero This type of cannon was occasionally carried on Spanish ships during the 16th and 17th centuries. Very little is known about it. At times, documents mentioned some firing balls of only a few pounds, being small

in size and weight, and at other times they were mentioned as firing 40 pound balls and weighing as much as two tons. The balls were always made of stone regardless.

Paleontology This science can be useful when human bones are found on a wreck. The bones can provide clues about the physical appearance of the people onboard. They can also be

A diver holding human bones found in the sunken city of Port Royal, Jamaica.

studied to determine what diseases the people had before they died. The approximate age and sex of the deceased can also be determine from bones and teeth.

Pasavolante This type of cannon was used on small Spanish vessels. It fired an iron ball weighing between two and 15 pounds and remained in use until the beginning of the 19th century.

Pewter, Identifying There are several different types of markings on pewterware which help identify its origin. The touchmark on all pieces identifies the manufacturer. After admission into the Pewterers' Guild, each pewtermaker was given permission to strike a mark of their own choice on all the pieces they made. Generally these marks were from half an inch to one inch in height. The marks of more than 6,000 English pewtermakers are recorded in a number of excellent books. The majority of marks consist of some type of design such as

Maker's name on a pewter plate identifies place and approximate date of manufacture of the object.

Pewterware recovered from a shipwreck.

a flower, animal or crown with the maker's name or initials around it. Even the place of manufacture is mentioned on many. In addition, many items were stamped with their date of manufacture. The first hallmark denoted the place of manufacture. The second mark consisted of a letter of the alphabet and denoted the year of manufacture. Every 27 years they would start the alphabet over again. The third hallmark denoted the fineness of the metal used in producing the object. The fourth hallmark denoted the identity of the maker and usually consisted of his initials. Many articles of pewterware bear hallmarks similar to those used on gold or silverware. These marks were not authorized by the Pewterers' Guild and were illegally struck by pewtermakers. They were struck in the shapes of shields or cartouches, averaging about three-eighths of an inch in height and were aligned in a straight row, unlike the marks mentioned above. Many books exist to identify the French, Dutch and German manufacturers of pewter and silverware as well as the English.

Pewter, Preservation Methods   If the pewter is recovered without corrosion, water and a mild detergent can be rubbed on it with a soft cloth to remove any black film that may exist on the surface. A paste of water and baking soda can then be used to polish the pewter. If small amounts of corrosion and calcareous deposits exist they can be removed by immersion in a bath consisting of a solution of 20 percent hydrochloric acid and 80 percent fresh water followed by thorough washings in running fresh water, generally for a period of several hours. The surface can then be rubbed gently with fine steel wool to remove the black patina, and the object should again be placed in a bath of running water for several hours. The same paste treatment is then used to restore the piece. Pewter is occasionally found badly corroded and the only means of preservation is to embed the object in plastic. Badly corroded pewter can be cleaned and preserved by the following method. A lye bath is prepared by dissolving a pint of lye in two gallons of boiling fresh water. When the object is placed in the bath, the bath is removed from the heat source and allowed to cool. Generally, a period of ten to 30 minutes is required to remove the corrosion. Caution must be observed to prevent the lye solution from coming in contact with the skin or eyes. The same procedure is then carried out as on pewter objects cleaned by the hydrochloric-acid process. If the object is bent out of its original shape, the best time to restore it is when it is taken out of the lye bath. The metal will be warm and easily reshapable; the reshaping is generally done with a rubber mallet.

Photographic Mosaic   A photographic mosaic of a shipwreck site, especially when it is in a compact area or is one on which some parts of the wooden hull remain, can be useful in trying to determine the type, size and sometimes the nationality of the ship. Experts on older ship construction can deduce a great deal from an accurate photographic record of this type. Mosaics can be made during different phases of the excavation but the most important will be those taken when the site has been completely uncovered and the anchors, cannon, ballast, wood and other remaining features and objects can be seen in relationship to one another.

A fast and efficient method of making a site mosaic and one which is not too expensive is to use a Pegasus, or underwater scooter, with a pulse camera mounted on it. A pulse camera is one that can be set to take photographs automatically at preset intervals. The focal width of the camera lens and the clarity of the water will determine the elevation above the site from which the photographs should be taken and the total number required. A handheld camera can be used to make a mosaic, but the diver must hold the camera at a constant elevation over the site while they swim a straight course. If not, the mosaic will not be accurate and the photographs will be difficult to piece together. If a hand-held camera is used to photograph objects on the bottom at a close range, less than ten feet away, the photographs will have some distortion unless the camera is held exactly vertical over the object. This is no easy feat when a diver is swimming and trying to hold a position. However, by attaching a plumb line with a weight from the side of the camera, the diver can note when the lines stop swinging and almost touches the object, and then shoot.

The following method of creating a mosaic has been successfully used by coauthor Robert Marx on one particular site. The wreck lay on a north-south axis in 30 feet of water and the visibility was about 80 feet. Taut lines were strung out running east and west at an elevation where they almost touched the highest points on the site. The lines were spaced ten feet apart and numbered plastic tags were attached at five-foot intervals along the lines, which allowed each photograph to be identified later. A photographic tower about 15 feet high with a wide-angle lens camera mounted on it was then constructed. From this elevation each photograph shot covered a width of 15 feet and overlapped the grid lines on both the top and bottom of the picture. The tower was moved from position to position, to ensure overlapping. The photographs were then blown up, cropped, and fit together to form the mosaic.

Photography, Underwater Underwater photography had its beginning in 1893 when Louis Bouton, a Frenchman, took the first underwater pictures. Most photography required on a site can be done with the Nikonos, a small, compact underwater 35mm still camera that is used by divers all over the world. On sites where the grid system is employed and the squares are perfectly square, a 35mm camera will not work since the film produces a rectangular negative. Instead, a camera such as a Rolliflex, which produces a perfectly square negative, should be used. A special housing called a Rollimarine is available to enclose this camera. The Rolliflex is a great deal bulkier than the Nikonos and difficult to maneuver underwater. The choice of film depends on light conditions. Black and white film is generally the best for recording or mapping since the cost is far less than color film. Daylight can penetrate clear seawater to great depths and has been known to reflect off the sea floor in 1,600 feet of water. However, even the cleanest seawater appears somewhat cloudy because of suspended plankton or mineral particles. To overcome this cloudy effect, the camera should be used as close as possible to the subject and a wide-angle lens used in most cases. A rule of thumb is that if the underwater visibility is 60 feet, one should not shoot a photograph more than one fourth this distance, or 15 feet from the

subject. The best time to shoot underwater is on a clear, nonwindy day between 10:00 a.m. and 2:00 p.m. when the sunlight most deeply penetrates the water. The blue-green color of the water acts as a filter absorbing colors at the red end of the spectrum. At only ten feet below the surface, red is considerably reduced in intensity. Orange and yellow are the next colors absorbed at greater depths. For black and white photography this is not much of a problem, but in using color film, one should partially compensate for the lack of warm colors by using a red filter over the camera lens. However, the filter is ineffective below 30 feet where red is totally absorbed by the water.

The type of day, angle of the sun, depth of the subject, turbulence of the water, amount of material and type of sea bottom all affect the choice of exposure. Cameras with automatic exposure control are simple to operate, but for better results, an exposure meter should be used. A reading should be taken close to the subject before backing away to snap the picture. It is a good idea to bracket each photograph by taking a shot at a stop slower and one at a stop faster than the meter indicates. Underwater objects appear slightly magnified and seem to be one-fourth closer than their actual distance. This means that a lens of normal focal length will produce a slight telephoto effect underwater. If the camera has a range finder or ground-glass focusing, the correct focusing scale can be set underwater as it is on land. However, in using a camera without a range finder, one must set the focus for about three-fourths the actual distance between the camera and the subject to eliminate the magnification effect underwater.

It may be necessary to use artificial light when visibility is limited. All cameras are adapted for use with either flash bulbs or electronic strobe units. However, the light fall off from artificial lighting underwater is great due to the water density. For all practical purposes, lighting should not be more than 12 feet from the subject. Powerful lighting units that are connected to surface power sources are most effective in such cases. It is also

a very good idea to use an underwater video camera to record the finds *in situ* and the excavation as it progresses.

Pistols Pistols were first used in England in 1521 and in most other European countries soon afterward. They were actually a smaller version of the harquebus and were lighter and easier to handle. They were primarily invented to be used by men on horseback who only had one free hand but became standard equipment for all officers aboard ships by the middle of the 16th century. The firing mechanisms on pistols, muskets and carbines changed at the same time as those of the harquebuses. In 1517, a German invented the wheel lock that replaced the matchlock. Another improvement on the firing mechanism was introduced around the end of the 16th century when the flintlock superseded the wheel lock. The flintlock remained in continuous use on all firearms until around 1820, when the percussion lock replaced it. Although it was invented near the end of the 16th century, some nations did not use the flintlock for many years. It was not used on a large scale in France until 1670.

Early 17th century flintlock Spanish pistol. *Courtesy of the Metro Museum of Art.*

Pneumatic Hammers A pneumatic hammer is used to chop through coral growth and free artifacts. The large pneumatic hammer is used to recover cannon and anchors. The medium hammer—only 12 inches long with a cutting chisel six inches long and two inches wide—is used to excavate basketball size chunks of coral. The smallest hammer, which has a chisel four inches long and three-fourths of an inch wide, is used for excavating fragile items such as glass and wine bottles, and small artifacts like brass medallions and crucifixes. When possible, conglomerates should be X-rayed before being broken apart to prevent any fragile objects from being damaged.

Porcelain   Large amounts of porcelain have been found on many different shipwrecks and most pieces can be identified and dated fairly accurately. Porcelain has the distinct feature of being translucent, unlike pottery which is opaque. All porcelain found on a 16th century shipwreck and the majority found on 17th century wrecks are of Chinese or Japanese manufacture. Some pieces bear marks of the province in which they were made in addition to the name of the reigning ruler of the country at the time. The first exact date or place where porcelain was manufactured in Europe is not known. However, it is believed to have been in Florence around the close of the 16th century where it was produced on a small scale and not for export. The English first began producing small amounts of porcelain about 1745. The Dutch began a few years later. Most of these pieces bear manufacturer's marks, making it possible to establish the date and place of manufacture. Most of the other European nations and the United States did not begin manufacturing porcelain until the 19th century. Due to porcelain's fragile nature and the many shallow-water wreck sites which are buffeted by wind, waves and currents, a salvor is more likely to find small fragments

Ming dynasty Chinese porcelain plate.

or shards of porcelain instead of intact pieces.

Porcelain, Preservation Methods
Of the different types of ceramics found on shipwrecks, porcelain survives the best, although the glazed exterior may have eroded. Because of its nonporous surface, porcelain is rarely found with any calcareous marine growth adhering to it. If there is growth found, it can be removed by gently tapping with a rubber tool or by bathing it in a ten percent solution of nitric acid. Iron or lead oxide stains can be removed by a bath in a five percent solution of sulfuric acid. If both calcareous deposits and oxide stains are present, the sulfuric-acid bath will remove both. The porcelain should be thoroughly washed in fresh water afterwards to remove all traces of alkalis.

Pottery, Preservation Methods
Glazed pottery survives much better than unglazed pottery due to its waterproof vitreous layer. If the glazed layer is incomplete or imperfect, soluble salts may have entered the body of the ware and crystallized. This process will result in the formation of efflorescence and the glaze may flake off. If the glazed layer on the piece is intact, the methods used on porcelain to remove calcareous deposits and oxide stains can be used here. If the glaze is not intact or if flaking is present, which occurs with many delftware items, acid should not be used to remove deposits or stains. Instead, the pieces should be thoroughly bathed in fresh water to remove sea salts, then air dried and coated with several layers of clear plastic or lacquer spray. Repairing or piecing together all types of ceramics is relatively simple. The joints should be cleared of any foreign bodies and the pieces then cemented together with Durofix or Elmer's Glue. The pieces should be held in place by tape or placed in a sandbox while the glue is drying.

Precious Stones, Preservation Methods   Hard gemstones such as sapphires, rubies and emeralds, and some semiprecious stones such as agate, do not suffer from immersion in

Gold kris handle with many precious stones. They were usually brought over on the Manila galleons.

salt water and are recovered in their natural state. Softer stones such as beryl are sometimes found scratched, due to the abrasive action of sand and other materials moving against them underwater. These scratches should be removed only by lapidary treatment.

Probe, Air   An air probe is used to search for a wreck when it is buried under more than four feet of compact sand or where the mud is hard and difficult to penetrate with a metal probe. Usually a 20 foot length of one-inch diameter galvanized iron water pipe is used. A hose connected to a surface air compressor is attached to the end, and sends down a continuous stream of air. This blows away the sand or mud around the mouth of the pipe and facilitates penetration into the sea floor. When a solid object is encountered, the sound of the contact can give a clue as to what the object is. Measuring the rod left above the seafloor will then give the depth of the object. The air probe is easily removed because of the compressed air blowing outward from the bottom of the pipe.

Probe, Metal   The metal probe is used to determine the perimeters and depth of a wreck site when it is located in very soft sand, silt or mud. A long iron rod, a quarter inch thick with a wooden handle, is driven into the sea floor until an object is struck. This method of determining site perimeters was used during the excavation of the sunken city of Port Royal, Jamaica, by coauthor Marx.

Prop-wash   The prop-wash, also called a "blaster" or "mail box," was invented in the early 20th century to blow away sediment covering oyster beds in the Chesapeake Bay. In 1962, salvors found that it was an effective excavation tool when working in murky water as it pushed clear water from the surface down to the seafloor. A prop-wash consists of an elbow-shaped metal tube several inches larger in diameter than the vessel's propeller diameter. It is attached to the transom of the salvage vessel so that the wash of the propeller is forced into the tube and deflected downward to the seafloor. Four anchors must be put out to hold the salvage vessel in place when the prop-wash is being used. Generally, the upper end of the tube is attached from one to three feet behind the propeller and a wire-mesh cage covers the propeller areas to prevent divers from being cut. On twin-screw vessels two prop-washes can be used side by side. Using twin screws creates a whirlpool action that forces water to the bottom at a high velocity and blasts away the sediment at a rapid rate. It is powerful enough to cut through coquina, a type of limestone coral growth, almost as fast as through sand. Once artifacts are reached under the seafloor, the prop-wash is stopped and other excavation methods are used, such as hand fanning or employing a small airlift, to avoid valuable and delicate artifacts and treasure being swept away.

The effective depth of a prop-wash depends on the size of the prop-wash tube and the highest velocity at which the vessel's propeller turns. A small prop-wash, such as that on an outboard engine, is effective to approximately 15 feet. A small prop-wash is only effective on a shallow-water site with a sandy bottom. A prop-wash with a propeller of two-thirds of a foot in diameter may be used up to 35 feet.

A view of the prop-wash before it is lowered and attached to the propeller.

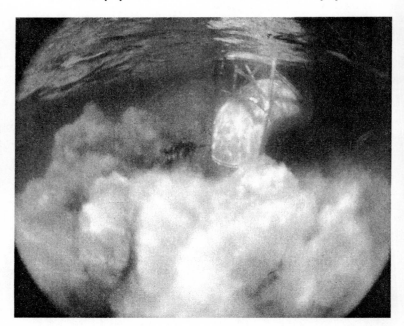

Prop-wash blowing away sand covering a shipwreck.

A propeller measuring a foot in diameter can be effective up to 50 feet. A prop-wash of two to three feet can excavate a hole 20 feet across and 15 feet deep in a few minutes. A larger prop-wash can excavate a hole 50 feet in diameter and 20 feet deep in the same period of time. The major disadvantage of using a prop-wash is that sediment is thrown or blasted over unexcavated areas, and may have to be removed later. The secret in using a prop-wash is being able to control its speed and knowing when to slow it down as the level of the wreck is reached.

Prop-wash, Hand-Held A hand-held "blaster" works at any depth a diver can reach. It is effective in depths greater than 50 feet, in digging in shallow water where there is deep sand and an airlift is not effective, and in areas where a salvage vessel can't approach. It can be constructed using a two-foot diameter piece of thick PVC pipe, four-foot long. It has two propellers, one pointing downward and another facing upward, and this prevents countertorque and counterthrust, enabling the diver to have fingertip control of the unit without having to fight the power of the blaster. It runs on hydraulic fluid circulated through two hoses connected to the middle of the blaster and to an oil reservoir and the engine on the boat. The blaster is given neutral buoyancy on the bottom by filling two small ballast cylinders with just the right amount of air from whatever breathing source the operator is using at the time. With this device, a diver can lie on the bottom and use one hand to control the blaster and the other to pick up artifacts

ROV armed with lights, cameras, suction pumps and manipulator arms.

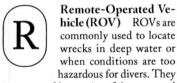 **Remote-Operated Vehicle (ROV)** ROVs are commonly used to locate wrecks in deep water or when conditions are too hazardous for divers. They are powered by a series of thrusters and carry low-light color television and still cameras. The units are connected to the surface by an umbilical cable which provides power and transmits commands down, and relays video images up to screens and recorders. The operator faces the video screen and controls the movements of the ROV and cameras by manipulating several joysticks. Many models come equipped with manipulator arms for picking up samples from the seafloor. ROV technology has advanced to include a model that is equipped with an integrated side-scan sonar and low-light level video camera that permits the operator to confirm sonar targets visually. This vehicle, which can also carry still cameras, a subbottom profiler sensor, and a magnetometer, operates at depths of up to 1,000 feet. A transponder beacon can also be attached to the

unit and dropped on a target. One of the most famous ROVs in shipwreck exploration was Jason Junior, used by Robert Ballard to explore and film the *Titanic* wreckage.

 Sakers This type of cannon fires balls weighing from five to ten pounds and is from five to eight feet in length and weighs between 3,000 and 4,000 pounds.

Scott, Norman Unlike most of the underwater explorers in this book, Norman Scott didn't have childhood dreams of becoming a famous underwater adventurer. In fact, his goal was to become a rich businessman, but within seconds of making his first dive on a coral reef in the crystal clear waters of the Virgin Islands, his plans changed. He lived around Richmond, Virginia most of his early life and graduated from the University of Virginia in 1952. He majored in economics but went on to start a business constructing and repairing swimming pools in the Washington, D.C. area.

The sport of skin diving fascinated him and in 1955 he took a vacation to St. Croix, where he fell in love with the underwater world. Like most divers, he was mainly interested in col-

lecting shells and coral, spearfishing and underwater photography. He returned to the Caribbean every chance he had. During a trip in 1956, while diving off St. John Island, he accidentally located a late 19th century shipwreck and recovered a collection of brass fittings, spikes and several portholes. This sparked his interest in old shipwrecks and when he returned home he read everything he could on the subject. The following year, after undertaking some serious research, he dove off Tortola, in the British Virgin Islands and discovered 11 Spanish silver coins. This persuaded him to become a professional treasure hunter with his own boat and salvage equipment.

His first serious expedition was not a stunning success, but he learned a great deal from it. He received permission from the Jamaican government to excavate part of the sunken city of Port Royal. He undertook the excavation even though the government was to receive everything he recovered. Unfortunately, the area that the Jamaican government authorized him to excavate was on the outer fringes of one of the least important areas of the sunken city. Two weeks of excavation produced very little and he returned home disheartened by the outcome of the expedition. His next

Norman Scott in the foreground aboard his salvage vessel in the Bahamas.

expedition to the Sacred Cenote of Chichén Itzá was a huge success. After selling his business in 1962, Scott headed to the Virgin Islands after hearing a legend concerning a French pirate who allegedly had hidden "millions in treasure" in a series of caves located near the islands. While exploring the caves, one of Scott's divers almost lost his life. A landslide of large rocks fell, blocking the entrance to the submerged cave, trapping the man. The diver managed to escape with only a few minutes of air remaining in his tank. This expedition taught Scott never to go after any treasure based on legends unless backed by substantial historical documents.

After returning home, he formed Expeditions Unlimited and began searching for a means to finance future projects. Texas millionaire F. Kirk Johnson financed all of Scott's expeditions from then until the millionaire's untimely death in 1968. His next project was the *Genovesa*, a Spanish galleon wrecked on Banner's Reef, off the south coast of Jamaica, which still had at least a half a million pesos in treasure left after being salvaged by contemporary salvors. The expedition was fruitless. Scott continued to dive on various wrecks including a wreck on Pedro Shoals which produced thousands of artifacts from a

merchant ship including: ivory combs, weapons, cannon and musket balls, brass navigational dividers, needles, knives, pewterware and ceramicware, but not one piece of treasure.

Norman Scott was followed by a string of unfortunate events over the years, including problems with his vessels and accidents to his divers with very little to show for it. He did continue to have finds, however. His biggest occurred in 1968, not in the Atlantic, but when he returned to the Sacred Cenote of Chichén Itzá. There he recovered more than 6000 important artifacts and items of treasure, including two intact ornate wooden stools, the first pieces of Mayan furniture ever discovered.

Shark Dart   Divers use the shark dart to ward off threatening sharks. It was invented in 1971 by a scientist at the Naval Undersea Research and Development Center in San Diego. The instrument fires a blast of carbon dioxide into the shark's flesh, which leaves it floating, belly up. The shark dart is silent and doesn't cause any bleeding, unlike other instruments used for the same purpose. Although the dart is not meant to harm the shark, it can kill if it penetrates the inner cavity of the shark's body.

Ships, Dating   Carbon dating can be used to date such materials as wood, bone, charcoal, peat, shell and plant, but it has certain disadvantages when dating wood. Many branches of science can help in dating ships, although sometimes more indirectly than directly. Dendrologists, scientists who study trees, can be helpful in establishing the origin of wood found on the shipwreck. Botany is another science that can be used to identify the origin of vegetable material found on a site. Zoologists can be helpful in identifying bones of animals, birds and fish. When large numbers of human bones are found on a shipwreck, it may indicate that either there was a sea battle or the ship sank in a storm. Paleontologists can be of particular assistance here. Geologists can help to establish the source of ballast rock found on a shipwreck in some cases, though there are always exceptions to this rule. Scientists specializing in metallurgy can determine, through microscopic study and other means, the exact origin of minerals and alloys used in metallic artifacts. This may not necessarily identify the particular nationality of a wreck but will give the precise origin of the metallic objects carried on it. Where metal fastenings were used in the construction of the ship's hull, information regarding them is especially useful, since these fittings were probably manufactured near the source of the minerals of which they are composed. Dr. Robert Brill developed a method of precisely determining the length of time glass has been under the sea, by counting the number of layers of weathered crust on the glass. Thermoluminescence and archaeomagnetic dating can be helpful in determining the dates of ceramic materials such as tableware and building bricks.

Ships, Identifying   There are many problems associated with identifying a shipwreck and its artifacts and cargo. Some items can't be positively identified because not enough is known about them, nothing has been published on them or because there are no experts on such subjects. Contamination of artifacts in the years following a shipwreck is always possible. Items

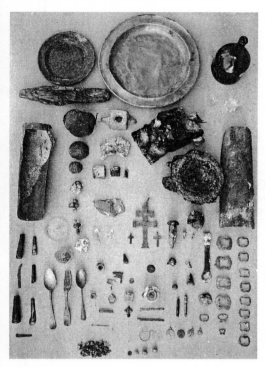

Artifacts recovered from a Spanish merchant ship lost in 1741.

from various wrecks that were lost in the same area may be mixed in with one another as well. Articles thrown off a passing ship or from a ship salvaging the shipwreck may also contaminate a site. Dredging operations, fishing and relocating beaches have also contaminated many shipwrecks. Besides contamination many sites have

Diver examining the keel of a Spanish ship lost in 1571.

items predating the period of the shipwreck. From reading old documents, coauthor Marx has found many instances in which items carried on ships were much older than the ships and men sailing them. In one instance a captain reported in 1682 that because he was unable to procure the required number of cannon for his voyage to Mexico, he had hired divers to recover several from a shipwreck in Cadiz Bay dating from the mid–16th century.

Establishing the nationality of a shipwreck from its cargo is often impossible. The majority of cargoes brought from Spain to the New World were manufactured in many different countries. This also applies to ships of other nationalities. Even during times of war, when the rulers prohibited trade between their subjects and the enemy, commerce continued as usual, sometimes through merchants of neutral countries acting as middlemen. Many ships of different nations sailing from Europe to the New World made it a practice to stop at one of the Canary Islands to take on fresh water and victuals before making the long ocean crossing. Since they often purchased Spanish wine and other spirits, it would not be unusual to find large numbers of Spanish jars in which such liquids were carried on non–Spanish ships. The highly prized swords made in Toledo and other items manufactured in Spain were also

available in the Canaries. Ships of all nations returning from the Western Hemisphere to Europe also carried goods from various countries. Items such as navigational equipment might be carried throughout the life of the ship, whereas other items might be obtained by trade in ports it visited. Items were also obtained when one ship captured another. Discovering Spanish specie or bullion on a shipwreck cannot identify it as Spanish either. Spanish coinage was the chief currency circulated by European nations with settlements in the New World. In fact, it circulated around the globe and was legal tender in the United States into the late 19th century. It was widely circulated because of the vast amount of silver and gold mined and minted by the Spaniards and the scarcity of these precious metals in all the other European nations.

Ships, Determining Size and Nationality   The table on page 40 can aid in establishing both the size and draft of a ship, and even help in identifying any ship in use throughout the world between 1500 and 1820. It was devised by coauthor Robert F. Marx, after studying hundreds of documents concerning size and tonnage of ships of different types and nationalities.

The salvor may know from documentary sources that the ship they have located was 500 tons. With this information it can be determined that the length of the keel should be about 92 feet. The information in the table can also be used in reverse. If the salvor discovers that the keel length was 120 feet, this would indicate that the ship was 1,400 to 1,500 tons.

Establishing the nationality of a ship from a visual inspection of the remains is difficult for many reasons. Ships were subject to a change of flag throughout the colonial era when European nations in varying patterns of alliances were almost constantly at war with one another. As a result of conflicts, privateering and piracy, a ship built in Spain may have been captured by French corsairs and then in turn lost to English privateers. Captured ships were used in navies and merchant fleets, while others were bought

Tonnage	Length of keel (in ft.)	Width of beam (in ft.)	Draft (in ft.)
100	52	19	7 ½
200	66	24	9 ½
300	76	27 ⅓	10 ½
400	84	30	12
500	92	33	13
600	98	35	14
700	102	36 ¾	14 ⅝
800	104	37 ½	15
900	107 ½	38 ½	15 ¼
1,000	109	39 ⅓	15
1,100	110	40	15 ½
1,400–1,500	120	44	16
1,600	132	48	16
2,000	152	60	18

or hired from different nations. A scarcity of Spanish shipping in 1593 caused the king to seize all foreign ships in Spanish ports so that a full fleet could sail on schedule to the New World. Of the 62 ships in this fleet, only 14 were Spanish-built. The others came from 12 nations, including Greece and Sweden. On almost all shallow-water sites very little of the shipwreck remains which can aid in establishing the place where it was constructed. Even if the origin of the ship can be established, it would not indicate the nationality of the ship at the time it was lost. The spikes, nails, tacks and other metal fastenings found in association with a shipwreck are of little use in identifying a ship's date or nationality since the shapes and sizes changed very little over the centuries. The only change that occurred in treenails or wooden pegs over the centuries was the method in which they were produced. Before 1825, treenails were shaped by hand. After 1825, they were turned on a lathe. The type of wood used to construct a ship also provides very few clues for a salvor: it was only what was available at the time. The earliest mention of a ship built in Europe using teakwood was in 1821. Honduras was the major source of mahogany in the old days, thus a ship built with mahogany planking may have been built nearby.

Preventing boring of the teredo and the accumulation of barnacles on the hulls was a constant problem. One method used by most European nations was to careen the ship and burn the bottom. A number of protective compounds, basically consisting of a tar and pitch base, were then applied to the hull. The Spaniards generally used a mixture of tar and lime. Some Spanish ships in the 18th century used a layer of wooden sheathing, then placed a compound of tar and animal hair between the sheathing and hull. The English used too many different mixtures to enumerate here. In 1745, the mix consisted of 100 parts of pitch, 30 parts of brimstone and 35 parts of brick or marble dust. The earliest mention of Spanish ships sheathed in lead dates to 1508. This practice was continued until 1567 when the king ordered it to cease, claiming that the added weight caused the ships to sail too slowly. In 1605, lead sheathing was again applied to Spanish ships sailing to the New World, but only to those traveling to Mexico. Those going to other Spanish settlements were still forbidden to use it. The only other nation to use lead sheathing was England, and only on a small scale. It was used mainly as an experiment on its warships in the Caribbean during different periods. There is a brief mention in 1735, of 20 sheathed English warships, but the material used was not mentioned. In 1766, several English warships were sheathed with copper. By 1780, all English ships were sheathed in copper, including both naval and merchant. The first French ships to use copper sheathing sailed in 1775. The Spaniards and Portuguese did not use copper sheathing until the first decade of the 19th century.

The majority of masts, yards, spars and rigging used on all ships came from the Baltic region. The shapes differed so little over the years that they cannot aid in identifying a ship's nationality or age. However, the dimensions can aid in determining the size of a ship.

Ships, Determining Types Sometimes, a shipwreck can be identified by establishing the size of the vessel and the objects found on it but caution must be exercised since there are many exceptions to confuse a salvor. Small caravels and pinnaces used by early explorers should be fairly easy to identify by the cannon they carried, as they differed a great deal in size and construction from all types on later period

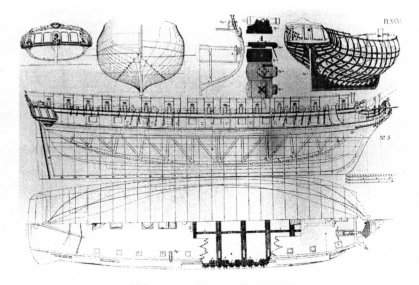

Mid-seventeenth century Spanish galleon.

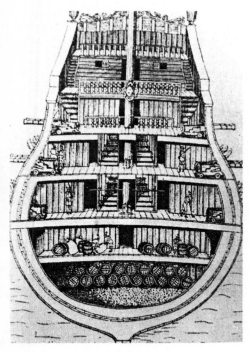

Cross-section of a Spanish warship c. 1650.

ships. Because of the risk involved in sailing in uncharted waters, the officers and crew usually avoided bringing such valuable items as silverware or glassware. Instead they ate and drank from wooden or ceramic objects. An exception occurred when one of these ships carried colonists or government officials to a newly settled area, in which case they brought all their possessions with them. Such a ship also carried agricultural, mining, masonry and carpentry tools. These items should enable the salvor to differentiate between an exploratory vessel and one transporting colonists. If any treasure is found on one of the early shipwrecks which was homeward bound, it will most likely be gold or silver of an unrefined and unminted nature or items manufactured by Indians.

Advice boats, mail boats and even reconnaissance boats for that matter, are very similar in appearance under water. Unlike the early exploratory or colonizing vessels, these carried more armament, which aids in identification. They were not armed to fight large vessels but rather to repel ships their own size and smaller ones that might overtake them. Their lightness and construction enabled them to outrun larger vessels. Since these vessels had to be light to maintain speed, they rarely carried any cargo at all. On occasion, advice boats returning to Spain carried small amounts of treasure to drop off at places along the way to pay officials or garrisons. Sometimes, too, they carried it to a hard-pressed Spanish king to tide him over until the treasure fleets arrived. Small pirate and privateering vessels also fit this description and are difficult to positively identify.

Salvage vessels also carried a substantial amount of armament to protect treasure they might have recovered. Finding diving bells or any of the many instruments used in early salvage operations might aid the modern-day salvor in identifying the type of ship they have located. If the early salvors were successful, a diversified cargo of treasure and artifacts might also be found on such a wreck. Because of the constant shortage of artillery throughout the Western Hemisphere during this period, very few small trading vessels carried any. If they did, the pieces were rarely ever larger than swivel guns, used for repelling boarders. Since this lack of armament and slow speeds from the weight of their cargoes made trading vessels vulnerable to attack by all other shipping, they sailed only when it was safe. Even when they did sail, they usually carried cargoes of relatively little value because of the risk of capture involved. Small Spanish vessels were forbidden by the crown from carrying any treasure; however, documents telling of many lost with treasure aboard reveal that this rule was not always strictly enforced. These small trading vessels were occasionally used to carry large amounts of treasure, but only when they were guarded by armed galleys or other warships.

The gold and emeralds that were sent annually from Bogota to Cartagena for transshipment to Spain were brought down the Magdalena River in small vessels, which then sailed along the coast to Cartegena. When the Chagres River was used to transport the treasure by raft from the Pacific to the Caribbean side of the isthmus, small trading ships carried the treasure from the mouth of the river to Nombre de Dios or Porto Bello. Virtually all nonprecious cargoes, such as lumber and agricultural products that these small ships carried, would have disappeared long ago from a shipwreck with few traces remaining, especially if the ship carried no armament or ballast. The cargoes on many of the larger merchant ships that wrecked on their way back to Europe suffered the same fate over the years, since they were comprised of perishable products such as tobacco, cocoa, sugar, rum, cotton, drugs, indigo, cochineal and lumber.

Finding a shipwreck that fits this description could lead a salvor to mistakenly think that they have found a ship which sailed without cargo, since only shipboard items—cannon, anchors, weapons, and cooking and eating utensils—would be found. However, when no trace of cargo, colonists or treasure is found on a wreck, the ship was most likely a warship. Generally, warships of all nations were forbidden to carry cargo of any description, and the scarcity of artifacts normally found on merchantmen will aid in identifying a wreck as a warship. In most cases, it is impossible to distinguish between a Spanish treasure galleon sailing from Europe or a New World port, and a warship. Neither would be carrying cargo and both would be carrying large numbers of cannon and hand weapons. Since mercury was occasionally shipped from Spain to the New World on treasure galleons, discovery of this on a wreck site would normally identify it as a treasure galleon arriving from Spain. British warships are easily identifiable because of the broad-arrow mark on many objects found on shipwrecks of this type. These arrows have been found on cannon, weapons, copper sheathing, cutlery, bottles and many other articles. The origin of the mark is obscure, but was in regular use by the second half of the 16th century to denote all crown property and continued until the end of the 19th century. Finding a few items with the broad arrow on a shipwreck will certainly indicate that the items once belonged to the British admiralty, but not necessarily that the shipwreck is British. Items marked with the broad arrow were found not only on several of the 1715 Spanish shipwrecks but also on wrecks that proved to be non–British.

Slave ships sailing to and from the New World are usually identified by the equipment found on them. A slave ship found near Panama contained hundreds of leg and arm bracelets attached to chains, used on the human cargoes these ships carried. Because every inch of the ship was used to carry slaves and water and victuals to maintain them, most ships of this type carried only a few cannon. Other than slaves, these ships also carried ivory and gold dust obtained on the African coast. After selling the slaves on the western side of the Atlantic, the ships returned to Europe with gold and silver specie or bullion received as payment.

Shipwreck Laws   All but 21 nations throughout the world have specific laws concerning shipwrecks. Up until 1981 in the United States, 27 states had laws concerning the laying of claims to sunken historical sites, but they differed widely from state to state. In 1981, these laws were challenged in the Supreme Court by Mel Fisher, a Florida treasure hunter, and states lost the rights to shipwrecks. Federal laws give the federal government control over natural resources within the 200-mile limit except for State ownership of resources within the coastal three-mile area. However, these laws do not cover shipwrecks or other man-made objects. Until recently, in the absence of a law recognizing the special nature of ancient shipwrecks, these sites were covered by the "finders-keepers" principle that applies to modern wrecked and abandoned commercial vessels. It meant that federal admiralty law took precedence over state laws.

During the next seven years, Congress labored over the passage of a new law granting states the right to jurisdiction over all shipwrecks 100 years old or older within three miles of the coast. The "Abandoned Shipwreck Act of 1987" was signed and went into effect on April 28, 1988. The new law covers five to ten percent of the estimated 50,000 shipwrecks inside the three-mile limit. Other shipwrecks, both within and outside this limit, continue to be covered by federal admiralty law. The shipwrecks affected by the new law are: (a) those defined as historical abandoned shipwrecks that are substantially buried in submerged state beds; (b) those held in coral formation; and (c) wrecks listed in the National Register of Historic Places (fewer than 100 are currently designated).

Each state has the right to determine how recovered artifacts and treasure are to be divided and to establish guidelines for search and excavation of shipwrecks. Some states have very different laws pertaining to salvaging shipwrecks. Many other countries also claim ownership of the shipwrecks in waters anywhere from three to 200 miles offshore and their laws vary a great deal as well. Some nations even have severe penalties for diving on wrecks under their jurisdiction. The Bahamas is one of the easiest foreign countries in which to obtain a salvage permit. A permit is not required for search activities and they abide by the customary 75/25 split of treasure and artifacts. Some nations are not content with claiming shipwrecks located in their own territorial waters. The Netherlands has laid claim to all its historical Dutch East Indiamen wrecks worldwide and has successfully defended this assertion in the International Court.

Silver, Preservation Methods   On some occasions, when large amounts of silver coins or items are found together, the majority will be in a very good state of preservation with only a black silver-sulfide patina on them. This can be cleaned by rubbing with a paste of baking soda and water. When silver has been protected by electroly-

sis it will survive intact, sometimes with only a superficial amount of corrosion which can be removed by various methods. The silver can be cleaned in an electrochemical bath, as is used for preserving ferrous metals.

Another method is electrolytic reduction. The semicorroded silver object is made the negative electrode (cathode) and is placed between two plates of sheet iron (acting as the positive electrode or anode) in a glass or plastic container filled with water and a five percent amount of caustic soda, which acts as the electrolyte. Electrical current, generally from a six- or 12-volt battery, is also required. The object is connected by copper wire to the negative pole of the battery. The iron anodes are connected to the positive pole through an ammeter and adjustable resistance unit. When current passes into the bath, hydrogen is evolved at the cathode, with the result that the corrosion is gradually reduced. As the reduction progresses, chlorides are transferred from the cathode to the iron anode. The length of the process depends on the amount of corrosion on the object. The object should be removed and inspected periodically until all corrosion has been removed. When this has been completed, there will be a smaller layer of insoluble oxides and metallic powder on the object. These can be removed by brushing under running water. The silver can then be rubbed with a paste of baking soda and water.

A silver coin lying on the sea floor and not protected by electrolysis from other metals, even other silver coins, may be converted to silver sulfide. When this occurs, it may weigh as little as one-fifth its original weight and may be two or three times its original thickness. Caution must be exercised in handling silver in this fragile condition, as it will easily disintegrate into powder form. Nothing can be done to preserve it other than casting it in plastic.

Site Lease   Depending on the country or site where the shipwreck is located, a search lease may be required before a salvor can begin surveying a wreck site. After a wreck is located, a

An electrochemical reduction bath used to remove corrosion from metallic objects.

Coauthor Robert F. Marx, on the right, and Dr. Harold Edgerton holding the sensor head of a side-scan sonar.

salvage lease gives the salvor permission to excavate the wreck and provides for a division of the recovered artifacts between the salvor and the state or country claiming ownership of the shipwreck. Most countries and states require a bond be put up to insure that the salvors abide by the lease requirements and doesn't run off with the treasure recovered.

Site Survey A site survey allows the salvor to judge whether the excavation of a shipwreck is economical or realistic. It will also indicate the best excavation techniques, equipment and tools, along with the best area to begin excavation. A site survey may include digging test holes or using probes to determine the depth, perimeters and type of bottom sediment covering a shipwreck.

Snuff Boxes Snuff came into general use in the 1700s. The discovery of snuffboxes on a wreck would date it from that time on.

Sonar, Hand-Held The hand-held sonar unit, which is no larger than an underwater camera, can locate objects up to 200 feet away. The device is used once a target area has been chosen and the underwater visibility is poor. A diver descends to an area where a buoy marks a spot worth examining closely. They sweep the surrounding area in a 360° circle until the sonar unit emits a beep, which indicates the direction of an object protruding above the sea floor. The closer they get to the object, the stronger the beep. Some models have an illuminated scope to show the distance between the target and the diver.

Sonar, Side-scan Side-scan sonar is mainly used for ships lost in water deeper than 100 feet since most remains of such a ship will be lying on the sea floor and not buried under bottom sediment. All the major deep-water discoveries such as H.M.S. *Edinburgh* and the S.S. *Central America* were found with side-scan sonar. However, exceptions occur that may make this type of sonar useful for shallow-water shipwrecks. When the *Atocha* was found, it was described as a "reef of silver bars" sticking up above the seafloor. The *Atocha* might have been found years earlier if side-scan sonar had been used.

Side-scan sonar operates on the same principle as the echo finder except that the sonic signal is directed obliquely toward the bottom. The instrument sends out a sound, called a "ping," and then counts how long it takes for the sound to hit the bottom of the sea and bounce back. The depths of the ocean floor are recorded on graph paper as the ship moves through the water. The result is a map of the sea floor. A sensitive side-scan sonar unit can cover an area 1,200 feet wide on each pass over deep water if the bottom is flat or gen-

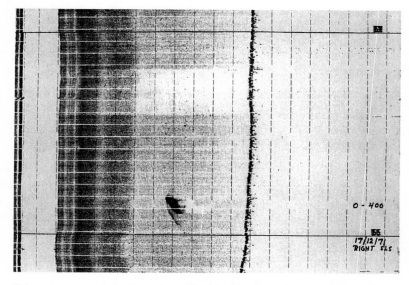

Side-scan sonar graph showing an intact Spanish galleon located in over 3,000 feet of water.

tly sloping. Up to 500 feet can be covered in depths of less than 50 feet. Thus, if a boat is moving at ten knots, one square mile of sea floor can be covered in a little over an hour. Unlike visual search systems, which are affected by bad weather, dirty water and darkness, side-scan sonar can be operated regardless of conditions and around the clock and cover large areas in a short period of time. New sophisticated units produce images of targets so clearly they appear like photographs.

Sonar, Sub-bottom Profiler The subbottom profiler is a special sonar instrument used to locate shipwrecks buried under mud or silt which have no ferrous material on them and can't be located with a magnetometer. The profiler must pass directly over a buried object to detect it. It has been used to pinpoint many wrecks when the approximate location has been determined and no other way to locate the wreck exists. Using a profiler to search for shipwrecks buried in sand has limitations. It can only penetrate to a depth of ten feet in coarse, compact sand. The profiler is also useless when a wreck is covered in coral. Prior to his death, Dr. Harold Edgerton was developing a profiler designed for use in deep sand. It is hoped that someone will continue this important work.

The subbottom profiler works on the same principle as other types of sonar, except that by using a lower frequency signal it can penetrate through sediment on the ocean floor. The profiler produces a three-dimensional seismic sonar profile that shows the object's size and shape and how deep it is buried. It also indicates the depth of water, the thickness and types of matter lying in the sediment and on the bedrock. Klein Microprofiler has developed an extremely efficient high-resolution profiler, which is superior to similar instruments available to the wreck hunter. By using a much higher frequency, a narrower beam and shorter pulses, and by having the sensor head towed close to the bottom, it produces a more sharply detailed outline of the seafloor topography and objects hidden in the sediment. Subtle features, such as bronze cannon, which are barely distinguishable from other bottom features on other profilers, are more clearly defined and identifiable with this subbottom profiler.

The subbottom profiler was an extremely valuable tool used to map the famous sunken city of Port Royal, Jamaica. With the aid of several draftsmen, hundreds of feet of sonar-recording paper was used to produce four large charts covering the entire site and showing the precise positions of hundreds of walls of the old buildings as well as of several shipwrecks.

Submanaut The Submanaut, a submersible vehicle, was built in 1956. It was designed to operate at 2,500 feet but installation of a three-inch window for photography decreased this depth to 600 feet. The Submanaut was used to shoot underwater movies and was featured in the movie *Around the World Undersea.*

Submersible Vehicle, Manned These vehicles have been used successfully on several deep water archaeological sites. Their cost is prohibitive, however, and they require a tremendous amount of maintenance.

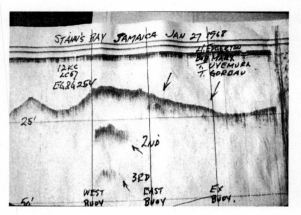

Sonar graph showing the remains of one of Columbus's ships in St. Ann's Bay, Jamaica.

A two-man submersible used by coauthor Robert F. Marx to explore deep-water wrecks.

Submersible Vehicle, Self-Propelled
Power-towing devices, known as sea scooters, allow divers to search the seafloor without being connected to a surface vessel. This enables them to travel four times faster and to travel ten times farther on one tank of air because they consume 50 percent less air. The diver holds onto the unit with both hands and is pulled through the water in any direction they choose. The units are lightweight and can be used as deep as 150 feet. They are especially practical for searching around reefs or shallow water or where it would be hazardous for a boat to maneuver. The only disadvantage to using these types of vehicles is that the longest they can operate is two hours, after which the batteries require from eight to 24 hours of recharging. However, extra batteries can be kept on hand to avoid loss of time.

A more sophisticated and rather expensive self-contained underwater vehicle called the "Pegasus" can carry a diver at three knots. They lie on the unit as on a sled and actually "fly" it through the water. It has a navigational module similar to the dashboard of a light plane, enabling the operator to follow a prescribed course and know their depth at all times. In addition, a magnetometer can be mounted on it to locate metallic deposits hidden from sight. Powerful lights for searching in dirty water are available and cameras can be attached for photographing a site, especially when a mosaic is required. The "Pegasus" has the same battery recharging limitations as the scooter.

Open or "wet" submarines, which can carry one or two divers in scuba equipment, are useful as well. However, they offer no advantage over any of the above self-contained water vehicles other than some protection against sharks. Like scooters, they can only cruise for two hours at three knots before they need recharging.

Surface Air Supply, (SAS) The SAS consists of an engine and air compressor assembly encased and floated on the surface with an inflatable tube. The 2-hp, 2-cycle engine delivers 2.5 cfm (cubic feet per minute) of clean air to each diver up to a depth of 25 feet, the length of the two hoses provided with the unit. The SAS's compact size and light weight are especially advantageous when working in a remote area. The unit also eliminates the need for a boat if the site is close to shore. This type of air supply has the advantage of relatively low maintenance. The chief drawback to the unit is that it has a small fuel tank. It should be noted that the SAS should never be used when excavating with a prop-wash, due to the danger of the air hose catching in the turning propeller and cutting off the diver's air supply or a diver being pulled into the propeller.

Swords, Daggers, Rapiers and Poniards Swords, daggers, rapiers and poniards were worn by all the officers and wealthy passengers aboard ship. Many of these weapons have been dis-

Mid-seventeenth century Dutch swords. *Courtesy of Metro Museum of Art.*

covered on shipwrecks over the years. Cutlasses were used by the seamen and marines during battles from about the middle of the 16th century onward. Bayonets were introduced by the Spaniards in 1580, but not adopted by the French until 1647 and the English until 1690.

 Tableware, Made of Gold, Brass, Silver and Pewter Large serving forks were in use as early as 1300, but small forks to

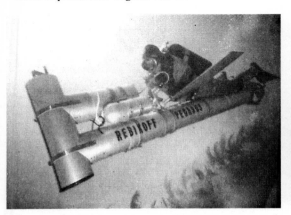
Diver using a Pegasus scooter to visually search for a shipwreck.

A surface air supply in use.

Coral embedded brass table spoons from a mid 18th century French wreck off Antigua.

transfer food from the plate to the mouth are not mentioned in documents until the latter part of the 16th century. This is when they came into general use with the upper class. They did not catch on with the lower classes until the end of the 17th century. Cutlery used by the lower classes was usually made of iron or brass until late in the 18th century. Because only the very rich could afford articles of gold or silver, small quantities of such items will be found on shipwrecks. The majority of upper and middle classes used items made of pewterware. Pewterware was first used by the Romans and has remained in continuous use until the present time. More than 95 percent of these types of artifacts found on shipwrecks are of English manufacture. The English also manufactured a vast majority of these types of artifacts found on Spanish shipwrecks. A small quantity of silver items—mainly spoons, forks, plates and cups of Spanish and French manufacture—has been found on various shipwrecks. Silver plating on copper items was first introduced in 1743, but not on a large scale until 1833, when electroplating was invented. Tableware made of pewter, silver or gold is usually easy to identify and date. Some of the objects bore the name of the owner and a majority is stamped with the owner's initials. These can often be matched to names found in historical archives or on a ship's passenger and crew lists. Gold and silverware had the same kinds of hallmarks as pewterware, in addition to other distinctive marks that can be easily identified. American-made silverware of the 17th and 18th centuries contained just the maker's mark, so these pieces can only

be dated from sometime during the life span of the known craftsman. There is a great deal published on these types of artifacts to help a salvor establish a precise date and place of manufacture.

Test Holes   Test holes are often made when surveying a shipwreck to determine the overall perimeters of the wreck site. In soft sand, silt or sediment the most effective way to make test holes is with an airlift, hydrolift or small prop-wash. Treasure hunter Art McKee developed a simple method of making test holes in deep sand by using a long metal tube and an airlift. The diameter of the tube used is a few inches wider than the diameter of the air lift tube. The tube is driven into the sand by hand as far as possible. The airlift is then employed to allow the tube to be driven into the seafloor until objects are located. The length of the metal tube remaining above the seafloor is measured and subtracted from the total length of the tube to determine the depth of the wreck below the seafloor. The tube can be recovered with the aid of lifting bags, or lifting equipment from a boat such as an anchor winch. When the shipwreck is located under soft coral growth, either a strong water jet or coring device is used to make the test holes. When the coral growth is hard, pneumatic hammers, sledge hammers and chisels are often used.

Thermoluminescence   This process was developed at the Oxford Research Laboratory in England and can be helpful in determining the dates of ceramic materials, such as dinnerware or building bricks. The process is based on the fact that radioactivity from certain isotopes in clay is trapped in the material until the object is fired in a kiln. The firing releases the electrons in a thermoluminescent glow. When the object cools, the electrons are again trapped but with the process of decay, they are increasingly released over time. An approximate date of origin can be established by measuring the number of remaining electrons in the object.

Thompson, Tommy G.   Tommy Thompson, an oceanographic engineer specializing in deep-sea mining, developed a consuming interest in deepwater shipwrecks in the early 1980s. He and Bob Evans, a geologist, spent several years researching various deepwater wrecks before selecting the S.S. *Central America* as their target. The sinking of the side-wheel steamer was the worst American maritime disaster of the 19th century. It claimed 425 lives and more than three tons of gold. The ship was a luxurious packet plying between New York and Panama, where she took on California gold and miners returning from the gold fields. The loss of the ship and gold onboard touched off a wave of bank failures across the United States and contributed to the panic of 1857, one of the country's most severe economic depressions.

In 1985, Thompson formed the Columbus-American Discovery Group to locate and salvage the famous steamship. Before the first dollar was raised to finance the project Thompson and the group were designing the Nemo, a revolutionary ROV, built to perform every function necessary to recover the *Central America's* treasure. Research in 19th century records and newspapers led them to focus on an area encompassing 1,400 square miles, ten times the search area for the *Titanic*. Using sonar, they completed their survey in a mere 40 days. They found a target 160 miles off Charleston, South Carolina, in 8,000 feet of water, which produced a lump of anthracite coal on July 8, 1987. The United States District Court in Norfolk, Virginia, granted Thompson and his group exclusive rights to the wreck and its treasure. While they were surveying and mapping the wreck several rival salvage groups appeared on the scene, claiming that the wreck lay outside government jurisdiction. It wasn't until July of 1989 that the challenging salvors lost their appeal in the United States Court of Appeals and the Columbus-America Discovery Group were allowed to salvage the sunken treasure.

They began salvage work on July 20, 1989. After probing a large part of the twisted remains of the wreck, they were beginning to wonder if there really was any gold. Then, on August 27, those monitoring the color television screens in the control center saw what they described as "the yellow brick road." The screen revealed a dazzling array of hundreds of gold coins and bars. The largest bar recovered the first day weighed 62 pounds. A dazed Thompson said, "It's like a storybook treasure in a kid's book. I never dreamed it would be like this." By the end of the summer Thompson and his group had recovered more than three tons of gold bars and coins. The gold coins were especially valuable because of their extreme rarity. Many had been made by private mints in San Francisco that had been hastily set up to meet the needs of gold miners as they traded in their gold dust and nuggets. Others came from the United States Mint at San Francisco. All the coins were in beautiful condition, many still in their original rolls or storage boxes. Within weeks of the team's arrival in port with the treasure, new legal problems flared up. Thirty-eight insurance companies that had paid claims on the gold now joined forces asserting that all the recovered gold belonged to them. In June of 1991, the United States Circuit Court of Appeals in Richmond, Virginia, awarded a small portion of the gold to the insurance companies and the rest to Thompson's group.

Thruster This excavation tool can be used in excavating a deep-water shipwreck. It is mounted on the bow of a submersible and worked in the same manner as the prop-wash used on shallow-water sites. Coauthor Marx successfully used this method in excavating the 1715 fleet shipwreck in 1,200 feet of water off St. Augustine, Florida.

Towvane A towvane is one of the devices used when it is necessary to visually cover an extensive area in deep water. This self-contained diving chamber is capable of searching in depths of up to 600 feet. One or two observers can be comfortably towed and can control their elevation over the seafloor with ailerons mounted on both sides of the chamber. When a target is sighted, the observers notify the surface by telephone and a buoy is dropped.

Transponders, Beacon Treasure hunters often use underwater beacon transponders to mark the position of a shipwreck and at the same time conceal the wreck's location from pirate

Diver setting up an underwater transponder.

divers who make a living poaching wreck sites belonging to others. These devices eliminate the problems of relocating a wreck and repositioning buoys, which are frequently lost due to heavy seas or because their lines are cut by passing boats. The beacon transponder can be hidden and attached to any part of the wreck site. It is easily activated from the salvage vessel and the site quickly located. It has an operational life of up to several years depending on the size of the battery power source.

Traverse Sweep Search Once a shipwreck target has been narrowed down through an aerial search by a small airplane, helicopter or hot air balloon, an underwater visual search can be performed. In areas where the current is strong, the best way to visu-ally locate a target is with the traverse sweep search. An anchor and line are dropped upstream of the likely area. The diver then operates in the same manner they would in executing the circular sweep method, except that to avoid fighting the current on each sweep, they swim in a relatively flat arc, which increases in size the farther they move from the starting point near the anchor. After each sweep, the diver drops back a bit further until they reach the next marker and then start on another sweep in the opposite direction.

Tucker, Teddy Teddy Tucker, who claims that he would prefer to have lived several centuries ago as a pirate, has led an exciting and interesting life as a treasure hunter. In addition to being one of the best-known residents of Bermuda he is a knowledgeable and successful underwater treasure hunter who has spent most of his life exploring the Bermuda Reefs. In 1938, at the age of twelve he convinced a helmet diver working in Hamilton Harbor to teach him to dive. Tucker became so fascinated with the underwater environment that he fashioned a diving helmet from a small boiler tank connected by a garden hose to a hand-operated air pump on the surface. With some of his school

Teddy Tucker smoking a clay pipe found on a ship that was lost in 1609 in Bermuda.

chums he explored miles and miles of the reefs surrounding Bermuda. They earned spending money by selling coral, sea fans and shells to tourists. Tucker loved the sea and hated school so much that his parents had to physically take him each day. When he was 15, he stowed away on a merchant ship to England where he lied about his age and joined the Royal Navy for the duration of World War II. While stationed at Plymouth, England, he was ordered to clean up the base's mascot, a jackass. Given methylated spirits to clean the animal's hooves, he mixed the spirits with beer instead and drank the mixture, ending up in the brig for several weeks. Tucker claims he spent most of his navy years in jail. He supported himself after the war by working as a commercial diver, salvaging modern shipwrecks, among other jobs. This gave him a chance to see the underwater world in such exotic places as the Malacca Straits, Gulf of Siam, Bay of Bengal and elsewhere in the Indian Ocean.

Returning to Bermuda in 1948, Teddy Tucker decided it was time to become a respectable citizen. In 1949, with diver Bob Canton, who became his brother-in-law, Tucker started a commercial salvage firm. They recovered brass, lead and other metals from modern shipwrecks. When the salvage business was slow, Tucker and Canton worked as commercial fishermen. While searching for one of his fish traps with a glass-bottom bucket in 1950, Tucker spotted two iron cannon on the bottom. A few days later, he returned to the same spot and raised the cannon as well as a large copper kettle full of lead musket balls. He and Canton planned to sell the cannon for scrap, but members of the Bermuda Monuments Trust Commission heard of his discovery and bought the cannon for more than he would have gotten by selling them as scrap. They went back to the wreck and recovered four more cannon, an anchor and a pewter plate. While the wreck was interesting, Tucker and Canton decided to stick to their normal salvage work.

After a storm in the summer of 1955, the two men stopped at the same wreck site. With excellent underwater

visibility, he noticed that the storm had removed a great deal of sand on the bottom. He pulled out a piece of metal, a beautifully decorated bronze apothecary's mortar bearing the date 1561. Excited by this find, Tucker returned to the boat, started the air compressor, and jumped back in. With a small board he began fanning the sand away in the area where he had found the mortar and in five minutes had a handful of blackened silver coins. He dug a trench about eighteen inches deep and a bright object fell out. It was a gold cube weighing about two ounces. Tucker was so excited that he bumped his head on the bottom of the boat while surfacing. Right then and there, he and his brother-in-law decided to forget about their salvage company and become full-time treasure hunters. It was during that week that they struck it rich, finding more gold cubes and larger gold bars in addition to gold buttons studded with pearls and other jewelry. At the end of the week, Tucker and Canton were forced to quit for the season. On their last day, Tucker discovered one of the most valuable single items of treasure ever recovered from an old shipwreck. It was a magnificent emerald-studded gold cross, subsequently valued at $200,000. Of course, this find hooked them for good. They became two of the most successful treasure hunters in the business. Teddy Tucker and his brother-in-law, Bob Canton, continued searching the waters around Bermuda well into their seventies, which is considered an advanced age for a diver.

U **Utilityware** The most common type of pottery discovered on shipwrecks is utilityware, which was made from a coarse hard paste, usually red but sometimes gray or brown. Only small amounts of utilityware were glazed, and then generally green. This pottery, used by the lower classes, was rarely decorated and seldom bore any other distinctive features that would facilitate identifying its origin or date of manufacture. The shapes of various vessels of this type—provided they are found intact or enough pieces of them

are found to establish their original shapes—can be used to fix approximate dates of manufacture.

 Versos This type of cannon was also called a swivel gun. They were either cast in bronze or made of iron in the same manner as the Lombards. Around 1552, they were made with trunnions and were about the same size and weight as the earlier types. By the end of the 16th century they were also cast in iron. They were mounted on a pivoting frame and attached to the bulkwarks of a ship. Versos varied in length from four to ten feet and weighed between 150 and 1,800 pounds. These small-caliber cannon fired a stone or iron ball between one and three inches in diameter and were mainly used to attack the personnel on the decks and castles of an enemy ship rather than a ship's hull, which could resist the shock of small projectiles. Versos were carried on ships of all types and nations as late as the end of the 18th century. They were also used as a signal gun and by officers in the suppression of mutiny.

Visual Search Once a shipwreck target has been narrowed down through an aerial search by a small airplane, helicopter or hot air balloon, an underwater visual search can be performed. A diver can use a submersible vehicle equipped with metal detectors to visually search for traces of a shipwreck, or visually comb the seafloor while being towed on a line behind a small boat which is following a predetermined search pattern. The visual search is the best method to use when hunting for an ancient wreck where a magnetometer is useless, such as a wreck which carried bronze cannon and lost its anchors in another area. It is also the best method to use when searching areas with a rocky bottom, whose irregularity prevents the effective use of sonar. In some zones, pinnacles of jagged rock called "secs" rise precipitously from the bottom to within several feet of the surface. Many ships have torn out their bottoms on these pinnacles and sunk nearby. In some of these areas the seafloor is relatively flat and sandy so that sonar could be used. Strange formations in coral or patch reefs located separately may indicate a shipwreck in shallow water. The color of coral may indicate a shipwreck as well. Over time, chemical changes in iron will turn coral brown or black. Brass, bronze and copper turn coral greenish while lead tends to turn it white or gray. There are no chemical changes in gold, pottery or ballast rock. However, these and other objects can be spotted by a trained eye that can detect strange shapes in coral formations. Unless a search site is small, diving is not practical. When it is necessary to visually cover an extensive area in deep water, there are several techniques to select from. A towvane can be used or a closed-circuit television. Manned submersibles or submarines have also been used successfully on several deep-water wrecks but their cost is prohibitive and they require a tremendous amount of maintenance.

Wagner, Kip   The late Kip Wagner started as a professional treasure hunter rather late in life, but this had little effect on his success. In fact, Wagner was the first treasure hunter to become a millionaire by recovering sunken treasure, before retiring in the early seventies. Wagner was born in Ohio and spent most of his life there. He had absolutely no interest in treasure or shipwrecks until he moved to Florida after World War II to start a construction business. He heard stories of people finding gold and silver coins on the beaches, usually after storms, but scoffed at them as idle tales. When one of his employees showed up drunk for work, Wagner would take him for a walk on the beach where fresh salt air could sober him up. As they walked along, the man bent down and picked up what appeared to be a piece of rusty metal. It was a silver coin. During the next half-hour, he found six more and told Wagner he had found hundreds over the years.

Kip Wagner's interest was aroused.

Kip Wagner seated and reading microfilm from the Spanish archives.

He learned through research about the fleet of 12 Spanish treasure galleons that had been wrecked in the area in the hurricane of 1715. He also learned that millions of dollars in treasure still lay in the remains. With local divers, he formed the Real Eight Company. All were amateurs and never having seen a shipwreck, they learned the ropes by trial and error. They located the sites of most of the shipwrecks from the 1715 disaster by finding coins on nearby beaches. After exploratory dives in the spring of 1960, Real Eight's salvage project got under way. The task that immediately concerned them on their first target was to move tons of ballast stones by hand before they could reach the treasure. At first everyone worked enthusiastically, but after spending several weekends at the backbreaking labor, they grew skeptical. Just as they approached the point of calling off the effort, a diver found a large wedge of silver ... the beginning of one of the major treasure finds of the century. During the next decade, Wagner and the Real Eight Company recovered over $10 million in treasure and artifacts. The 1715 wrecks are still producing treasure, and every diving season ten to 20 boats work on them.

Weapons   Weapons of many different types were carried on all ships. Even passengers were required to carry at least one hand-held weapon on ships of every flag. Full suits of armor were not used aboard ships; however, armored breast plates and helmets were until the end of the 16th century. At that time, other primitive weapons still in use were boarding axes, pikes, lances and shields. Crossbows were used until the end of the 16th century, but generally only small numbers of these weapons were carried aboard ships, since the arquebus or harquebus and the musket were considered better weapons. Harquebuses were introduced in the 14th century. Muskets were introduced in 1521 and were the largest guns fired by a single man. They gradually decreased in size over the years and by 1690 the average musket was about five feet in length. From around 1700 onward the term "musket" was used to identify any type of firearm shot from the shoulder. Carbines, which are similar to muskets, were introduced by the English during the second half of the 16th century. Pistols were first used in England in 1521 and in most other European countries soon afterward. Actually a smaller version of the harquebus, they

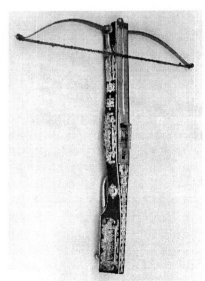

Midsixteenth century Spanish crossbow.
Courtesy of Metro Museum of Art.

were lighter and easier to handle. By the middle of the 16th century they became standard equipment for all officers aboard ships. Hand grenades were used on ships as early as 1467 and remained in use until the middle of the 19th century, but very few of these have been found to date. It is relatively simple to identify weapons and estab-lish their date and place of manufac-ture by using the many excellent books available on the subject.

 Zoology Zoologists can help to identify ani-mal, fish and fowl bones found on a wreck site. While excavating a ship-wreck near Jamaica, coauthor Marx found a great many fish bones mixed in with the ballast. At the time, he as-sumed they were either from local fish that had died or the remains of meals eaten by the ship's crew. The latter case proved correct when a marine zoolo-gist identified the bones as those of North Sea herring.

Part II
THE SHIPWRECKS

The Bahamas

The archipelago of the Bahamas is unquestionably one of the best areas for working on shipwrecks in the Western Hemisphere. It has a marvelous combination of clear water, close to ideal year-round weather conditions, and a vast number of ancient shipwrecks. Its proximity to the United States is a big advantage for American divers, since there is less expense involved in working a wreck site close to home. For this reason, the Bahamas runs a close second to Florida for shipwreck search and salvage.

As early as a century before Nassau was first settled by the English in the early 1700s, Bermudan wreckers established bases in different areas of the Bahamas and carried out salvage work. After Nassau was settled, wreck salvage work, or "wracking" as they called it, was the principal occupation of the island's inhabitants until as late as the end of the American Civil War. Many of today's wealthy Bahamian families began in the "wracking" business. Even now Bahamian fishermen use their glass-bottom buckets not only to locate

conch and turtles but in the hope of stumbling across a treasure wreck. Tales of these fishermen's discoveries are as numerous as the Bahamas' islands and cays, but rarely can they be verified.

Permission is not required for divers to explore shipwrecks in the Bahamas. However, a permit to salvage a wreck must be obtained from the Ministry of Transportation. Permits are granted on each wreck site for periods of five years. Salvors keep 75 percent of their recoveries and the Bahamian government receives 25 percent. Several years ago an American diver who salvaged a shipwreck without a permit was arrested and sentenced to a year in prison.

The biggest discovery of treasure in the Bahamas was the wreck *Maravillas*, discovered by coauthor Robert F. Marx. Marx recovered approximately $20 million from the wreck before having a falling out with the Bahamian government. Since then several other firms followed behind Marx and made significant finds.

Marx's files contain over 3,000 Bahamian shipwrecks, but due to the lim-

ited space in this book the wrecks listed are those which have a fairly accurate location or those of special importance.

SHIPWRECKS IN THE BAHAMAS' WATERS

Acress, American ship, Captain Lynch
   Location: Near Little Caicos Island
   History: The ship was lost near Little Caicos Island on July 25, 1801, while sailing from New York to Jamaica.

Active, English merchantman, Captain Howard
   Location: Cat Cay
   History: The merchantman wrecked at Cat Cay, south of Bimini, in 1794 while sailing from Jamaica to London. Part of her cargo was saved.

Adeline, ship of unknown registry, Captain Marre
   Location: Great Abaco Island
   History: The ship was lost near Great Abaco Island in 1817 while sailing from

51

Treasure recovered from the *Nuestra Señora de Maravillas*.

Savannah to Havana. The crew and part of her cargo were saved.

Adventure, American merchantman, Captain Bashford
   Location: Great Abaco Island
   History: The merchantman wrecked on Great Abaco Island in 1803 while sailing from Charleston to Havana.

Agnes, English slave ship, Captain Kitts
   Location: Near New Providence Island
   History: This slave ship was lost near New Providence Island in 1802 while coming from Africa. The slaves and crew were saved.

Albert, English ship, Captain Philip
   Location: Great Abaco Island
   History: The ship wrecked on Great Abaco Island in 1824 while sailing from Gibraltar to Mexico. Part of her cargo was saved.

Aldbro, English merchantman, Captain Suthoff
   Location: Memory Rock
   History: The vessel was totally lost on September 28, 1816, near Memory Rock while sailing from Honduras to London. The crew was saved.

Alexander, French merchantman
   Location: New Providence Island
   History: The merchantman was wrecked in March of 1818 near New Providence Island while sailing from France to Havana. The crew and part of the cargo were saved.

Alexander, schooner of unknown registry, Captain Stewart
   Location: Silver Shoals
   History: The schooner was totally lost on August 7, 1818, on Silver Shoals while coming from Jamaica.

Alompre, American ship, Captain Prior
   Location: Great Abaco Island
   History: The ship was lost near Great Abaco Island in 1816 while sailing from New York to New Orleans. The crew was saved.

Altezara, American sloop, Captain Glover
   Location: Great Abaco Island
   History: The sloop was totally lost at Hole in the Wall on Great Abaco Island in 1819.

Amwell, English ship, Captain Hawkins
   Location: Great Caicos
   History: The vessel wrecked at Great Caicos on December 19, 1816, while sailing from London to Jamaica. The crew and part of the cargo were saved.

Ann, English merchantman, Captain Robins
   Location: Berry Islands
   History: The merchantman wrecked in the Berry Islands on October 27, 1810, while sailing from Santo Domingo to Bristol. The crew and part of the cargo were saved.

Ann, American ship, Captain Grant
   Location: Caicos Bank
   History: She wrecked on the Caicos Bank on December 25, 1816, while sailing from South Carolina to Jamaica. The crew was saved.

Ann, Canadian ship
   Location: Great Abaco Island
   History: The vessel wrecked on Great Abaco Island prior to February 21, 1822, while sailing from Jamaica to New Brunswick, Canada.

Ann, Canadian ship, Captain Mackie
   Location: Turks Island
   History: The ship wrecked on Turks Island in 1806 while sailing from Quebec to Jamaica. Part of her cargo was saved.

Ann, American ship, Captain Nixon
   Location: Turks Island
   History: The vessel wrecked on Turks Island on May 15, 1809, while sailing from Amelia Island, Florida to Jamaica. Her crew and cargo were saved.

Divers holding an 80-pound silver bar recovered from a galleon in the Bahamas.

Anna Maria, French merchantman
Location: Crooked Island
History: The merchantman wrecked in 1754 at Crooked Island while sailing from Hispaniola to France with a cargo of indigo and sugar.

Anns, English ship, Captain Hodnett
Location: Great Inagua
History: She wrecked on May 6, 1821, near the northeastern end of Great Inagua Island while sailing from Bermuda to Jamaica.

Antelope, Bahamian ship, Captain Teder
Location: Atwood Key
History: The ship wrecked in October 1816 at Atwood Key while sailing from Nassau to St. Vincent Island.

Argonauta, Spanish merchantman
Location: Little Bahama Bank
History: The ship was totally lost at Mantanilla Reef on the Little Bahama Bank in the year 1802 while carrying a very rich cargo.

Atlantic, American ship, Captain Homer
Location: Crooked Island Passage
History: The ship was totally lost on December 30, 1820, in the Crooked Island Passage while sailing from Boston to Hispaniola. The crew was saved.

Auspicicus, English merchantman, Captain Procton
Location: Great Inagua Island
History: Six English merchantmen were wrecked at the same time on August 10, 1801, on the reefs of Great Inagua Island: the *Auspicicus, Milton, Jason, Bushy Park, Fanny* and an unidentified ship.

Bahama, Bahamian ship
Location: Bimini
History: She was totally lost during a gale at Bimini on March 4, 1786, while sailing from Honduras to Nassau.

Barbados, English packet boat
Location: Great Inagua Island
History: The boat wrecked on December 28, 1705, on Great Inagua Island. The ship's mail and money were saved.

Barcelones, Spanish merchantman
Location: Little Bahama Bank

History: The merchantman was lost on the Little Bahama Bank on January 6, 1815, while sailing from Cadiz to Havana. Part of her cargo was salvaged.

Beggars Benizon, American ship, Captain Rogers
Location: Caicos Bank
History: The vessel was lost on May 31, 1768, on the Caicos Bank while sailing from Charleston, South Carolina to Jamaica.

Bella Dolores, Spanish ship
Location: Caicos Bank
History: The ship was captured by a Colombian privateer and then wrecked on the Caicos Bank on June 9, 1823.

Benjamin, American ship, Captain Cushman
Location: Grand Bahama Island
History: The ship wrecked on September 21, 1816, near Grand Bahama Island while sailing from Boston to Havana. The crew and part of the cargo were saved.

Betsey, American merchantman, Captain Hilton
Location: Double Headed Key
History: The merchantman was totally lost on Double Headed Key in the year 1825 while sailing from New England to Cuba. All of the crew except one were murdered by pirates.

Bom Successo, Portuguese ship
Location: Little Island
History: The ship wrecked in 1819 at Little Island, near Rum Key while coming from Brazil with a cargo of sugar, cotton, rice and hides. Most of the cargo was salvaged.

Bonne Mère, French ship, 350 tons, Captain David
Location: San Salvador
History: The vessel was totally lost on San Salvador in 1789 while sailing from Hispaniola to France.

Brandy Wine, American ship, Captain Miller
Location: Great Inagua Island
History: The ship wrecked on Great Inagua Island in 1806 while sailing from New York to Jamaica.

Bridget & Kitty, English merchantman, Captain Minshall

Location: Little Inagua Island
History: The merchantman wrecked on the island in 1731 while sailing from Jamaica to Liverpool. Her crew was saved.

Britannia, English ship, Captain Middlemas
Location: Ackland Key
History: The vessel wrecked on December 24, 1816, on Ackland Key while sailing from Jamaica to New York. Part of her cargo was saved.

Britannia, English merchantman, Captain Preble
Location: Sugar Key
History: She was totally lost on November 19, 1822, on Sugar Key while sailing from Haiti to Wilmington.

British Trader, English brig, Captain Gemmell
Location: Memory Rock
History: The brig wrecked near Memory Rock on March 22, 1818, while coming from Jamaica. She was able to float again after throwing part of her cargo overboard.

Brown, English merchantman, Captain Brough
Location: Little Caicos Bank
History: The merchantman wrecked on October 5, 1812, on the Little Caicos Bank while sailing from Santo Domingo to London. The crew was saved.

Bushy Park, English merchantman, Captain Brown
Location: Great Inagua Island
History: Six English merchantmen were wrecked at the same time on August 10, 1801, on the reefs of Great Inagua Island: *Auspicicus, Milton, Jason, Bushy Park, Fanny* and an unidentified ship.

Caesar, Spanish ship
Location: Annagabes Island
History: The ship was lost on Annagabes Island in 1758 while sailing from Havana to Spain. This island has a different name today since no island by this name is shown on any of the current Bahamas charts.

Calcutta, American ship, Captain Orange
Location: Atwood Keys
History: The vessel was lost on the

Atwood Keys in 1794 while sailing from New York to Havana.

Camelcon, ship of unknown registry
   Location: Great Abaco Island
   History: She was lost on Great Abaco Island in 1815 while sailing from Norfolk to Havana.

Carlton, American ship, Captain Davis
   Location: Abaco Island
   History: The ship was lost near Abaco Island on February 18, 1812, while sailing from Virginia to Havana, Cuba. The crew and part of the cargo were saved.

Caroline, American ship, Captain Seymour
   Location: Great Abaco Island
   History: She wrecked on March 4, 1818, on Great Ab'co Island while sailing from Norfolk to New Orleans.

Catherine Rogers, American ship, Captain Griffiths
   Location: Great Abaco Island
   History: The vessel wrecked on Great Abaco Island in 1823 while sailing from New York to Mobile.

Cecilia, English merchantman, Captain Roach
   Location: Hogsty
   History: The merchantman was lost on the Hogsty in 1799 while sailing from Jamaica to Liverpool. Her crew was saved.

Chace, ship of unknown registry, Captain Anderson
   Location: Great Abaco Island
   History: The ship wrecked on Great Abaco Island in 1824 while sailing from Charleston, South Carolina to Havana. Her crew was saved.

Charlotte, English merchantman, Captain Potter
   Location: Nassau
   History: The merchantman was lost at Nassau in 1787 while sailing to London.

Charter, American merchantman
   Location: Great Isaac Key, Bimini
   History: The vessel wrecked near Great Isaac Key in 1816 while sailing from Baltimore to Havana. The crew was saved.

Christiansand, German merchantman, Captain Berge

Location: Guinches Key
   History: The merchantman wrecked near Guinches Key in the Old Bahama Channel on June 28, 1817, while sailing from Hamburg to Havana. The crew and some of the specie were saved.

Clarendon, English merchantman
   Location: Atwood Key
   History: She was lost on December 11, 1810, at Atwood Key while sailing from Jamaica to London. The crew was saved.

Cleo, English ship, Captain Heath
   Location: Grand Bahama Island
   History: The ship was lost on February 23, 1824, on Grand Bahama Island while sailing from Bath to Havana, Cuba. Part of her cargo was saved.

Cohen, English merchantman, Captain Davis
   Location: Fish Key
   History: The merchantman was lost near Fish Key in 1792 while sailing from Jamaica to Liverpool.

Conck, English ship
   Location: Eleuthera Island
   History: The ship wrecked on Eleuthera Island during a violent gale on July 26, 1813, while sailing from Nassau to Jamaica.

Concord, English merchantman, Captain Forresdale
   Location: Great Abaco Island
   History: The merchantman was lost close to Great Abaco Island in 1791 while sailing from London to Nassau. Part of her cargo was saved.

Constantia, ship of unknown registry, Captain Johnson
   Location: Ginger Key
   History: She wrecked on April 22, 1819, on Ginger Key while sailing from Haiti to France. Her cargo was saved.

Convention, American merchantman, Captain Allen
   Location: Great Abaco Island
   History: The merchantman wrecked near Great Abaco Island on October 24, 1810, while sailing from New York to Havana.

Cooler, American merchantman
   Location: Mouchoir Bank
   History: The merchantman wrecked on Mouchoir Bank, near Turks Island,

in 1816 while sailing from Philadelphia to Jamaica. The crew was saved.

Corriero Lisbonere, Portuguese mail boat
   Location: Little Bahama Bank
   History: The boat was totally lost on January 27, 1814, on the Little Bahama Bank while sailing from Liverpool to Havana.

Count de Paix, French merchantman, Captain Lewis Doyer
   Location: Great Inagua Island
   History: The merchantman wrecked in 1713 on Great Inagua Island while sailing from Hispaniola to France with a cargo of gold dust, ambergris, sugar, indigo, and other products. Only the gold dust and ambergris were saved.

Cuba, English merchantman, Captain M'Gowan
   Location: Mayaguana Island
   History: The merchantman was totally lost on October 15, 1821, on Mayaguana Island while sailing from Liverpool to Havana. The crew was saved.

Dart, English ship, Captain Sweeting
   Location: Nassau
   History: Over 40 ships were wrecked, sunk or cast ashore during a violent gale at Nassau on July 26, 1813. Only one was identified; the *Dart*, which was sailing from Jamaica to Nassau. Most of her cargo was saved.

Dartmouth, English brig, Captain Kimm
   Location: Near the northeastern end of Turks Island
   History: The brig was lost near the northeastern end of Turks Island on October 26, 1791.

David, ship of unknown registry, Captain Boyd
   Location: New Providence Island
   History: The ship was lost on April 30, 1784, at New Providence Island.

Defiance, English merchantman, Captain Carock
   Location: Little Bahama Bank
   History: The ship was lost on March 21, 1768, while sailing from Honduras to London. Her crew was saved.

Delight, ship of unknown registry
   Location: Nassau

History: The vessel wrecked near Nassau in 1823 while sailing from Jamaica to Philadelphia. Part of her cargo was saved.

Do, Bahamian ship, Captain Miller
Location: Great Abaco Island
History: The ship was lost near Great Abaco Island on November 7, 1817, while sailing from Philadelphia to Nassau. The crew and part of her cargo were saved.

Doris, English ship, Captain White
Location: Great Inagua Island
History: The vessel was totally lost near Great Inagua Island in 1825 while sailing from Santo Domingo to England. The crew was saved.

Doudswell, English merchantman, Captain M'Lean
Location: New Providence Island
History: The merchantman was lost at New Providence Island in the year 1800 while coming from London. Her crew was saved.

Draper, English ship, Captain Brown
Location: Caicos Bank
History: The ship was lost on the Caicos Bank on November 28, 1822 while sailing from Bermuda to Jamaica. The crew and passengers were saved.

Duke of Cumberland, English merchantman, Captain Prenton
Location: Acklin Key
History: The vessel was lost on March 27, 1750, while sailing from Jamaica to London. The crew and part of the cargo were saved.

Duncanon, English merchantman, Captain Elphinston
Location: Hogsty
History: She wrecked on the Hogsty in the Windward Passage in 1751 while sailing from Jamaica to London.

Eagle, American merchantman, Captain Toby
Location: Caicos Bank
History: The ship was lost on Caicos Bank on July 27, 1806, while sailing from Boston to Jamaica.

Eagle, American ship, Captain Byrnes
Location: Great Inagua Island reef
History: The vessel was lost on the Great Inagua Island reef in 1796 while

sailing from Santo Domingo to Baltimore. A small part of her cargo was saved.

Eagle Gally, English merchantman, Captain Nash
Location: Hogsty
History: She wrecked on the Hogsty in 1761 while sailing from Jamaica to Bristol. Her crew was saved.

Echo, Spanish merchantman, Captain Rodriques
Location: Memory Rock
History: The merchantman wrecked near Memory Rock in 1818 while sailing from Veracruz to Venezuela. The crew and over $100,000 in specie were saved.

Eliza, ship of unknown registry, Captain Huggins
Location: Crooked Island Reef
History: The ship was lost on the Crooked Island Reef in 1794 while sailing from Nassau to Santo Domingo.

Eliza, ship of unknown registry, Captain Grant
Location: Grand Caicos Island
History: She was lost on September 21, 1798, on Grand Caicos Island while sailing from the Azores to Santo Domingo. Her crew was saved.

Eliza Ann, English merchantman, Captain Little
Location: Memory Rock
History: The merchantman wrecked at Memory Rock in 1815 while sailing from Honduras to London.

Elizabeth, English ship
Location: Memory Rock
History: The vessel wrecked near Memory Rock on March 22, 1818, while sailing from Jamaica to Liverpool.

Elizabeth and Mary, English ship, Captain Graff
Location: Grand Caicos Island
History: The ship wrecked on April 23, 1808, on Grand Caicos Island while sailing from Haiti and Jamaica to London.

Elizabeth Ann, American merchantman, schooner, Captain Blake
Location: Great Abaco Island

History: The schooner wrecked near Great Abaco Island on November 1, 1810, while coming from Haiti.

Elizabeth Elenor, Belgian merchantman, Captain Rose
Location: Caicos Bank
History: The merchantman wrecked on the Caicos Bank on April 2, 1819, while sailing from Antwerp to Havana. The crew and part of the cargo were saved.

Endeavour, American ship, Captain Russel
Location: Long Island
History: She was lost on Long Island in 1801 while sailing from North Carolina to the Bahamas.

Eolus, French ship, Captain Dickinson
Location: Eleuthera Island
History: The ship wrecked on Eleuthera Island in 1824 while sailing from Morlaix, France to Mobile.

Essex, American merchantman, Captain Ladiew
Location: Great Abaco Island
History: The vessel wrecked on Great Abaco Island in 1823 while sailing from Rhode Island to Havana.

Estrella, Spanish brig
Location: Great Isaac Key
History: The brig was lost near Great Isaac Key in 1823 while sailing from Puerto Rico to Havana.

Europa, ship of unknown registry, Captain Allen
Location: Caicos Bank
History: The ship wrecked on the Caicos Bank on June 14, 1824, while sailing from Liverpool to Havana, Cuba. The crew and cargo were saved.

Expectation, ship of unknown registry, Captain Wake
Location: Long Island
History: She was lost on August 10, 1775, on the windward side of Long Island. Part of the cargo was saved.

Expedition, American merchantman, Captain Clare
Location: Great Isaac Key, Bimini
History: The merchantman wrecked near Great Isaac Key in 1816 while sailing from Baltimore to Havana. The crew was saved.

Fabius, American ship, Captain Higgins
 Location: Caicos Bank
 History: The ship was totally lost on the Caicos Bank in 1823 while sailing from Wilmington to Haiti. Her crew was saved.

Fair Bahamian, Bahamian ship, Captain Graham
 Location: Cat Cay
 History: The ship was totally lost on August 26, 1813, at Cat Cay, south of Bimini, while sailing from Nassau to Havana.

Fairfield, English merchantman, Captain Elias
 Location: Atwood Key
 History: The merchantman wrecked on March 28, 1819, on a reef at Atwood Key while sailing from Haiti to Liverpool. The crew and some of the cargo were saved.

Fair Trader, ship of unknown registry, Captain Haze
 Location: North Caicos Reef
 History: The ship wrecked on the North Caicos Reef on September 23, 1816, while sailing from Philadelphia to Cuba.

Falmouth, American merchantman
 Location: Exuma Keys
 History: The merchantman wrecked near the Exuma Keys in 1822 while sailing with a cargo of soap, lumber and candles.

Fame, American merchantman, Captain Salisbury
 Location: Harbor Island
 History: She was lost on January 12, 1817, near Harbor Island while sailing from Boston to Havana. The crew was saved.

Fancy, American ship, Captain Wilson
 Location: New Providence Island
 History: The vessel was lost near New Providence Island in 1802 while coming from Philadelphia.

Fanny, English merchantman, Captain Warden
 Location: Great Inagua Island
 History: Six English merchantmen were wrecked at the same time on August 10, 1801, on the reefs of Great In-agua Island: the *Auspicicus, Milton, Jason, Bushy Park, Fanny* and an unidentified ship.

Farmer, American merchantman, Captain Thompson
 Location: Wood Key
 History: The merchantman was lost on June 19, 1815, on Wood Key during a severe gale while sailing from Nassau to South Carolina. The crew was saved.

Favorite, Scottish merchantman, Captain Davis
 Location: Ragged Island
 History: She wrecked on May 7, 1822, on Ragged Island while sailing from Glasgow to Canada.

Felicity, Canadian ship, Captain Doty
 Location: Turks Island
 History: The ship was lost near Turks Island in 1792 while coming from New Brunswick.

Forest, Irish ship, Captain Lascell
 Location: Exuma Island
 History: The vessel was totally lost on December 2, 1815, on Exuma Island while coming from Norfolk. The crew was saved.

Forester, English ship, Captain Jackson
 Location: Turks Island
 History: The ship was lost on September 26, 1813, on Turks Island while sailing from Bermuda to Jamaica. The crew was saved.

Four Friends, American ship, Captain Jouffet
 Location: Caicos Bank
 History: The ship was lost on the Caicos Bank in 1807 while sailing from South Carolina to Jamaica. The crew and cargo were saved.

Fox, American ship, Captain Lippcatt
 Location: Turks Island
 History: The ship was lost on December 23, 1811, while sailing from New York to Jamaica. The crew was saved.

Frances Mary, American merchantman, Captain Jennings
 Location: Great Abaco Island
 History: The merchantman was lost on February 12, 1817, near Great Abaco Island while sailing from New York to New Orleans.

Franklin, American schooner, Captain Stevenson
 Location: Caicos Bank
 History: The schooner wrecked on the Caicos Bank in 1824 while sailing from Boston to South America.

Franklin, American ship, Captain Taper
 Location: Great Abaco Island
 History: The ship wrecked on Great Abaco Island in 1823 while sailing from Philadelphia to Venezuela.

Franklin, American ship
 Location: Great Inagua Island
 History: She was lost on February 26, 1807, on Great Inagua Island while sailing from New York to Jamaica. The crew was saved.

Friendship, ship of unknown registry, Captain Wells
 Location: Castle Island
 History: The vessel wrecked at Castle Island in 1823 while sailing from Jérémie, Haiti to Portsmouth, New Hampshire. The crew and most of the cargo were saved.

Friendship, English ship, Captain Riche
 Location: Great Caicos Reef
 History: The ship was lost on the Great Caicos Reef on the Caicos Bank in 1792 while sailing from Philadelphia to Jamaica.

Gambia, English merchantman, Captain Whiting
 Location: West Caicos Island
 History: The merchantman was lost on West Caicos Island in 1762 while sailing from Jamaica to Bristol. The crew was saved.

General Oglethorp, American ship
 Location: On a reef six miles north of Whale Key
 History: She wrecked on the reef and quickly went to pieces in the year 1802. Ten crewmen and 13 slaves drowned. In the same area five or six other ships were lost, one of which was an African slave ship.

George, slave ship
 Location: Nassau

History: Over 120 ships of various descriptions and sizes were wrecked, sunk or thrown on the beach near and at Nassau during a hurricane in July 1801. Only a slave ship named *George* was identified.

George Washington, American merchantman, Captain Brethoff
Location: Great Abaco Island
History: The merchantman wrecked on Great Abaco Island on January 1, 1819, while sailing from New York to Havana. The crew and a small part of her cargo were saved.

George Washington, American ship
Location: Great Abaco Island
History: The ship wrecked on Great Abaco Island in the year 1824 while sailing from Philadelphia to Havana. Her cargo was saved.

George Washington, American brig, Captain Baker
Location: Green Turtle Cay
History: The brig totally wrecked at Green Turtle Cay, near Great Abaco Island, in 1819 while sailing from New York to New Orleans.

Golden Fleece, English ship
Location: Long Key
History: The vessel wrecked in January of 1819 on Long Key while sailing from Jamaica to Liverpool. The crew and cargo were saved.

Good Hope, English ship, Captain Folger
Location: San Salvador Island
History: She was totally lost near San Salvador Island on October 30, 1810, while sailing from London to Baltimore.

Hamilton, American ship, Captain Noval
Location: Caicos Bank
History: The ship was lost on the Caicos Bank in 1799 while sailing from Savannah to Jamaica.

Hannah, American ship, Captain Larson
Location: Little Caicos Island
History: She was lost near Little Caicos Island in 1801 while sailing from Philadelphia to Jamaica.

Hannah, American ship, Captain Bright

Location: Long Island
History: The vessel was lost on Long Island in 1793 while sailing from Hispaniola to Wilmington.

Hanover Planter, English ship, Captain M'Cullock
Location: Great Inagua Island
History: The ship was lost on Great Inagua Island in 1774 while sailing from Jamaica to Philadelphia. The crew and cargo were saved.

Harmony, English merchantman
Location: Berry Islands
History: The merchantman was totally lost in the Berry Islands in 1807 while sailing from Bristol to the West Indies. The crew was saved.

Harmony, Canadian ship, Captain Penniston
Location: Turks Island
History: The ship was lost near Turks Island in 1811 while sailing from Newfoundland to Jamaica.

Harnet, English merchantman, Captain Curry
Location: Turks Island
History: She wrecked on Turks Island in 1806 while sailing from Jamaica to Halifax, Nova Scotia, Canada.

Harriet, English brig
Location: Ginger Cay
History: The brig wrecked on Ginger Cay in 1821 after sailing from Savannah. The crew was saved.

Harriet, Canadian ship, Captain Hitchins
Location: Mira Por Vos Keys
History: She wrecked on April 26, 1822, on the Mira Por Vos Keys while sailing from Jamaica to Halifax. Her crew was saved.

Harriet Newell, Canadian ship, Captain Corfield
Location: Turks Island
History: The ship totally wrecked at Turks Island on December 1, 1822, while sailing from New Brunswick, Canada to Jamaica. The crew and part of the cargo were saved.

Havana Packet, English mail boat, Captain Jenkins
Location: Caicos Bank

History: The boat wrecked on March 13, 1825, on the Caicos Bank while sailing from England to Jamaica.

Hazard, American ship, Captain Crocker
Location: Nassau
History: The vessel wrecked on January 3, 1819, near Nassau while sailing from Boston to Mobile. The crew and part of the cargo were saved.

Herman, Canadian ship, Captain Milne
Location: Caicos Bank
History: The ship wrecked on the Caicos Bank in 1819 while sailing from New Brunswick to Jamaica. Part of her cargo was saved.

Hero, ship of unknown registry, Captain Riebeiro
Location: Great Abaco Island
History: The vessel was lost on Great Abaco Island in June of 1821, while sailing from New York to Havana, Cuba. The crew and most of her cargo were saved.

Heron, American ship, Captain Cullum
Location: Turks Island
History: The ship wrecked on Turks Island in 1806 while sailing from Wilmington to Jamaica.

Hestor, English merchantman, Captain Pearson
Location: Great Inagua Island Reef
History: The merchantman was lost on the Great Inagua Island reef in July 1796 while sailing from Santo Domingo to London. The crew was saved.

Hinchinbrook, English packet boat
Location: San Salvador Island
History: The boat wrecked at San Salvador Island on July 19, 1813, while sailing from Jamaica to England. Only one person drowned.

Hiram, American ship, Captain Anner
Location: Great Abaco Island
History: The ship was lost on July 21, 1808, on Great Abaco Island while sailing from New York to Havana. The crew and part of the cargo were saved.

H.M.S. *Algerine*, English warship, cutter, Captain Carpenter
Location: Great Abaco Island

History: The cutter wrecked on May 20, 1813, near Great Abaco Island. The crew was saved.

H.M.S. *Bermuda*, 18-gun English warship, schooner, Captain William Henry Byam
Location: Memory Rock
History: The warship wrecked on April 22, 1808, at Memory Rock on the Little Bahama Bank. The crew was saved. Note: within a 300-yard radius of Memory Rock, there are seven old shipwrecks; all appear to have been thoroughly salvaged.

H.M.S. *Endymion*, English warship, Captain Woodriff
Location: Four miles southwest of Sand Key
History: The warship wrecked on a shoal four miles southwest of Sand Key, near Turks Island, in nine feet of water in the year 1790. The crew was saved.

H.M.S. *Laurestinus*, 22-gun English warship, Captain Alexander Gordon
Location: Silver Shoals
History: The vessel wrecked on Silver Shoals on October 22, 1813. The crew was saved.

H.M.S. *Lowestoffe*, English warship
Location: Great Inagua Island
History: The warship totally wrecked on Great Inagua Island in August 1800, along with eight merchantmen carrying cargoes of colonial produce valued at over 600,000 pounds sterling.

H.M.S. *Narcissus*, 24-gun English warship, Captain Percy Fraser
Location: Sandy Key
History: The warship wrecked on Sandy Key, near Nassau, in 1796. Her crew was saved.

H.M.S. *Persian*, 18-gun English warship, sloop, Captain Charles Bertram
Location: Silver Shoals
History: The sloop wrecked on Silver Shoals in 1813 in seven fathoms of water. Her crew of 121 men survived.

H.M.S. *Southampton*, 32-gun English warship, frigate, Captain Sir James Lucas Yeo
Location: 24.03.00 N, 69.57.00W
History: The vessel wrecked in 1812 on a reef three leagues from Conception Island in 24 degrees and 3 minutes of north latitude and 69 degrees and 57 minutes of west longitude.

H.M.S. *Sterling Castle*, English warship
Location: Silver Shoals
History: The warship wrecked on Silver Shoals and went to pieces in a few minutes on October 6, 1780. Only a small number of people were saved after floating on wreckage for days.

H.M.S. *Wolfe*, 18-gun English warship, sloop, Captain G.C. Mackenzie
Location: Great Inagua Island
History: The sloop wrecked on Great Inagua Island on September 4, 1806, with a crew of 121 persons; none were lost.

Hope, Canadian merchantman, Captain Tucker
Location: Great Inagua Island
History: The merchantman wrecked on September 13, 1821, near Great Inagua Island while sailing from Jamaica to New Brunswick, Canada.

Hope, brig of unknown registry, Captain Tooker
Location: Great Inagua Island
History: She wrecked near Great Inagua Island in 1822 while coming from Jamaica. Her crew was saved.

Hope, American ship, Captain Edmoundson
Location: Little Caicos Island
History: The ship was lost near Little Caicos Island in 1801 while sailing from Philadelphia to Jamaica.

Hope Sherrer, English transport
Location: New Providence Island
History: The ship was totally lost at New Providence Island during a hurricane in September 1785.

Horizon, American ship, Captain Johnson
Location: Fish Key
History: The vessel wrecked on Fish Key near Great Abaco Island in 1818 while sailing from Philadelphia to New Orleans.

Hotspur, English merchantman, Captain Marshall
Location: Atwood Key
History: The merchantman wrecked on July 25, 1813, at Atwood Key while sailing from Santo Domingo to London, England. The crew was saved.

Incle, English ship, Captain Thatcher
Location: Caicos Bank
History: The ship wrecked on the Caicos Bank in 1815 while sailing from Bermuda to Jamaica.

Industry, American ship, Captain Sweet
Location: Great Abaco Island
History: She was lost near Great Abaco Island on March 22, 1817, while coming from Boston.

Infanta, 18-cannon Spanish brigantine-of-war, Captain Casmiro de Madrid
Location: Reefs of Little Inagua Island
History: The brigantine wrecked on the reefs in 1788. Only the crew was saved.

Intrepid, American ship, Captain Martin
Location: Great Inagua Island
History: The ship was lost near Great Inagua Island in 1815 while sailing from Jamaica to Baltimore. Her crew and part of her cargo were saved.

Irmelinda, Scottish ship, Captain Graham
Location: Great Abaco Island
History: The vessel was lost near Great Abaco Island on November 9, 1812, while sailing from Clyde to Nassau.

Isaac, American merchantman, Captain Pearson
Location: Great Inagua Island
History: The merchantman wrecked on Great Inagua Island on September 15, 1806, while sailing from Philadelphia to Jamaica.

James Munroe, Irish ship, Captain Harwood
Location: St. Nicolas Key
History: The ship wrecked on St. Nicolas Key in 1821 while carrying a cargo of salt. The crew was saved.

Jane, English merchantman, Captain Caton
Location: Acklin Key

History: The merchantman wrecked off Acklin Key in 1751 while sailing from Jamaica to London. A French vessel saved the crew.

Jane, Canadian ship, Captain Boyd
   Location: Caicos Bank
   History: The ship was lost on the Caicos Bank on February 19, 1806, while sailing from Halifax to Jamaica. The crew was saved.

Jane, American schooner, Captain Miller
   Location: Castle Island
   History: She was lost on Castle Island in 1822 while sailing from Boston to Havana, Cuba. Part of her cargo was saved.

Jane, American ship, Captain Woodward
   Location: Crooked Island
   History: The ship wrecked on August 16, 1818, near Crooked Island while sailing from Savannah to Jamaica. Some of her cargo was saved.

Jane, American schooner, Captain M'Williams
   Location: Great Abaco Island
   History: The schooner wrecked on Great Abaco Island in 1823 while sailing from South Carolina to Havana. The crew and cargo were saved.

Jane, English ship
   Location: Great Inagua Island
   History: She was lost on Great Inagua Island in 1787 while coming from Jamaica.

Jason, English merchantman, Captain Watt
   Location: Great Inagua Island
   History: Six English merchantmen were wrecked at the same time on August 10, 1801, on the reefs of Great Inagua Island: the *Auspicicus, Milton, Jason, Bushy Park, Fanny* and an unidentified ship.

Jefferson, American ship
   Location: Mayaguana Reef
   History: The vessel was totally lost on February 14, 1806, on the Mayaguana Reef while sailing from New York to Jamaica.

Jemima, English brig
   Location: Castle Island

History: The brig was lost on Castle Island in 1822 while coming from Maracaibo, Venezuela. The crew was saved.

Jemima, Scottish ship, Captain Doyle
   Location: Reef near Crooked Island
   History: The vessel wrecked on April 2, 1822, on a reef near Crooked Island. Part of the cargo was saved.

Jenny, American ship, Captain Knox
   Location: Mantanilla Reef
   History: The ship wrecked on Mantanilla Reef on the Little Bahama Bank in 1798 while sailing from Havana, Cuba to Philadelphia. Her crew was saved.

Jerome Maximillian, American ship
   Location: Turks Island
   History: The ship, sailing from New York to Haiti, wrecked at Turks Island on December 30, 1824, with no one aboard.

John, American packet, Captain Sabe
   Location: Caicos Bank
   History: The packet was lost on the Caicos Bank on April 14, 1807, while sailing from Washington to Jamaica.

John, Jamaican ship, Captain Williams
   Location: Fortune Island
   History: The *John* was bound for the United States when it was lost at Fortune Island in 1805.

John, English merchantman, Captain Madge
   Location: Gun Cay
   History: The merchantman was lost off Gun Cay, to the south of Bimini, in 1773, while sailing from Jamaica to Bristol. Her crew was saved.

John, ship of unknown registry
   Location: Silver Shoals
   History: The ship wrecked on Silver Shoals on October 10 or 12 in the year 1818 while bound for Jamaica. The crew was saved.

John, English merchantman, Captain Yates
   Location: Turks Island
   History: The merchantman wrecked on August 13, 1809, on Turks Island while sailing from Liverpool to Nassau. The crew and part of the cargo were saved.

John and Rebecca, ship of unknown registry, Captain Rice
   Location: Inagua Island
   History: The vessel was lost on June 8, 1755, on Great Inagua Island while sailing from Jamaica to Philadelphia.

Jonus, American ship
   Location: Caicos Bank
   History: The ship wrecked on the Caicos Bank in 1819 while sailing from New York to Haiti. The crew and part of the cargo were saved.

Joseph, American ship, Captain Holdrige
   Location: Little Bahama Bank
   History: The vessel was totally lost on June 3, 1824, on the Little Bahama Bank, near Memory Rock while sailing from Mobile to New York.

Jufron Gertrud, Dutch merchantman, Captain Derrick Loffrey
   Location: Great Isaac Cay
   History: The merchantman wrecked near Great Isaac Cay in 1694 while carrying 74,000 pieces of eight and a great quantity of merchandise. The survivors reached Nassau in a small boat and salvors returned to the wreck recovering all her treasure and most of the cargo. They sighted another wreck nearby and again recovered things of value.

Juncta, Spanish merchantman, Captain Capillo
   Location: Little Bahama Bank
   History: The merchantman was lost on the Little Bahama Bank on December 26, 1815, while sailing from Havana to Cadiz. The crew was saved.

Jupiter, Spanish ship, Captain de Minchaca
   Location: Great Abaco Island
   History: The ship wrecked on Great Abaco Island in 1822 while sailing from Malaya to Havana. The crew and part of the cargo were saved.

Katherine, English merchantman, Captain Richards
   Location: Great Inagua Island
   History: The vessel was lost on the island in 1751 while sailing from Jamaica to Bristol. The crew was saved.

Keddington, English merchantman, Captain Bacon

Location: Atwood Key

History: The merchantman was lost on April 1, 1818, at Atwood Key while sailing from Jamaica to London. The crew and part of the cargo were saved.

King George, English ship, Captain Cook

Location: Bimini

History: The ship was lost on a cay near Bimini in 1818 while sailing from Jamaica to London. Most of her cargo was saved.

Lady Warren, English merchantman, Captain Kingsbury

Location: Caicos Bank

History: The merchantman was lost on the Caicos Bank on November 28, 1807, while sailing from Santo Domingo to London. The crew and passengers were saved.

La Fouvette, 20-gun French warship

Location: Great Inagua Island

History: The warship wrecked on Great Inagua Island on November 26, 1791, while sailing from Hispaniola to France. After jettisoning all her guns, provisions, water casks and part of her ballast, she was able to get off the reef and sail to Jamaica for repairs.

Lardegable, American merchantman, Captain Leon

Location: Little Isaac Key, Bimini

History: She was totally lost on Little Isaac Key in 1816 while sailing from Charleston, South Carolina to Havana. The crew was saved.

Lark, American ship, Captain Barry

Location: Great Inagua Island

History: The ship wrecked on Great Inagua Island in 1792 while sailing from Santo Domingo to New England.

Lark, American ship, Captain Swan

Location: Great Inagua Island

History: The vessel wrecked on Great Inagua Island on February 16, 1804, while sailing from Virginia to Jamaica.

L'Armitie, French slave ship, Captain Jabalet

Location: Cay Santo Domingo

History: The slave ship was lost near Cay Santo Domingo in the Old Bahama Channel in 1792 while sailing

from Africa to Havana with a cargo of slaves and ivory.

Le Belisaire, French ship, Captain Kelly

Location: Salt Pond Reef

History: The ship was lost in 1790 on Salt Pond Reef while sailing from Hispaniola to Philadelphia. Part of the cargo was saved.

Le Bernard, French ship

Location: Turks Island

History: This large French ship was totally lost on July 4, 1764, on Turks Island while sailing from Hispaniola to France.

Leopard, American brig

Location: Great Exuma Island

History: The brig wrecked during a gale on September 14, 1821, near Great Exuma Island.

Lilly, American merchantman, Captain M'Camen

Location: Great Abaco Island

History: The merchantman wrecked on Great Abaco Island on December 5, 1803, while sailing from Georgia to Nassau.

Lily, American schooner

Location: Andros Island

History: The schooner wrecked on Andros Island in 1818 while sailing from Port-au-Prince, Haiti to Great Exuma Island. The crew was saved.

Live Oak, American ship, Captain Brill

Location: Harbour Island

History: The ship wrecked on December 1, 1824, near Harbour Island while sailing from Gibraltar to Havana. The crew and cargo were saved.

Lord Duplin, English merchantman, Captain Thompson

Location: Hogsty

History: The merchantman wrecked on the Hogsty in 1752 while sailing from Jamaica to Liverpool. The crew was saved.

Lord North, English merchantman, Captain Maver

Location: San Salvador Island

History: She was lost on San Salvador Island in 1788 while sailing from Liverpool to Nassau. Part of her cargo was saved.

Louisa, American merchantman, Captain Hayes

Location: Great Abaco Island

History: The merchantman was lost near Great Abaco Island in April of 1817 while sailing from Philadelphia to Havana. Part of the cargo was saved.

Loyalty, English merchantman, Captain Atkinson

Location: Hogsty

History: The vessel wrecked on January 27, 1822, on the Hogsty while sailing from Jamaica to London. The crew and part of the cargo were saved.

Margaret, American ship, Captain Hughes

Location: Inagua Island

History: The ship wrecked on March 1, 1818, near Little Inagua Island while sailing from Haiti to New York. The crew and cargo were saved.

Maria, Bahamian sloop, Captain Bartlett

Location: Caicos Bank

History: The sloop wrecked on the Caicos Bank in 1824.

María Antonia, Spanish merchantman

Location: Great Abaco Island

History: The merchantman was lost in February of 1814 on a reef near Great Abaco Island while sailing from Florida to Havana, Cuba. The crew was saved.

Marquis de Castries, French ship

Location: Caicos

History: The ship was totally lost on the Caicos in 1785 while sailing from Cape François, Hispaniola to France.

Mars, English merchantman, Captain Patterson

Location: Hogsty

History: The merchantman wrecked on the Hogsty in 1802 while sailing from Jamaica to London. Part of her cargo was saved.

Martha, English ship, Captain Yates

Location: Caicos Bank

History: The ship was lost on the Caicos Bank in 1806 while coming from Liverpool.

Martha, ship of unknown registry, Captain Jackson

Location: Caicos Bank

History: The ship was lost on the Caicos Bank in 1807 while coming from St. Vincent Island. The crew was saved.

Martha, English ship, Captain M'Intosh

Location: Great Inagua Island

History: She was lost on Great Inagua Island in 1774 while sailing from Jamaica to London. Most of her cargo of rum and sugar was saved.

Mary, ship of unknown registry, Captain Jerault

Location: Berry Islands

History: The vessel wrecked on the Berry Islands in 1816 while coming from the Virgin Islands. The crew and part of the cargo were saved.

Mary, American merchantman, Captain Smith

Location: Caicos Bank

History: The merchantman was totally lost on the Caicos Bank in 1809 while sailing from Cape François, Hispaniola to Philadelphia.

Mary, ship of unknown registry

Location: Great Inagua Island

History: The ship was lost near Great Inagua Island on August 30, 1816, while sailing from Haiti to Baltimore.

Mary, American brig, Captain Telfair

Location: Turks Island

History: The brig was lost near the northeastern end of Turks Island on October 25, 1791, while sailing from New York to Jamaica.

Maryland, American merchantman

Location: Great Bahama Bank

History: The merchantman wrecked on the Great Bahama Bank in 1822. The crew was saved.

Medway Planter, English merchantman, Captain Leslie

Location: Near Cat Island

History: The merchantman was lost on April 25, 1765, while sailing from Jamaica to London, England. Her crew was saved.

Mentor, English ship, Captain Bellowly

Location: Bahamas

History: The ship wrecked in 1806 while carrying the cotton and stores salvaged from the wreck of the *Speedwell*.

Mercury, American ship, Captain Hemsley

Location: Great Inagua Island

History: The vessel was lost on Great Inagua Island in 1787 while sailing from Charleston, South Carolina to Jamaica.

Merredith, English merchantman, Captain Peacock

Location: San Salvador Island

History: The merchantman was lost on San Salvador Island in 1772 while sailing from Jamaica to London, England. The cargo was totally lost but the crew was saved.

Merrimack, ship of unknown registry, Captain Miltimore

Location: Turks Island

History: She totally wrecked at Turks Island in 1822 while sailing to Haiti. The crew and part of the cargo were saved.

Meylor, English merchantman, Captain Tyler

Location: Caicos

History: The merchantman was lost at Caicos in 1769 while sailing from Bristol and Boston to Jamaica. Her crew was saved.

Milford, American merchantman, Captain Dukehard

Location: Great Inagua Island

History: The merchantman was lost near Great Inagua Island on December 23, 1816, while coming from Baltimore. The crew and part of the cargo were saved.

Milton, English merchantman, Captain Robley

Location: Great Inagua Island

History: Six English merchantmen were wrecked at the same time on August 10, 1801, on the reefs of Great Inagua Island: the *Auspicicus, Milton, Jason, Bushy Park, Fanny* and an unidentified ship.

Minerva, American ship, Captain Robinson

Location: Great Abaco Island

History: The vessel was totally lost on March 8, 1816, near Great Abaco Island while sailing from New York to Havana.

Minerva, Canadian ship, Captain Potter

Location: Turks Island

History: The ship was lost at Turks Island in January 1802 while coming from New Brunswick.

Miriam, American ship

Location: Great Inagua Island

History: She wrecked on March 27, 1817, on Great Inagua Island while sailing from Baltimore to Jamaica. Her cargo was saved.

Mohawk, American ship, Captain Harding

Location: Crooked Island

History: The vessel wrecked in August of 1817 on Crooked Island while sailing from New York to Haiti. The crew and part of the cargo were saved.

Moreau, ship of unknown registry, Captain Crosby

Location: Nassau

History: The ship was lost on the Nassau Bar in 1814 while sailing from Amelia Island, Florida to Nassau.

Morne Fortunee, English ship, Captain Dale

Location: Crooked Island

History: The vessel was lost on December 5, 1804, at Crooked Island.

Morning Star, American ship, Captain Bishop

Location: Great Bahama Bank

History: The ship wrecked on the Great Bahama Bank on January 20, 1817, while sailing from South Carolina to Havana.

Nancy, American merchantman

Location: Great Bahama Bank

History: The merchantman wrecked on the Great Bahama Bank in 1822. The crew was saved.

Nancy, American ship, Captain Nevesin

Location: Turks Island

History: The ship was lost at Turks Island on October 28, 1802, while sailing from Virginia to Jamaica.

Nancy Gaer, American ship

Location: Great Inagua Island

History: The ship was lost on May 17, 1769, on Great Inagua Island while sailing from Hispaniola to Georgia. Her crew was saved.

Natchez Belle, American ship
Location: Great Abaco Island
History: The vessel was lost on March 23, 1817, near Great Abaco Island while sailing from New York to New Orleans. The crew and cargo were saved.

Neckar, French ship, Captain Voltearo
Location: Hogsty
History: The ship was wrecked on the Hogsty in 1792 while sailing from Santo Domingo to France.

Nelly, Jamaican privateer
Location: Great Inagua Island
History: She was lost on Great Inagua Island in 1797 while sailing from Jamaica to Nassau.

Neptune, ship of unknown registry, Captain Hallowell
Location: Eleuthera Island
History: The ship totally wrecked on February 5, 1818, near James Point on Eleuthera Island while sailing from France to New Orleans. The crew was saved.

Neptune, English ship, Captain Foller
Location: Turks Island
History: The ship was lost on September 29, 1818, at Turks Island while coming from Antigua.

Neutrality, American ship, Captain Kimball
Location: Cats Key
History: The vessel was lost on January 13, 1812, at Cats Key, south of Bimini, while sailing from Jamaica to Georgia. The crew was saved.

New Orleans, American ship, Captain Booth
Location: Great Abaco Island
History: The ship was lost near Great Abaco Island in 1816. The crew and cargo were saved.

Nile, American ship, Captain Turnley
Location: Great Inagua Island
History: She was lost near Great Inagua Island on March 26, 1816, while sailing from New York to Jamaica. The crew and cargo were saved.

North America, American ship
Location: Bimini
History: The ship wrecked near Bimini in 1825 while sailing from Nassau to Key West.

Nuestra Señora de la Concepción, galleon belonging to the Nueva España Flota (fleet) of Captain-General Juan de Campos, 680 tons, Captain Hernando Rodriques
Location: Silver Shoals
History: The galleon was separated from the convoy during a storm in the Bahama Channel in 1641, and drifted without masts or rudder until wrecking on the north side of Silver Shoals. Most of the 600 persons aboard managed to swim to a nearby sandbar. Makeshift rafts and boats were constructed from the shipwreck, which carried about 200 survivors toward Santo Domingo. However, only a few ever made it to safety. By the time a

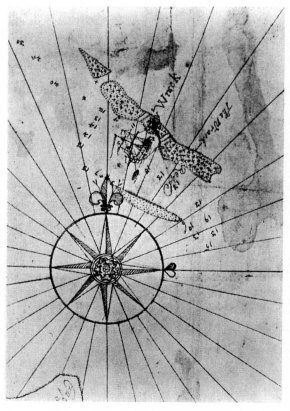

Chart showing the location of the *Concepción*.

rescue vessel reached the shipwreck all of the remaining shipwreck survivors had perished on the sandbar. Bad weather prevented salvage operations for several months. When the weather finally moderated, the sandbar had been washed away and the rescuers could not locate the wreck site. The Spaniards searched for the wreck for many years. Then in 1687, Sir William Phips discovered the galleon. Over a period of weeks, divers brought up more than 32 tons of silver, vast numbers of coins, gold, chests of pearls, and leather bags containing precious gems. There was a constant struggle to bring up the treasure while fighting off encircling pirates. Ultimately, bad weather and a shortage of provisions put an end to the salvage operations. The total value of Phips' recovery in today's money was more than $50 million. He was knighted by the grateful monarch, who later made him governor of the Massachusetts colony. Phips' share of the treasure made him one of the richest men in America. Even though the story of his recovery was well known, a myth still persisted that he did not recover all the treasure from the wreck. In fact, he recovered almost twice the amount that the ship's register stated she carried. Some of the salvors who visited the site within a few decades of Phips were successful in varying degrees. The exact location of the wreck was eventually lost and the galleon forgotten until the advent of scuba diving. Burt Webber, who grew up fascinated with the shipwreck after reading about Phips and the *Concepción*, finally found the wreck in 1978. What started with a single coin quickly became a steady flow. His team found coins by the bucketful in a depression in the sand that they dubbed the "money hole." They removed over 45 tons of coral to clean out the areas of the "money hole," and found more than 60,000 silver coins, numerous gold chains, several gold coins, and thousands of other priceless artifacts, including three astrolabes and a collection of fragile Ming Dynasty porcelain. They worked seven days a week for 11 months before the wreck was completely salvaged. The entire find from the *Concepción* was valued at $10 million, proving that Phips had indeed left plenty of treasure behind.

Nuestra Señora de la Maravillas, *almiranta* of the Tierra Firme Armada of Captain-General Marques de Montenegro, 650 tons, Admiral Mathias de Orelanas

Location: Little Bahama Bank

History: During 1656, the whole convoy found itself in shallow water one night and veered seaward. The *Maravillas* collided with another galleon and sank in five to six fathoms of water on the Little Bahama Bank about 20 miles north of Memory Rock. Of the more than 700 persons aboard the ship only 56 were saved. The Spaniards began salvage operations soon afterward and during the next three years recovered over 1,500,000 pesos of the five million pesos of treasure on

Spanish gold treasures recovered from the *Nuestra Señora de la Maravillas*.

the wreck. However, shifting sand soon covered the wreck over completely and salvage operations were abandoned. In 1657, two small salvage vessels carrying some of the treasure from the wreck to Puerto Rico themselves wrecked on the south side of Gorda Cay. The survivors buried some of the treasure on the cay and most of it, like most of what still remained on the wrecks, was recovered the following year. Later, in 1681, Sir William Phips searched the shipwreck site and recovered only a small amount of silver specie due to the sand over the wreck. In modern times many treasure hunters have searched for the wreck with most looking in the Florida Keys, where other authors had placed the site of the shipwreck. In 1960, coauthor Robert F. Marx discovered the true location of the wreck while researching in Spain's archives. Marx himself located the wreck site in 1972. He recovered tons of silver bars, thousands of silver coins, gold disks, uncut emeralds and tons of other artifacts. The most stirring find was a silver plate bearing the coat of arms of the author of the book that led Marx to discover the treasure galleon. Soon after salvaging part of the wreck, the Bahamian government rescinded his salvage permit. Rumors that inevitably plague any treasure operation were circulating that Marx and his team had found more than five tons of gold, as well as the Golden Madonna, and spirited it all away so as to cheat the Bahamians. No amount of reasoning could persuade the Bahamian officials otherwise. Marx lost the rights to the rest of the wreck and had to wait more than four years to obtain his share of what he had found. Every year thereafter, one treasure hunting firm or another received a permit for the *Maravillas* and set out to find the main section. Inevitably, after weeks and months of futile search, each group resorted to reworking the area of the bow section where Marx had recovered treasure. Some were more successful than others. Since 1986, Maritime Archaeological Research, Ltd., a firm headed by Tennessee businessman Herbert Humphreys, has been working around the bow section and

the "hot spot" from which Marx removed the anchor years ago. In 1988, they recovered an emerald weighing over ten carats, valued at $1 million. The following year they found 5,000 silver coins, 13 feet of gold chain, dozens of gold lockets, rings, pendants, and several gold bars. The 1991 season was the best of all, with the discovery of 29 gold ingots, the largest weighing over 35 pounds, 4,000 silver coins, and dozens of silver bars. The three silver bars discovered in recent years on Gorda Cay by Art McKee and the one bar discovered by Rosco Thompson and Howard Lightbourn came from the two small *Maravillas* salvage vessels, wrecked there in 1657.

Olympus, ship of unknown registry
   Location: New Providence Island
   History: The ship wrecked at New Providence Island in November 1810 while sailing from New Orleans to England.

Orient, American ship, Captain Hunter
   Location: Turks Island
   History: The vessel was lost at Turks Island in 1810 while sailing from New York to Jamaica. The crew was saved.

Orion, American ship, Captain Smith
   Location: Mayaguana Reef
   History: She wrecked on December 8, 1823, on the Mayaguana Reef while sailing from Haiti to Wilmington. The crew and cargo were saved.

Orion, ship of unknown registry, Captain Brown
   Location: Pelican Key
   History: The ship wrecked on October 28, 1810, on Pelican Key while sailing from Philadelphia to Havana. Four of the crew drowned.

Palliser, ship of unknown registry
   Location: New Providence Island
   History: The vessel was lost in 1774 on New Providence Island.

Panopea, American ship, Captain Bogle
   Location: Turks Island
   History: The ship wrecked at Turks Island on December 25, 1824, while sailing from South Carolina to Jamaica. Most of her cargo was saved.

Patrice, French merchantman, Captain Largement

Location: Great Inagua Island

History: The merchantman wrecked on Great Inagua Island in 1792 while sailing from Hispaniola to France.

Patty, English merchantman, Captain Clark

Location: Nassau

History: The merchantman was lost near Nassau in 1763 while sailing from Bristol.

Perseverance, American brig

Location: Great Abaco Island

History: The brig was lost on Great Abaco Island on June 9, 1821, while sailing from Charleston, South Carolina to Havana. The crew was saved.

Peter Beckford, English ship, Captain Lovelace

Location: Reef at San Salvador Island

History: The ship was lost on a reef at San Salvador Island in 1763 while sailing from Jamaica to London.

Phoenix, English ship

Location: Mantanilla Reef

History: The ship wrecked in March of 1816 on the Mantanilla Reef while sailing from Havana to Nassau. The crew was saved.

Pink, American ship, Captain Hasrwen [*sic*]

Location: Silver Shoals

History: The vessel was lost in January 1781 on Silver Shoals while sailing from New York to Jamaica. Her crew was saved.

Polly, American merchantman, Captain Bigby

Location:

History: The merchantman was lost on September 13, 1806, while sailing from Jamaica to Wilmington.

Polly, American merchantman, Captain Walker

Location: Silver Shoals

History: The ship was lost in 1753 on Silver Shoals near the *Nuestra Señora de la Concepción,* which wrecked there in 1641. The *Polly* was sailing from Rhode Island to Jamaica when she foundered.

Pomona, Scottish merchantman, Captain M'Naught

Location: Caicos Bank

History: The merchantman was lost on April 10, 1818, on the Caicos Bank while sailing from Jamaica to Glasgow. The crew, rum and sails were saved.

Porgey, American merchantman, Captain Dickson

Location: Turks Island

History: The merchantman was lost at Turks Island in 1786 while sailing from New York to Jamaica.

Port Morant, English merchantman, Captain Raffles

Location: Hogsty

History: The ship was lost on Hogsty in 1775 while sailing from Jamaica to London with a cargo of rum and sugar. The crew clung to the rocks for ten days before being rescued.

Port Royal, English ship, Captain John Russel

Location: 26.14.00 N latitude at Munsake Island near Abaco

History: The ship wrecked on the island on January 12, 1669. Current charts do not show an island by this name.

Port Royal, ship of unknown registry

Location: Great Inagua Island

History: She was lost near Great Inagua Island in 1815 while sailing from New York to Jamaica.

Posthumous, English merchantman, Captain Fisher

Location: Saynee Island

History: The merchantman was lost at Saynee Island in 1821. The crew was saved. There is no Bahamian island by this name today.

Prince Ferdinand, ship of unknown registry, Captain Caznean

Location: Great Inagua Island

History: The ship was lost on January 17, 1760, on Great Inagua Island while sailing from Boston to Jamaica. The crew was saved.

Prince of Wales, English packet boat, Captain Paquet

Location: Great Inagua Island Reef

History: This packet wrecked on the Great Inagua Island Reef on July 19, 1811, while coming from Jamaica. The crew, passengers, mail and specie were saved.

Prince Regent, Canadian ship, Captain Wickes

Location: Cat Cay

History: The ship was lost near Cat Cay, south of Bimini, on September 5, 1821, while sailing from Jamaica to Halifax. The crew was saved.

Princess Charlotte, English packet boat

Location: Hogsty Reef

History: The boat wrecked in early April of 1819 on Hogsty Reef while sailing from Jamaica to England. The crew, passengers, mail and specie, with the exception of about $30,000, were all saved.

Providence, English brig, Captain Dunn

Location: Great Exuma Island

History: The brig wrecked on August 8, 1824, near Great Exuma Island while sailing from Gibraltar to Havana.

Pyomingo, American merchantman, Captain Latimer

Location: Berry Islands

History: The merchantman wrecked in the Berry Islands in 1806 while sailing from London to New Orleans.

Ranger, American ship, Captain Eldridge

Location: Great Abaco Island

History: The vessel was totally lost on January 26, 1822, on Great Abaco Island while sailing from South Carolina to Havana.

Ranger, English merchantman, Captain Lea

Location: New Providence Island

History: The merchantman was lost near New Providence Island in 1802 while arriving from London.

Rapid, German ship, Captain Hinman

Location: Cat Cay

History: The ship was lost near Cat Cay, south of Bimini, in 1821, while sailing from Havana to Hamburg.

Rattlesnake, American ship, Captain Bessel

Location: Great Inagua Island

History: The vessel wrecked in September of 1806 on Great Inagua Island while sailing from Jamaica to North Carolina.

Remittance, ship of unknown registry, Captain Heter
Location: Great Abaco Island
History: She wrecked on Great Abaco Island in 1823 while sailing from New York to Havana.

Richard, American schooner, Captain Harvey
Location: Turks Island
History: The schooner was lost on September 11, 1823, on Turks Island while sailing from New York to Jamaica. The crew and most of the cargo were saved.

Rio, Cuban ship
Location: Berry Islands
History: The ship wrecked in the Berry Islands in 1823 while sailing from Philadelphia to Havana.

Rival, American ship
Location: Great Abaco Island
History: The vessel wrecked on Great Abaco Island on November 18, 1818, while sailing from Boston to Mobile. The crew, passengers and cargo were saved.

Robert, English ship, Captain Wilkes
Location: Egg Island
History: She wrecked on a reef off Egg Island in 1816 while sailing from Nassau to Liverpool.

Robert & Mary, American ship, Captain Cameron
Location: Near Great Abaco Island
History: The ship was lost on the North Cay near Great Abaco Island in 1791 while sailing from Wilmington to Barbados.

Robert Potter, American merchantman
Location: Great Abaco Island
History: The merchantman was lost on April 17, 1817, near Great Abaco Island while sailing from Norfolk to Havana.

Rodney, American ship, Captain Jenkins
Location: Samphire Reefs
History: The ship sprang a leak and sank on the Samphire Reefs near Nassau in 1785 while sailing from Florida to Jamaica.

Rosa, Spanish ship
Location: Great Abaco Island
History: She was lost near Great Abaco Island in 1816 while sailing from Africa to Havana with 300 slaves onboard. All the people were saved.

Rosa, Spanish merchantman
Location: Little Isaac Island
History: The merchantman wrecked near Little Isaac Island (called Las Profetas by the Spanish) in October 1817. She ran aground on a reef 13 nautical miles, and bearing 73 degrees, from the island.

Rose, ship of unknown registry, Captain Morris
Location: Atwood Key
History: She was totally lost in August 1814 at Atwood Key while sailing from Haiti to Hamburg, Germany.

Ruby, Jamaican ship, Captain M'Intosh
Location: Fortune Island
History: The *Ruby* was bound for the United States when it was lost at Fortune Island in 1805.

Sally, ship of unknown registry, Captain Croskill
Location: Nassau
History: The vessel wrecked at Nassau on October 24, 1785.

Sally, American merchantman, Captain Alexander
Location: Turks Island
History: She was lost at Turks Island in 1786 while sailing from Jamaica to Maryland.

San Francisco de Paula (alias *Orionon*), Spanish ship, Captain Pugol
Location: Mayaguana Island
History: This ship wrecked on the reefs near Mayaguana Island in 1825 while sailing from Barcelona to Havana, Cuba. The crew was saved.

San Juan Evangelista, galleon belonging to the Armada de Barlovento
Location: Twenty-seven degrees latitude in four fathoms of water near Grand Bahama Island

Drawing of a Spanish galleon c. 1650.

History: The galleon, sailing with the armada in 1714 from Veracruz to Puerto Rico and Santo Domingo, was carrying 300,000 pesos in treasure to pay the royal officials and military at both islands when it was struck by a storm in the Bahama Channel and wrecked. Salvors recovered all the treasure and the ship's cannon.

Santa Clara, galleon belonging to the Tierra Firme Armada of Captain-General Estevan de las Alas, 300 tons, Captain Juan Diaz
Location: El Mime Shoal
History: The galleon ran aground on October 6, 1564, on the El Mime Shoal. Other ships in the convoy saved all of the people, gold and silver. On 16th century charts, this shoal was situated several miles north of Memory Rock on the Little Bahama Bank. Later on the Spaniards called the shoals Mimbres.

Santa Rosa, Spanish ship, Captain Torres
Location: Egg Island
History: The ship was lost in March 1821 on Egg Island while sailing from Philadelphia to Havana. The crew was saved.

Sarah Ann, Bahamian schooner, Captain Bannatyne
Location: Green Key
History: The schooner wrecked on March 5, 1823, on Green Key while coming from Cuba.

Savannah, American packet boat, Captain Fowler
Location: Great Abaco Island

History: The boat wrecked on Great Abaco Island on October 14, 1818, while sailing from New York to Mobile. The crew, passengers and cargo were saved.

Savannah, American ship, Captain Bowers
   Location: Macories Reef
   History: The vessel was totally lost on Macories Reef in the Old Bahama Channel in 1816 while sailing from Liverpool, England to New Orleans. The crew was saved.

Savannah Packet, American merchantman
   Location: Great Bahama Bank
   History: The merchantman wrecked on the Great Bahama Bank in 1822. The crew was saved.

Sceptre, American ship, Captain Simpson
   Location: New Providence Island
   History: The ship was lost on New Providence Island in 1815 while sailing from Philadelphia to New Orleans.

Schomer, English ship, Captain Howe
   Location: Turks Island
   History: The vessel was lost at Turks Island on September 20, 1810, while sailing from Haiti to London. The crew was saved.

Sero, ship of unknown registry, Captain Murdock
   Location: Turks Island
   History: The ship was totally lost on July 27, 1819, at Turks Island while sailing from Philadelphia to Cuba.

Shakespeare, ship of unknown registry
   Location: Great Abaco Island
   History: The vessel wrecked on Great Abaco Island in March of 1818 while sailing from Le Havre to America.

Simon Taylor, English merchantman
   Location: Great Inagua Island
   History: The merchantman wrecked on Great Inagua Island on May 25, 1791, while carrying a cargo of rum and cotton. The passengers and crew were saved.

Sir Charles Hamilton, English merchantman
   Location: Turks Island
   History: The merchantman was to-

tally lost on Turks Island in 1807 while sailing from Liverpool to Santo Domingo.

Sir James Yeo, English ship, Captain Humble
   Location: Bird Rock
   History: The vessel wrecked on Bird Rock near Crooked Island in 1814 while sailing from Jamaica to Halifax. Most of her cargo was salvaged.

Sir John Doyle, English merchantman, Captain Watts
   Location: Great Abaco Island
   History: The merchantman wrecked on September 13, 1818, on Great Abaco Island while sailing from Havana to Santiago de Cuba. Part of her cargo was saved.

Sovereign, English ship, Captain Pierson
   Location: Hogsty
   History: The ship totally wrecked on November 17, 1821, on the Hogsty while sailing from Jamaica to London. The crew and cargo were saved.

Speedwell, English ship, Captain Fairbotham
   Location: Bahamas
   History: The vessel was lost on September 13, 1806, during a hurricane while sailing from Jamaica to Liverpool.

Speedy Peace, American merchantman
   Location: Great Bahama Bank
   History: The merchantman wrecked on the Great Bahama Bank in 1822 while sailing from Mobile to New York. The crew was saved.

Statira, American frigate
   Location: Great Inagua Island
   History: The frigate was lost near Great Inagua Island on February 27, 1815. The crew was saved.

St. Francis, ship of unknown registry
   Location: Sandy Cay
   History: The *St. Francis* was sailing from Philadelphia to Antigua when it was forced ashore on Sandy Cay by a French privateer in 1758.

St. George, American ship, Captain Vincent
   Location: Great Inagua Island

History: The ship wrecked on Great Inagua Island in 1791 while sailing from Jamaica to North Carolina. Part of her cargo was saved.

Strong, American ship, Captain McGill
   Location: Mayaguana Island
   History: The vessel wrecked on the reefs near Mayaguana Island in 1825 while sailing from Haiti to Baltimore. Part of her cargo was saved.

Supply, English merchantman, Captain Wallace
   Location: Mohairs Key, near New Providence Island
   History: The merchantman wrecked at Mohairs Key in 1801 while sailing from Honduras to London.

Swallow, ship of unknown registry, Captain Mossop
   Location: North end of Eleuthera Island
   History: The ship wrecked on December 10, 1816, on a reef at the north end of Eleuthera Island while sailing from Savannah, Georgia to Jamaica. The crew was saved.

The Charm, American ship, Captain Peggy Stinton
   Location: Caicos Bank
   History: The vessel was lost on the Caicos Bank in 1768 while sailing from North Carolina to Jamaica.

Thomas, American ship, Captain Cobb
   Location: Great Inagua Island
   History: The ship wrecked at Great Inagua Island on February 5, 1804, while sailing from Virginia to Jamaica.

Three Brothers, English ship
   Location: New Providence Island
   History: The ship wrecked at New Providence Island in 1810.

Three Sisters, American ship, Captain Spears
   Location: Guana Cay
   History: She was lost on Guana Cay in 1792 while sailing from South Carolina to Nassau. Her crew was saved.

Three Sisters, American schooner, Captain Allen
   Location: Hogsty
   History: The schooner wrecked on the Hogsty in 1824 while coming from Jamaica.

Transit, French ship, Captain Vaux
   Location: Great Inagua Island
   History: The ship was totally lost on a reef off the southwestern end of Great Inagua Island in 1810 while coming from Haiti.

Treasure
   Location: Large cay in the Bahamas
   History: A Spanish merchant ship, owned by Hernando del Castillo, was sailing to Havana in 1599 when it was captured by pirates. The pirates took the Spaniards and their cargo aboard and soon after anchored at Great Inagua Island. The Spaniards escaped in a small boat and headed for Cuba. En route they stopped at a large cay for water and accidentally discovered an enormous treasure of gold and silver bars and pieces of artillery from ships that must have wrecked there. They took some of the treasure with them, and Cuba sent other vessels, which picked up the remainder later.

Triton, English merchantman
   Location: Hogsty
   History: The merchantman was lost on June 19, 1790, on the Hogsty while sailing from Jamaica to England. The crew and part of the cargo were saved.

Twin Sisters, American ship, Captain Owen
   Location: Great Abaco Island
   History: The ship was lost near Great Abaco Island on February 18, 1812, while sailing from Baltimore to Havana, Cuba. The crew and most of the cargo were saved.

Two Brothers, English merchantman, Captain Holmes
   Location: Memory Rock
   History: The merchantman wrecked near Memory Rock in 1818 while sailing from New Orleans to Liverpool. The crew was saved.

Two Sisters, Irish merchantman, Captain Sedley
   Location: Royal Island, near Providence Island
   History: The merchantman was lost at Royal Island in 1791 while sailing from Cork to Nassau.

Unidentified, ships (2)
   Location: Bahamas

Sixteenth century galleon rescuing survivors from another galleon.

   History: Two unidentified ships carrying a great amount of silver suffered from a storm in the Bahama Channel and soon after were wrecked on one of the Bahama islands near Hispaniola in 1554. All the people and treasure made it ashore. A small frigate was made from the remains of both wrecks and sent to Cuba, but sank on the way. Only two people survived the foundering. Salvors were sent from Cuba but they were unable to locate the island where the survivors and silver were marooned.

Unidentified, ships (5 or 6)
   Location: Six miles north of Whale Key
   History: The *General Oglethorp* wrecked on a reef six miles north of Whale Key in the year 1802. In the same area five or six other ships were lost, one of which was an African slave ship.

Unidentified, merchant brig
   Location: Ackland Key
   History: The brig wrecked at Ackland Key in 1822. The crew was saved.

Unidentified, English merchantman
   Location: Acklins Key
   History: A large three-decked English merchantman wrecked on the south end of Acklin Key in 1787.

Unidentified, English privateers (3)

   Location: Arcas Reef, Old Bahama Channel
   History: The privateers sailing in the squadron of General Jacob Jackson wrecked on Arcas Reef in 1644.

Unidentified, ship
   Location: Bimini
   History: The ship identified in documents only by the name "Petatch," which may be an alternative English spelling for patache, wrecked near Bimini in 1723.

Unidentified, merchantman
   Location: Caicos Bank
   History: A three-decked merchantman was lost on the southwest cay of the Caicos Bank in 1772.

Unidentified, merchantman
   Location: Caicos Bank
   History: The vessel was lost on the southwestern part of the Caicos Bank in 1792.

Unidentified, ships (4)
   Location: Caicos Bank
   History: These four vessels were lost on the Caicos Bank in 1806.

Unidentified, Dutch brig
   Location: Caicos Bank
   History: The brig wrecked on the Caicos Bank on April 13, 1819, with a valuable cargo of silks while sailing from Hamburg to Havana.

Unidentified, American schooner
   Location: Caicos Bank
   History: The schooner wrecked on the Caicos Bank in 1819.

Unidentified, *urca*, Captain Gonzalo de Peñalosa
   Location: Cayo Romano
   History: The ship wrecked on Cayo Romano in the Little Bahama Channel in 1567.

Unidentified, caravels (2)
   Location: Crooked Island
   History: In July or August of 1500, two unidentified caravels of the four sailing in the squadron of Vicente Yanez Pinzón from Brazil to Spain, wrecked near Crooked Island.

Unidentified, brig
   Location: Crooked Island
   History: A large brig wrecked on the Crooked Island Reef before April 15, 1819.

Unidentified, English ship, Captain Sayle
   Location: Eleuthera Island
   History: The ship wrecked in 1660 on the island. Captain Sayle then sailed to Virginia in a small boat, returning later in a larger vessel to rescue the survivors.

Unidentified, American brigantine
   Location: Eleuthera Island
   History: In 1702, pirates forced the brigantine to run aground on Eleuthera Island where they plundered her.

Unidentified, French merchantman
   Location: Great Abaco Island
   History: In 1704, a Bermudan privateer commanded by Captain Peniston captured the French merchantman, which was sailing from Martinique to France with a cargo of sugar, indigo cocoa, and drugs. After transferring some of the cargo to their vessel, the privateers wrecked the French ship on Great Abaco Island.

Unidentified, Dutch ship
   Location: Great Bahama Bank
   History: The Dutch ship wrecked on the south edge of the Great Bahama Bank in July 1817. She was sailing from Amsterdam to Havana when she foundered.

Unidentified, French brig
   Location: Great Inagua Island
   History: The brig was lost on Great Inagua Island in 1787. Most of the crew and part of the cargo were saved.

Unidentified, French frigate
   Location: Great Inagua Island
   History: The frigate wrecked on May 10, 1791, while sailing from Hispaniola to France. The troops onboard and crew were saved.

Unidentified, merchantmen (8)
   Location: Great Inagua Island
   History: These eight unidentified merchantmen were totally wrecked on Great Inagua Island in August of 1800, along with eight other merchantmen carrying cargoes of colonial produce valued at over 600,000 pounds sterling.

Unidentified, English merchantman
   Location: Great Inagua Island
   History: Six English merchantmen were wrecked at the same time on August 10, 1801, on the reefs of Great Inagua Island: the *Auspicius, Milton, Jason, Bushy Park, Fanny* and an unidentified ship.

Unidentified, ships (3)
   Location: Great Inagua Island
   History: The three were lost near Great Inagua Island during June 1816. One of the ships was carrying a considerable amount of money.

Unidentified, ship of unknown registry
   Location: Great Inagua Island
   History: The ship wrecked near Great Inagua Island in 1822.

Unidentified, French ship
   Location: Hogsty
   History: The ship was lost in 1775 on the Hogsty while coming from Port-au-Prince.

Unidentified, English merchantman
   Location: Hogsty
   History: In December 1801, a large English merchantman coming from Jamaica, wrecked on the Hogsty but slipped off the reef and sank in deeper water before she could be identified.

Unidentified, Jamaican vessels (2)
   Location: Hogsty

History: A brig and a schooner were wrecked on the Hogsty in 1823.

Unidentified, ships (3)
   Location: Little Bahama Bank
   History: Three unidentified ships were wrecked in 1774 on the Little Bahama Bank north of Memory Rock, but the current was too strong for several passing ships to send rescue boats to them.

Unidentified, ships (3)
   Location: Little Bahama Bank
   History: A chart, drawn in 1687, was found in the archives, and on it a Captain Salman had indicated three shipwreck locations on the Little Bahama Bank: the *Copper Wreck*, bearing ten degrees from Memory Rock in latitude 27.02.11 N and about one and a half miles from the edge of the bank; the *Genovees Wreck*, bearing northwest by about three and a half English leagues from the *Copper Wreck* in latitude 27.10.11 N, and about a mile from the edge of the bank; and the *Plate Wreck*, bearing 15 degrees and ten nautical miles from the *Genovees Wreck* in about six fathoms of water in latitude 27.20.11 N, and about three nautical miles from the edge of the bank.

Unidentified, Spanish warship
   Location: Little Bahama Bank
   History: The ship was sailing from Havana to St. Augustine, Florida with 200 men aboard and chests of silver specie to pay the garrison there, when it wrecked in 1715 on the Little Bahama Bank. Salvors recovered all the treasure and then burnt the wreck.

Unidentified, Spanish *nao*
   Location: Lobos Cay
   History: The vessel wrecked in 1741 on Lobos Cay near the Old Bahama Channel.

Unidentified, merchant sloop
   Location: Long Key
   History: The large sloop wrecked on a reef at Long Key in 1770. Salvors recovered several chests of Spanish silver specie from the wreck.

Unidentified, Spanish galleons (2)
   Location: Lucaya Beach
   History: In 1628, two unidentified Spanish galleons carrying treasure were

wrecked during the night near Golden Rock on the south side of Grand Bahama Island. They had been captured in Matanzas Bay, Cuba by Piet Heyn and were sailing in the Dutch fleet under his command when they wrecked. A section of one of these two ships was discovered several years ago off Lucaya Beach. A considerable amount of silver coins were recovered; however, a great amount of treasure surely remains undiscovered.

Unidentified, ship
   Location: Mayaguana Island
   History: In 1702, this vessel was forced to wreck at Mayaguana Island by pirates. There, they burnt her to the waterline after plundering her.

Unidentified, ships (several)
   Location: Nassau
   History: Several unidentified ships were lost at Nassau in 1787.

Unidentified, ships (120+)
   Location: Nassau
   History: Over 120 ships of various descriptions and sizes were wrecked, sunk or thrown on the beach near and at Nassau during a hurricane in July 1801. Only a slave ship named *George* was identified.

Unidentified, ships (40+)
   Location: Nassau
   History: Over 40 ships were wrecked, sunk or cast ashore during a violent gale at Nassau on July 26, 1813. Only one was identified: the *Dart*.

Unidentified, ships (many)
   Location: Nassau
   History: Many ships were wrecked and sunk on December 14, 1818, at Nassau during a bad gale.

Unidentified, ships (several)
   Location: Rum Key
   History: Several unidentified ships were wrecked at Rum Key during a hurricane on September 11, 1824.

Unidentified, Spanish galleon
   Location: Seven miles southwest from Beak Cay
   History: According to an English historian writing in 1775, a very rich unidentified Spanish galleon was wrecked in 1765 on a shoal of sand located seven miles southwest from Beak Cay,

the southernmost cay in the Riding Rock Chain, in 17 feet of water. Some treasure was recovered at the time of the disaster but the wreck sanded over before the majority of it could be recovered.

Unidentified, French frigate
   Location: Silver Cay
   History: The frigate wrecked in 1724 at Caye de Argent (or Silver Cay) on the Caicos Bank.

Unidentified, galleons (2) belonging to the Nueva España Flota (fleet) of Captain-General Sancho de Viedma
   Location: Silver Shoals
   History: Two galleons owned by the viceroy of Mexico, Don Luis de Velasco, separated from the convoy during a storm in 1551 and wrecked on Silver Shoals. The ship then sank in deeper water. Divers were able to recover only 150,000 pesos of the treasure it carried.

Unidentified, Spanish merchantman, 300 tons
   Location: Sugar Cay
   History: The ship was forced ashore on Sugar Cay in 1744 by the famous American privateer Captain Lamprier, whose ship was also wrecked nearby. She was sailing from Cadiz to Mexico while carrying 200 men and a cargo valued at over 300,000 pounds sterling when she was forced ashore.

Unidentified, Dutch ship
   Location: Sugar Key
   History: The ships wrecked on Sugar Key in 1823 while sailing from Hamburg to Havana with a very valuable cargo. Most of the cargo was saved.

Unidentified, ships (many)
   Location: Windward Passage
   History: At least 11 merchantmen and several English warships were lost in the Windward Passage near the Caicos Islands in a hurricane on November 2, 1775.

Union, American merchantman, Captain M'Keown
   Location: Great Caicos Reef
   History: The merchantman wrecked on January 21, 1811, on the Great Caicos Reef while sailing from Virginia to Jamaica. The crew was saved.

Urbana, ship of unknown registry, Captain Brittain
   Location: Turks Island
   History: The ship was lost on Turks Island in 1815 while sailing from New York to Jamaica. The crew was saved.

Victoria, ship of unknown registry, Captain M'Killop
   Location: Mayaguana Reef
   History: The vessel wrecked on the Mayaguana Reef. She was able to get off the reef, but then wrecked off the western end of Crooked Island on November 10, 1823, where she went to pieces. She was sailing from Jamaica to Halifax when she was lost.

Victorina, English merchantman
   Location: New Providence Island
   History: The ship wrecked on the west end of New Providence Island on December 9, 1809, while sailing from Liverpool to this island.

Ville de St. Pierre, French ship, Captain Scolan
   Location: Sugar Key
   History: The vessel wrecked on Sugar Key in 1823 while sailing from France to Havana. The crew and most of the cargo were saved.

Walton Grey, American schooner
   Location: Berry Islands
   History: The schooner wrecked in 1819 in the Berry Islands while sailing from Baltimore to Havana. Most of her cargo was saved.

Wanderer, English ship
   Location: Double Headed Shot Key
   History: She totally wrecked on Double Headed Shot Key on June 3, 1823. The crew and passengers were saved.

Warren, ship of unknown registry
   Location: Sugar Key
   History: The ship wrecked on Sugar Key in 1823 while sailing from France to Havana with 400 tons of wine. Most of the cargo was saved.

Warrior, American ship, Captain Dickenson
   Location: Great Bahama Bank
   History: The vessel was lost on June 30, 1815, on the Great Bahama Bank to the west of Andros Island while sailing from New York to Havana. The crew was saved.

Warwick, English ship, Captain Manepenny

Location: Atwood Key

History: The ship was lost on August 8, 1751, at Atwood Key while sailing from Philadelphia to Hispaniola. The crew was saved.

Washington, American ship, Captain Taylor

Location: Great Abaco Island

History: The ship wrecked on Great Abaco Island in 1822 while sailing in ballast from New York to New Orleans.

Washington, American ship, Captain Berry

Location: Turks Island

History: The ship totally wrecked at Turks Island on October 17, 1822, while sailing from New York to Haiti. Her crew was saved.

Westmoreland, ship of unknown registry, Captain Majoribanks

Location: Caicos Bank

History: The vessel was totally lost on the Caicos Bank on December 5, 1822, while sailing from Quebec to Jamaica. Her crew was saved.

William, American schooner

Location: Great Inagua Island

History: The schooner was lost on Great Inagua Island in 1797 while sailing from Baltimore. Most of her cargo was saved.

William & Mary, American ship, Captain Cooper

Location: Great Abaco Island

History: She was lost near Great Abaco Island on October 17, 1816, while sailing from Philadelphia to Havana.

William & Mary, American merchantman, Captain Ross

Location: Hogsty

History: The merchantman wrecked on August 23, 1815, on the Hogsty while sailing from Haiti to Baltimore. The crew was saved.

Woodstock, English merchantman, Captain Paton

Location: Mayaguana Island

History: The merchantman wrecked on the reefs near Mayaguana Island in 1825 while sailing from Jamaica to London. A small part of her cargo was saved.

Workenston, American merchantman, Captain Wilkens

Location: North Caicos Key

History: The ship wrecked on North Caicos Key in 1817 while sailing from New England to Veracruz. The crew and part of her cargo were saved.

Zephyr, American ship, Captain Pace

Location: Grand Caicos Island

History: The vessel was lost on Grand Caicos Island in 1805 while sailing from Virginia to Jamaica.

Bermuda

Bermuda, in relation to its size, has more shipwrecks than any other area in the Western Hemisphere, with the possible exceptions of the Florida Keys and Cape Hatteras, North Carolina. Although the islands are nothing more than a dot on charts, located 800 miles from the United States, Bermuda played an important role in early navigation. All the Spanish ships, as well as those of other European nations sailing in the waters of the New World, attempted to pass within sight of Bermuda on their homeward-bound voyages, using it as a checkpoint in their haphazard navigation.

Most of the ships bringing colonists to North America either made stops there or passed within sight of the islands. Because they are very low in elevation and generally concealed by mist or haze, sighting the islands of Bermuda was not an easy task and many

ships ran up on reefs, some of which are as far as ten miles out.

From the earliest days many Bermudans have engaged in salvaging wrecks in their own waters. Teddy Tucker, a Bermudan and descendant of the first governor of Bermuda, has been responsible for locating many notable wrecks in his home waters, including the *San Antonio, Eagle, Virginia Merchant, Sir George Arthur, Ceasar* and the *L'Herminie.*

Although Bermudans generally work on shipwrecks during the summer, work on many sites can be carried out most of the year, except when passing hurricanes cause huge swells to break on the reefs. Certain areas are now restricted and are under control of the Bermudan Maritime Museum. In many areas no permits are necessary to explore wreck sites, but application for salvage leases must be made to

the Receiver of Wrecks. The salvor may keep all that he recovers, but the Bermudan government has the right to purchase any or all of it at a fair price. Most shipwrecks in Bermudan waters are stated in documents as being merely "at Bermuda," so there is no category "Location" for the following wrecks. If a more specific location is known, it is given in the category "History."

SHIPWRECKS IN BERMUDA'S WATERS

Actif, English warship, Captain John Harvey

History: The ship foundered off Bermuda on November 26, 1794.

Admiral Durham, English merchantman

Ornate clay pipe bowls from a 1776 British warship.

History: The merchantman wrecked on a reef off the west side of the islands during a gale on December 23, 1818, while sailing from Demerara to Bermuda. One of the crew drowned and some of her cargo of rum was saved.

Alfred the Great, English merchantman
History: The merchantman wrecked on a reef on the west side of the islands on September 8, 1818, while sailing from Jamaica to London. Part of the cargo was saved.

Allitude, English ship, Captain Rains
History: An unidentified vessel and the ship *Martin* were wrecked on a reef five or six miles northwest of Bermuda in December 1769 while sailing from Jamaica to London. A few days later, the English ship *Allitude*, sailing from Carolina to Tortuga was wrecked nearby.

Antonia, Spanish ship
History: The vessel wrecked on a reef to the north of the islands on October 24, 1812, while sailing from Havana to Tenerife in the Canary Islands. The crew and a small part of the cargo were saved.

Batavia, ship of unknown registry, Captain Houghton
History: She was lost on the Bermuda bar in 1808 while sailing from Trinidad to Liverpool. Only the crew was saved.

Betsey, Scottish brig, Captain Camarn [*sic*]
History: The merchantman wrecked on a reef while sailing from St. Kitts to

Cork, Ireland in March of 1784. The crew and most of the cargo were saved.

Britannia, English ship, Captain Sorogham
History: The Britannia struck on a bar while leaving Bermuda for London in 1758. The ship sank in eight fathoms of water.

Caesar, English merchantman, Captain James Richardson
History: The merchantman wrecked on a reef on May 17, 1818, while sailing from Newcastle, England to Baltimore. She carried a cargo of bricks, bottles and grindstones. Part of her cargo and rigging were saved. Teddy Tucker discovered the wreck and partially salvaged the site in 1962.

Collector, American schooner, Captain Hall
History: The schooner wrecked on the reefs in 1823 while sailing from St. Johns, New Brunswick to Bermuda and South America. She was carrying a general cargo.

Commerce, American brig, Captain English
History: The brig wrecked on a reef on January 1, 1802, due to fog. She was sailing from New England to St. Croix Island. The crew and part of the cargo were saved.

Cyno, American ship, Captain Dessey
History: The ship was totally lost on a reef off the northwestern part of the islands on August 5, 1824. She had been sailing from New York to St. Croix.

Dispatch, American merchantman, Captain Ramsey
History: The merchantman wrecked on a reef while sailing from Nevis Island to New England in 1801. The crew and part of the cargo were saved.

Dorothy and Elizabeth, either American or British registry, Captain Simpson
History: The ship was lost on the reefs off Bermuda in 1747 while sailing from Boston for the Leeward Islands.

Duke, snow of unknown registry, Captain French

History: She wrecked on a reef in 1765 while sailing from South Carolina to Oporto, Portugal.

Duke of Wellington, English ship, Captain Williams
History: The ship wrecked on a reef off the west side of the island in March of 1816 while sailing from London for Bermuda and Jamaica. Only a small part of her stores was saved.

Eagle, English merchantman, Captain Whitby
History: The ship, owned by the Virginia Company and sister ship to the *Virginia Merchant*, was sailing from Plymouth, England to Jamestown, Virginia with trade goods and passengers when it wrecked on January 12, 1659, on a reef off Bermuda. The shipwreck was discovered by Teddy Tucker in 1961. A tremendous number of trade-good artifacts were discovered on this wreck. During the excavation, Tucker and Donald Canton almost lost their lives. They were using the airlift next to a massive coral ridge that almost rose to the surface of the water. While digging at the base of the coral formation they uncovered a large wooden chest filled with thousands of clay pipes. Digging deeper, they found a copper teapot, then a slate and stylus, which were probably used by the ship's navigator in plotting its position. Suddenly, Tucker felt a strong tremor. Years of working underwater had taught him to act fast. He grabbed Canton and they scrambled out of the hole seconds before a huge piece of coral, weighing at least a ton, toppled into it. After a large shark harassed them the following day, Tucker decided the wreck was jinxed and spent the rest of the season salvaging the *San Antonio*. In 1965 and 1966, Tucker returned to the wreck and recovered a large number of artifacts.

Ebenezer, ship of unknown registry, Captain Sharman
History: The ship was lost while sailing to Santo Domingo in 1801.

El Galgo, *pattachuelo* belonging to the Tierra Firme Armada of Captain-General Gerónimo Gómez de Sandoval

History: The *El Galgo*, a prize vessel captured by the Spaniards, wrecked at Bermuda on October 22, 1639, along with the *urca*, *La Viga*. The survivors from both wrecks reached shore carrying some silver with them. The wreck site of the *La Viga* was given as three leagues from the main village in Bermuda.

Eliza, merchantman of unknown registry, Captain Lord
History: The merchantman wrecked on reefs on April 30, 1811, while sailing from New York to Guadeloupe. Her cargo was saved.

Elizabeth, English ship, Captain Trattle
History: The ship wrecked at Bermuda while sailing from New England to Antigua in 1766.

Elizabeth, ship of unknown registry, Captain Largie
History: The vessel was lost on February 19, 1817, while sailing from Barbados to America.

Emma, ship of unknown registry, Captain Morgan
History: The ship wrecked on a reef on October 5, 1817, while sailing from New York to St. Vincent's Island. Part of her cargo was saved.

Fairfax, English merchantman, Captain Copithorn
History: The merchantman wrecked at Bermuda while sailing from Virginia to Bristol in 1766. Part of her cargo was saved.

Frederick, merchantman of unknown registry, Captain White
History: She wrecked on reefs on February 1, 1811, while sailing from New York to the West Indies.

Friendship, English merchantman, Captain Hooper
History: The ship was driven off course by a storm while sailing from St. Kitts to Barbados and lost near Bermuda in 1744.

George Douglas, merchantman of unknown registry
History: The vessel wrecked in 1794 on a reef on the north side of the islands, then slid off into deeper water.

The vessel was en route from Havana to Newfoundland when it wrecked. She was lost about the same time as the *Harriet*.

Grand Annibal, French ship, Captain Caisergues
History: The ship was lost off Bermuda while sailing from Santo Domingo to Marseilles in 1792. This may be the same wreck listed in documents as the *Le Grand Aanictl*.

Griffin, 20-gun English man-of-war
History: The ship was lost off Bermuda on October 25, 1761. Fifty of her crew drowned.

Hamilton, English merchant ship, Captain Adams
History: She wrecked on the east side of the islands in 1819 while coming from Antigua.

Harriet, merchantman brig of unknown registry, Captain Monteath
History: The vessel wrecked on the south side of the islands 1794. She was lost about the same time as the *George Douglas*.

H.M.S. *Barbados*, 28-gun English warship, Captain Thomas Huskinsson
History: The warship wrecked on reefs at Sable Island on September 29, 1812. Only one out of the 195 crew members was lost.

H.M.S. *Cerberus*, 32-gun English warship, frigate, Captain Sir Jacob Wheate
History: The warship wrecked shortly after leaving Castle Harbor in 1783.

H.M.S. *Dominica*, 14-gun English warship, Captain Richard Crawford
History: She wrecked on a reef on August 15, 1815.

H.M.S. *Mentor*, sixteen-gun English warship, Captain R. Tullidge
History: The warship wrecked in 1783 on a reef.

H.M.S. *Pallas*, 36-gun English warship, Captain Christopher Parker
History: The ship ran ashore on St. George's Isle in 1783.

H.M.S. *Repulse*, 32-gun English warship, Captain Henry Davies
History: She foundered off Bermuda in 1777.

H.M.S. *Subtle*, eight-gun English warship, Captain William Dowers
History: The ship wrecked on the reefs near Somerset Island on October 26, 1807.

Hope, American merchantman
History: The merchantman wrecked at the islands on August 30, 1818, during a gale while coming from New York.

Humber, American brig, Captain Clough
History: The brig wrecked on a reef prior to April of 1800 while sailing from New York to Havana.

Hunter, American ship, Captain Slout
History: The vessel wrecked on November 30, 1805, while sailing from New York to Martinique Island. The crew and part of the cargo were saved.

Hunters Galley, American sloop, Captain Clement Conyers
History: The sloop was lost at Bermuda on January 11, 1757 while sailing from St. Eustatius Island to South Carolina with a general cargo.

Indian Chief, American brig, Captain M'Vicar
History: The brig wrecked at a reef on the north end of the islands on January 12, 1822, while en route from Jamaica to New Brunswick, Canada.

Industry, English merchant, Captain Lowes
History: The ship wrecked on April 13, 1774, while sailing from Limerick to Virginia. Part of her cargo was saved.

Judith Maria, English merchantman, Captain Ball
History: The ship wrecked at Bermuda in August 1762 while sailing from Jamaica to Bristol, England. The crew, some of the cargo, and the ship's stores were saved.

Katherine, English brigantine, Captain Simondson
History: The brigantine wrecked on April 4, 1763, on a reef while sailing from Philadelphia to Jamaica. Four of the crew drowned.

Kingston, American ship, Captain Farrer

History: This vessel was lost off Bermuda in 1786 while sailing from North Carolina to Grenada Island. Her people were saved.

La Bermuda, Spanish ship
History: According to noted 19th century British historian, Defroy, Bermuda is named after a Spanish ship, *La Bermuda*, that wrecked there not long after Columbus's discovery of the New World, sometimes in the years between 1500 and 1510. Other historians claim that the islands are named after their discoverer, a Spaniard named Juan Bermúdez.

La Viga, *urca* belonging to the Tierra Firme Armada of Captain-General Gerónimo Gómez de Sandoval, Captain Mathew Lorenzo
History: The *El Galgo*, a prize vessel captured by the Spaniards, wrecked at Bermuda on October 22, 1639, along with the *urca*, *La Viga*. The survivors from both wrecks reached shore carrying some silver with them. The wreck site of the *La Viga* was given as three leagues from the main village in Bermuda.

Lady Emily, English packet
History: The packet wrecked on a reef and was lost in June of 1813, but the crew and passengers were saved.

Le Grand Aanictl, French brig, 350 tons
History: The ship struck a reef on July 4, 1792, off the west side of Bermuda at a great distance from shore, then slid off into deep water. She was sailing from Hispaniola to Marseilles with a rich cargo. The captain and several passengers drowned but other survivors reached the island in a boat with only the clothes on their backs. This may be the same wreck listed in documents as the *Grand Annibal*.

Leoftoffe, English ship, Captain Fielding
History: She was lost off Bermuda in 1749 while coming from Jamaica.

L'Hermoine, French frigate
History: The ship was lost in 1838. Teddy Tucker located the wreck during the summer of 1962. The French vessel yielded a large number of weapons, shot, uniform buttons, copper powder cans, porcelain objects, and glass bottles, many containing their original contents.

Lord Frederick, English merchantman
History: This vessel wrecked at Bermuda in 1781 while sailing from the Clyde in Scotland to Charleston, South Carolina.

Loyal Sam, English merchantman
History: The merchantman wrecked due to a gale in December 1806 while coming from London with a valuable cargo.

Lydia, French merchant ship
History: She was lost near the islands in 1819 while sailing from Bordeaux to New York. The crew, passengers and part of her cargo were saved.

Mancheoneal, English ship, Captain Morgan
History: The ship wrecked on the west side of the island while sailing from London to Bermuda in 1760. Part of the cargo was saved.

Margaret, American merchantman, Captain Muir
History: The mercahntman was lost near the islands on January 19, 1803, while sailing from Virginia to Barbados.

Marie Thérèse, French ship, Captain Guathier
History: The ship was lost near Bermuda while sailing from Santo Domingo to Bordeaux, France in 1700. Only a few bales of cotton were saved.

Mark Antonio, Spanish privateering vessel, Captain Jean-Bautist Hugonne
History: She wrecked on the islands on July 18, 1777, while sailing from St. Eustatius to Cape Henlopen.

Martin, ship, Captain Mitchell
History: An unidentified vessel and the ship *Martin* were wrecked on a reef five or six miles northwest of Bermuda in December of 1769 while sailing from Jamaica to London. A few days later, the English ship *Allitude*, sailing from Carolina to Tortuga, was wrecked nearby.

Mary, American merchantman
History: The merchantman was wrecked on reefs off the southwestern point of the main island on December 25, 1818, while sailing from New York to St. Thomas.

Mary, American merchantman, Captain Cambell
History: She wrecked on the reefs off the northern part of the islands on August 15, 1823, while sailing from Philadelphia to St. Thomas. Her crew and part of the cargo were saved.

Mary, English ship, Captain Daniel
History: The ship was lost near Bermuda in 1757 while sailing from Philadelphia to Antigua.

Mary and Hannah, English ship, Captain Savage
History: The ship was lost at Bermuda in 1744 while sailing from Genoa, Italy to Carolina. Both North and South Carolina were often called Carolina at this time.

Mary Ann, ship of unknown registry, Captain Greave
History: The ship was lost in 1801 while sailing from New York to Montserrat Island. Only the crew was saved.

Merchant, ship of unknown registry, Captain Day
History: The vessel wrecked on the reefs on March 21, 1807, while coming from New London, Connecticut to Bermuda.

Minerva, merchatman of unknown registry, Captain Arnet
History: She wrecked on a reef prior to June 1795 while sailing from Norfolk, Virginia to Tobago. The crew and part of the cargo were saved.

Montgomery, merchantman of unknown registry, Captain Bignell
History: The merchantman wrecked on reefs in 1811 while coming from Bristol. Four of the crew were saved and three drowned.

Nancy, English ship, Captain Manley
History: The ship was lost entering a port in Bermuda in 1779 while sailing from Jamaica to Bristol.

Nancy, American ship, Captain Mitchell

History: The vessel was lost in 1796 while sailing from Philadelphia to Jamaica. The crew was saved.

Nuestra Señora de la Limpia Concepción, Spanish *nao* belonging to the Nueva España Flota (fleet) of Captain-General Fernando de Sousa, 116 tons, Captain Juan Calzado
History: Two of the fleet's *naos* were lost off Bermuda during a storm in 1622: the *San Ignacio* and *Nuestra Señora de la Limpia Concepción.*

Pacific, English merchantman
History: The merchantman wrecked on a reef and was lost on December 27, 1813. She was sailing from Halifax, Nova Scotia to Barbados. Only the crew was saved.

Pallas, American ship
History: The ship was lost on June 17, 1821, while coming from Savannah.

Pamela, French ship, Captain Demeul
History: The ship was lost prior to March of 1806 while sailing from Quebec to Jamaica.

Peggy, English ship, Captain M'Carthy
History: The ship wrecked on a reef on March 18, 1764, while sailing from South Carolina to Lisbon. Her hull slid off into seven fathoms of water. All the people onboard were saved.

Penn, American ship
History: The vessel wrecked on reefs off Bermuda in 1768 while sailing from North Carolina to Bristol.

Pensacola del Sol, Spanish ship
History: The ship struck on a reef on the west side of the islands on March 29, 1812, while sailing from Pensacola, Florida to London. Her cargo was saved.

Peter, ship of unknown registry, Captain Chadwick
History: She wrecked on a reef in February 1817 while coming from East Florida.

Polly, American schooner
History: The schooner was lost in 1796 while coming from Norfolk.

Providence, English merchantman, Captain Burnet (or Barnick)
History: The merchantman was lost

on October 20, 1804, while sailing from Havana to Spain. Only the crew was saved.

Roebuck, American schooner, Captain Forester
History: The schooner wrecked on reefs on January 1, 1802, due to fog while sailing from Boston to the West Indies. The crew and part of the cargo were saved.

Rosannah, American ship, Captain Mull
History: The ship wrecked on reefs on February 23, 1807, while sailing from Baltimore to Venezuela.

San Antonio, 12-cannon merchant *nao,* 300 tons
History: The ship, owned by Simón de Vidacar, wrecked in a storm in 1621 while the rest of the convoy it was sailing with rode out the foul weather storm within sight of Bermuda. The vessel's cargo consisted of 5,000 hides, 1,200 quintals of brazilwood, 6,000 pounds of indigo, 30,000 pounds of tobacco, 5,000 pounds of sarsaparilla, and gold and silver worth 5,000 pounds sterling in English currency. Bermudans, under the direction of the governor, recovered most of its cargo. The survivors were shipped to England several months later. Teddy Tucker discovered the wreck in 1958. While searching from the bow of a boat, Tucker sighted an iron cannon barely visible on the sandy bottom. During the few remaining hours of daylight, the men dug a few holes on the site with an airlift. They discovered two dozen silver coins, several fragments of gold chain, a pair of brass navigational dividers, lead musket shot, and many ceramic shards. The finds indicated that it was an old Spanish ship, so Tucker devoted the remainder of the season to the wreck. Each day they uncovered more of the ship's timbers and made wonderful finds: a gold ring with a large emerald mounted on it, more silver coins, swords, pulley blocks, bits of rigging, leaf tobacco, and many pieces of ceramicware. Research identified the wreck as the *San Antonio,* the Spanish merchant vessel lost in 1621. Work continued intermittently on the ship until 1961, whenever Tucker and

his team were not engaged in locating and salvaging other wrecks. They found a large part of the ship's cargo of indigo and cochineal dyes and recovered several thousand cowrie shells, commonly used to purchase slaves in Africa. Tucker completed the salvage work in 1961.

San Ignacio, Spanish *nao* belonging to the Nueva España Flota (fleet) of Captain-General Fernando de Sousa, 150 tons, Captain Domingo Hernández
History: Two of the fleet's *naos* were lost off Bermuda during a storm in 1622: *San Ignacio* and *Nuestra Señora de la Limpia Concepción.*

San Pedro, merchant *nao* belonging to the Nueva España Flota of Captain-General Pedro Menéndez Márques, 350 tons, Captain Hierónimo de Porras
History: The vessel wrecked near the islands in 1596 while sailing between Mexico and Spain. Documents do not indicate the type of cargo or the amount of treasure she carried, or if any attempts were made by the Spaniards to salvage her. Teddy Tucker discovered the wreck in 1955 and made the first major treasure recovery from an old wreck in this century. His finds included a magnificent emerald-studded gold cross containing seven emeralds, each about the size of a musket ball, valued at $200,000, bars and cubes of gold, gold and pearl buttons, a ceremonial spear made by Carib Indians, several pewter plates, porringer bowls, hand grenades, swords, muskets, a breast plate, small brass weights used by the ship's surgeon, a pair of navigational dividers, hourglasses, a pottery cruet for oil or vinegar, buckles, buttons, and hundreds of cannonballs and musket balls. Tucker established a museum on the islands to house the treasure he recovered from the wreck. Then, in 1961 he sold the museum and all the treasure to the Bermuda government for only $100,000.

San Salvador, Spanish *navío,* Captain Pedro de Aruide, 567 tons
History: The ship, owned by Admiral Manuel Casadeite, sprung a bad leak and wrecked at Bermuda in 1684. After the survivors reached shore in

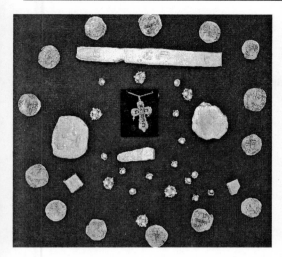

Treasure recovered from the wreck of the *San Pedro* which was lost in Bermuda in 1595.

small boats the Spaniards set the ship afire to prevent the Bermudans from salvaging her cargo.

Santa Ana, merchant *nao*, 200 tons
History: The *nao* sank in 1605 while sailing from Honduras to Spain with a general cargo. Only the people onboard were saved.

Santa Barbola, ship belonging to the Tierra Firme Armada of Captain-General Sancho de Viedma, Captain Alvarez de los Rios, 400 tons
History: After it cleared the Bahama Channel in 1551, the fleet was struck by a hurricane that lasted for ten days. The *capitana* (flagship) of the fleet sprang a leak and was deliberately run up on a reef, where her cannon and 150,000 ducats in treasure were saved. *Santa Barbola*, of the same fleet, also wrecked on a reef and all her treasure was saved.

Sea Venture, English vessel, Admiral Sir George Somers
History: A squadron of nine English vessels sailed from Plymouth, England, with colonists and supplies for Jamestown, Virginia. The flagship *Sea Venture* wrecked at Bermuda in 1609. The survivors reached Virginia in May 1610. Some of the survivors returned to Bermuda and a colony, part of the Virginia Company, was founded there. In 1953, the government asked treasure

hunter Teddy Tucker to locate the site of this important shipwreck. Tucker found a shipwreck site that initially appeared to be that of the *Sea Venture*; however, when artifacts from it were analyzed at the British Museum in London, they were identified as being from a later period and the project was abandoned. Then, in 1978 Allen "Smokey" Wingood, a retired professional diver and a keen student of Bermuda history, decided to locate the ship. After three years of research and searching he came to the conclusion that the wreck Tucker had found in 1959 was indeed the *Sea Venture*. Re-examination of the artifacts Tucker had submitted for identification proved that they had been mistakenly attributed to a later period. Excavation of the shipwreck differed from previous underwater projects in Bermuda. The wreck, such an important part of Bermuda's cultural legacy, was surveyed, mapped and excavated over a period of six summers by a team led by underwater archaeologists from the United States and England. Today, thousands of fascinating artifacts that were found on the site are on display in Bermuda's Maritime Museum.

Stadt Cortrycht, Dutch merchantman, Captain Harmong
History: The ship wrecked on a reef while attempting to enter a harbor on June 24, 1783. She was sailing from Dominica Island to Ostend, Holland, and carrying a cargo of sugar when she foundered.

St. Helena, ship of unknown registry
History: The ship wrecked on a reef on May 18, 1819, while sailing from Jamaica to Quebec. Only a small part of her cargo was saved.

Surprise, ship of unknown registry, Captain Renshaw
History: The ship was lost prior to

July 1804 while sailing for the Cape of Good Hope from Philadelphia.

Swift, ship of unknown registry, Captain M'Donald
History: The ship was lost off Bermuda in 1787 while sailing from Grenada Island to Newfoundland. The crew was saved.

Three Friends, English merchantman, Captain Pullinge
History: The merchantman wrecked due to a gale in December 1806 while coming from Philadelphia.

Tryton, English merchantman, Captain Gibbons
History: The merchantman, sailing from Carolina to London, was lost near Bermuda in 1747.

Unidentified, *capitana* (flagship) of the Firme Armada of Captain-General Sancho de Viedma
History: After it cleared the Bahama Channel in 1551 the fleet was struck by a hurricane that lasted for ten days. The *capitana* of the fleet sprang a leak and was deliberately run up on a reef, where her cannon and 150,000 ducats in treasure were saved. *Santa Barbola*, of the same fleet, also wrecked on a reef and all of her treasure was saved.

Unidentified, *capitana* (flagship) of the Tierra Firme Flota (fleet) of Captain-General Pedro de la Roelas
History: A storm struck in 1560 while the Tierra Firme Flota was in sight of Bermuda. The *capitana* disappeared without a trace, either sinking in deep water or on the reefs of Bermuda.

Unidentified, Spanish merchant *nao*
History: An unidentified Spanish merchant *nao* owned by a merchant named Johan de León and carrying an undisclosed amount of gold and pearls was lost on the reefs in 1533. Three years later, two ships sailing from Santo Domingo for Spain passed close to Bermuda and sighted fires on the island but the wind and current prevented them from investigating. They recommended to the king that a small ship be sent to pick up the survivors and treasure, but no documents reveal if this was done.

Unidentified, Portuguese slave ship
History: The slave ship was sailing

from Santo Domingo with seven Spanish merchantmen when it wrecked in 1543. The 30 shipwreck survivors made it ashore in the ship's boat and made many return trips to the wreck, bringing ashore supplies and part of its cargo. After they spent 60 days on the island they sailed for Santo Domingo in a vessel they had constructed from timbers of the shipwreck. They reported sighting the remains of several other shipwrecks on the reefs.

Unidentified, capitana (flagship) of the Nueva España Flota (fleet) of Captain-General Juan Menéndez

History: The *capitana* and several merchant *naos* of the fleet disappeared without a trace in 1563 while in the vicinity of Bermuda. One of these ships is believed to be the Spanish wreck dated 1560 that treasure hunter Teddy Tucker located. Toward the close of the 1962 season, Tucker sighted a few ballast rocks on a sandy bottom. His discovery turned out to be the oldest ship ever found in Bermuda waters. While digging an exploratory hold on the site, he uncovered a vast amount of ballast rock buried not far under the sand, as well as a small clump of badly sulfated silver coins, some of which bore mid–16th century dates. Historical research indicates that the ship is most likely the *capitana*. Tucker and his team devoted the summers of 1963 and 1964 to excavating the site. With the exception of the small clump of silver coins discovered in the exploratory hole, no other treasure was found on this wreck. In fact, it yielded very few significant artifacts, indicating that the Spaniards probably salvaged it. Nevertheless, the ship's early date and the fact that a large section of the lower hull was intact and remarkably well preserved, convinced a man called Peterson, who was working with Tucker, that the wreck should be excavated. The project was funded by a grant and furnished valuable archaeological data regarding the ship's construction. Coauthor Robert F. Marx spent most of the summer of 1963 working with Tucker on this site.

Unidentified, merchant *nao* of Pedro Menendez

History: An unidentified merchant

nao carrying a cargo of indigo, cochineal, logwood, and a small amount of silver specie was wrecked on a reef in 1588.

Unidentified, French ship

History: The ship, owned by Monsieur Charles de la Barbotière, wrecked on December 17, 1593, on a reef in the northwestern part of Bermuda after sailing from Laguna, Hispaniola. Twenty-six of the 50 persons onboard reached shore in a makeshift raft. They later made a small vessel from the wreck and reached France.

Unidentified, galleon in the Tierra Firme Armada, Captain-General Luís Fernández de Cordova

History: The galleon separated from the convoy during a storm and wrecked at Bermuda in 1603. Most of the treasure onboard was recovered, and together with the survivors, was rescued 22 days later. The crew reported seeing many earlier shipwrecks on the islands.

Unidentified, pinnace

History: An unidentified pinnace returning from a privateering voyage in the West Indies wrecked on the northwest shoals of Bermuda in 1619. The ship was manned mostly by Dutchmen, but there were a few Englishmen aboard. The vessel quickly went to pieces before anything could be saved.

Unidentified, ship

History: A large unidentified ship sank in Castle Harbor during a hurricane in 1669.

Unidentified, Spanish ship

History: The following information was taken from an English chart of Bermuda dated 1740: "Among these rocks which extend above three leagues to the northeast of the island[s] are a great number of wrecks and amongst others, that of a rich Spanish ship lost about the year 1644. It was once discovered, but it is now fished for in vain. Off the southwest and west-northwest section of the island[s] are great numbers of rocks at three to four leagues distance from land, whereby an abundance of ships have been lost."

Unidentified, vessel

History: An unidentified vessel and the ship *Martin* were wrecked on a reef five or six miles northwest of Bermuda in December 1769 while sailing from Jamaica to London. A few days later, the English ship *Allitude,* sailing from Carolina to Tortuga, wrecked nearby.

Unidentified, ships (50+)

History: Over 50 ships were wrecked or driven aground on the islands during a terrible hurricane on October 18, 1780.

Unidentified, ships (large number)

History: A large number of ships were wrecked on the southwestern side of Bermuda during a hurricane on July 26, 1788.

Unidentified, brig of unknown registry, Captain Clark

History: The unnamed brig wrecked on the north side of the island prior to June of 1795 while sailing from Newhaven, England to St. Vincent Island.

Unidentified, ships (large number)

History: A large number of ships were driven ashore or sank during a hurricane on August 15, 1815.

Unidentified, English brig

History: The brig wrecked on reefs off the southwestern point of the main island on December 25, 1818 while making its way from Barbados to Bermuda.

Unidentified, merchant *nao* belonging to the Nueva España Flota (fleet)

History: The vessel was badly damaged in a storm about 70 leagues west of Bermuda in 1550, and drifted until it struck one of the islands reefs. The *nao,* owned by Rodrigo Vago, carried a large amount of gold and silver, none of which was reported recovered.

Unidentified, Danish ship

History: The vessel, which was carrying 700 hogsheads of sugar, was lost on the reefs of Bermuda in 1753.

Unidentified, merchantman of unknown registry

History: The ship was lost around the islands prior to June 1795 while sailing from Madeira Island to Baltimore.

Virginia Merchant, English merchantman, Captain Robert Burk

History: The ship, owned by the Virginia Company, wrecked on March 26, 1660, while sailing from Plymouth to Jamestown. Of the 189 persons aboard, only ten were saved. The wreck was discovered by Teddy Tucker in 1961 and partially salvaged. Several weeks of excavation produced clay pipes, tools, weapons, house bricks, writing utensils, pieces of silverware, pewter plates, and many fragments of chinaware and pottery. Tucker discovered a new area of the wreck in 1967 using a magnetometer.

Vriendscaap, Dutch merchantman, Captain de Jong
History: The merchantman wrecked on the reefs off the west end of the main island on May 2, 1823, while sailing from Surinam to Amsterdam.

Warwick, English merchant brig
History: The vessel, owned by the Virginia Company, arrived from England in Castle Harbor on October 20, 1619, with the fledgling colony's first governor and badly needed supplies. A month later the brig wrecked in Castle Harbor during a storm. Teddy Tucker and several people from the Smithsonian Institution in the U.S. discovered the wreck in 1967 with the help of a magnetometer. A preliminary survey of the wreck revealed extensive timber remains. The wooden hull was found to be more complete than that of any other wreck yet discovered in the Western Hemisphere. The ship had settled quickly in the harbor silt, which preserved it from keel to gunwale. Tucker and his associate, Peterson, devoted the next two summers to excavating the ship, which furnished a wealth of archaeological data.

William & Mary, English merchantman, Captain Clifton
History: The merchantman wrecked in February 1810 with a cargo of sherry wine. The crew and part of the wine were saved.

William Grey, English ship, Captain King
History: The ship wrecked on a reef on the west side of the islands on August 29, 1809, while sailing to Jamaica. The crew and most of the cargo were saved.

Canada

One of the greatest concentrations of shipwrecks in Canadian waters is around Sable Island, located 150 miles off the coast of Nova Scotia. At least 500 ships have wrecked on Sable Island, an area where several ocean currents flow from different directions. Working conditions in these waters, however, are extremely difficult and shifting sands tended to cover most of the ships very soon after they were wrecked.

Bad weather, rough seas and cold water throughout most of the year make Canada one of the least attractive areas in the Western Atlantic for underwater exploration and salvage work. The hostile diving conditions are further compounded by extremely high tides, which produce currents of several knots in some areas.

Despite these difficult diving conditions significant discoveries have been made in Canadian waters. In 1914, a helmet diver located the 18th century French warship *Le Chameau*. He planned to recover the treasure but unfortunately drowned a few days later, taking the ship's location with him. Then in the 1960s, three divers, Alex Storm, David MacEachern and Harvey MacLeod, discovered the shipwreck again. When they began work on the *Chameau*, there were no laws concerning the discovery of sunken treasure. Soon after they brought up their first finds, the Canadian government ordered them to turn everything over to officials while the matter was investigated. This prevented them from selling anything to raise more capital to carry on their work. A court battle over the legal ownership of the treasure and artifacts dragged on into 1968 when the courts decided that the government should retain ten percent of the finds and ordered the return of the rest to the salvors.

The government has since passed a law stating that work on an old shipwreck cannot be undertaken without permission from the National Historical Park Service. The law also requires that a competent archaeologist supervise all such salvage operations. Each province in Canada has different laws regarding treasure hunting and underwater archaeology. People should be sure to check the regulations when preparing for any diving expedition.

SHIPWRECKS IN CANADA'S WATERS

Adventure, English merchantman
Location: Lost on the shore near the Port of St. John's
History: The *Adventure*, sailing from St. Eustatius Island to Newfoundland, was forced onshore by an American privateer near the Port of St. John's in 1780. The vessel and cargo were totally lost.

Andrea Gail, commercial swordfish longliner, 70 feet, Captain Billy Tyne
Location: Sable Island
History: The offshore fishing boat was lost in a monstrous gale, termed the "perfect storm," on October 28, 1991, near Sable Island. All six hands aboard perished. The storm produced

Above: Buckles, buttons, nails and musket balls recovered from a mid–18th century English wreck off Halifax, Novia Scotia. *Right:* German stoneware tankard from the first half of the 17th century.

winds of over 90 mph and 100 foot waves. The *Andrea Gail* was heading back toward Gloucester from Canada's Grand Banks when the storm occurred. The tale of the ship's demise was told in a book by Sebastian Junger and later made into a motion picture called *The Perfect Storm.*

Ann, English ship, Captain M'Clue
Location: Isle of Orleans
History: The English ship, sailing from Quebec to Barbados, was wrecked on the Isle of Orleans in the Gulf of St. Lawrence in 1781.

Apollon, 50-gun French ship
Location: Louisburg Harbor
History: The *Apollon* was one of four ships scuttled by the French in Louisburg Harbor on June 28, 1758, due to the fact that they did not have enough hands to man them in an impending attack by the English.

Atlanta, English merchantman, Captain Gammell
Location: Torbay
History: The merchantman, sailing from Grenada Island to Halifax, was wrecked at Torbay on January 29, 1805. Part of the cargo was saved.

Augusta, English ship, Captain Cole
Location: St. Lawrence River
History: The ship was burnt by accident in the St. Lawrence River on October 24, 1794, while sailing from Quebec to the West Indies.

Aurora, English ship
Location: Sable Island
History: The ship was lost on Sable Island in 1777. The survivors of the *Aurora* found seven black women living on the island who had been stranded there for 16 years after a previous French shipwreck.

Betsey, English merchantman, Captain Young
Location: Nova Scotia
History: The vessel was lost on the coast of Nova Scotia in 1788 while sailing from Scotland to Halifax, Nova Scotia. The crew was saved.

Betsey, brig of unknown registry
Location: Halifax Harbor
History: The *Betsey* was among many ships that sank during a gale in Halifax Harbor on September 25, 1798. Total loss of shipping was over 100,000 pounds sterling that day.

Betsey, English merchantman, Captain Anderson
Location: Hare Island
History: The merchantman was sailing from Quebec to Barbados when a violent gust of wind caused it to totally wreck on Hare Island on October 24, 1783. One crew member was lost.

Biche, 16-gun French warship
Location: Louisburg Harbor
History: The *Biche* was one of four ships scuttled by the French in Louisburg Harbor on June 28, 1758, due to the fact that they did not have enough hands to man them in an impending attack by the English.

Bienfaisant, 22-gun French warship
Location: Chaleur Bay

History: During an attack on July 8, 1760, by an English fleet commanded by Captain Byron, the *Bienfaisant* was sunk in Chaleur Bay along with two other warships, the *Marchault* and the *Marquis Marloze*, and 22 smaller provisioning and supply vessels.

Bonetta, English ship, Captain Feampton
Location: Near St. Mary's
History: The *Bonetta*, was lost near St. Mary's in 1763 while sailing to Poole, England. Her crew and cargo were completely lost.

Bosphorus, English ship
Location: St. Lawrence River
History: The victualer was lost on the St. Lawrence River in 1776.

Britannia, English merchantman, Captain Adney
Location: New Brunswick
History: The merchantman was lost at New Brunswick but the crew was saved in 1798.

Buchanan, English merchantman, Captain Lawrence
Location: Sable Island
History: The merchantman was captured by a French privateer while sailing from Gibraltar to Maryland. The ship wrecked on April 22, 1757, on Sable Island, Nova Scotia on her passage to Louisburg.

Caesar, Troop-transport ship, sloop, Captain Jeremiah Tay (or Taye)
Location: Digby Cut
History: In late August 1710, a fleet of New Englanders set out to capture Port Royal, a port in eastern Canada, but one of the transport ships from Rhode Island, the *Caesar*, ran ashore on Digby Cut. Twenty-six men aboard were lost.

Capricieux, 64-gun French warship
Location: Louisburg Harbor
History: The *Capricieux* was one of three ships accidentally burnt and sunk in the harbor while waiting for an impending attack by the English on June 28, 1758.

Charlotte, English merchantman, Captain Godfrey
Location: Labrador
History: The *Charlotte* was lost on

the coast of Labrador while coming from Dartmouth England in 1794.

Charlotte, English schooner
Location: St. Lawrence River
History: The schooner was lost on the river while sailing from Quebec to Halifax in 1794.

Charming Nancy, English merchantman, Captain Hume
Location: Quebec
History: The ship sank at Quebec after arriving from London in 1762. Most of her cargo was recovered.

Charming Nancy, English ship, Captain Haynes
Location: Port of Halifax
History: The vessel was lost entering port in 1762 while sailing from London to Halifax. Nothing was saved from her.

Chérre, 16-French warship
Location: Louisburg Harbor
History: The *Chérre* was one of four ships scuttled by the French in Louisburg Harbor on June 28, 1758, due to the fact that they did not have enough hands to man them in an impending attack by the English.

Christie, English ship, Captain Bodfield
Location: St. Lawrence River
History: The *Christie* was lost while making its way up the St. Lawrence River in 1782.

Cilibre, 64-gun French warship
Location: Louisburg Harbor
History: The *Cilibre* was one of three ships accidentally burnt and sunk in the harbor while awaiting an impending attack by the English on June 28, 1758.

Coleman, English merchantman, Captain Pickmore
Location: Newfoundland
History: The merchantman wrecked on Newfoundland in 1785 but the crew was saved.

Cupid, English merchantman, Captain Trimett
Location: St. John's Harbor
History: The ship, sailing from Newfoundland to the Leeward Islands, was lost while returning to St. John's Harbor due to bad weather.

Dalrymple, English merchantman, Captain Marsh
Location: St. Lawrence River
History: The merchantman was lost in the river in 1801 while sailing from Barbados to Quebec. Part of the cargo was saved.

Delight, English warship belonging to the fleet of Admiral Sir Humphrey Gilbert
Location: Sable Island
History: The ship sank sometime before 1583 on a shoal near Sable Island, off Nova Scotia.

Diana, English merchantman, Captain Greaves
Location: Newfoundland
History: The ship was wrecked on the coast of Newfoundland in 1793 while sailing from Dartmouth, England. The crew was saved.

Dolphin, English ship, Captain Thomas
Location: Near Halifax
History: The *Dolphin*, sailing from Newfoundland to Halifax, was lost near the port of Halifax in 1776.

Doncet, English schooner
Location: St. Lawrence River
History: The vessel was totally lost in the St. Lawrence River in 1807 while coming from Halifax. The crew was saved.

Duc de Fronfac, 20-gun French warship
Location: St. Lawrence River
History: The ship wrecked in 1759.

Eagle, English merchantman
Location: Cape Sable
History: The ship, sailing to the West Indies, was lost at Cape Sable in 1802 but the crew was saved.

Elizabeth, English merchantman, Captain Carter
Location: Fogo Harbor
History: The merchantman was lost in the harbor of Fogo in 1752 while coming from Poole, England.

Elizabeth and Mary, English merchantman, Captain Lethbrige
Location: Newfoundland
History: The vessel was lost at Newfoundland in 1788.

Empress of Ireland, Canadian Pacific ocean liner, Captain Kendall
Location: Twenty kilometers east of Rimouski in the Gulf of the St. Lawrence River
History: The *Empress of Ireland* collided with the Norwegian collier *Storstad* in fog on May 29, 1914. The ship sank in 14 minutes in the St. Lawrence River. The loss of 1,012 passengers and crew onboard made this one of Canada's worst maritime disasters. Salvage divers recovered mail and the purser's safe in 1914. The ship was declared a historical site in April 1999. The shipwreck is also protected under Canada's merchant marine legislation. The Canadian Coast Guard has marked the watery grave of the *Empress* with a buoy warning visitors that they must have a government permit to remove anything from the shipwreck.

Endeavour, English merchantman, Captain Simpson
Location: Twenty-five leagues east of Halifax
History: The *Endeavour* was sailing from Exeter, England to Quebec when it wrecked near Halifax, in December 1782. Part of the vessel's cargo was saved.

Enterprize, English merchantman, Captain Cummings
Location: Anticosti Island
History: The merchantman was lost on Anticosti Island in November of 1800 while sailing from London to Quebec.

Entreprenant, 74-gun French warship
Location: Louisburg Harbor
History: The *Entreprenant* was one of three ships accidentally burnt and sunk in the harbor while waiting for an impending attack by the English on June 28, 1758.

Euphrates, English transport ship, Captain Gordon
Location: Port of Halifax
History: The transport, which was arriving from London, was lost while entering the port of Halifax in 1776.

Fame, English merchantman, Captain Meggetson
Location: St. Pierre Island
History: The ship was sailing from London to Quebec when it wrecked

on St. Pierre Island, near Newfoundland, in 1791. The crew and part of her cargo were saved.

Fame Murphy, ship of unknown registry
   Location: Sable Island
   History: Wrecked on Sable Island in 1779.

Fanny, English merchantman, Captain Bugs
   Location: St. Andrews
   History: The *Fanny*, arriving from Grenada Island, burnt at St. Andrews in 1791.

Favorite, English merchantman, Captain Robertson
   Location: Lost on the lower part of the St. Lawrence River
   History: The vessel was lost while sailing from London to Quebec in 1788.

Favorite, English transport ship, Captain Bishipprick
   Location: Gulf of St. Lawrence
   History: Lost in the Gulf of St. Lawrence in 1776.

Fidile, 26-gun French ship
   Location: Louisburg Harbor
   History: The *Fidile* was one of four ships scuttled by the French in Louisburg Harbor on June 28, 1758 due to the fact that they did not have enough hands to man them in an impending attack by the English.

Francis, English ship
   Location: Sable Island
   History: The ship was totally lost on Sable Island in the year 1800 while sailing from London to Halifax. The entire crew perished.

General Gage, English merchantman
   Location: St. Lawrence River
   History: The *General Gage* wrecked in 1761 in the St. Lawrence River after leaving Quebec for London.

General Haldemand, English ship, Captain Love
   Location: St. Lawrence River
   History: The ship sank in the St. Lawrence River in 1781. Only one man perished in the wreck.

Good Intent, English merchantman, Captain Wood
   Location: St. Lawrence River
   History: The *Good Intent* wrecked in the St. Lawrence River in 1763 while sailing from London to Quebec. Most of her cargo was saved.

Grampus, 32-gun English transport warship, Captain John Frodsham
   Location: Newfoundland
   History: The armed transport foundered off the coast of Newfoundland in 1778.

Grandy (or *Granby*), English merchantman sloop, Captain Hay
   Location: Lighthouse Rocks in Halifax Harbor
   History: The *Grandy* wrecked off the Lighthouse Rocks in Halifax Harbor in 1771. She was carrying military stores and 3,000 pounds sterling in coins for the Halifax Navy Yards. All 16 men onboard perished.

Greyhound, English merchantman, Captain Shaw
   Location: Gulf of the St. Lawrence
   History: The *Greyhound* was lost out of sight of land while sailing from Liverpool to Quebec in 1764. However, her crew was saved.

Hamilton, English merchantman, Captain Gilchrist
   Location: St. Lawrence River
   History: The *Hamilton* was lost in 1808 on the St. Lawrence River while sailing from Clyde, Scotland to Quebec. Most of the cargo was saved.

Harvey, English ship, Captain Harvey [*sic*]
   Location: St. Lawrence River
   History: The crew was saved after the ship sank on the St. Lawrence River in 1781.

Hermoine, English packet boat
   Location: Cape Sable
   History: The packet wrecked on Cape Sable in 1785 while making its way from Halifax to Port Roseway.

H.M.S. *Active*, 32-gun English warship, Captain Edward Leverson Gower
   Location: St. Lawrence River
   History: She wrecked in the St. Lawrence River on July 5, 1796.

H.M.S. *Atalante*, 18-gun English warship, Captain Frederick Hickey

   Location: Off Halifax
   History: The warship wrecked on November 10, 1813, off Halifax, Nova Scotia.

H.M.S. *Avenger*, 16-gun English warship, Captain Urry Johnson
   Location: Wrecked off St. John's
   History: She wrecked on October 8, 1812.

H.M.S. *Banterer*, 22-gun English warship, Captain Alexander Shippard
   Location: St. Lawrence River
   History: She was lost December 4, 1808, on the St. Lawrence River.

H.M.S. *Barbadoes*, 28-gun English warship, Captain Thomas Huskisson
   Location: Sable Island
   History: The *Barbadoes* wrecked on Sable Island on September 28, 1812. She was carrying over $500,000 in gold and silver specie and bullion when she went down.

H.M.S. *Bold*, 12-gun English warship, Captain John Skekel
   Location: Prince Edward Island
   History: The warship was wrecked on Prince Edward Island on September 27, 1813.

H.M.S. *Chubb*, four-gun English warship, Captain Samuel Nisbett
   Location: Lost off Halifax
   History: The warship capsized off Halifax on August 14, 1812. All hands were lost.

H.M.S. *Cupid*, 16-gun English warship, Captain William Carlyon
   Location: Newfoundland
   History: The warship foundered in 1778 off the coast of Newfoundland.

H.M.S. *Cuttle*, four-gun English warship
   Location: Halifax
   History: She foundered near Halifax in 1814. The day of the loss is not known.

H.M.S. *Dispatch*, 14-gun English warship, Captain J. Botham
   Location: Gulf of St. Lawrence
   History: The warship capsized in 1778 in the Gulf of St. Lawrence.

H.M.S. *Drake*, ten-gun English warship, Captain Charles Adolphus Baker
   Location: Newfoundland

History: She wrecked with the loss of many lives off Newfoundland on June 20, 1822.

H.M.S. *Dutchess of Cumberland*, 16-gun English ship, Captain Edward March
  Location: Newfoundland
  History: The vessel wrecked at Newfoundland in 1781.

H.M.S. *Emulous*, 18-gun English warship, Captain Williams Howe Mulcaster
  Location: Sable Island
  History: She wrecked at Sable Island on August 3, 1812.

H.M.S. *Eurus*, 20-gun English warship, Captain John Elphinstone
  Location: St. Lawrence River
  History: She wrecked in 1760 in the St. Lawrence River.

H.M.S. *Fantome*, 18-gun English warship, Captain Thomas Sykes
  Location: Halifax
  History: The vessel was lost near Halifax on November 24, 1814.

H.M.S. *Ferret*, ten-gun English warship, Captain Arthur Upton
  Location: Louisburg Harbor
  History: The H.M.S. *Tilbury* and the H.M.S. *Ferret* were sunk in Louisburg Harbor during a hurricane on September 24, 1757.

H.M.S. *Fly*, 14-gun English warship, Captain Thomas Duvall
  Location: Newfoundland
  History: The ship foundered off Newfoundland in 1802 with the loss of all crew.

H.M.S. *Hector*, 74-gun English warship, Captain John Bourchier
  Location: Grand Banks
  History: The ship sank on the Grand Banks of Newfoundland in 1782.

H.M.S. *Herring*, four-gun English warship, Captain John Murray
  Location: Halifax
  History: She foundered near Halifax in 1814. The day of the loss is not known.

H.M.S. *Leopard*, 50-gun English troopship, Captain Edward Lowther Crofton
  Location: Anticosti Island

History: The vessel was wrecked on Anticosti Island on June 28, 1814.

H.M.S. *Lowestoft*, 28-gun English warship, Captain Joseph Deane
  Location: St. Lawrence River
  History: She wrecked on May 17, 1760, in the St. Lawrence River.

H.M.S. *Lynx*, English warship
  Location: Halifax Harbor
  History: The H.M.S. *Lynx* was among many ships that sank during a gale in Halifax Harbor on September 25, 1798. Total loss of shipping was over 100,000 pounds sterling that day.

H.M.S. *Mars*, 64-gun English warship, Captain John Amherst
  Location: Halifax
  History: The warship wrecked at Halifax in June 1755.

H.M.S. *Pegasus*, 16-gun English warship, Captain J. Hamilton Gore
  Location: Newfoundland
  History: She foundered off the coast of Newfoundland in 1777.

H.M.S. *Penelope*, 36-gun English troopship, Captain James Galloway
  Location: Newfoundland
  History: She wrecked off Newfoundland on May 1, 1815.

H.M.S. *Placentia*, 14-gun English warship
  Location: Newfoundland
  History: She wrecked near the island in 1782.

H.M.S. *Placentia*, English warship, Captain Alexander Shippard
  Location: Newfoundland
  History: The vessel was lost in 1794 near Newfoundland.

H.M.S. *Plumper*, 12-gun English warship, Captain W. Frissel
  Location: St. Lawrence River
  History: The warship foundered in the St. Lawrence River in November 1810.

H.M.S. *Rover*, 16-gun English warship, Captain George Irwin
  Location: Gulf of St. Lawrence
  History: She wrecked on June 23, 1798, in the Gulf of St. Lawrence.

H.M.S. *Savage*, eight-gun English warship, Captain Hugh Bromelge

Location: Near Louisburg, Cape Breton Island
  History: The vessel was lost in 1775 near Louisburg.

H.M.S. *Scout*, 18-gun English warship, Captain Henry Duncan
  Location: Newfoundland
  History: She foundered off Newfoundland in 1802. The crew was totally lost.

H.M.S. *Spy*, 12-gun English warship, Captain Thomas Lenox Frederick
  Location: Newfoundland
  History: The ship wrecked near the island of Newfoundland in 1778.

H.M.S. *Terrible*, 74-gun English warship
  Location: St. Lawrence River
  History: She wrecked in 1759.

H.M.S. *Tilbury*, 60-gun English warship, Captain Henry Barnsley
  Location: Louisburg Harbor
  History: The H.M.S. *Tilbury* and the H.M.S. *Ferret* were sunk in Louisburg Harbor during a hurricane on September 24, 1757.

H.M.S. *Tilbury*, English frigate
  Location: Louisburg Harbor
  History: The English wrecked the *Tilbury*, payship for Admiral Edward Boscawen's fleet, on a reef near Louisburg Harbor during an attack on the French on June 28, 1758.

H.M.S. *Tribune*, 32-gun English warship, Captain Scory Barker
  Location: Halifax
  History: She wrecked near Halifax on November 16, 1797.

H.M.S. *Tweed*, 18-gun English warship, Captain William Mather
  Location: Shoal Bay
  History: The vessel wrecked in Shoal Bay on November 5, 1813.

H.M.S. *Vestal*, 20-gun English warship, Captain James Shirley
  Location: Newfoundland
  History: The warship foundered off the coast of Newfoundland in 1777.

H.M.S. *Viper*, 16-gun English warship, Captain John Augustua
  Location: Gulf of St. Lawrence
  History: She wrecked on October 11, 1780, in the Gulf of St. Lawrence.

H.M.S. *William*, 12-gun English storeship, Captain John Foxton
   Location: Gut of Canso
   History: The vessel wrecked on November 11, 1807, in the Gut of Canso.

Hope, English merchantman, Captain Anderson
   Location: Coast of Newfoundland
   History: The merchantman was wrecked on the coast of Newfoundland while arriving from London in 1791.

Hope, English merchantman, Captain Cameron
   Location: Two leagues below Tadefase
   History: The merchantman was lost in the St. Lawrence River in 1783 while sailing from Tortola to Quebec. Part of the vessel's cargo was saved.

Hornett, English merchantman, Captain Priddes
   Location: Coast of Newfoundland
   History: She wrecked on the coast of Newfoundland in 1793 while coming from St. Ubes, England.

Industry, English merchantman, Captain Young
   Location: St. Lawrence River
   History: The Industry was lost in the river in 1801 while sailing from Quebec to Leith, Scotland.

Isaac and William, English ship, Captain Gregory
   Location: Orleans Shoals, St. Lawrence River
   History: The ship was lost on the Orleans shoals in 1761 after leaving Quebec for London. Her cargo was saved.

Jane, English merchantman, Captain Wilson
   Location: Sable Island
   History: The vessel was lost on Sable Island in 1780 while sailing from London to Halifax. The crew was saved.

Jersey, English merchantman, Captain Giffred
   Location: Newfoundland
   History: The merchantman was wrecked on the coast of Newfoundland in 1755 while coming from Jersey, off the coast of France.

L'Américaine, French ship
   Location: Lake Wallace, Sable Island
   History: The ship was lost off Lake Wallace on Sable Island in 1822 in a depth of 72 feet. She was carrying over $1 million in gold and silver bullion and specie when she went down.

Le Chameau, French frigate-of-war, transport, 600 tons
   Location: Cape Lorenbed
   History: The frigate sailed from Louisburg, a French stronghold on the eastern tip of Cape Breton Island, Nova Scotia in 1725. She was en route to Quebec and carrying about 30,000 livres in gold and silver as well as a large number of passengers. As the ship was rounding Cape Lorenbec, Nova Scotia on August 26th, a squall struck. The *Chameau* capsized and sank with a loss of all 310 persons onboard. Many of the bodies washed ashore, but nothing of the ship was ever found. The wreck was forgotten for two centuries. Then, in 1914 the steamship SS *Ragna* struck Chameau Rock and sank. A diver working for an insurance company surfaced after his first dive shouting that he had seen a great number of gold and silver coins. He vowed to salvage the coins after surveying the *Ragna*, but never got the chance. He drowned several days later. Two other salvage firms went after the *Chameau* treasure soon afterward. One firm found nothing and the other only recovered several iron cannon. A few days later, a fisherman snagged a chest. It was so heavy that he could barely pull it to the surface. Just as he was lifting the chest into his boat it split apart. The fisherman watched forlornly as a cascade of gold and silver coins fell back into the sea. In 1965, the *Chameau* finally surrendered her treasure, or at least some of it, to Alex Storm, David MacEachern and Harvey MacLeod, three sport divers who had grown up listening to tales of the *Chameau*. When they began salvaging the *Chameau*, there were no laws concerning the discovery of sunken treasure. Soon after they brought up their first finds, the Canadian government ordered them to turn everything over to officials while the matter was inves-

tigated. This prevented them from selling anything to raise more capital to carry on their work. A court battle over the legal ownership of the treasure and artifacts lasted until 1968 when the courts gave the government ten percent of the finds and returned the rest to the salvors.

Léopard, 60-gun French warship
   Location: St. Lawrence River
   History: The warship was burnt at Quebec in 1761 after arriving with the plague onboard.

Le Sinecterre, 24-gun French warship
   Location: St. Lawrence River
   History: The ship wrecked in 1759.

Le Soleil Royal, 24-gun French warship
   Location: St. Lawrence River
   History: The warship wrecked in 1759.

Liberty, ship of unknown registry, Captain Clark
   Location: St. Lawrence River
   History: The ship was lost in the St. Lawrence River in 1806 while sailing from Quebec to Plymouth, England.

Liberty, American ship
   Location: Halifax Harbor
   History: The *Liberty* was among many ships that sank during a gale in Halifax Harbor on September 25, 1798. Total loss of shipping was over 100,000 pounds sterling that day.

Lion, English ship, Captain Davis
   Location: Cape Sable
   History: The vessel was lost near Cape Sable in 1783.

Lizard, English ship
   Location: Quebec
   History: The *Lizard* was lost at Quebec in 1780.

Lock, English merchantman, Captain Gowland
   Location: St. Lawrence River
   History: The merchantman sank in the St. Lawrence River while arriving from London in 1777.

London, English ship, Captain M'Cullough
   Location: St. Lawrence River
   History: The ship sank in 1781 in the

St. Lawrence River. Her crew was saved.

Lord Elbank, English merchantman, Captain Warrell

Location: Gulf of the St. Lawrence

History: The *Lord Elbank*, sailing from New York to Quebec, was lost near Gaspé, New Brunswick in 1764. Part of her cargo was saved.

Loyal Pitt, English troop-transport, Captain Davis

Location: Between the islands of Caudre and Travers

History: The *Loyal Pitt* was lost in a strong gale on the St. Lawrence River on August 6, 1765, while sailing from London to Quebec.

Lucy, English merchantman

Location: Labrador coast

History: The *Lucy* was lost on September 11, 1799, on the coast of Labrador while sailing from Quebec to Greenock, Scotland in 1799. Part of her cargo was saved.

Lynx, English ship Captain Murphy

Location: Laun Island

History: The *Lynx*, sailing from Newfoundland to Cape Breton, was lost near Laun Island in the Gulf of St. Lawrence on July 9, 1790.

Manacles, English merchantman, Captain Jones

Location: Newfoundland coast

History: She wrecked on the coast of Newfoundland in 1793.

Marchault, 32-gun French warship

Location: Chaleur Bay

History: The *Marchault* was sunk in Chaleur Bay along with two other warships, the *Bienfaisant* and the *Marquis Marloze*, and 22 smaller provisioning and supply vessels during an attack on July 8, 1760, by an English fleet commanded by Captain Byron.

Margaret & Harriot, English merchantman, Captain Cordova

Location: Gulf of the St. Lawrence

History: The ship was lost on rocks in 1764 near the island of Anticosti while sailing from Plymouth, England to Quebec. One member of the crew drowned and the rest were forced to spend six months in great misery on the deserted island.

Margaretta Christina, English ship

Location: Between Halifax and Newfoundland

History: The ship foundered on a voyage between Halifax and Newfoundland. The crew was saved.

Marquis Marloze, 18-gun French warship

Location: Chaleur Bay

History: The *Marquis Marloze* was sunk in Chaleur Bay along with two other warships, the *Marchault* and the *Bienfaisant*, and 22 smaller provisioning and supply vessels during an attack on July 8, 1760, by an English fleet commanded by Captain Byron.

Mars, English merchantman, Captain Clemente

Location: Cape Sable

History: The merchantman, sailing to India, was lost at Cape Sable in 1802 but the crew was saved.

Mary, Captain Montburne

Location: St. Lawrence River

History: During the winter months of 1802, ten ships were lost on the river, but only one was identified: the *Mary*, sailing from Newfoundland to Quebec.

Mary & Frances, English ship, Captain Sutton

Location: Bay of Canso

History: The *Mary & Frances* was lost in 1777 while sailing from Cork, Ireland to Quebec.

Mary & Susannah, English ship, Captain Muire

Location: St. Lawrence River

History: She became a total loss in the St. Lawrence River while sailing from London to Quebec in 1768.

Matilda, English ship, Captain Blyth

Location: St Lawrence River

History: The vessel was lost on October 18, 1773, in the St. Lawrence River after being on rocks for five days. She was sailing from Philadelphia to Quebec when she was foundered.

Minehead, American or English ship, Captain Gwyn

Location: Sable Island

History: The *Minehead* was sailing from Bristol, England to Boston, Massachusetts when she was totally wrecked on Sable Island in 1766. Fifteen crew-members perished.

Minerva, brig of unknown registry

Location: St. Lawrence River

History: The brig was lost in the river on March 19, 1806, while heading to Quebec.

Monkey, English merchantman, Captain Palmer

Location: Newfoundland

History: The merchantman was a total loss on the banks of Newfoundland in 1791. However, the crew was saved.

Mont Blanc, steam-powered French freighter, 430 feet with a 44 foot beam

Location: Halifax

History: When the *Mont Blanc* left New York, it was carrying 5,000 tons of TNT. Her cargo was bound for the raging war in Europe. On December 6, 1917, the *Mont Blanc* steamed into Halifax harbor, the staging point for many transatlantic voyages. A Norwegian steamship of the same length, the *IMO*, was heading out of the harbor at the same time. After some confusion over who had the right of way and a series of mixed signals, the two vessels collided. When *Mont Blanc's* captain saw that a collision was imminent, he maneuvered the ship so that the forward hold, which was empty of explosives, would strike the *IMO*. However, after the collision a fire started which found its way to the stores of TNT. The explosion that resulted equaled a small nuclear blast in the harbor. The *Mont Blanc* was completely destroyed and the *IMO* was thrown ashore. So violent was the blast that most of the crews working on other boats in the harbor were instantly killed. The enormous explosion devastated a portion of the town of Halifax as well. In the wake of the accident 3,000 dwellings were destroyed. Over 1,600 residents were left dead, most of them children, and 9,000 people were injured. Due to the Halifax explosion, the United States empowered the Coast Guard to provide logistical supervision, security, law enforcement, and safety measures in all major ports during World War II. Although there is nothing left of the *Mont Blanc*, the collision between the freighters will be remembered as one of the worst maritime disasters of all time.

Nassau, English merchantman, Captain Smith
   Location: Near Canso
   History: The *Nassau* was totally wrecked while sailing from London to Boston in 1771. Her crew was saved.

Noble, English merchantman, Captain Taylor
   Location: Near Quebec
   History: The *Noble* was lost near Quebec while sailing from Halifax to Quebec in 1783. All of its cargo was saved.

North, 20-gun English armed transport, Captain George Selby
   Location: Nova Scotia
   History: She wrecked near the coast of Nova Scotia in 1779.

Orb, English merchantman, Captain Brigs
   Location: Sable Island
   History: The vessel wrecked on Sable Island on January 6, 1795, while sailing from Liverpool to Halifax.

Peggy (also known by the alias *Wolf*), English merchantman
   Location: St. Peter's Island
   History: The *Peggy*, arriving from Liverpool, wrecked on St. Peter's Island in 1780.

Penelope, American ship
   Location: Halifax Harbor
   History: The *Penelope* was among many ships that sank during a gale in Halifax Harbor on September 25, 1798. Total loss of shipping was over 100,000 pounds sterling that day.

Peter, English merchantman, Captain Bruce
   Location: Near the port of Halifax
   History: She was lost at Nova Scotia in 1783, while sailing from St. Lucia Island to Halifax.

Polly, English merchantman, Captain Graves
   Location: Labrador
   History: The vessel was lost on the coast of Labrador in 1794.

Potowmack, English ship, Captain Mitchell
   Location: Sable Island
   History: The English ship, sailing from London to Quebec, was captured by an American privateer and later wrecked on Sable Island, off the coast of Nova Scotia, in 1781.

Providence, English merchantman, Captain Pinkham
   Location: St. Lawrence River
   History: The vessel wrecked in the St. Lawrence River in 1763 while sailing from Quebec to Ireland and London. Her crew and some of the cargo were saved.

Rambler, ship of unknown registry, Captain Kaquet
   Location: Sable Island
   History: The ship was lost while sailing from Philadelphia to Boston under in 1792.

Renuse, English ship, Captain Bully
   Location: Newfoundland
   History: The ship was lost at Newfoundland in 1786.

Rose, ship of unknown registry, Captain King
   Location: St. Lawrence River
   History: She was lost in the St. Lawrence River in 1771 while sailing from Quebec to Cork, Ireland.

Sally, English merchantman, Captain Brame
   Location: Lost off Newfoundland
   History: The vessel was lost while sailing from London to Quebec in 1775.

Sampon, English ship, Captain Wood Whitehove
   Location: Cape Breton Island
   History: The *Sampon*, sailing to Quebec, was totally wrecked on Cape Breton Island in 1783. Three of the crew members drowned.

San Juan, Basque whaling vessel
   Location: Red Bay
   History: In 1978, a team of underwater archaeologists from Parks Canada discovered this whaling ship in the harbor of Red Bay, Labrador. They had been led to the site by sleuthing on the part of historian Selma Huxley Barkham, who came across information in the Spanish archives regarding the loss of a whaling vessel called the *San Juan* in 1565. The archaeologists found the wreck, which is Canada's oldest, on their first exploratory dive. The whole lower hull was intact—the frigid water had protected it from sea worms. The following summer, a team of 50 underwater archaeologists and support staff invaded Red Bay, as excavation of the wreck began. Directed by Dr. James Tuck and Robert Grenier, the excavation continued for seven summers. The Canadian archaeologists removed the mud and marl covering the site and found they had one of the best preserved lower hulls in the Western Hemisphere. Instead of bringing the material to the surface, they made latex molds of all the wooden remains *in situ*. Later these molds were used to construct a model of the ship. When the excavation was completed, the entire site was reburied and left intact for future study. The *San Juan* has furnished modern scholars with tens of thousands of fascinating 16th century maritime artifacts, many of them rare, including half of a brass navigator's astrolabe, the ship's compass, intact wooden barrels for storing whale oil, and even the ship's whaleboat, the only one of its kind in existence. In general, after ballast stones, iron items account for the greatest quantity of artifacts found on old shipwrecks. However, the only iron objects found on the *San Juan* site were an anchor and a small swivel gun. No one is sure why this is so, although the extremely low water temperature that preserved the wreck's oak timbers so well that they still have a honeyed hue, may be a factor. In 1983 and 1984, two other Basque whaling ships of the same vintage were discovered in Red Bay by Parks Canada divers. Preliminary investigation indicated that they are in an excellent state of preservation and they will be excavated when and if funds become available.

Sharp, English ship
   Location: Quebec
   History: The *Sharp* was lost in 1780.

Sophia, English merchantman, Captain Hastington
   Location: Sable Island
   History: The *Sophia* was lost on Sable Island while sailing from Philadelphia to Quebec in 1773.

Sovereign, English merchantman, Captain Ramshaw
Location: Cape Breton
History: She was lost at Cape Breton in May of 1801 while sailing from London to Quebec.

Speedwell, English merchantman, Captain Lawson
Location: St. Lawrence River
History: The vessel was lost on the river while sailing from Madeira Island to Quebec in 1808. Most of its cargo was saved.

Stag, English ship
Location: Halifax Harbor
History: The ship overset and was lost while leaving Halifax Harbor in 1797 for Jamaica.

St. George, English ship, Captain Gill
Location: Red Island
History: The ship wrecked on Red Island in the St. Lawrence River in 1776. The crew was saved.

St. Joseph, ship of unknown registry, Captain Barnveth
Location: Newfoundland coast
History: The *St. Joseph* was lost onshore at Newfoundland shortly after sailing from there in 1790.

Success, English ship, Captain Friend
Location: St. Lawrence River
History: The *Success* wrecked on the river while approaching Quebec in 1761 after leaving London, England.

Susannah, English merchantman, Captain Doucett
Location: St. Lawrence River
History: The *Susannah* was lost in the St. Lawrence River while sailing from Quebec to Halifax in 1798.

Swansey, English merchantman, Captain David
Location: Sable Island
History: The vessel was lost on Sable Island while sailing from Rhode Island to Newfoundland in 1771.

Telemachus, ship of unknown registry, Captain Sargeant
Location: Sable Island
History: The ship was lost on Sable Island while sailing from Georgia to Amsterdam in 1786. Most of her cargo was lost as well.

Terpsichore, ship of unknown registry, Captain Burge
Location: Flatt Island
History: The ship was lost on Flatt Island in 1802 while sailing from Quebec to the West Indies but its crew was saved.

Titanic, British luxury ocean liner
Location: Ninety-five miles off the coast of Newfoundland
History: On April 14, 1912, the *Titanic* tragically foundered and captured the world's attention. Most people know the story of the luxury liner, considered unsinkable, that collided with an iceberg on its maiden voyage. The ship then took 1,513 of its 2,224 people onboard down with it. Many passengers onboard the *Titanic* that night would never know the profound effect the loss of the liner or their lives would have on history and on safety at sea. Due to the accident the International Maritime Organization (IMO) was created along with the first Safety of Life at Sea (SOLAS) conference, and safety at sea changed forever. The legendary *Titanic* captured the world's attention again when it was discovered 95 miles off the coast of Newfoundland by Dr. Robert Ballard of the Woods Hole Oceanographic Institution. Ballard and the joint American-French expedition found the ship lying at a depth of two and a half miles, deeper than any previous shipwreck project. The following summer, Ballard returned to the site with the manned submersible Alvin, which was capable of reaching the *Titanic*. It took the Alvin two hours to travel to the bottom of the sea. Once there, the crew took some excellent photographs and recovered objects by using the Alvin's two manipulator arms. A small, tethered robot called Jason, Jr. was used to get inside the *Titanic*. The ROV was controlled by the Alvin's pilot and was invaluable in obtaining data from areas inside the immense wreck where twisted metal made other methods of inspection too dangerous. The explorers made 60 hours of video film and took 60,000 still photographs during a 12-day period. Ballard, who believes the *Titanic* should not be disturbed further, ended his explorations when bad weather set in at the end of the summer. In the summer of 1987, a well-financed French expedition used a submersible similar to the Alvin and several sophisticated ROVs to obtain additional video and still photographs of the *Titanic*. They also recovered an assortment of artifacts. They proved that even shipwrecks at such an immense depth could be successfully salvaged. Many people regarded the removal of artifacts as plundering and there was an international outcry.

Tom, English merchantman, Captain Smart
Location: Entrance to the port of Halifax
History: The ship was lost at the entrance to the port of Halifax in 1782 while sailing from Antigua to Halifax. All of its cargo was saved.

Tortoise, 32-gun English armed transport, Captain Jahleel Brenton
Location: Off the coast of Newfoundland
History: The transport foundered off Newfoundland in 1779.

Turk, English merchantman, Captain Thomas
Location: Banks of Newfoundland
History: The vessel was lost on the Banks of Newfoundland while sailing from Bristol, England to Newfoundland in the year 1800.

Unidentified, ships (over 50)
Location: Louisburg Harbor
History: Over 50 merchant ships and warships were driven ashore or sunk during a hurricane that struck Louisburg Harbor on October 1, 1752.

Unidentified, ships (many)
Location: Louisburg
History: During a very violent gust of wind on February 26, 1748, nearly every French merchantman and warship in the harbor of Louisburg, Cape Breton Island, Nova Scotia sank.

Unidentified, ships (over 40)
Location: Cape Breton Island
History: Over 40 large ships were wrecked at Cape Breton Island, Nova Scotia during a very bad storm on October 7, 1753.

Unidentified, English transport
  Location: St. Lawrence River
  History: An unidentified transport was lost while traveling up the St. Lawrence River in 1782.

Unidentified, ships (9)
  Location: St. Lawrence River
  History: During the winter months of 1802, ten ships were lost on the river, but only one was identified: the *Mary*, sailing from Newfoundland to Quebec.

Unidentified, vessels (12)
  Location: St. Lawrence River
  History: Twelve unidentified vessels were lost on the St. Lawrence River in 1803.

Unidentified, English merchantman
  Location: Cape Ray
  History: The ship was sailing from Liverpool to Quebec when it was lost in 1791 off Cape Ray.

Unidentified, English merchantmen (2)
  Location: Grand Banks
  History: The merchantmen were lost on the Grand Banks in 1795. Both crews were saved.

Unidentified, Danish ship
  Location: Halifax Harbor
  History: The Danish ship was among many ships that sank during a gale in Halifax Harbor on September 25, 1798. Total loss of shipping was over 100,000 pounds sterling that day.

Unidentified, ship of unknown registry
  Location: Sable Island
  History: She was lost on Sable Island in 1792.

Unidentified, small American schooner
  Location: South shoal of George's Bank
  History: The schooner foundered while acting as a tender for the frigate H.M.S. *Maidstone* in 1765. All 12 of her crew perished.

Union, English merchantman, Captain Hooper
  Location: Sable Island
  History: The merchantman wrecked on Sable Island on July 10, 1802, while sailing from Spain for Boston. The crew was saved.

Valiant, English ship
  Location: Quebec
  History: The *Valiant* was lost at Quebec in 1780.

Venus, English merchantman, Captain Millet
  Location: Cape Ray
  History: The merchantman wrecked at Cape Ray while sailing from Jamaica to Quebec in 1781. The crew and cargo were completely lost.

Warrior, English merchantman, Captain M'Donough
  Location: Merrygomish
  History: The merchantman wrecked at Merrygomish on December 28, 1785, while sailing from St. John's Island to Cadiz. Her cargo was completely lost but the crew was saved.

White, English merchantman, Captain Gill
  Location: Seaton off Cape Breton Island
  History: The vessel was lost at Seaton off Cape Breton Island in 1788 while sailing from Cowes, England to Quebec.

William, English merchantman, Captain Washman
  Location: Newfoundland
  History: The vessel wrecked on the coast of Newfoundland in 1780. The entire crew perished.

William, English merchantman, Captain Losh
  Location: Cape Breton
  History: The vessel was lost near Cape Breton on April 28, 1788, while sailing from London to Quebec.

York, English merchantman, Captain Norton
  Location: Cape Negro
  History: Wrecked at Cape Negro while sailing from Liverpool to Boston in 1792.

Cayman Islands

Crystalline waters, abundant marine life and friendly people who welcome visitors have made the Cayman Islands a mecca for divers. They go there primarily for underwater photography and spear fishing, but ballast piles and many iron cannon located around all three of the Caymans have attracted treasure hunters also.

Over the years, amateur and professional divers have discovered a substantial amount of sunken treasure in the Caymans. One of the most valuable and historically important finds was also the most serendipitous. In 1970, a young couple from Dalton, Georgia were snorkeling off the beach in front of the Holiday Inn on Grand Cayman Island when they spotted a metallic glint on the sandy bottom in water no more than waist deep. It turned out to be a gold cross covered with diamonds. They began fanning the fine white sand and within minutes had uncovered a few links of what proved to be a 13-foot gold chain.

What they pulled out of the crystal clear water that day ranks as one of history's most phenomenal treasure finds. Under a thin layer of sand they found a large bar of platinum dated 1521, seven bars of silver, many pieces of silver jewelry, and a cache of more than 300 pounds of gold objects. The wreck was eventually identified as the *Santiago*, a conquistadors' ship laden

Artifacts such as this silver penknife with the owner's name on it are useful in identifying a shipwreck.

with Aztec plunder that disappeared in 1522 while en route from Mexico to Spain.

There have been more than 325 documented cases of ships around the Cayman Islands. This relatively large number can be explained by the fact that the islands lay in the path of sailing vessels plying between Cuba—the last stop before setting out on the open ocean for Europe—and the Spanish Main.

All of the wrecks in Cayman Islands waters are Crown property. A search permit must be obtained to look for a wreck. If a salvage permit is granted, anything recovered from a wreck must be turned over to the British government, which will give a share to the salvor.

SHIPWRECKS IN CAYMAN ISLAND WATERS

Allegator, ship of unknown registry, Captain Rust
    Location: Grand Cayman Island
    History: The ship was lost on Grand Cayman Island in 1806 while sailing from France to New Orleans. The crew was saved.

Augustus Caesar, English merchantman, Captain Duffell
    Location: Grand Cayman Island
    History: The merchantman was lost on Grand Cayman Island in 1764 while sailing from Jamaica to London. The crew was saved.

Cambria, English merchantman, Captain Robertson
    Location: Grand Cayman Island
    History: The vessel was lost on Grand Cayman Island in 1810 while sailing from Jamaica to London.

Catherine, English merchantman, Captain Miller
    Location: Cayman Islands
    History: The merchantman was lost in the Cayman Islands in 1783 while sailing from Jamaica to Bristol. A small part of her cargo was salvaged and sold in Jamaica.

Constantine, English merchantman, Captain Allen
    Location: Grand Cayman Island
    History: The ship wrecked on Grand Cayman Island at the end of July 1819 while sailing from Jamaica to London. Most of her cargo of coffee was saved.

Convert, 32-gun English warship, Captain John Lawford
    Location: Grand Cayman Island
    History: The ship was originally the French warship *Inconstant* until it was captured by the English. It then wrecked on Grand Cayman Island on February 8, 1794. The crew was saved.

Cygnet, English merchantman, Captain Bale
    Location: Grand Cayman Island
    History: The merchantman was lost on Grand Cayman Island in 1808 while sailing from Jamaica to London.

Dorchester, Canadian schooner
    Location: Grand Cayman Island
    History: The schooner wrecked on Grand Cayman Island in 1822 while coming from St. John, New Brunswick.

Duncan, Scottish merchantman
    Location: Grand Cayman Island
    History: The merchantman was lost on Grand Cayman Island in 1810 while sailing from Jamaica to Dublin.

Fidelity, English merchantman, Captain Hewson
    Location: Grand Cayman Island
    History: The vessel was lost on Grand Cayman Island in 1783 while sailing from Jamaica to London. The crew and part of the cargo were saved.

Fortune, English merchantman, Captain Merryman
    Location: Grand Cayman Island
    History: The ship was lost on Grand Cayman Island in 1794 while sailing from Jamaica to Bristol. The crew was saved.

Grove, ship of unknown registry, Captain Reid
    Location: Grand Cayman Island
    History: She was lost on June 1, 1823, at Grand Cayman Island while sailing from Cadiz to Veracruz. Her crew was saved.

H.M.S. *Jamaica,* English sloop
    Location: Grand Cayman Island
    History: The sloop lost her mast in a storm in 1715 and drifted on the rocks on Grand Cayman Island where she was lost. The crew was saved.

Infante, Spanish merchantman, Captain Aspillage
    Location: Little Cayman Island
    History: The merchantman was lost at Little Cayman Island in 1774 while sailing from Bilbao, Spain to Havana. Her crew was saved.

Lion, English merchantman, Captain Wilmot
    Location: Grand Cayman Island
    History: The vessel was lost on Grand Cayman Island on June 4, 1812 while sailing from London to Honduras. The crew was saved.

Maria, English merchantman, Captain Allison
    Location: Cayman Islands
    History: The merchantman was lost in the Cayman Islands in 1795 while sailing from Jamaica to Liverpool. Part of her cargo was saved.

Mary, English merchantman, Captain Sullivan
    Location: Grand Cayman Island
    History: The vessel wrecked on Grand Cayman Island in 1766 while sailing from Jamaica to London.

Morning Star, pirate ship, Captain George Bradley
    Location: Grand Cayman Island
    History: The ship was totally lost on the reefs of Grand Cayman Island during a hurricane about the beginning of September 1722. The crew was saved.

Rodney, English snow
  Location: Grand Cayman Island
  History: The snow was lost on Grand Cayman Island in 1783 while sailing from Jamaica to London.

Señor San Miguel, Spanish patache belonging to the Nueva España Flota (fleet) of Admiral Rodrigo de Torres, Captain Juan Bautista de la Hondel y Zevallos
  Location: Little Cayman Island
  History: The ship wrecked on Little Cayman Island in 1730 while sailing in the *flota* en route to Veracruz from Spain. None of the cargo of mercury was salvaged.

Sisters, English merchantman, Captain Swiney
  Location: Grand Cayman Island
  History: The merchantman was lost on August 3, 1817, on Grand Cayman Island while sailing from Jamaica to London. The crew was saved.

Three Brothers, American merchantman, Captain Jeffries
  Location: Cayman Islands
  History: Totally lost on December 17, 1807, off the Cayman Islands while sailing from Jamaica to New York.

Unidentified, Dutch ship
  Location: Grand Cayman Island
  History: The ship, owned by the Dutch West India Company and carrying 30 iron cannon, wrecked on Grand Cayman Island in 1631.

Unidentified, American schooner
  Location: Grand Cayman Island
  History: The large schooner was wrecked on Grand Cayman Island in September 1823 while sailing from the Mediterranean to New Orleans. Part of her cargo of wine and silks was saved.

Zamore, Spanish merchantman
  Location: Grand Cayman Island
  History: The merchantman wrecked on Grand Cayman Island in 1824 while sailing from France to Mexico. Her crew was saved.

Cuba

Cuba was considered the most strategically located island in the Caribbean for more than three centuries. Virtually all shipping en route to Mexico, Central America and the southern sections of the present United States from Europe or Africa—and all shipping to Europe or ports in North America coming from the Caribbean, Mexico and Central and South America—had to sail close by the island.

When Old World countries were at war with one another, their privateering vessels generally cruised in search of enemy ships off the western tip of Cuba, which all Europe-bound ships using the Bahama Channel had to pass. The Windward Passage between the eastern tip of Cuba and Haiti was used by shipping at times to avoid capture, but because of the difficult navigation through the Bahamian Archipelago, this route was a last resort. Storms, faulty navigation and sea battles caused the loss of more than 700 ships in Cuban waters between the beginning of the 16th century and 1825. The ships listed in this chapter are only those for which accurate locations

were given in the archives or those of major importance.

Under the Castro government, no foreigners are permitted to salvage shipwrecks. Since Castro came to power, three American treasure-hunting expeditions had the misfortune of accidentally shipwrecking in Cuban waters. In two of these cases the divers were held captive for several months, even though their original destinations were not in Cuban waters.

Cuban patrol vessels extend their cruising grounds well out of their own territorial waters, ostensibly to try and intercept Cuban-exile raiders working out of Florida and the Bahamas. Recently a shrimp-boat captain reported sighting a large number of bronze cannon on a reef in Cay Sal Bank, which is in Bahamian waters, but when a group of Miami divers went there to recover these cannon, they were chased away by a Cuban gunboat. There are several unconfirmed stories of American divers recovering treasure in the vicinity of the Isle of Pines prior to Castro's takeover, but these reports cannot be verified. Castro's people are currently searching the waters around Cuba.

SHIPWRECKS IN CUBA'S WATERS

Actif, French ship, Captain Belliard
  Location: Nuevitas
  History: The ship was lost near Nuevitas in the year 1822 while sailing from Havana to Le Havre.

Albert, American merchantman, Captain Hall
  Location: Cape Maize
  History: The merchantman wrecked at Cape Maize while sailing from Boston to Jamaica in 1806. Part of her cargo was saved.

Albion, English merchantman, Captain Mentor
  Location: Cape San Antonio
  History: The ship sank off Cape San Antonio after colliding with another ship while en route from Jamaica to Bristol in 1793. Her crew was saved.

Alexander, American ship, Captain Hall
  Location: Cape Cruz
  History: She was totally lost on Cape Cruz at the end of May of 1811

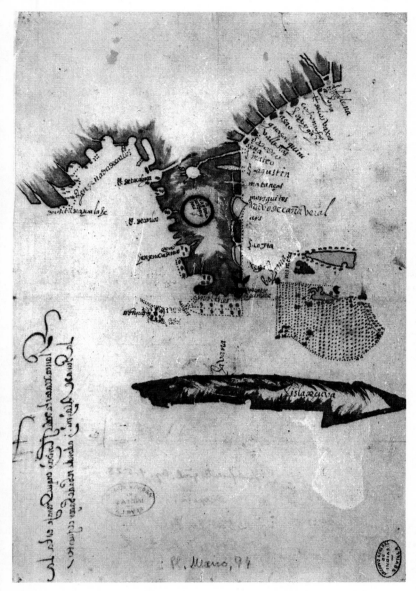

Sixteenth century chart of Florida, Cuba and the Bahamas. *Courtesy of the Archivo General de Indias, Seville.*

while sailing from Jamaica to the United States.

Ally, ship of unknown registry, Captain Sparling

Location: Cayo Romano

History: The vessel wrecked on Cayo Romano in 1791 while sailing from Africa and Dominica to Havana, Cuba. The crew and cargo were saved.

Almiranta Nuestra Señora de las Mercedes, galleon, Captain Juan Velez de Larres

Location: Havana

History: The treasure-laden galleon wrecked at Simarina, near Havana in 1695. Most of her treasure was recovered.

Amelia, Scottish merchantman, Captain Williams

Location: Jardines Reef

History: The merchantman wrecked on the Jardines Reef, near the Isle of Pines on May 2, 1818, while sailing from Jamaica to the Clyde, Scotland.

Amie, French ship, Captain Falvey

Location: Isle of Pines

History: The ship was lost off the Isle of Pines on September 13, 1821, while sailing from Haiti to Havana. Only the crew was saved.

Andromeda, 28-gun English warship

Location: Jardines Reefs, on the south coast of the island

History: During a hurricane on October 3, 1780, 13 English warships were lost on Jardines Reefs. They belonged to a squadron, commanded by Sir Hyde Park, sailing from Jamaica to Pensacola, Florida. The 13 were: the *Thunderer, Stirling Castle, Phoenix, La Blanche, Laurel, Andromeda, Deal Castle, Scarborough, Beaver's Prize, Barbadoes, Camelon, Endeavour,* and *Victor.* Most of the crews on these ships were lost.

Ann Phillippa, Scottish ship

Location: Near the Isle of Pines

History: She wrecked on January 22, 1809, while sailing from Jamaica to Glasgow.

Arinthea Bell, American ship, Captain Pearson

Location: Matanzas Bay

History: The ship was lost on the coast near Matanzas Bay while sailing from Baltimore to Havana in 1825. The crew and part of her cargo were saved.

Aristides, English merchantman

Location: Cape San Antonio

History: The merchantman was first captured by pirates while sailing from Liverpool to New Orleans in 1821. She was then wrecked near Cape San Antonio.

Artifacts

Location: Havana

History: Many houses and warehouses were carried into the sea by torrential floods during a hurricane that struck Havana in 1636. A large number of cannon and some of the ramparts of Morro Castle were also flung into the sea.

Artifacts
Location: Puestes Grandes

History: The house of a count named Barretos was swept into the sea at Puestes Grandes during a hurricane on June 21, 1791. He had died the same day and his coffin was swept into the sea as well.

Asia, 64-gun Spanish galleon, Captain Francisco Garganta
Location: Havana

History: Shortly before the Spaniards surrendered Havana to the English on June 3, 1762, they sank their three largest warships at the entrance to the harbor: the *Neptuno, Asia,* and *Europa.* During the attack, the *La Victoria* sank in the port.

Atocha, Spanish frigate-of-war, Captain Lorenzo Noriega
Location: Havana Harbor

History: The ship caught on fire and sank in Havana Harbor on July 4, 1816.

Azores, ship of unknown registry, Captain Bedford
Location: Trinidad de Cuba

History: The vessel was lost while entering port on March 2, 1824, while sailing from Jamaica to Trinidad de Cuba. Her crew was saved.

Barbadoes, 14-gun English warship
Location: Jardines Reefs, on the south coast of the island

History: During a hurricane on October 3, 1780, 13 English warships were lost on Jardines Reefs. They belonged to a squadron, commanded by Sir Hyde Park, sailing from Jamaica to Pensacola, Florida. The 13 were: the *Thunderer, Stirling Castle, Phoenix, La Blanche, Laurel, Andromeda, Deal Castle, Scarborough, Beaver's Prize, Barbadoes, Camelon, Endeavour,* and *Victor.* Most of the crews on these ships were lost.

Beaver's Prize, 16-gun English warship
Location: Jardines Reefs, on the south coast of the island

History: During a hurricane on Oc-

tober 3, 1780, 13 English warships were lost on Jardines Reefs. They belonged to a squadron, commanded by Sir Hyde Park, sailing from Jamaica to Pensacola, Florida. The 13 were: the *Thunderer, Stirling Castle, Phoenix, La Blanche, Laurel, Andromeda, Deal Castle, Scarborough, Beaver's Prize, Barbadoes, Camelon, Endeavour,* and *Victor.* Most of the crews on these ships were lost.

Berkeley, American ship, Captain Dent
Location: Colorado Reef

History: The ship wrecked on the Colorado Reef during a gale on November 17, 1818, while sailing from Jamaica to Virginia. After being plundered by Spaniards she was set afire, but her crew was saved.

Black River, English merchantman, Captain M'Taggart
Location: Isle of Pines

History: The merchantman wrecked on the Isle of Pines while en route from Jamaica to London in 1768. The crew was saved.

Blandford, Scottish merchantman, Captain Troup
Location: Isle of Pines

History: This vessel was totally lost on the Isle of Pines in 1783 while sailing from Jamaica to Scotland.

Britannia, English merchantman, Captain Lawrie
Location: Colorado Reef

History: The merchantman was lost on the reef in 1770 while coming from the Bay of Honduras.

Caesar, ship of unknown registry, Captain Jars
Location: Cayo Romano

History: The ship wrecked on Cayo Romano in 1823 while sailing from Hamburg, Germany to Havana. Her cargo was saved by wreckers and carried to Nassau.

Camelon, 14-gun English warship
Location: Jardines Reefs, on the south coast of the island

History: During a hurricane on October 3, 1780, 13 English warships were lost on Jardines Reefs. They belonged to a squadron, commanded by Sir

Hyde Park, sailing from Jamaica to Pensacola, Florida. The 13 were: the *Thunderer, Stirling Castle, Phoenix, La Blanche, Laurel, Andromeda, Deal Castle, Scarborough, Beaver's Prize, Barbadoes, Camelon, Endeavour,* and *Victor.* Most of the crews on these ships were lost.

Carlota, Spanish brigantine
Location: Matanzas Bay

History: She sank at the entrance of Matanzas Bay on December 23, 1784.

Carmen, Spanish schooner
Location: Punta Sabanilla, near Havana

History: The schooner wrecked in 1788.

Carso, Bermudan ship, Captain Peabody
Location: Two leagues east of Havana

History: The ship wrecked two leagues east of Havana on January 5, 1822 while sailing from Jamaica to Bermuda.

Catalena, ship of unknown registry, Captain Ferrer
Location: White Key, near Trinidad de Cuba

History: The ship wrecked on White Key on July 24, 1813, while sailing from San Andrés Island to Jamaica. The crew and part of the cargo were saved.

Charming Mary, Scottish merchantman, Captain English
Location: Jardines Reef

History: The merchantman was lost on the Jardines Reef in 1792 while sailing from Jamaica to Dublin. Part of her cargo of sugar, rum, coffee, ginger and castor oil was saved.

Churrieca, large Spanish ship, Captain Aspurua
Location: Morro Castle, Havana

History: The ship was totally destroyed by fire near Morro Castle in April 1823 while sailing from Cadiz, Spain to Veracruz. Her cargo was worth over $100,000.

Clara, ship of unknown registry
Location: Santiago de Cuba

History: While sailing from Rio de la Hacha, Columbia to Jamaica in the year 1816, the Clara put into Santiago de Cuba in distress and sank soon after.

Clementine, French ship
   Location: Havana Harbor
   History: The vessel wrecked in Havana Harbor during a storm on December 15, 1818, after arriving from St. Malo, France. The crew and part of the cargo were saved.

Cyrus, Canadian ship, Captain Lovitt
   Location: Cape Comentes
   History: The vessel was lost on Cape Comentes while sailing from Jamaica to Halifax in 1809.

Deal Castle, 24-gun English warship
   Location: Jardines Reefs, on the south coast of the island
   History: During a hurricane on October 3, 1780, 13 English warships were lost on Jardines Reefs. They belonged to a squadron, commanded by Sir Hyde Park, sailing from Jamaica to Pensacola, Florida. The 13 were: the *Thunderer, Stirling Castle, Phoenix, La Blanche, Laurel, Andromeda, Deal Castle, Scarborough, Beaver's Prize, Barbadoes, Camelon, Endeavour,* and *Victor.* Most of the crews on these ships were lost.

Delight, American merchantman, Captain Fry
   Location: Los Colorados Reefs
   History: Two American merchantmen, the *Salisbury* and *Delight*, both sailing from Honduras to New York, were wrecked on the Los Colorados Reefs in 1755. The *Delight*, after throwing part of her cargo overboard, was able to get off the reef. The *Salisbury* foundered and lost all its crew, except for a boy.

Devon, ship of unknown registry, Captain Carlisle
   Location: Cape Corrientes
   History: The ship was wrecked on a reef off Cape Corrientes on September 16, 1821 while sailing from Jamaica to Cork. Only some of her crew were saved.

Diamante, French frigate
   Location: Bajos de Santa Isabel
   History: In 1707, both the *Diamante* and *El Conde Torigin* wrecked on the Bajos de Santa Isabel, about three leagues from Bahía Honda and a half a league from shore. One carried a cargo of logwood and the other 30 tons of iron bars as ballast.

Diana, English merchantman, Captain Williams
   Location: Isle of Pines
   History: She wrecked on the Isle of Pines on July 19, 1802. The crew was saved.

Dorado, Spanish frigate
   Location: Havana
   History: During a hurricane that struck Havana on October 15, 1768, 69 ships were sunk, of which 17 belonged to the king. Of these, only five were identified: the *Tridente, Nancy, Perle, Dorado* and *San Francisco de Paula.* Over 5,000 buildings were also destroyed in the city and the surrounding countryside.

Duke of Bedford, English merchantman
   Location: Cape San Antonio
   History: The merchantman wrecked near Cape San Antonio in 1821 and quickly went to pieces. She was sailing from Jamaica to London when she foundered.

Edward Foote, English ship, Captain Smart
   Location: Havana
   History: The ship was lost off Havana in February 1811 while sailing from Jamaica to London. Her crew was saved.

El Bueno, French man-of-war
   Location: Castle de la Punta
   History: A French fleet, commanded by Admiral Ducase, was sent to Havana to escort Spanish ships back to Spain. The *El Bueno* from the French fleet wrecked at Castle de la Punta in Havana in 1703.

El Conde Torgin, French frigate
   Location: Bajos de Santa Isabel
   History: In 1707, both the *Diamante* and *El Conde Torigin* wrecked on the Bajos de Santa Isabel, about three leagues from Bahía Honda and a half a league from shore. One carried a cargo of logwood and the other 30 tons of iron bars as ballast.

Eliza & Polly, ship of unknown registry, Captain Forsyth
   Location: Havana
   History: The ship wrecked a few miles west of Havana after leaving port in 1823.

Eliza Partridge, Scottish ship, Captain Trenham
   Location: Jardines Reef
   History: The ship was lost on the Jardines Reef in 1792 while sailing from Jamaica to Dublin. Her crew and part of the cargo were saved.

Endeavour, 14-gun English warship
   Location: Jardines Reefs, on the south coast of the island
   History: During a hurricane on October 3, 1780, 13 English warships were lost on Jardines Reefs. They belonged to a squadron, commanded by Sir Hyde Park, sailing from Jamaica to Pensacola, Florida. The 13 were: the *Thunderer, Stirling Castle, Phoenix, La Blanche, Laurel, Andromeda, Deal Castle, Scarborough, Beaver's Prize, Barbadoes, Camelon, Endeavour,* and *Victor.* Most of the crews on these ships were lost.

Esther, English ship, Captain Newman
   Location: Havana
   History: The vessel was totally lost near Havana on February 2, 1814, while sailing from London to Havana.

Europa, 60-gun Spanish galleon, Captain Joseph Vicente
   Location: Havana
   History: Shortly before the Spaniards surrendered Havana to the English on June 3, 1762, the English sank Spain's three largest warships at the entrance to the harbor: the *Neptuno, Asia,* and *Europa.* During the attack, the *La Victoria* sank in the port.

Fleetwood, ship of unknown registry, Captain Herring
   Location: Cape Corrientes
   History: The ship wrecked at Cape Corrientes while sailing from Jamaica to London on June 2, 1824.

Flor, Spanish warship
   Location: Havana
   History: Seventy-six ships were totally lost and others damaged during a

hurricane on August 27 and 28, 1794. Of those lost, 12 were Spanish warships and the others were merchantmen of different nationalities. Only two ships were identified: the *Flor*, a Spanish warship, and *Sandown*, an English ship. Most of the cargoes were later salvaged.

Flora, English merchantman, Captain Fatheringham
Location: Jardines Reef, near the Isle of Pines
History: She was lost on the reef in 1790 while sailing from Jamaica to Leith.

Freetown, ship of unknown registry
Location: Santiago de Cuba
History: The ship was lost in 1823 while arriving from Jamaica in ballast and entering Santiago de Cuba.

Friendship, Scottish merchantman, Captain Curry
Location: Havana
History: The vessel was lost in the harbor in 1785 while sailing from Jamaica to Dublin.

General Palafox, Spanish ship, Captain Abente
Location: Isle of Pines
History: The ship was totally lost near the Isle of Pines in 1824 while sailing from Cadiz to Havana.

General Wolfe, English warship, 440 tons
Location: Havana
History: After the English captured the city of Havana in 1762, three of their warships were sunk at the entrance of the port while leaving for England with plunder. These three were the *Providence*, *General Wolfe* and *Lion*.

George, English merchantman, Captain Stenton
Location: Colorado Reef
History: The merchantman wrecked on the reef in 1773 while sailing from Jamaica to London.

Good Intent, English merchantman, Captain Kennedy
Location: Jardines Reef
History: The merchantman was lost on the Jardines Reef in 1792 while sailing from Jamaica to London.

Griffin, English merchantman, Captain Brown
Location: Cape San Anton
History: The ship was lost off Cape San Anton in 1753 while sailing from Jamaica to London.

Guadalupe, Spanish frigate, Captain José de la Encina
Location: Cape San Antonio
History: The frigate wrecked on Cape San Antonio on March 15, 1799. One hundred and forty persons perished.

Hall, English ship
Location: Havana
History: The ship wrecked at Havana on April 30, 1821, during a gale while sailing from Jamaica to Liverpool. A small part of her cargo was saved.

Hanna, Irish merchantman, Captain Williamson
Location: A few leagues northeast of the Colorado Reef
History: The ship struck on a rock a few leagues northeast of the Colorado Reef on August 2, 1787. The crew reached Havana in 13 days in the ship's boat.

Hanna, English merchantman, Captain Ellis
Location: Isle of Pines
History: Two English merchantmen were wrecked at the Isle of Pines on January 29, 1811. The *Louisa* and *Hanna* were both sailing from Jamaica to London.

Hannah, American merchantman, Captain Lewis
Location: Colorado Reef
History: The merchantman wrecked during September 1821 while sailing from Santiago de Cuba to Philadelphia.

Hare, English merchantman, Captain Colly
Location: Colorado Reef
History: She wrecked on the reef while en route from Jamaica to Liverpool in 1765. The crew was saved.

Havana, ship of unknown registry, Captain Hale
Location: Cape Maize
History: The vessel wrecked off

Cape Maize in 1763 while sailing from New England to Jamaica.

Hawke, English merchantman, Captain Caine
Location: Los Colorados Reef
History: The merchantman wrecked on November 3, 1757, on the Los Colorados Reef while sailing from Jamaica to London in 1757.

Hercules, merchant *urca*
Location: Cayo de Libizas
History: In 1639, the ship sank during a storm near Cayo de Libizas, located 22 leagues west of Havana, due to being overloaded. Four frigates with divers, sent from Havana, recovered all 20 of her cannon, eight of which were bronze.

Hercules, ship of unknown registry
Location: Havana
History: The ship wrecked near Havana during February of 1817.

H.M.S. Barracouta, ten-gun English warship, Captain Joel Orchard
Location: Jordan Key
History: The warship wrecked on Jordan Key on October 2, 1805. The crew was saved.

H.M.S. Bonetta, 18-gun English warship, Captain Thomas New
Location: Jardines Reef
History: She wrecked on Jardines Reef on October 25, 1801. The crew was saved.

H.M.S. Briseis, ten-gun English sloop-of-war, Captain George Domett
Location: Punta Pedras
History: The sloop wrecked on a reef on November 5, 1816, near Punta Pedras. The crew was saved.

H.M.S. Chesterfield, English warship
Location: Cayo Confite, north of Havana
History: The warship wrecked on Cayo Confite in 1762 along with four transports bringing reinforcements to hold the city of Havana for England. No lives were lost.

H.M.S. Diligence, 18-gun English warship, Captain Charles Baynton Hodgson
Location: Havana
History: She wrecked in September

1800 on a shoal near Havana. The crew was saved.

H.M.S. *Harwich*, 50-gun English warship, Captain William March
Location: Isle of Pines
History: The warship wrecked on October 4, 1760, on the Isle of Pines.

H.M.S. *Jamaica*, English warship, Captain Talbot
Location: Colorado Reef
History: The warship wrecked on the reef in 1770. The crew was saved.

H.M.S. *Mordaunt*, 46-gun English warship, Captain Francis Maynard
Location: Los Colorados Reefs
History: She wrecked on the Los Colorados Reefs on November 21, 1693, with a total loss of life.

H.M.S. *Muros*, 24-gun English warship, Captain Archibald Duff
Location: Bahía Honda
History: The warship was lost at the entrance to Bahía Honda in 1808. The crew was saved.

***Invencible*,** galleon belonging to the squadron of Admiral Rodrigo de Torres
Location: Havana Harbor
History: The large galleon was at anchor in the harbor in 1740 when it was struck by lightning and blew up. A great amount of damage was done to the city as well. The ship carried four million pesos in treasure, none of which was recovered.

***Jane*,** English ship, Captain M'Bride
Location: Cape Corrientes
History: The ship wrecked near Cape Corrientes on June 9, 1817, while sailing from Jamaica to Greenock, Scotland.

***Jesús Nazareno y Nuestra Señora de Guadaloupe*,** merchant *nao*, 112 tons, Captain Bartolome Antonio Garrote
Location: Guarico
History: Sometime prior to 1518, the vessel, owned by Tomás José Caro, was carrying a cargo of tobacco. It developed a bad leak after leaving Havana for Spain and sank in the port of Guarico. Most of its cargo was removed.

***Joan*,** American ship
Location: Colorado Reef

History: The ship wrecked on the Colorado Reef on July 4, 1818, while sailing from Jamaica to Norfolk. The crew and part of the cargo were saved.

***La Blanche*,** 42-gun English warship
Location: Jardines Reefs, on the south coast of the island
History: During a hurricane on October 3, 1780, 13 English warships were lost on Jardines Reefs. They belonged to a squadron, commanded by Sir Hyde Park, sailing from Jamaica to Pensacola, Florida. The 13 were: the *Thunderer, Stirling Castle, Phoenix, La Blanche, Laurel, Andromeda, Deal Castle, Scarborough, Beaver's Prize, Barbadoes, Camelon, Endeavour,* and *Victor.* Most of the crews on these ships were lost.

***La Concepción*,** *nao* belonging to the Tierra Firme Armada of Captain-General Alvaro Sánchez de Aviles, 220 tons, Captain Juan Diaz Bozino
Location: Between Cape San Anton and Havana
History: The *La Concepción,* carrying treasure onboard, wrecked on the coast between Cape San Anton and Havana on May 24, 1556, during a storm. The *La Magdalena* and two unidentified caravels belonging to the same fleet were also wrecked.

***La Concepción*,** advice boat, 50 tons, Captain Francisco Rodriquiz
Location: Cayo del Visal
History: The boat wrecked on Cayo del Visal, near the entrance to Rio de Puercos, in 1621 while sailing from Veracruz to Spain. Most of the crew drowned but the mail was recovered.

***La Gallardino*,** frigate, Captain Juan Gómez Brito
Location: Twelve to 14 leagues north of Rio de Puercos
History: The frigate, sailing from Puerto Rico, wrecked in 1660 on a small reef where waves are always breaking. The reef is described as about half the size of the main plaza of Havana and is located 12 to 14 leagues north of Rio de Puercos.

***La Magdalena*,** *nao* belonging to the Tierra Firme Armada of Captain-General Alvaro Sánchez de Aviles, 220 tons, Captain Cristobal García

Location: Between Cape San Anton and Havana
History: The *La Magdalena,* carrying treasure onboard, wrecked on the coast between Cape San Anton and Havana on May 24, 1556, during a storm. The *La Concepción* and two unidentified caravels belonging to the same fleet were also wrecked.

***Lancaster*,** English ship, Captain Andrews
Location: Havana
History: The ship wrecked at Havana on July 21, 1813, while bound for Liverpool.

***Lark*,** ship of unknown registry, Captain Knight
Location: Nuevitas Reef
History: The vessel wrecked on September 17, 1817, while sailing to Havana. Part of the cargo was saved.

***Laurel*,** 28-gun English warship
Location: Jardines Reefs, on the south coast of the island
History: During a hurricane on October 3, 1780, 13 English warships were lost on Jardines Reefs. They belonged to a squadron, commanded by Sir Hyde Park, sailing from Jamaica to Pensacola, Florida. The 13 were: the *Thunderer, Stirling Castle, Phoenix, La Blanche, Laurel, Andromeda, Deal Castle, Scarborough, Beaver's Prize, Barbadoes, Camelon, Endeavour,* and *Victor.* Most of the crews on these ships were lost.

***La Victoria*,** frigate, Captain Carlos Joseph de Sarria
Location: In the port of Havana on "La Colonia del Sacramento"
History: Shortly before the Spaniards surrendered Havana to the English on June 3, 1762, they sank their three largest warships at the entrance to the harbor. The three were the *Neptuno, Asia,* and *Europa.* During the attack, the *La Victoria* sank in the port.

***Lewis Williams*,** American ship, Captain O'Brien
Location: Colorado Reef
History: The ship wrecked on the reef on March 23, 1807, while sailing from New Orleans to New York.

***Liberty*,** English brig
Location: Havana

History: The brig wrecked near Havana on December 20, 1817. Her cargo was completely salvaged.

Ligera, 40-gun Spanish frigate-of-war
Location: Port of Santiago de Cuba
History: The frigate sank in the port in the year 1822.

Lion, English warship, 293 tons
Location: Havana
History: After the English captured the city of Havana in 1762, three of their warships were sunk at the entrance of the port while leaving for England with plunder. These three were the *Providence, General Wolfe* and the *Lion*.

Lion, English ship, Captain Brown
Location: Isla Blanca
History: The ship wrecked on Isla Blanca on the northern coast of Cuba in 1758 while sailing from Jamaica to Bristol.

Los Peligros, galleon
Location: Havana
History: The treasure-laden galleon caught fire and sank in Havana Harbor in 1613 while preparing to sail for Spain.

Louisa, English merchantman, Captain Folger
Location: Isle of Pines
History: Two English merchantmen were wrecked at the Isle of Pines on January 29, 1811: the *Louisa* and *Hanna*, both sailing from Jamaica to London.

Mable, American ship, Captain Reynolds
Location: Colorado Reef
History: The vessel was lost on the reef while sailing from Jamaica to New York in 1798. The crew was saved.

Mariner, English ship, Captain Whillis
Location: Colorado Reef
History: The ship wrecked on the reef in 1818 while sailing from London to Havana. The crew, silver and gold specie, and a small part of the cargo were saved.

Mary, English ship, Captain Aspinal
Location: Isle of Pines
History: The vessel wrecked on the Isle of Pines in 1773 while sailing from

Jamaica to London. Eight of the crew reached Grand Cayman Island in the ship's longboat.

May, ship of unknown registry, Captain Laughton
Location: Havana
History: The ship was burnt at Havana on July 25, 1810. The crew was saved.

Mercury, English ship, Captain Taylor
Location: Jardines Reef
History: She wrecked on the reef while sailing from Africa and Jamaica to Bristol in 1784.

Merry Quaker, American ship, Captain Brown
Location: Colorado Reef
History: The ship wrecked on the reef on January 9, 1807, while sailing from Jamaica to New York.

Minerva, Bahamian ship, Captain Whitehead
Location: Cape Maize
History: The vessel was lost on Cape Maize in 1816 while sailing from Jamaica to the Bahamas.

Nancy, Spanish frigate
Location: Havana
History: During a hurricane that struck Havana on October 15, 1768, 69 ships were sunk, of which 17 belonged to the king. Of these, only five were identified: the *Tridente, Nancy, Perle, Dorado* and *San Francisco de Paula*. Over 5,000 buildings were also destroyed in the city and the surrounding countryside.

Nancy, English ship, Captain Bowden
Location: Havana
History: The ship wrecked at Havana on October 8, 1813, while sailing from Jamaica to London. Very little of her cargo was saved.

Navigator, English ship, Captain Preda
Location: Havana
History: The vessel was totally lost near Havana on February 2, 1814, while sailing from London to Havana.

Neptune, ship of unknown registry, Captain Hodgson
Location: Bahía Honda
History: The ship was lost in Bahía

Honda in 1768 while sailing from Honduras to Leghorn, Italy. The crew was saved.

Neptuno, 70-gun Spanish galleon, Captain Pedro Bermudas
Location: Havana
History: Shortly before the Spaniards surrendered Havana to the English on June 3, 1762, they sank their three largest warships at the entrance to the harbor. The three were the *Neptuno, Asia,* and *Europa*. During the attack, the *La Victoria* sank in the port.

Nonsuch, American ship, Captain Hall
Location: Colorado Reef
History: She was lost on the reef in 1770 while sailing from Jamaica to South Carolina. The crew was rescued from a raft they constructed from the wreck.

Nuestra Señora de Arancacu, Spanish galleon belonging to the Tierra Firme Armada of Captain-General Carlos de Ibarra, 600 tons, Captain Sancho de Urdaniva
Location: Bahía Honda
History: A Dutch privateering fleet, commanded by the famous Dutch admiral known by the nickname "Wooden Leg," attacked the fleet in 1638. The battle raged for two days while the armada attempted to reach Havana. The *Nuestra Señora de Arancacu* was so badly damaged by cannon fire that after all its treasure had been transferred to other galleons, it was taken into the port of Bahía Honda and set afire. Later, divers retrieved 15 of the 20 large cannon from the burnt hulk, but the other five were not raised as they were buried under sand. All the other Spanish ships in the fleet made it to port safely.

Nuestra Señora de Atocha y San Josef, nao belonging to the Nueva España Flota (fleet) of Admiral Juan de Campos, 400 tons, Captain Geronimo Beleno
Location: A musket-shot distance from the Port of La Puntal
History: After the *flota* set sail from Havana for Spain, it was struck by a hurricane in the Bahama Channel in 1641. Many of the ships were lost. Four of the *flota*'s ships were driven back to Cuba where two were wrecked near

Havana. Another ship was wrecked six leagues from Santiago de Cuba. The *Nuestra Señora de Atocha y San Josef* reached the port of Santiago de Cuba. After making repairs, she left port and set out for Havana in January 1642. Within sight of Havana, a bad storm struck and the ship was wrecked only a musket-shot distance from the Port of La Puntal.

Nuestra Señora de la Concepción, *nao* belonging to the Nueva España Flota (fleet) of Captain-General Pedro de las Roelas, 250 tons, Captain Pedro del Corro

Location: Twenty-one degrees of north latitude and 12 leagues from the Isle of Pines

History: In 1563, a large convoy of ships sailed from Spain for the New World and, after stopping for water at Guadeloupe, those going to South America and those to Mexico split up into two groups. On July 18, 1563, six of the *flota's* ships wrecked on the Jardines Reefs on the southern coast of Cuba. All six were carrying large amounts of mercury as well as cargoes of general merchandise. The *capitana* (flagship) was also carrying Archbishop Salcedo, who was said to have been transporting a great amount of church and personal treasure. The wrecks were reportedly in 1½ to 4 fathoms of water. Ships were sent from Havana to rescue the survivors and undertake salvage operations, but only a small part of the mercury and merchandise was recovered and none of the treasure of Archbishop Salcedo. The vessels lost were the *San Juan Bautista* (the *capitana*), *San Juan, Nuestra Señora de la Consolación, Nuestra Señora de la Concepción, San Salvador,* and *Santa Margarita.*

Nuestra Señora de la Concepción y San Francisco, merchant *navío*, Captain Juan Ignacio de Cuellar

Location: Havana Harbor

History: The ship was accidentally burnt in Havana Harbor in 1672.

Nuestra Señora de la Concepción y San Ignacio, merchant *navío* belonging to the Nueva España Flota (fleet) of Captain-General Fernando Ponce

Location: Los Organos

History: The ship wrecked in 1681 on the shoals of Los Organos, located 14 leagues from Havana.

Nuestra Señora de la Consolación, *nao* belonging to the Nueva España Flota (fleet) of Captain-General Pedro de las Roelas, 300 tons, Captain Juan de Barrios

Location: Twenty-one degrees of north latitude and 12 leagues from the Isle of Pines

History: In 1563, a large convoy of ships sailed from Spain for the New World and, after stopping for water at Guadeloupe, those going to South America and those to Mexico split up into two groups. On July 18, 1563, six of the *flota's* ships wrecked on the Jardines Reefs on the southern coast of Cuba. All six were carrying large amounts of mercury as well as cargoes of general merchandise. The *capitana* (flagship) was also carrying Archbishop Salcedo, who was said to have been transporting a great amount of church and personal treasure. The wrecks were reportedly in 1½ to 4 fathoms of water. Ships were sent from Havana to rescue the survivors and undertake salvage operations, but only a small part of the mercury and merchandise was recovered and none of the treasure of Archbishop Salcedo. The vessels lost were the *San Juan Bautista* (the *capitana*), *San Juan, Nuestra Señora de la*

Sixteenth century Spanish diving bell. *Courtesy of the Archivo General de Indias, Seville.*

Consolación, Nuestra Señora de la Concepción, San Salvador, and *Santa Margarita.*

Nuestra Señora de la Limpia Concepción, *capitana* (flagship) of the Nueva España Flota (fleet) of Captain-General Juan de Vega Bazan, 600 tons, Captain Alonso Hidalgo

Location: Near Morro Castle, Havana

History: When the *flota* arrived from Veracruz and entered Havana in 1636, the *Nuestra Señora de la Limpia Concepción*, carrying a large amount of treasure, hit a rock near Morro Castle and sank. Due to the rapid action of many nearby ships, all the treasure and artillery was saved before she went down.

Nuestra Señora de las Mercedes, advice boat, Captain Ramon Ortis Delgado

Location: Cape San Anton

History: The small advice boat, sent from Spain, wrecked at Cape San Anton on January 26, 1763.

Nuestra Señora de la Soledad y San Ignacio de Loyola, galleon

Location: Havana

History: The treasure-laden galleon wrecked near the entrance of the port of Havana in 1695. All her treasure was recovered.

Nuestra Señora del Rosario, *nao* belonging to the Nueva España Flota (fleet) of Captain-General Martín Pérez Olozabal, 220 tons, Captain Cristobal Castellanos

Location: Havana

History: The treasure-laden ship was lost near Havana in 1593 along with the *Santa María de San Vicente* of the same fleet. The treasure from both ships was taken off before they sank.

Nuestra Señora del Rosario, San José y Las Animas, *nao* belonging to the Nueva España Flota (fleet)

Location: Five leagues west of Havana

History: Five ships of the *flota* were wrecked during a "norther" on December 16, 1711, about five leagues west of Havana. One was the *almiranta*, the *Santisima Trinidad*, which carried a large treasure; the other four were *naos*

Spanish grappling line being used to pull a shipwreck closer to shore for salvaging, c. 1620.

of which only one was identified, the *Nuestra Señora del Rosario, San José y Las Animas*. Divers were quickly employed and by January 4, they had recovered over 1,700,000 pesos in treasure from the wrecks. The total amount of treasure carried on these ships was not stated in the documents.

Nuestra Señora del Rosario y San Joseph, galleon, 424 tons
Location: Havana
History: The galleon, owned by Governor Francisco Blanco, was built in Havana and sank while entering Havana after her sea trials in 1687.

Olive, Canadian ship, Captain Vandirey
Location: Isle of Pines
History: The ship was lost on September 17, 1813, while sailing from Jamaica to Halifax. The crew was saved.

Olive Branch, American schooner, Captain Smith
Location: Port of Gibara
History: The *Olive Branch* and four unidentified Spanish vessels were lost in the port of Gibara during a gale on September 13, 1821.

Pacific, American ship, Captain Clark
Location: Jardines Reef
History: The vessel was lost on July 13, 1815, on Jardines Reef while sailing from Santo Domingo to Boston.

Paget, English merchantman, Captain Straycock
Location: Cape San Antonio
History: The merchantman wrecked at Cape San Antonio in 1805 while sailing from Jamaica to London.

Palas, 34-gun Spanish frigate-of-war, Captain Pedro Saenz de la Guardia.
Location: In two fathoms on "el placer de Cayo Blanco," near the Colorado Reef
History: The frigate was part of a Spanish squadron going after an English squadron in 1797 when it wrecked near Colorado Reef. The ship was later completely salvaged.

Peña de Francia, galleon belonging to the Armada de Barlovento
Location: Six leagues from Havana
History: The galleon sank in a bad storm in January of 1642 just six leagues from Havana with a total loss of lives. When salvors located the wreck eight months later they were unable to recover anything since it was completely buried in sand.

Perle, Spanish frigate
Location: Havana
History: During a hurricane that struck Havana on October 15, 1768, 69 ships were sunk, of which 17 belonged to the king. Of these, only five were identified: the *Tridente, Nancy, Perle, Dorado* and *San Francisco de Paula*.

Over 5,000 buildings were also destroyed in the city and the surrounding countryside.

Phoebe, American schooner, Captain Murray
Location: Santiago de Cuba
History: The schooner burnt off Santiago de Cuba in 1811. The crew was saved.

Phoenix, 44-gun English warship
Location: Jardines Reefs, on the south coast of the island
History: During a hurricane on October 3, 1780, 13 English warships were lost on Jardines Reefs. They belonged to a squadron, commanded by Sir Hyde Park, sailing from Jamaica to Pensacola, Florida. The 13 were: the *Thunderer, Stirling Castle, Phoenix, La Blanche, Laurel, Andromeda, Deal Castle, Scarborough, Beaver's Prize, Barbadoes, Camelon, Endeavour,* and *Victor.* Most of the crews on these ships were lost.

Piedad, Spanish schooner, Captain José Fernández de la Peña
Location: Baní
History: The ship ran aground on January 19, 1807, in Baní while sailing from Cartagena to Havana with mail. The people, mail and cannon were saved.

Port Maria, English merchantman, Captain Potter
Location: Jardines Reefs on the south side of the island
History: The merchantman was totally lost on the Jardines Reefs in 1785 while sailing from Jamaica to London.

Prince Regent, English brig
Location: Havana
History: The brig wrecked near Havana during a gale on March 3, 1817. The ship was arriving from the Bahamas with a cargo of salt.

Providence, English warship, Captain Strenham
Location: Havana
History: After the English captured the city of Havana in 1762, three of their warships were sunk at the entrance of the port while leaving for England with plunder. These three were the *Providence, General Wolfe* and *Lion*.

Ranger, English merchantman, Captain Patterson

Location: Colorado Reef

History: The merchantman was lost on the Colorado Reef in 1787 while sailing from Jamaica to Bermuda. Five men were drowned.

Rebecca, English merchantman, Captain Stott

Location: Colorado Reef

History: The merchantman wrecked on the reef while sailing from Jamaica to Bristol in 1776. The crew was saved.

Rebecca, English schooner, Captain Pedro Anson

Location: Shoals of Santa Isabel

History: The schooner wrecked in 1771 on the Shoals of Santa Isabel. The crew was rescued by a boat from Havana and carried to its port.

Réparateur, French ship, Captain Freore

Location: Cape Corrientes

History: The ship wrecked on June 1, 1824, while sailing from Cuba to Bordeaux, France.

Salisbury, American merchantman, Captain Ash

Location: Los Colorados Reefs

History: Two American merchantmen, the *Salisbury* and *Delight*, both sailing from Honduras to New York, were wrecked on the Los Colorados Reefs in 1755. The *Delight*, after throwing part of her cargo overboard, was able to get off the reef. The *Salisbury* foundered and lost all its crew, except for a boy.

Sally, American merchantman, Captain Thompson

Location: Jardines Reef

History: The merchantman was totally lost on the Jardines Reef in 1777 while sailing from Jamaica to New York. Some of the crew were saved.

San Andrés, nao, 300 tons, Captain Marco de Nápoles

Location: Havana Harbor

History: The vessel wrecked in Havana Harbor in 1563 while sailing from Cartagena and Panama with treasure.

San Anton, merchant *nao*, 100 tons, Captain Gonzalo Rodríguez

Location: Northwest coast

History: The ship was lost on a reef on the northwest coast of the island in 1521 while sailing from Havana to Spain.

San Antonio de Padua (alias *Hercules*), merchant *navío*, 174 tons, Captain Pedro Sanz y Sagardia

Location: Bahía Mangle

History: The vessel wrecked in 1731 in Bahía Mangle, located between Puerto de Principe and Bayano. She carried a cargo of mercury.

San Antonio y San Felix, galleon, Captain Ocana

Location: Between San Anton and Corrientes

History: The galleon was between capes San Anton and Corrientes during a storm on the coast in 1751. The crew and 400,000 pesos were saved.

Sandown, English merchantman, Captain Apsey

Location: Havana

History: Seventy-six ships were totally lost and others damaged during a hurricane on August 27 and 28, 1794. Of those lost, 12 were Spanish warships and the others were merchantmen of different nationalities. Only two ships were identified: the *Flor*, a Spanish warship, and *Sandown*, an English ship. Most of the cargoes were later salvaged.

San Francisco, frigate, 80 tons, Captain Juan d'Esquibel

Location: Matanzas Bay

History: The frigate was lost during a storm in 1618 as it attempted to enter Matanzas Bay. She was sailing as an advice boat between Veracruz and Spain. Everyone onboard survived and divers recovered the vessel's mail and cargo.

San Francisco de Paula, Spanish packet boat

Location: Havana

History: During a hurricane that struck Havana on October 15, 1768, 69 ships were sunk, of which 17 belonged to the king. Of these, only five were identified: the *Tridente*, *Nancy*, *Perle*, *Dorado* and *San Francisco de Paula*. Over 5,000 buildings were also destroyed in the city and the surrounding countryside.

San Gabriel, merchant *navío* belonging to the Nueva España Flota (fleet) of Captain-General Marcos de Aramburi, 140 tons, Captain Pedro de Morillo

Location: Havana Harbor

History: The vessel wrecked in Havana Harbor in 1595. The silver onboard was recovered by divers.

San José y Nuestra Señora del Rosario, galleon, 230 tons, Captain Francisco Blanco

Location: Havana Harbor

History: The galleon sank at the entrance of Havana Harbor in 1689. Divers recovered her 42 cannon and cargo of tobacco.

San Josef y San Francisco de Paula, *capitana* (flagship) of the Tierra Firme Armada of Captain-General Pedro de Ursua, 400 tons, Captain Jacobo de Oyanguren

Location: Havana Harbor

History: The *capitana* and an unidentified patache of the armada sank at the entrance to Havana Harbor in 1647 while the armada was arriving from Cartagena with large amounts of treasure.

San Juan, nao

Location: Five leagues east of Havana

History: The *nao* was lost five leagues east of Havana in 1537 during a hurricane while arriving from Spain with a valuable cargo of merchandise.

San Juan, nao belonging to the Nueva España Flota (fleet) of Captain-General Pedro de las Roelas, 250 tons, Captain Gaspar Luys

Location: Twenty-one degrees of north latitude and 12 leagues from the Isle of Pines

History: In 1563, a large convoy of ships sailed from Spain for the New World and, after stopping for water at Guadeloupe, those going to South America and those to Mexico split up into two groups. On July 18, 1563, six of the *flota's* ships wrecked on the Jardines Reefs on the southern coast of Cuba. All six were carrying large amounts of mercury as well as cargoes of general merchandise. The *capitana* (flagship) was also carrying Archbishop Salcedo, who was said to have been transporting a great amount of church and personal treasure. The wrecks were reportedly in 1½ to 4 fathoms of water. Ships were sent from Havana to rescue the survivors and undertake salvage operations, but only a small part of the mercury and merchandise was recovered and none of the treasure of Archbishop Salcedo. The vessels lost were the *San Juan Bautista* (the *capitana*), *San Juan, Nuestra Señora de la Consolación, Santa Nuestra Señora de la Concepción, San Salvador,* and *Santa Margarita.*

San Juan, galleon, Captain Francisco Maldonado
    Location: Havana Harbor
    History: The treasure-laden galleon was lost while entering Havana Harbor in 1721.

San Juan Agustin, galleon, Captain Bartolome de Larriba
    Location: Fifteen leagues from Havana
    History: The galleon was part of a four-galleon squadron commanded by Captain Sancho de Urdaniba which was escorting the Nueva España Flota (fleet) back to Spain. The vessel wrecked during the night in a storm in 1634 and sank about 15 leagues from Havana, between Rio de Puercos and Bahía Honda. Forty of the crew perished.

San Juan Bautista, *capitana* (flagship) of the Nueva España Flota (fleet) commanded by Captain-General Pedro de las Roelas, 150 tons, Captain Juan de Arenas
    Location: Twenty-one degrees of north latitude and 12 leagues from the Isle of Pines
    History: In 1563, a large convoy of ships sailed from Spain for the New World and, after stopping for water at Guadeloupe, those going to South America and those to Mexico split up into two groups. The Nueva España Flota was commanded by Captain-General Pedro de las Roelas. On July 18, 1563, six of the *flota's* ships wrecked on the Jardines Reefs on the southern coast of Cuba. All six were carrying large amounts of mercury as well as cargoes of general merchandise. The *capitana* (flagship) was also carrying

Archbishop Salcedo, who was said to have been transporting a great amount of church and personal treasure. The wrecks were reportedly in 1½ to 4 fathoms of water. Ships were sent from Havana to rescue the survivors and undertake salvage operations, but only a small part of the mercury and merchandise was recovered and none of the treasure of Archbishop Salcedo. Besides the *San Juan Bautista*, the vessels lost were the *San Juan, San Salvador, Nuestra Señora de la Consolación,* and *Nuestra Señora de la Concepción,* and *Santa Margarita.*

San Salvador, *galera* (gallery) belonging to the Nueva España Flota (fleet) of Captain-General Pedro de las Roelas, 350 tons
    Location: Twenty-one degrees of north latitude and 12 leagues from the Isle of Pines
    History: In 1563, a large convoy of ships sailed from Spain for the New World and, after stopping for water at Guadeloupe, those going to South America and those to Mexico split up into two groups. On July 18, 1563, six of the *flota's* ships wrecked on the Jardines Reefs on the southern coast of Cuba. All six were carrying large amounts of mercury as well as cargoes of general merchandise. The *capitana* (flagship) was also carrying Archbishop Salcedo, who was said to have been transporting a great amount of church and personal treasure. The wrecks were reportedly in 1½ to 4 fathoms of water. Ships were sent from Havana to rescue the survivors and undertake salvage operations, but only a small part of the mercury and merchandise was recovered and none of the treasure of Archbishop Salcedo. Besides the *San Salvador*, the vessels lost were the *San Juan Bautista* (the *capitana*), *San Juan, Nuestra Señora de la Consolación, Nuestra Señora de la Concepción,* and *Santa Margarita.*

Santa Catalina, *nao,* 200 tons, Captain Francisco López
    Location: Havana Harbor
    History: The vessel sank in Havana Harbor in the year 1537. She was carrying gold and silver from Mexico when she went down.

Santa Margarita, *nao* belonging to the Nueva España Flota (fleet) of Captain-General Pedro de las Roelas, 300 tons, Captain Gonzalo Monte
    Location: Twenty-one degrees of north latitude and 12 leagues from the Isle of Pines
    History: In 1563, a large convoy of ships sailed from Spain for the New World and, after stopping for water at Guadeloupe, those going to South America and those to Mexico split up into two groups. On July 18, 1563, six of the *flota's* ships wrecked on the Jardines Reefs on the southern coast of Cuba. All six were carrying large amounts of mercury as well as cargoes of general merchandise. The *capitana* (flagship) was also carrying Archbishop Salcedo, who was said to have been transporting a great amount of church and personal treasure. The wrecks were reportedly in 1½ to 4 fathoms of water. Ships were sent from Havana to rescue the survivors and undertake salvage operations, but only a small part of the mercury and merchandise was recovered and none of the treasure of Archbishop Salcedo. The vessels lost were the *San Juan Bautista* (the *capitana*), *San Juan, Nuestra Señora de la Consolación, Nuestra Señora de la Concepción, San Salvador,* and *Santa Margarita.*

Santa María de Finisterra, *nao,* 200 tons, Captain Juan Rodríguez Zarco
    Location: Havana Harbor
    History: The treasure-laden *nao* wrecked in Havana Harbor in 1552 while arriving from Panama.

Santa María de la Isla, *nao,* 180 tons, Captain Vicente Martín
    Location: Near Havana
    History: The ship wrecked on the coast near Havana in 1544 while sailing from Nombre de Dios to Havana with treasure onboard.

Santa María de San Vicente, *nao* belonging to the Nueva España Flota (fleet) of Captain-General Martín Pérez Olozabal, 180 tons, Captain Miguel de Alcata
    Location: Near Havana
    History: The treasure-laden ship was lost near Havana in 1593 along with *Nuestra Señora del Rosario* of the

same fleet. The treasure from both ships was taken off before they sank.

Santa María de Villacelan, *nao*, 220 tons, Captain Mateo de Vides
Location: Matanzas Bay
History: The vessel wrecked on the coast near Matanzas Bay in the year 1555. She was carrying treasure from Panama and Cartagena to Spain when she foundered.

San't Andrés, *nao*, 210 ton, Captain Vicente Hernández
Location: Havana Harbor
History: The treasure-laden vessel, owned by Sebastián González, wrecked in Havana Harbor in 1552 while arriving from Honduras. Most of her treasure was salvaged.

Santa Tecla, Spanish frigate-of-war, Captain Carlos Chacón
Location: Havana Harbor
History: The ship burnt completely in Havana Harbor in 1786.

Santiago, *nao*, 400 tons, Captain Andrés de la Calde
Location: Near Havana
History: A Dutch privateer forced the ship to run aground near Havana in 1629 where it was totally lost. The ship was coming from Honduras.

Santiago, merchant *navío*, 228 tons, Captain Salvador Vanegas
Location: Los Jardines Reef
History: The vessel, returning to Spain in 1699 with a cargo of no great value, was wrecked on the Los Jardines Reef, near the Isle of Pines.

Santísima Trinidad, *almiranta* of the Nueva España Flota (fleet), Captain Diego de Alarcón y Ocaño of the Armada de Barlovento
Location: Five leagues west of Havana
History: Five ships of the *flota* were wrecked during a "norther" on December 16, 1711 about five leagues west of Havana. One was the *almiranta*, the *Santísima Trinidad*, which carried a large treasure; the other four were *naos* of which only one was identified, the *Nuestra Señora del Rosario, San José y Las Animas*. Divers were quickly employed and by January 4, they had recovered over 1,700,000 pesos in treasure

from the wrecks. The total amount of treasure carried on these ships was not stated in the documents.

Santísima Trinidad, Spanish ship
Location: Los Pasajes Shoals
History: There is a brief mention in documents of a Spanish ship named *Santísima Trinidad* which was lost on Los Pasajes Shoals near Havana in 1715.

Sara, English merchantman
Location: Jardines Reef
History: The merchantman wrecked on the Jardines Reef in 1792 while sailing from Jamaica to Liverpool. Her cargo of sugar was lost but some rum and lumber was saved.

Sarah, ship of unknown registry, Captain Kelly
Location: Havana Harbor
History: She was lost entering Havana Harbor on January 14, 1815, while sailing from Jamaica to Halifax.

Scarborough, 20-gun English warship
Location: Jardines Reefs, on the south coast of the island
History: During a hurricane on October 3, 1780, 13 English warships were lost on Jardines Reefs. They belonged to a squadron, commanded by Sir Hyde Park, sailing from Jamaica to Pensacola, Florida. The 13 were: the *Thunderer, Stirling Castle, Phoenix, La Blanche, Laurel, Andromeda, Deal Castle, Scarborough, Beaver's Prize, Barbadoes, Camelon, Endeavour,* and *Victor.* Most of the crews on these ships were lost.

Scorpion, English merchantman, Captain Quay
Location: Jardines Reef, near the Isle of Pines
History: The merchantman wrecked on the Jardines Reef, near the Isle of Pines, in 1761 while sailing from Jamaica to Liverpool.

Sir Thomas Graham, Scottish ship, Captain Thomson
Location: Jardines Reef
History: The ship was lost in March of 1819 on the Jardines Reef while sailing from Jamaica to Havana.

Spanish Junta, ship of unknown registry, Captain Murray

Location: Stoney Point Reef, located three miles from Guazava Key on the north side of Cuba
History: The vessel was lost on the reef while sailing from London to Havana in 1809. The crew was saved.

Stirling Castle, 60-gun English warship
Location: Jardines Reefs, on the south coast of the island
History: During a hurricane on October 3, 1780, 13 English warships were lost on Jardines Reefs. They belonged to a squadron, commanded by Sir Hyde Park, sailing from Jamaica to Pensacola, Florida. The 13 were: the *Thunderer, Stirling Castle, Phoenix, La Blanche, Laurel, Andromeda, Deal Castle, Scarborough, Beaver's Prize, Barbadoes, Camelon, Endeavour,* and *Victor.* Most of the crews on these ships were lost.

Syren, English merchantman, Captain Clark
Location: Cape San Antonio
History: The merchantman totally wrecked on a rocky point near Cape San Antonio on June 9, 1819, while sailing from Jamaica to London. Only her crew was saved.

Tartaruga, ship of unknown registry, Captain Smith
Location: Twelve leagues east-southeast of the Isle of Pines
History: The vessel wrecked on the reef in 1809 while sailing from Bahía, Brazil to Havana.

Telegraph, ship of unknown registry, Captain Dixon
Location: Havana
History: She wrecked near Havana in 1825 after leaving Alvarado, Mexico.

Thunderer, 74-gun English warship
Location: Jardines Reefs, on the south coast of the island
History: During a hurricane on October 3, 1780, 13 English warships were lost on Jardines Reefs. They belonged to a squadron, commanded by Sir Hyde Park, sailing from Jamaica to Pensacola, Florida. The 13 were: the *Thunderer, Stirling Castle, Phoenix, La Blanche, Laurel, Andromeda, Deal Castle, Scarborough, Beaver's Prize, Barbadoes,*

Camelon, Endeavour, and *Victor.* Most of the crews on these ships were lost.

Tridente, Spanish *navío*
Location: Havana
History: During a hurricane that struck Havana on October 15, 1768, 69 ships were sunk, of which 17 belonged to the king. Of these, only five were identified: the *Tridente, Nancy, Perle, Dorado* and *San Francisco de Paula.* Over 5,000 buildings were also destroyed in the city and the surrounding countryside.

Trinidad, merchant *nao*
Location: Havana
History: The vessel wrecked near Havana in 1605. Only a few persons aboard were saved.

Two Brothers, American ship, Captain Blackman
Location: Cayo Blanco
History: The ship wrecked in the year 1821 on Cayo Blanco, located about 30 miles east of Matanzas, while sailing from Charleston, South Carolina to Matanzas Bay.

Unidentified, ships (5)
Location: Havana Harbor
History: Five ships were totally lost in Havana Harbor during a hurricane on October 2 and 3, 1796.

Unidentified, ship
Location: Coast of Cuba
History: In the early 16th century, the famous Spanish historian Oviedo mentions, without giving the year, that a ship sailing from Santo Domingo to Cuba was wrecked on the coast of Cuba and that Juan de Rojas and his wife, María de Lobera, were aboard.

Unidentified, Spanish caravel
Location: Cumanacan
History: Prior to 1515, a small Spanish caravel, carrying a valuable cargo, was lost in the port of Cumanacan at the mouth of the Bani River.

Unidentified, caravel
Location: Northern coast of Cuba
History: A caravel, sailing from the port of Santa María del Antigua, Colombia, for Santo Domingo was forced by bad weather to pass the northern coast of Cuba where it wrecked in 1519.

Large waves later tossed the ship over 100 yards ashore.

Unidentified, ship commanded by Juan de Avalos, a relative of Cortez
Location: West of Havana
History: The ship wrecked west of Havana at the end of October 1525 during a hurricane, while en route to Veracruz with supplies for the conquistadors. Only eight aboard survived.

Unidentified, ships belonging to the fleet of Admiral Pánfilo Narváez (2)
Location: Port of Trinidad
History: The ships were lost during a hurricane on October 14, 1527, in the port of Trinidad after arriving from Santo Domingo.

Unidentified, caravels belonging to the Tierra Firme Armada of Captain-General Alvaro Sánchez de Aviles (2), 220 tons
Location: Between Cape San Anton and Havana
History: Both the caravels wrecked on the coast between Cape San Anton and Havana on May 24, 1556, during a storm. The *La Magdalena* and *La Concepción,* of the same fleet and carrying treasure onboard, were also wrecked.

Unidentified, Spanish warships (3)
Location: Cuba
History: Three unidentified Spanish warships under the command of Admiral Esteban de las Alas went to the Caribbean to destroy enemy privateers and wrecked on Cuba in 1565. Only the crews were saved.

Unidentified, urca, 300 tons Captain Gonzales de Peñalosa
Location: Near Cayo Romano
History: The ship was lost near Cayo Romano in 1567 while sailing from Veracruz to Santo Domingo. She was carrying several chests of silver to pay the officials and soldiers garrisoned in Santo Domingo.

Unidentified, nao belonging to the Tierra Firme Armada of Captain-General Cristobal de Eraso
Location: Puerto Escondido
History: The ship was separated from the convoy in a storm in 1577 and forced to enter Puerto Escondido, where it

sank. The gold and silver onboard were recovered.

Unidentified, nao belonging to the Nueva España Flota (fleet) of Captain-General Francisco de Novoa
Location: Cape San Anton
History: The ship was lost at Cape San Anton around the end of September 1586 while sailing from Spain to Veracruz.

Unidentified, small mail boat, Captain Diego Ruiz
Location: Havana Harbor
History: The boat sank in Havana Harbor in 1605 after striking on the mast of another shipwreck.

Unidentified, warship belonging to the Armada de Barlovento of Admiral Juan Alvarez
Location: Los Jardines Reefs
History: The ship went to the Caribbean to capture foreign shipping. However, it was wrecked on the Los Jardines Reefs, near the Isle of Pines, in 1606.

Unidentified, English privateering vessel
Location: Isle of Pines
History: The vessel, sailing from Plymouth, England, sank in the year 1610 near the Isle of Pines while carrying a large amount of treasure captured from Spanish shipping. Only eight men of the 150 onboard survived.

Unidentified, small advice boat
Location: Isle of Pines
History: The boat wrecked in 1612 while sailing from Cartagena to Spain.

Unidentified, ships (more than 30)
Location: Oriente Province
History: During a hurricane at the end of September 1616, more than 30 ships sank in several ports of Oriente Province. Many of the ships sank after being dashed to pieces against other ships.

Unidentified, Portuguese merchantman belonging to the Nueva España Flota (fleet) of Captain-General Vallecillas
Location: Havana
History: For some unknown reason, the merchantman caught fire and sank

Sixteenth century Portuguese *nau*.

as the convoy was entering the port of Havana in 1618.

Unidentified, Honduras galleon
Location: Cabo San Anton
History: In 1628, a small squadron of privateers owned by the Dutch West India Company attacked two galleons near Cabo San Anton, forcing one ashore and capturing the other. The cargo of the wrecked ship consisted mainly of indigo and a small amount of silver specie, but only a small part of the indigo was recovered by divers from Havana.

Unidentified, Spanish ships (24) belonging to the Nueva España Flota (fleet) of Captain-General Juan de Benevides y Bazan
Location: Matanzas Bay
History: A Dutch West India Fleet commanded by Admiral Piet Heyn cornered the *flota* near Havana and forced it into Matanzas Bay on September 8, 1628. All 24 of the Spanish ships were wrecked on the shoals.

Some of the treasure on the *flota*'s ships was thrown overboard before the Dutch fleet entered the bay, and the Spaniards fled ashore without firing a shot to protect the treasure or their ships. The Dutch estimate the value of the treasure they took from the ships at 15 million Dutch guilders. This amount was greater than all that had been captured from Spanish shipping by privateers and pirates since the discovery of the New World. The treasure was so great that it could not be carried aboard the 28 ships of Piet Heyn, so four of the largest Spanish ships were refloated and used to carry some of the treasure back to Holland. Two of these Spanish ships were separated from the Dutch fleet in bad weather and wrecked near present Freeport, Grand Bahama Island. A small part of the treasure carried onboard one of these two ships was discovered several years ago.

Unidentified, advice boat
Location: Cabo de Cruz
History: The vessel was forced ashore near Cabo de Cruz in 1629 by a Dutch privateer while sailing between Spain and Veracruz. The crew escaped with the mail.

Unidentified, Portuguese galleon belonging to the Tierra Firme Armada of Captain-General Antonio de Oquendo
Location: Havana Harbor
History: The large galleon hit a reef and sank at the entrance to Havana Harbor in 1633. The crew was saved and her artillery was later recovered by divers.

Unidentified, merchant *nao*
Location: Port of Muriel
History: The ship, carrying the Mas-ter of Campo Francisco Riano y Gamboa to Spain, was sunk in the port of Muriel on October 5, 1634.

Unidentified, merchant *urca*
Location: Cape Corrientes
History: The vessel, owned by Captain Diego de Larrasa, was attacked by a Dutch warship off Cape Corrientes and wrecked on the shore in 1635. The crew escaped.

Unidentified, *urca*, Captain Juan de Urrutia
Location: Cape San Anton
History: The *urca* was forced to run aground at Cape San Anton by two Dutch privateers in 1636 while sailing from Maracaibo to Havana with a cargo of cocoa. After her crew reached shore, the Dutch stripped everything of value from the ship.

Unidentified, warships belonging to the famous Dutch Admiral "Wooden Leg" (7)
Location: Cuba
History: Admiral "Wooden Leg" returned to the Caribbean in 1640 in an attempt to duplicate Piet Heyn's feat of capturing a treasure fleet in 1628. (See: Unidentified, Spanish ships (24) belonging to the Nueva España Flota (fleet) of Captain-General Juan de Benevides y Bazan.) However, while cruising near Havana in wait for the Nueva España Flota, a hurricane wrecked seven of his warships on the coast near Xaimanita, Baru, Mosquitos, and La Herradura, located three, seven, nine and 11 leagues, respectively, from Havana. The Spaniards captured many of his men and recovered some cannon from a few of the wrecks.

Unidentified, ships (many) belonging to the Nueva España Flota (fleet) of Admiral Juan de Campos
Location: Cuba
History: After the *flota* set sail from Havana for Spain in 1641, it was struck by a hurricane in the Bahama Channel. Many of the ships were lost. Four of the vessels in the *flota* were driven back to Cuba where two were wrecked near Havana. Another ship was wrecked six leagues from Santiago de Cuba. The *Nuestra Señora de Atocha y San Josef* reached the port of Santiago de

Cuba and made repairs, but was wrecked in a bad storm near the Port of La Puntal in 1642.

Unidentified, merchantman ships (2)
   Location: Near Havana
   History: When a pirate ship was sighted cruising off Havana in 1648, the governor armed two large merchantmen and sent them out to capture or destroy it. Both ships ran aground at a small port near Havana and were totally lost. The pirate ship entered the port and its crew cut the throats of many of the Spanish survivors.

Unidentified, Spanish bark
   Location: Boga Pavillion
   History: In 1672, a Jamaican privateer, commanded by Captain Robert Hewytt, captured the bark, which was later wrecked at Boga Pavillion, one of the small cays on the south coast of Cuba.

Unidentified, ship
   Location: Havana Harbor
   History: A French fleet of warships commanded by Chateaurenault was sent to Havana to escort some Spanish treasure galleons back to Spain, but the vice-admiral's ship was burnt in Havana Harbor in 1702.

Unidentified, 24-gun Spanish ship, 600 tons
   Location: Baracoa
   History: In 1705, the *New York*, an American privateer commanded by Captain Tongerlou, chased the Spanish ship, coming from the Canary Islands, and forced it to run aground about one league from Baracoa. The ship's cargo of wine and brandy was saved.

Unidentified, Spanish warships (4)
   Location: Havana Harbor
   History: Four large Spanish warships, along with most of their crews, were lost in Havana Harbor in 1705 during a hurricane.

Unidentified, ship
   Location: Jaimanita
   History: A ship bringing 85 chests of silver and 50 silver bars was wrecked during a storm at Jaimanita, located five leagues from Havana in 1715, but divers recovered all its treasure. The ship was salvaged in 1970.

Unidentified, French merchant brigantine
   Location: Cabo Francés
   History: The brigantine ran aground at Cabo Francés in 1727 while sailing to the Mississippi River. The majority of her cargo was salvaged.

Unidentified, French warships (2)
   Location: Jardines de la Reina
   History: The two warships, commanded by Admiral du Rochet, were wrecked in 1727 on the reefs of Jardines de la Reina, on the southern coast of the island a bit to the east of Jaqua. When salvors were sent there they reported sighting several other wrecks in the same area.

Unidentified, Spanish frigate
   Location: Cayo Lobos
   History: A small frigate was wrecked on Cayo Lobos in 1741.

Unidentified, Spanish privateering vessels (2)
   Location: Santiago de Cuba
   History: The two vessels were run ashore near Santiago de Cuba by two New England privateering ships in 1744.

Unidentified, Spanish sloop
   Location: Matanzas Bay
   History: Two American privateering ships from Philadelphia drove the sloop ashore at Matanzas Bay in 1745 and carried her cargo away.

Unidentified, *almiranta* of the Nueva España Flota (fleet) of Captain-General Spinola
   Location: Near Havana
   History: An English squadron of warships commanded by Admiral Knowles attempted to capture the Nueva España Flota in 1748. During the battle near Havana, the *almiranta* of the *flota* lost her masts and was forced to run aground on the coast, where the Spaniards set her afire. Within an hour she blew up, scattering the beach with many of the more than ten million pesos in treasure she was carrying. A merchant *nao* of this same *flota* in attempting to escape from the English warships was lost in Ensenada de Vixiras, 95 leagues from Havana.

Unidentified, merchant *nao* belonging to the Nueva España Flota (fleet) of Captain-General Spinola
   Location: in Ensenada de Vixiras
   History: An English squadron of warships commanded by Admiral Knowles attempted to capture the Nueva España Flota in 1748. During the battle near Havana, the *almiranta* of the *flota* lost her masts and was forced to run aground on the coast, where the Spaniards set her afire. Within an hour she blew up, scattering the beach with many of the more than ten million pesos in treasure she was carrying. A merchant *nao* of this same *flota* in attempting to escape from the English warships was lost in Ensenada de Vixiras, 95 leagues from Havana.

Unidentified, ship
   Location: Jardines Reefs
   History: A large ship was wrecked on the Jardines Reefs, near Cape San Anton in 1749.

Unidentified, ships (16)
   Location: Havana
   History: Sixteen unidentified ships were lost near Havana during a hurricane on September 26, 1752.

Unidentified, ships (more than 150)
   Location: Cuba
   History: More than 150 ships of various sizes and nationalities were destroyed in the ports and on the coast during a hurricane on July 20, 1772.

Unidentified, ships (7)
   Location: Cuba
   History: During a hurricane on October 29, 1792, an unidentified brig was carried 100 yards ashore at Alarés Castle in Havana, two ships were wrecked near Batabanó, and four others wrecked along the coast.

Unidentified, English ship, Lieutenant John Payne
   Location: Twenty-two degrees of north latitude and four leagues from Cape Buena Vista, Colorado Reef
   History: The English hydraulic ship wrecked in 1770. The Spaniards rescued the crew and took them to Havana. From there, they were embarked on a ship for Jamaica, which also wrecked at Cape San Antonio on February 19, 1770.

Unidentified, *navío*

Location: Seven leagues east of Havana in 35 feet of water

History: The *navío* wrecked at Playa de Sabarimar during a storm in 1696. She was completely salvaged soon afterward.

Unidentified, English transports (4)

Location: Cayo Confite, north of Havana

History: The warship wrecked on Cayo Confite in 1762 along with four transports bringing reinforcements to hold the city of Havana for England. No lives were lost.

Unidentified, ships (74)

Location: Havana

History: Seventy-six ships were totally lost and others damaged during a hurricane on August 27 and 28, 1794. Of those lost, 12 were Spanish warships and the others were merchantmen of different nationalities. Only two ships were identified: the *Flor*, a Spanish warship, and *Sandown*, an English ship. Most of the cargoes were later salvaged.

Unidentified, ships (32)

Location: Havana

History: Thirty-two ships sank or wrecked at Havana during a hurricane from October 23 to 26, 1810. The city's pier and church and 60 of its buildings were also carried into the sea.

Unidentified, patache belonging to the Tierra Firme Armada of Captain-General Pedro de Ursua

Location: Havana Harbor

History: The *capitana* (flagship) and an unidentified patache of the armada sank at the entrance to Havana Harbor in 1647 while the armada was arriving from Cartagena with large amounts of treasure.

Unidentified, Spanish *nao*

Location: Havana Harbor

History: An unidentified *nao* carrying the cargo of the *El Nuevo Constante* (which had sunk 75 leagues from the mouth of the Mississippi River) sank between El Morro and La Punta in Havana Harbor in 1766.

Unidentified, ships (many)

Location: Havana Harbor

History: Many ships were lost in and around Havana Harbor during a hurricane in 1778 (date not stated).

Unidentified, English merchantmen (2)

Location: Isle of Pines

History: Both ships wrecked near the Isle of Pines in 1792.

Unidentified, English merchantmen (2)

Location: Los Colorados Reef

History: Lost on the Los Colorados Reef in 1758 while sailing from Jamaica to England.

Unidentified, Dutch ship

Location: Matanzas Bay

History: Lost on the coast near Matanzas in 1825. The large Dutch ship was found with no crew aboard and the decks running with blood. It is believed to have been plundered and set adrift by pirates.

Unidentified, Spanish vessels (4)

Location: Port of Gibara

History: The *Olive Branch* and four unidentified Spanish vessels were lost in the port of Gibara during a gale on September 13, 1821.

Unidentified, French ship

Location: Shoals of Los Jardines del Rey

History: The ship wrecked in 1803.

Unidentified, ships (a number of)

Location: Trinidad de Cuba

History: A number of unidentified ships were sunk during a hurricane on October 14, 1812, at Trinidad de Cuba.

Unidentified, ships (12 or 14)

Location: Trinidad de Cuba Harbor

History: Twelve or 14 ships were wrecked in the harbor during a violent gale on June 14, 1816.

Union, ship of unknown registry, Captain Munro

Location: A reef 16 leagues from Matanzas Bay

History: The ship was lost on a reef 16 leagues from Matanzas Bay in 1822 while sailing from Jamaica to Novia Scotia.

Ventura, Spanish warship, Captain Luis Cabaleri

Location: Punta del Palo

History: The warship wrecked at Punta del Palo in 1797 while chasing a pirate ship. Several of the men were drowned.

Victor, ten-gun English warship

Location: Jardines Reefs, on the south coast of the island

History: During a hurricane on October 3, 1780, 13 English warships were lost on Jardines Reef. They belonged to a squadron, commanded by Sir Hyde Park, sailing from Jamaica to Pensacola, Florida. The 13 were: the *Thunderer*, *Stirling Castle*, *Phoenix*, *La Blanche*, *Laurel*, *Andromeda*, *Deal Castle*, *Scarborough*, *Beaver's Prize*, *Barbadoes*, *Camelon*, *Endeavour*, and *Victor*. Most of the crews on these ships were lost.

Villorius, ship of unknown registry, Captain M'Kernly

Location: Baracoa

History: The ship wrecked at Baracoa at the end of September 1821 while sailing from the Plate River, Argentina to Havana. Most of her cargo was saved.

Westmoreland, English merchantman, Captain Smellie

Location: Isle of Pines

History: The merchantman wrecked in 1802. Her crew was saved.

Florida

Florida is the world center for underwater treasure hunting. More work has been done on shipwrecks in Florida waters than throughout the whole of the rest of the Western Hemisphere. There are several reasons for this activity. The Florida Keys and the east coast of Florida are lined with off-lying reefs and shoals which have claimed an extraordinary number of vessels. Because there are no safe refuges from bad weather, more ships have been lost in storms here than in many other areas. From the time of Columbus until the introduction of steamships almost all ships returning to Europe from the New World chose to sail up the dangerous Bahama Channel. Even in good weather, the prevailing winds and the Gulf Stream pushed all shipping toward the coast of Florida.

During the 20th century, Florida was one of the first places in the United States where skin diving and scuba diving caught on. Even before skin diving there were a handful of professional treasure hunters doing most of their exploring and salvaging in the Florida Keys. For years controversy raged between the State of Florida and salvors. When a group led by Tom Gurr discovered the Spanish merchant ship the *San José* outside the three-mile limit in 1968, the state passed a law extending its control over coastal waters from three miles to ten miles. Gurr was forced to stop his salvage operations until the state finally gave him a lease on the site. Mel Fisher also faced similar battles with the state after discovering the *Atocha*.

The State of Florida has very strict laws for locating and recovering objects from shipwrecks. In areas not covered by groups holding Admiralty Arrest Act permits, people must deal with the Division of Historical Resources in Tallahassee, which controls all wrecks inside the three-mile zone. For the last few years the state has been trying unsuccessfully to extend this area out to 200 miles. In the old days

it was a simple process to get a search permit, which encompassed 18 square miles, or a pinpoint salvage permit which covered a one–mile radius. However, it appears that the state wants to put an end to all shipwreck work in Florida waters, and many in the business fear it may eventually succeed. Early in 1992, the state shut down all shipwreck activities in the Florida Keys citing environmental concerns. There is now discussion about prohibiting shipwreck work along the east coast as well.

Today a salvor requesting even something as simple as a search permit must deal with four different state and federal agencies. Severe restrictions by these agencies are driving many salvors to work in other countries or in deep water where no permission is required —at least, that is the situation at this time.

Those fortunate enough to obtain a permit from the State of Florida must adhere to strict archaeological procedures. The state claims 25 percent of everything recovered, but has the right to buy part or all of the salvor's remaining share. After the division has

been made between the state and the salvors, they are free to dispose of their share in any way they wish, but must keep in mind that the IRS will also take its cut.

Many treasure hunters working in Florida waters have made valuable contributions to the public—contributions of historical significance. They have set up museums and donated thousands of artifacts for public display.

SHIPWRECKS IN FLORIDA'S WATERS

1622 Treasure Fleet, Spanish fleet including the Armada de Tierra Firme and the Tierra Firme Flota (fleet) of Marqués de Cadereita
Location: Florida Keys
History: On September 4, 1622, the armada and the *flota* set sail for Spain from Havana Harbor. The convoy sailed, despite the warnings of an imminent hurricane by the main pilots of the convoy. On September 6th (some accounts give the date as the 7th), the

Sixteenth century Spanish galleys and galleons.

convoy was struck by a fierce hurricane which caused the ships to scatter over a wide area. Nine of the ships were lost in the Florida Keys and several others were most likely lost on the high seas, as they were never accounted for. The surviving ships made it back to Havana in battered condition. Of those that reached Havana, all had lost their masts and many had been forced to jettison cannon and parts of their cargoes. This disaster was considered the worst to have occurred to the *flotas* in over 50 years. Of the nine ships that were wrecked in the Florida Keys, three were treasure-laden galleons, five were merchant *naos*, of which one was identified as the *Jesús y Nuestra Señora del Rosario*, one was a patache that served as a reconnaissance boat for the convoy. Only the locations of three galleons and the patache are given in documents; and only four of the nine are identified, including the *Nuestra Señora de Atocha, La Margarita* and *Nuestra Señora del Rosario*.

1715 Treasure Fleet, convoy composed of the New Spain Flota (fleet) of Captain-General Don Juan Esteban de Ubilla and the Squadron of Tierra Firme of Captain-General Don Antonio de Echeverz y Zubiza and a French ship, *Griffon*, commanded by Captain Antonio Daire

Location: Florida coast

History: The treasure-laden convoy was composed of six ships of the New Spain Flota: *capitana, almiranta, Nuestra Señora de Concepción, El Ciervo* and two other ships. There is a possibility that there were actually seven ships in Echeverz's squadron, but the documents are confusing. The Squadron of Tierra Firme ships in the convoy were the *capitana, almiranta, Refuerzo* (also called the *Urca de Lima*), a patache and a small frigate. The convoy set sail from Havana Harbor for the long voyage back to Spain on July 24, 1715.

All the ships in the convoy except for the *Griffon* wrecked on the coast of Florida on the night of July 30th during a fierce hurricane. Over 1,000 persons lost their lives. About 1,500 reached shore by floating on pieces of wreckage or swimming. Some perished from exposure, thirst and hunger before aid reach them from Havana and St. Augustine. The total value of treasure carried on the convoy was 6,466,066 pesos and 955 castellanos. According to records there were virtually no gold coins carried on any of the ships. Salvage efforts on the wrecks began immediately. By the end of December the officials in charge of operations reported that they had already recovered all the king's treasure and the major part of the treasure be-

Spanish gold doubloons recovered from the flagship of the 1715 fleet.

longing to private persons, totaling 5,241,166 pesos in silver specie and bars, but not the gold specie and bars, silverware and general cargoes. When the Spaniards ended their salvage operations, there supposedly remained a total of 1,244,900 pesos of registered treasure, but the amount will never be known, as survivors and salvors robbed an unknown amount. The Real Eight Company has completely worked all the wrecks of this convoy. According to records, there were virtually no gold coins carried on any of the ships, which means that those being recovered by the Real Eight Company were contraband. This is substantiated by the fact that most of the gold disks being recovered by Real Eight are not marked the way registered gold bars had to be during this period.

1733 Treasure Fleet, the Nueva España Flota (fleet) of Don Rodrigo de Torres

Location: Florida Keys

History: On July 13, 1733, the *flota* set sail for Spain. Documents give either 21 or 22 as the total number of ships in this fleet. The names of the ships are also confusing, as some ships had two names, a religious name and an alias. However, the majority of the documents reveal that the following ships sailed from Havana: the *El Rubi;* the *Nuestra Señora de Balvaneda* (alias the *El Gallo*); the *Nuestra Señora de Balvanedo* (alias *El Infante*); the *Nuestra Señora del Populo* (alias the *El Pinque);* the *San José de las Animas* (sometimes listed as the *San José y las Animas*); the *Nuestra Señora del Rosario* (the *San Francisco Javier y San Antonio de Padua*); the *Nuestra Señora del*

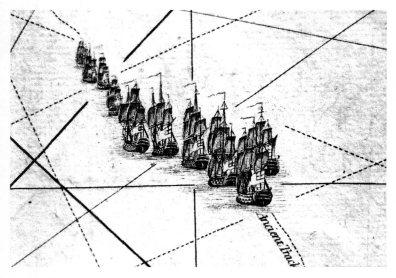

Spanish treasure fleet under sail.

Diorama of Spanish galleons sinking.

Rosario, San Antonio y San Vicente Ferrer; the *Nuestra Señora del Carmen, San Antonio de Padua y las Animas;* the *Nuestra Señora de Belem y San Juan Bautista;* the *Nuestra Señora de los Dolores y Santa Isabel* (alias the *El Nuevo Londres*); the *Nuestra Señora del Rosario y Santo Domingo;* the *Nuestra Señora de los Reys, San Fernando y San Francisco de Paula;* the *San Pedro;* the *San Felipe;* the *Señora de las Angustias y San Rafael;* the *El Gran Poder de Dios y Santa Ana* (alias the *Aná Agustina*); the *San Ignacio;* the *San Francisco de Asis;* the *San Fernando;* the *Floridana;* and a vessel only identified as a balandra (or schooner), which may be the reason for the different accounts stating that there were 21 or 22 ships in the fleet when it set sail. After setting sail, the fleet sighted the Florida Keys the following day. Around nine that evening, the wind blew very strong from the north. By the following morning, the wind had swung around to the south at hurricane force and prevented the ships from trying to reach the safety of Havana. By nightfall of this same day, all or most of the ships had wrecked on the Florida Keys, scattered in different areas between Key Bis-

cayne and Vaca Key. Many documents as well as charts showing the locations of the wrecks differ as to the names of the shipwrecks, their locations and the total number of ships lost. To add to the confusion, documents and charts mention the following ships as being wrecked in different places; they may also be aliases for some of the ships that were wrecked or for those whose fate was not mentioned in documents, or they may be ships that were not even part of the fleet, but were sailing separately: the *El Sueco,* at Cayo de Bacas del Leste; the *Sánchez,* which is probably the *El Poder de Dios y Santa Ana,* wrecked at Cayo de Bacas del Leste; *Murguia,* at Cayo de Matacumbe el Mozo; the *Ledieque,* at Cayo de Tavanos (probably the same place that is listed as Cayo Tabamos); the *Valandrita,* at Matacumbe el Grande. The *Nuestra Señora de los Dolores y Santa Isabel* is not mentioned as being lost in documents or shown on any chart, but it may have been mentioned by one of the above aliases. The *San Felipe* is not mentioned in any documents as being lost or returning to Havana; nor is it shown on any wreck chart. It may be one of the above aliases as well. The

San Fernando is not mentioned in documents or shown on any chart as being lost, but it was probably mentioned by its alias. The *Nuestra Señora del Rosario y Santo Domingo* made it safely back to Havana. The Spaniards carried out thorough salvage operations on all of these wrecks. Several others which were not identified by name were refloated. Fifteen which could not be refloated were burnt to their waterlines after salvage operations were completed. Within three months of the disaster, the king was informed by royal officials in Havana that not only had all of the registered treasure been recovered but a substantial amount of unregistered treasure as well. Most of the other cargo was also recovered, but a great amount of it was destroyed by the salt water, especially the sugar, indigo and cochineal. What little the Spaniards failed to recover has been searched for in the past few decades, but very little of real value has been discovered other than various items of historical and archaeological worth. Small amounts of silver coins have been found by modern-day salvors.

Acasta, British merchantman, Captain Parkin
   Location: Dry Tortugas
   History: The merchantman wrecked sometime before December 5, 1818, on the Dry Tortugas while sailing from Jamaica to Liverpool. The crew and most of the cargo were saved.

Adelaide Baker, American three-masted iron-rigged and reinforced wooden-hull bark, 153 feet with a beam of 35 feet and a depth of hold of 21 feet
   Location: 24.42.140 N, 80.53.56 W. Coffins Patches Reef in the Florida Keys
   History: The *Adelaide Baker,* originally called the *F.W. Carver,* was built in 1863 in Bangor, Maine. Her double-decked hull was constructed of oak and hackmatack. Two years after being built she was sheathed with copper. After being sold to the British she was renamed the *Adelaide Baker.* The wreck report documents that on January 28, 1889, she was bound for Savannah with a load of timber when she wrecked. On the night of the disaster,

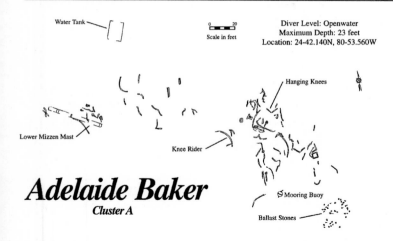

Water Tank

Scale in feet

Diver Level: Openwater
Maximum Depth: 23 feet
Location: 24-42.140N, 80-53.560W

Hanging Knees

Lower Mizzen Mast

Knee Rider

Adelaide Baker
Cluster A

Mooring Buoy

Ballast Stones

The site of the *Adelaide Baker* in the Florida Keys. *Courtesy of the Florida Keys National Marine Sanctuary.*

wreckers in the area assisted the captain and crew to safety. There was no loss of life. The remains of the shipwreck are scattered along a northnorthwest path 1,400 feet long. Large iron hold-beam-knee riders and deck beam hanging knees dominate the edge of the reef where she is believed to have first been "holed." The iron main mast, 77 feet long, the remains of a bilge pump, knee-riders, iron deck bit, hawsehole frames and miscellaneous rigging and tackle are located farther away where she finally came to rest. The widely dispersed wreck site and identifiable ship components make the wreck an excellent site for sports divers.

African, merchantman of unknown nationality, Captain Garcia
    Location: Florida shore
    History: Four ships were lost about October 25, 1810, on the Florida shore: the *Caroline*, *Union*, *African* and *Triton*. The *African* was sailing from Havana to New York when she was lost.

Albinia, British merchantman
    Location: Florida coast
    History: The merchantman wrecked on the coast of Florida in 1763 while sailing from Jamaica to London. The crew was saved.

Alexander, British merchantman, Captain Johnson
    Location: Florida Keys

History: The merchantman was lost in the Florida Keys in 1763 while sailing from Jamaica to London, England.

Alexander, British merchantman, Captain Mundis
    Location: Lost in the Gulf of Florida
    History: The following ships were lost in the Gulf of Florida during a hurricane on October 22, 1752: the *Alexander*, *Lancaster*, *Dolphin*, *Queen Anne*, *May*, *Rhode Island*, *Statea*, an unidentified Spanish man-of-war, an unidentified Spanish schooner, and three other ships of unknown identity. The *Alexander* was sailing from Jamaica to London when it was lost.

Almiranta, of the Flota de Nueva España
    Location: Bahama Channel
    History: The king ordered the armada and the Flota de Tierra Firme and the Flota de Nueva España to meet in Havana and form a convoy for protection against an English squadron that was known to be waiting for the return of the Spanish ships from the West Indies. The convoy of about 100 ships sailed from Havana on September 9, 1589. Soon after entering the Bahama Channel the convoy was struck by a hurricane. The *almiranta* of the Flota de Nueva España developed a bad leak and fired cannon for assistance, but she sank with a great treasure aboard at the mouth of the Bahama Channel in very deep water

before aid could reach her. There is no mention of what the cargo consisted of but it is certain that the *almiranta* was carrying treasure.

Almiranta de Honduras, ship
    Location: Miami
    History: A large convoy, sailing from Havana to Spain, was making its way up the Bahama Channel when two of its ships became separated and wrecked. The two ships were forced too close to the coast of Florida by currents and wrecked on the coast on April 2, 1632. One was the *Almiranta de Honduras* and the other was an unidentified frigate coming from Maracaibo, Venezuela with a cargo of mainly cocoa. The location of the two wrecks is probably in the vicinity of present-day Miami, since an advice boat passing that area a few days later reported sighting two ships wrecked shortly after clearing the head of the Florida Keys.

Amaranthe, 14-gun British sloop-of-war, Captain John Blake
    Location: Florida coast
    History: The sloop wrecked on the coast of Florida on October 25, 1799. Twenty-two out of the crew of 86 were lost.

Americano, Spanish merchantman, Captain Abrew
    Location: Florida Keys
    History: The vessel wrecked on July 26, 1814, on a reef in the Florida Keys while sailing from Havana to Lisbon.

Amesbury (DE–66), steel hulled U.S. Naval Destroyer Escort
    Location: 24.37.397 N, 81.58.912 W. Five miles west of Key West
    History: The *Amesbury (DE–66)*, locally known as "Alexander's Wreck," was launched and commissioned in 1943 as a destroyer escort. She was named for Lt. Stanton Amesbury who was killed in enemy action over Casablanca on November 9, 1942, while attached to an aviation squadron in the Atlantic Area. The *Amesbury's* first assignment was duty with the Atlantic Convoy 7; this was followed by participation in the Normandy invasion. Returning to the U.S. in August, 1944, she was assigned temporary duty with the Fleet Sonar School in Key West. In 1945, she was one of 104 destroyer

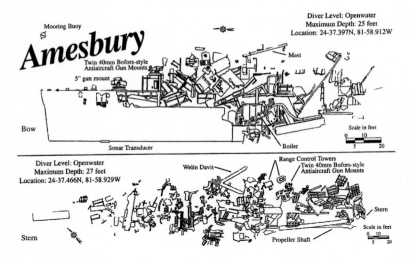

The *Amesbury*, **locally known as "Alexander's Wreck," in the Florida Keys.** *Courtesy of the Florida Keys National Marine Sanctuary.*

escorts converted to high-speed transports at the Philadelphia Navy Yard. The *Amesbury* was then assigned hull number *APD–46* and equipped with a five-inch turret gun and three twin-mount 40-millimeter antiaircraft guns. Proceeding to the Pacific she supported landings in Korea and China during 1945, carrying Underwater Demolition Team Twelve. The *Amesbury* returned to Florida in 1946, was decommissioned and never performed active service again. Chet Alexander Marine Salvage of Key West purchased her in 1962 for scrap. The vessel was being towed to deep water to be sunk as an artificial reef when she grounded and broke up in a storm. The shipwreck is now part of the Florida Keys National Marine Sanctuary.

Amiable Antoinetta, ship
  Location: St. Augustine
  History: The ship, identified only by its name, wrecked on December 26, 1816, near St. Augustine. She was sailing from Charlestown when she wrecked. The crew and cargo were saved.

Andromache, ship of unknown nationality, Captain Hickles
  Location: Florida Keys
  History: The vessel wrecked on December 6, 1805, in the Florida Keys while sailing from Jamaica to New

York. The principal part of her cargo was salvaged and carried to Nassau.

Andromache, ship
  Location: Florida Keys
  History: The ship wrecked on November 18, 1823, on a reef in the Florida Keys while sailing from Jamaica to New York. She was only identified in documents by her name.

Anie of Scarbro [*sic*], ship of unknown nationality, Captain Stanley
  Location: Florida Keys
  History: The ship was en route to England when it was lost on a reef in the Florida Keys on June 29, 1819. Only five of the crew were saved.

Ann of London, British merchantman, Captain Campbell
  Location: Florida Keys
  History: The merchantman was lost around the end of April in 1822 on the east Florida Keys while sailing from Havana to Buenos Aires. Only part of her cargo was saved.

Anna Maria, ship
  Location: Bason Bank off east Florida
  History: The ship, identified only in documents by its name, was wrecked on Bason Bank off east Florida on March 23, 1817. The crew was saved along with the few dry goods she had onboard. She had been en route from

New Orleans to Philadelphia when she was wrecked.

Anna Theresa, British packet boat, Captain Dyer
  Location: Florida Keys
  History: The *Anna Theresa* wrecked on the Florida Keys on July 30, 1768, while sailing from Pensacola to Falmouth. The British ship *Prince George*'s Captain Collier, was sailing past the Florida Keys when he saw the *Anna Theresa* aground on a reef and afire. Seeing three sloops anchored near the wreck, he sent a boat to investigate. He was told that the crew of the ship had been carried to New Providence in the Bahamas. He was also told that a Spanish ship and a brig from Boston, whose captain's name was Bostley, had been lost in the same area a few days earlier.

Apollo, ship, Captain Cragg
  Location: Cape Florida
  History: The British merchantman, *Elizabeth*, commanded by Captain Sims, ran aground on the coast of Florida in 1790 while sailing from Jamaica to Bristol. The crew were able to refloat the vessel by throwing part of its cargo overboard. The captain reported that he had seen four ships on the Florida reef on August 12, 1790, while in 25 degrees and four minutes of latitude. On August 19th he saw two other ships at Cape Florida wrecked on the reef: the *Apollo* and *Edmund & George*, both bound for London. Two other ships had been onshore in Florida but were refloated after throwing parts of their cargoes overboard.

Araucana, Spanish ship, Captain Benito de la Rigada
  Location: Elliot Key
  History: On October 17, 1811, Captain Benito de la Rigada, with an official rank of Teniente de Fragata, sailed from Havana with mail for Spain. The ship was totally wrecked on October 26 of the same year on Elliot Key due to a hurricane. The crew made it to shore and were picked up by a vessel and taken to Nassau and then Havana.

Atlas, ship of Glasgow, Captain Thompson
  Location: Florida Keys in the Gulf of Florida

History: The following vessels were wrecked in the Gulf of Florida during the violent gales between June 5 and 8, 1816: the *Atlas, Martha Brae, Cossack, General Pike* and the *Zanga*. The *Atlas*, en route from Jamaica to Glasgow, wrecked on a reef in the Florida Keys.

Barilla, American brig, Captain Jones
   Location: Florida Keys
   History: The ship was driven over a reef and lost in the Florida Keys in 1819 while sailing from New Orleans to Philadelphia. The cargo was saved.

Belieze [*sic*], British ship, Captain Gillis
   Location: East coast of Florida
   History: The ship was lost on October 12, 1776, on the east coast of Florida while sailing from Honduras to London.

Benwood, Norwegian merchant marine freighter, 360 feet with a 51-foot beam
   Location: 25.03.144 N, 80.19.930 W. Located approximately one mile northeast of the French Reef within the Florida Keys in 25 to 45 feet of water.
   History: The *Benwood*, built in England in 1910, was owned by a Norwegian shipping company. She carried ore and was armed with 12 rifles, one four-inch gun, six depth charges and 36 bombs. On the night of April 9, 1942, under the command of Captain

Torbjorn Skjelbred, the *Benwood* was making a routine voyage from Tampa, Florida to Norfolk, Virginia with a cargo of phosphate rock. Rumors of German U-boats in the area required the *Benwood* to travel completely blacked out with the Florida Keys coastal lights three miles abeam. The *Robert C. Tuttle*, also blacked out, was traveling in the same area and bound for Atreco, Texas. Both ships were on a collision course. The bow of the *Benwood* collided with the port side of the *Tuttle*. The *Tuttle* was not in immediate danger, but the *Benwood's* bow was crushed and she was taking on water. The captain turned her toward land and a half-hour later gave orders to abandon ship. The next day the keel was found to be broken and the ship was declared a total loss. Salvage operations began soon after the sinking and continued into the 1950s. It is believed that she was dynamited as a navigational hazard and was used by the U.S. Army for aerial target practice after World War II. This shipwreck is a popular dive site in the Florida Keys National Marine Sanctuary.

Betsey, British ship, Captain Telley
   Location: Amelia Island
   History: The ship was totally lost at Amelia Island in 1812 after sailing from St. Vincent.

Betsey, American merchantman, Captain Grafton

Location: Florida Keys
   History: The merchantman was lost on a reef in the Florida Keys in 1818 while sailing from Havana to Rhode Island. Part of her cargo was saved and carried to Nassau.

Betsey, British merchantman, Captain Slater
   Location: Lost in the Gulf of Florida
   History: The vessel was lost in the Gulf of Florida in 1750 while sailing from Jamaica to Bristol. A passing vessel picked up the crew.

Betsey, British ship, Captain Grant
   Location: Mosquito bar on the coast of Florida
   History: The ship was lost on the bar in 1788 while sailing from Nassau to Florida.

Bonee Adelle, ship
   Location: Coast of east Florida
   History: The ship wrecked on the coast of east Florida on February 5, 1819, while coming from Havana. Only her crew was saved.

Britannia, British merchantman, Captain Wright
   Location: Florida Keys
   History: The merchantman was lost on the Florida Keys in 1803 while sailing from Jamaica to London. Part of her cargo was saved by wreckers and carried to Nassau.

Burroughs (**or** *Smith*), British merchantman
   Location: North of Jupiter Inlet
   History: The merchantman, from the port of Bristol, was sailing in a convoy of 12 or 13 merchant ships from Port Royal, Jamaica, when it wrecked on September 23, 1696. The ship was lost north of Jupiter Inlet. The *Reformation* and *Nantwitch* of the same convoy also sank at different locations.

Cabinet, British merchantman, Captain Montgomery
   Location: Florida Keys
   History: The vessel was lost on October 26, 1811, on a reef of the Florida Keys while sailing from New Orleans to Liverpool. The crew and most of the cargo were saved.

Calliope, American merchantman, Captain Nash

Benwood

Diver Level: Openwater
Maximum Depth: 45 feet
Location: 25-03.144N, 80-19.930W

Scale in feet
0   20
10   50

Mooring Buoy

Mooring Buoy

Stern

Engine Mounts

Bow

Mooring Buoy

Mooring Buoy

The remains of the *Benwood* in the Florida Keys. *Courtesy of the Florida Keys National Marine Sanctuary.*

Location: Florida Keys

History: The merchantman was lost on the reefs of the Florida Keys in 1804 while sailing from Jamaica to Virginia.

Caroline, merchantman of unknown nationality, Captain Curtis

Location: Florida shore

History: Four ships were lost about October 25, 1810, on the Florida shore: the *Caroline*, *Union*, *African* and *Triton*. The *Caroline* was sailing from New Orleans to Liverpool when she foundered.

Catherine Green, British merchantman, Captain Rose

Location: Florida Keys

History: The merchantman wrecked on August 8, 1794, on a reef in the Florida Keys while sailing from Jamaica for London. Most of her cargo was saved.

Catherine Osmond, ship of unknown nationality, Captain Vicaiz

Location: "at Florida"

History: The ship wrecked "at Florida" in 1816 while sailing from Havana to Salem. Part of her cargo was saved and carried to Nassau.

Ceres, ship

Location: Dry Tortugas

History: The ship, identified in documents only by its name, wrecked on the Dry Tortugas in 1824 while coming from New Orleans. The crew was saved and taken to Havana.

City of Washington, two-masted American passenger and cargo sailing vessel

Location: 25.08.786 N, 80.15.354 W. Located east of Key Largo on Elbow Reef within the Florida Keys.

History: The *City of Washington* was built at Roach's Shipyard in Chester, Pennsylvania and launched in 1887. She transported passengers and cargo between New York, Cuba and Mexico. In 1889, she was refitted with a 2,750 h.p. steam engine, which dramatically reduced her sailing time. The *City of Washington's* moment in history came the night of February 15, 1898. Because of deteriorating relations between the United States and Spain over the rebellion in Cuba, the *USS Maine* was moored in Havana Harbor

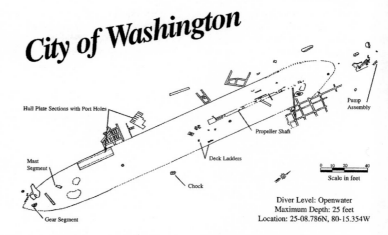

The *City of Washington's* final resting place in the Florida Keys. *Courtesy of the Florida Keys National Marine Sanctuary.*

to protect American interests. That night the *Maine* exploded. The *City of Washington* was moored close by and suffered damage to her awnings and deckhouses by flying debris. Her crew assisted in the rescue of the *Maine* survivors. This was the final event leading up to the Spanish-American War. During the war, the *City of Washington* was used as a transport ship to carry troops. She returned to her passenger and cargo runs following the war until retirement in 1908. Three years later she was purchased and converted into a coal transporting barge. On July 10, 1917 the tugboat *Luchenbach #4*, towing the *City of Washington* and the *Seneca*, ran aground on Elbow Reef. The *Luchenbach #4* and the *Seneca* were soon refloated, but the *City of Washington* broke up and was a total loss within a few minutes. The shipwreck is a popular dive site and protected as part of the Florida Keys National Marine Sanctuary.

Claudina, British ship, Captain Valliant

Location: Coast of Florida

History: The ship was totally lost on the coast of Florida in 1777 while sailing from London to Pensacola.

Cosmopolite, ship of unknown nationality, Captain Selliman

Location: Florida Keys

History: The ship was wrecked during a gale on September 14, 1821, in

the Florida Keys while sailing from Charlestown to New Orleans.

Cossack, vessel

Location: Florida Keys

History: The following vessels were wrecked in the Gulf of Florida during the violent gales between June 5 and 8, 1816: the *Atlas, Martha Brae, Cossack, General Pike* and *Zanga*. The *Cossack* was lost in the Florida Keys while sailing from Havana to Hamburg. The crew and part of the cargo were saved.

Despatch, American merchantman, Captain Field

Location: Carysford Reef

History: The merchantman wrecked on June 15, 1817, on Carysford reef while sailing from Havana for Charlestown. The crew and cargo were saved.

Diana, British ship, Captain Buckley

Location: Cape Florida

History: The ship was lost on Cape Florida in 1774 while sailing from Jamaica to Rhode Island. The crew was saved, but the cargo and ship were a total loss.

Dolphin, British merchantman, Captain Pedrick

Location: The Gulf of Florida

History: The following ships were lost in the Gulf of Florida during a hurricane on October 22, 1752: the *Alexander, Lancaster, Dolphin, Queen Anne, May, Rhode Island, Statea,* an unidentified Spanish man-of-war, an unidentified Spanish schooner, and three other ships of unknown identity. The *Dolphin* was sailing from Jamaica to Liverpool when it foundered.

Dolphin, British merchantman, Captain Smith
  Location: The coast of Florida
  History: The merchantman was lost on the coast of Florida in 1748 along with several other vessels while sailing from Carolina to Antigua.

Dove, British ship
  Location: The coast of Florida
  History: The ship was lost October 18, 1773, on the coast of Florida while en route from Africa to St. Augustine with slaves. The captain, two of the crew, and eight out of the 100 slaves onboard were lost.

Duane, U.S. Coast Guard Treasury Class Cutter, 327 feet
  Location: 24.59.388 N, 80.22.888 W. One mile south of Molasses Reef off Key Largo in 120 feet of water.
  History: The *Duane* was built in 1936 at the U.S. Naval Yard in Philadelphia, Pennsylvania. She was one of only seven such vessels and was named for William J. Duane, Secretary of the Treasury under Andrew Jackson. She had various assignments before being sent to the Atlantic in 1941, where she served with the U.S. Atlantic Fleet. Her service included an impressive wartime and peacetime record. On April 17, 1943, she and her sister ship, the *Spencer*, sank the German U-Boat *U–77*. She participated in four rescues at sea, picking up a total of 346 survivors. In 1980, she was an escort vessel for thousands of Cuban refugees coming to the United States. Her last assignments included Search and Rescue work and Drug Enforcement. After being decommissioned on August 1, 1985, as the oldest active U.S. military vessel, the *Duane* was donated to the Florida Keys Association of Dive Operators for use as an artificial reef. On November 27, 1987, she was towed to Molasses Reef in the Florida Keys. Her hatches were opened and her holds pumped full of water until she sank. As part of the Florida Keys National Marine Sanctuary, The *Duane* is a protected dive site.

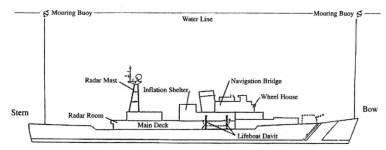

Diver Level: Advanced Openwater
Maximum Depth: 125 feet
Location: 24-59.388N, 80-22.888W

The *Duane* wreck site in the Florida Keys. *Courtesy of the Florida Keys National Marine Sanctuary.*

Due Bill, schooner of unknown nationality
  Location: St. Augustine
  History: The schooner wrecked near St. Augustine in early June 1816.

Eagle, Dutch-built conventional hull freighter
  Location: 24.52.184 N, 80.34.217 W. Three miles northeast of Alligator Reef Light in the Florida Keys in 110 feet of water.
  History: The *Eagle*, then known as the *Raila Dan*, was launched at Werf-Gorinchem, Holland, in December 1962 as a conventional hull freighter.

She had several owners and seven name changes after her launching. On October 6, 1985, she caught fire. Two U.S. Coast Guard cutters responded to her distress call, but the ship's superstructure was destroyed. After being declared a total loss, the Florida Keys Artificial Reef Association purchased her for $30,000 and Joe Teitelbaum, a private citizen, donated another $20,000 to help create an artificial reef out of her. The ship was then named the *Eagle Tire Company*; she was cleaned and gutted of all wooden parts, and all oil and fuel were removed to protect the marine life in the area. On the

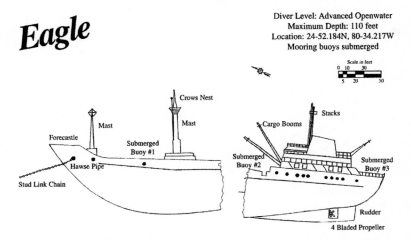

Diver Level: Advanced Openwater
Maximum Depth: 110 feet
Location: 24-52.184N, 80-34.217W
Mooring buoys submerged

The wreck site of the *Eagle*, in the Florida Keys. *Courtesy of the Florida Keys National Marine Sanctuary.*

night of December 19, 1985, while waiting to be sunk as an artificial reef next to the *Alexander Barge*, the *Eagle* broke from her moorings. Her port anchor was dropped to prevent further drifting in the current and she was sunk at that spot. The shipwreck is protected as part of the Florida Keys National Marine Sanctuary.

Eagle, ship
   Location: Amelia Island bar
   History: The *Eagle, Maria* and five or six other vessels, names unknown, were lost on the bar in October of 1811.

Eagle, American ship, Captain Dennet
   Location: Maranzie Reef, Florida Keys
   History: The ship wrecked on December 15, 1801 on the Florida side of the Maranzie Reef in the Florida Keys. She was sailing from Havana to Philadelphia when she wrecked. Her crew and cargo were saved.

East Florida Merchant, British merchantman, Captain Losthouse
   Location: St. Augustine bar
   History: The merchantman was lost on the bar in 1773 while sailing from London to St. Augustine. Two-thirds of the cargo was saved.

Edmund & George, ship, Captain Rainy
   Location: Cape Florida
   History: British merchantman, *Elizabeth*, commanded by Captain Sims, ran aground on the coast of Florida in 1790 while sailing from Jamaica to Bristol. The crew was able to refloat the vessel by throwing part of its cargo overboard. The captain reported that he had seen four ships on the Florida reef on August 12, 1790, while in 25 degrees and four minutes of latitude. On August 19th he saw two other ships at Cape Florida wrecked on the reef: the *Apollo* and *Edmund & George*, both bound for London. Two other ships had been on shore in Florida but were refloated by throwing parts of their cargoes overboard.

El Ciervo, Spanish ship belonging to the Squadron of Tierra Firme of Captain-General Don Antonio de Echeverz y Zubiza

   Location: Florida coast
   History: The *El Ciervo* belonged to the 1715 fleet, which wrecked on the coast of Florida during a hurricane on the night of July 30, 1715. The ship was carrying 96 tons of brazilwood when it foundered. The Real Eight Company has completely worked the wrecks of this convoy.

El Gran Poder de Dios y Santa Ana (alias Aná Agustina), German-built merchant *nao* belonging to the 1733 Spanish Treasure Fleet of Don Rodrigo de Torres, 181¾ tons, Captain and owner Francisco Sánchez de Madrid (Note: same name as the captain of the *Nuestra Señora de las Angustias y San Rafael* of the same fleet)
   Location: Florida Keys
   History: The *nao* belonged to the 1733 Spanish treasure fleet, which was caught by a hurricane and sank in the Florida Keys on July 15, 1733. The ship carried 14,000 pesos in silver specie and bullion, 139 marcos in worked silver, and a general cargo. The ship is listed by this name and that of *Sánchez de Madrid*, the name of the captain and owner, and is listed as being wrecked at Cayo de Bocas del Leste (Vacas Key). The Spaniards carried out extensive salvage operations of the shipwrecks of the 1733 fleet, and claim to have recovered all of their treasure. Several ships, not identified by name, were refloated. Fifteen, which could not be refloated, were burnt to their waterlines after salvage operations were completed.

Eliza, ship of unknown nationality, Captain Murphey
   Location: Carysford Reef
   History: The ship was lost on the reef in 1818 while sailing from Jamaica to Philadelphia. The crew and six boxes of dollars were saved.

El Mulato, Spanish privateer
   Location: Fort Pierce
   History: The richly laden vessel wrecked near Fort Pierce sometime before 1570. The Indians recovered a great deal of her treasure.

El Nauva Victoriosa, Spanish merchant *nao*, Captain Josef Varan
   Location: Entrance of the Bahama

Channel, on the head of the Florida Keys in the vicinity of Key Largo
   History: The ship, which had sailed from Cadiz on November 3, 1770, in a *flota* (fleet) going to Veracruz, sank some time in 1771. Only her crew was saved.

El Rubi, 60-cannon *capitana* (flagship) of the 1733 Spanish Treasure Fleet of Don Rodrigo de Torres, Captain Baltazar de la Torre y Alfaro
   Location: Florida Keys
   History: The ship was a member of the 1733 Spanish treasure fleet, which was caught by a hurricane and sank in the Florida Keys on July 15, 1733. This ship carried 104 castellanos in worked gold, 3,200 pesos in gold specie, 5,080,285 pesos in silver specie and bullion, and 6,099 marcos in worked silver, all the property of private citizens. In addition, the *El Rubi* and the *almiranta* of the *flota* (fleet) carried 1,519,527 pesos in silver specie and bullion, 4,110 "granos" in gold, an unspecified amount of worked gold and silver and copper ingots, all of which was the property of the king. The precise percentage of what each of the ships carried is not given in the documents, but there is an implication that it was equally divided aboard both ships. Documents also state that unspecified amounts of gold and silver specie and bullion were carried on both ships which were the property of the Church of Spain. The *El Rubi* is listed as being wrecked at Cayo Tabamos in most documents and at Cayo Largo (Key Largo) in a few others. The Spaniards carried out extensive salvage operations of the shipwrecks of the 1733 fleet and claim to have recovered all of their treasure. Several ships, not identified by name, were refloated. Fifteen, which could not be refloated, were burnt to their waterlines after salvage operations were completed.

Empecinada, six-gun Spanish ship, Captain Juan Villacencio
   Location: Amelia Island bar
   History: The ship left Havana on December 19, 1814, with four other Spanish ships. It wrecked at Amelia Island bar on January 8, 1815, while trying to enter port in bad weather.

The ship immediately went to pieces but the crew and cargo were saved.

Espíritu Santa el Mayor, Spanish galleon belonging to the Tierra Firme Flota (fleet) of Captain-General Antonio de Oquendo, 480 tons, Captain Antonio de Soto

Location: Bahama Channel

History: The *flota* set sail from Havana on April 26, 1623. Upon reaching the mouth of the Bahama Channel it was struck by a storm that created waves so huge that the ships were tossed about like corks. The treasure-laden galleon *Espíritu Santa el Mayor* opened up and sank so quickly that other ships could save only 50 of the 300 persons aboard. Her treasure of over one million pesos was totally lost. The *Santisimi Trinidad*, *Almiranta* of the *flota*, also sank but not as quickly. There was time for several pataches to recover all of her treasure, which amounted to one million pesos. Everyone onboard the *Santisima Trinidad* survived. Contemporary accounts differ as to where the ships were lost. Several state that they wrecked on the coast of Florida in the vicinity of Ais and others say that they sank on the high seas.

Europa, ship of unknown nationality, Captain Rich

Location: Florida Keys

History: The ship wrecked on a reef in the Florida Keys in May 1817 while sailing from St. Jago de Cuba for America.

Evenly, British merchantman, Captain Hebden

Location: Florida Keys

History: The merchantman wrecked on the Florida Keys in 1788 while sailing from Honduras to London.

Fair Weather, ship of unknown nationality

Location: Amelia Island bar

History: The ship was lost on the bar in 1811 while sailing from Amelia Island to England.

Fame, American merchantman, Captain Bennett

Location: Florida coast

History: The merchantman was lost on the coast of Florida in 1810 while sailing from New Orleans to Liverpool, England. The crew was saved.

Fanny, British ship, Captain Farquar

Location: North of Cape Florida

History: The ship ran aground to the north of Cape Florida on March 7, 1782, while sailing from Jamaica to Liverpool. She broke up quickly but a privateer from Nassau rescued the people and some cargo.

Flor de Guadiana, Spanish merchantman

Location: Amelia Island

History: The ship was driven onshore and broke up at Amelia Island during a violent storm on September 17, 1813. She had between 800 and 900 bags of cotton aboard when she wrecked.

Flora, British merchantman, Captain Adams

Location: Florida coast

History: The merchantman wrecked on the coast of Florida in 1807 while sailing from New Orleans to Liverpool.

Flora, British ship, Captain Scott

Location: Florida Keys

History: The ship was lost on the Florida Keys in 1798 while sailing from Charlestown to Havana.

Floridana, frigate belonging to the 1733 Spanish Treasure Fleet of Don Rodrigo de Torres

Location: Florida Keys

History: The frigate was part of the 1733 Spanish treasure fleet, which was caught by a hurricane and sank in the Florida Keys on July 15, 1733. There is no data available on the *Floridana*. This ship is listed in some documents as having escaped and in some others as being wrecked at Cayo de Vivoras. The Spaniards carried out extensive salvage operations of the shipwrecks of the 1733 fleet, and claim to have recovered all of their treasure. Several ships, not identified by name, were refloated. Fifteen, which could not be refloated, were burnt to their waterlines after salvage operations were completed.

Fly, British ship, Captain Walker

Location: Florida Keys

History: The ship was lost on the Florida Keys in 1789 while sailing from Jamaica to Africa.

Fortune, British ship, Captain Richardson

Location: Florida coast

History: The ship was lost on November 18, 1772, near the coast of Florida while sailing from Jamaica to London. Only two men drowned.

Frances & Lucy, British merchantman, Captain Barnaby

Location: Florida Keys

History: The merchantman was lost on a reef in the Florida Keys on January 14, 1822, while sailing from Jamaica to Halifax.

Franklin, American merchantman, Captain Taper

Location: Florida Keys

History: The ship wrecked in the Florida Keys in 1823 while sailing from Philadelphia to Pensacola. The crew and the principal part of the cargo were saved and taken to Nassau.

Frolic, American merchantman, Captain Kennedy

Location: Anastasia Island

History: The vessel wrecked on Anastasia Island in 1816 while sailing from Havana to Charlestown.

Fuerte, 60-cannon Spanish galleon

Location: Florida Keys near the H.M.S. *Tyger*

History: The H.M.S. *Tyger* was lost in the Florida Keys in 1742. The crew built a small fort from the timbers of the wreck. The Spanish Admiral Torres sent several small vessels to make prisoners of the survivors but they were not successful, as the Englishmen beat them off. When Admiral Torres learned that the crew of the *Tyger* had repelled his forces, he sent the larger *Fuerte* with a great number of Spanish soldiers aboard, but they themselves wrecked.

General Clark, British merchantman, Captain Lilburn

Location: Florida Keys

History: The merchantman was totally lost on a reef of the Florida Keys in 1793 while sailing from Jamaica to Savannah. The crew was saved.

General Conway, British ship, Captain Bail
  Location: Florida Keys
  History: The ship was lost in the Florida Keys in 1766 while sailing from Jamaica. The crew was saved.

General Jackson, American ship, Captain Taylor
  Location: Cape Florida
  History: The ship was sailing from New Orleans to Rotterdam when it wrecked on Cape Florida in 1819. Most of her cargo was saved.

General Jackson, American sloop
  Location: Florida coast
  History: The sloop wrecked on the coast of Florida in 1821. The crew was saved and arrived in Havana on October 5.

General Pike, vessel, Captain Emery
  Location: Sound Point
  History: The following vessels were wrecked in the Gulf of Florida during the violent gales between June 5 and 8, 1816: the *Atlas, Martha Brae, Cossack, General Pike* and *Zanga*. The *General Pike* was lost at Sound Point while sailing from Charlestown to Matanzas. Part of its cargo was saved.

George, British merchantman, Captain Decone
  Location: Amelia Island
  History: Two British merchantmen were lost on Amelia Island on October 20, 1810, while sailing from Liverpool to Amelia Island: the *Hanover* and *George*.

George III, British merchantman, Captain Danning
  Location: Carysford Reef
  History: The merchantman was lost February 24, 1824, on Carysford Reef while sailing from Honduras to Dublin. Only her crew was saved.

Grenville Packet, British ship, Captain Curlett
  Location: Dry Tortugas
  History: The ship ran ashore and was lost on the Dry Tortugas on February 27, 1765, while carrying mail from Falmouth to Pensacola. The crew was saved.

Hambro, ship, Captain Patterson
  Location: Twelve miles to the south of St. Augustine

  History: The ship wrecked on March 12, 1817, while sailing from St. Ubes to Savannah. The crew was saved but the cargo was a total loss.

Hanover, British merchantman, Captain Baxter
  Location: Amelia Island
  History: Two British merchantmen were lost on Amelia Island on October 20, 1810, while sailing from Liverpool to Amelia Island: they were the *Hanover* and *George*.

Hazard, British merchantman, Captain New
  Location: Cape Florida
  History: The ship was totally lost near Cape Florida in 1789 while sailing from Honduras to London. The crew was saved.

Hector, ship of unknown nationality
  Location: Florida Keys
  History: The ship was lost on a reef in the Florida Keys in the year 1800 while sailing from Havana to Nassau.

Henrietta Marie, British merchant slave ship, 120 tons, 80 feet, Captain Chamberlain
  Location: Florida Keys
  History: The slave ship left London in September 1699 en route to Africa's Guinea Coast to capture slaves. After anchoring off the coast between Sierra Leone and Lagos in Nigeria, the crew used longboats to travel upriver, raid villages and capture slaves. The slaves' mouths were bound with oakum and they were tossed into the lifeboats. Others were tied together like logs and floated out to the ship. They were then taken to Goree Island. According to historians, the slaves were crammed into airless stone chambers for up to three months. They were shackled by the neck and ankles and flogged and raped, and some were murdered. The slaves who survived were then taken out to the slave ship. Records show that 250 men, women and children were loaded onto the *Henrietta Marie* at the end of January 1700 when it set sail for Port Royal, Jamaica. Sixty slaves had died by the time the ship reached Jamaica. As it neared land the slaves were fed more food, shaved, oiled and their wounds dressed. On May 18, 1700, the slaves, naked and branded

with the ship's initials HM, were taken off the ship and into Port Royal where they were auctioned off in the town square. A few weeks later, Chamberlain set course for England. The ship met its end in a fierce hurricane that struck the Florida Straits at the end of June. The entire crew was washed overboard and the ship sank. The shipwreck was discovered in 1972 by Mo Molinar, a successful black treasure hunter who was working for Mel Fisher at the time. The *Henrietta Marie* became the world's first slave ship to be positively identified. Artifacts recovered from the ship include the ship's bell, shackles, cannonballs, elephant tusks, glass trading beads and an assortment of pewter. Altogether more than 7,000 artifacts were recovered from the ship, some of which are now part of a touring national exhibit.

H.M.S. *Carysford*, 28-gun British warship, frigate, Captain Francis Laforey
  Location: Carysford Reef, Florida Keys
  History: The warship was lost on the reef in the year 1793.

H.M.S. *Fly*, British warship, Captain Powoll Bast Pellew
  Location: Carysford Reef
  History: The ship wrecked in May 1805 on the Carysford Reef. All of the 121 crew onboard were saved. This wreck may have occurred on March 3, 1805.

H.M.S. *Fowey*, 20-gun British warship, Captain Francis William Drake
  Location: Fowey Rocks, Florida Keys
  History: The warship, along with the *Judith*, wrecked in the Florida Keys in 1748 in an area now known as Fowey Rocks. The *Judith* was carrying $57,000 in pesos and a large cargo of cocoa. The crew of both ships and the Spanish prize were all saved and transferred to a sloop and carried to Carolina.

H.M.S. *Looe* (sometimes called *Loo*), 44-gun British man-of-war, Captain Uting
  Location: Lost in the Florida Keys
  History: The man-of-war (called a frigate in some accounts) was lost in the Florida Keys on February 5, 1744,

along with a Spanish ship she had captured shortly before. All the men on both ships were saved. The Spaniards called the site of the wreck La Pareda, but shortly afterward the area was referred to as Looe Reef, as it is still called today.

H.M.S. *Otter*, ten-gun British warship, Captain John Wright
    Location: East coast of Florida
    History: The *Otter* wrecked off the east coast of Florida in 1778.

H.M.S. *Tyger*, British man-of-war
    Location: Lost in the Florida Keys
    History: The man-of-war was lost in the Florida Keys in 1742. The crew built a small fort from the timbers of the wreck. The Spanish Admiral Torres sent several small vessels to make prisoners of the survivors but they were not successful, as the Englishmen beat them off. When Admiral Torres learned that the crew of the *Tyger* had repelled his forces, he sent the larger *Fuerte* with a great number of Spanish soldiers aboard, but they themselves wrecked.

H.M.S. *Wolf*, 14-gun British war sloop
    Location: East coast of Florida
    History: The sloop wrecked in March 1741 on the east coast of Florida. This type of sloop generally carried eight regular iron cannon and 12 swivel guns, also called patereroes.

H.M.S. *Zenobia*, ten-gun British schooner
    Location: Florida coast
    History: The schooner wrecked on the coast of Florida in 1806. The crew perished.

***Highlander*,** British merchantman, Captain Cuthbert
    Location: Carysford Reef
    History: The ship was lost on July 15, 1812, on Carysford Reef while sailing from Jamaica to London. The crew was picked up by the ship *Hopewell*.

***Hope*,** brig of unknown nationality, Captain West
    Location: Cape Florida
    History: The brig was lost near Cape Florida in 1796 while sailing from Havana to a port in America.

***Hope*,** British merchantman, Captain Chappel
    Location: Coast of Florida
    History: The merchantman was lost on the coast of Florida in 1790 while sailing from Jamaica to Charlestown.

***Hope for Peace*,** American ship, Captain Baker
    Location: Florida coast
    History: The ship was dismasted and overset in the Gulf Stream on January 25, 1821, while sailing from New Orleans to Charlestown. The ship then drifted and wrecked on the coast of Florida on January 30. The crew was saved.

***Horatio*,** ship of unknown nationality, Captain Turner
    Location: Amelia Island
    History: The ship was totally wrecked at Amelia Island in 1811.

***Howlet*,** American merchant vessel
    Location: Cape Florida
    History: The vessel, on a trading voyage from Boston to the Gulf of Mexico, was driven ashore by strong winds near Cape Florida in 1748. Indians captured the crew and put them to death, except for a black slave who escaped.

***Huron*,** ship of unknown nationality, Captain Snow
    Location: St. Augustine
    History: The ship was lost near St. Augustine in early June 1816 while sailing from Charlestown to St. Mary's.

***Industry*,** British ship, Captain Lawrence
    Location: St. Augustine bar
    History: The ship was lost on the St. Augustine bar in 1764 while sailing from New York to east and west Florida. The ship, in the service of the government installed in Charleston, South Carolina, carried onboard a number of craftsmen and other settlers and their families. The crew and all the passengers were saved.

Jazo e Santa Ana (alias ***La Nimsa del Puerto***), Spanish ship
    Location: Florida Straits
    History: The ship was lost in the Florida Straits in 1768 while sailing from Havana, Cuba to Cadiz.

***Jerusalem*,** Spanish ship
    Location: Florida Keys
    History: The vessel was lost on November 13, 1815, on a reef of the Florida Keys while sailing from Havana to Africa. The crew and cargo were saved.

***Jesús María*,** merchant *nao*, 400 tons, Captain Francisco Salvago
    Location: Thirty degrees of latitude in the Bahama Channel
    History: Three merchant *naos* sank in 30 fathoms of water in about 30 degrees of latitude while running up the Bahama Channel in 1589. Only the names of two were given in archive documents: the *Santa Catalina*, owned by Fernando Ome and coming from Mexico, and the *Jesús María*, owned by Domingo Sauli, also coming from Mexico. There is no mention of what their cargoes consisted of.

***Jesús y Nuestra Señora del Rosario*,** Spanish *nao*, built in Portugal, belonging to the Armada de Tierra Firme and the Tierra Firme Flota (fleet) of Marqués de Cadereita, 117 tons, Captain Manuel Diaz
    Location: Florida Keys
    History: On September 4, 1622, the armada and the *flota* set sail for Spain from Havana Harbor. The convoy sailed, despite the warnings of an imminent hurricane by the main pilots of the convoy. On September 6 (some accounts give the date as the 7th), the convoy was struck by a fierce hurricane causing the ships to scatter over a wide area. Nine of the ships were lost in the Florida Keys and several others were most likely lost on the high seas, as they were never accounted for. The surviving ships made it back to Havana in battered condition. Of those that reached Havana, all had lost their masts and many had been forced to jettison cannon and parts of their cargoes. This disaster was considered the worst to have occurred to the *flotas* in over 50 years. Of the nine ships that were wrecked in the Florida Keys, three were treasure-laden galleons, five were merchant *naos*, of which one was identified as the *Jesús y Nuestra Señora del Rosario*, and one was a patache that served as a reconnaissance boat for the

Divers holding clumps of Spanish pieces of eight.

convoy. Only the locations of three galleons and the patache are given in documents; and only four of the nine are identified, including the *Nuestra Señora de Atocha, La Margarita,* and *Nuestra Señora del Rosario.*

Johan Carl (or *Carl John*), ship
    Location: Florida Keys
    History: The ship, identified only by its name, was lost on a reef in the Florida Keys in 1825 while sailing from Havana to the Mediterranean. Only 74 boxes of sugar out of a thousand onboard were saved.

Jolly Tar, ship of unknown registry
    Location: Florida coast
    History: The ship wrecked on the coast of Florida in 1796 while sailing from Jamaica to Norfolk. The crew and cargo were saved.

Judith (or *Judan*), Spanish merchantman
    Location: Fowey Rocks, Florida Keys
    History: The H.M.S. *Fowey* along with the *Judith* wrecked in the Florida Keys in 1748 in an area now known as Fowey Rocks. The *Judith* was carrying

$57,000 in pesos and a large cargo of cocoa. The crew of both ships and the cargo of the Spanish prize were all saved and transferred to a sloop and carried to Carolina.

Julian, ship
    Location: Anastasia Island
    History: The ship, identified only by its name, was sailing from St. Ubes to Savannah when it was lost on March 15, 1817, at Anastasia Island. The crew, passengers and part of the cargo were saved.

Juno, American ship, Captain Pratt
    Location: Carysford Reef
    History: The ship was lost on June 16, 1812, on the reef while sailing from New Orleans to Boston.

Lady Provost, British merchantman, Captain Clary
    Location: Amelia Island
    History: The merchantman struck on a bar at Amelia Island and was lost on May 9, 1811.

La Margarita, Spanish galleon belonging to the Armada de Tierra Firme and the Tierra Firme Flota (fleet) of Marqués de Cadereita, 600 tons, Captain Pedro Guerrero de Espinosa
    Location: Florida Keys
    History: On September 4, 1622, the armada and the *flota* set sail for Spain from Havana Harbor. The convoy sailed, despite the warnings of an imminent hurricane by the main pilots of the convoy. On September 6 (some accounts give the date as the 7th), the convoy was struck by a fierce hurricane causing the ships to scatter over a wide area. Nine of the ships were lost in the Florida Keys and several others were most likely lost on the high seas, as they were never accounted for. The surviving ships made it back to Havana in battered condition. Of those that reached Havana, all had lost their masts and many had been forced to jettison cannon and parts of their cargoes. This disaster was considered the worst to have occurred in the *flotas* in over 50 years. Of the nine ships that were wrecked in the Florida Keys, three were treasure-laden galleons, five were merchant *naos,* of which one was

identified as the *Jesús y Nuestra Señora del Rosario,* and one was a patache that served as a reconnaissance boat for the convoy. Only the locations of three galleons and the patache are given in documents, and only four of the nine are identified, including the *Nuestra Señora de Atocha, La Margarita,* and *Nuestra Señora del Rosario.* Sixty-eight of the 330 persons onboard the *La Margarita* perished. She was also carrying over half a million pesos in silver bullion and specie, and a small amount of tobacco belonging to private merchants. Contemporary salvors spent four years searching for the ships before locating the *La Margarita.* They spent four more years salvaging most of her cargo before it sanded over. The salvors reported locating a ballast pile from an older shipwreck nearby, from which they recovered several silver bars. The *La Margarita* was rediscovered in 1980 by treasure hunter Mel Fisher. The wreck continued to produce treasure, ultimately valued at $5 million. The finds included 43 elaborate gold link chains measuring a total of 180 feet, 56 gold bars weighing a total of 118 pounds, 56 gold coins, dozens of beautiful pieces of jewelry, 15,000 silver coins, and 18 large silver ingots. The most valuable item Fisher recovered from the wreck was a gold plate about eight inches in diameter embossed with a neo–Moorish design and valued at $100,000.

Lancaster, British merchantman, Captain Lowry
    Location: The Gulf of Florida
    History: The following ships were lost in the Gulf of Florida during a hurricane on October 22, 1752: the *Alexander, Lancaster, Dolphin, Queen Anne, May, Rhode Island, Statea,* an unidentified Spanish man-of-war, an unidentified Spanish schooner, and three other ships of unknown identity. The *Lancaster* was en route from Jamaica to Lancaster when it was lost.

Ledbury, British merchant snow, Captain John Lorain
    Location: About 15 leagues north of Cape Florida
    History: The snow was driven ashore in a violent gale of wind on September 29, 1769, while sailing from Jamaica to

Bristol. The crew and part of her cargo were saved.

Leopard, American sloop
  Location: Florida Keys
  History: The sloop was lost in the Florida Keys in 1823 while sailing from St. Augustine to Havana, Cuba. The crew was saved and taken to Havana.

Lively, British merchant brig, Captain Morse
  Location: Florida Keys
  History: The brig was lost in the Florida Keys in 1791 while sailing from Jamaica to Bristol. Most of her cargo was saved.

Lively, American schooner, Captain Avery
  Location: Florida Keys
  History: The ship was driven over a reef and lost in the Florida Keys in 1819 while sailing from New Orleans to Baltimore. The cargo was saved.

Lovely Ann, American merchantman, Captain Green
  Location: Florida Keys
  History: The ship was lost in the Florida Keys in 1792 while sailing from Jamaica to New York.

Magdalen, British merchantman, Captain Sawyer
  Location: Florida Keys
  History: The merchantman wrecked on a reef in the Florida Keys in 1816 while sailing from New Orleans to Liverpool. The cargo was saved.

Maria, British merchantman, Captain Forster
  Location: Amelia Island
  History: The ship was blown up at Amelia Island in 1811 while sailing from London to Amelia Island.

Maria, ship
  Location: Amelia Island bar
  History: The *Eagle*, *Maria* and five or six other vessels, names unknown, were lost on the bar in October of 1811.

Maria, ship of unknown nationality, Captain Rundle
  Location: Dry Tortugas
  History: The ship wrecked on the Dry Tortugas in 1806 while sailing from Jamaica to Halifax.

Maria, British merchantman
  Location: Florida coast
  History: The ship was wrecked on the Florida coast in 1803 while sailing from Honduras to Charlestown. The crew, materials and cargo were saved.

Maria, British naval transport, Captain Giltchrist
  Location: Ludberry Reef, Florida Keys
  History: The transport was lost on the reef in 1796 while sailing from Jamaica.

Maria Beckford, British merchantman, Captain Boyd
  Location: Cape Florida
  History: The merchantman wrecked at Cape Florida in 1772 and was a total loss.

Marquis de Pombal, Portuguese ship
  Location: Florida Keys
  History: While sailing from Penambuco to Oporto, the ship was captured by the *Patriola*, an insurgent privateer, but was run aground on May 5, 1817, on a reef in the Florida Keys. Her cargo was saved and carried to Nassau.

Martha Brae, vessel, Captain Farish
  Location: Cape Florida
  History: The following vessels were wrecked in the Gulf of Florida during the violent gales between June 5 and 8, 1816: the *Atlas, Martha Brae, Cossack, General Pike* and *Zanga*. The *Martha Brae* was lost near Cape Florida while sailing from Jamaica to Whitehaven. There was a total loss of cargo and two men perished.

Mary, British merchantman, Captain Forbes
  Location: Amelia Island
  History: The merchantman was totally lost at Amelia Island in October 1811.

Mary, British ship, Captain Horncastle
  Location: Cape Florida
  History: The ship was lost in December 1778 off Cape Florida while trying to escape from two American privateers. She was sailing from Jamaica to London.

Mary, British ship, Captain Stafford
  Location: St. Augustine bar

History: The ship was lost on the bar on April 19, 1783, while sailing from St. Augustine to London.

Mary & Jane, British merchantman, Captain Pennymont
  Location: Florida shore
  History: The merchantman was lost on the Florida shore in 1788 while sailing from Jamaica for Liverpool. The crew was saved.

May, British merchantman, Captain Crawford
  Location: The Gulf of Florida
  History: The following ships were lost in the Gulf of Florida during a hurricane on October 22, 1752: the *Alexander, Lancaster, Dolphin, Queen Anne, May, Rhode Island, Statea*, an unidentified Spanish man-of-war, an unidentified Spanish schooner, and three other ships of unknown identity. The *May* was sailing from Jamaica to Glasgow when it foundered.

Merrimack, American brig
  Location: Florida Keys
  History: The brig wrecked in the Florida Keys in 1817 while sailing from Havana to New York. Her cargo was completely lost but her crew was saved and taken to Nassau by wreckers.

Mill, ship, Captain Hays
  Location: Cape Florida
  History: Captain Addis of the ship *Green River* reported that he saw a ship wrecked at Cape Florida without a main or mizzen mast on April 23, 1774, while he was sailing from Jamaica to London. He believed it was the *Mill*, which was sailing in ballast from Jamaica to Boston.

Minerva, British merchantman, Captain M'Nelly
  Location: Amelia Island
  History: The merchantman was lost on Amelia Island on March 2, 1811, while sailing from Londonderry to Amelia Island. The crew was saved.

Minerva, ship of unknown nationality, Captain Callahan
  Location: East coast of Florida
  History: The ship was lost on the coast in 1777.

Modeste, French ship, Captain D'Barron

Location: Key Largo
History: The ship wrecked at Key Largo on May 21, 1819.

Montague, British merchantman, Captain Pickels
Location: Cape Florida
History: The merchantman was lost at Cape Florida in 1774. She was sailing from Jamaica to Liverpool when she wrecked. The crew and about 30 hogsheads of sugar were saved and carried to New Providence Island in the Bahamas.

Naffaw, British merchantman, Captain Bradshaw
Location: Florida Keys
History: The merchantman was lost in the Florida Keys in 1741 while sailing from Jamaica to Bristol, England. The crew was saved by a vessel bound for Virginia.

Nantwitch, British merchant bark, Captain John Smith
Location: South of Fort Pierce Inlet, about one-third of the distance between Fort Pierce and St. Lucie inlets
History: The ship sank in 1696 while sailing in a convoy of 12 or 13 merchant ships from Port Royal, Jamaica. The *Burroughs* and *Reformation* of the same convoy also sank, at different locations.

Nelly, American or British ship, Captain Smith
Location: St. Augustine bar
History: The ship was lost on the bar in 1766 while sailing from Philadelphia to St. Augustine. The crew and part of the cargo were saved.

Nelson, English brig
Location: Florida shore
History: The brig wrecked on the Florida shore on January 31, 1822. The crew was saved and taken to Jamaica.

Neptune, British merchantman, Captain Conolly [*sic*]
Location: Amelia Island bar
History: The ship wrecked on the Amelia Island bar and went to pieces in the year 1816 while sailing from Amelia Island to Jamaica.

Neptune, British ship, Captain Cushley
Location: Florida coast

History: The ship was lost on the coast of Florida in 1802 while sailing from New Orleans to Nassau. The crew and most of her cargo were saved.

Neptune, ship of unknown nationality, Captain Cosbury
Location: Florida coast
History: The ship was en route from New Orleans to Greencock in 1802 when she wrecked. She was lost on the coast of Florida 14 days after leaving New Orleans. The crew and a small part of the cargo were saved.

Neptune, British merchantman, Captain Duncan
Location: Florida shore
History: The merchantman wrecked on the east Florida shore in 1822 and broke up quickly. She was sailing from Jamaica to Dublin.

Nicholas Adolph, ship of unknown nationality, Captain Hoas
Location: Amelia Island
History: The ship was lost on November 10, 1814, on the Amelia Island bar. Part of her cargo was saved.

Noah's Ark, American merchantman
Location: Florida Keys
History: The merchantman was lost in the Florida Keys in 1795 while sailing from New Orleans to Philadelphia.

Noble Bounty, British ship
Location: Cape Florida Reef
History: The ship was sailing from Jamaica to London in 1787 when it wrecked on the Cape Florida Reef. The crew was saved by the *Friendship*, commanded by Captain Black.

North America, three-masted, square-rigged American vessel, 130 feet with a beam of 29 feet
Location: 24.38.270 N, 81.05.605 W. North of Delta Shoals, and just east of Sombrero light in the Florida Keys in 14 feet of water.
History: Although not confirmed, this shipwreck may be the *North America,* built in Bath, Maine in 1833 and lost on November 25, 1842, while carrying dry goods and furniture. Three ships were reported lost on Delta Shoals one mile east of Sombrero Light in the 19th century. Admiralty Court Records show that a three-masted, square rigged vessel by the name of *North America,* carrying dry goods and furniture, was lost on November 25, 1842, on Delta Shoals while en route from New York to Mobile, Alabama. Records also show that local wreckers provided assistance to Captain Hall and his crew during a three-day salvage effort. Although four ships were registered by the name of *North America* during this period, the size of the ship's remaining wreckage and Captain

Diver Level: Openwater
Maximum Depth: 14 feet
Location: 24-38.270N, 81-05.605W

Scale in feet

The *North America* **wreck site in the Florida Keys.** *Courtesy of the Florida Keys National Marine Sanctuary.*

Hall's name in the court records suggest that this wreck may indeed be the *North America*.

North Star, ship

Location: Amelia Island

History: The ship, identified only by name, was wrecked at Amelia Island in 1811.

Nuestra Señora de Atocha, Spanish galleon belonging to the Armada de Tierra Firme and the Tierra Firme Flota (fleet) of Marqués de Cadereita, 112 feet, 600 tons, Captain Jacome de Veider

Location: 24.00 N, 82.00 W. Florida Keys

History: The *Atocha* belonged to the 1622 Treasure Fleet. The ship wrecked in the Florida Keys during a hurricane on September 6, 1622. Two hundred and sixty people onboard perished. Five survivors who held onto the broken mizzenmast, the only part of the galleon remaining above water, were rescued by one of the fleet's other galleons. The *Atocha* was one of the richest galleons of the fleet. Her manifest listed cargo that included: 24 tons of silver bullion in 1038 ingots, 180,000 pesos of silver coins, 582 copper ingots, 20 bronze cannons, 525 bales of tobacco, 125 gold bars and discs, 350 chests of indigo, and 1,200 pounds of silverware. Besides the cargo listed on the manifest, the *Atocha* carried an enormous amount of unregistered jewelry and goods, mostly consisting of silver bullion and specie, and a small amount of tobacco belonging to the king. The wreck location was lost soon after the disaster when the buoy that was placed over the wreck disappeared in bad weather. The wreck sanded over

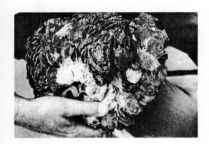

Hundreds of Spanish silver pieces of eight recovered from the *Atocha*.

before it could be relocated and was never salvaged. The arrival of the treasure onboard the *Atocha* was crucial to the faltering Spanish government. Archive records in Seville show that Spain looked for the *Atocha* for nearly 60 years before abandoning the search. On July 20, 1985, after 16 years of searching for the *Atocha*, Mel Fisher finally located the main section of the ship, which contained the largest portion of her treasure. The State of Florida soon stepped in and claimed ownership of the *Atocha* and her treasure. However, the U.S. Supreme Court eventually awarded salvage rights to Fisher. Significant recoveries from the *Atocha* include five bronze cannon, 127,000 silver coins, more than 900 silver bars averaging 70 pounds apiece, and over 250 pounds of gold bars, discs, bits and lengths of heavy gold chain, along with hundreds of pieces of jewelry, silverware, crucifixes and gold coins. Thousands of high quality contraband emeralds taken from South America's mines are also being recovered from the *Atocha*. The emeralds range in size from ½ carat to 77 carats. It is estimated that 69 pounds of Colombian emeralds were smuggled onboard the *Atocha* before she departed on her final voyage. Mel Fisher's group, Treasure Salvors Inc., continues to recover treasure and artifacts from the Atocha. In July 2000, the group located another rich pocket of the ship's treasure. Diving on the wreck is still off limits to anyone except Treasure Salvors Inc. However, Atocha Dive Expeditions headed by Fisher's group offers dive tours to certified open-water divers to certain areas of the wreck site that have been completely excavated. Divers can see the *Atocha's* ballast piles along with scattered timbers from her hull. Divers can also watch the continued excavation of the wreck nearby. Much of *Atocha's* treasure is on display in The Mel Fisher Maritime Museum in Key West, Florida as well as the Mel Fisher Museum located in Sebastian, Florida.

Nuestra Señora de Balvaneda (alias *El Gallo*), 60-cannon *almiranta* of the 1733 Spanish Treasure Fleet of Don Rodrigo de Torres, Captain Bernardo de Maturana

Location: Florida Keys

History: This ship was the *almiranta* of the 1733 Spanish Treasure Fleet, which was caught by a hurricane and sank in the Florida Keys on July 15, 1733. The ship, owned by the king, carried 196 castellanos in worked gold, 3,200 pesos in gold specie, 4,895,216 pesos in silver specie and bullion, 2,579 marcos in worked silver, and 285 marcos of "plata pasta," all property of private citizens. In addition, the *capitana*, (flagship) and the *almiranta* of the *flota* (fleet) carried 1,519,527 pesos in silver specie and bullion, 4,110 "granos" in gold, an unspecified amount of worked gold and silver, and copper ingots, all of which was the property of the king. The precise percentage of what each of the ships carried is not given in the documents, only that it was equally divided aboard both ships. Documents also state that unspecified amounts of gold and silver specie and bullion were carried on both ships as the property of the Church of Spain. This ship is listed as being wrecked at Cayo de Vivoras in all the documents and charts. The Spaniards carried out extensive salvage operations of the shipwrecks of the 1733 fleet, and claim to have recovered all of their treasure. Several ships, not identified by name, were refloated. Fifteen, which could not be refloated, were burnt to their waterlines after salvage operations were completed.

Nuestra Señora de Balvaneda (alias *El Infante*), Spanish galleon belonging to the 1733 Spanish Treasure Fleet of Don Rodrigo de Torres, Captain Domingo de Sanz

Location: Florida Keys

History: This galleon belonged to the 1733 Spanish Treasure Fleet, which was caught by a hurricane and sank in the Florida Keys on July 15, 1733. The ship, owned by the king, carried 562,509 pesos in silver specie and bullion and 643 marcos in worked silver. In addition it carried large amounts of indigo, vanilla and ceramic jars, jugs and plates. This ship is listed as being wrecked at Cayo Tabamos in all documents and charts. The Spaniards carried out extensive salvage operations of the shipwrecks of the 1733 fleet and

Spanish galleon c. 1720.

claim to have recovered all of their treasure. Several ships, not identified by name, were refloated. Fifteen, which could not be refloated, were burnt to their waterlines after salvage operations were completed.

Nuestra Señora de Belem y San Antonio de Padua, English-built Spanish merchant *nao* belonging to the 1733 Spanish Treasure Fleet of Don Rodrigo de Torres, 242¼ tons, Captain and owner Don Luis de Herrer
   Location: Florida Keys
   History: This *nao* belonged to the 1733 Spanish Treasure Fleet, which was caught by a hurricane and sank in the Florida Keys on July 15, 1733. The ship carried 12,000 pesos in sliver specie and bullion, 359 marcos in worked silver, and a cargo similar to that of the *San José.* It is listed as being wrecked at Cayo de Matacumbe el Viejo (upper Matacumbe Key), but on the charts it is not shown by the above name. However, the charts do list a shipwreck by

the name of *Herrera*, which is probably the same ship, as the captain and owner of this ship was named Herrera. The Spaniards carried out extensive salvage operations of the shipwrecks of the 1733 fleet and claim to have recovered all of their treasure. Several ships, not identified by name, were refloated. Fifteen, which could not be refloated, were burnt to their waterlines after salvage operations were completed.

Nuestra Señora de Belem y San Juan Bautista, foreign-built Spanish merchant *nao* belonging to the 1733 Spanish Treasure Fleet of Don Rodrigo de Torres, 212⅜ tons, Captain Diego de la Corte y Andrade
   Location: Florida Keys
   History: The *nao*, owned by Francisco Lebrum, belonged to the 1733 Spanish Treasure Fleet, which was caught by a hurricane and sank in the Florida Keys on July 15, 1733. This ship carried no treasure, only a general cargo similar to those of the other ships in the *flota.* The ship is probably better known by an alias, which is not revealed in documents. It is listed in documents as being wrecked at Cayo de Matacumbe el Viejo (Upper Matacumbe) but is not shown on any charts by the above name. However, the charts do show a ship named *Tres Puentes* as being lost at Upper Matacumbe, and this was probably the ship's alias. The Spaniards carried out extensive salvage operations of the shipwrecks of the 1733 fleet and claim to have recovered all of their treasure. Several ships, not identified by name, were refloated. Fifteen, which could not be refloated, were burnt to their waterlines after salvage operations were completed.

Nuestra Señora de Concepción, Spanish ship belonging to the Squadron of Tierra Firme of Captain-General Don Antonio de Echeverz y Zubiza
   Location: Florida coast
   History: The *Concepción* belonged to the 1715 Treasure Fleet, which wrecked

on the coast of Florida during a hurricane on the night of July 30, 1715. When it wrecked, the ship was carrying 3,000 pesos in gold doubloons, four gold bars valued at 5,703 pesos, 15 serons of cocoa, one chest of vanilla, 15¾ tons of brazilwood, 1,440 cured half-hides, and some tobacco. The Real Eight company has completely worked the wrecks of this convoy.

Nuestra Señora de Concepción y San Josefe, frigate
   Location: Key Largo
   History: The frigate was lost at Key Largo in 1689.

Nuestra Señora de las Angustias y San Rafael, English-built merchant *nao* belonging to the 1733 Spanish Treasure Fleet of Don Rodrigo de Torres, 328½ tons, Captain Francisco Sánchez de Madrid
   Location: Florida Keys
   History: The *nao*, owned by José Sanchez de Madrid, was part of the 1733 Spanish Treasure Fleet, which was caught by a hurricane and sank in the Florida Keys on July 15, 1733. The ship carried 27,000 pesos in silver specie and bullion, 605 marcos of worked silver, and a general cargo, plus an unspecified amount of Chinese porcelain. The ship was wrecked at Cayo de Vivoras. The Spaniards carried out extensive salvage operations of the shipwrecks of the 1733 fleet and claim to have recovered all of their treasure. Several ships, not identified by name, were refloated. Fifteen, which could not be refloated, were burnt to their waterlines after salvage operations were completed.

Nuestra Señora del Carmen, San Antonio de Padua y las Ánimas, Genovese-built Spanish merchant *nao* belonging to the 1733 Spanish Treasure Fleet of Don Rodrigo de Torres, 220⁹⁄₁₀ tons, Captain and owner Don Antonio de Chaves
   Location: Florida Keys
   History: This *nao*, owned by Captain Juan Arizon, was part of the 1733 Spanish Treasure Fleet, which was caught by a hurricane and sank in the Florida Keys on July 15, 1733. This ship carried no treasure, only a general cargo similar to those of the other

ships in the *flota* (fleet). It is listed in both documents and charts as being wrecked at Cayo de Matacumbe el Viejo, or Matacumbe Grande, both names for Upper Matacumbe. In the documents, this ship was sometimes called simply *Chaves*, the name of the captain and owner. On all the charts it was also called *Chaves*. The Spaniards carried out extensive salvage operations of the shipwrecks of the 1733 fleet and claim to have recovered all of their treasure. Several ships, not identified by name, were refloated. Fifteen, which could not be refloated, were burnt to their waterlines after salvage operations were completed.

Nuestra Señora de los Dolores y Santa Isabel (alias ***El Nuevo Londres***), English-built Spanish merchant *nao* belonging to the 1733 Spanish Treasure Fleet of Don Rodrigo de Torres, 296 tons, Captain Antonio de Loaysa

Location: Florida Keys

History: The *nao*, owned by Nicolas Fernández del Castillo, belonged to the 1733 Spanish Treasure Fleet, which was caught by a hurricane and sank in the Florida Keys on July 15, 1733. The ship carried a general cargo such as the other ships in this *flota* (fleet) did, plus an unspecified small amount of silver specie. The Spaniards carried out extensive salvage operations of the shipwrecks of the 1733 fleet and claim to have recovered all of their treasure. Several ships, not identified by name, were refloated. Fifteen, which could not be refloated, were burnt to their waterlines after salvage operations were completed. This ship is not mentioned in documents or shown on any of the charts, but she may have been referred to by an alias.

Nuestra Señora de los Reyes, San Fernando y San Francisco de Paula, Genovese-built merchant *nao* belonging to the 1733 Spanish Treasure Fleet of Don Rodrigo de Torres, 328 tons, Captain José Cabeza

Location: Florida Keys

History: The *nao*, owned by Francisco de Soto y Posada, was part of the 1733 Spanish Treasure Fleet, which was caught by a hurricane and sank in the Florida Keys on July 15, 1733. The ship carried 16,000 pesos in silver (it

was not disclosed if this was in specie or bullion or both), along with 226 marcos of worked silver and a general cargo. The ship wrecked at Cayo de Vivoras. The Spaniards carried out extensive salvage operations of the shipwrecks of the 1733 fleet and claim to have recovered all of their treasure. Several ships, not identified by name, were refloated. Fifteen, which could not be refloated, were burnt to their waterlines after salvage operations were completed.

Nuestra Señora del Populo (alias ***El Pinque***), Spanish pink belonging to the 1733 Spanish Treasure Fleet of Don Rodrigo de Torres, Captain Francisco Ibernon

Location: Florida Keys

History: The small pink belonged to the 1733 Spanish Treasure Fleet, which was caught by a hurricane and sank in the Florida Keys on July 15, 1733. This ship was owned by the king. Documents do not reveal the number of cannon, tonnage or what cargo this small vessel carried. It is listed as being wrecked at Cabeza de los Martires (head of the Florida Keys) and at Key Biscayne in different documents and charts. The Spaniards carried out extensive salvage operations of the shipwrecks of the 1733 fleet and claim to have recovered all of their treasure. Several ships, not identified by name, were refloated. Fifteen, which could not be refloated, were burnt to their waterlines after salvage operations were completed.

Nuestra Señora del Rosario, Spanish galleon belonging to the Armada de Tierra Firme and the Tierra Firme Flota (fleet) of Marqués de Cadereita, 600 tons, Captain Francisco Rodríguez Rico

Location: Florida Keys

History: On September 4, 1622, the armada and the *flota* set sail for Spain from Havana Harbor. The convoy sailed, despite the warnings of an imminent hurricane by the main pilots of the convoy. On September 6 (some accounts give the date as the 7), the convoy was struck by a fierce hurricane causing the ships to scatter over a wide area. Nine of the ships were lost in the Florida Keys and several others were

most likely lost on the high seas, as they were never accounted for. The surviving ships made it back to Havana in battered condition. Of those that reached Havana, all had lost their masts and many had been forced to jettison cannon and parts of their cargoes. This disaster was considered the worst to have occurred to the *flotas* in over 50 years. Of the nine ships that were wrecked in the Florida Keys, three were treasure-laden galleons, five were merchant *naos*, of which one was identified as the *Jesús y Nuestra Señora del Rosario*, and one was a patache that served as a reconnaissance boat for the convoy. Only the locations of three galleons and the patache are given in documents; and only four of the nine are identified, including: the patache, the *Nuestra Señora de Atocha, La Margarita*, and *Nuestra Señora del Rosario*. The *Rosario* wrecked at the Dry Tortugas with about half a million pesos of silver bullion and specie aboard. Salvors recovered all of the treasure and 20 cannon from the wreck.

Nuestra Señora del Rosario, San Antonio y San Vicente Ferrer, Spanish merchant *nao* belonging to the 1733 Spanish Treasure Fleet of Don Rodigo de Torres, Captain Juan José de Arizon

Location: Florida Keys

History: This *nao*, owned by Captain Juan Arizon, was part of the 1733 Spanish Treasure Fleet, which was caught by a hurricane and sank in the Florida Keys on July 15, 1733. The ship carried 24,000 pesos in silver specie and bullion, and a general cargo such as the *San José* carried. In addition, an item listed as tinta, which could be either coffee or some type of dye, was onboard. The shipwreck is not listed in any documents or shown on the charts. However, on two charts a shipwreck named *Arizon*, the name of the Captain and owner of this ship, is shown. On another chart in the same location, a shipwreck named *Terri* is shown as being lost at Cayo de Vivoras. Several documents also mention a ship named *Terri* (or *Terry*) as being lost at Cayo de Vivoras, and it is probably the same ship as above. The Spaniards carried out extensive salvage operations of the shipwrecks of the 1733 fleet and claim to have recovered all of their treasure. Several ships, not identified by name, were refloated. Fifteen, which could not be refloated, were burnt to their waterlines after salvage operations were completed.

Nuestra Señora del Rosario, San Francisco Javier y San Antonio de Padua, French-built Spanish merchant *nao* belonging to the 1733 Spanish Treasure Fleet of Don Rodrigo de Torres, 205⅓ tons, Captain and owner Don Luis Lozana

Location: Florida Keys

History: This *nao* was part of the 1733 Spanish Treasure Fleet, which was caught by a hurricane and sank in the Florida Keys on July 15, 1733. The ship carried 12,000 pesos in silver specie and bullion, and a cargo similar to that of the *San José de las Animas.* The above vessel is listed in some documents as being wrecked at Cayo de Vivoras, and in others as having survived the hurricane and safely returning to Havana. The Spaniards carried out extensive salvage operations of the shipwrecks of the 1733 fleet and claim to have recovered all of their treasure. Several ships, not identified by name, were refloated. Fifteen, which could not be refloated, were burnt to their waterlines after salvage operations were completed.

Nuestra Señora del Rosario y San Cristobal, merchant *nao*

Location: Lost on the coast of Florida in 30.20.0 N latitude

History: The ship was lost on the coast of Florida in 1711 while sailing from Havana, Cuba to Spain.

Ohio, American merchantman, Captain Hall

Location: Cape Florida

History: The merchantman wrecked on January 15, 1808, near Cape Florida while sailing from Jamaica to New York. The crew and a great part of the cargo were saved.

Orion, American merchantman, Captain Brown

Location: Florida Keys

History: The ship was lost on February 20, 1812, on a reef in the Florida

Keys while sailing from Aux Cayes to Philadelphia.

Oscar, ship

Location: Amelia Island

History: The ship was burnt at Amelia Island in 1814. She was bound for Liverpool.

Pearl, British merchantman, Captain Johnson

Location: Cape Florida

History: The merchantman was lost near Cape Florida on March 8, 1821, while sailing from Havana to Gibraltar. Only four of the crew and the captain survived.

Phoebus, American schooner, Captain Dominique

Location: St. Augustine bar

History: The schooner was lost on the bar in 1802 while sailing from Norfolk.

Pointe-à-Petre, French merchantman

Location: Florida Keys

History: The merchantman was lost on a reef in the Florida Keys on February 7, 1825, while sailing from New Orleans to Bordeaux. The crew and part of the cargo were saved.

Prince George, British ship

Location: St. Augustine

History: The ship was lost while sailing into St. Augustine in 1769 after coming from London.

Providence, ship of unknown nationality, Captain Gibson

Location: Florida Keys

History: The ship wrecked on September 17, 1805, in the Florida Keys while sailing from New Orleans to Bordeaux.

Quebec, British merchantman, Captain Foitt

Location: Florida Keys

History: The merchantman was totally lost on a reef in the Florida Keys on August 7, 1818, while sailing from Jamaica to London. Only her crew was saved.

Queen Ann, British merchantman, Captain Rymer

Location: The Gulf of Florida

History: The following ships were lost in the Gulf of Florida during a

hurricane on October 22, 1752: the *Alexander, Lancaster, Dolphin, Queen Anne, May, Rhode Island, Statea,* an unidentified Spanish man-of-war, an unidentified Spanish schooner, and three other ships of unknown identity. The *Queen Ann* was sailing from Jamaica to Bristol when it foundered.

Rattler, British merchantman, Captain Balmond

Location: Carysford Reef

History: The ship was totally lost on the reef in 1805 while sailing from Honduras to London. Only a small part of her cargo was saved.

Rebecca, ship of unknown nationality

Location: "at Florida"

History: Wrecked "at Florida" in 1816 while sailing from Cadiz and Havana to Savannah. Parts of its cargo were saved and carried to Nassau.

Reformation, British barkentine, Captain Joseph Kirle

Location: 27.08.000 N latitude, close to the shore and a bit north of Jupiter Inlet

History: The ship sank on September 23, 1696, while sailing in a convoy of 12 or 13 merchant ships from Port Royal, Jamaica. She carried 25 passengers and crew, and her cargo consisted of sugar, rum, beef, molasses and some Spanish money. The *Burroughs* and *Nantwitch* of the same convoy also sank, at different locations.

Refuerzo (also called the ***Urca de Lima***), ship belonging to the New Spain Flota of Captain-General Don Juan Esteban de Ubilla

Location: Florida coast

History: The ship belonged to the 1715 Treasure Fleet, which wrecked on

Three Spanish pieces of eight recovered from the flagship of the 1715 fleet.

the coast of Florida during a hurricane on July 30, 1715. The ship had a general cargo much like those of the *capitana* (flagship) and *almiranta* of the fleet. The ship carried no royal treasure but did carry 81 chests of loose sacks of silver specie valued at 252,171 pesos belonging to private persons. In addition it carried 13 chests of worked silver. It also carried snuff and balsam. The Real Eight Company has completely salvaged all the wrecks of this convoy.

Rhee Galley, British ship, Captain Hunter
  Location: Florida Keys
  History: The ship was lost in the Florida Keys in 1774 while sailing from Honduras to Bristol.

Rhode Island, American merchantman, Captain Ball
  Location: The Gulf of Florida
  History: The following ships were lost in the Gulf of Florida during a hurricane on October 22, 1752: the *Alexander, Lancaster, Dolphin, Queen Anne, May, Rhode Island, Statea*, an unidentified Spanish man-of-war, an unidentified Spanish schooner, and three other ships of unknown identity. The *Rhode Island* was sailing from Jamaica to New York when it went down.

Royal Desire, French ship, Captain Feuardant
  Location: Florida coast
  History: The ship was lost early in June 1821 near the Florida coast while sailing from Havana to Le Havre.

Sally, ship of unknown nationality, Captain Mathews
  Location: Near St. Augustine
  History: The ship was lost on February 22, 1773, in a snowstorm near St. Augustine while sailing from Lisbon to South Carolina. Everyone onboard except the mate perished.

San Anton, Spanish merchant *nao*, 100 tons, Captain Gonzalo Rodríquez
  Location: Florida Keys
  History: The *nao* was lost in the Florida Keys in 1521 after leaving Cuba en route to Spain.

San Antonio, Spanish ship, Captain Font
  Location: On a reef near Key West

History: The ship was lost on a reef near Key West on January 22, 1768, after leaving Havana, Cuba. The crew and passengers survived 22 days on the reef and were rescued by a turtling sloop and taken back to Havana.

Sancta Salbador, *naos* (2), 120 tons
  Location: Florida
  History: Three *naos* under the command of Captain Gonzalo de Carbajal were lost on the coast of Florida in the year 1556. Only two were identified: both carried the same name, *Sancta Salbador*. One was commanded by Captain Guillen de Lugo and the other by Captain Martin de Artaleco. They were en route from Puerto Rico to Spain when they foundered.

San Francisco de Asis, English-built merchant *nao* belonging to the 1733 Spanish Treasure Fleet of Don Rodrigo de Torres, 264⅔ tons, Captain and owner Cristobal de Urquijo
  Location: Florida Keys
  History: The *nao* was part of the 1733 Spanish Treasure Fleet, which was caught by a hurricane and sank in the Florida Keys on July 15, 1733. There is no mention in any document of what this ship's cargo was, but it can be assumed that it was a general cargo as generally carried in the fleet. This ship is listed as being wrecked at Cayo de Vivoras. The Spaniards carried out extensive salvage operations of the shipwrecks of the 1733 fleet and claim to have recovered all of their treasure. Several ships, not identified by name, were refloated. Fifteen, which could not be refloated, were burnt to their waterlines after salvage operations were completed.

San Ignacio, English-built merchant *nao* belonging to the 1733 Spanish Treasure Fleet of Don Rodrigo de Torres, 181¾ tons, captain not identified
  Location: Florida Keys
  History: The *nao*, owned by Francisco de Alzaibar, was part of the 1733 Spanish Treasure Fleet, which was caught by a hurricane and sank in the Florida Keys on July 15, 1733. The ship carried 12,000 pesos in silver specie and bullion, 696 marcos of worked silver in six boxes, a general cargo, plus some boxes containing gifts from

China. This ship is listed as being wrecked at Cayo de Bocas and Cayo de Vacas. One document calls this ship *San Ignacio de Urquijo*—Urquys was the name of the captain of the *San Francisco de Asis*. As the documents do not reveal the name of the captain of the *San Ignacio*, it is possible that Urquijo was his name as well. The Spaniards carried out extensive salvage operations of the shipwrecks of the 1733 fleet and claim to have recovered all of their treasure. Several ships, not identified by name, were refloated. Fifteen, which could not be refloated, were burnt to their waterlines after salvage operations were completed.

San José de las Ánimas (sometimes listed as *San José y las Ánimas*), Spanish merchant *nao* belonging to the 1733 Spanish Treasure Fleet of Don Rodrigo de Torres, 326½ tons, Captain Cristobal Fernández Franco
  Location: Florida Keys
  History: This *nao* was part of the 1733 Spanish Treasure Fleet, which was caught by a hurricane and sank in the Florida Keys on July 15, 1733. The ship carried 30,435 pesos in silver specie and bullion, plus sugar, chocolate, indigo, cochineal, dyewoods, cocoa,

A diver inspects the wooden timbers of the *San José*.

Complete silver service set recovered from the 1733 galleon *San José*.

hides, ceramicware, tobacco, vanilla, and various types of drugs. It is listed as being wrecked at Cayo Tabamos. On one chart showing the locations of the shipwrecks of this fleet, a shipwreck verified as *Africa* is shown in the same location the *San José de las Animas* is shown in on other charts, which means it is probably her alias. The Spaniards carried out extensive salvage operations of the shipwrecks of the 1733 fleet and claim to have recovered all of their treasure. Several ships, not identified by name, were refloated. Fifteen, which could not be refloated, were burnt to their waterlines after salvage operations were completed.

San Martín, *almiranta* of the Honduras Fleet
   Location: Fort Pierce Inlet
   History: On October 10, 1618, the governor of St. Augustine received news from Indians that a very large ship had sunk near the Fort Pierce Inlet. He sent men to aid the survivors—there were only 53. They identified the ship as the *San Martín, almiranta* of the Honduras Fleet. The ship's main cargo of indigo, cochineal and some hides was washed all over the coast. At the same time, a smaller unidentified *nao* also sank nearby. The governor sent a frigate to locate both wrecks. There were no other documents identifying the latter shipwreck, or if the Spaniards located either ship. In 1993 a rare bronze astrolabe was recovered from *San Martin* by Kane Fisher.

San Nicolas, *nao*, 200 tons, Captain Juan Christoval

Location: Fort Pierce
   History: The *nao* wrecked in 1551 near Fort Pierce. The Indians recovered a great deal of what the ship carried. The ship was en route from Nombre de Dios and Cartagena to Spain, but there is no mention in documents of whether it stopped in Havana or of its cargo.

San Pedro, Dutch-built vessel belonging to the 1733 Spanish Treasure Fleet of Don Rodrigo de Torres, 287 tons, Captain Gaspar López Gonzales
   Location: 24–51.802 N, 80–840.780 W. One and a quarter miles south of Indian Key in the Florida Keys in 18 feet of water.
   History: The *San Pedro* was a member of the 1733 Spanish Treasure Fleet, which was caught by a hurricane and sank in the Straits of Florida on July 15, 1733. The *San Pedro* carried 16,000 pesos in Mexican silver specie and bullion, and numerous crates of Chinese porcelain. The Spaniards carried out extensive salvage operations of the shipwrecks of the 1733 fleet and claim to have recovered all of their treasure. The wreck of the *San Pedro* was found in the 1960s in Hawk Channel. At this time treasure hunters heavily salvaged

Diver bringing up a Spanish sword from one of the 1733 wrecks.

the site. Silver coins dating between 1731 and 1733 were recovered from the pile of ballast and cannons that marked the place of her demise. Elements of the ships rigging and hardware as well as remnants of her cargo were unearthed and removed. In 1989, the site became part of the State of Florida Underwater Archaeological Preserve. Replica cannon, an anchor from another 1733 shipwreck, and a bronze plaque were placed on the site to enhance it.

Sandwich, British merchantman, Captain Fraser
   Location: Florida Keys
   History: The merchantman wrecked in the Florida Keys in 1819 while sailing from Havana to Guernsey. Only a small part of her cargo was saved.

Santa Ana María, *nao*, 180 tons, Captain Goncalo de la Rocha [*sic*]
   Location: Florida coast
   History: The *nao* was sunk in a storm on the high seas off the coast of Florida in 1622 while sailing alone from Santo Domingo and Havana for Spain.

Santa Anna, ship
   Location: Amelia Island
   History: The ship was lost on March 7, 1815, off Amelia Island while coming from Bermuda.

Santa Catalina, merchant *nao*, 350 tons, Captain Domingo Ianez Ome
   Location: Bahama Channel, 30 degrees latitude
   History: Three merchant *naos* sank in 30 fathoms of water in about 30 degrees of latitude while running up the Bahama Channel in 1589 before a hurricane. Only the names of two were given in archive documents: the *Santa Catalina* and the *Jesús María*. There is no mention of what their cargoes consisted of.

Santa Maria del Camino, *nao* belonging to the Armada de Tierra Firme of Captain-General Bartolome Carreño, 350 tons, Captain Diego Diaz
   Location: Fort Pierce
   History: The vessel, which belonged to Sr. Bolaños, was lost on the coast of Florida in 1554. The Spaniards salvaged everything the ship carried.

Santa Marie, ship of unknown nationality, Captain Wicks

Location: St. Augustine bar

History: The ship was lost on the St. Augustine Bar in 1790 while sailing from St. Augustine to Havana, Cuba.

Santa Rosa, ship

Location: Amelia Island bar

History: The vessel was lost on the bar in 1814 while coming from Liverpool.

Santisima Trinidad, *almiranta* of the Tierra Firme Flota (fleet) of Captain-General Antonio de Oquendo, 600 tons, Captain Ysidro de Cepeda

Location: Bahama Channel

History: The *flota* sailed from Havana on April 26, 1623. Upon reaching the mouth of the Bahama Channel it was struck by a storm that created waves so huge that the ships were tossed about like corks. The treasure-laden galleon *Espíritu Santa el Mayor* opened up and sank so quickly that other ships could save only 50 of the 300 persons aboard. Her treasure of over one million pesos was totally lost. The *Santisimi Trinidad*, *almiranta* of the *flota*, also sank but not as quickly. There was time for several patches to recover all her treasure, which amounted to one million pesos. Everyone onboard the *Santisima Trinidad* survived. Contemporary accounts differ as to where the ships were lost. Several state that they wrecked on the coast of Florida in the vicinity of Ais, and others say that they sank on the high seas.

Santo Cristo de Maracaibo, ship

Location: Eight leagues southwest of St. Augustine

History: The governor of Florida wrote the king on January 31, 1706, and stated that one of the two ships sent by the viceroy of Mexico to bring supplies to St. Augustine sank eight leagues southwest of St. Augustine during a storm.

Sarah, British brig, Captain Rowe

Location: Eight miles from St. Johnson's bar, east Florida

History: The brig, laden with logwood and mahogany, was wrecked eight miles from St. Johnson's bar, east Florida, in 1824.

Seaflower, ship of unknown nationality, Captain Pitch

Location: East coast of Florida

History: The ship was lost on the east coast of Florida in 1807 while sailing from Jamaica and Havana to New York.

Sir John Sherbroke, ship of unknown nationality, Captain Cowan

Location: Dry Tortugas

History: The ship struck a reef off the Dry Tortugas in 1816 and went to pieces. She was sailing from Jamaica to New York with a general cargo and $60,000 in specie. The crew was saved and made off with the specie.

Sisters, British merchantman, Captain Swiney

Location: Grand Cayman Island

History: The *Sisters* was lost on August 3, 1817, on Grand Cayman Island while sailing from Jamaica to London, England. The ship *Unity*, sailing from Jamaica to London, picked up her crew. The *Unity* was then lost on August 13, 1817, on Carysford Reef. The crews of both ships were saved by another passing ship.

Solway, British merchantman, Captain Bennett

Location: Florida Keys

History: The ship wrecked on August 10, 1818, on a reef of the Florida Keys while sailing from Jamaica to Withsharon. Eighteen different wrecking vessels were reported to have recovered the greatest part of her cargo.

Speedwell, British merchantman, Captain Brownlow

Location: Carysford Reef

History: The merchantman was lost on August 28, 1796, on Carysford Reef while sailing from Honduras to Charlestown. The crew and ship's materials were saved.

Statea, American merchantman, Captain Jones

Location: Gulf of Florida

History: The following ships were lost in the Gulf of Florida during a hurricane on October 22, 1752: the *Alexander*, *Lancaster*, *Dolphin*, *Queen Anne*, *May*, *Rhode Island*, *Statea*, an unidentified Spanish man-of-war, an unidentified Spanish schooner, and three other ships of unknown identity. The *Statea* was sailing from Honduras to Rhode Island when it went down.

Supply, ship of unknown nationality, Captain Fisher

Location: 26.20.000 N latitude

History: The ship was totally lost on the coast of Florida at the latitude of 26 degrees and 20 minutes during a heavy gale on January 26, 1821. She was sailing from Jamaica to Havana and heading for the Cape Verde Islands when she wrecked. The crew was saved.

Susan, British merchantman, Captain Beard

Location: Amelia Island

History: The merchantman was lost at Amelia Island in 1810 while sailing from Amelia Island to Clyde. The crew and cargo were saved.

Swift, ship of unknown nationality, Captain Miller

Location: Long Island

History: The ship was wrecked at night on Long Island in 1924 while coming from Havana, Cuba. The 900 boxes of sugar and all of the indigo and cochineal she had onboard were saved by wreckers and landed at Key West.

Three Sisters, British ship

Location: Carysford Reef, Florida Keys

History: The ship was lost on the reef in 1816 while en route from New York to Nassau.

Three Sisters, American ship, Captain Arnington

Location: Carysford Reef, Florida Keys

History: The *Three Sisters* wrecked on August 30, 1816, on Carysford Reef. The ship, of New York, was bound for New Orleans when she wrecked.

Thunderbolt, built under contract for the U.S. Army during World War II, 189 feet in length

Location: 24.39.663 N, 80.57.784 W. Four miles south of Marathon and Key Colony Beach in the Florida Keys in 120 feet of water.

History: The *Thunderbolt* was built, along with 15 sister ships, by Marietta Manufacturing Company at Point

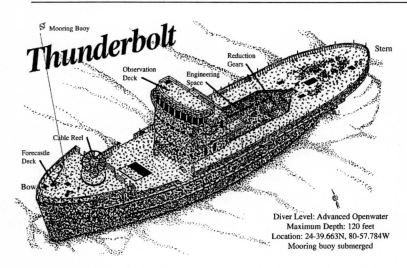

A map of the wreck site of the *Thunderbolt*. *Courtesy of the Florida Keys National Marine Sanctuary.*

Pleasant, West Virginia. The *Thunderbolt*, then named *Randolph*, was launched on June 2, 1942. It was built to plant and tend defensive coastal minefields for the Army's Coast Artillery Corps. However, in 1949 this function and the *Randolph* were transferred to the Navy. While in the Navy, the vessel was never commissioned and remained in the Naval Reserve Fleet, first in South Carolina and then in Florida. Caribbean Enterprises of Miami purchased the vessel in 1961, and later Florida Power and Light bought her for research on the electrical energy in lightning strikes—hence her new name: *Thunderbolt*. Eventually, Florida Power and Light donated the vessel to the Florida Keys Artificial Reef Association. On March 6, 1986, she was intentionally sunk in the Keys. Prior to being sunk the ship was stripped of all but a few major pieces of equipment. She now lies intact and upright on the ocean floor.

Tony, British merchantman, Captain Welsh

Location: St. Augustine bar

History: The merchantman was lost on the bar in 1783 while sailing from Charlestown to St. Augustine and London.

Treasure,

Location: Cape Canaveral

History: Indians of the King of Ais were reported to have recovered over a million pesos in bars of gold and silver along with many precious pieces of jewelry near Cape Canaveral. The jewelry, made by the Indians of Mexico, was from a ship or ships belonging to the Nueva España Flota, of which it is said the general was the son of Pedro de Menendez. The document containing this information is dated 1570 and although the Indians made this recovery in 1556, the ship or ships might have wrecked at an earlier date. The wording of the document makes it impossible to determine if only one ship, several or the whole fleet sank. However, it was probably only one or several ships, otherwise there would have been a great deal more mentioned in other contemporary documents.

Triton, merchantman of unknown nationality, Captain Hand

Location: Florida

History: Four ships were lost about October 25, 1810 on the Florida shore: the *Caroline, Union, African* and *Triton*. The *Triton* was sailing from Havana, Cuba to Richmond when she was lost.

Unidentified, patache belonging to the Armada de Tierrra Firme and the Tierra Firme Flota (fleet) of Marquis de Cadereita

Location: Near the *Nuestra Señora del Rosario* at the Dry Tortugas

History: On September 4, 1622, the armada and the *flota* set sail for Spain from Havana Harbor. The convoy sailed, despite the warnings of an imminent hurricane by the main pilots of the convoy. On September 6 (some accounts give the date as the 7th), the convoy was struck by a fierce hurricane causing the ships to scatter over a wide area. Nine of the ships were lost in the Florida Keys and several others were most likely lost on the high seas, as they were never accounted for. The surviving ships made it back to Havana in battered condition. Of those that reached Havana, all had lost their masts and many had been forced to jettison cannon and parts of their cargoes. This disaster was considered the worst to have occurred to the *flotas* in over 50 years. Of the nine ships that were wrecked in the Florida Keys, three were treasure-laden galleons, five were merchant *naos*, of which one was identified as the *Jesús y Nuestra Señora del Rosario*, and one was a patache that served as a reconnaissance boat for the convoy. Only the locations of three galleons and the patache are given in documents; and only four of the nine are identified, including the *Nuestra Señora de Atocha, La Margarita*, and *Nuestra Señora del Rosario*.

Unidentified, ships (5 or 6)

Location: Amelia Island bar

History: The *Eagle, Maria* and five or six other vessels, names unknown, were lost on the bar in October 1811.

Unidentified, frigate

Location: Cape Canaveral

History: The frigate, en route from Havana to St. Augustine, sank on the coast near Cape Canaveral in 1592. All the men made it ashore, but the Indians killed all but one before aid could reach them. The one survivor was being tortured when soldiers from St. Augustine arrived and saved him.

Unidentified, ship

Location: Carysford Reef

History: A large plain ship with yellow sides and black-painted parts was seen wrecked on the Carysford Reef about August 15, 1818.

Unidentified, ship
  Location: Carysford Reef
  History: Captain M'Donald of the ship *Trelawney Planter* reported sighting a ship ashore on the Carysford Reef with several wreckers about her on August 14, 1792.

Unidentified, ship
  Location: Carysford Reef
  History: The ship wrecked on Carysford Reef on December 6, 1815.

Unidentified, vessel
  Location: Carysford Reef
  History: A large vessel was seen aground on the reef on August 12, 1819, with three small vessels nearby, presumably anchored.

Unidentified, ship
  Location: Carysford Reef
  History: A ship was seen wrecked and totally dismasted on Carysford Reef at the end of February in 1821.

Unidentified, ship
  Location: Carysford Reef
  History: A ship with plain yellow sides was reported wrecked on Carysford Reef on May 19, 1822.

Unidentified, American brig
  Location: Carysford Reef
  History: A large bright-sided deeply laden American brig was seen wrecked on the southwestern end of Carysford Reef on August 5, 1824, with several wreckers alongside.

Unidentified, ships (2)
  Location: Carysford Reef, Florida Keys
  History: The *Brandt*, coming from New Orleans, arrived in New York on June 3, 1817, and reported seeing a ship and a brig aground on Carysford Reef with eight wreckers around the ship.

Unidentified, Spanish frigate
  Location: Cayo de Lobos on the coast of Florida
  History: There is a brief mention in the archives of an unidentified Spanish frigate being lost at Cayo de Lobos on the coast of Florida in 1741.

Unidentified, English vessel, Captain Williams
  Location: Coast of Florida
  History: On May 16, 1777, the Spanish ship *Begona* entered Cadiz, coming from Veracruz. While en route, its crew had sighted an English vessel under the command of Captain Williams, which was ready to sink off the coast of Florida. The Spaniards rescued the crew from the ship and took them to Cadiz.

Unidentified, British ship
  Location: East coast of Florida
  History: A vessel that was sailing from Jamaica to London picked up the crew of a British ship wrecked on the east coast of Florida in 1787.

Unidentified, American vessels (many)
  Location: East coast of Florida
  History: A number of American vessels were cast away on the east coast of Florida during a hurricane on October 15 and 16, 1797.

Unidentified, ship of unknown nationality, Captain Pinder
  Location: East Florida coast
  History: The ship was lost on the east Florida coast in 1817 while sailing from Jamaica to New York. The crew and part of the cargo were saved.

Unidentified, ships (several) belonging to the Flota de Tierra Firme commanded by Cosme Rodríques Farfan
  Location: Bahama Channel
  History: Several ships were separated from the convoy in the Bahama Channel after a storm hit in 1555. They were never heard from again.

Unidentified, nao
  Location: Florida coast
  History: Three *naos*, under the command of Captain Gonzalo de Carbajal, were lost on the coast of Florida in the year 1556. Only two were identified: both carried the same name *Sancta Salbador*. They were en route from Puerto Rico to Spain when they foundered.

Unidentified, vessels (several)
  Location: Santa Maria Bay
  History: A fleet of 13 vessels sailed from Veracruz under the command of Don Tristán de Luna y Arellano, Governor of Florida, on June 11, 1559. They planned to found a new Floridian colony. On August 14, the fleet anchored in the Bay of Santa Maria. On the night of September 19, the bay was struck by a tempest from the north that lasted 24 hours. Five ships were shattered, along with a galleon and a bark, all of which went to pieces with a great loss of life. The tempest swept a caravel with cargo into a grove of trees more than the distance of a harquebus shot from the shore.

Unidentified, ships (3)
  Location: Florida coast
  History: A Spanish historian briefly mentions the loss of three ships of Don Juan Menéndez on the Florida coast near Fort Pierce in 1564.

Unidentified, French ships (2)
  Location: Between Matanzas and Mosquito Inlet
  History: Two ships of the Frenchman Ribaut were wrecked during a storm in 1565 along the shore between Matanzas and Mosquito Inlet. Some of both crews drowned in attempting to reach shore. Indians captured and killed most of the others.

Unidentified, nao
  Location: Florida coast
  History: One of the *naos* of Pedro Menendez de Aviles was lost on the coast of Florida in 1567.

Unidentified, ships (2)
  Location: Cape Canaveral
  History: Two ships that were en route from Mexico to Santo Domingo to receive a cargo of sugar and hides were lost in a storm off Cape Canaveral in 1571 or 1572. The Indians massacred most of the crews as they were making their way to St. Augustine, which was a distance of 30 leagues.

Unidentified, tenders (2)
  Location: Florida coast
  History: In 1572, Adelantado Pedro Menendez de Aviles left St. Augustine en route to Havana in two small tenders and a bark. The vessels were separated by a storm while sailing down the coast of Florida. The tender in which Aviles and some Jesuits were sailing wrecked near Cape Canaveral. All 30 persons onboard reached shore and constructed a small fort from the wreckage. Sometime later they walked safely back to St. Augustine. The other

tender wrecked onshore in the province of Ais, where the crew was killed and their vessel burnt. The bark reached Havana safely.

Unidentified, *nao* belonging to the Armada de Tierra Firme of Captain-General Cristobal de Eraso

Location: Puerto Escondido

History: In 1576, a few days after the armada left Havana, Cuba en route to Spain, it was struck by a tempest in the Bahama Channel. One of the fleet's *naos* was separated from the other ships and arrived in sinking condition at Puerto Escondido, which is near Puerto de las Palmas on the coast of Florida. Soon after entering port the ship sank. Salvage operations were soon under way and all its gold and silver was recovered.

Unidentified, ships (2)

Location: Florida Keys

History: Don Gutierres de Miranda wrote the king from Havana on February 13, 1578: "While I was coming in a boat from St. Augustine to this town, off the Florida Keys, three Indians came in a canoe out to me, from which I understood by signs, that two vessels had been wrecked, which had been sent from this town in the month of August last past. As I knew not their language, I brought one of them to this town, where they understand it, and he said that the loss of the ships was a fact and that the Indians had killed all the people except two, whom two caciques are holding captive."

Unidentified, frigate belonging to the *flota* (fleet) of General Francisco de Noboa

Location: Florida coast

History: Don Antonio Martínez Carvajal wrote to the king from Havana on November 3, 1579, stating that: "We set out for St. Augustine and by reason of a tempest, one of the two frigates we had was lost ... The General and the rest of the people were saved from the wreck of said frigate, whence he went by land to the fort of St. Augustine." The wreck occurred somewhere on the east coast of Florida.

Unidentified, merchant *nao* belonging to the *flota* (fleet) of General Francisco de Noboa

Location: Florida coast

History: The *nao* of *maestro* Hernán García Marín sank off the coast of Florida with a great quantity of gold, silver and pearls during a hurricane in 1587. Almost all were saved and carried to the *capitana* (flagstaff) in a launch before the unidentified ship sank.

Unidentified, merchant *nao*

Location: Thirty degrees of latitude in the Bahama Channel

History: Three merchant *nao* sank in 30 fathoms of water in about 30 degrees of latitude while running up the Bahama Channel in 1589 before a hurricane. Only the names of two were given in archive documents: the *Santa Catalina*, owned by Fernando Ome and coming from Mexico, and the *Jesús María*, owned by Domingo Sauli and also coming from Mexico. There is no mention of what their cargoes consisted of.

Unidentified, Spanish treasure ships (several)

Location: Florida

History: The Dutch historian Linchoten tells us that in 1589, all but one out of 100 large ships in the Tierra Firme Flota (fleet) were wrecked in the Florida Channel, and that of 220 ships sailing that year for Spain and Portugal from various possessions of the Spanish Crown (Portugal was under Spanish rule at this time), only 14 or 15 arrived safely. No doubt Linchoten is grossly incorrect. The Spanish historian Duro states that 1589 was not a particularly bad year and goes on to say that 14 ships were lost in 1590 at San Juan de Ulua in Veracruz due to a "norther." From the abundance of documents in the archives for this year, there is no doubt that Linchoten was mistaken, as only four Spanish ships were lost and only one Portuguese ship, returning from Goa, in India.

Unidentified, ships (many)

Location: Florida coast

History: A Spanish fleet of 75 ships left Havana after spending the winter of 1590-91 there. The king's orders were to leave all their treasure in Havana. The convoy, consisting of ships from Mexican South America suffered many storms after it left Havana on July 27, 1591. No fewer than 29 were lost, many off the coast of Florida. This information was obtained from English sources. Since the Spanish sources for this year are vague on the matter, it cannot be disputed. Only one Spanish document, dated March 26, 1592, briefly states that "due to the fact that so many ships were lost returning from the Indies during the past year there are very few ships available to be sent to the Indies for this year." Since the lost ships were not carrying treasure, at least not registered treasure or any belonging to the king, this could be the reason there is so little mention of them in the Spanish documents. His treasure did reach Spain safely in 1591, however, by passing an English blockade aboard small but fast *zabras*.

Unidentified, *nao*, 200 tons

Location: Florida coast

History: The unnamed *nao* of Captain Diego Rodríguez was originally built in France. It sank on the coast of Florida in the year 1600 while coming from Mexico in the Flota de Nueva España.

Unidentified, patache

Location: "la Boca de Matasissos"

History: The unnamed patache, sent as an advice boat from Veracruz, was wrecked in March 1618 at "la Boca de Matasissos" on the coast of Florida on its 28th day of sailing. Some of the survivors reached St. Augustine safely but the Indians killed the others. Some mail and cargo washed ashore and was recovered by the Indians.

Unidentified, patache

Location: Three leagues off the Dry Tortugas

History: In 1621, the small patache, serving as an advice boat on a voyage from Veracruz to Spain, was capsized by a large wave about three leagues off the Dry Tortugas and sank. The number of persons aboard was not given, but 30 drowned and the rest reached one of the cays of the Dry Tortuga group. They were soon rescued by a passing Spanish ship after signaling by making fires on the cay. The mailbags they had saved from the ship were also taken aboard.

Unidentified, *capitana* (flagship)
Location: Florida Keys, four leagues to windward of the *Atocha* shipwreck
History: In the early spring of 1623, two galleons were sent to the Florida Keys to protect the salvors at work on the *La Margarita* from attack by Dutch privateers who were reported to be cruising in that area. The *capitana* of this small squadron was wrecked on the Florida Keys, four leagues to windward of the shipwreck of the *Nuestra Señora de Atocha*. The crew survived and reached Havana ten days later aboard rafts made from their shipwreck. The two galleons carried 14 bronze cannon.

Unidentified, frigate
Location: Florida coast
History: The frigate sank on the coast of Florida sometime before July 30, 1624. Eight of the 12 iron cannon it carried as well as several anchors were recovered from the wreck.

Unidentified, English ship
Location: Seventy leagues south of St. Augustine
History: On November 15, 1633, the governor of Florida wrote to the king, stating: "On the 10th of November, my soldiers captured three Englishmen from London. Their ship was carrying supplies and aid to the English settlement at Alxacan [probably somewhere in Virginia or New England], but sank on our coast. Forty of them reached shore safely, but the Indians had killed all but three that my soldiers had captured. I will send them back to Spain for questioning on the first available vessel. The location of their shipwreck was 70 leagues south of our town [St. Augustine]."

Unidentified, ship belonging to the Flota de Nueva España of Captain-General Lope de Hoces
Location: Florida coast
History: On December 20, 1634, the governor of Florida wrote to Captain-General Antonio de Oquendo, who was wintering in Havana, Cuba with his Armada de Tierra Firme, stating: "I received news that a ship of the Flota de Nueva España, commanded by Captain-General Lope de Hoces, had wrecked on my coast. We found some Indians that told us that some other Indians had salvaged some treasure off this wreck. We stationed some soldiers opposite the site of the wreck and sent others after the Indians who had recovered the treasure, but they were never located. I went with several canoes and some divers to the said wreck and in one day's time we recovered the 100,000 pesos in bullion and specie which the ship had been carrying as registered cargo and we took this treasure to my fort, St. Augustine."

Unidentified, ships (several) belonging to the Nueva España Flota of Captain-General Juan de Campos and the Armada de Barlovento
Location: Florida coast
History: The *flota* (fleet) and the armada (squadron used for protecting returning *flotas* during time of war) were struck by a hurricane on September 27, 1641. Five ships of the *flota* were wrecked on the coast in the latitude of 30 degrees north. Four of the five ships were merchant *naos* and there were no survivors. Another was the patache of the *flota*, which was located by another patache from Havana some days later. They found the wrecked patache about five leagues from the shore with some survivors still aboard. Other survivors had tried to swim ashore, including a priest, but they were eaten by sharks. Other ships in this same convoy were in such bad condition that they sank on the high seas. The treasure-laden *almiranta* of the *flota* lost all her masts and developed such a bad leak that she eventually drifted and was wrecked on a reef in the Bahamas called Abreojos, now known as Silver Shoals as a result of this shipwreck. The majority of the silver on this wreck was recovered about 40 years later by Sir William Phips.

Unidentified, ships (2) of unknown nationality
Location: Forty leagues from New Providence
History: There is a brief mention in documents that in 1698 a notorious pirate named Kelly forced two ships of unknown nationality ashore on the coast of Florida about 40 leagues from the Island of New Providence, in the Bahamas.

Unidentified, Spanish ship
Location: Florida Straits
History: While passing through the Florida Straits in 1771, Captain Clutsam, aboard the British ship *Hope*, reported that he saw a Spanish man-of-war; sometime later it caught on fire and blew up.

Unidentified, French ship
Location: Matacumbe
History: Sometime before 1775 a historian wrote: "... a little cay lying before Matacumbe is a dreadful monument of this [the cannibalism of the Colossas Indians], it is called Matanca [i.e., "slaughter"], from the number near four hundred wretched Frenchmen, who being cast away, fell into the hands of these monsters...."

Unidentified, American ships (5)
Location: Florida shore
History: Five American ships were wrecked on the Florida shore and went to pieces during a hurricane at the end of October 1810. The greatest parts of their cargoes were recovered.

Unidentified, ships (2 or 3) of the Squadron of Tierra Firme of Captain-General Don Antonio de Echeverz y Zubiza
Location: Florida coast
History: Two and possibly three ships of the Tierra Firme belonged to what is known today as the 1715 Treasure Fleet, which wrecked on the coast of Florida during a hurricane on the night of July 30, 1715. These unidentified ships were not said to have been carrying any cargo or treasure onboard, but like all the other ships in this squadron, it is believed that they received a large cargo of tobacco in Havana. The Real Eight Company has completely worked the wrecks of this convoy.

Unidentified, *capitana* (flagship) of the Squadron of Tierra Firme of Captain-General Don Antonio de Echeverz y Zubiza
Location: Florida Coast
History: The *capitana* of the Tierra Firme belonged to what is known today

as the 1715 Treasure Fleet, which wrecked on the coast of Florida during a hurricane on the night of July 30, 1715. The ship was carrying royal treasure of 46,095 pesos, six reals and ten maravedis in gold doubloons (escudos), 300 castellanos, seven tomines, six grains of gold dust, and 646 castellanos in two small gold bars. Also onboard were 19 gold bars valued at 26,063 pesos, 2,650 pesos in gold doubloons, 1,485 pesos in silver specie, three gold chains valued at 747 pesos, 47 serons of cocoa, and 1½ tons of brazilwood. The Real Eight Company has completely worked the wrecks of this convoy.

Unidentified, *almiranta* of the Squadron of Tierra Firme of Captain-General Don Antonio de Echeverz y Zubiza

Location: Florida coast

History: The *almiranta* of the Tierra Firme belonged to what is known today as the 1715 Treasure Fleet, which wrecked on the coast of Florida during a hurricane on the night of July 30, 1715. When it wrecked, the ship was carrying eight gold bars valued at 8,978 pesos, 3,150 pesos in gold doubloons, 175 pesos in silver specie, two chests of ceramic jugs, one chest of gifts, 2½ tons of brazilwood, 28 serons of cocoa, one chest of vanilla, two chests of tortoise shells, and 650 cured half-hides. The Real Eight Company has completely worked the wrecks of this convoy.

Unidentified, *capitana* (flagship) of the New Spain Flota (fleet) of Captain-General Don Juan Esteban de Ubilla

Location: Florida coast

History: The *capitana* was the leading vessel of what is known today as the 1715 Treasure Fleet, which wrecked on the coast of Florida during a hurricane on July 30, 1715. The ship was carrying 611,409 pesos in silver specie for the king, 169,111 pesos in silver specie for the wages of the members of the Council of the Indies in Madrid, and 2,559,917 pesos in silver specie belonging to private persons. All this treasure was contained in 1,300 chests. The ship also carried a small amount of silver bars, 23 chests of silverware, one small chest containing an undis-

Chinese porcelain cups recovered from the flagship of the 1715 fleet.

closed number of gold doubloons, gold bars and pearls, a small chest containing jewelry for the queen, and another small chest of gold jewelry belonging to a nobleman. The cargo consisted of Chinese porcelain, indigo, cochineal, drugs, hides, brazilwood, gifts, copper disks, and ceramic drinking vessels. Along with the above, the ship was carrying 36,000 pesos worth of silver specie, gold disks and several other bars that had been salvaged from a ship that had sunk in 1711. The Real Eight Company has completely salvaged all the wrecks of this convoy.

Unidentified, *patache* belonging to the New Spain Flota (fleet) of Captain-General Don Juan Esteban de Ubilla

Location: Florida coast

History: The *patache* belonged to the 1715 Treasure Fleet, which wrecked on the coast of Florida during a hurricane on July 30, 1715. The ship, which was smaller than the other ships in the *flota*, carried no royal treasure, but did carry 44,000 pesos of silver specie in 12 chests and some loose sacks of leather. It also carried a general cargo much like those of the *capitana* and *almiranta* of the fleet; in addition, it was carrying a quantity of a type of incense. The Real Eight Company has completely salvaged all the wrecks of this convoy. The Real Eight members also found a sufficient number of gold coins on this shipwreck, which were undoubtedly contraband.

Unidentified, *almiranta* of the New Spain Flota (fleet) of Captain-General Don Juan Esteban de Ubilla

Location: Florida coast

History: The *almiranta* of the *flota* belonged to the 1715 Treasure Fleet,

which wrecked on the coast of Florida during a hurricane on July 30, 1715. The ship's cargo consisted of Chinese porcelain, indigo, cochineal, drugs, hides, brazilwood, gifts, copper disks, ceramic drinking vessels, sarsaparilla, cocoa, and three Chinese folding screens. The ship also carried 990 chests of silver specie, of which 611,408 pesos belonged to the king and 2,076,004 pesos to private persons. Other treasure consisted of 53 chests of silverware. The Real Eight Company has completely salvaged all the wrecks of this convoy. According to documents, the unidentified *almiranta* carried no gold treasure in any form, so the gold coins which Real Eight members found on this shipwreck must have been contraband.

Unidentified, frigate of the New Spain Flota (fleet) of Captain-General Don Juan Esteban de Ubilla

Location: Florida coast

History: The small frigate of the 1715 Treasure Fleet wrecked on the coast of Florida during a hurricane on July 30, 1715. Documents do not indicate whether the frigate carried any cargo or treasure, but it is unlikely that it carried any treasure. The Real Eight Company has completely salvaged all the wrecks of this convoy.

Unidentified, ships (7)

Location: Florida shores

History: After arriving in London early in October 1771, Captain Bratt reported seeing seven large ships wrecked on the shores of Florida.

Unidentified, ship

Location: Florida Keys

History: On March 24, 1619, a ship coming from Campeche sank in the Florida Keys with a cargo of hides and indigo. All the crew escaped to shore and reached St. Augustine.

Unidentified, galleons (2) belonging to the Armada de Tierra Firme under the command of Maestro de Campo Antonio de Oteyca

Location: Florida Keys

History: The two galleons were sent to carry supplies in 1630 from Havana to St. Augustine. Both ships wrecked at the head of the Florida Keys. All the men on the wrecks were saved, and 56 bronze and iron cannon on them were recovered and taken to Havana.

Unidentified, Spanish merchant *nao*
    Location: Florida Keys
    History: There was a brief mention in records for the year 1688 of an unidentified Spanish merchant *nao* being lost in the Florida Keys.

Unidentified, balandra (schooner) belonging to the 1733 Spanish Treasure Fleet of Don Rodrigo de Torres
    Location: Florida Keys
    History: The Treasure Fleet, including the balandra, was caught by a hurricane and sank in the Florida Keys on July 15, 1733. This vessel, only identified as a balandra (or schooner), may be the reason why the different accounts state that there were 21 or 22 ships in the fleet when it sailed. This type of vessel was quite small and in some accounts it may not have been included as a ship of the fleet. The wreck is probably the Key Biscayne shipwreck mentioned in documents and shown on the charts as *El Aviso* (an advice boat). The Spaniards carried out extensive salvage operations of the shipwrecks of the 1733 fleet and claim to have recovered all of their treasure. Several ships, not identified by name, were refloated. Fifteen, which could not be refloated, were burnt to their waterlines after salvage operations were completed.

Unidentified, ships (2)
    Location: Florida Keys
    History: The *Anna Theresa* wrecked on the Florida Keys on July 30, 1768, while sailing from Pensacola to Falmouth. The British ship *Prince George* was sailing past the Florida Keys when he saw the *Anna Theresa* aground on a reef and afire. Seeing three sloops anchored near the wreck, he sent a boat to investigate. He was told that the crew of the ship had been carried to New Providence, in the Bahamas. He was also told that a Spanish ship and a brig from Boston, whose captain's name was Bostley, had been lost in the same area a few days earlier.

Unidentified, Spanish ship
    Location: Florida Keys
    History: News reached London, England from Jamaica in 1770 that a large Spanish ship, sailing from Caracas, Venezuela for Cadiz, was wrecked in the Florida Keys during a violent gale of wind. The ship and cargo were totally lost.

Unidentified, ships (5)
    Location: Florida Keys
    History: After leaving Jamaica on July 26, 1771, the British ship *Eagle* arrived in Bristol. The captain reported seeing five large ships and one brig wrecked in the Florida Keys and on the coast of Florida. One of the ships had lost her main- and mizzenmast. He also noted that the current set very strong towards the Florida coast.

Unidentified, ship
    Location: Florida Keys
    History: There is a brief mention in documents that an English ship sank on the Florida Keys during the year 1782.

Unidentified, ship
    Location: Florida Keys
    History: While sailing from Honduras to England, Captain Earl of the ship *Joseph* reported seeing a large ship wrecked on the Florida Keys on August 31, 1785. Two small vessels were nearby on the inside of the reef.

Unidentified, ship
    Location: Florida Keys
    History: Captain Graham of the ship *Mary*, reported seeing a large ship wrecking on the Florida Keys on June 5, 1792. The ship was a total loss and although he was within a mile of her he could not establish her identity.

Unidentified, brig
    Location: Florida Keys
    History: A brig with a white bottom and a white streak was seen wrecked on a reef along the Florida Keys on February 24, 1819.

Unidentified, French brig
    Location: Florida Keys
    History: The brig, laden with indigo, logwood and mahogany, was wrecked on the east Florida Keys around the end of April 1822. She had been com-

ing from Honduras when she foundered.

Unidentified, vessel
    Location: Florida Keys
    History: A large vessel was seen wrecked on a reef in the Florida Keys with six large wreckers around her on June 27, 1822.

Unidentified, brig
    Location: Florida Keys
    History: A brig, painted black with a white streak, was seen wrecked on a reef in the Florida Keys on March 14, 1824.

Unidentified, British brig
    Location: Florida Keys
    History: The sloop *Theodore* reported that a British brig sailing from Honduras to England was wrecked on a reef in the Florida Keys in the year 1824. American wreckers drove the *Theodore* away from the wreck.

Unidentified, ships (4)
    Location: Florida reef
    History: British merchantman *Elizabeth*, commanded by Captain Sims, ran aground on the coast of Florida in 1790 while sailing from Jamaica to Bristol. The crew were able to refloat the vessel by throwing part of her cargo overboard. The captain reported that he had seen four ships on the Florida reef on August 12, 1790, while in 25 degrees and 4 minutes of latitude. On August 19, he saw two other ships at Cape Florida wrecked on the reef: the *Apollo* and *Edmund & George*, both bound for London. Two other ships had been on shore in Florida but got off the reef by throwing parts of their cargoes overboard.

Unidentified, vessel, Captain Codington
    Location: Florida Straits
    History: In 1768, the vessel was set on fire by lightning and entirely consumed while sailing from Montego Bay, Jamaica to Rhode Island with a cargo of rum. All lives were lost.

Unidentified, nao
    Location: Fort Pierce Inlet
    History: On October 10, 1618, the governor of St. Augustine received news from Indians that a very large ship had

sunk near the Fort Pierce Inlet. He sent men to aid the survivors—they were only 53. They identified the ship as the *San Martín, almiranta* of the Honduras fleet. The ship's main cargo of indigo, cochineal and some hides was washed all over the coast. At the same time, another smaller unidentified *nao* sank nearby. The governor sent a frigate to locate both wrecks. There were no documents indicating the identity of the latter shipwreck, or if the Spaniards located either ship.

Unidentified, Dutch ship
Location: Key West
History: On May 4, 1677, the governor of Cuba sent Don Martín de Melgar with a frigate to salvage cannon from a Dutch ship that had wrecked at Key West.

Unidentified, vessel
Location: Latitude of 25 degrees
History: On March 26, 1824, a long black vessel with painted ports was seen wrecked on a reef with her masts cut down. She was sighted in the latitude of 25 degrees, near Caesar Creek.

Unidentified, brigs (3)
Location: Ledbury Reef
History: A full-rigged brig was reported wrecked on Carysford Reef on April 25, 1822. Two other brigs were also aground on the Ledbury Reef. One appeared to be over the reef. There were six or seven wreckers around the two wrecks.

Unidentified, ship
Location: Located between Mount Tucker and Cape Kennedy (now Kennedy Space Center)
History: An unidentified shipwreck, shown on a chart as "A wreck in 1768," is located between Mount Tucker and Cape Kennedy.

Unidentified, merchant *nao*
Location: Rico Seco, on the coast of Florida
History: The *nao* was lost in 1733 while sailing alone back to Spain.

Unidentified, Spanish man-of-war
Location: Gulf of Florida
History: The following ships were lost in the Gulf of Florida during a hurricane on October 22, 1752: the

Alexander, Lancaster, Dolphin, Queen Anne, May, Rhode Island, Statea, an unidentified Spanish man-of-war, an unidentified Spanish schooner, and three other ships of unknown identity.

Unidentified, Spanish schooner
Location: Gulf of Florida
History: The following ships were lost in the Gulf of Florida during a hurricane on October 22, 1752: the *Alexander, Lancaster, Dolphin, Queen Anne, May, Rhode Island, Statea*, an unidentified Spanish man-of-war, an unidentified Spanish schooner, and three other ships of unknown identity.

Unidentified, ships (3) of unknown registry
Location: Gulf of Florida
History: The following ships were lost in the Gulf of Florida during a hurricane on October 22, 1752: the *Alexander, Lancaster, Dolphin, Queen Anne, May, Rhode Island, Statea*, an unidentified Spanish man-of-war, an unidentified Spanish schooner, and three other ships of unknown identity.

Unidentified, ship
Location: Rio Seco
History: There is a brief mention in the archives of a ship of Don Gerónimo Barroso being lost near Rio Seco on the coast of Florida in 1734. Barroso could have been the captain or owner, or both.

Unidentified, merchant *nao*
Location: St. John's River
History: The *nao* was lost on the coast of Florida near the mouth of the St. John's River in 1731 while on a voyage from Havana to Spain.

Unidentified, Spanish ship and a Spanish snow
Location: Mocus Reef
History: Both ships, from Cadiz, were wrecked and totally lost in January 1803 on the Mocus Reef on the Florida shore.

Unidentified, ship
Location: Mount Tucker, north of Cape Canaveral
History: Bernard Romans' map of Florida shows an unidentified shipwreck called "Wreck 1769," at Mount Tucker, north of Cape Canaveral.

Unidentified, brig
Location: North of Cape Florida
History: Captain Magness of the ship *Ann & Elizabeth* arrived in London from Jamaica and reported that on August 8, 1774, he saw a large brig onshore to the north of Cape Florida being stripped by several wreckers.

Unidentified, brig
Location: Palmerstone Inlet
History: A large brig was seen wrecked on the Florida coast near Palmerstone Inlet on August 29, 1824, with several small vessels around her.

Unidentified, ships (8)
Location: St. Augustine Harbor
History: Eight ships were sunk in St. Augustine Harbor during a fierce northeast gale on September 6 or 7, 1804.

Unidentified, frigates (2)
Location: St. Augustine
History: In 1626, a small frigate sent from Havana, Cuba with salaries and supplies for the officials and soldiers at St. Augustine ran aground on the bar at the entrance to the latter place. The frigate was a total loss. Only a few pipes of wine that washed ashore were recovered from this wreck. When the news of the loss reached the viceroy of Mexico he ordered a frigate sent from Veracruz with supplies and money to pay the garrison at St. Augustine, who were threatening to mutiny if they were not paid promptly. The governor of Florida, Don Luis de Rojas, wrote to the king on February 15, 1627, stating that the second frigate also wrecked on the same bar and was a total loss. The crew, along with 12,000 pesos in eight-real silver coins, was saved. Only 11 of the 200 barrels of flour aboard were salvaged, and only two iron cannon out of the four iron and four bronze cannon she carried could be salvaged, as mud covered over the wreck quickly.

Unidentified, American schooner, Captain Fowler
Location: St. Augustine
History: The schooner was laden with salt and cotton when she wrecked at St. Augustine in 1810. She was en route from New Orleans to Liverpool when she foundered.

Unidentified, vessels (several)
Location: St. Augustine
History: Several unidentified vessels were lost near St. Augustine in early June 1816.

Unidentified, French ships (several)
Location: St. Bernards Bay
History: Sometime before the year 1685, the governor of Cuba sent two brigantines, under the command of captains Martín de Riva and Pedro de Iriarte, to St. Bernards Bay on the coast of Florida to salvage what they could from several French ships that had been wrecked there. Divers recovered only four cannon and some other objects of little value.

Unidentified, caravel
Location: Cape St. Helen
History: A caravel, which was part of the expedition of Don Lucas Vasquez de Ayllon, sailed from Spain in 1524 and was lost the following year near Cape St. Helen. The natives massacred all of the 200 survivors.

Unidentified, ship
Location: Fort Pierce
History: The ship of Farfan (probably its owner) sank near Fort Pierce in 1554, richly laden with gold and silver. The Indians of the King of Ais recovered a great deal from the wreck.

Unidentified, vessel
Location: Florida coast
History: The vessel wrecked in 1545 upon the coast of Florida. Some of its crew of 200 were slain by natives and the remainder reduced to slavery.

Union, merchantman of unknown nationality
Location: Florida shore
History: Four ships were lost about October 25, 1810, on the Florida shore: the *Caroline, Union, African* and *Triton*. The *Union* was sailing from Havana, Cuba to London when she went down.

Unity, ship, Captain Lambourn
Location: Carysford Reef
History: The *Sisters* was lost on August 3, 1817, while sailing from Jamaica to London, England. The ship *Unity*, also sailing from Jamaica to London, picked up her crew, but was then lost itself on August 13, 1817, on Carysford Reef. The crews of both ships were saved by another passing ship.

Viscayo, ship
Location: Fort Pierce Inlet
History: The ship, on which Don Anton Granado was a passenger, wrecked sometime before 1570. The richly laden vessel foundered near Fort Pierce Inlet. The Indians of the King of Ais salvaged a great deal of her treasure.

Visitación, nao, 20 tons, Captain Pedro de la Torre
Location: Florida Keys
History: The *nao* wrecked in the Florida Keys in 1550 while sailing alone from Veracruz to Spain.

Waterloo, British ship, Captain Kelcher
Location: East Florida shore
History: The ship wrecked during October 1822 on the east Florida shore while sailing from Jamaica to Cork.

All of its cargo was saved and carried to Nassau.

Water Witch, ship of unknown nationality
Location: St. Augustine
History: The *Water Witch* of Savannah was wrecked in early June of 1816 near St. Augustine.

Watt, ship of unknown nationality, Captain M'Gee
Location: Florida Keys
History: The ship was lost on a reef in the Florida Keys in 1815 while sailing from Jamaica to New York.

Winchester, 50-gun British man-of-war, Captain John Soule
Location: Cape Florida
History: The man-of-war wrecked on some reefs near Cape Florida in 1695 while sailing from Jamaica to England.

Windsor, British merchantman, Captain Low
Location: Amelia bar, Amelia Island
History: The merchantman wrecked on the bar at Amelia Island in 1811 and was lost while sailing from Liverpool to Savannah.

Zanga, vessel, Captain Russell
Location: Sound Point
History: The following vessels were wrecked in the Gulf of Florida during the violent gales between June 5 and 8, 1816: the *Atlas, Martha Brae, Cossack, General Pike* and *Zanga*. The *Zanga* was lost at Sound Point. All of its cargo was saved.

Hispaniola

Although there are a great number of interesting shipwrecks around this huge island very little salvage work has been undertaken. Both the governments of Haiti and the Dominican Republic have laws regarding the salvaging of shipwrecks by foreigners.

Only about a dozen shipwreck projects have been undertaken in the past ten years.

In 1955, millionaire Edwin Link and Mendel Peterson of the Smithsonian Institution attempted to locate Columbus's *Santa Maria*, which wrecked

at Cape Haitian in 1492. Although they didn't locate the shipwreck, they claimed to have discovered an iron anchor from it.

Over the years, dredging operations in the port of Santo Domingo have exposed large numbers of artifacts and gold and silver coins. Naval Officers have reported that they recovered several thousand gold coins from a shipwreck a few miles east of the port.

In many articles and books concerning sunken treasure, authors claim that the port of Puerto Plata (Silver Port) on the north coast of the island was a staging and departure port for homeward-bound Spanish treasure ships. In reality, the port was named the Silver Port for another reason. When Columbus first sighted it, the large mountain behind it was covered with a silver-colored cloud.

Another erroneous tale which appears in sunken treasure literature concerns a large table made of solid gold and supposedly lost in 1502 near Mona Island. The truth is that a very large gold nugget was found on the island, and when the governor wrote to Spain telling of the loss of the ship carrying the nugget, he said that it was big enough to eat off of, meaning that it was as large as a plate, not a table.

Weather and working conditions on shipwreck sites in Hispaniola are about the same as they are throughout the rest of the Caribbean. The calmest months are during the hurricane season . Of the more than 430 shipwrecks that have been lost around the island, only those whose locations are fairly accurate or those of major interest are given here. In many cases documents in the archives state simply that ships were lost on or at Hispaniola.

SHIPWRECKS IN HISPANIOLA'S WATERS

Active, Scottish merchantman, Captain Douglas
  Location: Isle-à-Vache
  History: The large merchantman was lost on the Isle-à-Vache on March 7, 1790, while sailing from Glasgow to Jamaica. The crew and part of the cargo were saved.

Ann, American ship, Captain Berchier
  Location: Aux Cayes
  History: During heavy gales from September 2 to 4, 1821, four merchantmen were wrecked at the Aux Cayes:

the *Peace, Rover, Ann* and an unidentified vessel.

Arethusa, English merchantman, Captain Dods
  Location: Isle of Ash
  History: The merchantman wrecked on the Isle of Ash in 1802 while sailing from London to Jamaica. The crew and part of the cargo were saved.

Atlas, French merchantman, Captain Tegail
  Location: Cape Francés
  History: The merchantman was lost while leaving the port of Cape Francés in 1749 en route to Bordeaux. The crew was saved.

Caerwent, English merchantman, Captain Browner
  Location: Jacmel Harbor
  History: The merchantman was lost on May 31, 1810, while departing from Jacmel Harbor, Haiti en route to London.

Catherine, ship of unknown registry, Captain Dohlin
  Location: Saona Island
  History: The ship was lost on December 19, 1808, on the reef at Saona Island while sailing from St. Thomas, Virgin Islands to Jacmel, Haiti.

Clement, French merchantman, Captain Omalin
  Location: Santo Domingo
  History: The merchantman was lost while departing from the port of Santa Domingo in 1792. She was en route to Bordeaux when she went down.

Commerce, American ship, Captain M'Knight
  Location: Cape St. Nicolas Mole
  History: The vessel was totally lost on Cape St. Nicolas Mole on June 10, 1822, while sailing from St. Thomas, Virgin Islands to Hispaniola. Her crew was saved.

Cornelia, ship of unknown registry, Captain Gilbert
  Location: Port of Jérémie
  History: The ship was lost in the port of Jérémie, on the northwest Tiburon Peninsula of Haiti, in 1798. She

Spanish galleon c. 1700.

was sailing to Charleston, South Carolina when she foundered.

Cornwallis, English ship, Captain M'Gowan
  Location: Neve Bay
  History: The vessel wrecked and was totally lost in a hurricane on August 25, 1785, at Neve Bay. She was sailing from Antigua to Port Royal, Jamaica when she went down. The crew was saved.

Delight, ship of unknown registry, Captain Anderson
  Location: Tortuga Island
  History: The ship was sailing from Grenada Island to Havana when she wrecked on June 3, 1783, at Tortuga Island. Part of her cargo was saved.

Diomede, 74-gun French warship
  Location: Santo Domingo
  History: Two French warships, the *Imperial* and *Diomede*, were sunk in 1806 during action with an English fleet, commanded by Vice-Admiral Sir J.T. Duckwork, off the port of Santo Domingo.

Dragon, 64-gun French warship
  Location: Cape François
  History: The warship wrecked at Cape François in 1762.

El Breton, ship belonging to the fleet of the lawyer Lucas Vázquez de Ayllon
  Location: Puerto Plata
  History: After the fleet of Lucas Vázquez de Ayllon reached Santo Domingo from Spain, one ship—the *El Breton*—was sent to carry colonists to new lands. However, bad weather forced the ship into Puerto Plata in 1505, where it sank at anchor.

Ellen, English ship
  Location: Aux Cayes
  History: The ship wrecked near Aux Cayes during a gale on September 27, 1810.

Ellis, English slave ship, Captain Rylands
  Location: Isle of Ash
  History: The ship was lost on the Isle of Ash in 1774 while sailing from Africa and Barbados to Jamaica. Her crew and all 450 slaves onboard were saved.

Favorite, English ship, Captain Hayward
  Location: St. Jago
  History: She wrecked on April 19, 1821, at St. Jago port while coming from Jamaica. Her crew was saved.

Felix, ship of unknown registry, Captain Condon
  Location: Cape Engano
  History: The ship was lost on Cape Engano on July 2, 1821.

Frederick William, American merchantman, Captain Henchman
  Location: Isle-à-Vache
  History: The vessel wrecked on the Isle-à-Vache on May 17, 1812, while sailing from Lisbon to Boston. Four of the crew perished.

Friendship, ship of unknown registry, Captain Reily
  Location: Cape François
  History: The ship wrecked at Cape François in 1784 while sailing from Dublin to Philadelphia.

Gallega, caravel belonging to Columbus

  Location: North coast
  History: On Columbus' second voyage, he founded a settlement on the north coast of Hispaniola and named it Isabela. Two of his caravels, the *Marigalante* and *Gallega*, are believed to have been lost there during a hurricane in 1494.

H.M.S. *Tartar*, 28-gun English warship, Captain Charles Elphinstone
  Location: Puerto de Plata
  History: The warship wrecked on July 1, 1797, while departing the port of Puerto de Plata. Her crew of 195 was saved.

H.M.S. *Cormorant*, 18-gun English sloop-of-war, Captain Thomas Gott
  Location: Port-au-Prince
  History: The sloop accidentally blew up at Port-au-Prince in 1796. Ninety-five out of her crew of 121 men were lost.

H.M.S. *Dunkirk Prize*, 24-gun English warship, Captain George Purvis
  Location: Off Cape Francés
  History: The warship ran up on a rock off Cape Francés and broke into pieces on October 18, 1706, while in pursuit of a French ship.

H.M.S. *Flying Fish*, 12-gun English schooner-of-war, Captain J. Glassford Gooding
  Location: East of Point Salines
  History: The schooner wrecked on December 15, 1808, on a reef east of Point Salines. Her crew was saved.

H.M.S. *Garland*, 22-gun English warship, Captain Frederick Cottrell
  Location: Cape François
  History: The ship wrecked at Cape François in November 1803.

H.M.S. *Salisbury*, 50-gun English warship
  Location: Isle d'Avanche
  History: The warship wrecked on May 13, 1796, on the Isle d'Avanche. Her entire crew of 343 men was saved.

H.M.S. *Tiger*, 50-gun English warship, Captain Edward Herbert
  Location: Tortuga Island
  History: The warship wrecked on a small key near Tortuga Island on January 12, 1742.

Honest Seaman, English ship
  Location: Porto Pina
  History: The ship was cast ashore at Porto Pina during a hurricane in September 1652.

Impérial, 120-gun French warship
  Location: Santo Domingo
  History: Two French warships, the *Imperial* and *Diomede*, were sunk in 1806 during action with an English fleet, commanded by Vice-Admiral Sir J.T. Duckwork, off the port of Santo Domingo.

Intelligence, English merchantman, Captain Hubbert
  Location: Cape François
  History: The merchantman was lost on January 2, 1772, while entering Cape François. Twenty-one slaves drowned and most of the cargo was lost.

Intrepid, American merchantman, Captain Crofts
  Location: Jacmel Harbor
  History: The merchantman wrecked in Jacmel Harbor, Haiti during a gale on January 30, 1821, while arriving from Charleston, South Carolina.

Jamaica Merchant, English privateering ship, Captain Knapman
  Location: East side of the Isle-à-Vache
  History: The privateering ship, operating out of Port Royal, Jamaica, wrecked on February 25, 1673, with Henry Morgan onboard. The ship wrecked on the east side of the Isle-à-Vache (also called Vaca and Vacour), due to the pilot's faulty navigation. Five or six days later they were rescued by another Jamaican privateering vessel and carried back to Jamaica. The governor of Jamaica sent salvage sloops to the wreck site; 20 large cannon and 212 cannonballs were recovered.

Jean Marie, French ship, Captain Bowie
  Location: Samana Bay
  History: The ship wrecked on the coast near Samana Bay around the end of May 1817 while sailing from Marseilles to Hispaniola. The crew and part of the cargo were saved.

Jefferson, American ship, Captain Marlore

Location: Isle-à-Vache
History: She was totally lost on January 10, 1823, on the Isle-à-Vache while sailing from Philadelphia to Dominica Island. Her crew was saved.

***Jume Eiema*,** French merchantman, Captain Camden
Location: Cape François
History: The merchantman was lost in the harbor of Cape François in 1792 after arriving from Bordeaux.

***La Candelaria*,** *nao*, 300 tons, Captain Juan de Patermina
Location: La Saona Island
History: The *nao* had set sail from Santo Domingo for Spain with three other *naos*; in 1626 they were all carrying products of the island. When near La Saona Island, three enemy ships gave chase and forced the *nao* to run aground on the small island, where it broke into pieces and sank.

***La Salvadora*,** *nao*, Captain Juan Rodríquez
Location: On the coast near Monte Cristi
History: The treasure-laden *nao* was caught in a storm in the Bahama Channel in 1553. After losing all her masts, she drifted until she wrecked on the coast of Hispaniola near Monte Cristi. All of her gold and silver was recovered.

***La Tolosa*,** *almiranta* of the Nueva España Flota (fleet) of Captain-General Baltasar de Guevara
Location: Cape Samana
History: The *flota* set sail from Veracruz on August 25, 1724. After leaving the Bahama Channel, it headed towards Bermuda, but due to a hurricane, the ships were forced to head south. An undisclosed number of them, carrying a great amount of treasure, were lost in the area of Samana Bay. The ships included the *Nuestra Señora de Guadalupe y San Antonio*, which sank on September 12 in deep water near the Samana Bay; the *La Tolosa*, which wrecked at Cape Samana and other merchant *naos* which wrecked on the reefs of the bay. Over 120 lives were lost. All the ships, with the exception of the *Nuestra Señora de Guadalupe y San Antonio*, were completely salvaged.

***Latona*,** American ship, Captain Low
Location: Samana Bay
History: The ship was lost in Samana Bay in 1818 while sailing from London to New Orleans. Her crew was saved.

***Lord Belhaven*,** Scottish merchantman
Location: Port-au Prince
History: The merchantman was lost about 20 miles from Port-au Prince in 1819 while sailing for there from Glasgow.

***Marigalante*,** caravel belonging to Columbus
Location: North coast
History: On Columbus' second voyage, he founded a settlement on the north coast of Hispaniola and named it Isabela. Two of his caravels, the *Marigalante* and *Gallega*, are believed to have been lost there during a hurricane in 1494.

***Mecca*,** French merchantman, Captain Merle
Location: Cape François
History: The merchantman wrecked near Cape François in 1770 while sailing from Hispaniola to Bordeaux.

***Nuestra Señora de Guadalupe y San Antonio*,** *capitana* (flagship) of the Nueva España Flota (fleet) of Captain-General Baltasar de Guevara
Location: Samana Bay
History: The *flota* set sail from Veracruz on August 25, 1724. After leaving the Bahama Channel, it headed towards Bermuda, but due to a hurricane, the ships were forced to turn south. An undisclosed number of vessels, carrying a great amount of treasure, were lost in the area of Samana Bay. The ships included the *Nuestra Señora de Guadalupe y San Antonio*, which sank on September 12 in deep water near the Samana Bay; the *La Tolosa*, which wrecked at Cape Samana; and other merchant *naos* which wrecked on the reefs of the bay. Over 120 lives were lost. All the ships, with the exception of the *Nuestra Señora de Guadalupe y San Antonio*, were completely salvaged.

***Oxford*,** English privateering frigate, 240 tons

Location: Isle of Ash
History: The ship, anchored at the Isle of Ash on January 12, 1669, had just returned from a successful attack on Porto Bello, Panama when it caught fire and blew up. She was carrying a great deal of plunder when she went down. Over 200 lives were lost in the incident.

***Peace*,** ship of unknown registry, Captain Clarkson
Location: Aux Cayes
History: During heavy gales from September 2 to 4, 1821, four merchantmen were wrecked at the Aux Cayes: the *Peace*, *Rover*, *Ann* and an unidentified vessel.

***Queen*,** English merchantman, Captain Sherwood
Location: Aux Cayes
History: The merchantman wrecked near the Aux Cayes in 1809 while sailing to London.

***Rover*,** American ship, Captain Johnson
Location: Aux Cayes
History: During heavy gales from September 2 to 4, 1821, four merchantmen were wrecked at the Aux Cayes: the *Peace*, *Rover*, *Ann* and an unidentified vessel.

***Roxano*,** American schooner
Location: Isle of Ash
History: The schooner was lost on the Isle of Ash in 1817 while coming from Nantucket. The crew and part of the cargo were saved.

***Sally*,** ship of unknown registry, Captain Brockesby
Location: Puerto Principe
History: The ship was totally lost near Puerto Principe in 1819 while sailing from Amsterdam to Havana.

***San Bartolome*,** *nao*, 120 tons, Captain Blas Alonso
Location: On the coast close to the port of Santo Domingo
History: The *nao* was wrecked on the coast close to the port of Santo Domingo in 1556 shortly after sailing for Spain. Divers recovered her cargo of gold, silver and hides.

***San Juan*,** *nao*, 200 tons, Captain Martín de Zavalo

Location: Puerto Hermosa

History: The ship wrecked in Puerto Hermosa during a hurricane in 1547 while sailing from Spain to Nombre de Dios, Panama. Another account gives the date as 1549.

San Miguel, *nao* belonging to the fleet of Admiral Francisco de Montejo

Location: Cape Cabrón

History: The *nao* was lost in 1542 near Cape Cabrón, about 15 leagues from Puerto Plata, while sailing from Santo Domingo to Spain. She was carrying a large amount of gold and silver when she went down.

San Miguel, Spanish galleon, 200 tons, Captain Salvador Garrido

Location: Between Cape Francés and Cape Cabrón

History: The *flotas* (fleets) of the Nueva España and Tierra Firme joined in Havana with the Armada de Tierra Firme, commanded by Captain-General Sancho de Veidma for the return to Spain. After entering the Bahama channel in 1551, the galleon *San Miguel,* owned by the viceroy of Mexico, Don Luis de Velasco, lost her mainmast and rudder during a storm. The galleon drifted until it wrecked on a reef between Cape Francés and Cape Cabrón, about 30 leagues from Puerto de Plata. All the people onboard were saved, and divers recovered all of the valuable cargo of gold and silver specie and bullion onboard.

Santa Maria, caravel, Columbus' flagship

Location: In Caracol Bay, near Cape Haitian

History: Columbus' flagship, the *Santa Maria,* was wrecked on a reef in Caracol Bay, near Cape Haitian, in 1492. He had the survivors from the wreck completely strip the ship of all its wood, fittings and supplies. His intention was for them to use the materials to build a fort, to give them shelter and protection until he could return to rescue them on his second voyage. If anything of the wreck of this legendary vessel remains on the reef, it would probably only be ballast stone, if the ship carried any.

Santa María, *nao,* 110 tons, Captain Pedro Núñez

Location: Puerto Plata

History: The *nao* sank in 1526 in Puerto Plata after loading a cargo of sugar onboard. Other accounts place the sinking in 1524 and 1525.

Santa María de Guadalupe, *nao,* 250 tons, Captain Salvador Gómez

Location: Monte Cristi

History: In 1564, after receiving a cargo of gold and silver from a ship that had sunk in the Bahama Channel during a storm, *Santa María de Guadalupe* lost her masts and drifted until she wrecked near Monte Cristi. Divers later recovered all the treasure she carried.

Santiago, oared galley

Location: Puerto de Plata

History: The galley, sent from Santo Domingo to search for pirates, was wrecked on the reefs in front of Puerto de Plata in 1584. All the galley slaves perished.

San Vicente Ferrer, *navío,* 84 tons, Captain Gaspar Alvarez

Location: Near Samana Bay

History: The vessel wrecked near Samana Bay in 1609 while sailing from Puerto Rico to Havana and Spain. Only her crew was saved.

Scipion, 74-gun French warship

Location: Cape François

History: Two large English warships drove this French warship ashore near Cape François on October 18, 1782.

Shark, English ship

Location: Port-au-Prince

History: The ship was accidentally burnt at Port-au-Prince about February 4, 1816, while arriving from London.

Swallow, Jamaican cutter, Captain Robertson

Location: Isle-à-Vache

History: Due to strong currents, the cutter wrecked on Isle-à-Vache on November 12, 1824, while sailing from Jamaica to Barbados. The crew and part of the cargo were saved.

Tounant, French warship belonging to the fleet of the Count D'Estaing

Location: Cape François

History: The ship was badly damaged in a storm and sank a few days afterward at Cape François, around the beginning of December 1779.

Unidentified, ship

Location: Aux Cayes

History: During heavy gales from September 2 to 4, 1821, four merchantmen were wrecked at the Aux Cayes: the *Peace, Rover, Ann* and an unidentified vessel.

Unidentified, *naos* (undisclosed number)

Location: Cape Samana

History: The *flota* (fleet) set sail from Veracruz on August 25, 1724. After leaving the Bahama Channel, it headed towards Bermuda, but due to a hurricane, the ships were forced to turn south. An undisclosed number of vessels, carrying a great amount of treasure, were lost in the area of Samana Bay. The ships included the *Nuestra Señora de Guadalupe y San Antonio,* which sank on September 12 in deep water near the Samana Bay; the *La Tolosa,* which wrecked at Cape Samana, and other merchant *naos* which wrecked on the reefs of the bay. Over 120 lives were lost. All the ships, with the exception of the *Nuestra Señora de Guadalupe y San Antonio,* were completely salvaged.

Unidentified, ships (26)

Location: Hispaniola

History: A large fleet of 30 caravels and *naos* were in the port of Santo Domingo in 1502 and preparing to sail for Spain. Columbus was in the port at the same time and attempted to prevent their departure, claiming there were signs of a hurricane. However, Governor Bodadilla, who was his enemy, would not heed his advice, and the fleet sailed despite Columbus' warnings. The fleet, commanded by Admiral Antonio de Torres and carrying a large amount of gold (including a gold nugget the size of a plate) and other valuables left port around the beginning of July. About 30 or 40 hours later the hurricane struck and all but four ships were lost. Most of them were wrecked on the coast eight or ten leagues east of the port. Others sank on the high seas near Mona Island. Over 500 persons perished.

Unidentified, ships (18 or 20)
   Location: Hispaniola
   History: Eighteen or 20 ships of various sizes, including several that Columbus' son, Diego, had just brought from Spain, were sunk during a hurricane in 1509 in the port of Santo Domingo. A smaller vessel owned by Mariscal was wrecked on the small key of Alto Velo, located 50 leagues west of the port, with six of the eight persons aboard drowning.

Unidentified, ships (many)
   Location: Hispaniola
   History: Sixteen merchantmen, loaded and ready to set sail for Seville, were totally lost during a hurricane that struck the port of Santo Domingo in 1553. At the same time, three *naos* and one patache, commanded by Cristobal Colón (the nephew of the famous discoverer), were also lost on the coast.

Unidentified, ship
   Location: Hispaniola
   History: Pirates had been living on Tortuga for about six years when the Spaniards launched an attack on the island in 1635. During the attack, the Spaniards burnt two ships and one pinnace after murdering all the pirates and their families.

Unidentified, French pirate ship
   Location: Iaguana
   History: The pirate ship with a crew of 150 men was wrecked on the coast of Iaguana in 1551 with only a few escaping.

Unidentified, ships (3)
   Location: Isle-à-Vache
   History: Privateer Henry Morgan was waiting for other ships to join his fleet when a storm blew up in October 1670. Ten of his 11 ships were run ashore on the Isle-à-Vache. All but three of the ships were refloated.

Unidentified, Haitian vessels (about 10)
   Location: Jérémie
   History: Ten Haitian vessels were driven ashore at Jérémie during a gale on September 27, 1810.

Unidentified, Spanish merchantman
   Location: Mona Island

History: A small French pirate vessel, with a crew of only 35 men, captured and plundered a large Spanish merchantman and then wrecked it on Mona Island in 1541.

Unidentified, Spanish advice boat
   Location: Mona Island
   History: The boat was lost on Mona Island in 1605 while en route from Spain to Santo Domingo.

Unidentified, French privateer
   Location: Monte Cristi
   History: An English privateer forced the large French privateer to run ashore near Monte Cristi in 1747. Her crew was saved.

Unidentified, Dutch warship
   Location: Near the port of Santo Domingo
   History: The warship wrecked during a storm in 1631 near the port of Santo Domingo.

Unidentified, French ships (28)
   Location: Northwestern tip of Hispaniola
   History: Twenty-eight French ships were lost near the northwestern tip of the island during a violent gale at the end of August 1772. Two hundred eighty bodies were washed ashore the following morning.

Unidentified, caravels (six or seven)
   Location: Port of Isabela
   History: Six or seven caravels were reported lost in the port of Isabela due to a hurricane in October 1495. One account states that two of Columbus' ships, the *San Juan* and *Cordera*, and four ships of the explorer Juan Aquardo were lost. Another account states that these six plus another of Columbus' ships, named the *Gallega*, were lost. This second account may be confusing the loss of the *Gallega* during the hurricane in 1494.

Unidentified, ships (50+)
   Location: Port-au-Prince
   History: More than 25 ships were lost during a hurricane on August 16, 1788, at Port-au-Prince. Another 25 were wrecked on the coast nearby.

Unidentified, ships (many)
   Location: Port-au-Prince

History: All the shipping at Port-au-Prince was wrecked or sunk during a hurricane on September 19, 1816.

Unidentified, *naos* (2)
   Location: Puerto Principe
   History: Two unidentified *naos* of the captains Rodrigo de Bastidas and Juan de la Cosa were lost in Puerto Principe in 1501. They were carrying cargoes of gold nuggets and dust as well as brazilwood and other products when they went down.

Unidentified, brig
   Location: Puerto Principe
   History: The brig was lost on July 30, 1819, at Port-au-Prince while sailing to England.

Unidentified, ship of Captain Alonso Durán
   Location: Puerto Real
   History: The ship was wrecked in the port sometime before April 1528.

Unidentified, nao
   Location: Samana Bay
   History: The vessel wrecked in Samana Bay in 1721 while sailing from Spain to Veracruz.

Unidentified, caravels and *naos* (20+)
   Location: Santo Domingo
   History: Most of the town of Santo Domingo was leveled to the ground and more than 20 unidentified caravels and *naos* were sunk or wrecked in the port or along the nearby coast during a hurricane on August 3, 1508. When the hurricane first struck, the crews of many ships also threw their cannon overboard in the port to lighten them.

Unidentified, ships (18 to 20)
   Location: Santo Domingo
   History: Two hurricanes struck the town and port of Santo Domingo in 1545. The first occurred on August 20 and many ships in port were lost. The second, which was even worse, occurred on September 18. This hurricane destroyed all the ships that had not been lost in the first hurricane. Roughly ten ships were lost in the Ozama River in the port, five near the fort, several others by the house of Columbus, more on the coast near the port, and one ship of Captain Cruzado on Saona Island. The total number of

ships lost during this second hurricane was 18 to 20.

Unidentified, ships (large number)
  Location: Santo Domingo
  History: During a hurricane on October 5, 1737, the whole town at the port of Santo Domingo was leveled to the ground and a large number of ships were wrecked or sunk in the harbor.

Unidentified, merchantmen (12)
  Location: Santo Domingo
  History: Twelve merchantmen were wrecked and more than 1,700 hogsheads of sugar were lost with them at the port of Santo Domingo during a hurricane in September 1754.

Unidentified, Portuguese slave ship, Captain Juan Bautista Pluma

  Location: Santo Domingo Harbor
  History: The slave ship was sunk in Santo Domingo Harbor in 1658. The divers who recovered 12 iron cannon of six- to eight-pound shot from the wreck were paid 108 reals in silver.

Unidentified, caravels (2)
  Location: Shoals of Babura
  History: Two unidentified caravels of the explorer Vicente Yañez Pinzon were wrecked during a storm in 1500 on the Shoals of Babura.

Unidentified, merchant *nao* belonging to the Nueva España Flota (fleet) of Captain-General Fulgencio de Meneses
  Location: Southern coast of the island
  History: The ship wrecked in 1603

on the southern coast of the island while sailing from Spain to Veracruz.

Unidentified, French ships
  Location: The port of Petit-Gonâve
  History: A Dutch fleet attacked all the French ships in the port of Petit-Gonâve in 1677. After sacking the ships they burnt them.

Unidentified, ships (3)
  Location: Tiberoon Bay
  History: In 1757, the English warship, H.M.S. *Assistance*, chased two French privateering vessels, along with an English vessel they had captured, into Tiberoon Bay, where the French had a fort. The French burnt all three vessels near the shore under the guns of the fort.

Jamaica

Over 900 ships of many nationalities and descriptions have been lost in Jamaican waters. Of these, there are very few Spanish shipwrecks due to the fact that the island was one of the least important colonies in Spanish-America and very few ships visited the island. The inhabitants were very poor and unable to purchase goods from Spain. They did not have precious metals or other products to ship back to Spain either. There were ten-year periods during the 16th and 17th centuries when no large ship put in at Jamaica. It wasn't until the English captured the island in 1655 that it prospered; then large numbers of ships visited.

Jamaica does have one of the most important marine archaeological sites in the Western Hemisphere, the sunken city of Port Royal. An earthquake and a tidal wave struck there in 1692. They caused nine tenths of the city to sink or slide into the sea, creating a time capsule of history similar to the city of Pompeii, which was destroyed by a volcanic eruption.

In the past two decades, there have been at least ten large-scale treasure expeditions to Pedro shoals. Although many interesting artifacts have been recovered from wreck sites, very little treasure has been found. The Jamaican government has enforced strict laws concerning old shipwrecks. In 1967 and 1968, three American diving groups were arrested for illegally diving there. The government now requires a salvage group to apply for a permit and post a $10,000 bond as a guarantee that the shipwreck will be excavated properly and the salvors won't disappear with their recovery before splitting it with the government.

Jamaica offers one of the most unattractive agreements of any country in the Western Hemisphere. It receives 100 percent of all artifacts recovered, as well as 50 percent of any treasure that is recovered. It also has the right to purchase any or all of the 50 percent of the treasure belonging to the salvor at bullion value. Unless the Jamaican government makes a more attractive division arrangement with potential

salvors, there probably won't be any serious work undertaken on the numerous shipwrecks in these waters.

Due to the vast number of shipwrecks in Jamaican waters, only the wrecks for which a fairly exact location is given in the archives or those of special interest are listed in this chapter.

SHIPWRECKS IN JAMAICAN WATERS

Active, ship, Captain Williams
  Location: Montego Bay
  History: Seven ships were wrecked or sunk in a gale at Montego Bay in the year 1793. They were: the *Langrest*, *Active*, *Young Eagle*, and *Palliseer*, all arriving from London; and three others that were not identified.

Active, American merchantman
  Location: Near Port Royal
  History: The merchantman wrecked near Port Royal on May 14, 1811, while

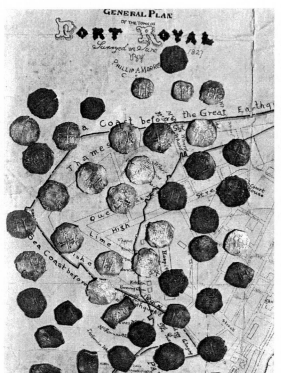

Old chart of Port Royal with Spanish pieces of eight recovered from the sunken city.

arriving from Boston. Part of her cargo was saved.

Agnes, American ship, Captain Livingston
  Location: Annotto Bay
  History: The ship wrecked entering Annotto Bay on December 23, 1816, while arriving from Charleston, South Carolina.

Almiranta, Spanish galleon belonging to the Tierra Firme Flota (fleet) of Marqués de Vado, Admiral Leonardo de Lara
  Location: Pedro Shoals
  History: Four galleons wrecked on Pedro Shoals in 1691 while sailing between Cartagena and Havana. Seven hundred and seventy-six persons were saved from the shipwrecks by fishing boats from Port Royal. The ships were the *Almiranta*, *Nuestra Señora del Carmen*, *Nuestra Señora de la Concepción*, and *Santa Cruz*. As soon as the Spaniards abandoned the wrecks a large

number of salvage sloops from Port Royal descended upon them and began salvage operations. England and Spain were at peace at this time and the Spaniards demanded all the treasure recovered. The British agreed that the treasure should be seized and turned over to the Spaniards; however, many chests of treasure were concealed by the salvors, so there is no way to know just how much was salvaged. The Spaniards also carried on their own salvage operations and as late as 1698 salvage boats from Havana were recovering cannon from the wrecks.

Anaconda, ship of unknown registry, Captain Pinel
  Location: Montego Bay
  History: The ship wrecked near Montego Bay in 1816 while sailing to Philadelphia. Part of its cargo was saved.

Ann, English merchantman, Captain Fortune
  Location: Near Oracabeza
  History: The ship capsized and sank near Oracabeza on August 1, 1819, while sailing to Cuba. The crew was saved.

Ann & Mary, English merchantman, Captain Graham
  Location: Kingston
  History: The merchantman wrecked on rocks while leaving Kingston in 1783, bound for London.

Aurora, English troop ship, Captain Milner
  Location: Old Harbour
  History: The ship wrecked at Old Harbour in 1798.

Blagrove, English merchantman, Captain M'Neil

Location: Buckness Bay
  History: The ship sank in Buckness Bay in 1782 due to a leak. She had a cargo of sugar products onboard.

Briseis, warship of unknown registry
  Location: Pedro Point
  History: The ship was lost on November 5, 1816, at Pedro Point while sailing to Nassau. The crew and a great part of her stores were saved.

Britannia, English merchantman, Captain Compton
  Location: Buckner's Bay
  History: The merchantman was lost at Buckner's Bay in 1800 while sailing to London. None of her cargo was saved.

Brutus, American sloop, Captain Brakenbridge
  Location: Downers Bluff
  History: The sloop was lost at Downers Bluff on September 19, 1821.

Caesar, English merchantman, Captain Raffes
  Location: West of Port Morant
  History: The merchantman was lost on a reef west of Port Morant on July 23, 1770, while en route to London.

Capitana, caravel belonging to Columbus
  Location: St. Ann's Bay
  History: Both of Columbus' ships, the *Capitana* and *Santiago*, were lost in St. Ann's Bay in 1504 during his fourth and last voyage of discovery. After spending some months exploring along Panama and Central America, where he was forced to abandon two of his caravels, he started for Santo Domingo. Both the *Capitana* and *Santiago* were leaking badly from sea worms. Contrary winds prevented him from heading toward his destination when he was off the northern coast of Jamaica. With both ships barely afloat from the great amount of water in them, he was forced to enter St. Ann's Bay where he ran both ships aground to prevent them from sinking. Columbus dispatched a dugout canoe with a few men to the town of Santo Domingo, where there was a governor and assorted officials, to notify authorities of his plight. The remaining Spaniards stripped both caravels, using what they

A caravel from the time of Columbus.

could to construct crude shelters on shore, and abandoned the two hulls, which eventually sank into the soft sediment of the harbor. It wasn't until June 29, 1504, a year and four days later, that Columbus and his 115 men were rescued by a ship from Santo Domingo. In 1940, Samuel Eliot Morison explored the gently curving bay, which Columbus had called Santa Gloria, to determine where the *Capitana* and *Santiago* had been lost. Morison's estimate of the hulls' location was published in a chart in his Pulitzer Prize–winning book *Admiral of the Ocean Sea*. Using Morison's chart as a guide, coauthor Robert F. Marx, assisted by Dr. Harold Edgerton of M.I.T., located both shipwrecks in February 1968 using sonar developed by Dr. Edgerton. They carried out a small excavation and positively identified Columbus' ships. Despite their significance, these wrecks have still not been explored. Since what little remains of them is deep in fine sediment, normal underwater excavation

methods are less effective than the procedure of building a cofferdam around the site, pumping the water out and excavating as if on land. Columbus' caravels will remain safely ensconced in the waters of St. Ann's Bay until the money to excavate and conserve the remains can be raised.

Carletch, English ship, Captain Hamilton
   Location: Jack's Bay
   History: The ship was lost near Jack's Bay in 1798 while arriving from New Brunswick, Canada. Part of her cargo was saved.

Caton, ship of unknown registry, Captain Glyn
   Location: Kingston
   History: The ship was lost at Kingston in 1776 due to fire, after departing from Africa with a cargo of slaves, ivory and beeswax.

Cecelia, English slave ship, Captain Dunn
   Location: Morant Keys
   History: The ship wrecked in the year 1770 in the Morant Keys after departing from Africa with a cargo of slaves.

Chance, Jamaican sloop
   Location: Port Royal Harbor
   History: The sloop sank in Port Royal Harbor during a gale on July 18, 1813, while arriving from Cuba with a cargo of cotton.

Charles and Martha, ship, Captain Elston
   Location: Montego Bay
   History: Seven large ships sank at Montego Bay during a hurricane on February 23, 1780: the *Echo*, from London; the *Petersfield*, from Bristol; the *Nancy*, from Bristol; the *Hero*, from New York; the *Cornelia*, from New York; the *Orangefield*, from New York; and the *Charles and Martha*, from Liverpool.

Columbus, English ship, Captain Mason
   Location: Bluefields
   History: The ship was burnt at Bluefields in 1790 while laden with sugar products for Leith, England.

Cornelia, ship, Captain Smith
   Location: Montego Bay

History: Seven large ships sank at Montego Bay during a hurricane on February 23, 1780: the *Echo*, from London; the *Petersfield*, from Bristol; the *Nancy*, from Bristol; the *Hero*, from New York; the *Cornelia*, from New York; the *Orangefield*, from New York; and the *Charles and Martha*, from Liverpool.

Countess of Bute, Scottish ship
   Location: Sandy Reef Key
   History: The vessel was lost on Sandy Reef Key on February 8, 1821, while sailing between Kingston and Montego Bay. The crew was saved.

Craven, English merchantman, Captain Stewart
   Location: St. Mary's harbor
   History: The merchantman was lost leaving St. Mary's harbor in 1757 while sailing to London with a cargo of sugar products.

Culloden, English merchantman, Captain Harris
   Location: Port Morant
   History: The ship was lost entering Port Morant on the eastern end of the island in 1747 while coming from London.

Daedalus, English frigate
   Location: Bare Bush Key
   History: Wrecked at Bare Bush Key in Old Harbour in the year 1808. Three men drowned.

Dragon, English merchantman, Captain Wall
   Location: Port Morant
   History: The merchantman was lost on May 14, 1749, at Port Morant. Only the crew was saved.

Dragon, English merchantman, Captain Lawson
   Location: St. Ann's Bay
   History: The merchantman wrecked while leaving St. Ann's Bay with a cargo of sugar and rum in the year 1748. She was en route to London when she wrecked.

Dryade, English ship, Captain Hoisbro
   Location: Manchaneal Harbour
   History: The ship was lost on the reefs at the entrance to Manchaneal Harbour on April 15, 1808, while sailing to

London. The crew and a small part of the cargo were saved.

Duke of Cumberland, ship of unknown registry, Captain Le Geyt
   Location: Montego Bay
   History: The ship was lost entering Montego Bay in 1781 while arriving from St. Eustatius Island.

Duke of Wellington, Bahamian ship, Captain Chancellor
   Location: Montego Bay
   History: The ship wrecked in Montego Bay on November 11, 1818, while arriving from Norfolk, Virginia.

Echo, ship, Captain Cragie
   Location: Montego Bay
   History: Seven large ships sank at Montego Bay during a hurricane on February 23, 1780: the *Echo*, from London; the *Petersfield*, from Bristol; the *Nancy*, from Bristol; the *Hero*, from New York; the *Cornelia*, from New York; the *Orangefield*, from New York; and the *Charles and Martha*, from Liverpool.

Eliza, English ship, Captain Johnston
   Location: Grand Reef at Negril
   History: The vessel wrecked on the Grand Reef at Negril on March 8, 1816, while arriving from Canada.

Emerald, English merchantman, Captain Kilgour
   Location: Martha Bay
   History: In 1793, the merchantman struck on her own anchor and sank in Martha Bay with 400 hogsheads of sugar onboard.

Enterprize, English slave ship, Captain Wilson
   Location: Near Port Royal
   History: The ship, arriving from Africa with a cargo of slaves, wrecked on the reefs near Port Royal in the year 1787.

Exuma, Scottish merchantman, brig, Captain Aylward
   Location: Oracabeza
   History: The brig was wrecked by strong winds onshore at Oracabeza in 1791 and quickly went to pieces. She was bound for Dublin and loaded with sugar and rum when she was lost.

Fanny, English merchantman, Captain Boyd

   Location: Pidgeon Island
   History: The merchantman sank at Pidgeon Island in Old Harbour on March 8, 1765, while coming from London.

Five Sisters, Canadian ship
   Location: St. Ann's Bay
   History: The ship wrecked in St. Ann's Bay on December 20, 1817, while arriving from Nova Scotia. Some of her cargo was saved.

Fly, Jamaican sloop, Captain Saise
   Location: St. Ann's Bay
   History: The sloop was driven onshore by wind in St. Ann's Bay on November 18, 1791.

Fortune, English ship, Captain Saunders
   Location: Oracabeza
   History: Three merchantmen were lost at Oracabeza during a gale in 1802. They were the *Generous Planter*, *Fortune* and *William*.

Friendship, English snow, Captain Johnson
   Location: Three miles west of Annotto Bay
   History: The snow wrecked onshore three miles west of Annotto Bay in 1766 after departing from Tortola, Virgin Islands. The crew and part of the cargo were saved.

Generous Planter, English ship, Captain Beattie
   Location: Oracabeza
   History: Three merchantmen were lost at Oracabeza during a gale in 1802. They were the *Generous Planter*, *Fortune* and *William*.

Genovesa, 54-gun Spanish galleon, Captain Francisco Guiral
   Location: Pedro Shoals
   History: While sailing alone from Cartagena to Havana in 1730, the galleon struck on a reef on Pedro Shoals. She was carrying over three million pesos in gold and silver along with many important passengers, several of whom drowned with the crew. An English frigate, the H.M.S. *Experiment*, arrived soon after the ship wrecked and took off the survivors and a large amount of the treasure. Other salvage vessels arrived from Port Royal and

recovered an undisclosed amount of treasure along with many of the ship's cannon. However, the ship broke up within a few weeks and a great deal of the treasure was scattered and buried under sand. Over the years, various treasure hunters claimed to have located this wreck. After examining all the artifacts these treasure hunters recovered, coauthor Marx was able to determine that they had located a different Spanish shipwreck in the same area, one that dates from at least 50 years later.

Grace, English merchantman, Captain Cook
   Location: Rio Bueno
   History: The merchantman wrecked at Rio Bueno in 1802 and was a total loss.

Graciosa, Spanish ship
   Location: Bajo Nuevo Shoals
   History: The ship wrecked on Bajo Nuevo Shoals in April 1823 while sailing from Cadiz to Honduras. A Dutch schooner rescued the crew.

Greyhound, English merchantman, Captain Palliser
   Location: Cape Morant
   History: The merchantman, with a cargo of sugar, molasses, rum and some silver specie, was chased ashore near Cape Morant by two Spanish privateers in 1748.

Griffin, American ship, Captain Vassey
   Location: Port Royal Bank
   History: The ship wrecked on the Port Royal Bank on December 19, 1792, while sailing to Savannah.

Hankey, English ship, Captain Kirky
   Location: Port Antonio
   History: The ship sank in Port Antonio in 1795 while sailing to London. The crew and cargo were saved.

Hanna, English troop transport, Captain Harrison
   Location: Montego Bay
   History: The transport ship was lost in Montego Bay on September 1, 1810. The crew was saved.

Hannah, English merchantman, Captain Lenox

Location: Buckner's Bay

History: The ship, from Greenock, Scotland, was lost in Buckner's Bay on March 16, 1802, during a violent gale.

Happy Return, Jamaican sloop
   Location: Port Maria Harbour
   History: The sloop was lost on June 11, 1817, while departing from Port Maria Harbour with a cargo of sugar. The crew was saved.

Happy Success, English merchantman, Captain Paterson
   Location: Port Antonio
   History: The merchantman was lost leaving Port Antonio in 1748. She was en route to London. Part of her cargo was recovered.

Henry Addington, English ship, Captain Lacey
   Location: Barebush Cay
   History: The ship wrecked on Barebush Cay in Old Harbour on April 14, 1804, as it was arriving from London.

Hercules, ship of unknown registry, Captain Cushing
   Location: Pedro Point
   History: The ship wrecked at Pedro Point on March 3, 1806, while arriving from Boston and sailing to the Spanish Main.

Hero, ship, Captain Logget
   Location: Montego Bay
   History: Seven large ships sank at Montego Bay during a hurricane on February 23, 1780: the *Echo*, from London; the *Petersfield*, from Bristol; the *Nancy*, from Bristol; the *Hero*, from New York; the *Cornelia*, from New York; the *Orangefield*, from New York; and the *Charles and Martha*, from Liverpool.

Hibernia, English ship, Captain Vaas
   Location: Morant Keys
   History: The ship was lost on the Morant Keys on November 17, 1814, while arriving from Halifax.

H.M.S. *Albans*, 50-gun warship, Captain William Knight
   Location: Kingston Harbour and Port Royal
   History: Nine warships and 96 merchantmen were wrecked or sunk in Kingston Harbour and Port Royal during a hurricane in October 1744. Many

of the wharves and warehouses in Kingston, which were full of merchandise, were also carried into the harbor. Only five of the warships that were lost have been identified: H.M.S. *Albans*, H.M.S. *Greenwich*, H.M.S. *Bonetta*, H.M.S. *Thunder* and H.M.S. *Lark*. Many of the ships were refloated and a great amount of their cargoes recovered. Coauthor Marx has dived on over 30 different wreck sites from the disaster and recovered a wide variety of artifacts including ceramicware, bottles, clay pipes and cannonballs.

H.M.S. *Badger*, ship
   Location: Lucea Harbour
   History: Many ships were lost at various ports during a hurricane in October 1780. The H.M.S. *Badger* was sunk at Lucea Harbour. At Port Morant three large ships were thrown over a quarter of a mile onshore and were totally lost.

H.M.S. *Bonetta*, 14-gun warship, Captain William Lea
   Location: Kingston Harbour and Port Royal
   History: Nine warships and 96 merchantmen were wrecked or sunk in Kingston Harbor and Port Royal during a hurricane in October 1744. Many of the wharves and warehouses in Kingston, which were full of merchandise, were also carried into the harbor. Only five of the warships that were lost have been identified: H.M.S. *Albans*, H.M.S. *Greenwich*, H.M.S. *Bonetta*, H.M.S. *Thunder* and H.M.S. *Lark*. Many of the ships were refloated and a great amount of their cargoes recovered. Coauthor Marx has dived on over 30 different wreck sites from the disaster and recovered a wide variety of artifacts including ceramicware, bottles, clay pipes and cannonballs.

H.M.S. *Colibri*, 18-gun English warship, Captain John Thompson
   Location: Port Royal Harbour
   History: The warship wrecked in Port Royal Harbour prior to July 1813.

H.M.S. *Dwarf*, ten-gun English cutter, Captain Nicholas Gould
   Location: Kingston
   History: The cutter wrecked on a pier at Kingston on March 3, 1824. One man was lost.

H.M.S. *Fox*, 20-gun warship
   Location: Kingston Harbour
   History: Twenty-four merchant ships and one man-of-war, H.M.S. *Fox*, were lost in Kingston Harbour and at Port Royal during a hurricane on September 25, 1751. Four of the merchantmen were American, one was Dutch and the rest were English.

H.M.S. *Glasgow*, 24-gun English warship, Captain Thomas Lloyd
   Location: Kingston
   History: The ship was accidentally lost due to fire on June 19, 1779, at Kingston.

H.M.S. *Greenwich*, 50-gun warship, Captain Edward Allen
   Location: Jamaica
   Location: Kingston Harbour and Port Royal
   History: Nine warships and 96 merchantmen were wrecked or sunk in Kingston Harbour and Port Royal during a hurricane in October of 1744. Many of the wharves and warehouses in Kingston, which were full of merchandise, were also carried into the harbor. Only five of the warships that were lost have been identified: H.M.S. *Albans*, H.M.S. *Greenwich*, H.M.S. *Bonetta*, H.M.S. *Thunder* and H.M.S. *Lark*. Many of the ships were refloated and a great amount of their cargoes recovered. Coauthor Marx has dived on over 30 different wreck sites from the disaster and recovered a wide variety of artifacts including ceramicware, bottles, clay pipes and cannonballs.

H.M.S. *Halcyon*, English warship
   Location: Annotto Bay
   History: The ship wrecked off Annotto Bay in May 1814. The crew was saved.

H.M.S. *Hinchinbrooke*, 20-gun English warship, Captain Nelson
   Location: St. Ann's Bay
   History: The warship wrecked on a reef off St. Ann's Bay in 1782. The wreck was reported as being located by a Jamaican diver in 1965.

H.M.S. *Lark*, warship, no guns
   Location: Jamaica
   History: Nine warships and 96 merchantmen were wrecked or sunk in Kingston Harbour and Port Royal

during a hurricane in October 1744. Many of the wharves and warehouses in Kingston, which were full of merchandise, were also carried into the harbor. Only five of the warships that were lost have been identified: H.M.S. *Albans*, H.M.S. *Greenwich*, H.M.S. *Bonetta*, H.M.S. *Thunder* and H.M.S. *Lark*. Many of the ships were refloated and a great amount of their cargoes recovered. Coauthor Marx has dived on over 30 different wreck sites from the disaster and recovered a wide variety of artifacts including ceramicware, bottles, clay pipes and cannonballs.

H.M.S. *Meleager*, 36-gun English warship, Captain Frederick Warren
Location: Bare Bush Key
History: The ship wrecked at Bare Bush Key in Old Harbour on July 30, 1808. The wreck was located and a large anchor raised, which is now on display in Port Royal.

H.M.S. *Orquijo*, 18-gun English warship, Captain Charles Balderson
Location: Jamaica
History: The warship foundered near Jamaica in October 1805.

H.M.S. *Pelican*, 24-gun ship, Captain Cuthbert Collingwood
Location: Morant Keys
History: Many ships were destroyed during a hurricane that struck Jamaica on August 1 and 2 in the year 1781. Ninety ships of various descriptions were wrecked or sunk in Kingston Harbour. Another 30 were lost at Port Royal and 73 more in other ports of the island. H.M.S. *Pelican* was wrecked on the Morant Keys. This wreck was discovered by a group of treasure hunters from Florida who recovered a small bronze cannon, one gold coin and other artifacts. They were only able to work on the site for one day before being driven away by a Jamaican naval launch.

H.M.S. *Redbridge*, ten-gun English warship, schooner, Captain Francis Blower
Location: Jamaica
History: The ship foundered near Jamaica in May of 1805.

H.M.S. *Rhodion*, English brig-of-war
Location: Port Royal

History: The brig wrecked onshore two miles from Port Royal on February 20, 1813, while arriving from Porto Bello.

H.M.S. *Rose*, 28-gun English warship, Captain Mathew Henry Scott
Location: Rocky Point
History: The warship wrecked on June 28, 1794, at Rocky Point.

H.M.S. *St. Pierre*, English warship, Captain Christopher Paule
Location: Point Negrille
History: The warship wrecked on February 12, 1796, on rocks off Point Negrille.

H.M.S. *Thunder*, eight-gun warship, Captain Thomas Gregory
Location: Jamaica
History: Nine warships and 96 merchantmen were wrecked or sunk in Kingston Harbor and Port Royal during a hurricane in October 1744. Many of the wharves and warehouses in Kingston, which were full of merchandise, were also carried into the harbor. Only five of the warships that were lost have been identified: H.M.S. *Albans*, H.M.S. *Greenwich*, H.M.S. *Bonetta*, H.M.S. *Thunder* and H.M.S. *Lark*. Many of the ships were refloated and a great amount of their cargoes recovered. Coauthor Marx has dived on over 30 different wreck sites from the disaster and recovered a wide variety of artifacts including ceramicware, bottles, clay pipes and cannonballs.

H.M.S. *Undaunted*, 38-gun English warship, Captain Robert Winthrop
Location: Point Negrille
History: The warship wrecked on August 27, 1796, in the Morant Keys. She was originally the French warship *Aréthuse* until the English captured her.

Hope, Scottish ship
Location: Palisadoes
History: The ship was lost on the Palisadoes, near Port Royal, in 1797 while arriving from Glasgow.

Humphreys, English ship, Captain Hastings
Location: Half Moon Key
History: The ship was wrecked on Half Moon Key near Old Harbour on

February 28, 1810, while sailing to Honduras.

Industry, English ship, Captain Haste
Location: Palisadoes
History: The ship wrecked on the Palisadoes, several miles east of Port Royal, while arriving from Liverpool in 1770. She was a total loss.

Industry, English merchantman, Captain Graham
Location: Port Morant
History: The merchantman was lost off Port Morant in 1748 while sailing from Boston to Kingston.

Isabella, American ship, Captain Roach
Location: Morant Keys
History: The ship wrecked on the Morant Keys in February 1817 while sailing to Philadelphia.

Jamaica, English merchantman, Captain Clarke
Location: John's Point
History: The ship was totally lost on John's Point on June 30, 1805, during a gale. Some of her cargo of rum was saved.

Jamaica Planter, American ship, Captain M'Fadzen
Location: Plumb Point
History: The ship was lost on Plumb Point, near Port Royal, in 1774 after departing from Boston with a cargo of trade goods.

Jane, American ship, Captain Rust
Location: Montego Bay
History: The vessel wrecked in Montego Bay on February 14, 1807, while arriving from Boston.

Jesús, María y José, Spanish advice boat, 80 tons
Location: North coast of Jamaica
History: The small advice boat, sent from Veracruz to Santo Domingo, wrecked on the north coast of Jamaica in the year 1699.

Johanna, English brig, Captain Caldwell
Location: Montego Bay
History: The brig wrecked in Morant Bay in 1817.

Johanna, Dutch ship, Captain Benoist
Location: Rocky Point
History: The ship wrecked on a reef

off Rocky Point in 1822 while sailing to Curaçao. The crew and cargo were saved.

John, English merchantman, Captain Churnside
Location: John's Point
History: The merchantman wrecked at John's Point, near the west end of the island, in 1785 while sailing to Bristol. Part of her cargo was saved.

John Shand, Jamaican cutter, Captain Tucker
Location: Port Morant
History: The cutter was totally lost in Port Morant on January 1, 1819.

Julian, Bermudan ship, Captain Brown
Location: Orange Bay
History: The ship wrecked at Orange Bay in 1819 while sailing to Bermuda. The crew and cargo were saved.

Jupiter, English merchantman, Captain Plank
Location: Rio Bueno
History: The ship was burnt at Rio Bueno in 1802 and was a total loss.

King David, English merchantman, Captain Broad
Location: Port Royal Harbor
History: The merchantman sank in 1770 in Port Royal Harbor when it struck upon a large anchor sticking up from the sea floor.

King George, English merchantman, Captain Eilbeck
Location: Pedro Point
History: The merchantman was lost on Pedro Point in the year 1800 while sailing from Kingston to London. The crew was saved.

La Andalucía, Spanish galleon
Location: Pedro Shoals
History: The large galleon wrecked on Pedro Shoals on June 9, 1755, while sailing alone from Cartagena to Spain. Her treasure and crew were saved.

Lady Milford, English ship, Captain Higgs
Location: Savanna la Mar
History: The ship was lost on a reef near Savanna la Mar in 1801 while sailing to London. The crew and part of the cargo were saved.

Langrest, ship, Captain Fitzhenry
Location: Montego Bay
History: Seven ships were wrecked or sunk in a gale at Montego Bay in the year 1793. They were: the *Langrest, Active, Young Eagle,* and *Palliseer,* all arriving from London; and three others that were not identified.

La Trinidad, *capitana* (flagship), 350 tons, Captain Manuel de Rodas
Location: South side of Jamaica
History: Captain-General Alvaro Manrique was traveling on this ship when it was lost on the south side of Jamaica in 1579. There were no details in documents on whether it was carrying any treasure at the time.

Leander, English merchantman, Captain Keen
Location: Alligator Pond
History: The ship was totally lost at Alligator Pond in 1812 as it was arriving from Liverpool.

London, English merchantman, Captain Hayes
Location: Old Harbour
History: The merchantman was almost fully loaded for her voyage to London in 1741 when she was accidentally destroyed by fire in Old Harbour.

Lowland Lass, Canadian ship, Captain Kyle
Location: St. Mary's Bay
History: The ship was totally lost in St. Mary's Bay in 1821 while arriving from New Brunswick. The crew was saved.

Lyon, English merchantman, Captain Irwin
Location: Oracabeza
History: The merchantman was lost in 1769 while departing from the harbor of Oracabeza and sailing to London.

Mackerel, English ship, Captain Thompson
Location: Port Morant
History: The ship wrecked on September 20, 1821, near Port Morant while sailing to the Spanish Main.

Margaret, English merchantman, Captain Goodwin

***Location:* Manchaneal Harbour
History: The merchantman was lost in Manchaneal Harbour on July 12, 1804, while sailing for London.

Maria, English merchantman
Location: Near Port Royal
History: The vessel was lost on a reef near Port Royal in 1796 while en route to Exeter, England.

Marianne, English merchantman
Location: Near Port Royal
History: She wrecked on the reefs near Port Royal in 1787 while arriving from Santo Domingo.

Mariner, English merchantman, Captain Allurd
Location: Oracabeza
History: The ship wrecked at Oracabeza in December 1812 while en route to London.

Marquis of Grandby, English ship, Captain Calvert
Location: Portland Bight
History: The ship struck a rock near Portland Bight in 1764 and quickly went to pieces. She was coming from London. Only her crew was saved.

Martins, English ship, Captain Ramsey
Location: Morant Keys
History: The ship wrecked on the Morant Keys on December 14, 1820, while sailing from Coro, Venezuela to Kingston. The crew and most of the cargo of mules were saved.

Mary, American schooner, Captain Eswell
Location: Morant Bay
History: The schooner wrecked in Morant Bay in 1817.

Mary, Jamaican schooner, Captain Brackenbridge
Location: Orange Bay
History: The vessel wrecked in Orange Bay in 1815 while sailing from Kingston.

Mary, English merchantman, Captain Stafford
Location: Port Maria
History: The merchantman, bound for London, wrecked at Port Maria during a gale on December 18, 1810. Her cargo of 167 hogsheads of sugar was lost.

Mary, American schooner, Captain White
   Location: St. Ann's Bay
   History: The schooner was totally lost in St. Ann's Bay on December 25, 1803.

Mary Ann, English merchantman, Captain Bannerman
   Location: Oracabeza
   History: The merchantman wrecked in a gale at Oracabeza in the year 1800.

Mary Charlotte, ship of unknown registry, Captain Richards
   Location: Montego Bay
   History: The ship was lost at Montego Bay in 1822. The crew was saved.

Mercater, Scottish merchantman
   Location: Port Royal Keys
   History: The merchantman wrecked on the Port Royal Keys prior to July 1813 while sailing to Glasgow.

Metcalf, English merchantman
   Location: Port Maria
   History: The merchantman, bound for London, was lost in April 1814 while sailing out of Port Maria.

Minerva, English merchantman, Captain Smith
   Location: Jamaica
   History: The merchantman was accidentally burnt on April 19, 1768, while loading for a voyage to London. She had 300 hogsheads of sugar and 17 puncheons of rum onboard when she was destroyed. Very little of the cargo was saved.

Minerva, American ship, Captain Harding
   Location: Plantain Garden
   History: The ship was lost at Plantain Garden in 1805 while sailing to Boston.

Montfort, English ship, Captain Clutson
   Location: Morant Keys
   History: The vessel wrecked on the Morant Keys in 1755 while sailing from Kingston to Bristol. Several chests of specie were recovered.

Nancy, ship, Captain Marshall
   Location: Montego Bay
   History: Seven large ships sank at Montego Bay during a hurricane on February 23, 1780: the *Echo*, from London; the *Petersfield*, from Bristol; the *Nancy*, from Bristol; the *Hero*, from New York; the *Cornelia*, from New York; the *Orangefield*, from New York; and the *Charles and Martha*, from Liverpool.

Nuestra Señora de la Concepción, Spanish merchant *nao*, Captain Joaquin Fernández
   Location: Morant Keys
   History: The ship wrecked on the Morant Keys on November 15, 1783, while sailing from Cartagena to Cadiz. Only a small part of her cargo was salvaged.

Nuestra Señora de la Concepción, Spanish galleon belonging to the Tierra Firme Flota (fleet) of Marqués de Vado, Captain Pedro Azpil Cueta
   Location: Pedro Shoals
   History: Four galleons wrecked on Pedro Shoals in 1691 while sailing between Cartagena and Havana. Seven hundred and seventy-six persons were saved from the shipwrecks by fishing boats from Port Royal. The ships were the *Almiranta, Nuestra Señora del Carmen, Nuestra Señora de la Concepción*, and *Santa Cruz*. As soon as the Spaniards abandoned the wrecks, a large number of salvage sloops from Port Royal descended upon them and began salvage operations. England and Spain were at peace at this time and the Spaniards demanded all the treasure recovered. The British agreed that the treasure should be seized and turned over to the Spaniards; however, many chests of treasure were concealed by the salvors, so there is no way to know just how much was salvaged. The Spaniards also carried on their own salvage operations and as late as 1698 salvage boats from Havana were recovering cannon from the wrecks.

Nuestra Señora del Amparo, Spanish warship
   Location: Morant Keys
   History: The large warship, carrying a valuable cargo of mercury and wine, wrecked in the Morant Keys in 1810 while sailing from Spain to Veracruz.

Nuestra Señora del Carmen, Spanish galleon belonging to the Tierra Firme Flota (fleet) of Marqués de Vado, Captain Salvador Velez de Guevara
   Location: Pedro Shoals
   History: Four galleons wrecked on Pedro Shoals in 1691 while sailing between Cartagena and Havana. Seven hundred and seventy-six persons were saved from the shipwrecks by fishing boats from Port Royal. The ships were the *Almiranta, Nuestra Señora del Carmen, Nuestra Señora de la Concepción*, and *Santa Cruz*. As soon as the Spaniards abandoned the wrecks, a large number of salvage sloops from Port Royal descended upon them and began salvage operations. England and Spain were at peace at this time and the Spaniards demanded all the treasure recovered. The British agreed that the treasure should be seized and turned over to the Spaniards; however, many chests of treasure were concealed by the salvors, so there is no way to know just how much was salvaged. The Spaniards also carried on their own salvage operations and as late as 1698 salvage boats from Havana were recovering cannon from the wrecks.

Ohio, American ship, Captain Sinclair
   Location: Plantain Garden River
   History: The ship wrecked in Plantain Garden River on November 14, 1811, while arriving from Portsmouth, England.

Old Dick, English slave ship, Captain Birdy
   Location: Near Morant Bay
   History: The vessel wrecked near Morant Bay in 1796 while arriving from Africa with a cargo of slaves, gold dust and ivory. The slaves and part of the cargo were saved.

Orangefield, ship, Captain Farris
   Location: Montego Bay
   History: Seven large ships sank at Montego Bay during a hurricane on February 23, 1780: the *Echo*, from London; the *Petersfield*, from Bristol; the *Nancy*, from Bristol; the *Hero*, from New York; the *Cornelia*, from New York; the *Orangefield*, from New York; and the *Charles and Martha*, from Liverpool.

Pallas, American ship
   Location: Port Morant
   History: The ship was lost entering

Port Morant on March 24, 1780, while arriving from Charleston, South Carolina with trade goods.

Palliseer, ship, Captain James
Location: Montego Bay
History: Seven ships were wrecked or sunk in a gale at Montego Bay in the year 1793. They were: the *Langrest, Active, Young Eagle,* and *Palliseer,* all arriving from London; and three others that were not identified.

Pembeston, English merchantman, Captain Nunns
Location: Port Morant
History: The ship was lost entering Port Morant on the eastern end of the island in 1747 while coming from Liverpool.

Petersfield, ship, Captain Thomas
Location: Montego Bay
History: Seven large ships sank at Montego Bay during a hurricane on February 23, 1780: the *Echo,* from London; the *Petersfield,* from Bristol; the *Nancy,* from Bristol; the *Hero,* from New York; the *Cornelia,* from New York; the *Orangefield,* from New York; and the *Charles and Martha,* from Liverpool.

Phebe, English merchantman, Captain Lawson
Location: Morant Keys
History: The ship wrecked on September 17, 1752, on the Morant Keys while coming from Liverpool with a rich cargo of trade goods and some pieces of artillery for the island's forts.

Planet (or **Patent**), American merchantman
Location: Near Frankfork Bay
History: The merchantman wrecked near Frankfork Bay during a gale on October 18 and 19, 1815, while arriving from New York.

Portland, English merchantman, Captain Kendal
Location: Manchaneal Bay
History: The merchantman was lost in Manchaneal Bay in 1766 after arriving from London.

Port Royal, sunken city
History: Port Royal was founded very shortly after the British captured Jamaica from the Spaniards in 1655. It first served as a base for the English invasion fleet and soon afterward became the principal army garrison on the island. During the next decade, Port Royal was the most important buccaneering base in the West Indies. Henry Morgan is only one of hundreds of successful privateers who brought immense riches in plunder into the boozy, bawdy town from raids on Spanish settlements and shipping. When in 1670 Spain and England signed a peace treaty, the heyday of the privateers ceased but Port Royal continued to prosper. By 1692, Port Royal had been transformed from a deserted cay into the most important trading center in the New World. The spacious harbor was always crowded with shipping and the amount and variety of goods that passed over its wharves was astonishing. Contraband trade with the Spanish colonies brought in even greater riches than the plunder obtained by privateers. From historical documents we know that the town consisted of 2,000 buildings, the majority of which were brick, and many two stories high. The population was about 8,000. Although most contemporary accounts claim that the vast majority of the inhabitants were "Godless men," there were several Protestant churches (including a Quaker meeting house), a Roman Catholic chapel and a synagogue. The wharves, warehouses and houses of the wealthy merchants were located on the harbor, or north side of the town, where the water was deep enough for ships of large tonnage to tie up against the shore. Three large forts, Charles, James and Carlisle (the last two of which sank during the earthquake), as well as several smaller batteries, protected the town. The most outstanding buildings were the king's house, where the island's council met; the governor's house; St. Paul's Church; the Exchange, the center for the town's main business transactions; the Marhsalsea, a prison for men; and Bridewell, a prison for women. At 20 minutes before noon on June 7, 1692, disaster struck the famous pirate haven of Port Royal. An earthquake followed by a tidal wave sent nine-tenths of the city into the harbor. More than 2,000 lives were lost that day. During the next month an additional 3,000 people died from epidemics that followed. Most of the survivors moved across the harbor and founded the town of Kingston. Salvage operations began on the very day of the disaster and continued for many years. However, the bulk of what was lost to the earthquake and tidal wave was missed by the salvors because of deep water or collapsed buildings. The sunken city of Port Royal is considered the most important marine archaeological site in the Western Hemisphere. Coauthor Robert F. Marx, employed as the government marine archaeologist from 1965 to 1968, carried on excavation of a section of the sunken city, which remains the largest underwater excavation undertaken anywhere in the world. Marx positively identified the sunken city by matching Jamaican records with personal possessions and artifacts recovered from the site. Working conditions during the excavation were terrible. Underwater visibility was never more than a few inches and constant landslides of sediment into a hole where divers were working resulted in 24 accidents requiring medical attention. However, an incredible number of artifacts were recovered during the expedition. There were 50,000 coral-encrusted iron objects alone, such as tools, weapons, apothecaries' items, household articles, ships' fittings, and thousands of these are still awaiting preservation. Other artifacts included 2,000 glass bottles, 12,000 clay smoking pipes, over 500 pewter and silver items, 2,500 copper and brass items, two silver hoards of silver coins, and numerous pieces of valuable jewelry. Marx's excavation of the sunken city barely scratched the surface of this unique site. Because this section of Jamaica was slated to be dredged for use as a deep-water port, Marx was only allowed to excavate what happened to be the least important part of the sunken city. Since the total area uncovered during the excavation was less than five percent of the overall site, there are still many years' worth of work left. A preservation laboratory was built to cope with the vast amount of material recovered. Still, before all

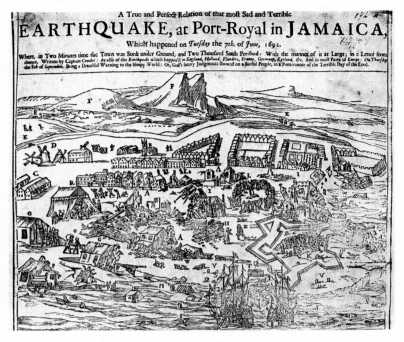

Contemporary newspaper with a drawing of Port Royal as it was hit by the earthquake.

the artifacts were preserved the government ran out of funding and threw many of them back into the sea.

Prince George, English merchantman
  Location: Martha Brae
  History: The ship was lost in a gale in 1762 while entering the harbor of Martha Brae after coming from London. Only the crew was saved.

Ritson, Irish merchantman, Captain Fairclough
  Location: Old Harbour
  History: The merchantman was lost due to fire on June 20, 1792, at Old Harbour.

Robert, Jamaican merchantman, schooner, Captain Clarke
  Location: Manchaneal Harbour
  History: The fully loaded schooner was lost on the reefs at the entrance to Manchaneal Harbour on June 16, 1808.

Rosemary, English merchantman, Captain Woodham
  Location: Jack's Bay
  History: The ship struck a reef and sank at Jack's Bay in 1792 while loaded with sugar.

Sally, English merchantman, Captain Bland
  Location: Near St. Ann's Bay
  History: The ship was lost on the reefs near St. Ann's Bay in 1760 while sailing for London. The crew and most of the cargo were saved.

Sampson, Scottish ship, Captain Bowie
  Location: Cow Bay
  History: The ship was lost in Cow Bay in 1794 while sailing to Santo Domingo and London.

Santa Cruz, Spanish galleon belonging to the Tierra Firme Flota (fleet) of Marqués de Vado, Captain Vicente López
  Location: Pedro Shoals
  History: Four galleons wrecked on Pedro Shoals in 1691 while sailing between Cartagena and Havana. Seven hundred and seventy-six persons were saved from the shipwrecks by fishing boats from Port Royal. The ships were the *Almiranta, Nuestra Señora del Carmen, Nuestra Señora de la Concepción,* and *Santa Cruz.* As soon as the Spaniards abandoned the wrecks, a large number of salvage sloops from Port Royal descended upon them and began

salvage operations. England and Spain were at peace at this time and the Spaniards demanded all the treasure recovered. The British agreed that the treasure should be seized and turned over to the Spaniards; however, many chests of treasure were concealed by the salvors, so there is no way to know just how much was salvaged. The Spaniards also carried on their own salvage operations and as late as 1698 salvage boats from Havana were recovering cannon from the wrecks.

Santiago de Palos, caravel belonging to Columbus
  Location: St. Ann's Bay
  History: Both of Columbus's ships, the *Capitana* and *Santiago*, were lost in St. Ann's Bay in 1504 during his fourth and last voyage of discovery. After spending some months exploring along Panama and Central America, where he was forced to abandon two of his caravels, he started for Santo Domingo. Both the *Capitana* and *Santiago* were leaking badly from sea worms. Contrary winds prevented him from heading toward his destination when he was off the northern coast of Jamaica. With both ships barely afloat from the great amount of water in them, he was forced to enter St. Ann's Bay, where he ran both ships aground to prevent them from sinking. Columbus dispatched a dugout canoe with a few men to the town of Santo Domingo, where there was a governor and assorted officials, to notify authorities of his plight. The remaining Spaniards stripped both caravels, and used what they could to construct crude shelters on shore. They abandoned the two hulls, which eventually sank into the soft sediment of the harbor. It wasn't until June 29, 1504, a year and four days later, that Columbus and his 115 men were rescued by a ship from Santo Domingo. In 1940, Samuel Eliot Morison explored the gently curving bay, which Columbus had called Santa Gloria, to determine where the *Capitana* and *Santiago* had been lost. Morison's estimate of the hulls' location was published in a chart in his Pulitzer Prize–winning book *Admiral of the Ocean Sea.* Using Morison's chart as a guide, coauthor Robert F. Marx,

assisted by Dr. Harold Edgerton of M.I.T., located both shipwrecks in February 1968 using sonar developed by Dr. Edgerton. They carried out a small excavation and positively identified Columbus' ships. Despite their significance, these wrecks have still not been explored. Since what little remains of them is deep in fine sediment, normal underwater excavation methods are less effective than the procedure of building a cofferdam around the site, pumping the water out and excavating as if on land. Columbus' caravels will remain safely ensconced in the waters of St. Ann's Bay until the money to excavate and conserve the remains can be raised.

Scarbro, English merchantman, Captain Scott
Location: Port Royal
History: The ship, bound for London, sprang a leak and sank at Port Royal in 1805.

Scipio, American merchantman, Captain Carr
Location: Annotto Bay
History: The merchantman wrecked at Annotto Bay during a storm on April 11, 1792, after arriving from Virginia. Most of her cargo of timber was washed ashore.

Sisters, American merchantman, Captain Richards
Location: The entrance to Port Royal
History: The ship was lost on the reefs at the entrance to Port Royal in 1804. She was arriving from the Canary Islands with a cargo of wine and brandy when she wrecked.

Solo, Spanish brig, Captain Dick
Location: Port Antonio
History: The brig was lost on the reefs at Port Antonio in 1815 while arriving from Cuba. Eight men drowned.

Speedwell, Jamaican schooner
Location: Manchaneal Bay
History: The schooner was lost in 1779 while leaving Manchaneal Bay on a sponging voyage to the Bahamas.

St. Andrew, English merchantman, Captain Howard
Location: Oracabeza
History: The merchantman, from

London, wrecked in a gale at Oracabeza in the year 1800.

Thomas & Edward, American merchantman, Captain Chevenick
Location: Near Kingston
History: The merchantman sank near Kingston in 1824 while arriving from Wilmington, North Carolina.

Three Brothers, Bahamian ship, Captain Hanson
Location: Off Port Antonio
History: The ship was lost off Port Antonio on February 14, 1821.

Triton, English ship, Captain Carzia
Location: Plumb Point
History: The ship was totally lost on December 5, 1818, off Plumb Point while arriving from Liverpool. The passengers, crew and part of her cargo were saved.

Triumph, English merchantman, Captain Johnson
Location: Kingston
History: While arriving at Kingston from New Brunswick in January 1804, the merchantman was burnt and became a total loss.

Two Friends, English merchantman, Captain Brookbank
Location: Old Harbour
History: The ship wrecked in Old Harbour in 1790 while sailing to England. Most of the cargo was saved.

Two Friends, Jamaican schooner
Location: Port Antonio
History: The schooner was lost on the reefs at Port Antonio in 1815.

Unidentified, ships (over 50)
Location: Jamaica
History: Over 50 ships of different descriptions were wrecked or sunk at Port Morant, St. Ann's Bay, Port Royal and Kingston Harbour during a hurricane on October 22, 1726. Several dozens of wooden houses were also blown into the harbor at Port Royal.

Unidentified, ships (105)
Location: Kingston Harbour and Port Royal
History: Nine warships and 96 merchantmen were wrecked or sunk in Kingston Harbour and Port Royal during a hurricane in October 1744. Many

of the wharves and warehouses in Kingston, which were full of merchandise, were also carried into the harbor. Only five of the warships that were lost have been identified: H.M.S. *Albans*, H.M.S. *Greenwich*, H.M.S. *Bonetta*, H.M.S. *Thunder* and H.M.S. *Lark*. Many of the ships were refloated and a great amount of their cargoes recovered. Coauthor Marx has dived on over 30 different wreck sites from the disaster and recovered a wide variety of artifacts including ceramicware, bottles, clay pipes and cannonballs.

Unidentified, ships (24)
Location: Kingston Harbour and Port Royal
History: Twenty-four merchant ships and one man-of-war, H.M.S. *Fox*, were lost in Kingston Harbour and at Port Royal during a hurricane on September 25, 1751. Four of the merchantmen were American, one was Dutch, and the rest were English.

Unidentified, ships (many)
Location: Jamaica
History: Many ships were lost at various ports during a hurricane in October 1780. H.M.S. *Badger* was sunk at Lucea Harbor. At Port Morant three large ships were thrown over a quarter of a mile onshore and were totally lost.

Unidentified, ships (many)
Location: Jamaica
History: Many ships were destroyed during a hurricane that struck Jamaica on August 1 and 2 in the year 1781. Ninety ships of various descriptions were wrecked or sunk in Kingston Harbour. Another 30 were lost at Port Royal and 73 more in other ports of the island. H.M.S. *Pelican* was also wrecked on the Morant Keys.

Unidentified, ships (over 80)
Location: Jamaica
History: Over 80 ships were destroyed or sunk in various ports around the island during a hurricane on July 30, 1784. Many houses were blown into the harbor at Port Royal as well.

Unidentified, ships (over 50)
Location: Jamaica
History: Over 50 ships were wrecked or sunk in Kingston Harbour and Port

Royal during a hurricane that struck the island prior to October 1785. Several others were lost at Savanna la Mar, Bulls Bay, and Bush Cay in Old Harbour.

Unidentified, ships (about 20)
Location: Jamaica
History: About 20 ships were lost at Kingston Harbour and several others at Montego Bay during a hurricane that struck the island on October 20, 1786.

Unidentified, ships (many)
Location: Jamaica
History: Both a hurricane and an earthquake struck Jamaica on July 13, 1813. Twelve large ships were lost at Kingston. Forty to 50 small vessels were lost at Port Royal, and eight ships at Morant Bay.

Unidentified, ships (3)
Location: Jamaica
History: During a bad gale in October 1815, two ships were lost at Port Maria, one in Orange Bay, one in Annotto Bay, and another at Goat Island.

Unidentified, Spanish merchant ship
Location: Bajo Nuevo Shoals
History: While sailing from Caracas, Venezuela to Veracruz in 1662, this Spanish merchant ship struck a reef and broke up quickly on Bajo Nuevo Shoals. Forty persons drowned and only a few reached Jamaica. The shoals are located about 150 nautical miles south of the western tip of Jamaica. Columbia claims jurisdiction over this area, so permission must be obtained from the Colombian government before any wreck can be salvaged there.

Unidentified, American schooner
Location: Buckner's Bay
History: The schooner was lost in Buckner's Bay on March 16, 1802, during a violent gale.

Unidentified, English warships and privateering vessels (a large number)
Location: Kingston Harbour
History: About 20 English warships and a large number of privateering vessels were wrecked in Kingston Harbour during a hurricane on October 7, 1670.

Unidentified, ships (several)
Location: Kingston Harbour
History: Several large English men-of-war, as well as several small trading sloops and schooners, were sunk during a hurricane that struck Kingston Harbour on August 9, 1714.

Unidentified, ships (17)
Location: Kingston Harbour
History: Seventeen ships were wrecked in Kingston Harbour and others lost at Black River, Savanna la Mar and Port Morant, during a hurricane on August 18, 1766.

Unidentified, ships (a great number)
Location: Kingston Harbour
History: A great number of ships were destroyed in Kingston Harbour during a hurricane from October 12 to 14 in the year 1812.

Unidentified, ships (3)
Location: Montego Bay
History: Seven ships were wrecked or sunk in a gale at Montego Bay in the year 1793. They were: the *Langrest, Active, Young Eagle,* and *Palliseer,* all arriving from London; and three others that were not identified.

Unidentified, ships (many)
Location: Montego Bay
History: Many ships were driven ashore at Montego Bay, Annotto Bay and Rio Bueno during a violent gale that struck the north coast of the island on February 23, 1802.

Unidentified, ship of unknown registry
Location: Montego Bay
History: The ship was lost at Montego Bay in 1822.

Unidentified, Dutch slave ship
Location: Morant Keys
History: After departing from Africa, the ship wrecked in the Morant Keys in 1774 with over 500 slaves onboard.

Unidentified, Spanish privateering vessel
Location: Pedro Point
History: The Spanish vessel was sunk by H.M.S. *Solebay* under the watchtower at Pedro Point in 1744. The present lighthouse is located near the ruins of the watchtower. There are four different old wrecks located in

this area in 30 feet of water, one of which may be this vessel.

Unidentified, caravel under the command of Valdivia, the regidor of Darien
Location: Pedro Shoals
History: The small caravel, sailing from Panama to Hispaniola for supplies and reinforcements in the year 1512, struck upon Pedro Shoals, located about 130 miles south of Jamaica. The caravel was carrying a great deal of treasure obtained from Indians when it wrecked. The ship broke up quickly and the crew escaped with nothing more than a small boat. They drifted for 13 days until reaching the Yucatán Peninsula.

Unidentified, merchant *nao* belonging to the Nueva España Flota (fleet) of Captain-General Alonso de Chaves Galindo
Location: Pedro Shoals
History: The large *nao* was accidentally separated from the convoy during bad weather and wrecked on Pedro Shoals in 1602. The ship was carrying a great deal of merchandise and missionaries from Spain to Yucatán when it was lost. After the ship broke up on the reef, the survivors made rafts of the debris and reached the southern section of Jamaica in a few days. The governor of Jamaica sent a salvage boat, but it could not locate the shipwreck. The owner of the ship was Tome Cano, one of the leading ship designers in Spain at that time.

Unidentified, vessel
Location: Plumb Point
History: The vessel, identified only by the captain's name, Todd, was lost on Plumb Point near Port Royal in 1774.

Unidentified, ships (2)
Location: Port Antonio
History: Two ships were totally lost at Port Antonio during a violent gale on March 16, 1802.

Unidentified, Spanish merchantman
Location: Port Morant
History: The ship wrecked on the coast near Port Morant in 1762 while sailing from Venezuela to Veracruz. She was laden with indigo, cocoa and

specie when she wrecked, but most of the cargo was salvaged.

Unidentified, American ship
   Location: Port Royal Harbour
   History: The ship sank in Port Royal Harbour prior to July 1813.

Vease Pink, English troop transport, Captain Horn
   Location: Morant Keys, off the south coast of Jamaica
   History: The ship hit a reef on the Morant Keys in July of 1741 and broke up quickly. Most of the persons onboard perished.

Venus, American ship, Captain Dony
   Location: Rio Bueno
   History: The ship was totally lost at Rio Bueno in December 1806 while arriving from New York.

Vulcan, English merchantman, Captain Gardner
   Location: Bar Bush Keys
   History: The merchantman was totally lost on Bar Bush Keys on July 26, 1806, while bound for Bristol.

Watson, American ship
   Location: Blue Hole
   History: The ship was driven ashore at Blue Hole on October 18, 1815, and went to pieces. She was arriving from New York. All the cargo was lost and 13 men drowned.

William, American brig, Captain Clark
   Location: Oracabeza
   History: Three merchantmen were lost at Oracabeza during a gale in 1802. The ships were the *Generous Planter, Fortune* and *William.*

William, English ship, Captain M'Iver
   Location: Plantain Garden
   History: The vessel was lost at Plantain Garden in 1805.

Young Eagle, ship, Captain Jones
   Location: Montego Bay
   History: Seven ships were wrecked or sunk in a gale at Montego Bay in the year 1793. They were: the *Langrest, Active, Young Eagle,* and *Palliseer,* all arriving from London; and three others that were not identified.

Young March, Jamaican sloop, Captain Brown
   Location: Healthshire Point
   History: The sloop wrecked at Healthshire Point on February 11, 1818. Part of her cargo was saved.

Lesser Antilles

Year-round working conditions in the Lesser Antilles are better than those of the other, larger islands of the Caribbean, which are subject to more hurricanes and storms. However, due to the prevailing northeasterly winds on the windward or eastern side of the Lesser Antilles they are continually battered by large ocean swells rolling in off the Atlantic, which generally makes diving difficult and hazardous. For example, off the eastern side of Barbados the average size of the swells is over 20 feet. Furthermore, since there are very few safe harbors or anchorages on the eastern side of most of these islands, a large vessel is needed for serious work on shipwreck sites. There are occasional days, generally during the hurricane season, when diving conditions are more favorable. Strong ocean swells still roll in and caution must be exercised. With the exception of a few harbors, such as Trinidad's Port of Spain and Bridgetown in Barbados, the underwater visibility is excellent around all of these islands.

The Dutch government prohibits shipwreck search and salvage around their islands, except by accredited archaeologists. The government takes 100 percent of all finds by a salvor. The French government has a law requiring that an archaeologist must supervise any work undertaken on shipwrecks in their waters. The salvor keeps 40 percent of their finds. The French government has the right to purchase all or any part of the 40 percent belonging to the salvor at a price determined by the government.

The British government requires a potential salvor to obtain a permit from the Admiralty Office in London before working on a site, but no ruling has been passed yet as to what percentage of the recovery a salvor will receive. The Admiralty Office claims to receive numerous requests for permission to salvage various wrecks around the British West Indian Islands. However, it has not granted any permits, since the laws governing the salvaging of ancient shipwrecks is not

clear and will have to be modified and rewritten.

SHIPWRECKS IN ANGUILLA'S WATERS

Brown Gally, English merchantman, Captain Belson
   Location: North side of the island
   History: The ship was lost on the north side of the island in 1755 while sailing from Rhode Island to the Leeward Islands.

Castle Shallop, English merchantman
   Location: South side of the island
   History: The ship, owned by Sir William Stapleton, wrecked on the south side of the island in 1733. She was sailing from St. Kitts to England with a cargo of sugar when she wrecked. Only the rigging was salvaged.

El Buen Consejo, 70-gun Spanish warship, galleon, Captain Julio de Urcullo
   Location: East end of the island

Top: **Spanish treasure chest with gold and silver coins.** *Bottom:* **Spanish silver pieces of eight dating from around 1590.**

History: Two large Spanish warships, escorting 18 merchant *naos* of the Flota (fleet) de Nueva España, were wrecked in 1772 off the east end of Anguilla: the *El Buen Consejo* and the *Jesús, María y Joseph.* The English from surrounding islands salvaged most of their cargoes.

Jesús, María y Joseph (alias *El Prusiano*), 40-gun Spanish warship, galleon, Captain Juan Baptista de Echeverria
Location: East end of the island
History: Two large Spanish warships, escorting 18 merchant *naos* of the Flota (fleet) de Nueva España, were wrecked in 1772 off the east end of Anguilla. The two ships were identified as the *El Buen Consejo* and the *Jesús, María y Joseph.* The English from surrounding islands salvaged most of their cargoes.

Temple, English merchantman, Captain Campbell
Location: Anguilla
History: The merchantman struck on a reef in 1763 at Anguilla and quickly went to pieces. She was en route from Liverpool to Jamaica when she wrecked. Most of the crew was saved.

Unidentified, American merchantmen (several)
Location: North side of Anguilla
History: Several unidentified American merchantmen were wrecked on the north side of the island in 1811.

Unidentified, Spanish merchant *nao*
Location: North side of the island
History: One of two unidentified *naos* sailing from Puerto Rico for Spain wrecked on the north side of Anguilla on December 12, 1628. Frenchmen from St. Kitts salvaged some of its cargo.

Unidentified, French merchantman
Location: North side of the island
History: The merchantman was lost on the north side of the island in 1755 while sailing from Martinique to France.

William, English merchantman, Captain Stoodley
Location: Wrecked at the island
History: The ship was wrecked in 1773 while sailing from London to the West Indies.

SHIPWRECKS IN ANTIGUA'S WATERS

Alice Bridger, American ship
Location: Reef near St. John's River
History: The ship wrecked on the reef near St. John's River in 1803 while coming from New York.

Alliance, French merchantman, Captain Gamare
Location: Long Island
History: The merchantman wrecked on Long Island, off Antigua, in 1791 while sailing from France to Hispaniola.

Britannia, English merchantman, Captain Brown
Location: Antigua
History: The merchantman wrecked in 1802 while coming from Demarara.

Cape Fear Merchant, English merchantman, Captain Allen
Location: Antigua
History: The ship wrecked on the bar while entering the main harbor in 1744 while coming from Bristol. Most of her cargo was saved.

Dorsetshire, English slave ship, Captain Traud
Location: Antigua
History: The ship wrecked on a reef in 1768 while coming from Africa. The slaves and crew were saved.

Eagle, English merchantman, Captain Long
Location: Antigua
History: The merchantman wrecked on a reef in 1740 while sailing from London to South Carolina.

Echo, English merchantman, Captain Johnson
Location: Antigua
History: The merchantman wrecked on Diamond Rock in 1802 while sailing from London to Jamaica. Most of her cargo was saved.

Europe, English merchantman, Captain Huddlestone

Location: Off St. John's Harbour

History: The merchantman was burnt on August 7, 1816, off St. John's Harbour while arriving from Liverpool. One man was lost.

Friends, English ship, Captain Gourley

Location: Antigua

History: The ship wrecked on a reef in 1809 while sailing from the Clyde to St. Thomas. Most of her cargo was saved.

Friendship, English merchantman, Captain Bowen

Location: Antigua

History: The merchantman wrecked on a reef in 1786 while sailing from Bristol to Honduras. Her crew was saved.

H.M.S. *De Ruyter*, 32-gun English warship, Captain Joseph Becket

Location: Deep Bay

History: The warship sank in Deep Bay on September 4, 1804. None of her crew of 250 were lost.

H.M.S. *Gloire*, English warship

Location: English Harbour

History: The ship was forced to cast all her guns overboard in the English Harbour during a hurricane on July 7, 1811.

H.M.S. *Guachapin*, ten-gun English warship, Captain Michael Jenkins

Location: Rat Island

History: The warship wrecked on Rat Island during a hurricane on July 7, 1811.

H.M.S. *Weymouth*, English warship, Captain Calmady

Location: Near Sandy Island off St. John's Road

History: The ship wrecked on February 16, 1745, on a reef near Sandy Island off St. John's road.

Hope, American schooner

Location: Little Bird Island on the north side of the island

History: She wrecked on the island in 1823.

Lively, English slave ship, Captain Bell

Location: East end of the island

History: The vessel wrecked on the east end of the island in 1797 while coming from Africa.

Nancy, English slave ship, Captain Bare

Location: Sandy Island

History: She was lost near Sandy Island in 1762 while coming from Africa. The slaves and crew were saved.

Nester, American ship, Captain Rowland

Location: Antigua

History: The ship wrecked on the island in 1773 while sailing from New England to Trinidad.

New Providence, Canadian ship, Captain Butler

Location: South side of the island

History: The ship wrecked on the south side of the island on October 17, 1817, while arriving from Halifax.

Parras, English merchantman, Captain Sleigh

Location: Guana Island

History: The merchantman wrecked on Guana Island in 1802 while coming from Bristol.

Phaeton, English merchantman, Captain Billings

Location: Boon Point

History: The vessel wrecked off Boon Point in 1802 while coming from Baltimore with a cargo of salt.

Philip & Emelie, German merchantman, Captain Rentz

Location: Belfast Reef on the north side of the island

History: The merchantman wrecked on the Belfast Reef on June 27, 1821, while sailing from Hamburg to St. Thomas. Only a small part of her cargo was saved.

Sarah & Rachel, Dutch merchantman, Captain Almers

Location: Antigua

History: The merchantman was lost near the island in 1779 while sailing from Amsterdam to St. Eustatius. Only her crew was saved.

Shirley, English ship, Captain Sherbourn

Location: Antigua

History: The ship was driven ashore by French privateers in 1747 while coming from Boston.

Sisters, English merchantman, Captain Douthwarte

Location: On the south side of the island

History: The merchantman wrecked on a reef on the south side of the island in 1823 while sailing from Demarara to London.

Successful Noney, English merchantman

Location: Sandy Island

History: The merchantman wrecked near Sandy Island on August 16, 1805, while sailing to Liverpool.

Unidentified, English ship, Captain Gadbury

Location: Antigua

History: The ship was totally lost in the main harbor during a hurricane on September 6, 1681.

Unidentified, Spanish privateer

Location: Antigua

History: An English warship forced the privateer ashore near the south shore and destroyed it in 1744.

Unidentified, sloop

Location: Antigua

History: The sloop was lost during a hurricane on September 21, 1747.

Unidentified, Spanish ship

Location: Antigua

History: The ship wrecked on the island in 1770. Only the crew was saved.

Unidentified, ships (several)

Location: Antigua

History: Several English merchantmen sank in St. John's Harbour and four or five English warships were lost in English Harbour during a hurricane on August 30, 1772.

Unidentified, French ship

Location: Antigua

History: The vessel wrecked on a shoal located three miles from the island in 1774 while sailing from Guadeloupe to France. Only a small part of her cargo of sugar was saved.

Unidentified, merchantman

Location: Antigua

History: The ship sank shortly after

leaving St. John's Harbour in 1782 while bound for Belfast.

Unidentified, English warships (2)
Location: English Harbour
History: Two unidentified English warships were lost in English Harbour during a hurricane in 1666 with great loss of life.

Unidentified, English vessels (2)
Location: Pope's Head
History: Two unidentified English vessels, a brig and a schooner, were wrecked and totally lost off Pope's Head in 1748.

Unidentified, ships (more than 10)
Location: St. John's Harbour
History: More than ten unidentified ships were wrecked off St. John's Harbour during a hurricane on September 13, 1754.

SHIPWRECKS IN BARBADOS' WATERS

Argo, English merchantman, Captain Alleyne
Location: Carlisle Bay
History: The ship wrecked shortly after leaving Carlisle Bay in 1751 while sailing for London. Her crew was saved.

Aurora, American merchantman, Captain Campbell
Location: Carlisle Bay
History: The following ships were wrecked or sunk in Carlisle Bay during a hurricane on August 23, 1758: an English privateer brigantine, the *Aurora, Jenny & Sally, Rose, Good Intent,* and *David & Susanna.* The *Aurora* was coming from North Carolina when it wrecked.

Barbadoes, English packet boat, Captain Twine
Location: The east side of the island
History: The boat burnt after running up on a reef on the east side of the island in 1772, while arriving from Bristol.

Betsey, American ship, Captain Brown
Location: East side of the island
History: The ship was totally lost on the east side of the island in 1790 while

sailing from Georgia to Grenada. Her crew was saved.

Blakeney, Scottish merchantman, Captain Murford
Location: East side of the island
History: While coming from Belfast in 1761, the ship was forced ashore on the east side of the island by a French privateer and quickly went to pieces. The crew and some of the cargo were saved.

Bridgetown, English merchantman
Location: Cobler's Rock
History: The merchantman wrecked on Cobler's Rock in 1807 while sailing from London to Jamaica.

Cato, Irish ship, Captain Houseman
Location: Near the entrance to Carlisle Bay
History: The ship wrecked on the island near the entrance to Carlisle Bay in 1762 while sailing from Cork to Guadeloupe. Only her crew was saved.

Chance, English merchantman, Captain Peters
Location: East side of the island
History: The merchantman wrecked on the east side of the island in 1801. The crew was saved.

Cicero, English ship, Captain Turner
Location: Cobler's Rock
History: The ship wrecked on Cobler's Rock in 1807 while sailing from London to Jamaica.

Commerce, English brig
Location: Barbados
History: The brig was totally lost on the island during a hurricane on September 15, 1816, while arriving from England

Cruden, Canadian merchantman
Location: Cobler's Rock
History: The vessel wrecked on Cobler's Rock on March 7, 1812, while sailing from Newfoundland to Grenada.

Cunriff, English merchantman, Captain Clapp
Location: East side of the island
History: The merchantman wrecked on the east side of the island in 1772 while arriving from London and Cork. Only a small part of her cargo was saved.

David & Susanna, ship of unknown registry, Captain Bartlett
Location: Carlisle Bay
History: The following ships were wrecked or sunk in Carlisle Bay during a hurricane on August 23, 1758: an unidentified brigantine, the *Aurora, Jenny & Sally, Rose, Good Intent,* and *David & Susanna.*

Duncannon, Scottish packet boat, Captain Goddard
Location: Near Carlisle Bay
History: The boat wrecked near Carlisle Bay during a gale on August 25, 1775, while arriving from England. The crew and mail were saved.

Economy, English sloop
Location: Barbados
History: The sloop was totally lost on the island during a hurricane on September 15, 1816, while arriving from St. Lucia.

Edward, English ship, Captain Peoples
Location: Barbados
History: Over 20 ships were wrecked around the island on October 10 during the famous hurricane of 1780. A large number of other ships were blown out to sea, most of them never to be heard from again. Two English ships, the *Happy Return* and the *Edward*, which had been blown away during the hurricane, made it back to the island, but sank upon returning. In addition, one of the main buildings of the Naval Hospital at Bridgetown was carried into the sea by large waves.

Edwards, English merchantman, Captain Wilson
Location: Cobler's Rock
History: The merchantman wrecked on Cobler's Rock in 1799 while arriving from England.

Elizabeth, Scottish merchantman, Captain Duncan
Location: East side of the island
History: She was lost on the east side of the island in 1815 while sailing from England to St. Vincent.

Euphrates, English merchantman, Captain Smith
Location: Eastern side of the island
History: The ship was totally lost on

a reef on the eastern side of the island in 1784 while coming from London. The crew was saved.

Francizhena, Portuguese merchantman, Captain Carros

Location: East side of the island

History: The richly laden merchantman wrecked on the east side of the island in 1804. Many men perished when the vessel wrecked.

Garland, English slave ship, Captain Sherwood

Location: Cobler's Rock

History: The vessel wrecked on Cobler's Rock in 1792 while arriving from Africa. The crew and slaves were saved.

Generous Planter, English merchantman, Captain Sands

Location: Carlisle Bay

History: Various accounts state "that every ship in Carlisle Bay was lost" during a hurricane on September 2, 1786. Only two were identified: the *Hibernia* and *Generous Planter*.

George, American ship, Captain Hardy

Location: Barbados

History: The ship wrecked on the island in November 1757 while coming from Philadelphia.

Good Intent, ship of unknown registry, Captain Tucker

Location: Carlisle Bay

History: The following ships were wrecked or sunk in Carlisle Bay during a hurricane on August 23, 1758: an unidentified brigantine, the *Aurora*, *Jenny & Sally*, *Rose*, *Good Intent*, and *David & Susanna*.

Grantham, English packet boat, Captain Ball

Location: East side of the island

History: The boat wrecked on the east side of the island in 1801 while sailing from England to Jamaica. The crew and passengers were saved.

Greyhound, English ship, Captain Walsh

Location: Barbados

History: The ship was driven ashore by a French privateer on January 8, 1762. Her cargo was saved.

Happy Return, English ship

Location: Barbados

History: Over 20 ships were wrecked around the island on October 10 during the famous hurricane of 1780. A large number of other ships were blown out to sea, most of them never to be heard from again. Two English ships, the *Happy Return* and *Edward*, which had been blown away during the hurricane made it back to the island, but sank upon returning. In addition, one of the main buildings of the Naval Hospital at Bridgetown was carried into the sea by large waves.

Hibernia, Scottish ship, Captain McConnel

Location: Carlisle Bay

History: Various accounts state "that every ship in Carlisle Bay was lost" during a hurricane on September 2, 1786. Only two were identified: the *Hibernia* and *Generous Planter*.

Hill, ship of unknown registry, Captain Coffin

Location: Bridgetown

History: The ship was struck by lightning and blew up off Bridgetown in 1773. Most of her crew perished.

H.M.S. *Glommen*, 18-gun English sloop-of-war, Captain Charles Pickford

Location: Carlisle Bay

History: The sloop wrecked in Carlisle Bay in November 1809. No lives were lost.

Industry, French ship, Captain Carcaud

Location: East side of the island

History: The vessel wrecked on the east side of the island in 1776 while sailing from Marseilles to Barbados. Her crew was saved.

Jane, English merchantman, Captain Ranof

Location: East side of the island

History: The merchantman was lost on the east side of the island in 1814 while sailing from London and Madeira to Dominica. The crew and cargo were saved.

Jenny & Sally, American ship, Captain Boulton

Location: Carlisle Bay

History: The following ships were wrecked or sunk in Carlisle Bay during a hurricane on August 23, 1758: an unidentified brigantine, the *Aurora*, *Jenny & Sally*, *Rose*, *Good Intent*, and *David & Susanna*. The *Jenny & Sally* was arriving from South Carolina when it wrecked.

Jonathan, English merchantman, schooner

Location: Marida Reef

History: The schooner was forced onto Marida Reef in 1814 by an American ship and then destroyed by cannon fire. Most of the cargo of dry goods and rum was lost.

Joseph, Scottish ship, Captain McNabb

Location: Bridgetown

History: The ship, ready to sail for Dublin, sank at Bridgetown in 1765. Her cargo was recovered.

King George, English slave ship, Captain Howard

Location: East side of the island

History: The vessel wrecked on the east side of the island in 1791 while arriving from Africa. Only 80 of the 360 slaves onboard were saved.

Kingston, Scottish merchantman

Location: Cabbin Rock Reef

History: The merchantman wrecked on Cabbin Rock Reef on the east side of the island in 1794 while coming from Glasgow.

Lady Georgiana, English packet boat, Captain Spencer

Location: Carlisle Bay

History: The boat was totally lost in Carlisle Bay on September 1, 1821.

Lady Spencer, English mail packet boat

Location: East side of the island

History: The boats, *Sprightly* and *Lady Spencer*, wrecked on the east side of the island on July 23, 1813.

Lark, English slave ship, Captain Blackhouse

Location: East side of the island

History: The ship wrecked on the east side of the island in 1782 while arriving from Africa. The crew and all of the 320 slaves onboard were saved.

Lark, American brig, Captain Worrel

Location: South part of the island

History: The brig wrecked on the

south part of the island in 1807 while arriving from Surinam.

Laura, Canadian schooner
Location: Pier Head
History: The schooner wrecked at Pier Head during a gale on August 12, 1810. The crew was saved.

Majestic, English troop transport
Location: Carlisle Bay
History: The ship was burnt and sunk in Carlisle Bay in 1808. No lives were lost.

Mary, English merchantman, Captain Leigh
Location: Cobler's Rock
History: The merchantman wrecked on Cobler's Rock in 1799 while arriving from Liverpool.

Maryann, English merchantman, Captain Mack
Location: Barbados
History: The ship wrecked on the island in 1806 while sailing from Newcastle to Grenada.

M'Dowall, ship of unknown registry
Location: Kettlebottom Rock
History: The ship was lost on Kettlebottom Rock in 1815 while coming from Dominica.

Nancy, English merchantman
Location: Bridgetown
History: Six ships were sunk near Bridgetown during a hurricane in October of 1749. Only the English merchantman *Nancy,* sailing from Bristol to Jamaica, was identified.

Nelly, English ship, Captain Adamson
Location: Near Bridgetown
History: She wrecked on the island near Bridgetown in 1807 while arriving from Trinidad.

Ostall, English ship, Captain Temple
Location: Barbados
History: The ship wrecked on the island on September 2, 1775, during a hurricane while coming from Newfoundland.

Patty, English slave ship, Captain Johnson
Location: East side of the island
History: The ship wrecked on the east side of the island in 1776 while arriving from Africa. The crew and slaves were saved.

Pickering, 20-gun privateer ship
Location: Barbados
History: In 1779, the ship was forced ashore by H.M.S. *Aurora* then burnt.

Rebecca, English slave ship, Captain Brodie
Location: Near Long Bay
History: The ship wrecked on a reef near Long Bay on November 17, 1767, while arriving from Africa. The crew, slaves and cargo of ivory and wax were saved.

Rose, English merchantman, Captain Elmore
Location: Carlisle Bay
History: The following ships were wrecked or sunk in Carlisle Bay during a hurricane on August 23, 1758: an unidentified brigantine, the *Aurora, Jenny & Sally, Rose, Good Intent,* and *David & Susanna.* The *Rose* was arriving from Bristol when it wrecked.

Rose, American ship, Captain Savage
Location: Round Rock
History: She wrecked at Round Rock in 1785 while coming from Philadelphia. Part of her cargo was saved.

Serpent, English sloop-of-war
Location: Barbados
History: The sloop wrecked on the island in 1748. Seven of her crew perished.

Sprightly, English mail packet boat
Location: East side of the island
History: The boats, *Sprightly* and *Lady Spencer,* wrecked on the east side of the island on July 23, 1813.

Star, English schooner
Location: Southern part of the island
History: The schooner wrecked in a gale on the southern part of the island on June 30, 1798, shortly after sailing for Trinidad.

Sylph, English merchantman, Captain Davidson
Location: Near the northern end of the island
History: The merchantman was totally lost on August 10, 1815, on a reef near the northern end of the island. She was sailing from Gibraltar to the West Indies at the time.

Unidentified, ships (many)
Location: Barbados
History: Many ships were wrecked on the island during a hurricane on November 1, 1669. Over 1,500 interred coffins from the island's main cemetery were swept into the sea as well.

Unidentified, ships (4)
Location: Barbados
History: Two large and two small unidentified ships were lost during a hurricane in 1700.

Unidentified, 24-gun pirate ship, Captain Martel
Location: Barbados
History: In 1776, the pirate ship of Captain Martel sank a sloop that was guarding the entrance to Carlisle Bay. The following day an English warship chased the pirate around the island and sank it by cannon fire off the eastern shore.

Unidentified, sloop
Location: Barbados
History: In 1776, the pirate ship of Captain Martel sank a sloop that was guarding the entrance to Carlisle Bay. The following day an English warship chased the pirate around the island and sank it by cannon fire off the eastern shore.

Unidentified, ships (over 20)
Location: Barbados
History: Over 20 ships were wrecked around the island on October 10 during the famous hurricane of 1780. A large number of other ships were blown out to sea, most of them never to be heard from again. Two English ships, the *Happy Return* and the *Edward,* which had been blown away during the hurricane, made it back to the island but sank upon returning. In addition, one of the main buildings of the Naval Hospital at Bridgetown was carried into the sea by large waves.

Unidentified, English merchantmen (12)
Location: Bridgetown
History: Twelve large unidentified English merchantmen were sunk at Bridgetown during a hurricane on September 1, 1675. Some of the ships were loaded with sugar and rum.

Unidentified, ships (5)
Location: Bridgetown
History: Six ships were sunk near Bridgetown during a hurricane in October 1749. Only the English merchantman *Nancy*, sailing from Bristol to Jamaica, was identified.

Unidentified, ships (6)
Location: Bridgetown
History: Six unidentified ships were lost at Bridgetown during a hurricane on August 23, 1758.

Unidentified, English merchantmen (26)
Location: Carlisle Bay
History: The merchantmen were sunk in Carlisle Bay during a hurricane on September 27, 1694. Over a thousand men perished.

Unidentified, ships (8)
Location: Carlisle Bay
History: Eight ships were lost at Carlisle Bay and Bridgetown during a hurricane in July 1757.

Unidentified, English privateer brigantine, Captain Franklin
Location: Carlisle Bay
History: The following ships were wrecked or sunk in Carlisle Bay during a hurricane on August 23, 1758: an unidentified brigantine, the *Aurora, Jenny & Sally, Rose, Good Intent,* and *David & Susanna.*

Unidentified, English merchantmen (7)
Location: Carlisle Bay
History: Seven large merchantmen were lost in Carlisle Bay during a gale or hurricane in August 1765.

Unidentified, ships (all in Carlisle Bay)
Location: Carlisle Bay
History: Various accounts state "that every ship in Carlisle Bay was lost" during a hurricane on September 2, 1786. Only two were identified: the *Hibernia* and *Generous Planter.*

Unidentified, English warship
Location: East side of the island
History: The warship wrecked on the east side of the island during a hurricane in July 1666.

Unidentified, French merchantman
Location: East side of the island
History: An unidentified richly laden French merchantman, sailing from France to Martinique, was wrecked on the east side of the island in 1748.

Unidentified, English merchantmen (17)
Location: In the vicinity of Bridgetown
History: The ships were sunk in the vicinity of Bridgetown during a hurricane in October 1693.

SHIPWRECKS IN BARBUDA'S WATERS

Adventure, English ship, Captain MacMillon
Location: Barbuda
History: The ship wrecked during August 1810 while sailing from Lancaster to St. Thomas. Her crew was saved.

Argo, ship of unknown registry, Captain Pindar
Location: Barbuda
History: The ship wrecked near the island in 1801 while sailing from Nassau to Surinam.

Betsey, American ship, Captain Woodman
Location: Barbuda
History: The ship was totally lost near the island in 1785 while coming from South Carolina.

Boscawen, ship of unknown registry, Captain Hawkins
Location: Barbuda
History: The ship wrecked in 1761 while sailing from Virginia to Barbados. Nothing of her cargo was saved.

Castle Semple, Scottish ship
Location: Barbuda
History: The ship was totally lost near the island in 1797 while sailing from Glasgow to the West Indies.

Ceres, English merchantman, Captain Howes
Location: Barbuda
History: The merchantman wrecked in 1780 while sailing from London to Antigua. Part of her cargo was saved.

Farmer, English merchantman, Captain Young
Location: Barbuda
History: The ship wrecked in 1809 while sailing from Newcastle to Honduras. Only the crew was saved.

Fortune Teller, English privateer, Captain Kay
Location: Barbuda
History: The privateer wrecked in 1780. The crew was saved.

Grand Sachem, American ship, Captain Cairnes
Location: Barbuda
History: She wrecked on a reef in 1793 while sailing from St. Helena to Massachusetts.

Hazard, French slave ship
Location: Barbuda
History: The ship wrecked in 1755 while sailing from Africa to Hispaniola. More than 80 slaves drowned.

H.M.S. Griffin, 20-gun English warship, Captain Thomas Taylor
Location: Barbuda
History: The warship wrecked during October of 1760.

H.M.S. Woolwich, 40-gun English warship, Captain Thomas Ball Sullivan
Location: Barbuda
History: The warship wrecked on November 6, 1813.

Hound, English merchantman, Captain Stronnack
Location: Off the southwest end of the island
History: The merchantman was lost in 1821 while sailing from St. Vincent to London. Her crew was saved.

Jeanette, American merchantman, Captain Anderson
Location: North side of the island
History: The ship wrecked in 1795 while sailing from New England to St. Thomas. The crew and some of the cargo were saved.

Jeune Adolphe, French ship
Location: Barbuda
History: The ship wrecked on August 2, 1817, while sailing from Guadeloupe to France. Her crew was saved.

John, English merchantman, Captain Simpson
Location: Barbuda

History: The merchantman wrecked in 1763 while sailing from England for the West Indies.

Julia, English merchantman, Captain Snow
   Location: Barbuda
   History: The vessel wrecked in 1809 while coming from Cadiz. Most of her cargo was saved.

Kingston, English merchantman, Captain Bruton
   Location: Barbuda
   History: She wrecked in 1809 while sailing from Liverpool to St. Croix.

Lanzerota, 24-gun Spanish warship, Captain Ignacio Perez
   Location: Barbuda
   History: The warship wrecked on July 23, 1792, with very little saved except the crew.

Martiniquin, French merchantman, Captain Garcin
   Location: Off the west end of the island
   History: The merchantman was lost off the west end of the island on July 24, 1821, while sailing from Martinique to France.

Monitor, American merchantman, Captain Whitter
   Location: Barbuda
   History: The merchantman wrecked on September 25, 1822, while sailing from Philadelphia to St. Eustatius.

Nancy, English merchantman, Captain Dlam
   Location: Barbuda
   History: The ship wrecked on November 2, 1749, while sailing from Bristol to Jamaica. Only a small part of her cargo was saved.

Nelly & Nancy, American merchantman, Captain Dennison
   Location: Barbuda
   History: The merchantman was lost on July 2, 1790, while sailing from North Carolina to Guadeloupe. The crew was saved.

Pearl, English slave ship, Captain Dighton
   Location: Barbuda
   History: The ship wrecked here in 1749 while coming from Africa with a cargo of slaves. Seventy slaves and 11 of the crew drowned.

Prince Charles, Scottish merchantman, Captain Walsh
   Location: South end of the island
   History: The merchantman wrecked on the south end of the island in 1752 while sailing from Dublin to Jamaica.

Royal Duke, English merchantman, Captain Tory
   Location: Barbuda
   History: The merchantman wrecked in 1763 while sailing from Guadeloupe to London.

San Josef, Spanish brig, 150 tons
   Location: Barbuda
   History: The brig wrecked on April 7, 1821, while coming from Spain with a cargo of olive oil, brandy, paper and almonds.

Seaforth, American merchantman, Captain Phelan
   Location: Barbuda
   History: The merchantman was captured by a French privateer in 1799 while sailing from New York to Barbados. Shortly after, she wrecked on a reef. Most of her cargo was lost.

Speculation, ship of unknown registry, Captain Colburn
   Location: North part of the island
   History: The ship was totally lost off the north part of the island on August 25, 1819, while coming from Bermuda.

Telemacko, English merchantman
   Location: Barbuda
   History: The merchantman wrecked on November 9, 1782, while sailing from London to Nevis. The crew and a small part of the cargo were saved.

Triton, English merchantman, Captain Newhall
   Location: Barbuda
   History: The merchantman wrecked on April 29, 1807, while en route to Antigua. The crew was saved.

Unidentified, sloop of unknown registry
   Location: Barbuda
   History: The sloop wrecked near the island in 1801 while sailing from Nassau to Surinam.

Unidentified, brig of unknown registry
   Location: Barbuda
   History: The brig wrecked near the island in 1801 while sailing from New England to Antigua.

Unidentified, Spanish merchant *nao*, Captain Francisco Morales
   Location: Off the east side of the island
   History: The merchant ship wrecked off the east side of the island in 1695 while carrying 13,000 pesos to pay the garrisons at Maracaibo. All the specie and a great deal of merchandise were recovered by divers.

SHIPWRECKS IN DOMINICA'S WATERS

Edward & Ann, English merchantman, Captain Adnet
   Location: Roseau
   History: Thirteen ships were totally destroyed at Roseau during a hurricane on July 26, 1769. Only one of the ships was identified: the *Edward & Ann.* Two unidentified sloops were also sunk at Prince Ruperts Bay.

El Espíritu Santo, *nao* belonging to the New Spain Flota (fleet) of Captain-General Juan Velasco de Barrio, 120 tons, Captain Juan de Rosales
   Location: Dominica
   History: Before the *flota* sailed from Veracruz for Spain in 1567, it received word that there were two English fleets waiting to intercept it. One was waiting near Havana and the other near the mouth of the Bahama Channel. To protect the treasure the *flota* decided to sail back to Spain by a very unusual route, hugging the coast of Yucatán and then turning south, passing south of Jamaica. They planned to sail toward the Virgin Islands then head directly for Spain. However, they were struck by a bad storm when nearing Puerto Rico and were forced to run before it. Six of the *flota's* major ships were wrecked near the northwest tip of Dominica: the *San Juan, Santa Barbola, San Felipe, El Espíritu Santo*, and two unidentified *naos*. They carried over three million pesos in treasure.

None of the other ships in the *flota* could stop to pick up the survivors or the treasure due to the storm. However, most of the survivors reached shore where the Carib Indians then cruelly massacred them. According to several Indians captured the following year by salvors who came to the island, the Cabris hid all the treasure in caves, but even under torture, they would not reveal its exact location. There is no record of it being recovered.

H.M.S. *Berbice*, 20-gun English warship, Captain John Tresakar
Location: Near the island
History: The ship wrecked during November 1796 on a reef near the island.

H.M.S. *Lark*, 18-gun English warship, Captain Robert Nicholas
Location: Point Palenqua
History: The warship wrecked off Point Palenqua during a gale on August 1 or 3, 1809. Three of her crew of 121 perished.

***Hunter*,** Scottish merchantman, Captain Robinson
Location: West side of the island
History: Two ships were wrecked on the west side of the island during a hurricane on September 6, 1776: the *Mary & Jane*, arriving from Lancaster, and *Hunter*. Some of the latter's cargo was recovered.

***Juno*,** forty gun French frigate
Location: East side of the island
History: The newly built frigate wrecked on the east side of the island during a hurricane on October 9, 1780. Over three hundred men perished.

***Mary & Jane*,** English merchantman, Captain Gerdner
Location: West side of the island
History: Two ships were wrecked on the west side of the island during a hurricane on September 6, 1776: *Mary & Jane*, arriving from Lancaster; *Hunter*, with some of her cargo recovered.

***Nufus*,** English merchantman, Captain Sandland
Location: Dominica
History: The merchantman wrecked in 1804 while coming from London with a valuable cargo.

***Olive*,** English merchantman
Location: West side of the island
History: Fourteen English ships were lost in various ports on the west side of the island during a hurricane on August 1, 1792. Only one was identified: the merchantman *Olive*, which was ready to sail for England.

***Phoenix*,** English merchantman, Captain Knight
Location: Roseau
History: Five English merchantmen were totally lost at Roseau during a hurricane in October 1766. The ships were the *Phoenix*, just arriving from Bristol; *Three Friends*, recently arrived from Newfoundland; and three unidentified vessels.

***San Felipe*,** galleon belonging to the New Spain Flota (fleet) of Captain-General Juan Velasco de Barrio, 120 tons, Captain Juan López de Sosa
Location: Dominica
History: Before the *flota* sailed from Veracruz for Spain in 1567, it received word that there were two English fleets waiting to intercept it. One was waiting near Havana and the other near the mouth of the Bahama Channel. To protect the treasure the *flota* decided to sail back to Spain by a very unusual route, hugging the coast of Yucatán and then turning south, passing south of Jamaica. They planned to sail toward the Virgin Islands then head directly for Spain. However, they were struck by a bad storm when nearing Puerto Rico and were forced to run before it. Six of the flota's major ships were wrecked near the northwest tip of Dominica: the *San Juan*, *Santa Barbola*, *San Felipe*, *El Espíritu Santo*, and two unidentified *naos*. The ships carried over three million pesos in treasure. None of the other ships in the *flota* could stop to pick up the survivors or the treasure due to the storm. However, most of the survivors reached shore where the Carib Indians then cruelly massacred them. According to several Indians captured the following year by salvors who came to the island, the Caribs hid all the treasure in caves, but even under torture they would not reveal its exact location. There is no record of it being recovered.

***San Juan*,** *capitana* (flagship) of the New Spain Flota (fleet) of Captain-General Juan Velasco de Barrio, 150 tons, Captain Benito de Santana
Location: Dominica
History: Before the *flota* sailed from Veracruz for Spain in 1567, it received word that there were two English fleets waiting to intercept it. One was waiting near Havana and the other near the mouth of the Bahama Channel. To protect the treasure the *flota* decided to sail back to Spain by a very unusual route, hugging the coast of Yucatán and then turning south, passing south of Jamaica. They planned to sail toward the Virgin Islands then head directly for Spain. However, they were struck by a bad storm when nearing Puerto Rico and were forced to run before it. Six of the *flota's* major ships were wrecked near the northwest tip of Dominica: the *San Juan*, *Santa Barbola*, *San Felipe*, *El Espíritu Santo*, and two unidentified *naos*. The ships carried over three million pesos in treasure. None of the other ships in the *flota* could stop to pick up the survivors or the treasure due to the storm. However, most of the survivors reached shore where the Carib Indians then cruelly massacred them. According to several Indians captured the following year by salvors who came to the island, the Caribs hid all the treasure in caves, but even under torture they would not reveal its exact location. There is no record of it being recovered.

***Santa Barbola*,** *almiranta* of the New Spain Flota (fleet) of Captain-General Juan Velasco de Barrio, 150 tons, Captain Vicencio Garullo
Location: Dominica
History: Before the *flota* sailed from Veracruz for Spain in 1567, it received word that there were two English fleets waiting to intercept it. One was waiting near Havana and the other near the mouth of the Bahama Channel. To protect the treasure the *flota* decided to sail back to Spain by a very unusual route, hugging the coast of Yucatán and then turning south, passing south of Jamaica. They planned to sail toward the Virgin Islands then head directly for Spain. However, they were struck by a bad storm when nearing

Puerto Rico and were forced to run before it. Six of the *flota's* major ships were wrecked near the northwest tip of Dominica: the *San Juan, Santa Barbola, San Felipe, El Espíritu Santo*, and two unidentified *naos*. The ships carried over three million pesos in treasure. None of the other ships in the *flota* could stop to pick up the survivors or the treasure due to the storm. However, most of the survivors reached shore where the Carib Indians then cruelly massacred them. According to several Indians captured the following year by salvors who came to the island, the Caribs hid all the treasure in caves, but even under torture they would not reveal its exact location. There is no record of it being recovered.

Stag, English merchant schooner, Captain Derbyshire
Location: Roseau
History: The schooner wrecked at Roseau during a gale on July 14, 1808. The crew and most of the cargo were saved.

Three Friends, English merchantman, Captain Reef
Location: Roseau
History: Five English merchantmen were totally lost at Roseau during a hurricane in October 1766. The ships were the *Phoenix*, just arriving from Bristol; the *Three Friends*, recently arrived from Newfoundland; and three unidentified vessels.

Unidentified, Spanish ship
Location: Dominica
History: An unidentified Spanish ship wrecked in 1565 on the island. The Carib Indians captured and ate most of the survivors. When John Hawkins stopped there for water a few months later he rescued the few remaining survivors.

Unidentified, naos (2) belonging to the New Spain Flota (fleet) of Captain-General Juan Velasco de Barrio, 120 tons
Location: Dominica
History: Before the *flota* sailed from Veracruz for Spain in 1567, it received word that there were two English fleets waiting to intercept it. One was waiting near Havana and the other near the mouth of the Bahama Channel. To

protect the treasure the *flota* decided to sail back to Spain by a very unusual route of hugging the coast of Yucatán and then turning south, passing south of Jamaica. They planned to sail toward the Virgin Islands then head directly for Spain. However, they were struck by a bad storm when nearing Puerto Rico and were forced to run before it. Six of the *flota's* major ships were wrecked near the northwest tip of Dominica: the *San Juan, Santa Barbola, San Felipe, El Espíritu Santo*, and two unidentified *naos*. The ships carried over three million pesos in treasure. None of the other ships in the *flota* could stop to pick up the survivors or the treasure due to the storm. However, most of the survivors reached shore where the Carib Indians then cruelly massacred them. According to several Indians captured the following year by salvors who came to the island, the Caribs hid all the treasure in caves, but even under torture they would not reveal its exact location. There is no record of it being recovered.

Unidentified, nao belonging to the New Spain Flota (fleet)
Location: Dominica
History: In 1605, the New Spain Flota approached Guadeloupe to stop for water. During the night an unidentified *nao* became separated from the *flota* and anchored at Dominica. While there, a large Dutch warship appeared and, after a brief battle, sank the *nao*. There were only a few survivors whom the Dutch rescued and placed ashore on Puerto Rico.

Unidentified, ships (several)
Location: Dominica
History: Dominica suffered from three different hurricanes in 1787. The first one occurred on August 3 and caused an English slave ship as well as several schooners to be totally lost. Another occurred on August 23 causing another English slave ship, three brigs and many smaller ships to be sunk. The third hurricane on August 29 caused another English slave ship and two brigs loaded with rum to sink at Roseau.

Unidentified, British ship
Location: Northern tip of the island

History: The ship wrecked on the northern tip of the island during a gale on August 1 or 3, 1809.

Unidentified, sloops (2)
Location: Prince Ruperts Bay
History: Thirteen ships were totally destroyed at Roseau during a hurricane on July 26, 1769. Only one of the ships was identified: the *Edward & Ann*. Two unidentified sloops were also sunk at Prince Ruperts Bay.

Unidentified, vessels (3)
Location: Roseau
History: Five English merchantmen were totally lost at Roseau during a hurricane in October 1766. The ships were the *Phoenix*, just arriving from Bristol; the *Three Friends*, recently arrived from Newfoundland; and three unidentified vessels.

Unidentified, ships (12)
Location: Roseau
History: Thirteen ships were totally destroyed at Roseau during a hurricane on July 26, 1769. Only one of the ships was identified: the *Edward & Ann*.

Unidentified, English merchantmen (18)
Location: Roseau
History: Eighteen unidentified English merchantmen were sunk or wrecked at Roseau during a hurricane on August 30, 1772. Several cannon from the fort were also washed into the sea.

Unidentified, American schooner
Location: Roseau
History: The schooner wrecked at Roseau during a gale on August 1 or 3, 1809.

Unidentified, ships (16)
Location: Roseau
History: Sixteen ships were totally lost near and in the port of Roseau during a hurricane in August 1813.

Unidentified, English ships (13)
Location: West side of the island
History: Fourteen English ships were lost in various ports on the west side of the island during a hurricane on August 1, 1792. Only one was identified: the merchantman *Olive*, which was ready to sail for England.

SHIPWRECKS IN GRENADA'S WATERS

Amelia, English merchantman, Captain Burgess
   Location: North end of the island
   History: The merchantman wrecked on the north end of the island in 1790.

Ann, English sloop, Captain Knotsford
   Location: Bacolet
   History: The sloop wrecked on a reef near Bacolet in 1773. Three men were lost.

Ann & Bridget, American merchantman, Captain Shaftoe
   Location: Grenada
   History: The ship wrecked on the island in 1791 while arriving from Boston.

Armida, Portuguese merchantman, Captain Silva
   Location: Point Saline
   History: The large merchantman wrecked at Point Saline on December 20, 1805, while sailing from Brazil to Venezuela. Most of her cargo was lost.

Arrow, English sloop, Captain Williams
   Location: La Bays Rock
   History: The sloop wrecked on La Bays Rock in 1824 but her crew was saved. The ship was in ballast at the time.

Champion, English merchantman, Captain Glover
   Location: St. George's Harbour
   History: The merchantman was lost at St. George's Harbour in 1772 while arriving from Bristol.

Charlotte, ship of unknown registry, Captain Cummings
   Location: East side of the island
   History: She was lost on the east side of the island in 1793.

Charlotte, English merchantman, Captain Buttery
   Location: South side of the island
   History: The vessel wrecked on the south side of the island in the year 1800 while arriving from London. Most of her cargo was saved.

Columbine, English merchantman, Captain Bannatyne

   Location: East side of the island
   History: The ship wrecked on the east side of the island in 1822. The crew and cargo were saved.

Comte de Durant, French privateer, Captain Lamster
   Location: Grenada
   History: The following ships were lost on October 10 during the famous hurricane of 1780: 19 unidentified Dutch merchantmen in Grenville Bay; the *Prince Frederick Adolph*, in St. George's Harbour; the *Two Sisters*, on the east side of the island; the *Comte de Durant*, on the south side of the island; and three French and seven other merchantmen, lost in various ports of the island.

Elizabeth, American ship
   Location: St. George's Harbour
   History: The ship wrecked on a reef near St. George's Harbour while arriving from New York in 1798. Most of her cargo was saved.

Fanny, English slave ship, Captain Moore
   Location: East side of the island
   History: The vessel was lost on the east side of the island while arriving from Africa in 1793. Only two of the crew were saved.

Four Brothers, English merchantman
   Location: East side of the island
   History: The merchantman wrecked on the east side of the island in 1813 while sailing for London.

Hope, English merchantman, Captain Blackman
   Location: Granada
   History: The ship wrecked on the island in 1790.

Industry, English ship, Captain Wilkinson
   Location: St. George's Harbour
   History: The following ships were sunk at St. George's Harbour during a hurricane on August 9, 1768: the *Industry*, arriving from Barbados; a Dutch ship, arriving from St. Eustatius; and three unidentified brigs.

Lady Hughes, English merchantman, Captain Dommet
   Location: Grenada
   History: The merchantman was to-

tally lost on the island in 1787. Her crew was saved.

Love, English ship, Captain Death
   Location: St. George's Harbour
   History: The ship wrecked entering St. George's Harbour in 1801 while arriving from England. All of her cargo was saved.

Mary, English merchantman, Captain Johnson
   Location: Grenville Bay
   History: The merchantman was totally lost in 1794 while leaving Grenville Bay en route to London.

Mary Ann, American ship, Captain Dale
   Location: North side of the island
   History: The ship wrecked on the north side of the island on December 2, 1788, while arriving from Virginia.

Molly, slave ship, Captain Woodburn
   Location: Grand Once
   History: The vessel wrecked at Grand Once on August 9, 1768, during a hurricane while coming from Africa.

Morris & Molly, Scottish merchantman, Captain Weatherhead
   Location: Grenada
   History: The ship was lost in 1774 while sailing out of Mergain for Dublin. Some of the cargo was saved.

Neptune, English sloop, Captain Hunt
   Location: Grenada
   History: The sloop wrecked on the island in 1807 while arriving from London.

Prince Frederick Adolph, Swedish merchantman, Captain Lonstroom
   Location: Grenada
   History: The following ships were lost on October 10 during the famous hurricane of 1780: 19 unidentified Dutch merchantmen in Grenville Bay; the *Prince Frederick Adolph*, in St. George's Harbour; the *Two Sisters*, on the east side of the island; the *Comte de Durant*, on the south side of the island; and three French and seven other merchantmen, lost in various ports of the island.

Rochard, English ship, Captain Bartlet
   Location: Grenville Bay

History: The ship was lost on August 3, 1774, while leaving Grenville Bay for London. Some of the cargo was saved.

Sally, English slave ship, Captain Tonkey
  Location: Grand Roy Bay
  History: The ship wrecked in Grand Roy Bay on June 19, 1769, while arriving from Africa. The crew and slaves were saved.

Sophia, English merchantman
  Location: East side of the island
  History: The merchantman wrecked on the east side of the island in 1822 while sailing from Tobago. The crew and cargo were saved.

Surprise, English brig
  Location: Grenville Bay
  History: The brig wrecked at the entrance to Grenville Bay in 1804 while leaving for Trinidad. All of her cargo of rum was saved.

Two Sisters, French ship, Captain Townseau
  Location: Grenada
  History: The following ships were lost on October 10 during the famous hurricane of 1780: 19 unidentified Dutch merchantmen in Grenville Bay; the *Prince Frederick Adolph,* in St. George's Harbour; the *Two Sisters,* on the east side of the island; the *Comte de Durant,* on the south side of the island; and three French and seven other merchantmen, lost in various ports of the island.

Unidentified, ships (many)
  Location: Grenada
  History: The following ships were lost on October 10 during the famous hurricane of 1780: 19 unidentified Dutch merchantmen in Grenville Bay; the *Prince Frederick Adolph,* in St. George's Harbour; the *Two Sisters,* on the east side of the island; the *Comte de Durant,* on the south side of the island; and three French and seven other merchantmen, lost in various ports of the island.

Unidentified, ships (4)
  Location: St. George's Harbour
  History: The following ships were sunk at St. George's Harbour during a hurricane on August 9, 1768: the *Industry,* arriving from Barbados; a Dutch ship, arriving from St. Eustatius; and three unidentified brigs.

Virgen del Rosario, Spanish merchant *nao,* Captain Gale
  Location: Point Saline
  History: The richly laden Spanish merchantman wrecked on January 22, 1816, at Point Saline while coming from Spain. Only a small part of her cargo was saved.

SHIPWRECKS IN THE GRENADINES' WATERS

Adventure Baptista, ship of unknown registry, Captain Blanckley
  Location: Carriacou Island
  History: The ship wrecked on a reef near Carriacou Island in 1794.

Lily, American schooner
  Location: Grenadines
  History: The schooner wrecked on one of the Grenadines in 1818. Only the captain was saved.

March, English merchantman
  Location: Carriacou Island
  History: The ship was totally lost at Carriacou Island in April 1821 while sailing from London to Grenada.

Nancy, English merchantman, Captain Hamilton
  Location: Grenadines
  History: The merchantman was lost on one of the islands in 1768 while sailing from Bristol to Nevis. Her crew was saved.

Rebecca, English merchantman, Captain Sim
  Location: East side of Bequia Island
  History: The merchantman was totally lost on the east side of Bequia Island in 1782 while sailing from Demarara to Barbados.

Rose, English merchantman, Captain Farr
  Location: East side of Carriacou Island
  History: She wrecked on the east side of Carriacou Island in 1769 while sailing from London and Madeira to Jamaica.

Unidentified, French slave ship
  Location: Grenadines
  History: The ship wrecked on one of the islands of the Grenadines in 1611 with over 400 slaves onboard. The Spaniards later killed all the Frenchmen and rescued most of the slaves.

Unidentified, French ship
  Location: Grenadines
  History: The large French ship was totally lost near one of the smaller cays in this chain of islands in July 1653.

Unidentified, Portuguese slave ship
  Location: Bequia Island
  History: The ship wrecked on Bequia Island during a hurricane in August 1675. A large amount of ivory went down with the ship.

SHIPWRECKS IN GUADELOUPE'S WATERS

Armstrong, English merchantman, Captain Muntford
  Location: Chatron Point
  History: The merchantman was chased ashore by the French near Chatron Point in 1760 and totally lost.

Catherine & Francis, English ship, Captain Smith
  Location: Maria-Galante Island
  History: The ship wrecked on the island in 1800 while sailing from Bermuda to Martinique.

Cornwallis, English merchantman
  Location: Off Pointe-à-Pitre
  History: The merchantman was sailing from Antigua to Liverpool when it was captured by the French. They then wrecked it off Pointe-à-Pitre in 1797.

Deliverance, English merchantman, Captain Whyte
  Location: Isle des Saintes
  History: The merchantman wrecked on the Isle des Saintes in 1760 while sailing from London to Virginia. Her crew was saved.

Didon, 44-gun French warship
  Location: Pointe-à-Pitre
  History: The warship was wrecked and was totally lost at Pointe-à-Pitre in 1792.

Divers using hammers and chisels to dig into coral on a wreck site off Guadeloupe.

France, French merchantman, Captain Gérard
 Location: Guadeloupe
 History: The merchantman wrecked on the main island in 1824 while departing for France.

Friendship, English merchantman, Captain Rivoira
 Location: Basse-Terre
 History: Seventeen English merchantmen were lost at Basse-Terre during a hurricane on July 31, 1765. Only one was identified: the *Friendship*.

H.M.S. Britannia, English troop transport
 Location: Basse-Terre
 History: The ship was accidentally burnt at Basse-Terre in 1794.

H.M.S. Carieux, 18-gun English warship, sloop, Captain Henry George Moysey
 Location: Petite Terre off Marie-Galante Island
 History: The warship wrecked on September 25, 1809, on the Îles de La Petite Terre off Marie-Galante Island.

H.M.S. Falcon, eight-gun English bomb vessel, Captain Mark Robinson
 Location: Isle des Saintes

History: The vessel wrecked on the Isle des Saintes in 1759.

H.M.S. Grouper, four-gun English warship, Captain James Atkins
 Location: Guadeloupe
 History: The warship wrecked on the main island on October 21, 1811.

H.M.S. Rapide, six-gun English warship
 Location: Isle des Saintes
 History: The warship wrecked on the Isle des Saintes in 1814.

H.M.S. Unique, 12-gun English warship, Captain Thomas Fellowes
 Location: Basse-Terre
 History: The ship was burnt at Basse-Terre on May 31, 1809.

Kate, ship of unknown registry, Captain Purdy
 Location: Désirade Island
 History: The ship was captured by pirates and scuttled near Désirade Island in 1821 while sailing to Halifax with a large amount of specie onboard.

La Rosa, nao belonging to the New Spain Flota (fleet) of Captain-General Fulgencio de Meneses, Captain Juan Diaz Canpillo

Location: Southwest side of Guadeloupe
 History: The *flota* was making its customary stop for water on the southwest side of the island in 1603. While anchored there, an onshore breeze caused three of the ships to wreck: the *Capitana San Juan Bautista* (flagship), *La Rosa*, and an unidentified vessel. The value of the cargoes lost on these ships was over one million pesos. Two hundred and fifty men were left behind to salvage the wrecks. Soon after the *flota* sailed, however, Carib Indians attacked the Spaniards. The men fled the island before they could recover anything. A few months later the Spaniards captured a French pirate vessel near Puerto Rico that had onboard ten of the bronze cannon lost on the *San Juan Bautista*. A different *San Juan Bautista*, a merchant *nao*, sank in the same area later, in 1609.

Loire, 40-gun French warship
 Location: Anse la Barque
 History: The British destroyed two French warships on December 18, 1809, at Anse la Barque. They were the *Loire* and *Seine*.

Nuestra Señora del Pilar, galleon belonging to the New Spain Flota (fleet) of Captain-General Roque Centeno, 1,100 tons, Captain Alonso García del Castillo
 Location: Close to shore off the south end of the island
 History: The galleon sank for no apparent reason quite close to the shore in 1630 while anchored for water along with the rest of the *flota*. The ship was completely salvaged.

Petit Louis, French merchantman, Captain Videau
 Location: Guadeloupe
 History: The merchantman wrecked on the main island in 1824 while arriving from France.

Pointe-a-Petre [sic] English merchantman
 Location: Pointe-à-Pitre
 History: She was lost during a gale off Pointe-à-Pitre on July 29, 1810, while sailing for London.

Prosperity, English merchantman, Captain Wilson

Location: Guadeloupe
History: The merchantman was chased onshore by a French privateer in 1760 and wrecked.

Richard, ship
Location: West side of the island
History: The ship was stripped and then scuttled on the west side of the island in 1595 because she was sailing too slowly during an English privateering voyage to the West Indies led by Francis Drake and John Hawkins.

Rose, English trading vessel, Captain Carline
Location: Grand Terre
History: The small English trading vessel wrecked at Grand Terre in 1774 while arriving from Dominica.

San Juan Baustista, 45-gun *capitana*, (flagship) of the New Spain Flota (fleet) of Captain-General Fulgencio de Meneses, 700 tons, Captain Domingo de Licona
Location: Southwest side of the island
History: The *flota* was making its customary stop for water on the southwest side of the island in 1603. While anchored there an onshore breeze caused three of the ships to wreck: the *Capitana San Juan Bautista* (flagship), *La Rosa*, and an unidentified ship. The value of the cargoes lost on these ships was over one million pesos. Two hundred and fifty men were left behind to salvage the wrecks. Soon after the *flota* sailed, however, Carib Indians attacked the Spaniards. The men fled the island before they could recover anything. A few months later the Spaniards captured a French pirate vessel near Puerto Rico that had onboard ten of the bronze cannon lost on the *San Juan Bautista*. A different *San Juan Bautista*, a merchant *nao*, sank in the same area later, in 1609.

San Juan Bautista, Spanish merchant *nao*, Captain José de Ybarra
Location: Southwest side of the island
History: The ship, sailing from Cadiz to Veracruz, sank in 1609 after anchoring in the same area where the *Capitana San Juan Bautista* (flagship), and *La Rosa* sank in 1603. Carib Indi-

ans prevented the Spaniards from salvaging the *nao's* valuable cargo.

Seine, 40-gun French warship
Location: Anse la Barque
History: The British destroyed two French warships on December 18, 1809, at Anse la Barque. They were the *Loire* and *Seine*.

Superior, American ship, Captain Shaw
Location: Marie-Galante Island
History: The ship wrecked on the island on December 20, 1823. The crew and cargo were saved.

Syren, French merchantman, Captain Rhode
Location: East side of the island
History: The merchantman wrecked on the east side of the island in 1801 while sailing from France to St. Thomas.

Unidentified, ship belonging to the New Spain Flota (fleet) of Captain-General Fulgencio de Meneses
Location: Guadeloupe
History: The *flota* was making its customary stop for water on the southwest side of the island in 1603. While anchored there an onshore breeze caused three of the ships to wreck: the *Capitana San Juan Bautista* (flagship), *La Rosa*, and an unidentified ship. The value of the cargoes lost on these ships was over one million pesos. Two hundred and fifty men were left behind to salvage the wrecks. Soon after the *flota* sailed, however, Carib Indians attacked the Spaniards. The men fled the island before they could recover anything. A few months later the Spaniards captured a French pirate vessel near Puerto Rico that had onboard ten of the bronze cannon lost on the *San Juan Bautista*. A different *San Juan Bautista*, a merchant *nao*, sank in the same area later, in 1609.

Unidentified, French ships (large number)
Location: Guadeloupe
History: A large number of French ships were totally lost at the port of Basse-Terre and around Marie-Galante Island during a hurricane in 1656.

Unidentified, ships (many)
Location: Guadeloupe

History: A major sea battle between a French fleet and an English fleet commanded by Lord Willoughby took place on August 12, 1666. The French lost over 12 major warships, and the English lost two near the Isle des Saintes. Two days later a hurricane struck and an additional 50 vessels were lost, including all 15 of Lord Willoughby's remaining fleet. In the terrible weather the walls of the Fort at Basse-Terre were also washed into the sea, carrying many 14-pound cannon with them.

Unidentified, English merchantmen (50+)
Location: Guadeloupe
History: Over 50 large English ships were lost at different ports around the island and 12 inbound slave ships from Africa were also totally lost near the Isle des Saintes during a hurricane on October 6, 1766.

Unidentified, ships (40+)
Location: Guadeloupe
History: Over 40 ships of various nationalities were wrecked around the island during a hurricane on September 6, 1776.

Unidentified, ships (over 40)
Location: Basse-Terre
History: Over 40 ships of different nationalities were lost at Basse-Terre and other nearby anchorages during a hurricane in September 1713.

Unidentified, English merchantmen (6)
Location: Basse-Terre
History: Six unidentified English merchantmen were sunk at Basse-Terre and several others at Marie-Galante Island during a hurricane in July 1762.

Unidentified, English merchantmen (16)
Location: Basse-Terre
History: Seventeen English merchantmen were lost at Basse-Terre during a hurricane on July 31, 1765. Only one was identified: the *Friendship*.

Unidentified, English ships (3)
Location: Basse-Terre
History: Three English ships were sunk at Basse-Terre during a hurricane on September 10, 1786.

Unidentified, French privateer
Location: East side of the island
History: The privateer wrecked on the east side of the island in 1618. The six survivors were rescued two years later by an English merchantman bound for Virginia.

Unidentified, French frigate belonging to Admiral De Casse's fleet
Location: Isle des Saintes
History: Several English warships forced the French frigate of Admiral De Casse's fleet ashore on the Isle des Saintes in 1691.

Unidentified, ship, 200 tons
Location: Isle des Saintes
History: The ship wrecked on the Isle des Saintes in 1760 while arriving from Virginia. Some of her crew perished.

Unidentified, slave ships (12)
Location: Isle des Saintes
History: Over 50 large English ships were lost at different ports around the island and 12 inbound slave ships from Africa were also totally lost near the Isle des Saintes during a hurricane on October 6, 1766.

Virginia, English ship, Captain Burt
Location: Isle des Saintes
History: The ship wrecked on July 20, 1822, on the Isle des Saintes. The ship was sailing from Dominica to Antigua with a large number of soldiers when it wrecked, but the crew and passengers were saved.

SHIPWRECKS IN ISLAS DE AVES' (BIRD ISLANDS) WATERS

Rising Sun, American slave ship, Captain Allanson
Location: Islas de Aves
History: The ship wrecked on the islands in 1774 while sailing from Africa to America with a cargo of slaves.

Santa Ana María, Spanish merchant *nao*
Location: Islas de Aves
History: The *nao* wrecked on the Islas de Aves in 1689 while carrying a valuable cargo of mercury and general merchandise from Cadiz to Veracruz.

Unidentified, 24-gun English merchantman
Location: Islas de Aves
History: The merchantman wrecked in 1705 with a main cargo of iron bars and barrels of nails. Eleven days later a French ship rescued the survivors and recovered most of her cargo.

SHIPWRECKS IN MARTINIQUE'S WATERS

Alfred, French ship, Captain Mony
Location: Diamond Rock
History: The ship wrecked on Diamond Rock in 1823 while arriving from France.

Amphitrite, 40-gun French warship
Location: Fort de France
History: The English sank the French warship on February 4, 1809, at Fort de France during an English attack against the French on the island.

Brilliant, English merchantman, Captain Boyd
Location: Off the south part of the island
History: The merchantman foundered off the south part of the island in 1762 while sailing from London to the West Indies. All her crew was saved.

Carnation, 18-gun French warship
Location: Fort de France
History: The French burnt two of their warships, the *Rossollis* and *Carnation*, in Fort de France on February 24, 1809, to prevent their capture by the English.

Caroline, French merchantman, Captain Monnier
Location: Martinique
History: The merchantman wrecked on the island in May 1816 while sailing from France to Louisiana. The crew was saved.

Diana, ship of unknown nationality, Captain Deare
Location: A port on the west side of the island
History: The ship, sailing from India to America, was forced to enter a port on the west side of the island in 1796. The vessel was then burnt to prevent

it from falling into the hands of some English warships.

Diligence, English merchantman, Captain Orr
Location: Fort Royal Bay
History: After departing from England, the merchantman was captured by a French privateer near the island in 1780 and taken into Fort Royal Bay. As ten English warships were coming to her rescue, she was burnt along with the ship that had captured her.

Dispatch, English merchantman, Captain McIntire
Location: Martinique
History: The vessel wrecked on the island in 1802 while sailing for Quebec. Part of her cargo was saved.

Edward, English merchantman, Captain Nash
Location: East side of the island
History: The merchantman wrecked on the east side of the island in 1801 while sailing from London to Honduras.

Endymion, supply ship
Location: Martinique
History: The hurricane that struck Martinique on October 12, 1780, was the worst to ever hit the island. A French convoy of 40 large troop transports, which had just reached Martinique, was totally destroyed in some port on the west side. Four large French warships were sunk in Fort Royal Bay with a total loss of life. Three of Admiral Rodney's English warships wrecked on the west side of the island. They were H.M.S. *Andromeda,* H.M.S. *Laurel,* and H.M.S. *Deal Castle.* An English ship, probably a supply ship of Admiral Rodney's fleet, the *Endymion,* was lost on the island as well. Some accounts in documents place the total number of ships of different nationalities lost on the island during the hurricane at over 150. However, no two accounts agree as to that number.

General Hunter, Canadian brig, Captain Perkins
Location: Fort de France
History: The brig was lost at Fort de France in 1814 while arriving from Halifax.

Generous Friends, English troop transport, Captain Harrison

Location: Martinique

History: The ship wrecked on the island in 1794 while arriving from London.

Geraundeau, French slave ship, Captain Duckerson

Location: South side of the island

History: While arriving from Africa in 1774 with 450 slaves aboard, the ship wrecked on the south side of the island. The slaves and crew were saved.

H.M.S. *Andromeda*, 28-gun English warship belonging to the fleet of Admiral Rodney

Location: Martinique

History: The hurricane that struck Martinique on October 12, 1780, was the worst to ever hit the island. A French convoy of 40 large troop transports, which had just reached Martinique, was totally destroyed in some port on the west side. Four large French warships were sunk in Fort Royal Bay with a total loss of life. Three of Admiral Rodney's English warships wrecked on the west side of the island. They were H.M.S. *Andromeda*, H.M.S. *Laurel*, and H.M.S. *Deal Castle*. An English ship, probably a supply ship of Admiral Rodney's fleet, the *Endymion*, was lost on the island as well. Some accounts in documents place the total number of ships of different nationalities lost on the island during the hurricane at over 150. However, no two accounts agree as to that number.

H.M.S. *Coventry*, English ship

Location: Bay of All Saints

History: In 1666, when the governor of Barbados heard that there were six richly laden French ships in the Bay of All Saints on Martinique, he sent H.M.S. *Coventry* and four other large English warships to capture them. When the French saw the English approaching the bay they set fire to all six of their vessels. The English managed to save all but one of the French ships; the sixth ship went down. The following day, while the English were transferring the plunder to their own vessels, a storm struck and all five sank. The French recovered over 80

large cannon from these wrecks as well as other items.

H.M.S. *Deal Castle*, 24-gun English warship belonging to the fleet of Admiral Rodney

Location: Martinique

History: The hurricane that struck Martinique on October 12, 1780, was the worst to ever hit the island. A French convoy of 40 large troop transports, which had just reached Martinique, was totally destroyed in some port on the west side. Four large French warships were sunk in Fort Royal Bay with a total loss of life. Three of Admiral Rodney's English warships wrecked on the west side of the island. They were H.M.S. *Andromeda*, H.M.S. *Laurel*, and H.M.S. *Deal Castle*. An English ship, probably a supply ship of Admiral Rodney's fleet, the *Endymion*, was lost on the island as well. Some accounts in documents place the total number of ships of different nationalities lost on the island during the hurricane at over 150. However, no two accounts agree as to that number.

H.M.S. *Laurel*, 28-gun English warship belonging to the fleet of Admiral Rodney

Location: Martinique

History: The hurricane that struck Martinique on October 12, 1780, was the worst to ever hit the island. A French convoy of 40 large troop transports, which had just reached Martinique, was totally destroyed in some port on the west side. Four large French warships were sunk in Fort Royal Bay with a total loss of life. Three of Admiral Rodney's English warships wrecked on the west side of the island. They were H.M.S. *Andromeda*, H.M.S. *Laurel*, and H.M.S. *Deal Castle*. An English ship, probably a supply ship of Admiral Rodney's fleet, the *Endymion*, was lost on the island as well. Some accounts in documents place the total number of ships of different nationalities lost on the island during the hurricane at over 150. However, no two accounts agree as to that number.

H.M.S. *Morne Fortunee*, 12-gun English warship, Captain John Brown

Location: Martinique

History: The warship was wrecked

on the island in 1809. Forty-one of her crew of 65 perished.

H.M.S. *Raisonable*, 64-gun English ship, Captain Molyneux Shuldham

Location: Near a battery several miles north of Fort de France

History: The ship, belonging to an English fleet commanded by Sir James Douglas, wrecked in 1761 near a battery several miles north of Fort de France during an attack on the island by the English. The crew and most of the stores were saved. The French later recovered her cannon.

H.M.S. *Thames*, English warship, Captain Willoughby

Location: Near Diamond Rock

History: The warship was captured by the French off Barbados, but wrecked in 1807 near Diamond Rock on the south side of the island.

Hope, English merchantman, Captain Thompson

Location: East side of the island

History: The merchantman wrecked on the east side of the island in 1801 while sailing from London to Tortola.

John, American sloop, Captain Richardson

Location: Martinique

History: The sloop wrecked on the island in 1794 while coming from Virginia.

Kennion, English slave ship, Captain Robinson

Location: Martinique

History: The vessel wrecked on the island in 1802 while sailing from Africa to Jamaica.

Madame Royale, French merchantman

Location: East side of the island

History: The merchantman was totally lost on the east side of the island on June 7, 1815, while arriving from France. There were no survivors.

Madona, English merchantman, Captain Vollum

Location: East side of the island

History: The ship wrecked on the east side of the island in 1801 while arriving from London.

Margaret, Canadian sloop

Location: Grand Passage Bay

History: The sloop was lost at Grand Passage Bay in 1814 while coming from New Brunswick. Her crew was saved.

New Hampshire, American ship, Captain Knight

Location: Fort de France

History: The ship wrecked entering the port of Fort de France in 1763 while coming from New England. The crew and cargo were saved.

Our Lady of Hope, French merchantman, Captain Serres

Location: Six miles off the east side of the island

History: The ship wrecked on a reef six miles off the east side of the island in 1687 while coming from Marseilles.

Pacific, English merchantman, Captain Wilson

Location: East side of the island

History: The ship wrecked on the east side of the island in 1801 while arriving from London.

Rossollis, 18-gun French warship

Location: Fort de France

History: The French burnt two of their warships, the *Rossollis* and *Carnation,* in Fort de France on February 24, 1809, to prevent their capture by the English.

San Salvador, Spanish warship, Captain Sancho de Urdanibia

Location: South side of the island, in two fathoms

History: The warship wrecked on the south side of the island in 1636 while carrying a cargo of war materials to Venezuela for an attack against the Dutch on Curaçao. Because Martinique was settled by their enemies, the French at the time, the Spaniards threw the 26 bronze cannon overboard, then set the ship afire before escaping in small boats. The French tried to reach the wreck, but it blew up before they could take any of its cargo off.

Spring Bird, American merchantman, Captain Lambert

Location: Martinique

History: The merchantman wrecked on the island early in the year 1811 while coming from New England.

Stanislaus, French merchantman, Captain Berthelet

Location: Martinique

History: The ship wrecked on the island on September 15, 1816, while arriving from France.

Susannah, English merchantman, Captain Stanton

Location: Martinique

History: She wrecked on the island in 1802 while sailing for Dublin.

Unidentified, ships (many)

Location: Martinique

History: Two accounts differ as to what happened on the island in 1667. One account states that a large English fleet commanded by Admiral Sir John Harman entered the main port, which was Fort de France, and burnt 20 French warships and merchantmen at anchor. The other account states that the event occurred at Governor's Bay, and that 19 French warships, three fireships and some Dutch merchantmen were burnt and sunk.

Unidentified, ships (many)

Location: Martinique

History: Two large French warships and many merchantmen were sunk or wrecked in different ports of the island during a hurricane in October 1740.

Unidentified, ships (many)

Location: Martinique

History: During a hurricane in October 1766, 28 French and eight English ships were lost at Fort de France; nine English ships were lost at Flemish Bay; 18 unidentified ships were totally lost at La Trinité Bay.

Unidentified, ships (over 150)

Location: Martinique

History: The hurricane that struck Martinique on October 12, 1780, was the worst to ever hit the island. A French convoy of 40 large troop transports, which had just reached Martinique, was totally destroyed in some port on the west side. Four large French warships were sunk in Fort Royal Bay with a total loss of life. Three of Admiral Rodney's English warships wrecked on the west side of the island. They were H.M.S. *Andromeda,* H.M.S. *Laurel,* and H.M.S. *Deal Castle.* An English ship, probably a supply ship of Admiral Rodney's fleet, the *Endymion,* was lost on the island as well.

Some accounts in documents place the total number of ships of different nationalities lost during the hurricane at over 150. However, no two accounts agree as to that number.

Unidentified, French ships (over 50)

Location: Martinique

History: Over 50 large French ships were totally destroyed in various ports of the island during a hurricane in September 1788. Most of the town of Caravel, along with the majority of its inhabitants, were swept into the sea as well.

Unidentified, ships (42)

Location: Martinique

History: A total of 42 ships of different nationalities were lost in various ports of the island during a hurricane in August 1813. Over 3,000 persons perished.

Unidentified, ships (10)

Location: Bay of All Saints

History: In 1666, when the governor of Barbados heard that there were six richly laden French ships in the Bay of All Saints on Martinique, he sent H.M.S. *Coventry* and four other large English warships to capture them. When the French saw the English approaching the bay they set fire to all six of their vessels. The English managed to save all but one of the French ships; the sixth ship went down. The following day, while the English were transferring the plunder to their own vessels, a storm struck and all five sank. The French recovered over 80 large cannon from these wrecks as well as other items.

Unidentified, ships (over 22)

Location: Cul-de-Sac Bay

History: Over 20 large French ships and two English ships were totally lost in Cul-de-Sac Bay during a violent hurricane on August 3, 1680. The loss of life was great.

Unidentified, ships (4 or 5)

Location: Cul-de-Sac Bay

History: Four or five unidentified ships were lost at Cul-de-Sac Bay during a hurricane on July 8, 1811.

Unidentified, French warship

Location: Fort de France

History: An English warship, commanded by Captain Arther forced an unidentified French warship to run aground near Fort de France in 1691.

Unidentified, merchantmen (over 100)
   Location: Point Petre Bay
   History: Over 100 French and Dutch merchantmen, all in a convoy preparing to sail for Europe, were totally lost at Point Petre Bay during a hurricane on September 6, 1776. Over 6,000 persons were drowned.

Unidentified, Spanish merchantman
   Location: South side of the island
   History: In 1744, the large merchantman, sailing from Cadiz to Cartagena, was forced ashore and destroyed on the south side of the island by several ships belonging to the English fleet commanded by Commodore Knowles.

Unidentified, French ships (32)
   Location: South side of the island
   History: The English fleet of admiral Townsend attacked a French fleet of 40 large merchantmen being escorted by two warships as it was making its way around the south side of the island in 1745. Thirty of the French merchantman and the two warships were forced ashore and destroyed by the English. The cargoes on the merchantmen were valued at over 15 million lives.

Unidentified, ships (8+)
   Location: West side of the island
   History: During a hurricane in October 1695, six or seven large French ships and several smaller ones were totally lost on the west side of the island and over 600 men aboard them perished.

Unidentified, merchantmen and small vessels (many)
   Location: West side of the island
   History: Thirty-three large French merchantmen and many small vessels were lost in different ports on the west side of the island during a hurricane in July 1765.

Unidentified, ships (over 70)
   Location: West side of the island
   History: Martinique had barely recovered from the hurricane of 1776 when an even worse one struck on Au-

gust 28, 1779. Over 70 ships were lost all over the west side of the island. Among the many people lost were some of the survivors from the previous hurricane.

SHIPWRECKS IN MONTSERRAT'S WATERS

Eliza, English merchantman, Captain Summers
   Location: Montserrat
   History: The merchantman wrecked during a gale on July 26, 1807, while bound for Bristol.

Friends Goodwill, English merchantman, Captain Lesley
   Location: Montserrat
   History: A sloop, several shallops and two English merchantmen, the *Friends Goodwill* and *Imperial Anne*, were lost during a hurricane on September 21, 1747.

Gill, English merchantman
   Location: Montserrat
   History: The ship sank during a hurricane on July 31, 1775, while sailing from St. Eustatius to St. Vincent Island.

Imperial Anne, English merchantman, Captain Butler
   Location: Montserrat
   History: A sloop, several shallops and two English merchantmen, the *Friends Goodwill* and *Imperial Anne*, were lost during a hurricane on September 21, 1747.

Lady Parker, English merchantman
   Location: Montserrat
   History: The merchantman wrecked during a gale on July 26, 1807, while bound for London.

London Packet, English ship, Captain Tirnam
   Location: Montserrat
   History: The ship was totally lost during a hurricane that struck on October 24, 1747.

Two Brothers, Irish merchantman, Captain Brown
   Location: Montserrat
   History: The merchantman wrecked

in 1744 while coming from Cork. Her cargo was saved.

Unidentified, French warships (large number)
   Location: Montserrat
   History: A large number of unidentified French warships were wrecked on the island during a hurricane in September 1666.

Unidentified, merchantman
   Location: Montserrat
   History: The merchantman wrecked on Montserrat during a hurricane in October 1681 while coming from New England.

Unidentified, ships (several)
   Location: Montserrat
   History: A sloop, several shallops and two English merchantmen, the *Friends Goodwill* and *Imperial Anne*, were lost during a hurricane on September 21, 1747.

Unidentified, English merchantmen (large number)
   Location: The west side of the island
   History: A large number of homeward-bound English merchantmen were totally lost on the west side of the island during a hurricane in October 1766.

Unidentified, English merchantmen (8)
   Location: Plymouth Harbour
   History: Eight merchantmen were wrecked in Plymouth Harbour during a hurricane on September 13, 1754. Plymouth is the main town and port of Montserrat.

SHIPWRECKS IN NEVIS' WATERS

Artifacts
   Location: Nevis
   History: An earthquake struck the whole island at 7:00 A.M. on April 6, 1690. Most of Charlestown, including the main fort, was cast into the sea. Records about the disaster are very brief and vague. There is no mention of the number of buildings lost, the value of the property destroyed, or the number of lives lost. During an exploratory

dive on the site in 1961, coauthor Robert F. Marx located at least 50 different brick buildings that were protruding above the sandy sea floor. There is no doubt that many more are buried on the site. Most of the site is in 20 to 30 feet of water; however, the walls of the main fort are near shore in only eight to ten feet of water, and over 20 huge iron cannon were sighted there at the time of Marx's dive.

Brutus, Venezuelan cruiser
   Location: Nevis
   History: The cruiser wrecked during a hurricane on September 21 and 22, 1819.

Cambell, English merchantman, Captain Goodwin
   Location: Nevis Point
   History: The merchantman was captured by a French pirate while coming from Bristol. The ship then wrecked in a gale at Nevis Point on September 10, 1728.

Friends, English merchantman, Captain Donald
   Location: On the island
   History: The merchantman wrecked on the island in 1804 while coming from London.

Grace, English merchantman, Captain Taylor
   Location: The northeast end of the island
   History: The merchantman was totally lost on a reef at the northeast end of the island in 1808 while coming from London. The crew and part of the cargo were saved.

H.M.S. Drake, 14-gun English warship, Captain William Ferriss
   Location: Near the island
   History: The warship wrecked on a reef near the island in 1804. None of the crew of 86 were lost.

H.M.S. Solebay, 28-gun English warship, Captain Charles Holmes Everritt
   Location: Nevis Point
   History: The English ship wrecked at Nevis Point on January 25, 1782, while trying to elude three French ships. The crew burnt the ship before they escaped ashore.

Mackey, mailboat of unknown registry
   Location: Nevis
   History: The mailboat was totally lost on January 16, 1823. Only the mail was saved.

Mary, English merchantman, Captain Herbert
   Location: Around the island
   History: Eight vessels were wrecked around the island during a hurricane on September 21, 1747, including five sloops, one schooner, a large prize snow, and the *Mary,* which was preparing to sail for London.

Princess Ann, English merchantman, Captain Tampert
   Location: Green Point
   History: The merchantman wrecked at Green Point in 1761 while sailing from Barbados to Ireland. Her cargo of rum was saved.

Rachael, ship of unknown registry
   Location: Nevis
   History: The ship was totally lost during a hurricane on October 7, 1811.

Sarah & Ann, English merchantman
   Location: Nevis
   History: The merchantman was totally lost during a hurricane on August 1, 1792, while sailing to London. Nothing of her cargo was salvaged.

Unidentified, English warship
   Location: Nevis Roads
   History: An English ship was accidentally blown up by her own crew during a battle between 30 French and ten English warships on April 10, 1667, in Nevis Roads.

Unidentified, English merchantman
   Location: Nevis
   History: A large unidentified English merchantman, carrying 500 hogsheads of sugar, was totally lost in 1772.

Unidentified, French warships (several)
   Location: Charlestown
   History: Several large French warships of the Count d'Estaing's fleet then anchored off Charlestown, were totally lost during a hurricane on September 4, 1779.

Unidentified, vessels (7)
   Location: Around the island
   History: Eight vessels were wrecked around the island during a hurricane on September 21, 1747, including five sloops, one schooner, a large prize snow, and the *Mary,* which was preparing to sail for London.

Unidentified, British privateer
   Location: Off Charlestown
   History: A large British privateer was totally lost off Charlestown, the island's main port and town, during a hurricane on August 16, 1669.

Unidentified, English merchantman
   Location: West side of the island
   History: The merchantman was wrecked on the west side of the island during an attack by the Spanish in the year 1629.

Unidentified, English merchantmen (20)
   Location: The vicinity of Charlestown and Nevis Point
   History: Twenty merchantmen wrecked in the vicinity of Charlestown and Nevis Point during a hurricane in August 1790.

SHIPWRECKS IN SABA'S WATERS

Bristol, English slave ship, Captain Payne
   Location: Saba
   History: The ship wrecked on the island during a hurricane in June 1733. The vessel was sailing from Africa to Jamaica with a cargo of slaves when it wrecked.

La Regla, four-gun Spanish advice boat, Captain Julio Rodríquez Espinosa
   Location: East side of Saba
   History: The advice boat wrecked on the east side of the island while sailing from Spain to Puerto Rico in 1567 with mail and passengers.

SHIPWRECKS IN ST. BARTHÉLEMY'S WATERS

Guernsey, French ship, Captain Collinette

Location: St. Barthélemy
History: The ship was totally lost in June 1811. Most of her crew perished.

H.M.S. *Subtle,* ten-gun English warship, Captain Charles Brown
Location: St. Barthélemy
History: The ship foundered near the island in 1813. The crew of 50 perished.

Nelly, American merchantman, Captain Shelly
Location: St. Barthélemy
History: The merchantman wrecked in 1792 while sailing from Antigua to America.

Unidentified, ship
Location: St. Barthélemy
History: A large unidentified ship was sunk in the harbor of St. Barthélemy during a hurricane on August 29, 1707.

Unidentified, ships (3)
Location: St. Barthélemy
History: Three ships were wrecked on the island during a severe gale in September 1791.

Unidentified, ships (10)
Location: St. Barthélemy
History: Ten ships were totally destroyed in the main harbor during a hurricane on August 1, 1792, with a great loss of life.

Unidentified, ships (40)
Location: St. Barthélemy
History: A total of 40 ships, most of which were American, sailed into the harbor for shelter from a hurricane on October 7, 1811. They all wrecked or foundered.

Unidentified, ships (60)
Location: St. Barthélemy
History: Sixty ships, mostly American, entered the harbor for shelter from a hurricane on September 18, 1815. All wrecked or went down. A Swedish sloop-of-war was also lost.

Unidentified, Swedish sloop-of-war
Location: St. Barthélemy
History: Sixty ships, mostly American, entered the harbor for shelter from a hurricane on September 18, 1815. All wrecked or went down. A Swedish sloop-of-war was also lost.

Unidentified, ships
Location: St. Barthélemy
History: A hurricane in September 1819 totally destroyed half the island's town and washed it into the sea, and rendered all the shipping a mass of ruins at the head of the bay.

Unidentified, ships (many)
Location: St. Barthélemy
History: Many unidentified sloops and schooners were totally lost in the port during a hurricane on September 10, 1821.

Shipwrecks in St. Eustatius' Waters

Artifacts
Location: Orange Town
History: All 400 houses in Orange Town were blown down and the Dutch church was thrown into the sea during a hurricane in August 1772.

Duke Compagni, Italian merchantman, Captain Lambaldi
Location: North side of the island
History: In 1758, the ship set sail from the island for Amsterdam after unloading a valuable cargo of merchandise for which it received many chests of silver specie. It then wrecked as it attempted to round the north side of the island. All the crew and most of the specie were saved.

Unidentified, treasure and artifacts
Location: West side of the island
History: More than half of the main town of St. Eustatius, which was located on the island's west side, was cast into the sea during an earthquake on April 6, 1690. Several hundred lives were lost. At the time of the earthquake, the town was used mainly as a base for privateers and contraband traders of various nationalities. Therefore, many of the buildings that fell into the sea were warehouses full of plunder and contraband, the overall value of which exceeded a million pounds sterling. The ruins of these sunken buildings are still visible and are located off the bluff of Orange Town, the island's only settlement. Coauthor Marx dove on the site in

1960 and recovered a large number of bottles, intact pieces of ceramic ware, clay smoking pipes, bricks, and two muskets.

Unidentified, English merchantmen (2)
Location: St. Eustatius
History: Two merchantmen were wrecked in June 1733 during a hurricane.

Unidentified, English merchantmen (20)
Location: Orange Town
History: A large fleet of homeward-bound English merchantmen sought shelter off Orange Town during a hurricane in 1737. Twenty of the vessels sank.

Unidentified, merchant ships (several)
Location: Orange Town
History: Several unidentified merchant ships were totally lost off Orange Town during a violent hurricane on September 21, 1766.

Unidentified, ships (7)
Location: North Point
History: Seven Dutch ships were totally lost on the coast at North Point during a hurricane on October 9, 1780, with everyone onboard perishing. Orange Town was leveled to the ground by the hurricane, and between 4,000 and 5,000 persons died.

Unidentified, ships (large number)
Location: St. Eustatius
History: A large number of ships of different nationalities were lost around the island during a hurricane in August 1786.

Unidentified, Dutch merchantmen (2)
Location: Orange Town
History: Two large Dutch merchantmen were lost off Orange Town during a hurricane around the end of October 1791.

Unidentified, ships (several)
Location: West side of St. Eustatius
History: One large Dutch ship and several of other nationalities were totally lost off the west side of the island in 1792.

Unidentified, Spanish brig
Location: St. Eustatius

History: The brig sank in 1792 while sailing between St. Kitts and the island. There were only two survivors.

SHIPWRECKS IN ST. KITTS' WATERS

Ancient Britain, English ship
Location: Basseterre
History: Twelve ships were sunk at Basseterre during a hurricane in June 1733. Three of them were identified as English ships: the *Nassau, Stapleton* and *Ancient Britain*.

Apollo, English merchantman, Captain Manning
Location: St. Kitts
History: Two ships were totally lost during a hurricane in the year 1772: the *Apollo* and *Thistle*.

Betsey, English merchantman, Captain Basdon
Location: Deep Bay
History: Five English merchantmen were wrecked in Deep Bay during a hurricane on August 26, 1785. Only three of them were identified: the *Thomas, Spooner* and *Betsey*.

Betsey, English merchantman, Captain Mathews
Location: Sandy Point
History: The English ship, ready to sail for England, was wrecked at Sandy Point during a gale on September 18, 1766. Only some of the rigging was salvaged from the wreck.

Bottle, English merchantman, Captain Ford
Location: St. Kitts
History: Seventeen ships were wrecked during a hurricane that struck on July 23, 1813. Ten were American ships that had been seized as war prizes; three were American coastal schooners; and four were English merchantmen. The last were: the *John & William*, just arrived from France; the *Britannia*, sailing to England; the *Colonest*; and the *Bottle*.

Britannia, English merchantman, Captain Woodyear
Location: St. Kitts
History: The merchantman was lost on the island before August 1, 1792, while sailing to London.

Britannia, English merchantman, Captain Paulson
Location: St. Kitts
History: Seventeen ships were wrecked during a hurricane that struck on July 23, 1813. Ten were American ships that had been seized as war prizes; three were American coastal schooners; and four were English merchantmen. The last were: the *John & William*, just arrived from France; the *Britannia*, sailing to England; the *Colonest*; and the *Bottle*.

Charlotte, English merchantman, Captain Williamson
Location: East side of the island
History: The merchantman wrecked off the east side of the island in 1773 while arriving from London.

Colonest, English merchantman, Captain Oliver
Location: St. Kitts
History: Seventeen ships were wrecked during a hurricane that struck on July 23, 1813. Ten were American ships that had been seized as war prizes; three were American coastal schooners and four were English merchantmen. The last were: the *John & William*, just arrived from France; the *Britannia*, sailing to England; the *Colonest*; and the *Bottle*.

Cornwally, English merchantman, Captain Sword
Location: Basseterre
History: During hurricanes on September 21 and October 24, 1747, a total of 24 English merchantmen were lost at Basseterre, most of them fully loaded with cargoes of sugar for England. Only these 12 were identified: the *Owen Gally, Rising Sun, Pretty Patsy, Duke of Marlborough, Cornwally, Rowlandson, Emma, Mary, Swallow, Plante, Parkham Pink*, and *Nisbitt*.

Dart, English merchantman
Location: St. Kitts
History: The Dart had just arrived from England when it was lost around the island in 1811. The crew was saved.

Douglas, English merchantman, Captain Webster
Location: Near Basseterre
History: The *Douglas*, recently arrived from London, was burnt near Basseterre in 1782 during an attack by several French warships.

Duke of Marlborough, English merchantman, Captain Denn
Location: Basseterre
History: During hurricanes on September 21 and October 24, 1747, a total of 24 English merchantmen were lost at Basseterre, most of them fully loaded with cargoes of sugar for England. Only these 12 were identified: the *Owen Gally, Rising Sun, Pretty Patsy, Duke of Marlborough, Cornwally, Rowlandson, Emma, Mary, Swallow, Plante, Parkham Pink*, and *Nisbitt*.

Earl of Cornwallis, eighteen gun American privateer
Location: Basseterre
History: The privateer sank at Basseterre in 1781 with 100 men onboard. A large number of the crew perished.

Emma, English merchantman, Captain Faulker
Location: Basseterre
History: During hurricanes on September 21 and October 24, 1747, a total of 24 English merchantmen were lost at Basseterre, most of them fully loaded with cargoes of sugar for England. Only these 12 were identified: the *Owen Gally, Rising Sun, Pretty Patsy, Duke of Marlborough, Cornwally, Rowlandson, Emma, Mary, Swallow, Plante, Parkham Pink*, and *Nisbitt*.

Flying Delight, English ship
Location: Around the island
History: Thirty merchantmen, both English and American, were lost around the island during a hurricane on August 12, 1793. Only a few of the English ships were identified by name: the *Hoppitt, Letitia, Flying Delight, Indian Castle, Polly* and *Nancy*.

Friendship, Irish merchantman, Captain Bodkin
Location: Basseterre
History: Several ships were wrecked at Basseterre during a violent gale on July 24, 1751. Only one was identified, the *Friendship*, sailing to Cork. None of the crew was saved.

George & Margaret, English merchantman, Captain Ashington
Location: On the island
History: The merchantman was lost before August 1, 1792, while sailing to London.

H.M.S. *Child's Play*, 24-gun English warship, Captain George Doyley
Location: Palmetto Point
History: The warship wrecked at Palmetto Point during a hurricane on August 30, 1707. The ship's cannon were salvaged.

H.M.S. *Supply*, 20-gun English storeship, Captain John Lockhart Nasmyth
Location: Basseterre
History: The storeship was accidentally burnt at Basseterre in the year 1779.

H.M.S. *Winchester*, English warship
Location: Sandy Point
History: The warship wrecked off Sandy Point during a hurricane on August 30, 1707. The ship's cannon were salvaged.

Hoppitt, English ship
Location: Around the island
History: Thirty merchantmen, both English and American, were lost around the island during a hurricane on August 12, 1793. Only a few of the English ships were identified by name: the *Hoppitt, Letitia, Flying Delight, Indian Castle, Polly* and *Nancy*.

Indian Castle, English ship
Location: Around the island
History: Thirty merchantmen, both English and American, were lost around the island during a hurricane on August 12, 1793. Only a few of the English ships were identified by name: the *Hoppitt, Letitia, Flying Delight, Indian Castle, Polly* and *Nancy*.

Isabella, English merchantman, Captain Carnage
Location: On the island
History: The merchantman was lost on the island before August 1, 1792, while sailing to Glasgow.

John & William, English merchantman
Location: St. Kitts
History: Seventeen ships were wrecked during a hurricane that struck on July 23, 1813. Ten were American ships that had been seized as war prizes; three were American coastal schooners; and four were English merchantmen. The last were: the *John & William*, just arrived from France; the *Britannia*, sailing to England; the *Colonest*; and the *Bottle*.

Letitia, English ship
Location: Around the island
History: Thirty merchantmen, both English and American, were lost around the island during a hurricane on August 12, 1793. Only a few of the English ships were identified by name: the *Hoppitt, Letitia, Flying Delight, Indian Castle, Polly* and *Nancy*.

Maria, English merchantman, Captain Williams
Location: On the island
History: Two schooners, two sloops and the merchantman *Maria* were wrecked on the island during a gale on July 26, 1807.

Mary, English merchantman, Captain Watson
Location: Basseterre
History: During hurricanes on September 21 and October 24, 1747, a total of 24 English merchantmen were lost at Basseterre, most of them fully loaded with cargoes of sugar for England. Only these 12 were identified: the *Owen Gally, Rising Sun, Pretty Patsy, Duke of Marlborough, Cornwally, Rowlandson, Emma, Mary, Swallow, Plante, Parkham Pink*, and *Nisbitt*.

Nancy, English ship
Location: Around the island
History: Thirty merchantmen, both English and American, were lost around the island during a hurricane on August 12, 1793. Only a few of the English ships were identified by name: the *Hoppitt, Letitia, Flying Delight, Indian Castle, Polly* and *Nancy*.

Nassau, English ship
Location: Basseterre
History: Twelve ships were sunk at Basseterre during a hurricane in June 1733. Three of them were identified as English ships: the *Nassau, Stapleton* and *Ancient Britain*.

Nisbitt, English merchantman, Captain Hall

Location: Basseterre
History: During hurricanes on September 21 and October 24, 1747, a total of 24 English merchantmen were lost at Basseterre, most of them fully loaded with cargoes of sugar for England. Only these 12 were identified: the *Owen Gally, Rising Sun, Pretty Patsy, Duke of Marlborough, Cornwally, Rowlandson, Emma, Mary, Swallow, Plante, Parkham Pink*, and *Nisbitt*.

Owen Gally, English merchantman, Captain Wood
Location: Basseterre
History: During hurricanes on September 21 and October 24, 1747, a total of 24 English merchantmen were lost at Basseterre, most of them fully loaded with cargoes of sugar for England. Only these 12 were identified: the *Owen Gally, Rising Sun, Pretty Patsy, Duke of Marlborough, Cornwally, Rowlandson, Emma, Mary, Swallow, Plante, Parkham Pink*, and *Nisbitt*.

Parkham Pink, English merchantman, Captain Aberdam
Location: Basseterre
History: During hurricanes on September 21 and October 24, 1747, a total of 24 English merchantmen were lost at Basseterre, most of them fully loaded with cargoes of sugar for England. Only these 12 were identified: the *Owen Gally, Rising Sun, Pretty Patsy, Duke of Marlborough, Cornwally, Rowlandson, Emma, Mary, Swallow, Plante, Parkham Pink*, and *Nisbitt*.

Plante, English merchantman, Captain Cains
Location: Basseterre
History: During hurricanes on September 21 and October 24, 1747, a total of 24 English merchantmen were lost at Basseterre, most of them fully loaded with cargoes of sugar for England. Only these 12 were identified: the *Owen Gally, Rising Sun, Pretty Patsy, Duke of Marlborough, Cornwally, Rowlandson, Emma, Mary, Swallow, Plante, Parkham Pink*, and *Nisbitt*.

Polly, English ship
Location: Around the island
History: Thirty merchantmen, both English and American, were lost around the island during a hurricane on August 12, 1793. Only a few of the

English ships were identified by name: the *Hoppitt, Letitia, Flying Delight, Indian Castle, Polly* and *Nancy*.

Pretty Patsy, English merchantman, Captain Hays
Location: Basseterre
History: During hurricanes on September 21 and October 24, 1747, a total of 24 English merchantmen were lost at Basseterre, most of them fully loaded with cargoes of sugar for England. Only these 12 were identified: the *Owen Gally, Rising Sun, Pretty Patsy, Duke of Marlborough, Cornwally, Rowlandson, Emma, Mary, Swallow, Plante, Parkham Pink,* and *Nisbitt*.

Rebbeca & Martha, Irish merchantman, Captain Copythorn
Location: East side of the island
History: The merchantman wrecked on the east side of the island in 1741 while coming from Cork.

Rising Sun, English merchantman, Captain Parker
Location: Basseterre
History: During hurricanes on September 21 and October 24, 1747, a total of 24 English merchantmen were lost at Basseterre, most of them fully loaded with cargoes of sugar for England. Only these 12 were identified: the *Owen Gally, Rising Sun, Pretty Patsy, Duke of Marlborough, Cornwally, Rowlandson, Emma, Mary, Swallow, Plante, Parkham Pink,* and *Nisbitt*.

Rowlandson, English merchantman, Captain Watson
Location: Basseterre
History: During hurricanes on September 21 and October 24, 1747, a total of 24 English merchantmen were lost at Basseterre, most of them fully loaded with cargoes of sugar for England. Only these 12 were identified: the *Owen Gally, Rising Sun, Pretty Patsy, Duke of Marlborough, Cornwally, Rowlandson, Emma, Mary, Swallow, Plante, Parkham Pink,* and *Nisbitt*.

Spooner, English merchantman, Captain Lorban
Location: Deep Bay
History: Five English merchantmen were wrecked in Deep Bay during a hurricane on August 26, 1785. Only three of them were identified: the *Thomas, Spooner* and *Betsey*.

Stapleton, English ship
Location: Basseterre
History: Twelve ships were sunk at Basseterre during a hurricane in June of 1733. Three of them were identified as English ships: the *Nassau, Stapleton* and *Ancient Britain*.

Sussex, English merchantman
Location: Around the island
History: The *Sussex* was partially loaded when it was lost around the island in 1811. The crew was saved.

Swallow, English merchantman, Captain Watts
Location: Basseterre
History: During hurricanes on September 21 and October 24, 1747, a total of 24 English merchantmen were lost at Basseterre, most of them fully loaded with cargoes of sugar for England. Only these 12 were identified: the *Owen Gally, Rising Sun, Pretty Patsy, Duke of Marlborough, Cornwally, Rowlandson, Emma, Mary, Swallow, Plante, Parkham Pink,* and *Nisbitt*.

Thistle, Scottish merchantman, Captain Hunter
Location: St. Kitts
History: Two ships were totally lost during a hurricane in the year 1772: the *Apollo* and *Thistle*.

Thomas, English merchantman, Captain Furber
Location: Deep Bay
History: Five English merchantmen were wrecked in Deep Bay during a hurricane on August 26, 1785. Only three of them were identified: the *Thomas, Spooner* and *Betsey*.

Thornhills Hill, English merchantman
Location: West side of the island
History: The merchantman wrecked on June 1, 1690, against rocks off the west side of the island.

Unidentified, ships (4)
Location: Basseterre
History: In 1629, four small ships were sunk during a Spanish attack led by Captain-General Fadrique de Toledo who was trying to dislodge the recently settled French and English.

The ships were sunk by Spanish cannon fire in the port of Basseterre, on the west side of the island.

Unidentified, ships (large number)
Location: St. Kitts
History: A large number of unidentified ships were lost during a hurricane in October 1775.

Unidentified, ships (over 100)
Location: St. Kitts
History: During a hurricane on October 11 and 12, 1780, described as the worst in over a century, more than 100 ships of different nationalities and sizes were totally lost all around the island. The loss of life was in the thousands.

Unidentified, ships (13)
Location: St. Kitts
History: Seventeen ships were wrecked during a hurricane that struck on July 23, 1813. Ten were American ships that had been seized as war prizes; three were American coastal schooners; and four were English merchantmen. The last were: the *John & William,* just arrived from France; the *Britannia,* sailing to England; the *Colonest*; and the *Bottle*.

Unidentified, merchantmen (28)
Location: Basseterre
History: A total of 28 merchantmen of different nationalities were lost in and near Basseterre in 1650 during two different hurricanes. There were a great number of lives and over a half million pounds sterling in cargoes lost.

Unidentified, ships (21)
Location: Basseterre
History: Nine English and 12 Dutch ships were wrecked in Basseterre during a hurricane in 1651.

Unidentified, ships (2)
Location: Basseterre
History: One French and one Dutch ship were burnt by an English squadron of warships while the English were trying to recapture the island from the French in 1667. Both ships were anchored at Basseterre when they were lost.

Unidentified, shallops (2)
Location: Basseterre
History: Two shallops were wrecked

at Basseterre during a hurricane on August 3, 1680.

Unidentified, English merchantman, Captain Sutton
  Location: Basseterre
  History: The merchantman was sunk at Basseterre during a hurricane in October 1737. Her main cargo consisted of rum and sugar. Only one of the crew survived.

Unidentified, ships (several)
  Location: Basseterre
  History: Several ships were wrecked at Basseterre during a violent gale on July 24, 1751. Only one was identified, the *Friendship*, sailing to Cork. None of the crew was saved.

Unidentified, ships (5)
  Location: Basseterre
  History: Five unidentified ships were wrecked at Basseterre during a hurricane on September 13, 1754.

Unidentified, ships (5)
  Location: Basseterre
  History: Two unidentified ships were wrecked and three others sank at Basseterre during a hurricane in 1776.

Unidentified, English ships (23)
  Location: Basseterre
  History: Twenty-three English ships of various sizes were wrecked at Basseterre during a hurricane in 1642. There was little loss of life, since most of the crews were ashore.

Unidentified, ships (several)
  Location: Basseterre
  History: Several ships were wrecked in and near Basseterre during a severe gale in 1791. Only one was identified, the *Yucatán*.

Unidentified, Spanish merchant *nao* belonging to the New Spain Flota (fleet) of Captain-General Miguel de Echazarreta
  Location: East side of the island
  History: The ship wrecked on the east side of the island in 1630. Among the many drowned was the new governor of Santiago, Cuba.

Unidentified, ships (more than 20)
  Location: Around the island
  History: More than 20 ships of different nationalities were lost around

the island during a hurricane on August 1 and 2, 1792.

Unidentified, English ships (24)
  Location: Around the island
  History: Thirty merchantmen, both English and American, were lost around the island during a hurricane on August 12, 1793. Only a few of the English ships were identified by name: the *Hoppitt*, *Letitia*, *Flying Delight*, *Indian Castle*, *Polly* and *Nancy*.

Unidentified, ships (10)
  Location: On the island
  History: Nine English merchantmen and one French mail boat were lost around the island during a hurricane in August 1765.

Unidentified, ships (4 or 5)
  Location: Sandy Point
  History: Four or five fully loaded English merchantmen were totally lost off Sandy Point on the west side of the island during a hurricane in 1652.

Unidentified, ship
  Location: Sandy Point
  History: A ship that had just arrived at Sandy Point from Philadelphia in June 1733, suffered a total loss of life and cargo during a hurricane.

Unidentified, English privateer
  Location: Sandy Point
  History: The English privateer sank at Sandy Point during a hurricane in 1758 with 200 persons onboard. Everyone perished.

Unidentified, English merchantmen (15)
  Location: West side of the island and at Basseterre
  History: Thirteen English merchantmen and two Dutch sloops were wrecked off the west side of the island and at Basseterre during a hurricane in October 1766.

Unidentified, ships (4)
  Location: On the island
  History: Two schooners, two sloops and the merchantman *Maria* were wrecked on the island during a gale on July 26, 1807.

Venus, English merchantman, Captain Moore
  Location: St. Kitts

History: The *Venus* was sailing to Quebec when it was lost around the island in 1811. The crew was saved.

Yucatán, English merchantman, Captain Barton
  Location: In or near Basseterre
  History: Several ships were wrecked in and near Basseterre during a severe gale in 1791. Only one was identified, the *Yucatán*, sailing from Cork to Jamaica.

SHIPWRECKS IN ST. LUCIA'S WATERS

Barbara, English merchantman, Captain Perry
  Location: Northern part of the island
  History: The merchantman wrecked on the northern part of the island in 1783 while arriving from Liverpool. The crew and part of the cargo were saved.

Beaver's Prize, 18-gun English warship
  Location: St. Lucia
  History: The warship sank during a hurricane on October 10, 1780.

Champion, American merchantman, Captain Hall
  Location: St. Lucia
  History: The merchantman sank during a hurricane on October 10, 1780, while arriving from New York.

Dolphin, English merchantman, Captain Morrison
  Location: St. Lucia
  History: The merchantman sank during a hurricane on October 10, 1780.

Dolphin, English schooner
  Location: East side of the island
  History: The schooner wrecked on the east side of the island in 1805 while coming from Barbados with rum.

H.M.S. *Cornwall*, 74-gun English warship, Captain Timothy Edwards
  Location: St. Lucia
  History: The warship sank during a hurricane on October 10, 1780.

H.M.S. *Thetis*, 32-gun English warship, Captain Robert Linzee

Location: West side of the island
History: The warship wrecked on the west side of the island in 1781.

H.M.S. *Vengeance*, 32-gun English warship
Location: St. Lucia
History: The warship sank during a hurricane on October 10, 1780.

Lancashire Witch, English merchantman
Location: East side of the island
History: The merchantman was totally lost on the east side of the island in 1809 while sailing from Liverpool to Barbados. Her crew was saved.

Prince John, English slave ship, Captain Hestor
Location: East side of the island
History: The vessel was lost on the east side of the island in the year 1800 while arriving from Africa. The crew and slaves were saved.

Suffolk, American merchantman
Location: East side of the island
History: The merchantman wrecked on the east side of the island on September 15, 1823, while sailing from Demarara to New York. Her crew was saved.

Unidentified, English merchantmen (7)
Location: West side of the island
History: Seven large English merchantmen were sunk on the west side of the island on October 21, 1817, during a hurricane. Over 200 men perished.

SHIPWRECKS IN ST. MARTIN'S WATERS

H.M.S. *Proselyte*, 32-gun English warship, Captain George Fowke (some accounts have a Henry Whitly as the captain)
Location: South side of the island in 15 to 50 feet of water.
History: The warship wrecked on a reef on the south side of the island in 1801, which is now named Proselyte Reef after this wreck. The entire crew of 215 survived. Coauthor Marx, spent several days exploring this wreck in

1960. He located six anchors, at least 20 cannon and several hundred tons of pig iron ingots, which were often used for ballast during the period this ship was lost. A great section of the wreck was covered over by thick coral growth but some parts of it were found off the reef on a sandy bottom.

Santissimo Trinidade, Portuguese merchantman, Captain Dos Santos
Location: St. Martin
History: The richly laden ship wrecked in 1781 while sailing from Brazil to Amsterdam. Only a small part of its valuable cargo was salvaged.

Unidentified, ship belonging to the Windward Armada of Admiral Azevelo
Location: St. Martin
History: Several ships of the Windward Armada, commanded by Admiral Azevelo, chased an unidentified Dutch merchantman until it wrecked off the south side of St. Martin in 1631. While the Spanish admiral's ship was cruising to pick up survivors from the Dutch wreck, a sudden storm struck, causing it to also sink. There were only eight survivors from both wrecks.

Unidentified, ships (several)
Location: St. Martin
History: Several unidentified ships were wrecked during a hurricane on October 7, 1811.

Unidentified, ships (2)
Location: Oyster Pond
History: Two unidentified ships foundered in Oyster Pond during a hurricane on August 1, 1792.

Unidentified, Dutch merchantman
Location: South side of St. Martin
History: Several ships of the Windward Armada, commanded by Admiral Azevelo, chased an unidentified Dutch merchantman until it wrecked off the south side of St. Martin in 1631. While the Spanish admiral's ship was cruising to pick up survivors from the Dutch wreck, a sudden storm struck, causing it also to sink. There were only eight survivors from both wrecks.

Wynhandelet, Dutch merchantman, Captain Froon
Location: South side of the island

History: The ship, sailing from St. Martin to Ireland, was totally lost at anchor on the south side of the island in 1780 during a hurricane.

SHIPWRECKS IN ST. VINCENT'S WATERS

Africa, English slave ship, Captain Brown
Location: Kingstown
History: The vessel wrecked entering the port of Kingstown in 1784 while arriving from Africa with a cargo of slaves. The crew and slaves were saved.

H.M.S. *Experiment*, 50-gun English warship
Location: East coast of the island
History: The *Juno* and H.M.S. *Experiment* were totally destroyed on the east coast of the island on October 10 during the famous hurricane of 1780. There was almost a total loss of life.

Juno, 40-gun French warship
Location: East coast of the island
History: The *Juno* and H.M.S. *Experiment* were totally destroyed on the east coast of the island on October 10 during the famous hurricane of 1780. There was almost a total loss of life.

Unidentified, Spanish merchant *naos* (2)
Location: East side of the island
History: Two *naos* wrecked on the east side of the island in 1635 while sailing from Spain to Cartagena. The first English settlers found survivors on the island in 1667.

Unidentified, ship
Location: East side of the island
History: A large unidentified ship, apparently English-built, drifted ashore on the east side of the island in 1793 and quickly went to pieces. No one was onboard at the time it wrecked.

Unidentified, English merchantmen (10)
Location: Kingstown
History: Ten large unidentified English merchantmen wrecked or sank at Kingstown during a hurricane on October 21, 1817.

William, English merchantman, Captain Landells
Location: East side of the island
History: The merchantman wrecked on the east side of the island on May 27, 1818, while sailing from Tobago to London. The crew and some of the cargo of rum were saved.

Willoughby Bay, English packet boat
Location: East side of the island
History: The boat wrecked on the east side of the island on September 21, 1792. The crew and mail were saved.

SHIPWRECKS IN TOBAGO'S WATERS

Catherine, English merchantman, Captain Bodkin
Location: North side of the island
History: The merchantman wrecked on the north side of the island in 1803 while arriving from London.

Eclipse, English merchantman, Captain Vaughan
Location: Courland Bay
History: The vessel was totally lost in Courland Bay in 1807. Her crew was saved.

Fame, English ship, Captain Mumford
Location: Tobago
History: The ship wrecked on August 21, 1812, on Tobago while sailing to the island from Madeira.

Mary Ann, English merchantman, Captain Craig
Location: Tobago
History: The merchantman wrecked on the island in the year 1800 while arriving from London. Some of the cargo was saved.

Rebecca, English ship, Captain Reed
Location: East side of the island
History: She wrecked on the east end of the island in 1801 while arriving from London. The crew was saved.

Recovery, English merchantman, Captain Abercromby
Location: Tobago
History: The vessel wrecked on the island in 1800 while sailing to London. Some of the cargo was saved.

Rosalia, English merchantman, Captain Ferguson
Location: Tyrrel Bay
History: She wrecked on a reef in 1805 while attempting to enter Tyrrel Bay. She was coming from London.

Tabago [*sic*], English sloop
Location: East of Englishman's Bay
History: The sloop was totally lost on August 16, 1787, on a reef east of Englishman's Bay on the north side of the island.

Trafalgar, English merchantman, Captain Pines
Location: East end of the island
History: The merchantman wrecked off the east end of the island in June 1813 while sailing for Bristol. Some of her cargo was saved.

Unidentified, Spanish merchant *naos* (5)
Location: Tobago
History: The vessels wrecked on the island in 1572 while sailing from Spain to Veracruz. Divers from Margarita Island later salvaged most of their cargoes.

Unidentified, French ship, Captain Steur
Location: Tobago
History: The ship wrecked on the island in 1792 while sailing from Demarara to Amsterdam.

Unidentified, ships (many)
Location: Palmit Bay
History: A large battle took place in Palmit Bay in 1677 between a French fleet, under Admiral Estres' command, and a Dutch fleet, under Vice-Admiral Herr Binkes' command. The French fleet was burnt and sunk. The number of ships and their identities are not known. The Dutch also lost several ships in the battle.

SHIPWRECKS IN TRINIDAD'S WATERS

Arrogante, 70-gun Spanish *almiranta*, Captain Rafael Bennazar
Location: Off Chaguaramas
History: On February 17, 1797, an English fleet of warships, commanded by Sir Henry Harvey, approached the island with the intention of capturing it from the Spanish. As the fleet neared, the Spaniards burnt five of their large warships off Chaguaramas to prevent them from falling into the hands of the English. The ships were the *San Vicente, Arrogante, Gallardo, San Damasco* and *Concha*. Amateur divers have located and recovered a few artifacts from these wrecks over the years.

Charlotte, English merchantman, Captain Crow
Location: Trinidad
History: The ship wrecked on the island in the year 1800 while arriving from Africa. The crew was saved.

Concha, 34-gun Spanish frigate, Captain Manuel Urtizabel
Location: Off Chaguaramas
History: On February 17, 1797, an English fleet of warships, commanded by Sir Henry Harvey, approached the island with the intention of capturing it from the Spanish. As the fleet neared, the Spaniards burnt five of their large warships off Chaguaramas to prevent them from falling into the hands of the English. The ships were the *San Vicente, Arrogante, Gallardo, San Damasco* and *Concha*. Amateur divers have located and recovered a few artifacts from these wrecks over the years.

Friends, English merchantman, Captain Wood
Location: East side of the island
History: The merchantman wrecked on the east side of the island in 1780 while arriving from Africa. Only a few of the crew were saved.

Gallardo, 74-gun Spanish galleon, Captain Gabriel Sorondo
Location: Off Chaguaramas
History: On February 17, 1797, an English fleet of warships, commanded by Sir Henry Harvey, approached the island with the intention of capturing it from the Spanish. As the fleet neared, the Spaniards burnt five of their large warships off Chaguaramas to prevent them from falling into the hands of the English. The ships were the *San Vicente, Arrogante, Gallardo, San Damasco* and *Concha*. Amateur divers have located and recovered a few artifacts from these wrecks over the years.

Governor Picton, Scottish ship
   Location: South side of the island
   History: The ship wrecked on the south side of the island on April 19, 1806, while arriving from the Clyde. Only her crew was saved.

H.M.S. *Dromedary*, 20-gun English warship, Captain Bridges W. Taylor
   Location: Trinidad
   History: The warship wrecked on the island on August 10, 1800, at Parasol Rock. The crew was saved.

H.M.S. *Rattlesnake*, English warship
   Location: Trinidad
   History: The warship wrecked on the island in 1782. One of the crew perished.

Kate, English slave ship, Captain Good
   Location: East side of the island
   History: She wrecked on the east side of the island in 1803 while arriving from Africa. Ten people were lost.

Lion, English merchantman, Captain Grove
   Location: East side of the island
   History: The merchantman wrecked on the east side of the island in 1816 while sailing to Demarara. Her crew was saved.

Nuestra Señora de la Concepción, Spanish merchant *nao*, Captain Gotibo
   Location: Trinidad
   History: The vessel wrecked on Maracas Bar in 1731. Only her crew was saved.

Polly, Canadian ship, Captain Bell
   Location: Port of Spain
   History: The ship sank at the Port of Spain in 1810 while arriving from Newfoundland, Canada. Her crew was saved.

San Damasco, 74-gun Spanish galleon, Captain José Jordan
   Location: Off Chaguaramas
   History: On February 17, 1797, an English fleet of warships, commanded by Sir Henry Harvey, approached the island with the intention of capturing it from the Spanish. As the fleet neared, the Spaniards burnt five of their large warships off Chaguaramas to prevent them from falling into the hands of the English. The ships were the *San Vicente, Arrogante, Gallardo, San Damasco* and *Concha*. Amateur divers have located and recovered a few artifacts from these wrecks over the years.

San Vicente, 80-gun Spanish *capitana*, (flagship), Brigadier Jerónimo Mendoza
   Location: Off Chaguaramas
   History: On February 17, 1797, an English fleet of warships, commanded by Sir Henry Harvey, approached the island with the intention of capturing it from the Spanish. As the fleet neared, the Spaniards burnt five of their large warships off Chaguaramas to prevent them from falling into the hands of the English. The ships were the *San Vicente, Arrogante, Gallardo, San Damasco* and *Concha*. Amateur divers have located and recovered a few artifacts from these wrecks over the years.

Swan, Scottish merchantman
   Location: Bocas
   History: The merchantman wrecked in the Bocas on September 20, 1802, while arriving from Glasgow.

Tamar, Spanish ship
   Location: Bocas
   History: The ship wrecked in the Bocas in 1821 while arriving from Puerto Rico. Some of the cargo was saved.

Puerto Rico

Compared with the majority of the other Caribbean islands, Puerto Rico has relatively few shipwrecks in her waters. There are various explanations for this. The island is high in elevation and can be sighted at quite a distance from the sea, which decreases the possibility of a ship running up on its shores. Unlike many of the other islands, there are very few dangerous offshore reefs, thus eliminating the danger of ships running aground. The waters surrounding virtually the whole coastline of Puerto Rico are quite deep and there are exceedingly few, if any, shoals or sandbanks. The question of how much maritime traffic there was around Puerto Rico must also be considered. Since the island lacked precious metals and other important export commodities and was never considered an important settlement by the Spaniards, there was very little shipping directed there during the 16th, 17th and 18th centuries.

Permits are required here for all shipwreck-related work. Puerto Rico enjoys relatively good weather year round, except during the hurricane season. The United States National Park Service has several archaeologists and historians working in San Juan and they, along with several historians at the University of Puerto Rico, can be helpful in identifying and dating artifacts recovered from shipwrecks in this area.

SHIPWRECKS IN PUERTO RICO'S WATERS

Carlos V, 50-cannon warship
   Location: Puerto Rico
   History: The warship was lost at Puerto Rico in 1720 during a hurricane. Over 500 men drowned.

Doña Juana, *nao* belonging to the Nueva España Flota (fleet) of Don C. Rodríguez Farfan

Location: San Juan

History: Three of the *flota*'s *naos* were lost in the port of San Juan in 1554 but their cargoes were largely salvaged. The vessels lost were the *San Salvador*, *Doña Juana*, and *Regina Caelis*.

Elizabeth, British merchantman, Captain Alexander

Location: Off Puerto Rico

History: The merchantman foundered off Puerto Rico in 1764 while sailing from Antigua to London. The crew and captain were saved.

Eugenia, two-cannon Spanish schooner, Captain Francisco Gómez

Location: Puerto Rico

History: The schooner was lost at Puerto Rico on August 13, 1818.

Fountain, British ship, Captain Howard

Location: On the island

History: The ship—of St. John, New Brunswick, Canada, and sailing from Trinidad to Boston—was lost on December 23, 1822, on the island of Puerto Rico. The crew was saved.

La Victoria, Spanish ship

Location: Bahía Anegada

History: The ship was lost in Bahía Anegada at Puerto Rico in 1720.

Nautilus, German ship, Captain (either) Korff or Miltenburg

Location: Northern coast

History: The ship was lost off the northern coast of Puerto Rico in 1818.

Nuestra Señora de Begoña, galleon belonging to the squadron of the Armada de Mar Oceano of Captain-General Thomas de Larraspuru

Location: San Juan

History: As the squadron was entering the port of San Juan in 1623, a rainsquall struck and caused the ship to run aground on the shallows inside the port and then sink in deeper water. She was carrying only war munitions as cargo, part of which was later salvaged along with some of the ship's cannon. No lives were lost in the disaster.

Nuestra Señora del Pilar y San Antonio, Spanish galleon, Captain Domingo Casares Goicochea

Location: Near Puerto Rico

History: The galleon was lost near Puerto Rico in 1739 while coming from Maracaibo and bound for Cadiz. The people and goods were saved.

Ogeron, pirate ship

Location: Near islands called Guadanillas

History: The French governor of the Island of Tortuga (Isle de la Tortue), which is located off the northern coast of Haiti, had a large warship built, which he named *Ogeron*. It was manned by 500 pirates of various nationalities and sent by the governor to aid in the capture of Curaçao. During a violent storm in 1673, the ship wrecked on the rocks near islands called Guadanillas. The ship broke up quickly. Most of the pirates made it ashore to Puerto Rico but were massacred the next day by the Spaniards.

Proserpina, ten-cannon Spanish brigantine schooner

Location: Aguadilla

History: The schooner was lost on the coast of Aguadilla in 1821.

Regina Caelis, *nao* belonging to the Nueva España Flota (fleet) of Don C. Rodríguez Farfan

Location: San Juan

History: Three of the *flota*'s *naos* were lost in the port of San Juan in 1554, but their cargoes were largely salvaged. The vessels lost were the *San Salvador*, *Doña Juana*, and *Regina Caelis*.

Revenge, British merchantman, Captain Kerr

Location: Puerto Rico

History: The ship was lost at Puerto Rico in 1780 while sailing from Newfoundland, Canada to Jamaica.

San Estevan, *nao*, 120 tons, Captain Lazaro Morel

Location: San Juan de Puerto Rico

History: The vessel was lost "at San Juan de Puerto Rico" in 1562.

San Nicolas, caravel, 80 tons, Captain Domingo de Guedin Bermeo

Location: San Juan

History: The caravel, owned by Antonio de Norcia of Seville, sank in the harbor of San Juan "en una isleta llamada Berberia" ("on a little island called Berberia") sometime before October 25, 1515. She was sailing from Spain for Puerto Rico and Santo Domingo at the time.

San Salvador, *nao* belonging to the Nueva España Flota (fleet) of Don C. Rodríguez Farfan

Location: San Juan

History: Three of the *flota*'s *naos* were lost in the port of San Juan in 1554, but their cargoes were largely salvaged. The vessels lost were the *San Salvador*, *Doña Juana*, and *Regina Caelis*.

Santa María de Jesús, merchant *nao*, Captain Diego Bernal

Location: One league from the port of San Juan

History: The *nao* was lost one league from the port of San Juan while en route from Spain to Mexico. The governor of Puerto Rico wrote stating that this ship was one of the richest galleons ever to come to the Indies. Some salvage work was undertaken on the wreck but the majority of the cargo was not recovered. The accident occurred shortly before August 27, 1550.

Sisters, British slave ship, Captain Alworthy

Location: Mona Passage

History: The ship was overset by a strong gust of wind while in the Mona Passage on May 17, 1787, while sailing from Africa to Havana with 500 slaves onboard. All except two crew members and three slaves perished.

Unidentified, caravel

Location: "On the coast"

History: The caravel was lost "on the coast of Puerto Rico" in 1550 and only the people were saved.

Unidentified, capitana (flagship)

Location: Puerto Rico

History: Two ships entered Saulúcar de Barrameda in Spain on January 10, 1606, and reported that on October 26, 1605, while sailing from Santo Domingo to Spain, the *capitana* of their fleet sank due to a leak when they were north and south of Punta de la Aguada and that only the men were saved.

Unidentified, French ship

Location: Off Puerto Rico

History: In a letter, an unidentified French ship was reported to have hit a reef and sunk off Puerto Rico during February 1673, although the location was not given. In another letter in the same *legajo* (file), there was a brief mention that a ship was wrecked this same year at El Arecibo. It was probably the same ship.

Unidentified, ships (2)
Location: Near the island
History: In 1720, the pirate Captain George Lowther captured two ships near Puerto Rico, a small ship from Bristol of Captain Smith and a Spanish privateer that had just captured the ship of Captain Smith. The pirate burnt both prizes near the island after stripping them.

Unidentified, Spanish privateer, sloop
Location: Onshore at Puerto Rico
History: The sloop was chased onshore and dashed to pieces in 1742.

Unidentified, 24-cannon Spanish privateer, sloop
Location: Off Puerto Rico
History: The sloop was sunk off Puerto Rico in an engagement with H.M.S. *Scarsborough*, Captain Liste, in the year 1742.

Unidentified, Swedish ship, 200 tons
Location: Isla Palominos
History: The ship wrecked on a small island near Puerto Rico named Isla Palominos in 1649. The ship carried sixteen cannon, two of which were brass. The Spaniards recovered all of them from the wreck and imprisoned the Swedes.

Unidentified, merchant ship
Location: Northern coast of the island
History: Sometime before September 22, 1623, eight merchant ships left Santo Domingo for Spain. One of them ran aground and was lost on the northern coast of Puerto Rico due to bad navigation.

Unidentified, ships (large number)
Location: Off the western end of the island
History: A large number of ships were sunk off the western end of Puerto Rico during a severe hurricane on September 3, 1804.

Unidentified, merchant *nao*, 300 tons
Location: San Juan
History: The Dutch totally destroyed a merchant *nao* of 300 tons by fire during their attack on San Juan in 1625.

Unidentified, Dutch *urca*
Location: San Juan
History: After the Dutch attack on San Juan in 1625, one of the Dutch *urcas* sank in the harbor as the enemy fleet was sailing from port. The Spaniards later salvaged six iron cannon from this wreck.

Unidentified, *aviso* (advice boat)
Location: San Juan
History: The advice boat, owned by Captain Francisco de Liende, was forced to enter San Juan due to a bad leak in 1659 or 1660 while sailing from Spain to Veracruz. The vessel sank soon after. Only a part of the mail, papal bulls and a little money was recovered.

Unidentified, 36-gun French ship
Location: San Juan
History: The ship was accidentally lost while entering the port of San Juan in 1745.

Unidentified, Spanish ships (2)
Location: West end of the island
History: H.M.S. *Lichfield* arrived at Kingston, Jamaica on November 8, 1743. She reported that she had sunk a Spanish privateer on the west end of Puerto Rico and burnt a Spanish sloop in Bahía La Aguada.

South America

The majority of shipping off the East Coast of South America was Portuguese during the 16th, 17th and 18th centuries. Hundreds of wrecks must have occurred, but relatively few locations are known today due to the almost total destruction of old Portuguese documents. Over 400 shipwrecks have been deleted from this section due to vague locations listed in documents.

All South American countries have laws regarding the salvaging of shipwrecks. Brazil has the law most favorable to salvors. The government takes only 20 percent of a find. Colombia's law is similar to Florida's: the salvor receives 75 percent and the country receives 25 percent of all treasure and artifacts recovered. In addition, a foreigner must post a bond of about $25,000. Although the salvor retains 75 percent of everything they receive, no gold in any form is allowed to leave Colombia; and, if a Colombian museum wishes to obtain anything belonging to a salvor, it can buy it at a price deemed reasonable.

SHIPWRECKS IN SOUTH AMERICA'S WATERS

"Roman Wreck"
Location: Ilha do Gobernador, Brazil
History: One of the most intriguing Roman shipwreck finds occurred in 1976 in Brazil. A young diver named José Robert Teixéira was spearfishing around a rock off Ilha do Gobernador when he discovered many intact amphorae on the sea floor and brought up three of them. He assumed that they were Portuguese jars from the colonial

Above: Dutch gold coins minted in Brazil in 1645. *Right:* Artifacts recovered from the *Hollandia* lost during the Dutch attack on Salvador, Brazil in 1627.

period and sold them to an antique dealer for a small amount. Some time later, the Brazilian Institute of Archaeology mistakenly identified one of the amphorae as of ancient Greek origin. News of the find soon spread and sport divers recovered dozens more amphorae. Local scholars, trying to solve the puzzle of how they had come to be in Brazilian waters, decided they most likely had been found in the Mediterranean and later thrown overboard by a vessel visiting Brazil. Five years later, in 1981, coauthor Robert F. Marx was asked to investigate the site by the director of the Maritime Museum of Rio de Janeiro. Marx learned that since the mid–1960s, fishermen in the area had snagged at least 50 intact amphorae, each over three feet in length. Having dived on many Roman wrecks, Marx identified the amphorae as Roman. Experts identified them as being from the third century A.D., and manufactured at Kouass, southwest of Tangiers, on the Atlantic coast of Morocco. Carbon-14 dating placed the marine growth found on the amphorae at up to 1,500 years old, making this a Roman shipwreck. There is no written record that Roman ships ever came to the Americas. However, there may have been accidental crossings, such as the one in which Portuguese explorer Pedro Álvares Cabral was given credit for the discovery of Brazil. In 1500, while attempting to sail to the Indian Ocean, Cabral was becalmed off the African coast. The ship was caught in a strong westbound current and carried across the South Atlantic to the shores of Brazil. In the past century alone, records indicate that more than

600 vessels have been unwillingly driven to the American coast by contrary winds and currents. A Roman ship could have suffered the same fate, entered the Bay of Guanabara in search of food and water after the long crossing, struck a submerged rock pinnacle and sunk. Marx spent more than 200 hours surveying the plundered site over a period of some months. He located several hundred shards, including the necks and handles of dozens of amphorae, and ceramic shards of smaller jugs and plates. He also recovered a circular stone with a center hole, resembling a grinding wheel, which may have been a small anchor. In December 1982, Marx enlisted the services of the late Dr. Harold E. Edgerton of the Massachusetts Institute of Technology (MIT). He conducted a three-day subbottom profiling sonar search of the area in an effort to pinpoint any wooden shipwreck remains. Shortly after Edgerton's report appeared, the Portuguese and Spanish governments expressed concern to the Brazilian government about the possibility that this discovery could displace Cabral as the discoverer of Brazil and Columbus as the discoverer of the New World. The Brazilian government decided that to do so would be too controversial. A dredge boat was employed to cover the entire site and the area was declared a restricted zone by the Brazilian government.

Africa, 60-gun Spanish warship, galleon
  Location: Castillo Grande, Cartagena, Colombia
  History: In 1741, an English fleet,

led by Admiral Vernon, attacked the town of Cartagena. On the first day of the attack, the Spaniards sank six of their own galleons, four large warships, several merchant *naos,* and a French merchantman. Only the warships and the French merchantman were identified: the *Galicia, San Carlos, Africa, San Felipe,* and the French ship *El Leon de Nantes.* These five and the other Spanish ships were scuttled across the mouth of the outer harbor near Castillo Grande to prevent the English from entering the port. The following day, two remaining Spanish warships, the *Conquistador* and *Dragon,* were also sunk, in the inner channel of the port. Most of the superstructures of the Spanish ships remained above the water and the Spaniards burnt these parts to prevent the English from obtaining anything of value from them. While the English were still at Cartagena, a large Spanish ship named the *Galicia* unsuspectingly entered the harbor and was captured by the English; they burnt her after stripping her first.

Amistad, Spanish schooner, Captain Manuel de Zaragosa
  Location: Magdalena River bar, Columbia
  History: The schooner wrecked on the bar in 1818. The captain and several of the crew perished.

Artifacts
  Location: Curaçao, Netherlands Antilles
  History: During a hurricane that struck the island of Curaçao on October 16, 1808, many of the buildings in the main town were carried into the

sea, as well as many graves in the churchyard and cannon from the forts.

Caledonia, ship of unknown registry
   Location: Los Roques Reefs, Venezuela
   History: The ship wrecked in 1824 on Los Roques Reefs while sailing from Philadelphia to La Guaira. Part of her cargo of soap and flour was saved.

Catheresa, galleon
   Location: Cartagena Harbor, Colombia
   History: The galleon sank in 1682 in sight of Cartagena Harbor. Records do not indicate whether she was in a convoy or carried any treasure. They do indicate, however, that in 1963 several bronze cannon were recovered from this wreck.

Cecila, American schooner, Captain Hampton
   Location: Curaçao, Netherlands Antilles
   History: The schooner sank off the west end of Curaçao in 1822 while sailing from the island with a valuable cargo which included dry goods, cocoa and indigo.

Ceres, Dutch merchantman, Captain Jucometti
   Location: Bonaire Island, Netherlands Antilles
   History: The ship wrecked on December 27, 1817, on Bonaire Island while sailing from Rotterdam to Curaçao. Only a small part of her cargo was saved.

Chalmers, ship of unknown registry, Captain Tyack
   Location: Cabo de la Vela
   History: The ship, carrying slaves from Africa to the West Indies, wrecked on February 24, 1808, near Cabo de la Vela. The crew and slaves were all saved.

Chalmers, English slave ship
   Location: Margarita Island, Venezuela
   History: The slave ship wrecked on Margarita Island in 1808 after leaving Africa.

Clara, English merchantman, Captain Roberts

Location: Gulf of Darien, Colombia
   History: The merchantman sank on September 23, 1814, off St. Blas, in the Gulf of Darien while making its way from Jamaica. The crew was saved.

Confeance, English merchantman, Captain Molloy
   Location: Cartagena, Colombia
   History: The ship was lost at the end of March 1813 near Cartagena while coming from Jamaica.

Conquistador, 60-gun Spanish warship
   Location: Cartagena, Colombia
   History: In 1741, an English fleet, led by Admiral Vernon, attacked the town of Cartagena. On the first day of the attack, the Spaniards sank six of their own galleons, four large warships, several merchant *naos*, and a French merchantman. Only the warships and the French merchantman were identified: the *Galicia, San Carlos, Africa, San Felipe,* and the French ship *El Leon de Nantes*. These five and the other Spanish ships were scuttled across the mouth of the outer harbor near Castillo Grande to prevent the English from entering the port. The following day, two remaining Spanish warships, the *Conquistador* and *Dragon,* were also sunk, in the inner channel of the port. Most of the superstructures of the Spanish ships remained above the water and the Spaniards burnt these parts to prevent the English from obtaining anything of value from them. While the English were still at Cartagena, a large Spanish ship named the *Galicia* unsuspectingly entered the harbor and was captured by the English; they burnt her after stripping her first.

Dragon, 60-gun Spanish warship
   Location: Cartagena, Colombia
   History: In 1741, an English fleet, led by Admiral Vernon, attacked the town of Cartagena. On the first day of the attack, the Spaniards sank six of their own galleons, four large warships, several merchant *naos*, and a French merchantman. Only the warships and the French merchantman were identified: the *Galicia, San Carlos, Africa, San Felipe,* and the French ship *El Leon de Nantes*. These five and the other Spanish ships were scuttled

across the mouth of the outer harbor near Castillo Grande to prevent the English from entering the port. The following day, two remaining Spanish warships, the *Conquistador* and *Dragon,* were also sunk, in the inner channel of the port. Most of the superstructures of the Spanish ships remained above the water and the Spaniards burnt these parts to prevent the English from obtaining anything of value from them. While the English were still at Cartagena, a large Spanish ship named the *Galicia* unsuspectingly entered the harbor and was captured by the English; they burnt her after stripping her first.

Éclatant, French bomb galliot
   Location: Castillo Santa Cruz, Cartagena, Colombia
   History: In 1697, a French fleet under the command of Admiral Point attacked Cartagena. The Spaniards sank two of their own large galleons near Castillo Santa Cruz to prevent the French from entering the harbor. When that stratagen failed, they burnt two other large ships, two galleys and many small vessels in the inner harbor to prevent their capture by the French. The French bomb galliot *Éclatant* was so badly damaged by the Spanish cannon fire that the French burnt her in the harbor before leaving.

Edward, English merchantman, Captain Darby
   Location: Aruba, Netherlands Antilles
   History: The merchantman wrecked on the island of Aruba in 1763 while sailing from Hispaniola to Curaçao.

Eliza, American ship, Captain Bicker
   Location: Bonaire Island, Netherlands Antilles
   History: The ship was lost on November 30, 1822, off Bonaire Island while sailing from New York to Curaçao.

El Leon de Nantes, French merchantman, Captain José Lesvin
   Location: Castillo Grande, Cartagena. Colombia
   History: In 1741, an English fleet, led by Admiral Vernon, attacked the town of Cartagena. On the first day of the attack, the Spaniards sank six

of their own galleons, four large warships, several merchant *naos*, and a French merchantman. Only the warships and the French merchantman were identified: the *Galicia, San Carlos, Africa, San Felipe*, and the French ship *El Leon de Nantes*. These five and the other Spanish ships were scuttled across the mouth of the outer harbor near Castillo Grande to prevent the English from entering the port. The following day, two remaining Spanish warships, the *Conquistador* and *Dragon*, were also sunk, in the inner channel of the port. Most of the superstructures of the Spanish ships remained above the water and the Spaniards burnt these parts to prevent the English from obtaining anything of value from them. While the English were still at Cartagena, a large Spanish ship named the *Galicia* unsuspectingly entered the harbor and was captured by the English; they burnt her after stripping her first.

Escape, ship of unknown registry
    Location: Curaçao, Netherlands Antilles
    History: The vessel was lost near Curaçao Island in 1802 while coming from Martinique Island.

Friendship, English merchantman, Captain Morgan.
    Location: Punta Gallinas, Colombia
    History: The merchantman wrecked off Punta Gallinas in 1765 while coming from Jamaica.

Galicia, Spanish warship, galleon
    Location: Castillo Grande, Cartagena, Colombia
    History: In 1741, an English fleet, led by Admiral Vernon, attacked the town of Cartagena. On the first day of the attack, the Spaniards sank six of their own galleons, four large warships, several merchant *naos*, and a French merchantman. Only the warships and the French merchantman were identified: the *Galicia, San Carlos, Africa, San Felipe*, and the French ship *El Leon de Nantes*. These five and the other Spanish ships were scuttled across the mouth of the outer harbor near Castillo Grande to prevent the English from entering the port. The following day, two remaining Spanish warships, the *Conquistador* and *Dragon*,

Coauthor Robert F. Marx, on the right, with cannon and anchor recovered from a Spanish merchant ship.

were also sunk, in the inner channel of the port. Most of the superstructures of the Spanish ships remained above the water and the Spaniards burnt these parts to prevent the English from obtaining anything of value from them. While the English were still at Cartagena, a large Spanish ship named the *Galicia* unsuspectingly entered the harbor and was captured by the English; they burnt her after stripping her first.

Good Hope, ship of unknown registry, Captain Dirks
    Location: Curaçao, Netherlands Antilles
    History: The ship was totally lost near the island of Curaçao in 1780 while coming from France.

Guipuscoa, 70-gun Spanish warship
    Location: Santa Marta, Colombia
    History: The ship was sent from Cartagena to search for English privateers operating near Santa Martha, but she wrecked near the entrance to Santa Martha in 1741 during a storm.

H.M.S. Bassora, 12-gun English warship, brig, Captain James Violett

    Location: Cartagena, Colombia
    History: The ship wrecked within sight of Cartagena on February 13, 1808. All her crew of 50 were saved.

H.M.S. Firefly, 12-gun English warship, Captain Thomas Price
    Location: Curaçao
    History: The warship foundered on November 11, 1807, near the island of Curaçao. Most of the crew perished.

H.M.S. Legere, 18-gun English warship, Captain Cornelius Quinton
    Location: Jamba Bay, Colombia
    History: The warship wrecked in Jamba Bay, east of Cartagena, on February 2, 1801. Only one of her crew of 121 men was lost.

H.M.S. Margaret, English warship
    Location: Punta de la Canoa
    History: The small sloop was lost at Punta de la Canoa in 1707 while giving chase to a small French sloop.

H.M.S. Pert, 14-gun English warship, Captain Donald Campbell
    Location: Margarita Island, Venezuela
    History: The warship wrecked on October 16, 1807, on Margarita Island.

H.M.S. *Raposa*, ten-gun English warship, frigate

Location: Cartagena, Colombia

History: The warship wrecked within sight of Cartagena on February 15, 1808. The crew was saved.

H.M.S. *Volador*, 16-gun English warship, Captain Francis George Dickens

Location: Gulf of Coro, Venezuela

History: The warship wrecked on October 24, 1808, in the Gulf of Coro.

***Hollandia*,** flagship of Piet Heyn

Location: Baia de Todos os Santos (All Saints Bay), Brazil

History: The *Hollandia* was the flagship of Piet Heyn, who prowled the seas and captured more treasure from the Spaniards and Portuguese than all other pirates and privateers of the 16th and 17th centuries combined. The town of Baia was a major entrepôt for commerce, a port of call for homeward-bound East Indiamen, and an irresistible lure to pirates and privateers. In 1624, Heyn descended on Baia with a fleet of 34 warships. He sacked the city and seized 15 richly laden Portuguese ships in the port. He returned to Baia in March 1627, sweeping boldly into the harbor, where 26 large merchant ships lay at anchor near

several forts. The dauntless Heyn took his flagship, the *Hollandia*, into the midst of the enemy, dropping anchor between the *capitana* (flagship) and *almiranta*, two of the largest and best armed of the Portuguese vessels. While half his men returned the enemy's fire, Heyn and the rest of the Hollanders scrambled into small boats and boarded the two ships. In less than ten minutes, both massive galleons struck their colors and surrendered. Heyn spurred his men on to take another 22 ships right under the noses of the Portuguese shore batteries. His flagship was left within range of the main fort to draw fire while the Dutch ships and the captured Portuguese vessels were moved farther from shore. The *Hollandia*'s guns slammed cannonballs into the fort without a break but took such return fire that by sunset the flagship was battered almost beyond recognition, riddled with more than 500 holes. At midnight, Heyn set the remains of his ship ablaze and escaped in a sloop with the surviving members of his crew. With the wreck's approximate position and permission from the Brazilian navy, coauthor Marx set out to locate the flagship in May 1979. Marx eventually located the ship in 1981. It was

buried under a 19th century shipwreck in the harbor. Seventeenth century divers had recovered the ships bronze guns, but Marx was able to recover six iron cannon as well as 5,000 artifacts and some treasure. His recoveries included cannon, cannonballs, pistols, muskets, swords, lead musket and pistol balls, glass hand grenades, cutlery, a fine collection of pewter and silverware, ceramic objects of all types including Bellarmine jugs, and many personal items such as buttons, buckles and leather boots. In the stern castle, several brass dividers, sounding leads, fragments of an hourglass, a lead compass rose from the ship's binnacle, hundreds of gold and silver coins, several gold buttons, and seven pounds of gold nuggets were also found. The most significant find was a collection of two hundred pounds of human bones, including a number of skulls. Marx took these remains back to Holland, where they were laid to rest with great ceremony. The most important artifacts are on permanent display in the maritime museum in Rio de Janeiro. The remainder were sold at an auction in Amsterdam and ended up in various museums throughout the Netherlands.

***Jason*,** Scottish merchantman, Captain Stewart

Location: Orchila Island, Venezuela

History: The merchantman wrecked on August 17, 1809, on Orchila Island while sailing to Curaçao. The crew and a small part of the cargo were saved.

***John & Stephen*,** Irish merchantman, Captain Kent

Location: Bonaire Island, Netherlands Antilles

History: The merchantman wrecked on August 10, 1766, on Bonaire Island while sailing form Cork to Curaçao. Most of her cargo was saved.

***La Armona*,** French merchantman

Location: Salmedina Reef, near Cartagena, Colombia

History: The French merchantman, which had permission to trade with the Spaniards, was wrecked on Salmedina Reef in 1705 while carrying a valuable cargo of merchandise.

Dutch warship c. 1640.

Los Tres Reyes, merchant *nao* belonging to the Tierra Firme Armada of Captain-General Antonio de Oquendo, 600 tons

Location: Cartagena, Colombia

History: Four of the armada's ships were lost while arriving at Cartagena from Porto Bello in 1634 with a vast amount of treasure onboard. The *San Juan Bautista* wrecked on Salmedina Reef but her treasure and cannon were recovered; the *Nuestra Señora del Carmen* wrecked at the entrance of Boca Chica but was totally salvaged later; the *Nuestra Señora del Rosario* and *Los Tres Reyes* both sank due to leaks shortly after entering the inner harbor at Cartagena.

Manuel, Spanish brigantine-of-war, Captain Martin María Espino

Location: Puerto Cabello, Venezuela

History: The ship sank in Puerto Cabello on April 27, 1813. The crew and some equipment were saved.

Mariposa, Spanish merchantman

Location: Islas de Aves, Venezuela

History: The ship was totally lost on Aves Islands in 1819 while sailing to Spain. Her crew was saved.

Martin, ship of unknown registry, Captain Bull

Location: Rio de la Hacha

History: The ship was lost on December 10, 1817, near Rio de la Hacha while sailing from Barcelona to Santa Marta. The crew and part of the cargo were saved.

Martins, English merchant ship, Captain Ramsey

Location: Cartagena, Colombia

History: The ship wrecked off Cartagena in 1822 while coming from Jamaica.

Mary, English merchantman, Captain Richardson

Location: Maracaibo bar, Maracaibo, Venezuela

History: The merchantman wrecked on September 17, 1822, on the bar in front of the port of Maracaibo while coming from London, England. The crew was saved.

Morning Star, American merchantman, Captain Waring

Location: Islas de Aves, Venezuela

History: The merchantman was totally lost on November 14, 1824 on Aves Islands while sailing from New York to Curaçao. Only the crew was saved.

Nuestra Señora de Cortijo (alias *La Serrana*), Spanish merchant *nao*

Location: Isla de Galera Zamba

History: The vessel wrecked on the north side of the point of Isla de Galera Zamba in 1793.

Nuestra Señora de la Asunción, merchant *nao* belonging to the Tierra Firme Armada of Captain-General Marqués de Brenes

Location: South America

History: After the armada sailed from Cartagena for Porto Bello, Panama, in 1681, four of the ships were lost: the *Santa Teresa, Nuestra Señora de la Soledad, Nuestra Señora de la Asunción*, and *Nuestra Señora de la Encarnación*. Neither the cause of the loss nor the location of the four ships is stated in documents. After receiving the treasure at Porto Bello, the armada returned to Cartagena, then sailed for Havana. Shortly after leaving Boca Chica, near Cartagena, four more ships were wrecked on nearby reefs: the *Santa Teresa* (another by the same name as the one above), *Santiago*, an unidentified small *nao*, and the armada's patache. The loss of treasure and life was great. Only four persons were rescued from the latter four ships.

Nuestra Señora de la Candelaria, galleon belonging to the Tierra Firme Armada of Captain-General Thomas de Larraspuru, 600 tons, Captain Juan de Campos

Location: Salmedina Reef, near Cartagena, Colombia

History: The treasure-laden galleon wrecked on Salmediana Reef in 1626 as the armada was leaving Cartagena en route to Havana, Cuba. Divers recovered most of her treasure.

Nuestra Señora de la Concepción y San Francisco, galleon, 550 tons

Location: Cartagena Harbor

History: The galleon sank in 1629 due to bad leaks while at anchor in Cartagena Harbor. She did not have any treasure or other cargo onboard when she foundered.

Nuestra Señora de la Encarnación, patache belonging to the Tierra Firme Armada of Captain-General Marqués de Brenes

Location: South America

History: After the armada sailed from Cartagena for Porto Bello, Panama, in 1681, four of the ships were lost: the *Santa Teresa, Nuestra Señora de la Soledad, Nuestra Señora de la Asunción*, and *Nuestra Señora de la Encarnación*. Neither the cause of the loss

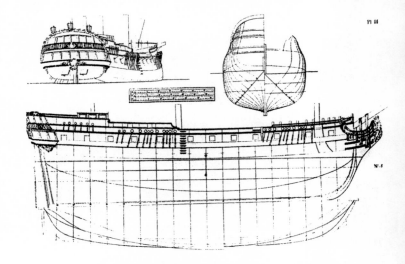

Drawing of a mid–17th century Spanish *nao*.

nor the location of the four ships is stated in documents. After receiving the treasure at Porto Bello, the armada returned to Cartagena, then sailed for Havana. Shortly after leaving Boca Chica, near Cartagena, four more ships were wrecked on nearby reefs: the *Santa Teresa* (another by the same name as the one above), *Santiago*, an unidentified small *nao*, and the armada's patache. The loss of treasure and life was great. Only four persons were rescued from the latter four ships.

Nuestra Señora de Lantigua, merchant *nao*, Captain Benito Sánchez
   Location: Tortuga, Venezuela
   History: The vessel sank on June 1, 1630, on the north side of the island of Tortuga (not to be confused with the island of the same name located off Hispaniola). The Dutch later salvaged the ship.

Nuestra Señora de la Soledad, galleon belonging to the Tierra Firme Armada of Captain-General Marqués de Brenes
   Location: South America
   History: After the armada sailed from Cartagena for Porto Bello, Panama, in 1681, four of the ships were lost: the *Santa Teresa, Nuestra Señora de la Soledad, Nuestra Señora de la Asunción,* and *Nuestra Señora de la Encarnación.* Neither the cause of the loss nor the location of the four ships is stated in documents. After receiving the treasure at Porto Bello, the armada returned to Cartagena, then sailed for Havana. Shortly after leaving Boca Chica, near Cartagena, four more ships were wrecked on nearby reefs: the *Santa Teresa* (another by the same name as the one above), *Santiago*, an unidentified small *nao*, and the armada's patache. The loss of treasure and life was great. Only four persons were rescued from the latter four ships.

Nuestra Señora del Carmen, patache belonging to the Tierra Firme Armada of Captain-General Antonio de Oquendo, 80 tons
   Location: Cartagena, Colombia
   History: Four of the armada's ships were lost while arriving at Cartagena from Porto Bello in 1634 with a vast amount of treasure onboard. The *San Juan Bautista* wrecked on Salmedina

Reef but her treasure and cannon were recovered; the *Nuestra Señora del Carmen* wrecked at the entrance of Boca Chica but was totally salvaged later; the *Nuestra Señora del Rosario* and *Los Tres Reyes* both sank due to leaks shortly after entering the inner harbor at Cartagena.

Nuestra Señora del Carmen (alias *Bristol*), Spanish merchant *nao*, Captain Joséph de Artecona
   Location: Sunzen Shoals, San Bernardo Island, Colombia
   History: The vessel wrecked in 1751 while coming from Cadiz.

Nuestra Señora del Rosario, merchant *nao* belonging to the Tierra Firme Armada of Captain-General Antonio de Oquendo, 450 tons
   Location: Cartagena, Colombia
   History: Four of the armada's ships were lost while arriving at Cartagena from Porto Bello in 1634 with a vast amount of treasure onboard. The *San Juan Bautista* wrecked on Salmedina Reef but her treasure and cannon were recovered; the *Nuestra Señora del Carmen* wrecked at the entrance of Boca Chica but was totally salvaged later; the *Nuestra Señora del Rosario* and *Los Tres Reyes* both sank due to leaks shortly after entering the inner harbor at Cartagena.

Nuestra Señora de Rosario, *nao*, 250 tons, Captain Baltazar Rodríquez Carreno
   Location: Cartagena Harbor, Cartagena, Colombia
   History: The vessel sank at anchor in 1615 in Cartagena Harbor shortly after arriving from Spain.

Penelope, English merchantman, Captain Boon
   Location: Curaçao, Netherlands Antilles
   History: The merchantman was lost near Curaçao in 1809 while sailing to the island from London. The crew and part of the cargo were saved.

Robert, English merchantman, Captain Neilson
   Location: Maracaibo, Venezuela
   History: The ship wrecked on a reef near the port of Maracaibo on May 20,

1822, while coming from Liverpool, England. Most of her cargo was saved.

San Antonio, Spanish advice boat
   Location: Bonaire Island, Netherlands Antilles
   History: The boat wrecked on June 4, 1779, on Bonaire Island while sailing from Caracas to Spain.

San Carlos, Spanish schooner, Captain Juan Casteneda
   Location: Islas de Aves, Venezuela
   History: The schooner was lost in May 1803 on Aves Islands during a voyage from Puerto Rico. The crew and some cannon were saved.

San Carlos, 70-gun Spanish warship, galleon
   Location: Castillo Grande, Cartagena, Colombia
   History: In 1741, an English fleet, led by Admiral Vernon, attacked the town of Cartagena. On the first day of the attack, the Spaniards sank six of their own galleons, four large warships, several merchant *naos*, and a French merchantman. Only the warships and the French merchantman were identified: the *Galicia, San Carlos, Africa, San Felipe,* and the French ship *El Leon de Nantes.* These five and the other Spanish ships were scuttled across the mouth of the outer harbor near Castillo Grande to prevent the English from entering the port. The following day, two remaining Spanish warships, the *Conquistador* and *Dragon,* were also sunk, in the inner channel of the port. Most of the superstructures of the Spanish ships remained above the water and the Spaniards burnt these parts to prevent the English from obtaining anything of value from them. While the English were still at Cartagena, a large Spanish ship named the *Galicia* unsuspectingly entered the harbor and was captured by the English; they burnt her after stripping her first.

San Filipe, galleon, 550 tons, Captain Galdomez
   Location: Isla Tesora
   History: The treasure-laden galleon caught fire while sailing between Nombre de Dios and Cartagena in 1572. It ran aground near Isla Tesora. The ship blew up before the majority

of the treasure she carried could be taken off.

San Filipe, 42-cannon *capitana* (flagship) of the Tierra Firme Armada of Captain-General Hierónimo, 850 tons, Captain Gaspar de Vargas

Location: Bonaire Island, Netherlands Antilles

History: The *capitana* and the patache of the armada were wrecked off the east side of Bonaire Island in 1610. Over a period of five years divers were able to recover all the cannon (which were bronze) from both shipwrecks, as well as a great amount of the cargo of the *capitana*.

San Filipe, 80-gun Spanish warship, galleon

Location: Castillo Grande Cartagena, Colombia

History: In 1741, an English fleet, led by Admiral Vernon, attacked the town of Cartagena. On the first day of the attack, the Spaniards sank six of their own galleons, four large warships, several merchant *naos*, and a French merchantman. Only the warships and the French merchantman were identified: the *Galicia, San Carlos, Africa, San Felipe*, and the French ship *El Leon de Nantes*. These five and the other Spanish ships were scuttled across the mouth of the outer harbor near Castillo Grande to prevent the English from entering the port. The following day, two remaining Spanish warships, the *Conquistador* and *Dragon*, were also sunk, in the inner channel of the port. Most of the superstructures of the Spanish ships remained above the water and the Spaniards burnt these parts to prevent the English from obtaining anything of value from them. While the English were still at Cartagena, a large Spanish ship named the *Galicia* unsuspectingly entered the harbor and was captured by the English; they burnt her after stripping her first.

San Francisco de Paula, Spanish ship

Location: Lake Maracaibo bar, Maracaibo, Venezuela

History: The ship was totally lost on the bar at the entrance to Lake Maracaibo in 1791.

San José, 64-gun *capitana* (flagship) of a treasure fleet of 17 ships

Location: Baru Island, off Cartagena, Colombia

History: The *San José* was the richest single Spanish galleon ever lost in the Western Hemisphere. She was carrying over 11 million pesos in treasure when she went down in 1708. Due to the War of the Spanish Succession, there hadn't been any treasure sent from South America to Spain in six years. This year, a fleet of 17 ships arrived at Porto Bello to receive the treasure. Since only four of the ships were heavily armed, all of the 22 million pesos in treasure received at Porto Bello was placed on these four: The the *San José* (*capitana*), the *San Martín* (*almirata*), the *Gobierno*, and an unidentified *urca*. As the Spanish fleet was approaching Cartagena, an English squadron commanded by Commodore Wager appeared on the horizon between the Spanish fleet and the port, and closed in on it. A battle ensued between the four Spanish ships and the English warships, and it continued into the night. The *San José* exploded and quickly sank with only five of her crew of 600 surviving. The English captured the *Gobierno*. The *urca* was run aground and set afire by the Spaniards on the tip of the Baru Peninsula. The 64-gun *almiranta*, the *San Martín*, managed to reach the safety of Cartagena, along with the other Spanish merchantmen. The exact location of the *San José* is not given in the records; they say only that it sank off Baru Island. The Spaniards later recovered most of the treasure on the *urca*.

San Joséph, Spanish *nao*, Captain Arestiqui

Location: Cartagena Harbor, Cartagena, Colombia

History: The vessel was lost entering the harbor in 1773 while arriving from Cadiz.

San Juan Bautista, galleon belonging to the Tierra Firme Armada of Captain-General Antonio de Oquendo, 600 tons, Captain Hernán Martínez de Velasco

Location: Cartagena, Colombia

History: Four of the armada's ships were lost while arriving at Cartagena from Porto Bello in 1634 with a vast amount of treasure onboard. The *San Juan Bautista* wrecked on Salmedina Reef but her treasure and cannon were recovered; the *Nuestra Señora del Carmen* wrecked at the entrance of Boca Chica but was totally salvaged later; the *Nuestra Señora del Rosario* and *Los Tres Reyes* both sank due to leaks shortly after entering the inner harbor at Cartagena.

San Miguel, Spanish warship, Captain Juan Elizalde

Location: Between Punta de la Canoa and El Palmarita

History: The warship struck a submerged rock on January 9, 1790, between Punta de la Canoa and El Palmarita and sank in 14 fathoms of water. Only one of her crew was lost.

San Miguel, Spanish *navío*

Location: Cumaná, Venezuela

History: The ship wrecked near the port of Cumaná in 1733. The English later salvaged the vessel.

San Pedro Alcantara, 64-gun Spanish warship, Captain Jávier de Salazar

Location: Coche Island, Venezuela

History: A large fleet of Spanish warships and troop transports was sent from Spain to suppress the revolution in Venezuela. After reaching the Caribbean, the fleet anchored off Coche Island, located near Margarita Island. On the afternoon of April 24, 1815, the largest warship in the fleet, the *San Pedro Alcantara*, caught on fire and blew up. Over 50 men lost their lives. There was also over 800,000 pesos in silver specie aboard, as well as tons of weapons and munitions. The explosion scattered the ship over a wide area. Salvage operations were started the following day and as late as 1871 salvors were still recovering treasure from the wreck. However, due to incomplete records, it is not known just how much was recovered or if anything remains. In recent years, amateur divers from Caracas have dived on the wreck and recovered a few cannon and artifacts.

Santa María de Begonia, *nao*, 250 tons, Captain Cosme Andrés

Location: Cartagena Harbor, Cartagena, Colombia

History: The treasure-laden ship ran aground entering Cartagena Harbor in 1562 and was lost. All of her treasure was saved.

Santa María de Villacelan, *nao* belonging to the Tierra Firme Armada of Captain-General Bartolome Carreno, 120 tons, Captain Martín García

Location: On the coast about ten leagues south of Cartagena, Colombia

History: After the armada sailed from Nombre de Dios with a great amount of treasure, the *Santa María de Villacelan* wrecked on the coast in 1553. Indian divers, brought from the pearl fisheries of Margarita Island, salvaged all of her treasure.

Santa Teresa, galleon belonging to the Tierra Firme Armada of Captain-General Marqués de Brenes

Location: South America

History: After the armada sailed from Cartagena for Porto Bello, Panama, in 1681, four of the ships were lost: the *Santa Teresa, Nuestra Señora de la Soledad, Nuestra Señora de la Asunción,* and *Nuestra Señora de la Encarnación.* Neither the cause of the loss nor the location of the four ships is stated in documents. After receiving the treasure at Porto Bello, the armada returned to Cartagena, then sailed for Havana. Shortly after leaving Boca Chica, near Cartagena, four more ships were wrecked on nearby reefs: the *Santa Teresa* (another by the same name as the one above), *Santiago,* an unidentified small *nao,* and the armada's patache. The loss of treasure and life was great. Only four persons were rescued from the latter four ships.

Santiago, galleon belonging to the Tierra Firme Armada of Captain-General Marqués de Brenes

Location: South America

History: After the armada sailed from Cartagena for Porto Bello, Panama, in 1681, four of the ships were lost: the *Santa Teresa, Nuestra Señora de la Soledad, Nuestra Señora de la Asunción,* and *Nuestra Señora de la Encarnación.* Neither the cause of the loss nor the location of the four ships is stated in documents. After receiving the treasure at Porto Bello, the armada

returned to Cartagena, then sailed for Havana. Shortly after leaving Boca Chica, near Cartagena, four more ships were wrecked on nearby reefs: the *Santa Teresa* (another by the same name as the one above), *Santiago,* an unidentified small *nao,* and the armada's patache. The loss of treasure and life was great. Only four persons were rescued from the latter four ships.

Thetis, Scottish ship

Location: La Guaira (the port of Caracas), Venezuela

History: The ship was lost near the port of La Guaira in 1822 while coming from the Clyde. Part of her cargo was saved.

Thetis, English frigate

Location: Cape Frio, Brazil. Depth of water 70 feet

History: In December 1830, the *Thetis* was sailing from Rio de Janeiro to England when she was driven against the rocks in a storm off Cape Frio, Brazil. Half the frigate crew drowned and $810,000 in gold and silver bars went down with the ship. A current of six knots and huge 27-foot waves made recovery of the treasure almost impossible. Thomas Dickinson, captain of a British sloop in Rio at the time, along with 50 seamen from his sloop, decided to salvage her cargo. They made a crude diving bell with two iron water storage tanks and converted a fire-fighting pump into a compressor to provide the bell with air. Unable to anchor over the wreck, Dickinson constructed a boom on a cliff nearby using the mast and spars from the Thetis. They returned to London with $750,000 worth of treasure, even after several bells failed. Dickinson's was the first important recovery of treasure by anyone except the Spanish up until that time. Litigation over the division of treasure left the salvors with only one-eighth of it to split among themselves, apportioned according to how much work they each had done.

Unidentified, *urca* belonging to a treasure fleet of 17 ships, Captain Francisco Neito

Location: The tip of the Baru Peninsula

Early 18th century Spanish naval sword. *Courtesy of the Metro Museum of Art.*

History: The *San José* was the richest single Spanish galleon ever lost in the Western Hemisphere. She was carrying over 11 million pesos in treasure when she went down in 1708. Due to the War of the Spanish Succession, there hadn't been any treasure sent from South America to Spain in six years. This year, a fleet of 17 ships arrived at Porto Bello to receive the treasure. Since only four of the ships were heavily armed, all of the 22 million pesos in treasure received at Porto Bello was placed on these four: The the *San José* (*capitana*), the *San Martín* (*almirata*), the *Gobierno,* and an unidentified *urca.* As the Spanish fleet was approaching Cartagena, an English squadron commanded by Commodore Wager appeared on the horizon between the Spanish fleet and the port, and closed in on it. A battle ensued between the four Spanish ships and the English warships, and it continued into the night. The *San José* exploded and quickly sank with only five of her crew of 600 surviving. The English captured the *Gobierno.* The *urca* was run aground and set afire by the Spaniards on the tip of the Baru Peninsula. The 64-gun *almiranta,* the *San Martín,* managed to reach the safety of Cartagena, along with the other Spanish merchantmen. The exact location of the *San José* is not given in the records; they say only that it sank off Baru Island. The Spaniards later recovered most of the treasure on the *urca*.

Unidentified, Spanish merchant *nao*
Location: Cartagena, Colombia
History: The *nao* wrecked on a reef near Cartagena in 1546. Thirteen of the 104 persons onboard perished.

Unidentified, caravel
Location: Paraguaná Peninsula, Venezuela
History: An unidentified caravel carrying the Count of Nieva, the new viceroy of Peru, and other important persons was lost on the coast of the Paraguana Peninsula in 1561. Everyone onboard perished.

Unidentified, galleon belonging to the Tierra Firme Armada of Captain-General Esteban de las Alas
Location: Cartagena, Colombia
History: The treasure-laden galleon wrecked on a reef near Cartagena in 1564. Thirteen people perished. The wreck fell off the reef into deeper water before her treasure could be saved. Divers were unable to recover anything due to the depth of water into which the ship sank.

Unidentified, *nao* and patache belonging to the Tierra Firme Armada of Captain-General Marqués de Brenes
Location: South America
History: After the armada sailed from Cartagena for Porto Bello, Panama, in 1681, four of the ships were lost: the *Santa Teresa, Nuestra Señora de la Soledad, Nuestra Señora de la Asunción,* and *Nuestra Señora de la Encarnación.* Neither the cause of the loss nor the location of the four ships is stated in documents. After receiving the treasure at Porto Bello, the armada returned to Cartagena, then sailed for Havana. Shortly after leaving Boca Chica, near Cartagena, four more ships were wrecked on nearby reefs: the *Santa Teresa* (another by the same name as the one above), *Santiago*, an unidentified small *nao*, and the armada's patache. The loss of treasure and life was great. Only four persons were rescued from the latter four ships.

Unidentified, patache
Location: Islas de Aves (Isle of Birds), Venezuela
History: The patache wrecked in 1613 on Aves Islands. She was carrying a large number of pearls. Two years later the owner of the vessel stated that it had not yet been salvaged.

Unidentified, French ships (16), fleet commanded by Count D'Estres
Location: Islas de Aves, Venezuela
History: The French fleet, consisting of 18 warships and two privateers, was sent to capture Curaçao from the Dutch. During the night of May 3, 1678, all but one of the warships and one of the privateers were totally lost on a reef on Aves Islands. Over 1,200 men perished, and 250 brass and 300 iron cannon were lost. The Dutch were able to salvage most of the cannon. Later, the French recovered most of those not recovered by the Dutch.

Unidentified, *naos* (4) belonging to the flotilla commanded by Captain Juan de la Cosa
Location: Bahía de Uraba, Colombia
History: The flotilla consisting of four large *naos* was sent to explore and map the coast of Colombia, but all four wrecked during a storm in 1504 in the Bahía de Uraba. One hundred and seventy-five of the 200 men onboard the *naos* were drowned.

Unidentified, patache belonging to the Tierra Firme Armada of Captain-General Hierónimo
Location: Bonaire Island, Netherlands Antilles
History: The armada's *capitana* (flagship) the *San Filipe*, and the patache of the armada were wrecked off the east side of Bonaire Island in 1610. Over a period of five years, divers were able to recover all the cannon (which were bronze) from both wrecks, as well as a great amount of the cargo of the *capitana*.

Unidentified, Spanish advice boat
Location: Cabo de la Vela
History: The advice boat wrecked off Cabo de la Vela in 1652. Her crew

reached shore but was captured and eaten by the Carib Indians. These same Indians recovered the mail from the wreck and sold it to the Spaniards.

Unidentified, merchant *nao*
Location: Cartagena, Colombia
History: The *nao*, from Santo Domingo, sank in 1634 after hitting the *Nuestra Señora del Carmen* that had sunk a week earlier at the entrance of Boca Chica near Cartagena.

Unidentified, Spanish warships
Location: Cartagena
History: Two large unidentified Spanish warships were wrecked in the harbor when a terrible storm struck Cartagena on December 12, 1761. Both went into the sea. During the same storm, many cannon from the two forts at Santa Marta were thrown into the sea as well.

Unidentified, ships (3)
Location: Cartagena Harbor, Cartagena, Colombia
History: Three ships carrying over half a million pesos in gold and silver were sunk in 1542 near Boca Chica, in Cartagena Harbor while entering the port. On the admiral's orders, the main pilot of the convoy was hanged. Later, divers were able to recover only a small part of the treasure, as it was reported to be in a depth too great for them to work in.

Unidentified, merchant *nao* of Captain Juan Estevan
Location: Cartagena Harbor, Cartagena, Colombia
History: The *nao* sank in 1556 while at anchor in Cartagena Harbor. Indian divers recovered all of her treasure.

Unidentified, galleons (2)
Location: Cartagena Harbor, Cartagena, Colombia
History: Shortly before the Tierra Firme Armada was to sail for Havana in 1575, two of its galleons collided while at anchor in Cartagena. One of the galleons, carrying an immense treasure in silver bullion and specie, sank. Divers were only able to recover some of the ship's rigging and a few bronze cannon because of the water's depth.

Unidentified, ships (many)
Location: Castillo Santa Cruz, Cartagena, Colombia
History: In 1697, a French fleet under the command of Admiral Point attacked Cartagena. The Spaniards sank two large galleons of their own near Castillo Santa Cruz to prevent the French from entering the harbor. When that stratagen failed, they burnt two other large ships, two galleys and many small vessels in the inner harbor to prevent their capture by the French. The French bomb galliot *Éclatant* was so badly damaged by the Spanish cannonfire that the French burnt her in the harbor before leaving.

Unidentified, frigate
Location: Coro, Venezuela
History: An unidentified frigate owned by the king of Spain and carrying 30,000 pesos worth of tobacco, sank near the port of Coro in the year 1622.

Unidentified, ships (several)
Location: Curaçao, Netherlands Antilles
History: During a hurricane in 1784, several large ships were wrecked in the main harbor on the island of Curaçao and others were forced to sea where they were lost without a trace.

Unidentified, Spanish merchant *naos* (3), commanded by Captain Diego de Ondas
Location: Gulf of Venezuela, Venezuela
History: The ships were lost in the gulf in 1531 near the entrance of Lake Maracaibo.

Unidentified, patache
Location: Isla Beata in Lake Maracaibo, Venezuela
History: The patache wrecked on the Isla Beata in 1622.

Unidentified, Spanish merchant *nao*
Location: Isla de los Sombreros
History: The *nao* was lost in 1740 near Isla de los Sombreros.

Unidentified, Spanish merchant *nao*
Location: Isla de los Sombreros
History: The *nao* was lost near Isla de los Sombreros in 1740.

Unidentified, patache
Location: Isla Tesora
History: The patache wrecked on Isla Tesora in 1632 with a valuable cargo of pearls. Divers recovered most of the pearls.

Unidentified, ships (20+)
Location: La Guaira (the port of Caracas), Venezuela
History: Over 20 large ships of different nationalities were lost during a bad gale that struck the port of La Guaira on December 22, 1822.

Unidentified, frigates (2) belonging to the Windward Armada of Admiral Alonso de Espinosa
Location: Lake Maracaibo, Venezuela
History: In 1669, three large Spanish frigates were sent to fight the pirate Henry Morgan while he was attacking and sacking various settlements on Lake Maracaibo. The three Spanish ships anchored under the guns of the fort at the entrance to Lake Maracaibo, where the pirates would have to pass to leave the lake. The pirates sank one of the vessels by using a fire ship. The Spaniards burnt another to prevent its capture. The pirates captured the third.

Unidentified, Spanish *naos* (3), commanded by Captain Antonio Campos
Location: Lake Maracaibo, Venezuela
History: The ships were lost in the year 1660.

Unidentified, galleon
Location: A bit south of Cartagena Harbor, Cartagena, Colombia
History: In 1559, a richly laden galleon, sailing from Nombre de Dios in Panama with over 900,000 pesos in gold and silver aboard, parted from its convoy and attempted to enter Cartagena Harbor at night. The pilot made a mistake as to where the entrance was and the ship ran aground a bit south of the port and quickly broke up. Only a small amount of the treasure was recovered.

Unidentified, large *nao*
Location: A bit west of Darien, Panama
History: A large *nao*, carrying a large number of colonists and supplies, was sent from Santo Domingo to the new Spanish settlement named Darien, located close to the present boundary of Panama and Colombia. The pilot erred in his navigation and the *nao* wrecked a bit west of Darien in 1513. There were only a few survivors.

Unidentified, merchant *nao*, Captain Bodes
Location: Mouth of the Medellín River
History: A merchant *nao*, coming from Margarita Island with a large number of pearls, wrecked in 1600 at the mouth of the Medellín River.

Unidentified, Spanish schooner
Location: Puerto de la Guayra, Venezuela
History: The schooner wrecked in 1734 on the reefs in front of Puerto de la Guayra at the mouth of the Orinoco River.

Unidentified, French pirate vessel
Location: Puerto Santo on Margarita Island, Venezuela
History: Two Spanish galleys were sent after a French pirate vessel anchored at Puerto Santo. During the eventual battle in 1586, the French pirate ship exploded. Forty-six of the 50 Frenchmen aboard were lost.

Unidentified, Dutch ships (22)
Location: Punta de Araya, Venezuela
History: A large armada of Spanish warships was sent after the Dutch several years after they had established a thriving salt industry at Punta de Araya. The Spanish armada surprised the 22 Dutch warships at Punta de Araya in 1605. They burnt and sank the vessels, and massacred all the Dutchmen.

Unidentified, Portuguese slave ship
Location: Punta de la Canoa
History: In 1660, the ship struck on a rock in 1½ fathoms of water near Punta de la Canoa, then sank into deeper water.

Unidentified, patache belonging to the Tierra Firme Armada of Captain-General Carlos de Ibarra
Location: Reef near Cartagena, Colombia

History: The patache wrecked on a reef near Cartagena in 1637 while sailing between Venezuela and Cartagena. Her cargo consisted of 60 tons of copper ingots. Salvors were able to recover most of the cargo.

Unidentified, flagship of Captain Cristobal Garcia
    Location: Reef near Punta de Canoas, which is between Cartagena and Barranquilla, Colombia
    History: The flagship of Captain Cristobal Garcia wrecked on a reef in 1504 during an exploration voyage along the coast of Columbia. The reef is located between Cartagena and Barranquilla. Two other vessels in the flotilla rescued the crew, but an undisclosed number of gold nuggets and emeralds that the explorers had traded from the natives went down with the ship.

Unidentified, Portuguese galleons (3)
    Location: Reef near the entrance of Boca Grande, Cartagena, Colombia
    History: Due to the outbreak of war between Spain and Portugal in 1640, the Spanish Tierra Firme Armada intercepted the richly laden Portuguese armada as it was sailing between Brazil and Portugal. The Spanish forced the armada to sail with them to Cartagena. The leader of the Portuguese armada, Admiral Rodrigo Lobad da

Ming dynasty plate recovered from a Portuguese wreck on the coast of Brazil.

Silva, had no idea that there was a war between the two countries but suspected foul play, so as both armadas were entering Cartagena Harbor, he deliberately wrecked his three richest galleons on a reef near the entrance of Boca Grande. The treasure onboard the three galleons, consisting of gold, diamonds and other precious stones, was estimated at over five million pesos. The records do not state if any of it was ever recovered.

Unidentified, patache belonging to the Tierra Firme Armada of Captain-General Thomas de Larraspuru
    Location: Reef off Isla Baru
    History: The patache wrecked on a reef off Isla Baru in 1631 while sailing

with the armada between Porto Bello and Cartagena.

Unidentified, advice boat
    Location: Salmedina Reef, near Cartagena, Colombia
    History: An advice boat arriving from Spain was totally lost on the reef in the year 1680.

Unidentified, Spanish *nao*
    Location: Santa Marta, Colombia
    History: A large *nao*, carrying a bishop to Cartagena from Spain along with a rich cargo of merchandise, wrecked on the coast near Santa Martha in 1544.

Unidentified, ship
    Location: Santa Marta
    History: A small unidentified ship, coming from Venezuela with a cargo consisting mainly of tobacco, ran aground entering the port of Santa Marta in the year 1616.

Victoria, ten-gun Spanish warship, Captain Francisco de Raula Escudero
    Location: Bajo de Negrillo, near Cartagena, Colombia
    History: The warship wrecked on March 28, 1795, on the shallows of Bajo de Negrillo, located near Cartagena. She was originally a French ship captured by the Spaniards.

The United States

Since the Abandoned Shipwreck Act of 1987 was passed, every state bordering the Atlantic Ocean has enacted laws relevant to shipwrecks and other underwater cultural resources within its jurisdiction. It is essential for someone to know both local and federal regulations before attempting to carry out salvage work in any body of water in the United States. This may prevent seizure of artifacts or treasure that is recovered.

A total of 1,167 shipwrecks have been excluded from the following list because their locations were too vague in archive documents. For example, over 300 were listed as being lost on "the New England coast." Others were lost on "the American Coast" or on "the North American Continent." Besides the ships identified in archive documents, significant shipwrecks that have been positively identified are also included in this section. Note: Florida

is given a separate section because its shipwrecks are so numerous.

SHIPWRECKS IN UNITED STATES WATERS

CONNECTICUT

Anion, Spanish merchantman
    Location: New London

History: She sank in October 1816 near New London due to a bad leak, while sailing from Italy to New York.

George, American merchantman, Captain Speeding
   Location: New London
   History: The vessel was lost on October 16, 1817, near New London while sailing to Granada. Her crew and cargo were saved.

Mary, American merchantman, Captain Hanly
   Location: Darien
   History: The merchantman was lost on March 25, 1817, while crossing the bar at Darien. The vessel was en route to Liverpool when it went down.

Osprey, American merchantman, Captain Cook
   Location: New London
   History: She wrecked during a gale in February 1812 near New London while sailing from Pernambuco to New York.

Unidentified, merchantmen (2)
   Location: New London
   History: Two large merchantmen were wrecked at New London during a hurricane on October 19, 1770.

DELAWARE

Adeline, American merchantman, Captain Israel
   Location: Cape Henlopen
   History: The merchantman wrecked on December 9, 1824, at Cape Henlopen while sailing from North Carolina to Philadelphia.

Adriana, American merchantman
   Location: Delaware Bay
   History: She sank in the bay in 1801 due to heavy ice while sailing from Philadelphia to Dublin.

Andrea Doria, 14-gun American warship
   Location: Delaware Bay
   History: Seven American warships were lost during a battle with the British in the Delaware Bay in 1777: the *Washington, Effingham, Sachem, Independence, Dolphin, Wasp* and *Mosquito.* Another American warship, the *Andrea Doria,* was burnt to prevent her capture, also in Delaware Bay.

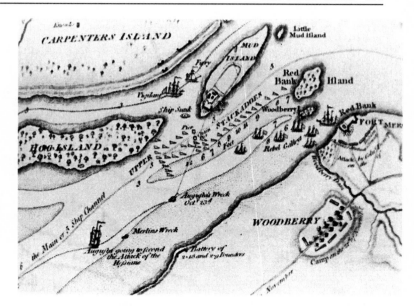

Chart showing the locations of three Revolutionary War wrecks on the Delaware River.

Charlestown, American merchantman, Captain Simpson
   Location: Branclawine Bank
   History: The vessel wrecked on January 25, 1766, on the Branclawine Bank while sailing from Hamburg to Philadelphia.

China, merchantman of unknown registry, Captain M'Pherson
   Location: Delaware Bay
   History: The merchantman sank in Delaware Bay in 1805 while sailing from Batavia to Philadelphia. Part of her cargo was saved.

Commerce, English merchantman, Captain Addis
   Location: Cape Henlopen
   History: The merchantman wrecked at Cape Henlopen in 1771 while sailing from England to New York. Very little of her cargo was saved.

Constellation, American merchantman
   Location: Delaware Bay
   History: The merchantman sank in the Delaware Bay in 1801 while sailing for New York.

Cornelia, English merchantman, Captain Smith
   Location: Between Capes Henlopen and May

History: The ship sank between Capes Henlopen and May in 1757 while sailing from Philadelphia to Gibraltar. Three of her crew perished.

Dolphin, ten-gun American warship
   Location: Delaware Bay
   History: Seven American warships were lost during a battle with the British in Delaware Bay in 1777: the *Washington, Effingham, Sachem, Independence, Dolphin, Wasp* and *Mosquito.* Another American warship, the *Andrea Doria,* was burnt to prevent her capture, also in Delaware Bay.

Effingham, 28-gun American warship
   Location: Delaware Bay
   History: Seven American warships were lost during a battle with the British in Delaware Bay in 1777: the *Washington, Effingham, Sachem, Independence, Dolphin, Wasp* and *Mosquito.* Another American warship, the *Andrea Doria,* was burnt to prevent her capture, also in Delaware Bay.

Endeavor, English merchantman, Captain Caldwell
   Location: Reedy Island
   History: The vessel caught on fire and sank off Reedy Island in the Delaware River in 1775 while sailing from Philadelphia to Londonderry. Most of her cargo was saved.

Faithful Stewart, Scottish immigrant ship, Captain M'Causland
Location: Cape Henlopen
History: The ship sank in 1785 near Cape Henlopen while sailing from Londonderry to Philadelphia. Over 200 persons perished.

Fanny, merchantman of unknown registry
Location: Delaware Bay
History: The merchantman sank in the bay in 1805 while sailing from France to Philadelphia.

Favorite, American merchantman
Location: Delaware Bay
History: The ship sank in the Delaware Bay in 1796 while sailing from Cadiz to Philadelphia.

George, English ship
Location: Philadelphia
History: This English ship sank at Philadelphia in the year 1800 while preparing to sail for England.

Henry & Charles, American merchantman
Location: Cape Henlopen
History: The vessel wrecked in 1796 near Cape Henlopen while sailing from Philadelphia to Hamburg.

H.M.S. *DeBraak*, 16-gun English warship, Captain James Drew
Location: Lewes
History: The warship capsized and sank near Lewes in 1798. Thirty-five of her crew perished. At the time of the disaster, she carried 70 tons of copper ingots and a large amount of gold and silver bullion and specie. Over the years, there were many attempts to locate this shipwreck. It was finally located in 1984. Among the recovered items are a large collection of copper-alloy bolts, fasteners, sheathing, and sheathing nails. The 20,000 artifacts recovered from the *DeBraak* were eventually bought by the State of Delaware, in order to preserve the entire collection.

Independence, ten-gun American warship
Location: Delaware Bay
History: Seven American warships were lost during a battle with the British in Delaware Bay in 1777: the *Washington*, *Effingham*, *Sachem*, *Independence*,

Dolphin, *Wasp* and *Mosquito*. Another American warship, the *Andrea Doria*, was burnt to prevent her capture, also in Delaware Bay.

Industry, American merchantman, Captain Carson
Location: Delaware Bay
History: The merchantman sank in Delaware Bay, near Cape May, in 1793 while sailing from France to Philadelphia.

John, American ship, Captain Folger
Location: Cape Henlopen
History: This ship wrecked near Cape Henlopen in 1797 while sailing from Hamburg to Philadelphia with over 300 immigrants.

John, English merchantman, Captain Staples
Location: Delaware River
History: She wrecked on December 5, 1790, on the Delaware River near Philadelphia while arriving from England. Some of her cargo was saved.

Kildare, ship of unknown registry, Captain Nicholson
Location: Delaware River
History: The vessel was lost at the mouth of the Delaware River in 1768 while sailing from Barbados to Philadelphia.

Lively, ship of unknown registry, Captain Lawrence
Location: Near Lewes
History: The ship sank near Lewes in 1795 while sailing from Amsterdam to New York. Only her crew was saved.

Matilda, American ship
Location: Delaware Bay
History: She wrecked on the north side of Delaware Bay in 1811 while sailing from the Canary Islands to Baltimore. The crew and part of the cargo were saved.

Mercury, English merchantman, Captain Hogg
Location: Delaware River
History: The merchantman was lost near the Delaware River in 1741 while sailing from Philadelphia to London.

Minerva, American merchantman
Location: Delaware River
History: The vessel wrecked near the

mouth of the Delaware River in 1796 while sailing from Lisbon to Philadelphia. Seven of her crew perished.

Molly, Scottish merchantman, Captain Stewart
Location: Delaware River
History: The merchantman sank in the Delaware River in 1760.

Mosquito, four gun American warship
Location: Delaware Bay
History: Seven American warships were lost during a battle with the British in Delaware Bay in 1777: the *Washington*, *Effingham*, *Sachem*, *Independence*, *Dolphin*, *Wasp* and *Mosquito*. Another American warship, the *Andrea Doria*, was burnt to prevent her capture, also in Delaware Bay.

New Jersey, American merchantman, Captain Clay
Location: Delaware Bay
History: The merchantman wrecked on the west side of Delaware Bay in 1799 while sailing from Puerto Rico to Philadelphia.

Peace, ship of unknown registry, Captain Star
Location: Hog Island
History: The ship wrecked on Hog Island in 1874 while sailing from London to Virginia. Some of her cargo was saved.

Peggy, American ship
Location: Delaware Bay
History: She was lost in the bay in 1794 while sailing from Philadelphia to Savannah.

Pitt Packet, English merchantman, Captain Montgomery
Location: Delaware Bay
History: The vessel foundered in Delaware Bay in 1763. She was carrying a large number of passengers, and all perished, along with the crew.

Pomona, English ship, Captain Hopkins
Location: Delaware Bay
History: She sank in Delaware Bay on October 30, 1789, while arriving from Quebec.

Pusey, English merchantman, Captain Good
Location: Reedy Island

History: The merchantman wrecked in 1757 on Reedy Island while arriving from Jamaica.

Sachem, ten-gun American warship
Location: Delaware Bay
History: Seven American warships were lost during a battle with the British in Delaware Bay in 1777: the *Washington, Effingham, Sachem, Independence, Dolphin, Wasp* and *Mosquito*. Another American warship, the *Andrea Doria*, was burnt to prevent her capture, also in Delaware Bay.

Sally, English merchantman, Captain Saze
Location: Brandy Wine on the Delaware River
History: The merchantman was lost at Brandy Wine in 1757 while sailing from Philadelphia to Antigua.

San Joseph, Spanish ship
Location: Delaware Bay
History: The ship was lost due to ice crushing her hull in Delaware Bay in 1794. She was sailing from Philadelphia to Cuba.

Santa Rosalea, Spanish merchantman, Captain Pardenus
Location: Cape Henlopen
History: The vessel wrecked in 1788 near Cape Henlopen while sailing from Baltimore to Havana. Some of her cargo was saved.

Severn, English merchantman, Captain Hathorn
Location: Delaware Bay
History: The merchantman wrecked in the bay in 1774 while sailing from Bristol to Philadelphia. All of her crew were saved.

Susannah, American ship, Captain Medlin
Location: Delaware Bay
History: She wrecked in Delaware Bay in 1800 while sailing from Hamburg to Philadelphia.

Unidentified, ship
Location: Philadelphia
History: A large newly arrived unidentified ship sank at Philadelphia during a hurricane on October 9, 1804.

Unidentified, ships (9)
Location: Cape Henlopen

History: During a severe gale in the fall of 1783, nine large unidentified ships were wrecked at Cape Henlopen. Many lives were lost.

Unidentified, ship
Location: Delaware River
History: An unidentified ship sank near the mouth of the Delaware River in the year 1800.

Vaughan, English merchantman, Captain Foster
Location: Delaware Bay
History: The merchantman wrecked in the bay in 1763 while sailing from Bristol to Philadelphia.

Washington, 32-gun American warship
Location: Delaware Bay
History: Seven American warships were lost during a battle with the British in Delaware Bay in 1777: the *Washington, Effingham, Sachem, Independence, Dolphin, Wasp* and *Mosquito*. Another American warship, the *Andrea Doria*, was burnt to prevent her capture, also in Delaware Bay.

Wasp, eight-gun American warship
Location: Delaware Bay
History: Seven American warships were lost during a battle with the British in Delaware Bay in 1777: the *Washington, Effingham, Sachem, Independence, Dolphin, Wasp* and *Mosquito*. Another American warship, the *Andrea Doria*, was burnt to prevent her capture, also in Delaware Bay.

GEORGIA

Achilles, English merchantman
Location: Martha's Industry Shoals
History: The ship was lost in 1815 on the Martha's Industry Shoals.

Active, American merchantman
Location: Savannah bar
History: The merchantman was totally lost at the end of November in 1811 on the Savannah bar while arriving from Lisbon.

Albion, English merchantman, Captain Stephenson
Location: St. Catherine's Island
History: The ship wrecked on the island in 1824 while sailing from Hon-

duras to London. There were only six survivors.

Braddock, English merchantman, Captain Johnson
Location: Savannah
History: The merchantman was lost near Savannah on November 21, 1816, while arriving from Liverpool.

Conception, ship of unknown registry, Captain Towers
Location: St. Simons Island
History: The ship wrecked on St. Simons Island in 1792 while arriving from Philadelphia.

Duchess of Argyle, Scottish merchantman, Captain Miller
Location: Cumberland Island
History: The merchantman wrecked on Cumberland Island in 1787 while sailing from Jamaica to Philadelphia. No lives were lost.

Edward, American merchantman, Captain Lewis
Location: Savannah bar
History: The merchantman was totally lost on the Savannah bar in 1811 while laden with timber and bound for England.

Eliza, English merchantman, Captain Shelburn
Location: Savannah bar
History: The ship was totally lost on the Savannah bar in 1791 while arriving from Barbados.

Friends Endeavour, English merchantman, Captain Wake
Location: Sunbury bar
History: The ship was lost crossing over the Sunbury bar in 1763 while sailing for London. Only her crew was saved.

Goleah, American merchantman, Captain Payne
Location: Savannah
History: The merchantman wrecked near Savannah in March 1817 while arriving from France.

Grenada, English packet boat
Location: Savannah Harbor
History: After being captured by a French privateer, the packet boat was brought into Savannah Harbor and burnt in 1794.

H.M.S. *Defiance*, 64-gun English warship, Captain Maximillian Jacobs
   Location: Savannah bar
   History: The warship wrecked on February 18, 1780, on the Savannah bar.

H.M.S. *Hope*, 16-gun English warship, Captain William Thomas
   Location: Savannah
   History: The warship wrecked off Savannah in 1781.

H.M.S. *Rose*, 20-gun English warship, Captain John Brown
   Location: Savannah bar
   History: The ship was deliberately sunk in September 1779 to block the bar at the entrance to Savannah.

Jamaica, English merchantman, Captain Redman
   Location: Savannah River
   History: The ship was lost on the Savannah River in 1780 while arriving from Jamaica.

Jason, English ship, Captain Thomson
   Location: South Breakers of the St. Simon Island bar
   History: The ship wrecked on the breakers in 1821 while arriving from England. No lives were lost.

Jupiter, American merchantman
   Location: Savannah
   History: The merchantman wrecked near Savannah in 1817 while arriving from Havana.

Mars, English merchantman, Captain Taylor
   Location: Savannah
   History: The merchantman was lost on December 2, 1815, near Savannah while arriving from London. No lives were lost.

Mary, American merchantman, Captain Firth
   Location: Savannah River
   History: The ship was lost as it was sailing down the Savannah River in 1806 while en route to Barbados. The crew and cargo were saved.

Minerva, American brig, Captain Bunker
   Location: St. Andrews Sound
   History: The brig was lost during April 1799 near St. Andrews Sound.

Pezzarro, ship of unknown registry, Captain Fosh
   Location: Savannah
   History: The ship was wrecked at Savannah in 1810 while sailing for Liverpool. The crew and cargo were saved.

Polly, English merchantman, Captain Newell
   Location: Savannah Harbor
   History: The ship was accidentally burnt in Savannah Harbor in 1785 while preparing to sail for London.

Prudence, English merchantman, Captain Smith
   Location: Cumberland Island
   History: The ship was totally lost on Cumberland Island in 1769 while arriving from Cadiz.

Rose in Bloom, English merchantman, Captain Lake
   Location: Savannah
   History: The merchantman wrecked near Savannah on May 6, 1817, while sailing from New Orleans to Amsterdam. The crew and a small part of the cargo were saved.

Speculator, English merchantman, Captain Hardy
   Location: Savannah
   History: The merchantman was lost on December 10, 1815, near Savannah. Seven of her crew perished.

Triton, ship of unknown registry, Captain Cox
   Location: Savannah
   History: The ship was totally lost near Savannah in 1808 while sailing from Amsterdam to Baltimore.

Unidentified, ships (large number)
   Location: Savanna Harbor
   History: A large number of unidentified ships were sunk in Savannah Harbor during a hurricane on September 11, 1804.

Velina, English merchantman, Captain Wickham
   Location: Savannah
   History: The ship was lost near Savannah on March 3, 1816, while arriving from England. Her crew and part of her cargo were saved.

Whydah, Scottish merchantman, Captain Balfour

   Location: Near Savannah
   History: The merchantman was lost on January 6, 1803, near Savannah while arriving from the Clyde. The crew and part of the cargo were saved.

MAINE

Charles, American merchant schooner, Captain Adams
   Location: Portland Lighthouse
   History: This vessel wrecked in 1807 on a reef of rocks to the west of the Portland Lighthouse. Only six of her crew of 22 were saved.

Diligent, 14-gun American warship, Captain Brown
   Location: Portland
   History: The British burned the *Warren, Diligent, Hazard* and *Tyrannicide* at Portland, Maine on August 14, 1779, to prevent their capture. Some of the cannon were recovered several years later.

Hazard, 16-gun American warship, Captain John Foster Williams
   Location: Portland
   History: The British burned the *Warren, Diligent, Hazard* and *Tyrannicide* at Portland, Maine on August 14, 1779, to prevent their capture. Some of the cannon were recovered several years later.

H.M.S. *Astrea*, English warship, Captain Robert Swanton
   Location: Piscataqua River
   History: The ship accidentally burnt at the mouth of the Piscataqua River in 1743. Several of the crew perished.

Phoenix, English merchantman, Captain Barter
   Location: Casco Bay
   History: The merchantman wrecked in Casco Bay while sailing from England to Boston in 1758.

Tyrannicide, 14-gun American warship, Captain Cathcart
   Location: Portland
   History: The British burned the *Warren, Diligent, Hazard* and *Tyrannicide* at Portland, Maine on August 14, 1779, to prevent their capture. Some of the cannon were recovered several years later.

Warren, 32-gun American warship, Captain Dudley Saltonstall
   Location: Portland
   History: The British burned the *Warren*, *Diligent*, *Hazard* and *Tyrannicide* at Portland, Maine on August 14, 1779, to prevent their capture. Some of the cannon were recovered several years later.

MARYLAND

Boyne, English merchantman, Captain Howard
   Location: Chesapeake Bay
   History: The merchantman wrecked in the Chesapeake Bay near Baltimore in 1770 while arriving from St. Kitts.

Earl of Chatham, Scottish merchantman, Captain Wolsey
   Location: Cambridge
   History: This vessel was lost near Cambridge in 1769 while sailing from Dublin to Maryland. Some of her cargo was salvaged.

Hannah, Canadian brig
   Location: Potomac River
   History: The brig wrecked at the mouth of the Potomac River at the end of May 1817 while arriving from St. John's.

Hawke, English merchantman, Captain Price
   Location: Chesapeake Bay
   History: Sank in the upper reaches of Chesapeake Bay in 1766 while sailing for Cadiz. All of her crew was saved.

H.M.S. *Charon*, 44-gun British ship, Captain Thomas Symonds
   Location: Chesapeake Bay
   History: Early in 1781, a storm severely damaged the British fleet and H.M.S. *Culloden* was lost in New York except for her masts, which were salvaged. Later in the year the British scuttled three of their warships in the northern part of Chesapeake Bay: H.M.S. *Guadeloupe*, H.M.S. *Charon*, and H.M.S. *Vulcan*.

H.M.S. *Guadeloupe*, 28-gun British ship, Captain Hugh Robinson
   Location: Chesapeake Bay
   History: Early in 1781, a storm severely damaged the British fleet and

H.M.S. *Culloden* was lost in New York except for her masts, which were salvaged. Later in the year the British scuttled three of their warships in the northern part of Chesapeake Bay: H.M.S. *Guadeloupe*, H.M.S. *Charon*, and H.M.S. *Vulcan*.

H.M.S. *Vulcan*, eight-gun British ship, Captain George Palmer
   Location: Chesapeake Bay
   History: Early in 1781, a storm severely damaged the British fleet and H.M.S. *Culloden* was lost in New York except for her masts, which were salvaged. Later in the year the British scuttled three of their warships in the northern part of Chesapeake Bay: H.M.S. *Guadeloupe*, H.M.S. *Charon*, and H.M.S. *Vulcan*.

Mary, ship of unknown registry, Captain Hunt
   Location: Baltimore
   History: The ship was lost at Baltimore during a gale on September 12, 1808.

Ruthy, English merchantman
   Location: Baltimore River
   History: The vessel wrecked at the mouth of the Baltimore River in 1806 after arriving from Liverpool. Her crew and some of her cargo were saved.

Swan, English merchantman, Captain Clarkson
   Location: Baltimore
   History: The merchantman was burnt shortly after leaving Baltimore in 1753. She was sailing from Baltimore to London with three hundred hogsheads of tobacco onboard.

Totness, English ship, Captain Waring
   Location: St. Mary's City
   History: The ship was set afire by Indians and totally destroyed in 1775 near St. Mary's City, but no lives were lost.

MASSACHUSETTS

Abeona, French merchantman, Captain Blunt
   Location: Cape Cod
   History: The merchantman was lost on Cape Cod in 1811 while sailing from Boston to Portsmouth. Her crew was saved.

Alert, French merchantman
   Location: Boston
   History: The vessel was lost near Boston on December 24, 1804, while arriving from France.

Alfred, American merchantman
   Location: Cape Ann
   History: She was lost on January 3, 1812, near Cape Ann while sailing from Russia to Boston. Her crew was saved.

Alknomack, Irish merchantman
   Location: Martha's Vineyard
   History: She was lost on Martha's Vineyard in 1811 while carrying immigrants from Ireland to New York. Her crew and all the passengers were saved.

Anne, English merchantman, Captain Goodridge
   Location: Martha's Vineyard
   History: The vessel was lost on Martha's Vineyard in 1731 while coming from Barbados.

Astrea, American merchantman
   Location: Cape Cod
   History: She was lost in the year 1802 on Cape Cod while sailing from Boston to the West Indies.

Betsey, Scottish merchantman, Captain MacFarlan
   Location: Race Point, Cape Cod
   History: She wrecked near Race Point on Cape Cod while sailing from Boston to London in 1767.

Britannia, English troop transport, Captain Walker
   Location: Boston Harbor
   History: The transport was accidentally burnt in Boston Harbor in 1773 after arriving from London. There was no loss of life.

Brutus, ship of unknown registry, Captain Brown
   Location: Cape Cod
   History: The vessel was lost on Cape Cod in 1802 while sailing from Salem to Europe.

Charming Betsey, American merchantman, Captain Foffey
   Location: Martha's Vineyard
   History: She wrecked on Martha's Vineyard in 1798 while arriving from Martinique.

Cibila, Spanish warship
　Location: Boston Harbor
　History: A Spanish chart of New England published in 1799 mentions that two Spanish warships—the *Magnífico* and *Cibila*—were sunk in Boston Harbor at a previous date.

Claremont, English merchantman, Captain Newton
　Location: Cape Cod
　History: She wrecked on Cape Cod in 1760 while sailing to Jamaica. Several of her crew perished.

Clarissa, English merchantman, Captain Scott
　Location: Nantucket Isle
　History: The vessel was lost in 1795 on Nantucket Isle while arriving from London. The crew and cargo were saved.

Clinton, American merchantman, Captain Hughes
　Location: No-man's Land
　History: She wrecked on August 12, 1757, on No-man's Land, a small island near Martha's Vineyard, while coming from Jamaica and South Carolina. Some of her cargo was saved.

Columbia, American ship, Captain Chauncey
　Location: Plymouth
　History: She was lost off Plymouth while arriving from Liverpool in 1792. Only two of her crew survived.

Commerce, English merchantman
　Location: Nantucket Shoals
　History: The ship was lost on Nantucket Shoals in 1798 while sailing from Havana to Bristol.

Delight, English merchantman, Captain Wilson
　Location: Cape Cod
　History: The vessel was lost on Cape Cod in 1798 while sailing from Virginia to London.

Delight, English merchantman, Captain Williams
　Location: Martha's Vineyard
　History: The merchantman wrecked on a shoal off Martha's Vineyard in 1800 while arriving from Gibraltar.

Dispatch, American packet boat, Captain Lovett

Location: Boston
　History: She wrecked near Boston in 1817 while arriving from the Virgin Islands.

Fanciculetta, ship of unknown registry
　Location: Nantucket Shoals
　History: She was lost on Nantucket Shoals in 1784 while arriving from Tobago Island.

Fanny, American merchantman, Captain Stevens
　Location: Martha's Vineyard
　History: The merchantman was totally lost on Martha's Vineyard in 1794 while arriving from Virginia.

Favorite, American merchantman, Captain Webster
　Location: Edgarton
　History: The vessel wrecked on May 7, 1822, near Edgarton while sailing from Honduras to Boston. Her crew was saved.

Federal George, American merchantman, Captain David
　Location: Scituate Lighthouse off Boston Harbor
　History: She was totally lost on January 20, 1824, near the Scititute Lighthouse while sailing from Philadelphia to Boston. Her crew and part of her cargo were saved.

Florenza, merchantman of unknown registry, Captain King
　Location: Cape Cod
　History: The ship was lost on Cape Cod in 1811 while arriving from London. Her crew and some of her cargo were saved.

Four Brothers, American merchantman
　Location: Cape Cod
　History: She was lost on Cape Cod in 1811 while arriving from Russia. All of her cargo was saved.

Fox, American merchantman, Captain Williams
　Location: Martha's Vineyard
　History: The vessel wrecked on January 18, 1817, on Martha's Vineyard while arriving from Guadeloupe Island.

Gertrude Maria, Danish merchantman, Captain Klein

Location: Boston
　History: She was lost near Boston in 1793 while arriving from Copenhagen. Some of her cargo was saved.

Hawke, American merchantman, Captain Norton
　Location: Shagg Rock
　History: The vessel wrecked on Shagg Rock near Boston in 1768 while carrying a cargo of salt from the Bahamas. All of her crew were saved.

H.M.S. *Astrea*, 20-gun English warship, Captain John Barker
　Location: Boston Harbor
　History: The warship accidentally burnt in Boston Harbor in 1744. No lives were lost.

H.M.S. *Blonde*, 32-gun English warship, Captain Edward Thornborough
　Location: Nantucket Shoals
　History: She wrecked on a rock on Nantucket Shoals in 1782. Several of her crew perished.

H.M.S. *Hazard*, English sloop-of-war
　Location: Green Bay
　History: The ship wrecked in Green Bay, about 30 miles from Boston, in 1714 while bringing munitions from England. All of her crew perished.

H.M.S. *Solebay*, 32-gun English warship
　Location: Boston Neck
　History: The warship was totally lost on December 25, 1709, at Boston Neck. All of her crew perished.

H.M.S. *Somerset*, 70-gun English frigate-of-war, Captain George Curry
　Location: Provincetown, Cape Cod
　History: The frigate wrecked near Provincetown in 1778 while carrying a large cargo of war materials.

Hopewell, English merchantman, Captain Harrison
　Location: Boston
　History: The merchantman wrecked near Boston in 1791 while arriving from London.

Industry, American ship, Captain Barnes
　Location: Cape Ann
　History: The ship was utterly lost near Cape Ann in 1795 with a total

loss of lives. She was sailing from Portsmouth to Boston when she went down.

John & Mary, English merchantman, Captain Quirk
Location: Boston
History: The ship was lost near Boston in 1731 while coming from Barbados.

Julianna, English ship, Captain Ingraham
Location: Nantucket Isle
History: Lost at Nantucket Isle in 1796 while arriving from South Carolina.

Julius Caesar, Spanish merchantman
Location: Cape Cod
History: The ship was lost on Cape Cod in 1784 while coming from Cadiz.

Magnifico, Spanish warship
Location: Boston Harbor
History: A Spanish chart of New England published in 1799 mentions that two Spanish warships—the *Magnífico* and *Cibila*—were sunk in Boston Harbor at a previous date.

Margaret, ship of unknown registry, Captain Mackay
Location: Cape Ann
History: The ship was lost in 1795 near Cape Ann while arriving from Amsterdam.

Marretta, American ship, Captain Barnes
Location: Cape Cod
History: The ship was lost on Cape Cod in 1792.

Mary, English merchantman, Captain Nain
Location: Boston
History: The vessel was lost near Boston in 1762 while sailing from Halifax to Gibraltar with a cargo of hides and furs.

Mary & Ann, English merchantman, Captain Evers
Location: Plumb Island
History: The merchantman wrecked on Plumb Island in 1789 while arriving from London. Four of her crew perished.

Mary Ann, American merchantman, Captain Robinson

Location: Cape Cod
History: The ship was lost on Cape Cod in 1818 while arriving from Baltimore. Part of her cargo was saved.

Matchless, English merchantman
Location: Boston Harbor
History: The merchantman sank at anchor in Boston Harbor during a gale on September 23, 1815, after arriving from London.

Minerva, English merchantman, Captain Phelim
Location: Cape Cod
History: She was lost on Cape Cod on January 11, 1802, after arriving from Madeira Island.

Neutrality, English merchantman, Captain Forster
Location: Cape Cod
History: The merchantman was lost on Cape Cod in 1811 while arriving from Liverpool.

Nordkoping, Swedish merchantman, Captain Nordstrom
Location: Nantucket Shoals
History: The vessel was lost on Nantucket Shoals in July of 1814 while sailing from Cuba to Boston.

Paragon, American merchantman, Captain Hardon
Location: Cape Ann
History: The ship was totally lost on February 16, 1821, near Cape Ann after arriving from Havana.

Peace & Plenty, American merchant, Captain Calahan
Location: Cape Cod
History: The merchantman was lost on Cape Cod in 1784.

Pembroke, English merchantman, Captain Taylor
Location: Lynn Beach near Boston
History: She wrecked on Lynn Beach near Boston in 1766 while arriving from England with a valuable cargo. Some of her cargo was saved.

Princess, American ship
Location: Cape Cod
History: The ship was totally lost on Cape Cod on April 27, 1813, while sailing from London to New York. Salvors failed to recover several chests of silver specie from the wreck.

Protecto, Spanish merchantman
Location: Cape Cod
History: The merchantman was lost on Cape Cod in 1804 while sailing from Boston to Lima, Peru.

Robert Todd, English merchantman, Captain Campbell
Location: Nantucket Shoals
History: The vessel was totally lost on the Nantucket Shoals on October 21, 1817, while arriving from Liverpool and the Bahamas.

Rodney, English merchantman, Captain Wytock
Location: Cape Cod
History: The ship was lost in 1792 on Cape Cod while sailing from Boston to the Caribbean.

Ross, American packet boat
Location: Boston Bay
History: The boat sank after entering Boston Bay in 1785 while sailing from Newfoundland to New York.

Semiramis, American merchantman, Captain Smith
Location: Nantucket Shoals
History: She was lost on Nantucket shoals in 1804. Only a small part of her cargo was saved.

Sparrow Hawk, English vessel
Location: Cape Cod
History: The small vessel, carrying settlers and supplies to the newly founded Virginia colony, wrecked in 1624 on the beach near the site of the present day town of Orleans on Cape Cod. She was recently excavated and many recovered items were placed in a museum.

Three Sisters, English merchantman, Captain Delano
Location: Cape Cod
History: The vessel wrecked on Cape Cod in 1797 while arriving from Liverpool. All of her crew was saved.

Ulysses, ship of unknown registry, Captain Cock
Location: Cape Cod
History: She was lost on Cape Cod in 1802 while sailing from Salem to Europe.

Unidentified, ships (3)
Location: Boston Harbor

History: Three unidentified ships sank in Boston Harbor during a gale on October 9, 1783.

Unidentified, ships (3)
Location: Buzzards Bay
History: Two unidentified merchantmen, arriving from the Leeward Islands, and a schooner from Virginia, were totally lost in Buzzards Bay during a gale in December 1774.

Unidentified, ships (7)
Location: Martha's Vineyard
History: Seven ships were wrecked on Martha's Vineyard during a hurricane on October 8, 1749. Many lives were lost.

Unidentified, French merchantman
Location: Nantucket Shoals
History: The ship was totally lost on Nantucket Shoals in 1678 while coming from Canada with a cargo of hides.

Unidentified, French brig
Location: Nantucket Shoals
History: The brig was lost on Nantucket Shoals on July 31, 1786, while sailing from the Caribbean to France. All of her crew were saved.

Warren, American merchantman, Captain Knowles
Location: Cape Cod
History: Lost during the month of November in 1818 while arriving from Brazil.

Whydah, pirate ship, Captain "Black Sam" Bellamy
Location: Cape Cod
History: The pirate captain Samuel Bellamy, who preyed on Caribbean shipping during the first two decades of the 18th century, was based near New Providence Island in the Bahamas. In 1717 "Black Sam" captured the slave ship *Whydah* after it unloaded slaves at Port Royal, Jamaica. He made the *Whydah* his flagship and captured five or six other ships within the next two months. After netting enough plunder, Bellamy headed to England where his wife and children lived. On April 26, 1717, the *Whydah* ran into a storm near Wellfleet, Cape Cod. The crew, drunk on plundered rum, ran the ship aground on a bar a shot distance off Wellfleet. The governor of the Mass-achusetts colony sent a Boston mapmaker, Captain Southack, to see what could be salvaged. Southack drew a chart of the wreck's position and wrote to the governor, "there have been two hundred men from twenty miles distance plundering the wreck," implying that whatever treasure was aboard the ship had been carried off by scavengers. Barry Clifford, who grew up nearby in Hyannis, first heard the story of the pirate ship when he was eight years old. Four years later he started diving and searching for the wreck. In 1984, he mounted a full-scale expedition and found the *Whydah* within an hour. She was exactly where Southack had reported—in 25 feet of water. However, she was covered over by an additional 18 feet of sand. He soon learned that the wreck was scattered over an area of several square miles. Clifford excavated the shipwreck over six summers. The total value of treasure and artifacts recovered was $5 million. The recoveries included the ship's bell, silver and gold coins, small gold ingots, dozens of pieces of gold jewelry and hundreds of artifacts, whose origins reflected the pirates varied prey. Divers also discovered another startling find that took them back to the reality of piracy, a pair of pistols tied at the ends of a silk sash. The most interesting find was the 200 unusual gold beads from Africa, which were made by the lost-wax process. They were probably taken from a slaver who had acquired them on the Ivory Coast from the Akan people in what is now Ghana. Soon after Clifford found the wreck the state of Massachusetts demanded the rights to it and its cargo. Clifford challenged the State and after a three-year court battle, won exclusive rights to the shipwreck. He is building a museum in Tampa, Florida to display its treasures and artifacts.

NEW HAMPSHIRE

Commerce, American merchantman, Captain Roberts
Location: Portsmouth Beach
History: The merchantman was totally lost on May 14, 1817, on Portsmouth Beach while sailing from Ja-maica to New York. The crew and some of her cargo of rum were saved.

Friends Adventure, English merchantman, Captain Hamilton
Location: Portsmouth Harbor
History: The merchantman was lost while leaving Portsmouth Harbor in 1760 when sailing for Jamaica.

Scripio, American merchantman, Captain Moore
Location: Fernands Point
History: She wrecked on a rock at Fernands Point in Piscataqua Harbor in 1774 while sailing for the West Indies.

Unidentified, American merchantmen (3)
Location: Appledore Island, on the Isle of Shoals
History: Three merchantmen returning from Jamaica with rum and sugar products were totally lost on Appledore Island, on the Isle of Shoals, in 1780. Many persons from the crews were lost.

NEW JERSEY

Amelia, English merchantman
Location: Sandy Hook
History: This merchantman wrecked on February 16, 1811, at Sandy Hook while sailing from England to New York.

Andrea Doria, Italian luxury ocean liner, 656 feet
Location: 40.29.24 N, 69.52.03 W, 150 miles east of Sandy Hook
History: The greatest rescue to ever take place at sea occurred on July 26, 1956, as the Italian ocean liner the *Andrea Doria* foundered 60 miles off the coast of Massachusetts. A total of 1,654 passengers and crew were rescued from the *Andrea Doria* following a collision with the Swedish-American ocean liner, the *Stockholm*. Fifty-two people lost their lives from the collision, five onboard the *Stockholm* and the remainder on the *Andrea Doria*. Both ocean liners were traveling towards Nantucket lightship when they collided. Although other factors, including right of way rules and last-minute course changes by both vessels were

considered, dense fog was cited as the official cause of the accident in the proceedings that followed the collision. The ill-fated *Andrea Doria* took nearly eleven hours to sink, leaving time for her passengers and crew to transfer to other vessels in the area. The *Stockholm*, with only her bow section damaged, remained afloat and took many of the *Andrea Doria's* passengers aboard. A New York-based documentary filmmaker named Peter Gimbel was the first to dive on the *Andrea Doria* after she foundered. Within 24 hours of the foundering, Gimbel had photographed the ship. It was rumored that the ocean liner's two safes held a fortune in cash and precious stones. It was also thought that the liner could have remained afloat if a crucial watertight door had been closed at the time of the collision. In 1981, Gimbel and his wife, Swedish actress Elga Anderson, began an expedition to make a documentary film about the *Andrea Doria*. They found that the seams had opened on both sides of the *Andrea Doria's* watertight door, so that closing the door would not have kept the liner afloat. The Gimbels also retrieved one of the ship's two safes before Hurricane Dennis cut their expedition short. The safe was opened on national television during a live broadcast. Stacks of redeemable United States silver certificates were found. Thousands of depreciated Italian lira bills were also retrieved from the safe. The *Andrea Doria*, once known as the Great Dame of the Sea, was also carrying a large amount of priceless artwork onboard when she sank. The walls of the luxurious ship were lined with artwork produced by some of Italy's finest artists at the time. Successful salvage attempts by salvor John Moyer have brought up two 750-pound mosaic friezes along with smaller ceramic pieces of an ornate mosaic. Part of the bronze statue of Admiral Andrea Doria and the ship's helm have also been recovered. Additional artwork carried onboard included wooden murals, ceramic panels, mirrors, mosaics and crystals. The *Andrea Doria* remains in fairly good condition today and is a popular site for recreational divers as well as continued salvage attempts.

Due to the low water temperature, variable ocean currents and depth of the wreck, only experienced divers should attempt to dive on the *Andrea Doria*.

Andrew, English merchantman, Captain Hathaway
  Location: Barnegat
  History: The ship wrecked at Barnegat in 1819 while sailing from Liverpool to Philadelphia. Her crew was saved.

Belle Air, ship of unknown registry, Captain Allen
  Location: Egg Harbor
  History: She wrecked near Egg Harbor in 1811 while sailing from Norway and Cork to Philadelphia. Her crew was saved.

Betsey, English merchantman, Captain Douglas
  Location: Barnegat
  History: The merchantman wrecked at Barnegat in 1791 while sailing from London to New York.

Betsey, merchantman, Captain Brown
  Location: Cape May
  History: Four ships were lost at Cape May during a gale on September 19, 1783: the *New York, Two Friends, Betsey* and *Mercury*. The *Betsey* was sailing to Philadelphia, Pennsylvania when it was lost.

Betsey, American merchantman, Captain Parke
  Location: Great Egg Harbor
  History: She wrecked at Great Egg Harbor in 1779 while sailing from Providence, Rhode Island to New York.

Boston & Liverpool, ship of unknown registry, Captain Laud
  Location: Barnegat
  History: The ship wrecked near Barnegat in 1791 while sailing from Liverpool to Philadelphia.

Caledonia, English merchantman, Captain Struthers
  Location: Ten miles south of Sandy Hook
  History: This vessel wrecked on December 28, 1820, about ten miles south of Sandy Hook while sailing from Liverpool to New York. Three persons drowned.

Castle del Rey, 18-gun privateer vessel, 130 tons, Captain Otto Van Tyle
  Location: Shoal near Sandy Hook
  History: The vessel was struck by a gale in 1704 while sailing from Manhattan and wrecked on a shoal near Sandy Hook. The ship quickly went to pieces. Of her crew of 145, only 13 survived.

Cato, American ship, Captain Darrell
  Location: Sandy Hook
  History: The ship was lost on November 11, 1808, at Sandy Hook while arriving from the Bahamas.

Charming Nancy, American merchantman, Captain Penkham
  Location: Cape May Roads
  History: The merchantman wrecked during a gale in 1784 at Cape May Roads. She was en route from Philadelphia to the West Indies when she foundered. Some of her cargo was saved.

Citizen, ship of unknown registry, Captain Loring
  Location: Brigantine Shoals, near Egg Harbor
  History: The vessel wrecked on April 9, 1822, on Brigantine Shoals, near Egg Harbor, but then drifted off and sank in five fathoms of water. She was sailing from Manila to New York when she wrecked. Her crew was saved.

Claredon, American ship, Captain Gainess
  Location: Sandy Hook
  History: She wrecked at Sandy Hook on April 7, 1815, while sailing from Bermuda to New York. Her crew and passengers were saved.

Columbia, American merchantman, Captain Lewis
  Location: Little Egg Harbor
  History: This vessel was totally lost on January 4, 1806, near Little Egg Harbor while sailing from Lisbon to New York.

Edward, American ship, Captain Goodrich
  Location: Barnegat Shoals
  History: She was lost on Barnegat Shoals in 1793 while arriving from Turk's Island, Bahamas.

Enterprize, English merchantman
  Location: Little Egg Harbor
  History: This merchantman was lost in May 1822 near Little Egg harbor while sailing from Maine to Philadelphia. Her crew was saved.

Fanny, merchantman of unknown registry, Captain Johnson
  Location: Cape May
  History: She wrecked at Cape May in 1792 while sailing from the Virgin Islands to Philadelphia.

Hannah, ship of unknown registry, Captain Askwith
  Location: Tom's River
  History: The ship wrecked on April 19, 1817, off Tom's River while sailing to New York. Her crew and cargo were saved.

Harnett, American merchantman, Captain Gardner
  Location: Sandy Hook
  History: She was lost on February 20, 1809, near Sandy Hook while arriving from Jamaica.

Hind, Scottish ship
  Location: Sandy Hook
  History: The ship wrecked on January 28, 1822, at Sandy Hook while sailing from Dundee to New York.

H.M.S. Zebra, 16-gun English warship, Captain Henry Collins
  Location: Egg Island Harbor
  History: The warship wrecked during October 1778 at Egg Island Harbor.

Hunter, merchantman of unknown registry
  Location: Cape May
  History: This vessel wrecked at Cape May in 1824 while sailing from France to Philadelphia. Her crew and cargo were saved.

Ida, English merchantman
  Location: Cape May
  History: She was lost on February 16, 1808, near Cape May while sailing from Lisbon to Philadelphia.

Jupiter, merchantman, Captain Rumage
  Location: Cape May
  History: The ship was totally lost off Cape May in 1783 while sailing from

Jamaica to New York. Two men perished.

Manchester, merchantman, Captain Clay
  Location: Egg Island Shoals
  History: The merchantman wrecked on the shoals in 1793 while sailing from Liverpool to Philadelphia.

Mary, American merchantman, Captain Peppard
  Location: Sandy Hook
  History: She sank in 1779 during a gale while arriving from St. Kitts. An unidentified ship carrying a cargo of rum was also lost near the *Mary* at the same time.

Mercury, merchantman, Captain Herpin
  Location: Cape May
  History: Four ships were lost at Cape May during a gale on September 19, 1783: the *New York, Two Friends, Betsey* and *Mercury*. The *Mercury* was sailing from Dunkirk to Philadelphia when she foundered.

New York, merchantman, Captain Fortey
  Location: Cape May
  History: Four ships were lost at Cape May during a gale on September 19, 1783: the *New York, Two Friends, Betsey* and *Mercury*. The *New York* was sailing from Glasgow to New York when she foundered. Her crew was saved.

Norbury, Irish merchantman, Captain Wood
  Location: Sandy Hook
  History: The merchantman wrecked at Sandy Hook in 1777 while sailing form Cork to New York. Her crew and most of her cargo were saved.

Nymph, American merchantman, Captain Palmer
  Location: Barnegat
  History: The merchantman wrecked during November 1789 near Barnegat while sailing from Oporto to New York.

Rebecca, merchantman of unknown registry, Captain Stairs
  Location: Sandy Point
  History: This vessel wrecked on December 2, 1824, at Sandy Point while

sailing from the West Indies to Halifax.

Recovery, English brig
  Location: Sandy Hook
  History: The brig wrecked at Sandy Hook in 1805 while sailing from England to New York.

Robert Walne, English merchantman
  Location: Sandy Hook
  History: She wrecked on Sandy Hook on August 22, 1816, while sailing from London to New York. A small part of her cargo was saved.

Rose in Bloom, American merchantman
  Location: Central New Jersey coast
  History: The merchantman sank off the central New Jersey coast during a hurricane on August 24, 1806.

Sally, ship of unknown registry, Captain Moffet
  Location: Barnegat
  History: The ship was totally lost on September 22, 1810, near Barnegat while sailing from England to New York.

Sally, English merchantman, Captain Rankin
  Location: Little Egg Harbor
  History: The vessel wrecked off Little Egg Harbor in 1768 while sailing from England to Philadelphia.

St. Francesco de Paula Costellina, Italian ship, Captain Genovese
  Location: Little Egg Harbor Bar
  History: This ship was lost on the bar in 1794 while sailing from France to New York.

Success, American merchantman, Captain Forbes
  Location: Sandy Hook
  History: She wrecked on January 16, 1811, near Sandy Hook while sailing from the Virgin Islands to New York.

Swallow, American ship, Captain Wright
  Location: Sandy Hook
  History: The vessel wrecked near Sandy Hook in 1793 while sailing from Antigua to New York.

Syren, English ship
  Location: Great Egg Harbor
  History: The vessel wrecked around

February 1821 at Great Egg Harbor while sailing from the Caribbean to Boston.

Thetis, Italian ship, Captain Granbury,
Location: Cape May
History: She wrecked on Cape May on February 16, 1808.

Trumbell, American merchantman, Captain Hitchcock
Location: Sandy Hook
History: The merchantman wrecked at Sandy Hook in 1825 while sailing from Trinidad to New York.

Two Friends, merchantman, Captain Bevan
Location: Cape May
History: Four ships were lost at Cape May during a gale on September 19, 1783: the *New York, Two Friends, Betsey* and *Mercury.* The *Two Friends* was sailing to Philadelphia when she foundered.

Unidentified, ship
Location: Absecon Beach (present-day Atlantic City)
History: A gale on October 9, 1804, caused an unidentified ship to wreck on Absecon Beach.

Unidentified, ships (4)
Location: Cape May
History: Two ships sank at Cape May and two others near Great Egg Harbor during a gale on October 8, 1783.

Unidentified, ships (large number)
Location: Cape May
History: A large number of unidentified ships sank in the vicinity of Cape May during a hurricane on September 3, 1821.

Unidentified, ship
Location: Sandy Hook
History: The ship was lost in 1779 near Sandy Hook while arriving from Antigua with a cargo of rum. The *Mary* was also lost at the same time near this ship.

Union, American ship, Captain Cotter
Location: Sandy Hook
History: This ship wrecked at Sandy Hook in 1823 while sailing from Lon-

donderry and Bermuda to New York. Her crew was saved.

Virginia, American ship, Captain Darby
Location: Sandy Hook
History: The ship was lost south off Sandy Hook in 1803 while sailing from London to New York. Several of her crew and passengers perished.

Walters, ship of unknown registry, Captain Homer
Location: Sandy Hook
History: She wrecked on January 16, 1807, near Sandy Hook while sailing from Amsterdam to New York. All of her crew were saved.

Wilhelmina, merchantman of unknown registry, Captain Steele
Location: North of Cape May
History: The vessel was sailing from New London to Dublin when it wrecked north of Cape May in 1792. Her crew was saved.

William, American merchantman, Captain Ashton
Location: Sandy Hook
History: The merchantman sank in 1804 near Sandy Hook while arriving from the Canary Islands.

NEW YORK

Adventure, Scottish merchantman, Captain Auld
Location: New York Bay
History: The vessel was lost in the lower New York Bay in 1760 while sailing from New York for Dublin.

Albert, American merchantman, Captain Salter
Location: Long Island
History: She wrecked on Long Island in 1821 while sailing from Portsmouth, New Hampshire to Philadelphia.

Albion, English merchantman, Captain Cox
Location: Coney Island
History: The merchantman wrecked on Coney Island in February of 1818. Her crew and cargo were saved.

Alstromer, Swedish ship
Location: Governor's Island

History: The ship wrecked on Governor's Island during a gale on September 29, 1785.

Ann, ship of unknown registry
Location: Long Island
History: She wrecked on Long Island, near Brookhaven, in the year 1801 while sailing from New York City to Liverpool.

Augusta, American merchantman, Captain Peterson
Location: Long Island
History: The vessel wrecked during a gale on October 27, 1822, at Shrewsbury Beach.

Betsey, English troop transport, Captain Obrien
Location: New York Bay
History: She wrecked on some rocks in the lower New York Bay in 1780. Many lives were lost.

Betsey & Amy, English merchantman, Captain Watts
Location: Long Island
History: The ship wrecked on Long Island while arriving from Liverpool in 1788.

Catherine Ray, ship of unknown registry, Captain Benthall
Location: Long Island
History: She wrecked on February 21, 1802, on Long Island while arriving from Lisbon. Part of her cargo was saved.

Cato, American merchantman, Captain Updell
Location: Long Island
History: The vessel wrecked on January 16, 1805, on Long Island while arriving from New York.

Cincinnati, American merchantman
Location: Governor's Island
History: The merchantman was bound for Lisbon when it wrecked on Governor's Island during a gale on November 10, 1810.

City of Werry, American ship, Captain Patterson
Location: New York Bay
History: The ship was sunk in the Narrows of New York Bay in 1761 while arriving from Boston. Her crew was saved.

Colpoys, American merchantman
   Location: Long Island
   History: The vessel was totally lost on Long Island in 1779 while arriving from St. Kitts. Only one man drowned.

Congress, 28-gun American warship
   Location: Hudson River
   History: The ship was burnt on the Hudson River in 1777 to prevent her capture by the British.

Diamond, Irish merchantman, Captain Lanning
   Location: East River
   History: The ship struck some rocks at the entrance to the East River and sank near a wharf close to Manhattan in 1777 while arriving from Cork.

Edward, Scottish merchantman, Captain Babcock
   Location: Long Island
   History: She was totally lost on Long Island in 1806 while arriving from Dublin. All of her crew were saved.

Edward Douglas, English merchantman, Captain Carlew
   Location: Long Island
   History: The ship wrecked on Long Island on September 14, 1824, while sailing to Haiti. No lives were lost.

Eliza, ship of unknown registry, Captain Hughes
   Location: Long Island
   History: She wrecked on Long Island in 1792 while arriving from Jamaica.

Elizabeth, Scottish merchantman, Captain Consy
   Location: Long Island
   History: The vessel was totally lost on the south side of Long Island in 1769 while arriving from Dublin.

Elizabeth, English supply ship, Captain Griffith
   Location: Long Island
   History: She wrecked on Staten Island in 1783.

Elizabeth, American merchantman, Captain Williams
   Location: Long Island
   History: This ship wrecked on Long Island while arriving from Amsterdam on May 22, 1822. All of her crew and part of her cargo were saved.

Enrique, Spanish merchantman, Captain Cuzana
   Location: Long Island
   History: The vessel wrecked on Long Island in 1797 while arriving from Cadiz. Some of her cargo was saved.

Experiment, American merchantman
   Location: Manhattan
   History: She sank shortly before reaching Manhattan in the year 1800 while arriving from Havana.

Flora, American merchantman, Captain Adams
   Location: East River
   History: The ship burnt on the East River in 1808 while arriving from New Orleans with a cargo of cotton.

Friendship, English merchantman
   Location: Staten Island
   History: She wrecked on Staten Island during a gale on September 23, 1815, while sailing from Halifax to Jamaica. Most of her cargo was saved.

Generous Friends, American troop transport
   Location: Coney Island
   History: The vessel sank near Coney Island in 1776, but no lives were lost.

George, ship of unknown registry, Captain Gregorio
   Location: Long Island
   History: She wrecked on Long Island in 1792 while arriving from Madeira Island.

Herbert, German ship
   Location: Long Island
   History: The vessel wrecked on July 7, 1710, on the east end of Long Island while bringing immigrants from one of the Palatinates. No lives were lost but only a small part of her cargo was saved.

H.M.S. *Culloden*, 74-gun British ship
   Location: Long Island
   History: Early in 1781, a storm severely damaged the British fleet and the H.M.S. *Culloden* was lost except for her masts, which were later salvaged. The intact remains of the *Culloden*, wooden British man-of-war, lie on the bottomlands of Fort Pond Bay, Long Island. It is owned by the British Government and listed in the National Register of Historic Places.

H.M.S. *Hussar*, 28-gun English warship, Captain Charles Maurice Pole
   Location: Hell's Gate, East River
   History: The ship sank at Hell's Gate in 1779, quite close to the *James & William*, which sank the same year. Although there have been several articles over the years stating that the *Hussar* was carrying a large amount of treasure, there has not been any documentary evidence discovered in the archives to support this claim as yet.

H.M.S. *Liverpool*, 28-gun English warship, Captain Henry Bellow
   Location: Long Island
   History: The warship wrecked in 1777 on the south side of Long Island.

H.M.S. *Mercury*, 24-gun English warship, Captain James Montagu
   Location: New York City
   History: She wrecked near New York City in 1778.

H.M.S. *Swallow*, 16-gun English warship, Captain Thomas Wells
   Location: Long Island
   History: The warship wrecked on Long Island in 1781.

H.M.S. *Sylph*, 18-gun English ship, Captain George Dickens
   Location: Southampton Bar, Long Island
   History: She was lost on the bar in 1815. Out of 121 crew, 115 perished. This is one of Long Island's 20 prominent shipwrecks.

H.M.S. *Thistle*, ten-gun English warship, Captain George McPherson
   Location: Long Island
   History: She was lost on March 6, 1811, on Long Island. Six of her crew of 50 perished.

Hope, Scottish merchantman, Captain Stewart
   Location: Staten Island
   History: She wrecked on Staten Island in 1773 while sailing from New York City to Dublin. Her crew was saved.

Hornet, American schooner
   Location: Long Island
   History: The schooner foundered off Long Island during a hurricane on June 3 or 4, 1825.

Huzzar, American merchantman, Captain Wilson

   Location: Long Island

   History: She wrecked on Long Island in 1783 while arriving from Jamaica. Part of her cargo was saved.

James & William, English troop transport

   Location: Hell's Gate, East River

   History: This transport was totally lost at Hell's Gate in 1779 while arriving from Rhode Island. Her crew was saved. The wreck lies quite close to the H.M.S. *Hussar* shipwreck.

Jenny, American merchantman, Captain Dickson

   Location: New York Bay

   History: The vessel wrecked in the Lower New York Bay in 1798 while sailing to Jamaica.

Jenny, American merchantman

   Location: Staten Island

   History: She wrecked on Staten Island during a gale in 1778 while sailing for London.

Ligera, Spanish schooner, Captain Rock

   Location: Montauk Point, Long Island

   History: The schooner wrecked at Montauk Point while arriving from Havana in 1823. Only a small part of the specie she carried was recovered.

Little George, American merchantman

   Location: Long Island

   History: The vessel wrecked on January 29, 1808, near Long Island while arriving from Newfoundland.

Lucy & Elizabeth, American ship, Captain Bray

   Location: New York Bay

   History: She was lost in the lower New York Bay in 1812 while arriving from Lisbon. All of her crew were saved.

Marey, American coastal schooner, Captain Samuel Vetch

   Location: Long Island

   History: The schooner wrecked at Montauk Point in 1763 while carrying a cargo of contraband goods from French Canada.

Mary, Dutch ship, Captain Seimen

   Location: New York Bay

   History: She was lost in the lower New York Bay in 1802 while arriving from Amsterdam.

Mary Ann, ship of unknown registry, Captain Stewart

   Location: Long Island

   History: The ship wrecked on Long Island in August 1786 while coming from the Far East.

Mercury, English ship, Captain Monkhouse

   Location: Long Island

   History: She was lost on Long Island on March 2, 1780, during a gale while sailing to Portugal.

Mississippi, merchantman of unknown registry, Captain Stedmore

   Location: New York Bay

   History: The ship wrecked in the lower New York Bay while arriving from London in 1807. Her crew and some of her cargo were saved.

Montgomery, 24-gun American warship

   Location: Hudson River

   History: The warship was captured and blown up on the Hudson River by the British in 1777.

Nelly, ship of unknown registry, Captain Nueller

   Location: Long Island

   History: The vessel wrecked on Long Island in 1804 while arriving from Newfoundland.

Nelson, English merchantman, Captain Scoffin

   Location: New York Bay

   History: The merchantman sank in the lower New York Bay in 1815 while arriving from London.

Neptune, American merchantman, Captain Wallace

   Location: Long Island

   History: She wrecked on the south side of Long Island in 1795 while arriving from Dominica Island. Some of her cargo was saved.

Nereus, merchantman of unknown registry, Captain Stowe

   Location: Long Island

   History: The ship wrecked on Long Island in 1807 while arriving from St. Vincent's.

Nestor, English merchantman, Captain Pease

   Location: Long Island

   History: She wrecked on Long Island while arriving from Liverpool on November 28, 1824.

Nuestra Señora del Rosario, Spanish merchantman, Captain Moratus

   Location: New York City

   History: The ship wrecked near New York City in 1785 while arriving from the Canaries. Part of her cargo was saved.

Ocean, German ship

   Location: Long Island

   History: The vessel wrecked on the south side of Long Island in 1800 while sailing from Bremen to Philadelphia. Only the captain perished.

Olive Branch, English merchantman, Captain Newman

   Location: Long Island

   History: The ship was lost on Long Island in 1811 while arriving from Liverpool. The crew and passengers were saved.

Patience, American privateer, Captain Chase

   Location: Long Island

   History: She wrecked on Long Island in 1780.

Pocahontas, American merchantman, Captain Grover

   Location: Long Island

   History: The ship wrecked on Long Island while arriving from Jamaica on April 11, 1824. One person drowned.

Prins Maurits, Dutch ship

   Location: Fire Island

   History: The vessel was lost on Fire Island in 1657 while carrying immigrants to Nieuw Amsterdam (New York City). Indians rescued all of the crew and passengers. The ship is Long Island's first recorded shipwreck and one of the island's 20 prominent wrecks.

Rose, American naval vessel, Captain Anderson

   Location: Staten Island

   History: She wrecked on Staten Island during a gale in December 1778.

Ruth, American merchantman, Captain Hughson
  Location: Long Island
  History: The ship wrecked near Mount Desart on Long Island on April 2, 1822, while sailing from South America to Canada.

Sally, American merchantman, Captain Mathews
  Location: Coney Island
  History: She wrecked on Coney Island in 1789 while arriving from Grenada.

Savannah, American merchantman, Captain Holdridge
  Location: Long Island
  History: The vessel wrecked in 1821 while arriving from Savannah. Most of her cargo was saved.

Savannah, American merchantman, Captain Cole
  Location: Long Island
  History: This ship wrecked on Long Island in October 1822 while arriving from Liverpool. There was a total loss of lives.

St. James, English troop transport
  Location: Staten Island
  History: This ship wrecked on Staten Island in 1783.

Selby, merchantman of unknown registry, Captain Pratt
  Location: Manhattan
  History: She wrecked on March 25, 1807, near Manhattan while arriving from Jamaica.

Thomas, English merchantman
  Location: East River
  History: The merchantman was totally lost on the East River in 1801.

Traveller, American ship, Captain Russell
  Location: Long Island
  History: The ship wrecked on Long Island in 1801 while sailing from the West Indies to Boston.

True American, American merchantman, Captain Newson
  Location: New York Bay
  History: The vessel wrecked on February 20, 1809, near The Narrows in upper New York Bay while arriving from Haiti.

Unidentified, 12-gun Spanish privateer
  Location: Long Island
  History: The ship had 133 men onboard when it was blown up during a battle with a New York privateer off the east end of Long Island in 1719. Ninety-one of the Spaniards perished.

Unidentified, French packet boat
  Location: Long Island
  History: This ship wrecked on January 15, 1784, on Long Island. Several of her crew perished.

Unidentified, ships (50 to 60)
  Location: Long Island
  History: Between 50 and 60 large unidentified ships were wrecked on the south side of Long Island during a violent storm on December 23 and 24, 1811.

Unidentified, ships (8)
  Location: New York City
  History: Eight unidentified ships sank at anchor or at the wharves, in New York City during a gale on January 11, 1796. One was an English packet boat.

Unidentified, ships (many)
  Location: New York City
  History: During a hurricane on September 4, 1821, New York City suffered severe damage. A large ferryboat sank at Whitehall Dock, a sloop sank at Coenties Slip, ten large ships sank at the Quarantine, 12 other large ships sank at Public Store Dock #12, four ships wrecked at Fountain Ferry, five ships wrecked at Kilm, and a large number were wrecked along the south side of Long Island.

Venezuela, Colombian warship
  Location: New York Harbor
  History: This warship wrecked in New York Harbor during a hurricane on June 3 or 4, 1825.

Vidette, English merchantman, Captain Hammond
  Location: Long Island
  History: She wrecked on October 28, 1815, on Long Island while arriving from Guadeloupe. Three persons drowned.

Watt, American ship, Captain Coulthard
  Location: Long Island

History: The ship was totally lost on Long Island in 1780 while sailing to Jamaica. Twenty-six men perished.

NORTH CAROLINA

#140, American gun boat
  Location: Ocracoke Island
  History: This vessel wrecked on September 23, 1814, on Ocracoke Island.

Top: A cast bronze bell recovered from the shipwreck believed to be the *Queen Anne's Revenge. Courtesy of N.C. Archives and History. Bottom:* Brass swivel mount recovered from the wreck presumed to be the *Queen Anne's Revenge. Courtesy of N.C. Archives and History.*

Adriatick, English merchantman, Captain Hanney
  Location: Cape Hatteras
  History: The merchantman wrecked in 1739 with a large loss of life while sailing from London to Virginia.

Anne, English merchantman, Captain Thresher
  Location: Cape Fear bar
  History: This ship was lost on the bar while arriving from Cadiz in 1760.

Atlanta, American brig
  Location: Diamond Shoals
  History: She was lost on November 8, 1815, on Diamond Shoals but the crew was saved.

Aurora, English troop transport, Captain Bishop
  Location: Cape Hatteras
  History: The transport was lost on November 11, 1777, off Cape Hatteras. There were very few survivors.

Aurora, brigantine of unknown registry
  Location: Portsmouth Island
  History: The vessel was lost on September 19, 1776, on Portsmouth Island.

Austin, English merchantman, Captain Sarrat
  Location: Cape Hatteras
  History: The ship was lost off Cape Hatteras in 1775 while sailing from Tobago to Liverpool.

Beggars Bennison, English merchantman, Captain Boyd
  Location: Cape Lookout Shoals
  History: She was lost in 1768 on Cape Lookout Shoals.

Betsey, ship of unknown registry, Captain Flynn
  Location: Cape Fear
  History: The ship was totally lost in 1784 near Cape Fear while sailing to Antigua.

Betsey, American sloop
  Location: Currituck Inlet
  History: The sloop was lost on September 6, 1797, at Currituck Inlet.

Betsey, English merchantman, Captain Leadbeater
  Location: Ocracoke Inlet
  History: The merchantman was lost in 1772 while crossing the Ocracoke Inlet bar.

Betsey, English merchantman, Captain Roberts
  Location: Old Topsail Inlet
  History: This vessel was lost at the inlet in 1771 while arriving from London. No lives were lost.

Bolina, American ship, Captain Lee
  Location: Boddy Island
  History: She wrecked on the island on September 26, 1816, while sailing from New York to Charleston. The crew and part of the cargo were saved.

Britannia, English ship, Captain Dunlop
  Location: Cape Fear River
  History: The ship wrecked south of the Cape Fear River in 1786 while arriving from England. No lives were lost.

Brunshill, English merchantman, Captain Bacon
  Location: Cape Hatteras
  History: The merchantman was lost on Cape Hatteras in 1802 while sailing from England to Virginia. Her crew was saved.

Caroline du Nord, French merchantman, Captain Grace
  Location: Ocracoke Inlet bar
  History: The vessel was lost on the bar on January 19, 1824. No lives were lost.

Charles K. Mallory, American merchantman, Captain Driver
  Location: Cape Hatteras
  History: The ship wrecked on Cape Hatteras on September 10, 1821, while arriving from St. Thomas. There was a total loss of lives.

Charming Betsey, Scottish merchantman, Captain Watts
  Location: Cape Hatteras
  History: The merchantman foundered off Cape Hatteras in 1760 while sailing from Lisbon to Virginia. Nine of the crew perished.

Charming Betsey, English merchantman, Captain Waugh
  Location: Ocracoke Island
  History: She wrecked on the island in 1774 while sailing from Baltimore to London. Only a small part of her cargo was saved.

Charming Polly, English merchantman, Captain Shoemaker
  Location: Cape Hatteras
  History: The ship was totally lost off Cape Hatteras in 1770 while arriving from London.

Christian, German immigrant ship, Captain Deetjen
  Location: Cape Lookout
  History: She was lost near Cape Lookout in 1799 while sailing from Bremen to Baltimore. No lives were lost and part of the cargo was saved.

Clementina, English merchantman, Captain Weir
  Location: Cape Hatteras
  History: The merchantman was lost in 1775 at Cape Hatteras while arriving from London.

Diomede, American schooner
  Location: Kitty Hawk
  History: The schooner was lost at Kitty Hawk on January 23, 1825.

Dolphin, English merchantman, Captain Cleavers
  Location: Cape Fear
  History: The merchantman sank at Cape Fear during a hurricane on October 7 and 8, 1749.

Eliza, American ship, Captain Steele
  Location: Ocracoke Island
  History: The ship was lost on Ocracoke Island in 1816 while sailing from Jamaica to Philadelphia. The crew and part of the cargo were saved.

Elizabeth & Mary, English merchantman
  Location: Cape Fear Inlet
  History: The ship was lost entering Cape Fear Inlet in 1775 while arriving from England.

El Salvador, Spanish galleon belonging to the New Spain Flota (fleet) of Captain-General Juan Manuel de Bonilla
  Location: Fifteen leagues north of Ocracoke Inlet
  History: Four of the *flota*'s ships were lost during a hurricane on August 18, 1750: the *Nuestra Señora de la Soledad*, wrecked ten leagues north of Ocracoke Inlet; the *El Salvador*, wrecked 15 leagues north of Ocracoke Inlet; an unidentified *nao* wrecked at Topsail Inlet; and another *nao* at Drum Inlet. The Spaniards and the English recovered the majority of the treasure.

Emperor of Russia, ship of unknown registry
   Location: Currituck Inlet
   History: The ship was lost on March 18, 1817, near Currituck Inlet while sailing from Amsterdam to Boston. The crew and part of her cargo were saved.

Emulous, American schooner
   Location: Kitty Hawk
   History: The schooner was lost at Kitty Hawk on January 22, 1825.

Enterprize, Scottish ship, Captain Reid
   Location: Linger Shoals, Cape Fear
   History: The ship was totally lost during a gale on February 3, 1768, on Linger Shoals, inside the Cape Fear bar.

Enterprize, American schooner
   Location: New Inlet
   History: The schooner wrecked on October 27, 1822, at New Inlet.

Expectation, English merchantman, Captain Baker
   Location: Cape Hatteras
   History: The merchantman was lost on Cape Hatteras in 1802 while sailing from Antigua to North Carolina.

Experiment, American ship, Captain McDonald
   Location: Cape Hatteras
   History: The ship was lost off Cape Hatteras in 1792 while sailing to New York.

Fly, English merchantman
   Location: Frying Pan Shoals
   History: The ship sank on Frying Pan Shoals during a storm on October 3, 1818.

Fortura, Portuguese merchantman, Captain Rhode
   Location: Cape Hatteras
   History: The merchantman was lost on Cape Hatteras in 1805 while sailing from Brazil to Baltimore. Part of her cargo was saved.

Four Lantons, ship of unknown registry, Captain Tasker
   Location: Edenton
   History: The ship was lost entering Edenton in 1760 while arriving from Jamaica.

Friendship, English merchantman, Captain Briscal
   Location: Cape Hatteras
   History: The merchantman was lost at Cape Hatteras in 1758 while arriving from England. No lives were lost.

George, American coastal trader, Captain Raitt
   Location: Oregon Inlet
   History: The ship wrecked near Oregon Inlet in 1743 while sailing from Boston to North Carolina. No lives were lost.

Georgia, English merchantman, brig, Captain Colesworth
   Location: Currituck Inlet
   History: The brig wrecked on July 15, 1818 at Currituck Inlet while coming from New York. Most of the cargo of wood was saved.

Good Intent, English slave ship, Captain Copeland
   Location: Cape Hatteras
   History: The ship was lost off Cape Hatteras in 1767 while arriving from Africa with over 300 slaves.

Greyhound, English merchantman, Captain Cook
   Location: Chowan River
   History: The merchantman wrecked in 1751 during bad weather near Salmon Creek in the Chowan River while sailing from Boston to North Carolina. The crew was saved.

Harvest, American schooner, Captain Murphy
   Location: Bodie Island
   History: The schooner was lost November 18, 1825, at Bodie Island.

Hector, English merchantman, Captain Quince
   Location: Frying Pan Shoals
   History: While arriving from London, the English merchantman was lost on the Frying Pan Shoals during a hurricane that struck the North Carolina coast on September 2, 1775. A large number of ships were lost, but only the *Hector* was identified.

Henry, American sloop
   Location: Ocracoke Island
   History: The sloop was lost during January 1820 on Ocracoke Island.

H.M.S. *Garland*, English warship
   Location: Small sandbar a little south of Currituck Inlet
   History: The small warship wrecked on November 29, 1710, with 15 of her crew perishing. The wreck sanded over before anything could be salvaged.

Horam, American merchantman, Captain Eldridge
   Location: Ocracoke Inlet bar
   History: The merchantman was lost on April 6, 1825, on the Ocracoke Inlet bar while sailing from Boston to Jamaica.

Horatio, American merchantman, Captain Martin
   Location: Diamond Shoals
   History: The merchantman was lost on the shoals during April 1820.

Hoylin, English merchantman, Captain Cunningham
   Location: Cape Hatteras
   History: This vessel was lost off Cape Hatteras in 1741 while arriving from Bristol. No lives were lost.

Industry, American merchantman, Captain Woodend
   Location: Cape Hatteras
   History: The merchantman was lost on Cape Hatteras in 1798 while sailing from St. Vincent to Virginia.

Islington, American merchantman, Captain Wilson
   Location: Cape Hatteras
   History: The merchantman was lost on March 16, 1820, at Cape Hatteras.

John Adams, American ship
   Location: Cape Hatteras
   History: The ship was lost on May 19, 1817, on Cape Hatteras while sailing from Charleston to Norfolk. The crew and some of the cargo were saved.

John & Jane, English merchantman, Captain Close
   Location: Nine leagues seaward of the Cape Fear bar
   History: The ship foundered nine leagues seaward of the Cape Fear bar during a hurricane on October 7 and 8, 1749.

Katherine & Elizabeth, English merchantman, Captain Webster

Location: Diamond Shoals

History: This vessel was lost on the shoals in 1744 while sailing for London.

Kingston, English ship, Captain Goodman

Location: Cape Fear

History: The ship foundered off Cape Fear in 1760 while sailing from Havana to Philadelphia. A passing ship rescued the crew.

Little Dick, American ship

Location: Wilmington bar

History: The ship was lost crossing the Wilmington bar in 1816 while sailing from Jamaica to Wilmington.

Lively, English merchantman, Captain Read

Location: Cape Hatteras

History: The merchantman was lost off Cape Hatteras in 1771 while arriving from Grenada.

Lively Lass, American ship

Location: Ocracoke Island

History: The ship, sailing from New Orleans to Liverpool, drifted onshore without anyone onboard at Ocracoke Island at the end of September 1810.

Lydia, English ship, Captain Hatton

Location: Cape Hatteras

History: The ship was lost on Cape Hatteras in 1804 while sailing from Wilmington to England.

Maria, French ship

Location: Cape Hatteras

History: The ship was lost on Cape Hatteras in 1810 while sailing from Martinique to New York.

Martha, English merchantman

Location: Currituck Sands

History: The vessel wrecked at Currituck Sands in 1821 while sailing from Bermuda to New London.

Mary, ship of unknown registry

Location: Currituck Beach

History: The ship wrecked on April 15, 1816, while sailing from Norfolk to Trinidad. Most of her cargo was saved.

Mary & Francis, American ship, Captain Marsh

Location: Cape Hatteras

History: The ship wrecked near Cape Hatteras in March 1817 while sailing from Madeira to Baltimore. Most of her cargo was saved.

Molly, English merchantman, Captain Baker

Location: Cape Hatteras

History: The ship wrecked at Cape Hatteras in 1789 while sailing from Dunkirk to Virginia.

Molly, American merchantman, Captain Mill

Location: Cape Hatteras

History: The merchantman wrecked near Cape Hatteras in 1804 while arriving from Jamaica.

Monitor, Federal ironclad

Location: Sixteen miles south-south-east of the Cape Hatteras lighthouse in 230 feet of water

History: The Civil War–era *Monitor*, dubbed the "Yankee cheese box on a raft," is a wreck of considerable historical interest. The Federal ironclad defeated the Confederate ironclad *Merrimack* at Hampton Roads, Virginia on March 9, 1862. This battle probably had little effect on the outcome of the Civil War, but it did mark a new era in naval warfare, since it was the first time that two ironclads fought. Later that same year, on December 29, the *Rhode Island*, a paddle-wheel steamer, towed the *Monitor* out of Fort Monroe, Virginia and headed south toward Charleston, South Carolina, where the *Monitor* was to participate in a blockade. The *Monitor* rode so low in the water that her decks were usually awash, and only her circular gun turret amidships was visible. Definitely not a seaworthy ship, she was designed for giving battle in calm, protected waters. The first night after leaving port, the two ships were off Cape Hatteras when a sudden squall came up. The *Monitor* began taking on water at an alarming rate. The towline parted and the captain gave orders to abandon ship. After sighting a flare, the *Rhode Island's* crew lowered lifeboats and rescued all but 16 of the sinking ironclad's crew. Soon after, the *Monitor* went to a watery grave. There was no salvage attempt at the time, although reports by both ship's officers gave a vague location. For more than a century, she was just another shipwreck in the

"Graveyard of the Atlantic," which has claimed countless ships over the years. Then in 1973, a multidisciplinary team was organized to locate her. The team was headed by underwater archaeologist Gordon Watts from East Carolina University, oceanographer John Newton of Duke University, geologist Robert Sheridan of the University of Delaware, and Dr. Harold Edgerton. The search focused on a hundred square mile area with a center about 17 miles southeast of Cape Hatteras. The *Monitor* was located in 230 feet of water using magnetometers, side-scan sonar, and a closed-circuit television camera. On January 30, 1975, President Richard Nixon signed a law designating the *Monitor* a National Marine Sanctuary to protect the site from plunderers. The *Monitor* lies beyond safe depths for scuba divers so in May 1974 the team returned to the site with the Alcoa Seaprobe, a specially designed oceanographic vessel capable of working on shipwrecks at depths of almost four miles. A tall derrick aboard the Seaprobe lowered lengths of drilling pipe into the sea through an opening in the center of the ship. A pod containing an array of electronic detection equipment and still and video cameras was attached to the bottom of the pipe. The operation was controlled in the ship's search control room. The team spent a week on the *Monitor* and produced hours of video film and more than 2,000 still photographs. From these a partial photomosaic of the wreck was made, to determine if the ship could be raised. Two years later, Gordon Watts returned to the wreck. Using the manned submersible, Johnson Sea-Link I, Watts and his team each made one four-hour dive per day for a month. The submersible divers were monitored on closed-circuit television by the observer in the forward sphere as they used a hydraulic dredge to remove the sediment covering the wreck. They learned that the hull had been damaged during World War II when the *Monitor* was apparently mistaken for an enemy submarine and depth-charged. The team collected a small number of artifacts, including a brass marine navigation lantern, and took samples of the ship's metal plating.

Turret of the U.S.S. *Monitor. Courtesy of Dr. Harold Edgerton.*

Analysis of the plating proved that the hull was too weak to raise without the danger of it breaking apart. The last mission to the *Monitor* was in 1983 when Watts led a successful expedition to recover the anchor. Not surprisingly, at a cost of $100,000 for the expedition, there was some furor in the media over the amount spent to recover a single anchor. Since then, the *Monitor* has rested undisturbed on the ocean floor. The Mariners' Museum in Newport News, Virginia is the principal museum housing the *Monitor* Collection. Updated information on current events, recreational diving on the ship and educational information can be found at the internet web site: http://monitor.nos.noaa.gov/education/tenq.html

Nancy, English merchantman, Captain M'Carroll
   Location: Cape Hatteras
   History: The merchantman wrecked in 1760 near Cape Hatteras while sailing from Philadelphia to Cape Fear.

Nancy, American merchantman, Captain Beacon
   Location: Currituck
   History: The merchantman wrecked on a shoal off Currituck in 1793 while sailing from Jamaica to Virginia. No lives were lost.

Nancy, English ship, Captain Scott
   Location: Newburn

History: The ship wrecked on January 23, 1816, near Newburn while sailing from the Virgin Islands to Edenton. The crew was saved.

Nancy, American ship, Captain Hatch
   Location: Ocracoke Inlet bar
   History: The ship was lost on the bar on February 21, 1825.

Neptune, English merchantman, Captain Knowler
   Location: Diamond Shoals
   History: The merchantman was lost on the shoals in 1744 while sailing for London.

Nereus, ship of unknown registry, Captain Bosse
   Location: Cape Hatteras
   History: The ship was totally lost on January 1, 1822, on Cape Hatteras while sailing from Bremen to Virginia.

Nuestra Señora de la Soledad, Spanish galleon belonging to the New Spain Flota (fleet) of Captain-General Juan Manuel de Bonilla
   Location: Ten leagues north of Ocracoke Inlet
   History: Four of the *flota's* ships were lost during a hurricane on August 18, 1750: the *Nuestra Señora de la Soledad*, wrecked ten leagues north of Ocracoke Inlet; the *El Salvador*, wrecked 15 leagues north of Ocracoke Inlet; an unidentified *nao* wrecked at Topsail Inlet, and another *nao* at Drum Inlet. The Spaniards and the English recovered the majority of the treasure.

Olympus, English ship
   Location: Wilmington
   History: The ship was totally lost near Wilmington at the end of November 1810 while arriving from England.

Patriot, American pilot boat
   Location: Nags Head
   History: The boat was lost in January 1813 at Nags Head.

Peggy, English merchantman, Captain Abercrombie
   Location: Cape Hatteras
   History: The merchantman was lost at Cape Hatteras in 1758 while sailing from Philadelphia to South Carolina.

Peggy, American merchantman, Captain McNeil
   Location: Cape Hatteras
   History: The merchantman was lost off Cape Hatteras in 1783 while sailing from the Virgin Islands to New York. Only a small part of her cargo was saved.

Peter Francisco, American ship, Captain Reerson
   Location: Bodies Island
   History: The ship wrecked on October 7, 1823, on Bodies Island while sailing from New York to Mobile. The crew, passengers and all of the cargo were saved.

Phoenix, American schooner, Captain Coffin
   Location: Cape Hatteras
   History: The schooner wrecked on May 13, 1819, on Cape Hatteras while sailing to Philadelphia.

Pitt, English ship, Captain Cook
   Location: Ocracoke Inlet bar
   History: She was lost on the bar in 1792 while arriving from Antigua.

Polly, American merchantman
   Location: Beaufort
   History: The ship wrecked in 1793 near Beaufort without any loss of life.

Princess Amelia, English merchantman, Captain Freizwell
   Location: Cape Hatteras
   History: The merchantman was lost at Cape Hatteras in 1758 while sailing from Halifax to South Carolina.

Pusey Hall, American ship, Captain Simpson
   Location: Cape Lookout
   History: The ship wrecked at Cape Lookout in 1790 while sailing from Jamaica to Virginia.

Queen Ann's Revenge, 40-gun pirate flagship, 300 tons, commanded by Edward Teach (known as "Blackbeard")
   Location: Beaufort Inlet in 20 feet of water

Eighteenth century rendering of Blackbeard.

caping to another ship, but died a month later after being trapped by British warships off Ocracoke. Mike Daniel of Intersal, Inc., working under the auspices of the North Carolina Department of Cultural Resources, discovered the ship in 1996 in Beaufort Inlet; it is now one of North Carolina's most historically significant shipwrecks. Artifacts raised from the excavation site include the ship's bronze bell, inscribed with the date 1709; several cannon; a bag shot grenade, which is a Molotov cocktail–style weapon; a sounding weight; pewter platters; 17th and 18th century gin bottles; a 1714 onion bottle; and three anchors, one of which has a partial wood shank. The most unusual object discovered on the wreck site is a blunderbuss. Intersal, Inc. has donated the entire find to the State of North Carolina. State archaeologists expect to finish salvage of the wreck in the year 2002.

Racehorse, English slave ship, Captain Barker
  Location: Frying Pan Shoals
  History: The slaver wrecked on June 22, 1760, while carrying slaves from Africa to South Carolina. Many lives were lost.

Revenge, American sloop
  Location: Currituck Inlet
  History: The sloop was lost during January 1819 at Currituck Inlet.

Revenge, English merchantman, Captain Whittingham
  Location: Two miles north of Currituck Inlet
  History: The merchantman wrecked in June 1765 while sailing from Curaçao to Norfolk. Only the crew was saved.

History: The *Queen Ann's Revenge* was originally the slave trader *Concord,* built in England around 1710, and captured by the French late in that year. In 1717, Blackbeard captured the ship and renamed it *Queen Ann's Revenge.* It became his flagship during the height of his reign of terror, which ended in the port of Charleston in May 1718. The following month, the pirate ship ran aground and sank in a storm. Blackbeard survived the foundering by es-

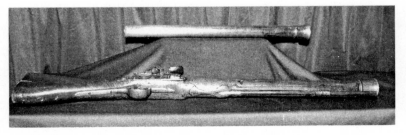

A blunderbuss was a muzzle loading weapon popular during the 17th and 18th centuries. *Courtesy of N.C. Archives and History.*

Rhine, English merchantman, Captain Turnly
   Location: Wilmington bar
   History: The merchantman was lost crossing the Wilmington bar in September 1810 while arriving from the Bahamas. No lives were lost.

Rosetta, ship of unknown registry, Captain Sissen
   Location: Ocracoke Inlet bar
   History: The ship was lost while crossing the bar on March 4, 1817, after arriving from New York. The crew and all of the cargo were saved.

Royal Charlotte, English merchantman, Captain Severy
   Location: Long Bay
   History: The merchantman wrecked at Long Bay in 1763 while sailing from Montserrat to Georgia.

Royal Exchange, English merchantman, Captain Daverson
   Location: Cape Lookout
   History: The merchantman was lost at Cape Lookout in 1775 while bound for London. All of her crew were saved.

Sally, English merchantman, Captain Keith
   Location: Cape Hatteras
   History: The merchantman was lost on Cape Hatteras in 1774 while sailing from Maryland to Gibraltar.

San Antonio, Spanish brig, Captain Fabre
   Location: Wilmington
   History: The brig was totally lost on February 18, 1813, near Wilmington. All of her crew were saved.

Santa Rosa, Spanish merchantman, Captain Fernandez
   Location: Wilmington
   History: The merchantman was lost about the middle of November 1804 near Wilmington. She was sailing from Havana to Bilbao with a great amount of treasure aboard when she foundered.

Sero, English merchantman, Captain Robinson
   Location: Cape Hatteras
   History: The merchantman wrecked on September 25, 1815, off Cape Hatteras while coming from Cuba.

Shannon, Scottish merchantman, Captain Williamson
   Location: Currituck Inlet
   History: The ship wrecked at the inlet in 1764 while sailing from Virginia to Glasgow. The crew and part of the cargo were saved.

Sophia, American merchantman, schooner, Captain Massey
   Location: Ten miles north of Currituck Inlet
   History: The schooner wrecked in 1821 while sailing from Philadelphia to Norfolk. There was only one survivor.

Statira, English merchantman
   Location: Frying Pan Shoals
   History: The merchantman was lost on the shoals in 1822 while sailing from Havana to London. No lives were lost.

St. James Planter, English merchantman, Captain Paxton
   Location: Cape Lookout
   History: The merchantman was lost near Cape Lookout in 1791 while sailing from Jamaica to London. Part of her cargo was saved.

Superior, American merchantman, Captain Spence
   Location: Cape Hatteras
   History: The vessel was lost on October 3, 1815, near Cape Hatteras while sailing from Martinique to Philadelphia. The crew and part of the cargo were saved.

Susan, American schooner
   Location: Ocracoke Inlet bar
   History: The schooner was lost on June 1, 1824, while sailing from Demarara to Philadelphia.

Tiger, English ship
   Location: Ocracoke Inlet
   History: The ship, on a voyage of exploration, wrecked on June 29, 1585, at Ocracoke Inlet. The crew was saved.

Tyrrel, English merchantman
   Location: Bacon Island Roads
   History: The merchantman wrecked on July 3, 1759, off Bacon Island Roads. All of the crew were saved.

Unidentified, English merchantmen (9)

   Location: Ocracoke Inlet
   History: During a hurricane on October 7 and 8, 1749, nine unidentified English merchantmen were totally lost: seven sank inside the bar at Ocracoke Inlet and two were wrecked five miles north.

Unidentified, *nao* belonging to the New Spain Flota (fleet) of Captain-General Juan Manuel de Bonilla
   Location: Drum Inlet
   History: Four of the *flota*'s ships were lost during a hurricane on August 18, 1750: the *Nuestra Señora de la Soledad*, wrecked ten leagues north of Ocracoke Inlet; the *El Salvador*, wrecked 15 leagues north of Ocracoke Inlet; an unidentified *nao* wrecked at Topsail Inlet, and another *nao* at Drum Inlet. The Spaniards and the English recovered the majority of the treasure.

Unidentified, *nao* belonging to the New Spain Flota (fleet) of Captain-General Juan Manuel de Bonilla
   Location: Topsail Inlet
   History: Four of the *flota*'s ships were lost during a hurricane on August 18, 1750: the *Nuestra Señora de la Soledad*, wrecked ten leagues north of Ocracoke Inlet; the *El Salvador*, wrecked 15 leagues north of Ocracoke Inlet; an unidentified *nao* wrecked at Topsail Inlet, and another *nao* at Drum Inlet. The Spaniards and the English recovered the majority of the treasure.

Unidentified, ships (large number)
   Location: North Carolina coast
   History: A large number of ships were lost during a hurricane that struck the North Carolina coast on September 2, 1775. Only the English merchantman *Hector*, lost on the Frying Pan Shoals while arriving from London, was identified.

Unidentified, Spanish brigantine
   Location: Cape Fear
   History: A small unidentified Spanish brigantine, which was sent from Cuba on a voyage of exploration along the eastern coast of America, was wrecked during the month of June in 1526 at Cape Fear. The survivors made a smaller vessel from the wreckage and managed to reach Santo Domingo with great hardship.

Unidentified, English flyboat
  Location: Cape Fear
  History: The boat wrecked at Cape Fear in 1665 but no lives were lost.

Unidentified, English brigantine, Captain Murray
  Location: Cape Fear
  History: The brigantine wrecked near Cape Fear in 1752 while sailing for London.

Unidentified, English merchantman
  Location: Cape Hatteras
  History: The merchantman was lost off Cape Hatteras during a hurricane on August 18, 1750, with a total loss of life.

Unidentified, American schooner, Captain Hayman
  Location: Cape Hatteras
  History: The schooner was lost at Cape Hatteras in 1757 while sailing to the Leeward Islands.

Unidentified, Spanish ships (undisclosed number)
  Location: Cape Hatteras
  History: Six unidentified ships were wrecked on the Ocracoke Inlet bar during a bad gale on August 2, 1795. During the same storm a fleet of 18 Spanish ships, sailing from Havana to Spain, were struck off Cape Hatteras. An undisclosed number of these ships were lost.

Unidentified, American merchantmen (2)
  Location: Cape Hatteras
  History: Two American merchantmen wrecked near Cape Hatteras during a storm on October 3, 1818.

Unidentified, English merchantman, about 125 tons
  Location: Cape Hatteras
  History: The merchantman wrecked at Cape Hatteras in September 1821 with a cargo of rum. There was a total loss of life.

Unidentified, English sloop
  Location: Cape Lookout
  History: The sloop wrecked at Cape Lookout in 1666. The survivors salvaged all of her cargo.

Unidentified, English ship
  Location: Six miles seaward from Ocracoke Inlet
  History: The ship wrecked during a hurricane in 1728. There were only a few survivors.

Unidentified, merchantmen, schooners (2)
  Location: Ocracoke Bar
  History: The merchantmen wrecked on the bar in 1752 while arriving from Virginia.

Unidentified, ships (17)
  Location: Ocracoke Inlet
  History: Seventeen ships were wrecked at Ocracoke Inlet during a hurricane on July 23 and 24, 1788. Only a few lives were lost.

Unidentified, ships (more than 20)
  Location: Ocracoke Inlet
  History: More than 20 ships were wrecked or sunk at Ocracoke Inlet on Ocracoke Island during a hurricane in early September 1815.

Unidentified, merchantmen (14–15)
  Location: Ocracoke Inlet bar
  History: Fourteen or 15 unidentified large merchantmen were totally lost near the Ocracoke Inlet bar during a hurricane at the beginning of September 1772.

Unidentified, ships (6)
  Location: Ocracoke Inlet bar
  History: Six unidentified ships were wrecked on the Ocracoke Inlet bar during a bad gale on August 2, 1795. During the same storm a fleet of 18 Spanish ships, sailing from Havana to Spain, were struck off Cape Hatteras. An undisclosed number of these ships were lost.

Unidentified, ships (more than 25)
  Location: Outer Banks
  History: More than 25 unidentified ships were wrecked north of Ocracoke Inlet on the Outer Banks on June 4, 1825 during a hurricane.

Union, English merchantman, Captain Blackburn
  Location: Cape Fear bar
  History: The merchantman was lost crossing the Cape Fear bar in 1763 while sailing from Barbados to North Carolina. The crew was saved.

Union, American merchantman, Captain Hammond

Location: Cape Hatteras
  History: The ship was lost at Cape Hatteras in January 1757 while coming from Rhode Island.

Victory, American schooner
  Location: Kitty Hawk
  History: The schooner was lost in December of 1825 at Kitty Hawk.

Virginia Packet, English packet boat, Captain Ball
  Location: Cape Hatteras
  History: The boat was lost at Cape Hatteras in 1757 while sailing from Bristol to Virginia.

Voucher, American ship, Captain Howland
  Location: Chicamacomico
  History: The ship wrecked on November 19, 1817, at Chicamacomico while sailing from New York to Charleston. All of her crew, passengers and cargo were saved.

Washington, American ship
  Location: Ocracoke Island
  History: The ship was lost at Ocracoke Island on January 24, 1825, while coming from Jamaica.

William Carlton, American merchantman
  Location: Kill Devil Hills
  History: The merchantman wrecked on May 15, 1818, at Kill Devil Hills.

Wilmington Packet, American packet boat
  Location: Bald Point
  History: The packet boat was lost at Bald Point on September 8, 1804, after first striking on Frying Pan Shoals.

Woolford, English merchantman, Captain Kenlock
  Location: Cape Hatteras
  History: The merchantman was lost off Cape Hatteras in 1741 while sailing from Jamaica to London.

Young Factor, English merchantman
  Location: Wilmington bar
  History: The ship was lost crossing the Wilmington bar in 1811 while sailing for London. There was no loss of life.

RHODE ISLAND

American, American merchantman, Captain Lincoln
  Location: Block Island
  History: The vessel was lost off Block Island on May 25, 1819, while sailing from the West Indies to Boston.

Ann, American merchantman, Captain McDonald
  Location: Barrington
  History: She wrecked in 1813 near Barrington. Her crew and cargo were saved.

Anna and Hope, ship of unknown registry
  Location: Block Island
  History: The ship was totally lost on Block Island in 1805 while coming from France.

Brutus, English ship, Captain Tobey
  Location: Block Island
  History: The vessel wrecked on Block Island in 1807 after arriving from Liverpool.

Golden Grove, Irish merchantman, Captain Chitty
  Location: Block Island
  History: She wrecked on the island in 1765 while sailing from Cork to Halifax with a cargo of dried meats and butter. The crew and some of her cargo were saved.

Governor Hopkins, American ship
  Location: Brenton's Reef
  History: The vessel wrecked during a storm in December 1818 on Brenton's Reef while arriving from Savannah. Most of her cargo was saved.

H.M.S. *Cerberus*, 28-gun English warship, Captain John Symons
  Location: Narragansett Bay
  History: Seven English warships were burnt and sunk in Narragansett Bay during the War of Independence in 1778: the H.M.S. *Kingfisher*, H.M.S. *Juno*, H.M.S. *Lark*, H.M.S. *Orpheus*, H.M.S. *Flora*, H.M.S. *Cerberus* and H.M.S. *Falcon*.

H.M.S. *Falcon*, 16-gun English warship, Captain Harry Harmood
  Location: Narragansett Bay
  History: Seven English warships were burnt and sunk in Narragansett Bay during the War of Independence in 1778: the H.M.S. *Kingfisher*, H.M.S. *Juno*, H.M.S. *Lark*, H.M.S. *Orpheus*, H.M.S. *Flora*, H.M.S. *Cerberus* and H.M.S. *Falcon*.

H.M.S. *Flora*, 32-gun English warship, Captain John Brisbane
  Location: Narragansett Bay
  History: Seven English warships were burnt and sunk in Narragansett Bay during the War of Independence in 1778: the H.M.S. *Kingfisher*, H.M.S. *Juno*, H.M.S. *Lark*, H.M.S. *Orpheus*, H.M.S. *Flora*, H.M.S. *Cerberus* and H.M.S. *Falcon*.

H.M.S. *Gaspee*, English warship
  Location: Newport Harbor
  History: The warship was lost near Newport Harbor on June 10, 1772.

H.M.S. *Juno*, 30-gun English warship, Captain Hugh Dalrymple
  Location: Narragansett Bay
  History: Seven English warships were burnt and sunk in Narragansett Bay during the War of Independence in 1778: the H.M.S. *Kingfisher*, H.M.S. *Juno*, H.M.S. *Lark*, H.M.S. *Orpheus*, H.M.S. *Flora*, H.M.S. *Cerberus* and H.M.S. *Falcon*.

H.M.S. *Kingfisher*, 16-gun English warship
  Location: Narragansett Bay
  History: Seven English warships were burnt and sunk in Narragansett Bay during the War of Independence in 1778: the H.M.S. *Kingfisher*, H.M.S. *Juno*, H.M.S. *Lark*, H.M.S. *Orpheus*, H.M.S. *Flora*, H.M.S. *Cerberus* and H.M.S. *Falcon*.

H.M.S. *Lark*, 32-gun English warship, Captain Richard Smith
  Location: Narragansett Bay
  History: Seven English warships were burnt and sunk in Narragansett Bay during the War of Independence in 1778: the H.M.S. *Kingfisher*, H.M.S. *Juno*, H.M.S. *Lark*, H.M.S. *Orpheus*, H.M.S. *Flora*, H.M.S. *Cerberus* and H.M.S. *Falcon*.

H.M.S. *Orpheus*, 32-gun English warship, Captain Charles Hudson
  Location: Narragansett Bay
  History: Seven English warships

were burnt and sunk in Narragansett Bay during the War of Independence in 1778: the H.M.S. *Kingfisher*, H.M.S. *Juno*, H.M.S. *Lark*, H.M.S. *Orpheus*, H.M.S. *Flora*, H.M.S. *Cerberus* and H.M.S. *Falcon*.

H.M.S. *Redbridge*, 12-gun English schooner-of-war, Captain Edward Burt
  Location: Providence
  History: The schooner wrecked on November 4, 1806, near Providence.

H.M.S. *Syren*, 20-gun English warship
  Location: Point Judith
  History: The warship wrecked near Point Judith on November 10, 1777.

H.M.S. *Triton*, Captain Woolcomb
  Location: Point Judith
  History: This vessel wrecked near Point Judith in the year 1777.

London, English merchantman, Captain Folger
  Location: Newport Harbor
  History: She was lost near Newport Harbor while sailing for London in 1772.

Minerva, American ship, Captain Cranston
  Location: Westerly
  History: She wrecked near Westerly while sailing to New York in 1779.

Montgomery, American merchantman
  Location: Sakonnet Point
  History: The vessel was lost in 1819 near Sakonnet Point while arriving from Honduras.

Princess Augusta, German ship, Captain Brook
  Location: Sandy Point, Block Island
  History: The ship wrecked on the northern tip of Sandy Point in 1738 while carrying German immigrants from Amsterdam to New York. Prior to the disaster, 250 of the 350 immigrants and some of the crew had died from contaminated water. The ship was reported to be carrying a considerable amount of personal treasure belonging to the immigrants.

Unidentified, ships (35)
  Location: Providence

History: Four large ships, nine brigs, seven schooners and fifteen sloops were wrecked or sunk at Providence during a hurricane on September 23, 1815.

SOUTH CAROLINA

America, English merchantman, Captain Jameson
  Location: Charleston bar
  History: The merchantman was lost on the bar in 1784 while arriving from Scotland.

Anamaboo, slave ship of unknown registry, Captain Ferguson
  Location: St. Helena Sound
  History: The ship was totally lost near St. Helena Sound in 1757 while sailing from Africa to Rhode Island with a cargo of slaves. Only a few of the crew survived.

Argus, English merchantman, Captain Johnson
  Location: Charleston bar
  History: The merchantman was lost on the Charleston bar in 1800 while sailing for Liverpool. Most of her cargo was saved.

Bennet, English merchantman, Captain Wadham
  Location: Charleston Harbor
  History: The ship was accidentally burnt in Charleston harbor in April 1752 while preparing to sail for London.

Benson, English ship, Captain Wilmot
  Location: Near Charleston
  History: The ship wrecked on March 23, 1811, near Charleston while sailing from Honduras to London.

Bricole, 44-gun American naval vessel
  Location: Charleston
  History: A British fleet, commanded by Vice-Admiral Arbuthnot, destroyed and sank three American naval vessels during a battle off Charleston in 1780. The ships were the *Bricole, General Moultrie* and *Notre Dame*.

Britannia, English ship, Captain Wilson
  Location: Rebellion Road, Charleston

History: Five ships were lost in Rebellion Road at Charleston during a hurricane on May 4, 1761: the *Polly & Betsey, Success, Daniel, Britannia* and an unidentified Bermudan schooner.

Caesar, English merchantman, Captain Sparks
  Location: Charleston bar
  History: The ship was forced to enter Charleston for repairs in 1750 but was lost crossing the bar of this port while sailing from the Bay of Honduras for England.

Calcutta, American ship, Captain Winslow
  Location: Folly Island
  History: The ship was wrecked on April 10, 1822, about four miles north of the lighthouse on Folly Island while arriving from Amsterdam.

Cracklow, English merchantman
  Location: South of Charleston Harbor
  History: The merchantman was lost several miles south of Charleston Harbor in 1810 while arriving from London.

Daniel, English merchantman, Captain Lake
  Location: Rebellion Road, Charleston
  History: Five ships were lost in Rebellion Road at Charleston during a hurricane on May 4, 1761: the *Polly & Betsey, Success, Daniel, Britannia* and an unidentified Bermudan schooner.

Dee, English ship, Captain Dixon
  Location: Charleston
  History: The ship was totally lost on December 24, 1820, to the south of the Charleston Lighthouse while arriving from Liverpool. The crew, four chests of specie and the mail were saved.

Despatch, English merchantman
  Location: Charleston
  History: The ship, arriving from Jamaica, was driven ashore near Charleston by several American privateers in 1781 and totally lost.

Dispatch, English merchantman, Captain Shields
  Location: Georgetown harbor
  History: The merchantman was totally lost at Georgetown harbor in

1785 while fully loaded and ready to sail for London.

General Hodgkinson, sloop of unknown registry
  Location: Charleston
  History: The sloop wrecked off Charleston on November 24, 1813, while arriving from Curaçao.

General Moultrie, 20-gun American naval vessel
  Location: Charleston
  History: A British fleet, commanded by Vice-Admiral Arbuthnot, destroyed and sank three American naval vessels during a battle off Charleston in 1780. The ships were the *Bricole, General Moultrie* and *Notre Dame*.

Governor Bickney, American ship, Captain Hall
  Location: Charleston bar
  History: The ship wrecked on the bar in 1791 while sailing to Hispaniola.

Grampus, English merchantman
  Location: South of Charleston
  History: The ship wrecked south of Charleston in 1796 while arriving from Liverpool.

Harriet, American ship, Captain Folson
  Location: Sullivan's Island
  History: The ship wrecked on August 6, 1816, on the island while sailing from Havana to Wilmington.

H.L. Hunley, American submarine, 40 feet
  Location: Off Sullivan's Island
  History: The historical *Hunley* was the first submarine to ever sink an enemy ship in wartime. This type of submarine was built by the confederates in honor of David Bushnell, an early American submarine inventor. "David Boats," as they were often called, were built from cylindrical steam boilers taken from Mississippi River boats. They were cigar shaped, ranged from 20 to 40 feet and could carry a crew of nine. The "David Boats" were propelled by hand turned screws and could make up to four knots in speed. They carried a spar torpedo, which was attached to the bow. The David boat attached the explosives to the hull of

an enemy vessel in attempt to sink the ship. The *Hunley* sank twice during tests, drowning both her crews. Then on February 16, 1864, the submarine made a late night attack on the Yankee ironclad U.S.S. *Housatonic*. The *Hunley* rammed the ironclad with a torpedo packed with explosive powder. The torpedo was detonated by a rope as the *Hunley* backed away. The *Housatonic* exploded and carried its five crew members to the bottom of Charleston Harbor. The explosion also sank the *Hunley* with its nine crew. After 14 years of searching and $130,000, the *Hunley* was located in May 1995 by noted author Clive Cussler and his team from the National Underwater and Marine Agency (NUMA). A federal oversight committee made up of the National Park Service, the U.S. Navy, the National Oceanic and Atmospheric Administration, the General Services Administration, and the Advisory Council on Historic Preservation, was formed to oversee the recovery proposals. After consideration, it was decided to raise the submarine by passing several slings under the sub and attaching them to an elaborate truss system. Divers are currently digging under the sub in preparation for attaching the slings. The total cost of recovering and preserving the submarine is estimated at $17 million.

H.M.S. *Acteon*, 28-gun English warship, Captain Christopher Atkins
   Location: Charleston Harbor
   History: The warship was burnt in Charleston Harbor by her crew on June 29, 1776.

H.M.S. *Cruiser*, eight-gun English warship, Captain Francis Parry
   Location: Charleston
   History: The ship was burnt in 1777 off Charleston by her crew to prevent its capture by the Americans.

H.M.S. *Peacock*, 18-gun English warship, Captain Richard Coote
   Location: Charleston
   History: The warship foundered off Charleston during August 1814 with a total loss of life.

Hercules, American merchantman, Captain Duncan
   Location: Charleston

History: The ship was totally lost off Charleston in 1815 while arriving from Jamaica and the Bahamas.

Hope, English merchantman, Captain Worsley
   Location: Charleston bar
   History: The ship was lost on the bar in 1787 while sailing to Hamburg.

Jack Park, English merchantman
   Location: Charleston bar
   History: The ship was lost while crossing the bar in 1805 after sailing for Liverpool.

Jamaica, ship of unknown registry, Captain McLeon
   Location: Charleston Harbor
   History: The ship capsized and sank in Charleston Harbor in 1781 while arriving from New York.

John, English slave ship, Captain Cummings
   Location: Charleston Harbor
   History: The *John* and *Swan*, both slave ships, wrecked while attempting to enter Charleston Harbor in 1806. No lives were lost.

Judith, English merchantman, Captain Martin
   Location: Cape Romain
   History: The merchantman wrecked in 1759 on Cape Romain while sailing from North Carolina to England.

Leeds Industry, English troop transport, Captain Hobkirk
   Location: Charleston Harbor
   History: The transport sank in Charleston Harbor in 1781.

London, English warship
   Location: Charleston
   History: Two English warships, the *Thetis* and *London*, sank at the Charleston docks during a hurricane on August 9, 1781.

Marcella, English merchantman, Captain Way
   Location: Three leagues from Charleston
   History: The merchantman wrecked on February 18, 1758, on a sandbank about three leagues from Charleston while arriving from Lisbon. No lives were lost and the wreck was totally salvaged.

Margaret, English merchantman
   Location: Charleston bar
   History: The merchantman wrecked on August 9, 1818, on the Charleston bar while sailing for Liverpool. The crew and cargo were saved.

Martha, Scottish merchantman, Captain Shea
   Location: Cape Romain
   History: The merchantman wrecked on Cape Romain in 1751 while arriving from the Canary Islands. All of the crew were saved.

Mary, English merchantman, Captain Loveday
   Location: Charleston
   History: The merchantman wrecked a bit south of Charleston in 1767 while arriving from London. The crew, rigging and sails were all saved.

Minerva, ship of unknown registry, Captain Neilson
   Location: Edisto Island
   History: The ship wrecked on Edisto Island on January 3, 1821, while arriving from France. Her crew was saved.

Monticello, American ship, Captain Newell
   Location: Morris Island
   History: The ship wrecked on the island in 1802 while coming from the Leeward Islands. Some of her cargo was saved.

Nancy, English merchantman, Captain Cummingham
   Location: Several leagues north of Charleston
   History: The merchantman wrecked several leagues north of Charleston in 1775 while sailing from London to North Carolina.

Northumberland, English merchantman, Captain Gibb
   Location: Charleston Harbor
   History: The merchantman was lost in Charleston Harbor while arriving from Jamaica on October 14, 1805. The crew was saved.

Notre Dame, 16-gun American naval vessel
   Location: Charleston
   History: A British fleet, commanded by Vice-Admiral Arbuthnot, destroyed and sank three American naval vessels

during a battle off Charleston in 1780. The ships were the *Bricole, General Moultrie* and the *Notre Dame.*

Patrick, English ship, Captain Salmon
   Location: Charleston bar
   History: The vessel was lost on the bar in 1801 while arriving from Honduras.

Plantagenet, English merchantman, Captain Key
   Location: Charleston bar
   History: The ship was totally lost on February 20, 1824, on the Charleston bar while arriving from Liverpool. Only her crew was saved.

Polly, American merchantman, Captain Higgins
   Location: Near Charleston
   History: The merchantman wrecked near Charleston in 1797 while arriving from Havana.

Polly & Betsey, English merchantman, Captain Muer
   Location: Rebellion Road, Charleston
   History: Five ships were lost in Rebellion Road at Charleston during a hurricane on May 4, 1761: the *Polly & Betsey, Success, Daniel, Britannia* and an unidentified Bermudan schooner.

Port Morant, English merchantman
   Location: Martin's Industry
   History: The merchantman wrecked on October 10, 1781, on a sandbank called Martin's Industry, to the east of Port Royal while sailing from Jamaica to London. No lives were lost.

Powhaton, English merchantman, Captain Shaw
   Location: Charleston bar
   History: The ship was lost on the Charleston bar in 1796 while sailing from Liverpool to Jamaica. Most of her cargo was saved.

Rising Sun, Scottish merchantman
   Location: Charleston bar
   History: The merchantman was lost on the Charleston bar during a hurricane on September 3, 1700.

Sarah, English merchantman, Captain Milner
   Location: Morris Island

History: The merchantman was lost on May 7, 1810, while sailing from Havana to Jamaica.

Seaflower, ship of unknown registry, Captain Williams
   Location: Georgetown bar
   History: The ship was lost on the bar in 1799 while arriving from Jamaica. Some of her cargo was saved.

Sergeant Glynn, English merchantman, Captain Mogridge
   Location: Port Royal Sound
   History: The merchantman was totally lost near Port Royal Sound in 1770 while arriving from London. No lives were lost.

Speedwell, English merchantman, Captain Redman
   Location: Charleston bar
   History: The ship was lost crossing the Charleston bar in 1766 while arriving from London.

Spring, English merchantman, Captain Smith
   Location: Cape Romain Shoals
   History: The ship was totally lost on Cape Romain shoals during August of 1815 while sailing from Liverpool to Wilmington. No lives were lost.

S.S. *Central America*, U.S. Mail Side-Wheel Steamship, Captain William Lewis Herndon
   Location: 160 miles off Charleston
   History: The *Central America*, originally named the *George Law*, was responsible for carrying at least one-third of the gold mined in the California Gold Rush back to the East Coast. During this era passengers made the trip on the steamer *Sonora* from California down to Panama. After a four-hour train ride across Panama, they boarded the *Central America* for the final leg of the trip to New York. On September 9, 1857, the *Central America*, commanded by Capt. William Lewis Herndon of the U.S. Navy, was confronted by an enormous hurricane off the Carolina coast. The *Central America* carried 101 crewmembers and 477 passengers including families, miners, immigrants, entrepreneurs, merchants and lawyers. Also onboard were 38,000 pieces of mail and tons of gold including several commercial ship-

ments of it. Many of the passengers carried gold as well in ingots, coins, nuggets and dust that had been collected during years of toiling in the hostile western environment. The captain and passengers fought to keep the steamer afloat for three days. After she began to take on water, every man onboard began to bail. The steamer continued to sink deeper and the boilers soon lost steam. The pumps ceased working when the boilers gave out. The *Central America* was now at the mercy of the sea. On Saturday, September 12, the vessel *Marine* was spotted. After making her way to the foundering steamer, the *Marine* began to drift downwind, unable to maintain her position near the stricken vessel, which now sat deep in the water. Capt. Herndon and the men onboard the *Central America* showed unequivocal honor by first putting every woman and child safely into lifeboats less one young boy who refused to go, for the transfer to the *Marine*. The lifeboats were able to make their way back to the *Central America* one more time before she foundered. The *Marine* rescued a total of 100 people before the *Central America* sank. Several hours later, a Norwegian bark named *Ellen* was able to rescue 50 more men. Three more men managed to find a lifeboat that had drifted away from the *Marine* and were also rescued. The loss of the commercial gold on the *Central America* that day set off the 1857 economic depression that spread across the nation. Tommy Thompson, a former senior engineer at Battelle Memorial Institute and his group, the Columbus-America Discovery Group, were awarded the salvage rights after finding the wreck on September 11, 1988. Recovering the gold lost during the California Gold Rush has made a significant contribution to America's rich historical background. Besides the gold, the many artifacts recovered thus far include a sealed trunk with clothes, books with papers still inside, the ship's bell, and pictures.

St. Anthony, Portuguese merchantman, Captain Arnold
   Location: Charleston
   History: The merchantman foundered soon after leaving port in 1767

while sailing from Charleston to Oporto. No lives were lost.

Success, English merchantman, Captain Clark
   Location: Rebellion Road, Charleston
   History: Five ships were lost in Rebellion Road at Charleston during a hurricane on May 4, 1761: the *Polly & Betsey, Success, Daniel, Britannia* and an unidentified Bermudan schooner.

Suffolk, English merchantman, Captain Warton
   Location: Charleston bar
   History: The merchantman was lost on the bar in 1784 while sailing for London. Part of her cargo was saved.

Swan, English slave ship, Captain Smith
   Location: Charleston Harbor
   History: The *John* and *Swan,* both slave ships, wrecked while attempting to enter Charleston Harbor in 1806. No lives were lost.

Swift, English merchantman, Captain Craig
   Location: Charleston bar
   History: The merchantman was lost on the bar in 1784 while arriving from St. Augustine.

Thetis, English warship
   Location: Charleston
   History: Two English warships, the *Thetis* and *London,* sank at the Charleston docks during a hurricane on August 9, 1781.

Three Friends, Scottish ship, Captain McElcheran
   Location: Charleston
   History: The ship wrecked near Charleston in 1787 while arriving from Tobago. Some of her cargo was saved.

Three Friends, English merchantman, Captain Bradford
   Location: Charleston bar
   History: The merchantman was lost on the bar in 1797 while sailing to London.

Unidentified, Spanish *nao,* Captain Lucas Vázques de Ayllon
   Location: Cape Romain
   History: The *nao* wrecked near Cape Romain in 1520 with no loss of life.

Unidentified, ships (8)
   Location: Charleston
   History: Eight ships were sunk in the harbor and 15 badly damaged during a hurricane on September 14, 1728. A great part of the town of Charleston was destroyed as well.

Unidentified, ships (large number)
   Location: Charleston
   History: A large number of ships were sunk in the river and harbor and others wrecked on the shore during a hurricane on August 27 and 28, 1813.

Unidentified, ships (large number)
   Location: Charleston Harbor
   History: A large number of ships were sunk and wrecked in Charleston Harbor during a hurricane in September 1713.

Unidentified, ships (23+)
   Location: Charleston Harbor
   History: More than 20 large English merchantmen and three warships were totally lost in Charleston Harbor during a hurricane on September 15, 1752.

Unidentified, ships (12)
   Location: Charleston Harbor
   History: Twelve newly arrived English merchantmen sank during a hurricane on September, 30, 1752.

Unidentified, merchantmen (several)
   Location: Charleston Harbor
   History: Several large unidentified merchantmen were lost in the harbor during a severe gale on October 30, 1792.

Unidentified, ships (5)
   Location: Charleston Harbor
   History: Five ships were sunk and 11 severely damaged in Charleston Harbor during a hurricane on September 11, 1804.

Unidentified, Bermudan schooner
   Location: Rebellion Road, Charleston
   History: Five ships were lost in Rebellion Road at Charleston during a hurricane on May 4, 1761: the *Polly & Betsey, Success, Daniel, Britannia* and an unidentified Bermudan schooner.

Vigilant, 20-gun British privateer, Captain Thomas Goldesbrough
   Location: Beaufort

   History: The ship was burnt at Beaufort in 1780.

York, English merchantman, Captain Randell
   Location: Charleston bar
   History: The ship was forced into Charleston for repairs in November 1768 while sailing from Jamaica to London, but was lost while crossing the bar of this port. All of her cargo was lost, but the crew was saved.

VIRGINIA

Adventure, American merchantman, Captain Smith
   Location: Cape Henry
   History: The merchantman wrecked on September 7, 1805, on Cape Henry while arriving from Jamaica. Her crew and some of her cargo were saved.

Antony Mangin, merchantman of unknown registry, Captain Stafford
   Location: Cape Charles
   History: The merchantman was lost near Cape Charles in 1798 while sailing from Hamburg to Baltimore.

Betsey, American merchantman, Captain Tredwell
   Location: Norfolk
   History: The ship was fully laden at Norfolk and ready to sail for Liverpool in 1807 when it was accidentally burnt at anchor and sank.

Brothers, English merchantman, Captain Morrison
   Location: Cape Henry
   History: This vessel wrecked in 1764 near Cape Henry after setting sail for London. Her crew was saved.

Charles, English merchantman, Captain Waterman
   Location: Cobb Island
   History: The merchantman was totally lost on Cobb Island in 1768 while arriving from London. Several of her crew perished.

Clotilda, American merchantman, Captain Brotherdon
   Location: Cape Henry
   History: The ship wrecked on Cape Henry on March 5, 1818, while sailing from New Orleans to Philadelphia. Eleven men drowned.

Congress, American war frigate
  Location: Norfolk
  History: During a hurricane that struck Norfolk on September 3, 1821, two American war frigates—the *Congress* and *Guerriere*—plus a large number of brigs, schooners and smaller vessels were sunk or wrecked.

Cox, ship of unknown registry, Captain Mason
  Location: Assateague Island
  History: The ship wrecked on Assateague Island in 1784 while sailing from Barbados to Philadelphia. Her crew was saved.

Duke, English merchantman, Captain Maitland
  Location: Off Virginia
  History: Foundered four days after setting sail for London in 1757.

Duke of Cumberland, English merchantman, Captain Ball
  Location: Nine leagues south of Cape Henry
  History: The merchantman was lost nine leagues south of Cape Henry in 1757 while sailing from the Canaries to Virginia. Twenty-five of her crew perished.

Fanny, French merchantman
  Location: Cape Charles
  History: She wrecked in 1790 near Cape Charles while arriving from the Channel Islands.

Five Oak, English merchantman, Captain Peaton
  Location: Hog Island
  History: The ship was totally wrecked on Hog Island in 1775 while arriving from the Leeward Islands. Only two of the crew were saved.

Flora, American merchantman, Captain Finlay
  Location: Twenty-five miles north of Cape Charles
  History: The vessel wrecked in 1790 while sailing from London to Philadelphia.

Flower of Cork, Irish merchantman, Captain Chip
  Location: Five leagues south of Cape Henry
  History: She wrecked on the coast five leagues south of Cape Henry in

1753 while arriving from Cork. The crew was saved.

Friendship, American schooner, Captain Clark
  Location: South of Cape Henry
  History: The schooner wrecked on November 25, 1764, a little south of Cape Henry while sailing from Barbados to Philadelphia. Two of her crew perished.

Glasgow, Scottish merchantman, Captain Montgomery
  Location: Cape Charles
  History: Two Scottish merchantmen, the *Prince George* and *Glasgow*, were captured near Cape Charles by a French warship in 1746. After the crews and cargoes were transferred to the French ship, both merchantmen were burnt.

Gorel, English merchantman, Captain Rymey
  Location: Three leagues north of Cape Charles
  History: The merchantman was lost three leagues north of Cape Charles in 1770 while arriving from Liverpool. Most of her cargo was saved.

Grange, English ship
  Location: Cape Charles
  History: The ship wrecked at Cape Charles in 1785 while arriving from England. All of her cargo was saved.

Guerriere, American war frigate
  Location: Norfolk
  History: During a hurricane that struck Norfolk on September 3, 1821, two American war frigates—the *Congress* and *Guerriere*—plus a large number of brigs, schooners and smaller vessels were sunk or wrecked.

Heroine, American ship, Captain Maxwell
  Location: Hog Island
  History: The ship wrecked on April 14, 1811, while sailing from Lisbon to Norfolk. No lives were lost.

Hibernia, English merchantman, Captain Morrison
  Location: Ten leagues south of Cape Henry
  History: The merchantman wrecked during a violent storm on September

2, 1775, while arriving from Londonderry.

H.M.S. *Deptford*, ten-gun English warship, Captain Thomas Berry
  Location: Cedar Island
  History: The warship wrecked on August 26, 1689, near Cedar Island but no lives were lost.

H.M.S. *Hunter*, 18-gun English warship, Captain Tudor Tucker
  Location: Hog Island
  History: The warship wrecked on December 27, 1797, on Hog Island. Seventy-five of her crew of 80 perished.

Impétueux, 74-gun French warship
  Location: Cape Henry
  History: The warship was forced ashore by two British frigates in 1806 and destroyed.

Inclination, merchantman of unknown registry, Captain Coster
  Location: Hog Island
  History: The ship wrecked on Hog Island in 1798 while sailing from Bremen to Baltimore.

Jane & Dianna, American merchantman, Captain Handwith
  Location: Cape Henry
  History: The ship was lost near Cape Henry while sailing from Norfolk to Spain in 1790.

Jan Pierre, Dutch merchantman, Captain Veffer
  Location: Cape Henry
  History: This vessel foundered on December 24, 1772, near Cape Henry while sailing from the Caribbean to Amsterdam. Her crew was saved.

Janus, Dutch ship, Captain Windt
  Location: Cape Henry
  History: The ship was totally wrecked in 1822 on Cape Henry while arriving from Bremen. The crew was saved.

June, English merchantman, Captain Rexburg
  Location: Hog Island
  History: The merchantman was totally lost on Hog Island in 1800 while sailing from Liverpool to Baltimore.

Juno, 34-gun Spanish warship
  Location: Off Assateague Island
  History: The ship was driven off course by strong winds while sailing

from Mexico to Spain. Documents state that due to many bad leaks, she sank on October 29, 1802, near Cape May, carrying all of her 425 persons and over 300,000 pesos in silver to the bottom. The wreck was located by Ben Benson, owner of Sea Hunt Inc. He pinpointed the wreck 1,500 feet from shore in twenty feet of water. Benson also located another Spanish warship, *La Galga*, which sank in 1850. The landmark battle over ownership of the two wrecks involved the Park Service, the Navy, the State Department, the Justice Department, and Spain. Initially, Spain was encouraged by the difference of opinion between federal agents and U.S. Park Service archaeologists, who disagree on ideological grounds about whether or not commercial salvaging of historic wrecks should be discontinued: the Park Service archaeologists believe it should; the federal agents believe it should not. Spain then challenged Virginia's claim that the *Juno* was covered under the U.S. 1987 Abandoned Shipwreck Act. Spain argued that the issue of ownership of the warships could jeopardize relations between her and the United States. The *Juno* was declared the property of Spain and the *La Galga* the property of Virginia. However, this decision was overturned in an unprecedented court ruling in July 2000, which gave Spain ownership of both frigates lying inside United States territory.

King's Fisher, English merchantman, Captain Biddy
   Location: Wallop's Island
   History: The ship was sailing from New England to South Carolina in 1751 with a cargo of prisoners. The prisoners captured the vessel, murdered the captain and crew, then wrecked the ship at Wallop's Island.

Kitty, American merchantman, Captain Shaw
   Location: Cape Charles
   History: The ship sank off Cape Charles during a gale in 1771 after setting sail for England.

Kitty & Alice, English merchantman
   Location: Cape Henry
   History: The merchantman was lost near Cape Henry while arriving from Jamaica in 1790.

La Galga, Spanish ship belonging to the New Spain Flota of Captain-General Juan Manuel de Bonilla
   Location: Coast of Virginia
   History: A hurricane on August 18, 1750, struck the *flota* off Cape Hatteras, North Carolina. Four of the ships were lost in this vicinity. Two other Spanish ships were lost on the coast of Virginia: the *Nuestra Señora de los Godos*, near Cape Charles, and the *La Galga*, 15 leagues north. The *capitana* (flagship) *Nuestra Señora de Guadalupe*, and the galleon *Zumaca*, reached Norfolk; however, both ships and 12 unidentified English merchantmen were lost during another hurricane several weeks later. The *La Galga* was located by Ben Benson, owner of Sea Hunt Inc., while he was searching for the *Juno*, another Spanish warship lost in 1802. The landmark battle over ownership of the two wrecks involved the Park Service, the Navy, the State Department, the Justice Department, and Spain. Initially, Spain was encouraged by the difference of opinion between federal agents and U.S. Park Service archaeologists, who disagree on ideological grounds about whether or not commercial salvaging of historic wrecks should be discontinued: the Park Service archaeologists believe it should; the federal agents believe it should not. Spain then challenged Virginia's claim that the *Juno* was covered under the U.S. 1987 Abandoned Shipwreck Act. Spain argued that the issue of ownership of the warships could jeopardize relations between her and the United States. The *Juno* was declared the property of Spain and the *La Galga* the property of Virginia. However, this decision was overturned in an unprecedented court ruling in July 2000, which gave Spain ownership of both frigates lying inside United States territory.

La Plata, Spanish ship
   Location: Cape Charles
   History: The ship was totally lost on October 22, 1822, near Cape Charles while sailing from Havana to Baltimore. No lives were lost.

Liverpool, English merchantman, Captain Nash
   Location: Cape Henry
   History: The merchantman was lost on March 10, 1824, to the south of Cape Henry while arriving from Jamaica. Her crew and part of the cargo were saved.

Lovely Ann, Scottish merchantman
   Location: Cape Charles
   History: The ship was wrecked near Cape Charles in 1790 while arriving from Glasgow.

Lucy, American merchantman, Captain Pickman
   Location: Cape Henry
   History: The merchantman wrecked on Cape Henry in 1810 while sailing from Madeira Island to Baltimore. The crew and some of the cargo of wine were saved.

Lucy, American merchantman
   Location: Middle Ground, between Capes Henry and Charles
   History: The ship wrecked on Middle Ground in 1753 while sailing from Maryland to Lisbon with a cargo of wheat.

Lydia, English merchantman, Captain Teague
   Location: Cape Henry
   History: The merchantman foundered near Cape Henry in 1757.

Martin, English merchantman
   Location: Hampton Roads
   History: The merchantman was lost at Hampton Roads in 1797 while sailing for London.

Mary & Ann, American merchantman, Captain Barlow
   Location: Hog Island Shoals
   History: The ship wrecked on November 19, 1824, while sailing from Havana to Philadelphia.

Maryland, American packet boat, Captain Brown
   Location: Cape Henry
   History: The boat wrecked while arriving from London in 1786. Her crew was saved.

Minerva, English merchantman, Captain Ewing
   Location: Cape Charles

History: She wrecked on September 4, 1775, at Cape Charles while arriving from Londonderry.

Molly, English merchantman, Captain Collins
Location: Norfolk
History: The ship was burnt in 1776 at Norfolk while preparing to sail for Liverpool.

Nanty, English merchantman, Captain Foster
Location: Hampton Roads
History: The merchantman was lost in Hampton Roads in 1791 while sailing to London.

Neptune, English merchantman, Captain Burdon
Location: Twenty-five miles south of Cape Henry
History: The *Neptune* and the *Thomas & Richard* wrecked south of Cape Henry in 1760 while arriving from London.

Nonsuch, English merchantman, Captain Wallace
Location: Middle Ground between Capes Charles and Henry
History: The vessel was lost on the Middle Ground in 1787 while arriving from London. Her crew was saved.

Nuestra Señora de Guadalupe, capitana (flagship) of the New Spain Flota of Captain-General Juan Manuel de Bonilla
Location: Virginia
History: A hurricane on August 18, 1750, struck the *flota* (fleet) off Cape Hatteras, North Carolina. Four of the ships were lost in this vicinity. Two other Spanish ships were lost on the coast of Virginia: the *Nuestra Señora de los Godos,* near Cape Charles, and the *La Galga,* 15 leagues north. The *capitana* the *Nuestra Señora de Guadalupe,* and the galleon *Zumaca,* reached Norfolk; however, both ships and 12 unidentified English merchantmen were lost during another hurricane several weeks later.

Nuestra Señora de los Godos, Spanish ship belonging to the New Spain Flota of Captain-General Juan Manuel de Bonilla
Location: Near Cape Charles

History: A hurricane on August 18, 1750, struck the *flota* (fleet) off Cape Hatteras, North Carolina. Four of the ships were lost in this vicinity. Two other Spanish ships were lost on the coast of Virginia: the *Nuestra Señora de los Godos,* near Cape Charles, and the *La Galga,* 15 leagues north. The *capitana* the *Nuestra Señora de Guadalupe,* and the galleon *Zumaca,* reached Norfolk; however, both ships and 12 unidentified English merchantmen were lost during another hurricane several weeks later.

Pearl, English ship
Location: Cape Charles
History: The ship caught fire and blew up in the vicinity of Cape Charles in 1754.

Prince George, Scottish merchantman, Captain Coulter
Location: Cape Charles
History: Two Scottish merchantmen, the *Prince George* and the *Glasgow,* were captured near Cape Charles by a French warship in 1746. After the crews and cargoes were transferred to the French ship, both merchantmen were burnt.

Rainbow, English merchantman, Captain Coward
Location: Cape Henry
History: The merchantman was lost near Cape Henry in 1791 while sailing from Newfoundland to Philadelphia. Her crew was saved.

Randolph, English merchantman, Captain Andrews
Location: Cape Henry
History: The merchantman wrecked off Cape Henry in 1769 while arriving from Bristol. All of her crew were saved.

Revanche du Cerf, French privateer
Location: Norfolk
History: The French privateer was captured by an American naval vessel and taken into Norfolk, where it was stripped and burnt on April 16, 1811.

Robert, American merchantman, Captain Stocking
Location: Cape Henry
History: The merchantman wrecked on August 31, 1809, at Cape Henry

while sailing from Jamaica to Philadelphia. Her crew was saved.

Rogers, English merchantman, Captain Wignell
Location: Middle Ground, between Capes Henry and Charles
History: This vessel wrecked on the Middle Ground in 1766 while arriving from Liverpool. The crew was saved.

Russel, English merchantman, Captain Calder
Location: Cape Henry
History: The merchantman was lost while passing Cape Henry in 1761 and sailing for Barbados. The crew and part of the cargo were saved.

Sally, English merchantman, Captain Pritchard
Location: Cape Charles
History: She was lost off Cape Charles in 1762 while sailing from Philadelphia to Lisbon.

Samuel Smith, ship of unknown registry, Captain Stiles
Location: Cape Henry
History: The ship wrecked south of Cape Henry in 1804 while arriving from the Far East with a valuable cargo. Many of her crew perished.

Seaflower, ship of unknown registry, Captain Bascombe
Location: Cape Henry
History: The ship was lost near Cape Henry in 1822 after arriving in ballast from St. Vincent. The crew and sails were saved.

Sea Nymph, English merchantman, Captain Ecles
Location: Hog Island
History: The merchantman was lost on Hog Island in 1741 while sailing for England. Many of her crew perished.

Shepherdess, English merchantman, Captain Wells
Location: Cape Henry
History: The merchantman wrecked near Cape Henry in 1806 while arriving from London. Her crew and passengers were saved.

Suffolk, American merchantman, Captain Doggett
Location: Middle Ground between Capes Henry and Charles

History: The merchantman was totally lost on the Middle Ground in 1801 while sailing from New York to Norfolk. The crew and passengers were saved.

Swan, English merchantman, Captain Dale
Location: Hog Island
History: She was lost on Hog Island in 1791 while sailing for London.

Tamerlane, French ship
Location: Cape Henry
History: After being captured, the French ship was totally lost on Cape Henry in 1813. Only a small part of the large amount of silver and gold specie onboard was saved.

Tamphough, English merchantman, Captain Brag
Location: Cobb Island
History: The ship wrecked on Cobb Island while arriving from England in 1749. Her crew was saved.

Thomas & Richard, English merchantman, Captain Wilkinson
Location: Twenty-five miles south of Cape Henry
History: The *Neptune* and *Thomas & Richard* wrecked 25 miles south of Cape Henry in 1760 while arriving from London.

Unidentified, ships (2)
Location: Cape Charles
History: Two unidentified ships were lost off Cape Charles in 1762 but both crews were saved.

Unidentified, ship
Location: Cape Charles
History: During a gale on August 2, 1795, a large unidentified ship sank off Cape Charles with a total loss of lives.

Unidentified, English ships (2)
Location: Cape Henry
History: A brig and a snow were lost in the area of Cape Henry in the year 1757. All of the snow's crew perished.

Unidentified, ship
Location: Cape Henry
History: An unidentified ship carrying over 300 immigrants from Germany to the James River wrecked off Cape Henry in January 1739. There were only ten survivors.

Unidentified, ships (several)
Location: James River
History: Several ships were wrecked on the James River during a hurricane on August 12, 1724. Most of their cargoes were saved.

Unidentified, merchantman
Location: Near the boundary of Virginia and North Carolina
History: The merchantman was wrecked near the boundary line of Virginia and North Carolina in 1822. No lives were lost.

Unidentified, English merchantmen (12)
Location: Norfolk
History: A hurricane on August 18, 1750, struck the New Spain Flota (fleet) of Captain-General Juan Manuel de Bonilla off Cape Hatteras, North Carolina. Four of the ships were lost in this vicinity. Two other Spanish ships were lost on the coast of Virginia: the *Nuestra Señora de los Godos,* near Cape Charles, and *La Galga,* 15 leagues north. The *capitana* (flagship) *Nuestra Señora de Guadalupe,* and the galleon *Zumaca,* reached Norfolk; however, both ships and 12 unidentified English merchantmen were lost during another hurricane several weeks later.

Unidentified, ships (many)
Location: Norfolk
History: Many unidentified ships were destroyed and sunk during a bad gale at Norfolk on July 23, 1788.

Unidentified, vessels (large number)
Location: Norfolk
History: During a hurricane that struck Norfolk on September 3, 1821, two American war frigates—the *Congress* and *Guerriere*—plus a large number of brigs, schooners and smaller vessels were sunk or wrecked.

Unidentified, merchantmen (14)
Location: Northern coast of Cape Charles
History: After setting sail for England, a fleet of 14 unidentified merchantmen were lost on the northern coast of Cape Charles during a hurricane in 1706.

Unidentified, ships (many)
Location: Portsmouth
History: Many severe storms struck the vicinity of Virginia during September and October 1785. Several large ships were sunk or destroyed along the coast and in the rivers. During one tremendous gale at Portsmouth, several large ships were carried a long way into the woods.

Unidentified, English merchantmen (6)
Location: Virginia
History: Four large English merchantmen were wrecked on the York River and two on the James River during a hurricane on September 7 and 8, 1769.

Unidentified, British warships (6+)
Location: Yorktown
History: At least six British warships and other smaller support vessels were sunk during the British siege of Yorktown in October 1781.

William, Scottish merchantman, Captain Church
Location: Cape Charles
History: The merchantman wrecked on Cape Charles in 1790 while sailing for Dublin. Her cargo was saved.

William Murdock, English merchantman, Captain Brooks
Location: Cape Charles
History: The ship wrecked in January 1808 on Cape Charles while sailing in ballast from Rotterdam to the Potomac River. No lives were lost.

Zumaca, Spanish galleon belonging to the New Spain Flota (fleet) of Captain-General Juan Manuel de Bonilla
Location: Virginia
History: A hurricane on August 18, 1750, struck the *flota* (fleet) off Cape Hatteras, North Carolina. Four of the ships were lost in this vicinity. Two other Spanish ships were lost on the coast of Virginia: the *Nuestra Señora de los Godos,* near Cape Charles, and *La Galga,* 15 leagues north. The *capitana* (flagship) *Nuestra Señora de Guadalupe,* and the galleon *Zumaca,* reached Norfolk; however, both ships and 12 unidentified English merchantmen were lost during another hurricane several weeks later.

Virgin Islands

The waters of both the American and British Virgin Islands offer a good cross-section of shipwrecks of various types and nationalities. The wrecks span the centuries, although there is only one documented 16th century shipwreck and only a few from the 17th century. Virtually no shipping of any kind passed near or through the Virgin Islands until the late 17th century, when sailing patterns of the Nueva España Flota (fleet) were changed. In the early days the *flota*, after making its Caribbean landfall at Guadeloupe or a nearby island, would head for Mexico, passing within sight of the southern coast of St. Croix. In later years, the *flota* made landfall at Anguilla or St. Barthélemy and passed around the northern edge of the Virgin Islands, generally sighting Anegada.

Several historians claim that prior to 1850, over 100 ships were wrecked off the low-lying Anegada, including some of the Nueva España Flota. The other islands in this group are considerably higher and could be spotted even in the night. Consequently, they were less of a hazard to navigation and have few shipwrecks. Most of the wrecks occurred in bad weather when the ships were driven by stress of wind and seas upon the reefs and islands.

The Virgin Islands have long been a major center for diving and although many wrecks have been accidentally discovered by amateurs, no serious attempts have been made to salvage any. The only major wreck discovered in these waters was in February 1969, when the harbor was being dredged at Roadtown. The dredge buckets brought up over 400 artifacts, which included silver and pewter plates, cutlery, a silver sword handle, a cutlass, carpenter's tools, various types of shot, clasp knives, a flintlock rifle, ship fittings, caulking tools, clay pipes, and different types of rigging.

No permits are required to work on shipwrecks in the American Virgin Islands. However, a permit must be obtained from the Keeper of Wrecks in Roadtown on the Island of Tortola to work on any shipwreck in the British Virgin Islands. The weather pattern for the Virgin Islands is about the same as that for Puerto Rico.

Dr. Edward Towle, former director of the Caribbean Research Institute, which is affiliated with the College of the Virgin Islands, created a department of Marine Archaeology on the islands during the Spring of 1968.

SHIPWRECKS IN THE VIRGIN ISLANDS' WATERS

Acadia, British ship, Captain Venham
  Location: Anegada Shoals
  History: The ship, of and for Trinidad from Puerto Rico, was lost on the Anegada Shoals on March 4, 1823. About 50 head of cattle were saved.

Aftrivedo, Spanish merchant ship, Captain Laporta
  Location: Anegada Island
  History: The ship was lost on July 22, 1810, on Anegada Island while coming from Tarragona. Part of the cargo was saved and carried to Tortola.

Agno, British ship, Captain Park
  Location: Hogland (may be Hog Island)
  History: The ship was lost on the south end of Hogland (may be Hog Island) in the Virgin Islands in 1819 while sailing from London to St. Petersburg.

Aimable Eulalie, French ship, Captain Alleaume
  Location: Anegada Shoals
  History: The ship was wrecked on the Anegada Shoals in May 1824 while sailing from Guadeloupe to Le Havre. Only a small part of the cargo was saved.

Ajax, English ship
  Location: Off Anegada

History: The ship wrecked off Anegada in September 1819. The captain and three men drowned.

Albion, British ship, Captain Robertson
  Location: Tortola
  History: The ship was lost at Tortola in 1801 while sailing from Montserrat to London.

Angelica, ship of unknown nationality, Captain Treby
  Location: Buck Island, off St. Croix
  History: The ship was totally wrecked on Buck Island, off St. Croix in 1824. The crew and a small part of the cargo were saved.

Anrora (correct spelling is probably *Aurora*), Spanish ship, Captain Aldayturriaga
  Location: Anegada
  History: The ship was totally lost on Anegada on November 29, 1813, while sailing from Cadiz to Veracruz. The crew was saved.

Arabella, ship of unknown nationality, Captain Spiller
  Location: St. Thomas
  History: The ship was totally lost near St. Thomas in 1817 while sailing from Pará, Brazil to New York.

Argus, British brig
  Location: Anegada
  History: The brig sank at Anegada in 1819.

Artifacts
  Location: Anegada
  History: A large unidentified Spanish ship with over 300 African slaves aboard ran aground on the horseshoe part of Anegada in 1817. After throwing many heavy objects overboard, she was light enough to be pulled off and proceeded on her voyage.

Astrea, 32-gun British frigate, Captain Edward Heywood
  Location: Anegada
  History: The ship was lost on a reef at the island of Anegada on May 23, 1808. Only four men were lost.

Bark, ship
 Location: One of St. John's harbors
 History: The *Bark*, commanded by
Jean Pinart, was carrying French settlers from St. Christopher's and was
burnt by Spaniards, most likely in one
of St. John's harbors in 1647.

Brothers, British ship, Captain Briggs
 Location: St. Croix
 History: While sailing from Virginia
for Lisbon in 1769, the ship sprang a
leak at sea and, bearing away for the
West Indies, it ran ashore upon a reef
off St. Croix. Both the ship and cargo
were lost but the crew was saved.

Bryon (or *Byron*), British ship, Captain Anderson
 Location: Anegada Shoals
 History: The ship, of and for Cork
from Trinidad, was totally lost on the
Anegada Shoals on November 23,
1821. The crew and passengers were
saved.

Bulwark, British ship
 Location: Anegada
 History: The ship wrecked on Anegada on December 13, 1818, while sailing from New Brunswick to Jamaica.

Caroline, ship of unknown nationality, Captain DaSilva
 Location: Tortola
 History: The ship was lost off Tortola on November 15, 1814, while sailing from Madeira to Jamaica. The
crew was saved and taken to Puerto
Rico.

Caroline, American brig
 Location: Anegada Shoals
 History: The brig, sailing from Boston to Puerto Rico, was totally lost on
the Anegada Shoals about November
25, 1822.

Christopher, ship of unknown nationality (but most likely French), Captain Mollyneaux
 Location: St. Croix
 History: The ship, from Africa,
struck on a submerged anchor in the
harbor of St. Croix in 1793 and sank.

Constantine, ship, Captain Langdon
 Location: Thatch Island
 History: The ship was lost in a hur-
ricane on August 26, 1785, on Thatch
Island, near St. Thomas while sailing

from Dominica to Bristol. The crew
was saved.

Cruger, American ship, Captain Williams
 Location: Horseshoe Reef, Anegada
 History: The ship wrecked on September 3, 1786, on Horseshoe Reef of
Anegada while sailing from Philadelphia to St. Croix.

Dash, British ship, Captain Falls
 Location: Anegada Reef
 History: The ship, of London, was
totally lost on May 23, 1816, on Anegada Reef while sailing from Puerto
Rico to Barbados. The crew, some of
the rigging and 20 of the 120 oxen onboard were saved.

Defiance, British ship, Prince Maurice
 Location: Anegada
 History: Prince Maurice, while privateering in the Caribbean in 1652 with
a convoy commanded by his brother,
Prince Rupert, wrecked off Anegada
in 1652. Rupert and Maurice were
both leading Royalists who had fought
for their uncle, King Charles I of
Great Britain, in the recent English
Civil War.

Dominica, ten-gun British war brig,
Captain Charles Welsh
 Location: Tortola
 History: The brig foundered near
Tortola in 1809. Sixty-two of her crew
of 65 perished, including the captain.

Dona Paulo, Portuguese ship, Captain
Viana
 Location: Anegada Shoals
 History: The ship, of Pará, was totally wrecked on the Anegada Shoals
on the night of September 3, 1819. Two
hundred and thirty-five African slaves
and the crew were saved.

El Cesar, Spanish merchantman, Cap-
tain Josef Bernabe Madero
 Location: Anegada
 History: The ship, owned by the
Marqués de Casa Madrid, was lost on
Anegada Island in 1757.

Eliza, British ship, Captain Filliul
 Location: Horseshoe Reef near Anegada
 History: The ship wrecked on Horseshoe Reef near Anegada in 1823 while

sailing from Liverpool to St. Thomas.
The cargo and crew were saved.

El Rayo, Spanish ship
 Location: Anegada
 History: The ship ran ashore on
Anegada in 1790 while sailing from
Bilbao to Puerto Rico. The crew aban-
doned her safely.

Falcon, American ship, Captain Broth-
off
 Location: Anegada
 History: The ship wrecked at Anegada on May 26, 1817.

Fox, British slave ship, Captain Jones
 Location: St. Thomas
 History: The ship was lost at St.
Thomas in 1776 while sailing from
Africa for America.

General Abercrombie, British ship,
Captain Booth
 Location: St. Croix
 History: The ship was lost at St.
Croix in 1803 while sailing from
Africa to the West Indies. Most of her
cargo was saved.

General Brown, American ship, Captain Godfrey
 Location: Anegada Shoals
 History: The ship was totally wrecked
on the Anegada Shoals while sailing
from New York to the west end of
Puerto Rico in 1821. Most of its cargo
was saved and sold at Tortola.

Good Hope, British ship, Captain Watson
 Location: Anegada
 History: The ship was lost near Anegada in 1809 while sailing from London to the Spanish Main. Most of the
cargo was saved.

Graham, British merchantman, Captain M'Intosh
 Location: St. Croix
 History: The ship was cast away off
the back reef of St. Croix in 1769 while
sailing from Grenada to London. Both
the ship and cargo were a total loss but
the crew was saved.

Hebe, British ship, Captain Gray
 Location: Tortola
 History: The ship was lost on the
rocks near Tortola in 1795 while sailing from Cork to Jamaica.

Henry, British merchant ship, Captain Retson
Location: Water Island, St. Thomas
History: The ship, of Liverpool, was lost off Water Island on April 26, 1807.

Jamaica, British ship, Captain Alexander
Location: St. Croix
History: The ship, sailing from Tobago and Grenada to London, was captured by the French and run ashore at St. Croix in 1796.

James Barron, American ship, Captain Fisher
Location: Anegada Reef
History: The ship, sailing from Charleston, South Carolina to Barbados, was totally lost on January 7, 1824, on the Anegada Reef.

James Edwards, American schooner
Location: Anegada
History: The schooner sank at Anegada in 1819.

Jane, British cutter
Location: Tortola
History: The cutter was lost on the north side of Tortola, her port of origin, at the end of February 1816.

Katherine, ship, Captain Richards
Location: Anegada
History: The ship was lost on Anegada while sailing from Jamaica to Bristol in 1751. The crew was saved.

La Trompeuse, 32-gun pirate ship of John Hamlin
Location: Charlotte Amalie Harbor
History: British naval officer Captain Carlile of H.M.S. *Francis* wrote: "31 July 1683, attacked a pirate ship at anchor in the harbor of Charlotte Amalie, of thirty-two guns and six patararoes, by the name of *La Trompeuse*, commanded by the Frenchman John Hamlin ... setting her afire and she blew up...."

Lavinia, ship of unknown nationality, Captain Elles
Location: Tortola
History: The ship was lost near Tortola in 1801. A great part of her cargo was saved.

Le Count de Poix, French ship, Captain Lewis Coyer

Location: Anegada
History: The ship wrecked on Anegada while sailing from Santo Domingo to Havre de Grace, France in 1713.

Lioness, American brig
Location: Anegada Reef
History: The ship wrecked on the Anegada Reef in 1811.

London, British ship, Captain Cromie (may be Cramie)
Location: Anegada Island
History: The ship was lost on Anegada Island in 1810 while sailing from London to Haiti.

Lord Mount Cathell, British ship, Captain Fisher
Location: St. Croix
History: The ship, previously commanded by the late Captain Taylor, was lost on the island of St. Croix in July 1773. Only part of the cargo was saved.

Marina, British ship, Captain Littlewood
Location: West of St. Thomas
History: The ship wrecked on a small island to the west of St. Thomas in 1815 while sailing from Barbados to St. John and New Brunswick. Part of her cargo was saved.

Martha, ship, Captain McIntosh
Location: Anegada
History: The vessel was lost on May 25, 1774, on Anegada while sailing from Jamaica to London.

Mary, British ship, Captain Hunter
Location: St. Croix
History: The ship, from Africa, was lost near St. Croix in 1797. Her cargo was saved.

Mary, ship of unknown nationality, Captain Autman
Location: Anegada
History: The ship was lost on Anegada in 1817 while sailing from Jamaica to Veracruz.

Mary, ship of unknown nationality, Captain Hellyer
Location: Anegada Shoals
History: The ship was lost on February 22, 1821, on Anegada Shoals while sailing from New York to St.

Thomas. The crew and cargo were saved.

Maxwell, American schooner
Location: Anegada
History: The schooner sank at Anegada in 1819.

Nancy Gaer, ship
Location: Anegada
History: The ship was lost off Anegada in 1769 but her crew was saved.

Neptune, British ship, Captain Casey
Location: St. John
History: The ship, of London, was lost at the island of St. John in 1789.

Neptune, Dutch ship, Captain Spranges
Location: Tortola
History: The ship was lost at Tortola in 1778.

Nevarro (probably correctly spelled *Navarro*), Spanish ship, Captain Belandia
Location: Anegada
History: The ship was lost at Anegada in 1792 while sailing from St. Andero (Santander), Spain to Havana.

Nuestra Señora de la Victoria, Spanish ship
Location: Anegada Reef
History: The ship was lost on December 5, 1812, on the Anegada Reef while coming from Málaga.

Nuestra Señora de Lorento y San Francisco Xavier, English-built ship converted to a Spanish galleon, 212 tons, Captain Juan de Arizon
Location: Anegada
History: The vessel sank on Anegada Island in 1730 while coming from Spain. She was sailing in convoy with a fleet of treasure galleons commanded by General Manuel López Pintado and bound for Cartagena and Porto Bello.

Ocean, British merchant ship, Captain Brown
Location: Tortola
History: The ship was lost near the island of Tortola in 1806 while sailing from St. Vincent Island to Bristol.

Ocean, British ship, Captain Stewart
Location: Anegada Reef
History: The ship was totally lost in February 1812 on the Anegada Reef

while sailing from London to Honduras. The crew was saved.

Ortello, ship, Captain Johnson
Location: Tortola
History: The ship was cast away in Tortola in 1783 while sailing to there from Africa. Two hundred and thirteen slaves were saved.

Partridge, British ship, Captain Miller
Location: Tortola
History: The ship was lost near Tortola in 1806 while sailing from Bristol and the Island of Madeira to St. Thomas. Part of her cargo was saved.

Paterson, ship
Location: Anegada
History: The ship sank at Anegada in 1818.

Perseverance, British ship, Captain Oriel
Location: Anegada
History: The ship was totally lost on the north side of Anegada near Tortola in 1795 while sailing from Dublin to Jamaica.

Prince Ferdinand, ship, Captain Caynoon
Location: Anegada Reef
History: The ship was lost on the Anegada Reef in 1760 while sailing from Boston to Jamaica. Her crew was saved.

Purcell, British merchantman, Captain Fuller
Location: Tortola
History: The merchantman was lost on the rocks near Tortola while sailing from Bristol for Tortola in 1749.

Ranger, British ship, Captain Stewart
Location: Tortola
History: The ship was lost on a reef of rocks near Tortola in 1784 while sailing from Tortola to London.

Recovery, British slave ship, Captain Walker
Location: Tortola
History: The ship was blown out of Nevis Roads (on Nevis Island) and driven by winds until it wrecked on Tortola Island in 1793.

San Ignacio, Spanish merchant ship
Location: Anegada

History: The ship, belonging to the newly formed Caracas Company, was lost on Anegada Island in 1742.

Santa Monica, British ship (originally Spanish), Captain John Linzee
Location: Tortola
History: The ship, originally a Spanish ship taken by the British on September 14, 1779, was lost near Tortola in 1782. All her crew but one were saved as well as many of her guns, stores and cargo.

Santa Rosa, Spanish merchantman
Location: Anegada
History: The merchantman wrecked on the reefs of Anegada in 1758.

Sector, British ship
Location: Anegada Shoals
History: The ship wrecked on the Anegada Shoals on May 6, 1824, while sailing from Trinidad to St. Thomas. Some of her cargo of dry goods was saved.

Sophia, British schooner
Location: Anegada Reef
History: The schooner, of Antigua and bound for Curaçao, ran onto the Anegada Reef in 1823 and was totally lost. The crew, rigging and part of the cargo of mahogany wood were saved.

Sophia Sarah, British ship, Captain Stairs
Location: Anegada Shoals
History: The ship, of and from Halifax and sailing to Jamaica, was totally lost in July 1822 on the Anegada Shoals. The crew and part of her cargo were saved.

Spirito Santo (Spanish spelling would be *Espíritu Santo*), Spanish snow
Location: Anegada
History: The snow wrecked on the night of March 19, 1775, on the rocks of Anegada at the point called the Horseshoe while bound for Harvard from La Coruña, Spain. The vessel was lost but the people and a great part of the cargo were saved.

St. Auguasies (English spelling of its name; possibly the same as the *San Ignacio* wrecked on this island), 30- to 60-gun Spanish warship
Location: Anegada

History: The ship wrecked on Anegada on March 20, 1742. Four hundred of the 600 persons onboard drowned. She was sailing with two other warships from San Sebastian, Spain for Havana; the squadron was carrying 2,000 troops and many supplies.

Swallow, British merchantman, Captain Heblethwaith
Location: Tortola
History: The ship, of Liverpool, was lost coming out of Tortola in 1781. The crew was saved.

Thomas, English ship
Location: Between Buck Island and St. Thomas
History: An unidentified brig struck a rock between Buck Island and St. Thomas and stuck there in 1813. The *Thomas*, of Bristol and coming from St. Vincent, struck the same rock on the same day and was run ashore to keep it from sinking.

Unidentified, merchant *naos* (2), Captain Francisco Vara
Location: Anegada
History: Two merchant *naos* were sailing from Spain for Santo Domingo when one was lost in the Virgin Islands in 1523. One was under the command of Captain Francisco Vara, and the other, Captain Diego Sanchez Colchero. The location of Vara's ship was given only as on some "shallows," but Colchero's was reported wrecked on the island of Anegada. After several days, Colchero was able to refloat his ship by throwing most of its cargo and anchors overboard. Then they located Vara's wrecked ship two leagues away but could only save the men onboard.

Unidentified, Spanish galleon
Location: Anegada
History: Written in 1775 on a chart of the Virgin Islands, which was printed in a book, was the following note: "On Anegada is Ye Treasure Point, so called by ye freebooters from the gold and silver supposed to have been buried there abouts after the wreck of a Spanish galleon."

Unidentified, vessels (3)
Location: Tortola
History: Two vessels wrecked on St.

Thomas and a packet boat ran aground at Tortola during a hurricane on August 1, 1792.

Unidentified, Spanish felucca
Location: Anegada
History: The ship was lost off Anegada in 1808. Three men drowned.

Unidentified, ship
Location: Anegada
History: An unidentified ship was lost off Anegada in the year 1810.

Unidentified, brig
Location: Between Buck Island and St. Thomas
History: The brig struck a rock between Buck Island and St. Thomas and stuck there. The incident took place the same day in 1813 that the *Thomas*, of Bristol and coming from St. Vincent, struck the same rock and was run ashore to keep it from sinking.

Unidentified, vessel
Location: Tortola
History: An unidentified vessel was driven onshore at Tortola during a hurricane in September 1819.

Unidentified, vessels (over 104)
Location: St. Thomas
History: A dreadful hurricane struck the Leeward Islands September 20–22, 1819. Over 100 vessels were totally lost at St. Thomas alone.

Unidentified, Spanish felucca
Location: Anegada
History: The felucca was lost on Anegada in the year 1822.

Unidentified, Spanish galleon
Location: Anegada
History: In a description of Anegada between 1692 and 1705, Pete Labat wrote: "It is said that a year ago a great Spanish galleon laden with treasure

was wrecked on Anegada, and that the treasure was buried on the island. There it still remains, or so they say, because most of the men who buried it were lost at sea, and the few survivors did know where the treasure was hidden and were never able to find it. This treasure has caused many men including several filibusters to waste their time. I knew a man who stayed four or five months on the island, digging and sounding. He said that he had found something but no one has yet found the real treasure...." Speaking of another shipwreck, he added, "...one of our priests was wrecked on L'Isle Noyee or Anegada and had been captured with the rest of his crew by the people of Panestown, also known as Virgin Gorda. He told me that he had remained a prisoner for two months with these Englishmen on Panestown...."

Unidentified, Spanish galleon
Location: Anegada
History: The galleon, carrying a very valuable cargo of mercury or quicksilver and destined for the silver and gold mines of Mexico, wrecked on the reefs of Anegada in 1731.

Unidentified, Spanish galleon
Location: Anegada
History: A document dated 1734 stated: "While I was in England, they [inhabitants of Anguilla, Spanish Town (Virgin Gorda), and Tortola] pirated upon a Spanish ship wrecked on the Anegadas...."

Unidentified, sloop
Location: Anegada
History: The sloop, returning from the wreck of the *Nuestra Señora de la Soledad* (lost on Cape Hatteras, North Carolina) and supposedly carrying the

valuables from that ship, wrecked off Anegada in 1750.

Unidentified, English ship, 70 tons
Location: Anegada Island
History: The governor of Puerto Rico wrote the king of Spain in 1625 stating that an English built ship with 18 men on it sank at Anegada Island. They had sailed from Virginia and were bound for Bermuda to salvage a wreck, but their ship was damaged in bad weather and driven onto the reefs of Anegada.

Unidentified, French frigate
Location: Crab Island
History: The frigate, part of the war fleet of Count D'Estrees, wrecked on Crab Island in 1678.

Union, British ship, Captain Purrington
Location: Anegada
History: The ship was lost on December 12, 1823, on Anegada while sailing from Barbados to Bath.

Victory, Spanish warship, Captain Don Carlos Casamara
Location: Anegada Shoals
History: The warship was cast away on the Anegada Shoals in the year 1738.

Volvent, Danish brig
Location: Anegada
History: The brig sank at Anegada in 1819.

Warwick, British ship, Captain Simpson
Location: Between Buck Island and St. Thomas
History: While sailing from Liverpool to St. Thomas in 1816, the ship struck on a rock between Buck Island and St. Thomas and was lost. The cargo was also lost but the crew was saved.

Index